Strategies and Tactics
of Behavioral Research
and Practice

Strategies and Tactics of Behavioral Research and Practice focuses on the most effective methods for measuring and evaluating changes in behavior. The authors provide the rationale for different procedures for measuring behavior and designing within-subject comparisons between control and intervention conditions. The text explains the strengths and weaknesses of methodological alternatives for every topic so that behavioral researchers and practitioners can make the best decisions in each situation.

This classic text has been extensively revised to be more accessible and practical. Not only does it feature much more discussion of how research methods are relevant to today's practitioners, it also includes additional examples based on field research and service delivery scenarios. With expanded coverage on creating experimental designs, as well as new chapters on behavioral assessment, the statistical analysis of data, and ethical issues associated with research methods, this book provides a strong foundation for direct behavioral measurement, within-subject research design, and interpretation of behavioral interventions.

Enriched with more pedagogical features, including key terms, tables summarizing important points, figures to help readers visualize text, and updated examples and suggested readings, this book is an invaluable resource for students taking courses in research methods. This book is appropriate for researchers and practitioners in behavior analysis, psychology, education, social work, and other social and health science programs that address questions about behavior in research or practice settings.

James M. Johnston is a Professor Emeritus of Psychology at Auburn University, USA.

Henry S. Pennypacker is a Professor Emeritus of the University of Florida, USA.

Gina Green is Chief Executive Officer at the Association of Professional Behavior Analysts, USA.

Strategies and Tactics of Behavioral Research and Practice

Fourth Edition

James M. Johnston
Auburn University

Henry S. Pennypacker
University of Florida

Gina Green
Association of Professional Behavior Analysts

Routledge
Taylor & Francis Group

NEW YORK AND LONDON

Fourth edition published 2020
by Routledge
52 Vanderbilt Avenue, New York, NY 10017

and by Routledge
2 Park Square, Milton Park, Abingdon, Oxon, OX14 4RN

Routledge is an imprint of the Taylor & Francis Group, an informa business

First edition published by Erlbaum Associates 1980
Third edition published by Routledge 2009

Library of Congress Cataloging-in-Publication Data
Names: Johnston, James M., author. | Pennypacker, H. S. (Henry S.), author. |
    Green, Gina, author.
Title: Strategies and tactics of behavioral research and practice / James M.
    Johnston, Auburn University, Henry S. Pennypacker, University of Florida,
    Gina Green, Association of Professional Behavior Analysts.
Other titles: Strategies and tactics of behavioral research
Description: Fourth edition. | New York, NY : Routledge, 2019. | Includes
    bibliographical references and index.
Identifiers: LCCN 2019006754 (print) | LCCN 2019009232 (ebook) |
    ISBN 9781315537085 (Ebook) | ISBN 9781138641235 (hardback) |
    ISBN 9781138641594 (pbk.)
Subjects: LCSH: Psychology–Research–Methodology.
Classification: LCC BF76.5 (ebook) | LCC BF76.5 J63 2019 (print) |
    DDC 150.72–dc23
LC record available at https://lccn.loc.gov/2019006754

ISBN: 978-1-138-64123-5 (hbk)
ISBN: 978-1-138-64159-4 (pbk)
ISBN: 978-1-315-53708-5 (ebk)

Typeset in Garamond
by Servis Filmsetting Ltd, Stockport, Cheshire

Dedicated to the memory
of Murray Sidman

Contents

List of Boxes

Preface

The original edition of *Strategies and Tactics of Behavioral Research* was published in 1980, which in the lifespan of textbooks is a very long time ago. It was the first effort since Murray Sidman's seminal 1960 volume, *Tactics of Scientific Research*, to attempt a comprehensive description of the research methods of the growing field of behavior analysis. Sidman's text explained what the field's basic research enterprise had taught us about experimental methods for studying behavior. Our volume broadened that treatment to include the challenges of studying behavior outside of the laboratory, particularly expanding discussion of behavioral measurement, among other topics. Our effort was verbose, and we struggled in some areas to explain things clearly, but that edition had a certain awkward charm and at least assured that students who persevered learned how to do behavior analytic research.

Our second edition in 1993 included less rhetoric and reflected our acknowledgment that perhaps a textbook did not need to probe every nook and cranny of behavior analytic research methods. We convinced the publisher to let us put the more esoteric material into a supplementary readings volume, allowing us to craft an improved instructional description of core content in the primary text.

The third edition, published in 2009, recognized that the behavior analysis practitioner community was developing at an increasing pace, spurred by well-accepted certification credentials offered by the Behavior Analyst Certification Board, Inc. That edition, therefore, had an increased focus on practitioner interests in research methods. The second edition reading volume was discontinued, and although the textbook chapter themes remained relatively unchanged, the context shifted somewhat to accommodate applied concerns. As before, familiar topics were addressed with mostly new writing, and many instructional features were added to make the volume a better textbook.

A field's research methods evolve fairly gradually, but the research issues driving their application and the circumstances in which the field operates reflect more rapidly changing influences. Since the third edition was published, behavior analysis has seen continued development of its applied community. There are now hundreds of graduate training programs focusing on preparing practitioners to meet the burgeoning demand for applied behavior analysis (ABA) services. The number of professionals earning the field's credentials continues to be positively accelerated from year to year, and many are now taking advantage of new state licensure laws. The demand for their expertise continues to exceed that growth, and a steady increase in third-party funding of ABA services has supported their career interests.

This fourth edition continues our effort to accommodate the interests of the large and growing practitioner cohort. The most obvious sign of the book's increasingly applied focus is its revised title – *Strategies and Tactics of Behavioral Research and Practice*. This updated title seems an appropriate way to accommodate the book's expanded support for the methodological needs of practitioners. Although their activities are diverse, practitioners are always investigators, whether pursuing applied research questions or delivering routine services. The methods by which they measure changes in target behaviors or evaluate the influence of environmental variables are fundamentally the same as those used by colleagues who focus on research careers. Practitioners are also consumers of the field's research output. They must keep up with the applied research literature, evaluate presentations at professional meetings, and appraise claims coming from all directions about treatment models and procedures.

Readers whose interests in research methods are not especially applied, much less focused on delivery of services, should be reassured that our effort to better serve practitioner needs has not required substantial changes in the core material for which the book is well known. We continue to not just describe basic methodological practices but to explain their underlying rationale. Although much of the writing is new – as it has been in every edition – the issues, procedures, and reasoning associated with methods of discovery do not appreciably differ across questions, settings, and participants. We have taken care to address that essential material in a way that encompasses the full range of behavior analytic interests. Among other changes, that required adding a chapter dealing with methodological issues associated with behavioral assessment and another addressing research ethics. The third edition's passing mention of statistically based options has now grown into a full chapter orienting behavior analysts to foundational issues in that approach to design and analysis. Additional revisions involved dividing single and multiple baseline designs into separate chapters. Of course, this fourth edition incorporates updated citations and more examples, tables, figures, and text boxes.

In this effort, we were fortunate to convince two knowledgeable and experienced colleagues to work with us. Dr. Ryan Zayac of the University of North Alabama developed most of the material at the end of each chapter, including chapter summaries, text and box study guides, discussion topics, and exercises.

Dr. Amy Polick of Florida State University Panama City took responsibility for developing some of the materials available to instructors and students on the publisher's website, including instructor slides for each chapter, as well as a comprehensive set of test questions in multiple-choice, fill-in and free-response formats. The online materials also include chapter outlines, study guides, discussion topics and exercises, tables, figures, definitions of key terms, and suggested readings references.

In this overview of the fourth edition, we have saved the best for last. This edition includes Dr. Gina Green as a co-author. In addition to expertise in research methods, she brings skills and experience as a clinician, researcher, teacher, and supervisor, not to mention superior writing skills. She is especially well known for her leadership in the area of public policy associated with the needs of the practitioner community. Our contributions are thoroughly intertwined.

—James M. Johnston
—Henry S. Pennypacker
—Gina Green

Those who fall in love with practice without science are
like a sailor who enters a ship without a helm or a compass,
And who never can be certain whither he is going.

—Leonardo da Vinci

PART ONE

THE NATURAL SCIENCE
OF BEHAVIOR

CHAPTER ONE

Discovery in Research and Practice

THE CHALLENGE OF DISCOVERY
  The Role of Scientific Method
  Scientific Methods in Behavior Analysis
SCIENTIFIC METHODS AS BEHAVIORAL CONTINGENCIES
  Methods as Behavior
  Examples of Methodological Alternatives
CONTROL BY THE SUBJECT MATTER
METHODS IN RESEARCH AND PRACTICE
  Distinguishing Between Research and Practice
  Research Methods and Service Delivery

THE CHALLENGE OF DISCOVERY

The Role of Scientific Method

Throughout our daily lives, we often wonder what is going on with someone's behavior or how to get someone to act in a particular way. We may even be that someone. Why is the person in front of me at the grocery store checkout only starting to look for a charge card after the clerk has rung up the total? How can I learn to interrupt less often when others are talking? Why do drivers fail to use their turn signal? How can I get my supervisor to accept my suggestions? Why do people vote for politicians who support policies that are obviously not in the voter's best interests? These everyday questions are usually no more than idle curiosities, and their answers may not matter very much at the moment.

It may be good that our personal questions about behavior are often pretty casual because few people are prepared to search for the real answers. Most simply depend on their experience with the situation at issue, filter it through everyday assumptions about how behavior works, guess at an answer, and make no effort to determine whether the answer is truly correct. How would we know anyway? If the answer is wrong, it will probably not make much difference if we are not really trying to solve a problem. Such curiosities are not actually going to result in a meaningful effort to come up with a substantive answer. Even when people are serious about resolving an issue, they are unlikely to appreciate what is required to convince nature to reveal its secrets, let alone have the resources to mount an effective attack on a problem.

This assessment should not be taken as a criticism. Discovering nature's secrets is a difficult task. It is only in the last two or three hundred years that the challenge has been eased by an approach called the **scientific method**. That approach encompasses tactics for learning about natural phenomena that have become the backbone of all of the natural sciences. Although each area of science uses specialized techniques required by its subject matter, all natural sciences adhere to the same core rules and methods. In brief, they include asking only answerable questions, developing explanatory hypotheses, testing hypotheses through measurement and experimentation, analyzing data in light of the hypothesis and question, and publishing results so that others can independently evaluate them. The reason for this shared approach is that it has proven remarkably effective in revealing the intricacies of natural phenomena. Regardless of differences among scientific specialties in their subject matters, research questions, and experimental circumstances, scientists have learned that if they pursue their curiosities in just the right way, they will be rewarded with revealing and useful answers.

> **Scientific method.** The established practices of scientific communities that have evolved over time because of their effectiveness in studying natural phenomena.

Over the years, guided by the power of the scientific method, discoveries resulting from basic research in each of the natural sciences led to the development of applied research agendas focusing on how the fruits of basic research might be used for real-world benefits. The resulting practical discoveries in turn spawned technologies (in the form of both hardware and techniques) that were useful in everyday life. Many of the methods of discovery that worked so well in basic research laboratories were carried over into those latter stages. That is, the same approach that resolved basic research issues was understandably used to address questions that were more applied in character. After all, the differences between basic and applied research primarily lie in the focus of the questions, not in how to go about answering them. The same approach to framing questions, formulating testable hypotheses, measuring natural phenomena, designing test conditions, and analyzing data assures the same benefits for all research endeavors, whether they lean toward elementary or practical outcomes.

The dependence on core scientific methods of discovery was further extended to developing and disseminating science-based technologies. The development, production, and delivery of practical products and services that flow from scientific discoveries involve many of the same features of scientific methods that were used in making those discoveries in the first place. That extension should not be surprising, because turning applied research findings into everyday technologies also involves discovery in which the focus is on learning how to use products and procedures to yield consistently effective practical outcomes. Although that kind of discovery is strictly aimed at achieving practical results, it still requires using such methods as testable questions, sound measurement, replication of results, and more. Even routine dissemination of mature technologies often carries with it some features of scientific methods. We are all familiar with the importance of measurement in medical practice, for example. Even when applied research has documented the health benefits of particular drugs, physicians often monitor their effects on each patient by repeatedly measuring the status of key physiological processes.

Scientific Methods in Behavior Analysis

The scientific study of behavior as a natural phenomenon fits squarely within this methodological tradition. The same rules and methods used by other natural sciences lie at the foundation of both basic and applied behavior analysis research, as well as the practical use of behavioral technologies. In fact, it is easy to argue that the productivity of basic and applied behavior analysis researchers and the effectiveness of applied behavior analysis practitioners depend on their shared commitment to the core methods of the natural sciences.

Guided by the early work of B. F. Skinner, starting in the late 1930s the young field of behavior analysis abandoned the methodological traditions of psychology and forged a fresh approach to measuring and evaluating behavior change (Johnston, 1993a). That approach adapted natural science methods to the study of behavior by directly measuring behaviors of individuals in baseline and experimental (intervention) conditions, controlling factors that could contaminate intervention effects, and comparing data from baseline and intervention conditions separately for each participant so that effects could be seen clearly. The approach taken by Skinner and his students and colleagues was, in hindsight, straightforward and revealing. It even seemed that way to Skinner. In reflecting on his early research, he wrote: "So far as I can see, I began simply by looking for lawful processes in the behavior of the intact organism" (1956, p. 80).

By the 1950s some researchers became interested in whether the laboratory findings that Skinner and others obtained with rats and pigeons could also be obtained with humans. Their early applied research most often took place in mental hospitals, developmental centers, and schools. Some of it involved individuals with significant behavioral challenges (e.g., see Cooper, Heron, & Heward, 2007; Morris, Altus, & Smith, 2013). Many of those investigators were experienced basic researchers and, buoyed by the young field's achievements in the laboratory, they understandably extended the same methodological practices to applied questions. As **applied behavior analysis** grew into a distinct research specialty with its own journals, its methodological style continued to include some of the same features that had made the basic research so powerful.

> **Applied behavior analysis.** A phrase that may refer to (a) the area of research that focuses on developing and evaluating procedures for changing behavior for practical purposes, (b) the behavior change technology resulting from behavior analytic research, or (c) the field encompassed by both applied behavior analysis research and the delivery of applied behavior analysis services.

By the late 1960s, opportunities for gainful employment were increasingly available for applied behavior analysts who were more interested in offering practical services than doing research. They evaluated the effects of those services using the same methods as applied researchers, even though the practical agenda focused on meeting the behavioral needs of individual clients rather than answering questions intended to apply to other individuals and circumstances. The methodological centerpiece of their approach was ongoing direct measurement of carefully defined target behaviors conducted separately for each individual throughout baseline and intervention conditions. Data analysis emphasized graphical displays of data separately for each individual, which made it easy to evaluate any modifications of intervention procedures as distinct phases in a quasi-experimental style. The everyday settings in which behavior change services occurred did not always allow practitioners to carefully control factors that might be intermingled with intervention procedures, however. That limited opportunities to identify exactly what was responsible for changes in behavior, but practitioners were focusing on improving their clients' lives, not publishing reports intended to represent accurate conclusions about the effects of interventions and what produced them.

In sum, all specializations in the field of behavior analysis – from basic research to applied research to everyday delivery of services – share a commitment to key features of natural science methods of discovery. The interests of investigators vary from one circumstance to another, of course, and each situation imposes different constraints on the methodological options that are available. Across all activities in the field, however, methods of measuring and evaluating behavior change are far more similar than different and are among the features that define behavior analysis as a distinct discipline. This book explains how those methods are used by investigators in basic and applied behavior analysis research as well as those involved in the routine delivery of practical services.

SCIENTIFIC METHODS AS BEHAVIORAL CONTINGENCIES

Methods as Behavior

The scientific method is customarily viewed as a body of general rules and practices that investigators follow in designing, conducting, and interpreting research. Because behavior is its subject matter, the field of behavior analysis focuses on the daily endeavors of scientists and practitioners as behavior. That approach to understanding the methods of discovery used in both science and practice - the explicit conviction that those methods involve nothing more than the behavior of investigators - underlies how behavior analysts adapt natural science methods of discovery in their work. Instead of talking about what is going on "in the scientist's head," behavior analysts focus on relations between the behavior of investigators and the circumstances they face in their daily work environments.

The scientific understanding of operant behavior provides the context for that focus. Informally described, the primary activities of investigators involve figuring out what they need to learn, planning and conducting experimental tests or interventions, and interpreting and communicating the results. When investigators are doing those kinds of things, they are behaving. Understanding those activities in terms of **operant** contingencies can help guide decision-making in research and service settings. Therefore, in this book we approach those domains of professional behavior in the same way behavior analysts approach any behavior - as our subject matter. We try to identify the **antecedent events** that may encourage investigators to engage in one course of action over another, for example, or the **consequences** that may reinforce some practices but not others.

BOX 1.1

But What about the Stuff that Isn't Behavior?

Does it seem that viewing methods of discovery as nothing more than the behavior of researchers and practitioners fails to acknowledge the contribution of more "intellectual" activities? If so, you have yet to learn about the philosophy of science that is part of the foundation of the field of behavior analysis. A field's philosophy of science includes such features as the nature of its language, the style with which it approaches explanation and prediction, the ways it defines and studies its subject matter, how it arrives at and validates its discoveries, and its implications for society (Moore, 2008).

The philosophy of science for behavior analysis is called **radical behaviorism**. It has been thoroughly described by Skinner and many others over the years in countless articles and books, which means that a few paragraphs cannot begin to do it justice. Skinner defined it as "the philosophy of a science of behavior treated as a subject matter in its own right apart from internal explanations, mental or physiological" (1989, p. 122).

In contrast with Skinner's statement, our culture teaches us that behavior is largely driven by causes that are said to exist only in a mental domain entirely lacking physical dimensions. The conflict between behavior as a physical phenomenon and the everyday tendency to look for mental or nonphysical causes has always been a challenge for psychology and other social sciences, which fully accept the cultural mandate.

Radical behaviorism is based on the proposition that as a physical phenomenon, behavior is influenced only by other physical events, which means that mental "events" cannot explain behavior. Furthermore, from a radical behavioristic perspective, the mental explanations that are implied by everyday dialect are largely invented or fictitious. They merely reflect the way we have been taught by the culture to talk about behavior. Radical behaviorism offers an alternative way of understanding human nature that addresses all of its physical features while avoiding the pitfalls of **mentalism**.

Without stepping outside of our everyday verbal repertoire, it is difficult to understand how a science that focuses only on behavior can begin to explain the complexity of human nature. If that is where you are, do not give up before you start. To begin the journey, you might begin by reading some of B. F. Skinner's book, *Science and Human Behavior* (Skinner, 1953). Moore (2008) offers a much more formal and systematic description of radical behaviorism, and Johnston (2014) has written a treatment aimed at practitioners. Other book-length treatments include Baum (2005) and Moore (2015).

Operant. A class of responses (a behavior) defined by a functional relation with a class of consequent events that immediately follow those responses.

Antecedent event. An environmental event that occurs immediately before a response. Used generically when it is not certain what function the event serves.

Consequent event. An environmental event that occurs immediately after a response. Used generically when it is not certain what function the event serves.

This is a good perspective for a text on methods of discovery because it helps highlight the many decisions investigators must make in conducting an experiment or managing an intervention. Each way of doing something – such as defining a target behavior or deciding what features of a behavior should be measured – involves some antecedent circumstances and some possible consequences. Different actions by the investigator may lead to outcomes that are reinforcing, punishing or neither, given the focus of the questions being asked, which will then make similar actions more or less likely in the future. Examining methodological contingencies can help reveal why some actions might be more effective than others under certain conditions. Although contingencies vary across circumstances for each investigator, if we step back and examine the actions most often taken in the study and management of

---

BOX 1.2

What is a Contingency?

A contingency is nothing more than a relation between events. To say that there is a contingency between events A and B only means that one is related to the other in some way, but there are many possible ways. For example, the relation might be causal, which means that one event is influenced by the other. On the other hand, two events might be related – for example, one might reliably follow the other – though neither influences the other (a third variable might be responsible for the relation, or the two events might just happen to occur close in time).

In behavior analysis, references to contingencies are usually of the causal variety because contingent relations between behavior and environment are the key to understanding how behavior works. Many of the technical terms in behavior analysis, such as reinforcement and punishment, refer to contingencies in which changes in the environment depend on – are contingent on – some aspect of responding. Those contingencies in turn influence the nature of the behavior that produced them. So when responding tends to be followed by a particular change in the environment, the contingency may affect the nature of that behavior in the future.

---

behavior, we can identify the established methodological traditions of behavior analysis. The reason those actions are preferred stems from their effectiveness for investigators who choose them, but the accumulated outcomes define the effectiveness of the entire field.

The objective of this book is to summarize what many behavior analysts have learned over the years about methods of studying behavior. One way this book differs from other books on similar topics is that it avoids presenting a set of methodological rules that might give a misleading impression of simplicity. Discovering things about behavior is not a matter of following some rules like recipes in a cookbook. Cookbooks may work quite well when the recipe is well tested, but discovering what is going on with behavior in research and service venues is more like creating the recipe in the first place. Answering questions about behavior involves many decisions, judgments, and even guesses. This book, therefore, describes methodological practices in terms of the behavior of investigators and the likely consequences of different courses of action. Although each investigation requires a unique series of decisions, the consequences of those decisions should always lead to a clear picture of the effects of certain conditions on target behaviors.

Examples of Methodological Alternatives

One of the first things investigators must do is decide what behavior should be measured and how to measure it. As Chapter 4 explains, there are different

---

BOX 1.3

Rule-Governed versus Contingency-Shaped Behavior

The goal of science is to describe regularities in nature so we may behave more effectively than would otherwise be the case. Scientific methods help researchers figure out those regularities, which are often expressed as rules. If what researchers learn is accurate and sufficiently detailed, the rules can lead others who have never experienced the contingencies to behave effectively.

A disadvantage of managing behavior with rules is that they are often less than fully accurate and complete. Furthermore, people may not follow the rules very well because their actions may be influenced by their experiences (contingencies). For instance, although following the rule "Do not smoke" is almost certain to decrease one's chance of contracting certain diseases, the immediate consequences of smoking usually have the effect of making smoking more likely.

Behavior shaped by contingencies is usually very closely attuned to those contingencies, but for such shaping to occur, each individual must experience the contingencies. That is not only less efficient than managing behavior with rules; sometimes the consequences are quite costly in one way or another (as in developing heart disease from smoking).

The distinction between rule-governed and contingency-shaped behavior is relevant to the methods used by researchers and practitioners. As we have already pointed out, describing research methods as a set of rules to be strictly followed would not necessarily bring the investigator's behavior under very good control of what is going on with the subject matter. A rule-based approach to teaching methods of discovery tends to lead to behavior that is too strongly influenced by theory, the research literature, or factors other than the data from the project. In contrast, the approach taken in this book emphasizes the contingencies between the actions of the researcher or practitioner and the characteristics of the resulting data. Such contingencies tend to shape sound decisions about designing and conducting a study or practical intervention and interpreting the data by encouraging close attention to what is going on with the target behavior. That in turn tends to lead to more accurate and complete descriptions of nature – that is, better rules.

---

ways of defining any behavior, which may yield different pictures of what is happening with the behavior. For instance, consider an evaluation of procedures to reduce the occurrence of tantrum behavior exhibited by a young boy diagnosed with autism spectrum disorder. The behavior might be defined as specific forms of crying and screaming or in terms of a broader collection of actions that is often effective in producing certain outcomes for the boy, such as getting what he wants. The other actions might include hitting, kicking, and throwing things in addition to crying and screaming, though any single episode might not include each kind of response. Both definitions might seem to capture tantrumming, but the two different definitions could result in differences in the data, which might then lead to different conclusions about the effects of the intervention procedures being evaluated. One of those pictures of tantrumming behavior may be more revealing or meaningful than the other. That is, one definition could be less useful than the other for evaluating the effects of intervention and achieving intervention goals. The decision about which definition to use is likely to have a big effect on the investigator, not to mention the boy and those around him.

Another set of measurement decisions involves choosing the particular features of a target behavior that need to be measured. In this example, measuring how often tantrum behavior occurs will provide a different picture of that behavior than measuring how long each tantrum lasts. One kind of data may be more useful than the other in revealing the effects of an intervention and guiding conclusions. Knowing that the boy has a meltdown four to six times a day may be important, but it may also matter whether each of those episodes lasts only a few minutes or close to an hour. Different intervention procedures may affect one aspect of the behavior (e.g., the frequency of tantrumming) more than another (e.g., the durations of tantrums).

Choices must also be made in designing procedures for observing and recording a target behavior. For example, investigators must decide when and how often observation will take place, as well as how long each observation period will last. Not surprisingly, those decisions can have a big impact on the picture of the behavior revealed by the data. Scheduling observation sessions at the wrong times can result in data that misrepresent what goes on at other times. Observing too infrequently can mislead as well, but observing all the time can be effortful and costly. Short observation sessions may sometimes be sufficient, but under other circumstances they may yield misleading data. Decisions about when and how often to measure depend not only on the nature of the target behavior but also on the intervention effects that might be expected and the interests of the investigator and others. In other words, it can get complicated.

Whether the discovery process involves designing a formal experiment or evaluating a practical treatment, it is essential to arrange comparisons between baseline and intervention phases in ways that will reveal important differences in responding under each condition. There are lots of alternatives, and each option has strengths and weaknesses. For instance, a single comparison between a baseline or non-intervention phase (A) followed by a treatment phase (B) is the minimum basis for describing any effects those conditions have on a participant's behavior, but it leaves important questions unanswered. If the baseline condition were repeated following the treatment condition (an ABA arrangement), would responding look like it did in the original baseline phase? If responding changed when the treatment condition was implemented, is that change reliable? That is, if a second treatment phase followed the second baseline phase (ABAB), would responding change the same way it did the first time the participant experienced it? Are any differences in one participant's behavior under the two conditions typical of what might be found with other participants?

Of course, practitioners do not always have the luxury of arranging carefully planned comparisons of baseline and treatment conditions. Their focus is on

improving behavior in some way, whatever the contributions of different features of treatment protocols. Nevertheless, tracking changes in target behaviors
is essential for making informed treatment decisions and may make it possible
to also draw more general conclusions about the effects of treatment protocols.
Practitioners might become increasingly skilled in drawing such conclusions
with experience but only if they evaluate interventions in ways that support
strong conclusions logically and empirically.

The methodological options just discussed are only a small sample of the
choices that are usually available to researchers and practitioners. Does it
already seem that making the best methodological decisions is going to be
challenging? It can be, but understanding when certain decisions are required,
as well as the relation between each option and how it may affect what can be
learned from the resulting data, usually makes the best choices fairly obvious.
The upcoming chapters systematically tackle the key issues one at a time, carefully pointing out the pros and cons of each option.

CONTROL BY THE SUBJECT MATTER

Earlier we pointed out that basic and applied natural sciences and their technologies depend on the same approach to discovery. As members of the natural
science community, behavior analysts share that approach. As the science of
behavior, however, our field is uniquely positioned to understand research
methods as part of its subject matter. This unique perspective embodies three
themes that are carried throughout this volume:

(a) The essence of behavior analytic discovery lies in the behavior of individual investigators, be they researchers or practitioners.

(b) That behavior results from the same kinds of environmental contingencies that influence all other behavior.

(c) Viewing investigator behaviors in terms of their antecedents and consequences highlights important distinctions among methodological
choices and helps investigators make sound decisions.

This point of view suggests that methodological decisions are controlled by
many environmental factors. In fact, the key to understanding natural science
methods of discovery lies in appreciating the role of control. Conducting an
evaluation, for example, requires the investigator to control the factors whose
effects are of clinical or research interest (the **independent variable**). At the
same time, the investigator must control all other factors that are not of interest
but that might interfere with seeing the effects of the independent variable
clearly (**extraneous variables**). In other words, the investigator must manage
not only the independent variable to make sure it operates as intended but
also the status of any extraneous variables whose influence might be confused
with the effects of the independent variable. All the while, the investigator

must manage procedures for accurately measuring the target behavior (the **dependent variable**) to see if it changes as the independent variable is systematically presented or terminated.

> **Independent variable.** An environmental event whose presence or absence is manipulated by the investigator in order to determine its effects on the dependent variable.
>
> **Extraneous variable.** An environmental event that is not of interest to the researcher but that may influence the participant's behavior in ways that obscure the effects of the independent variable.
>
> **Dependent variable.** In behavior analytic research, usually a behavior (response class). The objective is to see if changes in the behavior depend on manipulations of the independent variable.

These considerations apply to practitioners as well as researchers. Of course, achieving control over all factors that might affect a target behavior is often not feasible in service delivery settings, nor is it necessarily a priority. As we will see, however, the issue of control is still important in deciding whether target behaviors changed and, if so, what produced the change.

Although it may seem that the researcher or practitioner does all the controlling, ideally their behavior comes largely under control of the subject matter. In other words, data representing changes in target behaviors typically have a major influence on the investigator's decisions. Obtaining a clear picture of the effects of the independent variable on the dependent variable is a highly reinforcing consequence, and good investigators work hard to achieve that outcome. For instance, a researcher may try to eliminate an extraneous factor to improve the clarity with which data reflect the relation between the independent and dependent variables. A practitioner might work to insure that assistants or parents implement treatment procedures correctly so that she can be confident about decisions to continue or change the procedures.

As investigators attempt to produce a clear picture of the effects of intervention procedures on target behaviors, they use the accumulating data to make decisions. Although those efforts stem partly from the training and experience the investigator brings to a particular study, the picture of responding provided by the data in each phase is a primary source of ideas about how to make improvements as it moves along. In other words, the subject matter as represented by the data controls the behavior of those conducting the study by serving as feedback and as a prompt for needed improvements. When the project is finished, the data guide conclusions about what happened and why. Those conclusions reflect both the behavior of participants and how that behavior was influenced or revealed by all of the methodological decisions made by the investigator along the way.

The alternative is to allow other influences to dominate investigators' decision-making. Those influences may not be entirely appropriate – in fact, they are often quite inappropriate – and can result in poor decisions that limit the value of a study or the effectiveness of a treatment. The risk is especially high when questions about human behavior are involved because it is always difficult for investigators to be entirely free of the preconceptions about behavior everyone learns from growing up in the culture. For example, everyday language suggests that (a) behavior is generally motivated and controlled by events going on in the mind, (b) emotions control subsequent actions, and (c) people can make choices that are free of outside influences. Graduate training in behavior analysis is supposed to replace those preconceptions with the influences from the field's research and theoretical literatures. Those influences may overcome many pre-scientific assumptions and personal biases, but it is difficult to fully put aside pre-professional histories. Methods of measuring and evaluating behavior change that focus attention on what is happening with the behavior of each participant under each condition are the best safeguards against those risks.

METHODS IN RESEARCH AND PRACTICE

Distinguishing Between Research and Practice

As with other fields rooted in a natural science, behavior analysis may be divided into two major endeavors: research and delivery of practical services. A portion of the behavior analytic research literature focuses on understanding fundamental features of behavior. Those studies are typically conducted under relatively controlled conditions such as laboratories with human or nonhuman participants. Much of the applied behavior analysis research literature, however, has focused on developing ways of changing behavior for practical purposes. Although applied research also requires good control of critical variables and careful measurement, applied studies are often conducted under fairly typical everyday circumstances and involve participants appropriate to the applied focus of the study (for example, school children in a study of procedures for teaching reading or employees in a study of workplace safety).

Most applied behavior analysts are employed not as researchers but in positions that require them to provide behavior change services to a wide variety of individuals. The focus of those services is improving the lives of individuals – a very different objective from that of behavioral research, which is to discover useful relations between environment and behavior that hold up under varying situations (Johnston, 1996). Furthermore, practitioners do not typically work under circumstances where they can establish the degree of control necessary for drawing accurate conclusions about the role of experimental variables. (Differences between research and practice will be further explored in other chapters.)

Research Methods and Service Delivery

Although distinctions between research and practice may seem straightforward, the two undertakings are far more similar than different when it comes to how investigators make decisions about the methods they use in conducting experiments or evaluating services. In spite of what might appear to be a strictly real-world agenda, behavior analysis practitioners share with their research colleagues an interest in making sound methodological choices. It might seem that giving research methods a key role in the routine delivery of behavioral services involves more sophistication than is warranted. Professional behavior analysts, however, have repeatedly endorsed competence in research methods as essential for practitioners in job analysis studies conducted by the Behavior Analyst Certification Board (BACB; see Johnston, Mellichamp, Shook, & Carr, 2014; Shook, Johnston, & Mellichamp, 2004). As a result, completion of coursework in behavior analytic research methods is required to qualify to take BACB certification examinations, and those methods are included in the body of knowledge applicants must master in order to pass those examinations (see http://www.bacb.com).

Practitioners must also understand research methods because they are the primary consumers of applied behavior analysis research. That research is the foundation for practice, so it is essential for practitioners to be skilled in reading and interpreting it. It might seem that any study that survives the peer review process and gets published in a respected journal must be methodologically sound and its outcomes worthy of application. However, the task of deciding whether a study's methods and findings should guide practitioner decisions is complicated. The reality is that not all published studies are free of methodological problems. For example, published studies may include baseline and intervention phases that last only two or three days, but practitioners may know from experience that brief exposure to an intervention often does not forecast the effects that might be revealed over a week or two.

Even if a published study is methodologically sound, determining if its findings might be useful in a specific situation poses further challenges. The practitioner must determine whether a study's methods are relevant to the needs of the client, are feasible to implement given the practitioner's skills and the client's circumstances, and will yield beneficial outcomes for the client and those around him. Most studies have features that differ from conditions with which the practitioner must contend. For example, the target behavior might be different than the one at issue, so the published results might not be obtained. In fact, practitioners must usually consider many differences between the conditions under which a published study was conducted and the circumstances they face in service settings in deciding whether the study's findings might apply to a particular case. Understanding how methodological features may have influenced those findings is critical for making sound decisions about everyday services.

Another reason it is essential for practitioners to understand how to use research methods is that changing a client's behavior is at least as complex as answering research questions, may have profound effects on the client and others, and is anything but routine. Each situation practitioners face is unique, and not all applied behavior analysis procedures are so well developed that they consistently yield desired outcomes every time they are applied. Even the most thoroughly researched procedure implemented by the best-trained practitioner is likely to require ongoing adjustments in order to achieve treatment objectives. Those adjustments are best viewed as similar to the phase changes in a formal experiment. The practitioner must use accumulating data to evaluate the effects of each condition and decide whether they are satisfactory or further modifications in treatment procedures are necessary.

Sometimes practitioners want even more. In order to learn from their experience, they may also want to understand what features of an intervention are responsible for its effectiveness (or lack thereof). Exploring such questions systematically is a good way to improve one's professional expertise. When an intervention is associated with desired behavioral changes, it is understandably tempting to assume that the intervention was responsible for those changes. But it is important to remember that correlation is not causation. That is, just because a procedure was implemented and behavior then changed in a certain way, it does not follow that the procedure was responsible for the change. As other chapters will show, there are often other reasons the behavior changed. The only way out of this trap is to let comparisons of data from different conditions over the course of treatment guide conclusions.

In other words, practitioners are often – or should be – in the position of doing an informal experiment in order to figure out what must be done to meet treatment objectives. Although the effort will not usually lead to a journal publication, the practitioner's decisions are no less important than those of a researcher because of their impact on the lives of clients and others. A disappointing outcome may be frustrating to a researcher because it could require repeating a study in order to produce findings worthy of publication. For a practitioner and those she serves, however, the implications can be profound. A treatment plan cannot be abandoned just because a particular procedure did not work, so the practitioner is ethically bound to identify and evaluate alternatives that might be more effective.

Figure 1.1 illustrates how practitioners often find themselves straddling the fence between simply arranging intervention procedures and conducting the manipulations necessary to figure out if the procedures are effective and what to do if they are not. The objective of the project illustrated here was to reduce the amount of crawling by a young girl with profound intellectual disabilities in order to encourage her to walk instead. Three 10-minute training sessions were conducted each day. They involved an adult located in one corner of a large room encouraging the girl to come to them. When she got close to the adult, whether by walking or crawling, she was praised and given food reinforcers.

The graph shows the percentage of time spent crawling (as opposed to walking) over the course of the evaluation. During an initial baseline phase, there was no training or intervention, and the girl crawled most of the time she

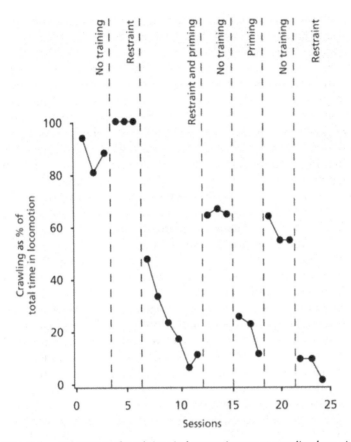

FIG. 1.1. Percentage of total time in locomotion spent crawling by a girl with profound mental retardation. Adapted from O'Brien, F., Azrin, N. H., & Bugle, C. (1972). Training profoundly retarded children to stop crawling. *Journal of Applied Behavior Analysis*, 5, 131–137, p. 134. Copyright 1972 by the Society of the Experimental Analysis of Behavior, Inc. Used by permission.

was moving. The first intervention involved making crawling ineffective. The trainer did that by holding the girl by the waist for five seconds each time she started crawling, which prevented her from making progress. Under that condition, the girl continued to try to crawl, although the authors reported that she attempted crawling less often. In the third phase, the trainer continued to hold the girl briefly when she started crawling and primed walking by raising her to a standing position. The data showed that the percentage of time spent crawling instead of walking immediately decreased by about half and continued to decline to near zero. The investigators next repeated the no-training baseline condition, but this time the child spent only about 60% of her time in motion crawling. Next they evaluated the effects of just priming walking by raising her to a standing position. The data showed that crawling immediately decreased to relatively low levels. Following another no-training phase, the investigators again tried the procedure that made crawling ineffective, and the proportion of time spent crawling instead of walking decreased still further.

This example shows the value of measuring behavior carefully and evaluating the effects of each change in procedures in a clinical intervention. Of course, the investigators could not know in advance the effects of each variation in procedures. By systematically comparing data from baseline and each intervention phase, they learned that the procedure to make crawling less effective worked best when it was combined with priming walking than when it was used alone. They also learned that priming alone could be effective, and that after that intervention, merely preventing crawling was much more effective than when it was first used. The availability of an ongoing picture of the child's locomotor behavior (crawling versus walking) allowed the investigators to make a series of informed judgments about what procedural changes might be most effective and to evaluate their predictions.

Because the evaluation just described was published, it might be tempting to assume that the procedures stand a good chance of being effective in similar cases. The study's findings are certainly worth considering, but how well its results will apply to different individuals under different circumstances is unknown. It would help if there were a dozen or more well-controlled studies addressing the same problem, each contributing to a coordinated understanding of what procedures were most effective under what conditions. That kind of evidence is not often available, however. Even if it were, practitioners know all too well that each client brings unique differences in history, present repertoire, and current influences. Those differences mean that each treatment challenge is also unavoidably unique.

The approach to behavioral measurement and evaluation in the example just described is fundamentally the same as the approach used by researchers whose interests are more narrowly scientific. Different practitioners faced with the challenge of getting a child with profound intellectual disabilities to walk instead of crawl might choose to try other procedures and arrange other sequences of conditions. In the absence of multiple studies addressing this particular clinical need, they would have little choice but to "feel their way" by analyzing the details of the behavior and possible controlling variables in a phase-by-phase experimental style.

Throughout this book, we will discuss methods for evaluating behavior and its relations to environmental variables in terms of the shared interests of researchers and practitioners. The questions guiding those interests, the circumstances under which the questions can be addressed, and the investigator's priorities certainly vary considerably from one project to another. What does not vary so much are the consequences of methodological decisions. Researchers and practitioners alike are at the mercy of the resulting data and the circumstances under which they were collected when it comes to learning what they want to know. The following chapters explain the methodological alternatives available and how they are likely to influence what the investigator learns.

CHAPTER SUMMARY

1. The scientific method is critical to studying and learning about natural phenomena. It provides researchers with a set of core rules and methods to utilize when conducting scientific activities in order to discover the laws of nature.

2. The use of the scientific method in addressing applied research questions has been beneficial, resulting in practical discoveries and the development of improved behavioral technologies.

3. Basic and applied behavior analysis research has been guided by many of the same fundamental methodological principles of other natural sciences. This has allowed applied behavior analysis practitioners to focus on changing individuals' behavior in targeted ways that solve problems in everyday living.

4. As applied behavior analysis grew as a science, practitioners utilized ongoing direct measurement of target behaviors for each individual during baseline and intervention conditions.

5. Scientists are organisms whose behavior is influenced by the same operant contingencies that underlie the behavior of other organisms. Understanding the antecedents and consequences that influence decision-making by researchers and practitioners can help to identify the established methodological traditions of behavior analysis and their overall effectiveness in the field.

6. An investigator's decision of how to define the target behavior(s), which dimensions to record, how often and when to measure the behavior, and other methodological decisions can often lead to different interpretations of the effects of intervention procedures. These decisions must be made carefully.

7. Practitioners must routinely measure target behaviors and evaluate the effects of behavior-change procedures as the intervention proceeds (e.g., baseline and treatment conditions).

8. There are three important themes throughout the book: (a) the essence of behavior analytic discovery lies in the behavior of individual investigators, be they researchers or practitioners, (b) that behavior results from the same kinds of environmental contingencies that influence all other behavior, and (c) viewing investigator behaviors in terms of their antecedents and consequences highlights important distinctions among methodological choices and helps investigators make sound decisions.

9. An investigator must control the factors whose effects are under study (independent variable), as well as those factors (extraneous variables) that are not of interest but may affect how clearly the independent variable's effects are seen. Additionally, the investigator must manage procedures for accurately measuring the target behavior (dependent variable) to see how it is impacted by the independent variable's presentation.

10. The investigator's behavior should come under the control of the subject matter (behavior) with the data guiding decision-making and interpretations. Investigators should avoid allowing personal biases and pre-professional preconceptions regarding behavior influence their decisions.

11. Basic researchers try to identify empirical generalizations about the relationship between behavior and environment by arranging conditions designed to answer experimental questions. Most applied behavior analysts are not researchers but work to change individual's behavior in socially significant ways. In spite of these differences, both share the same interest in methods of studying or changing behavior, and it is essential that each understands how methodological features may influence findings and, in turn, decision-making.

HIGHLIGHTED TERMS

Antecedent event. An environmental event that occurs immediately before a response. Used generically when it is not certain what function the event serves.

Applied behavior analysis. A phrase that may refer to (a) the area of research that focuses on developing and evaluating procedures for changing behavior for practical purposes, (b) the behavior change technology resulting from behavior analytic research, or (c) the field encompassed by both applied behavior analysis research and the delivery of applied behavior analysis services.

Consequent event. An environmental event that occurs immediately after a response. Used generically when it is not certain what function the event serves.

Dependent variable. In behavior analytic research, usually a behavior (response class). The objective is to see if changes in the behavior depend on manipulations of the independent variable.

Extraneous variable. An environmental event that is not of interest to the researcher but that may influence the participant's behavior in ways that obscure the effects of the independent variable.

Independent variable. An environmental event whose presence or absence is manipulated by the investigator in order to determine its effects on the dependent variable.

Operant. A class of responses (a behavior) defined by a functional relation with a class of consequent events that immediately follow those responses.

Scientific method. The established practices of scientific communities that have evolved over time because of their effectiveness in studying natural phenomena.

TEXT STUDY GUIDE

1. Describe the scientific method.

2. Discuss the differences between basic and applied research. Would the scientific method assure the same benefits for each type of research?

3. Briefly describe how the field of behavior analysis adapted the natural science methods to the study of behavior.

4. What is the methodological centerpiece of applied behavior analysts?

5. List the primary activities of investigators and their relationship to operant contingencies.

6. What is an antecedent event? What is a consequent event? Using a researcher attempting to publish their work (e.g., a journal article), provide an example of each.

7. Discuss the benefits of describing methodological practices in terms of the behavior of investigators and the likely consequences of their actions, as opposed to presenting a set of fixed rules.

8. Describe one of the first decisions investigators must make and why this decision is important.

9. How may selecting a procedure for observing and recording a target behavior impact the data that are collected?

10. Briefly discuss the importance of arranging comparisons between baseline and intervention phases when examining target behaviors.

11. Describe the three themes related to methodological decision-making the authors identify that are integrated throughout the text.

12. Distinguish between independent and dependent variables.

13. What are extraneous variables?

14. Discuss the importance of "control" for both researchers and practitioners. Is it more important for one group versus the other?

15. What does it mean to say "The data controls the behavior of those conducting the study?"

16. Provide an example of the difficulty that investigators face concerning preconceptions they may have about behavior.

17. Briefly discuss the difference between research and practice.

18. What is the objective of behavioral research, and how does this differ from the goals of applied behavior analysts?

19. Why must practitioners have a thorough understanding of research methods?

20. Briefly describe how practitioners often divide their time between arranging interventions and conducting manipulations to assess the effectiveness of particular variables.

BOX STUDY GUIDE

1. What is the central tenet of radical behaviorism?
2. What is a contingency? Provide an example of one in your own life.
3. Provide an example of a rule-governed behavior and a contingency-shaped behavior that you have experienced. What are the differences between behavior controlled by rules and behavior shaped by contingencies?

SUGGESTED READINGS

Johnston, J. M. (1993a). The development of behavioral research methods: Contributions of B. F. Skinner. In *Readings for strategies and tactics of behavioral research*, 2nd edition. Hillsdale, NJ: Lawrence Erlbaum Associates.

Johnston, J. M. (1993b). Why behavior analysis is a natural science. In *Readings for strategies and tactics of behavioral research*, 2nd edition. Hillsdale, NJ: Lawrence Erlbaum Associates.

Skinner, B. F. (1953). *Science and human behavior*. New York: The Free Press.

Skinner, B. F. (1956). A case history in scientific method. *American Psychologist*, 11, 221–233.

DISCUSSION TOPICS

1. Ask students to identify causal factors for examples of target behaviors (e.g., studying, exercising) and problem behaviors (e.g., procrastination, gossiping) they have engaged in recently. Use their responses to discuss how we could use the scientific method to examine their hypotheses. This may also be a good introduction to discussing how to avoid the pitfalls of mentalism.
2. Why does the text choose not to provide a set of methodological rules? Using the responses from the previous discussion topic, lead students in a discussion on how blindly following methodological rules can lead to an incomplete understanding of behavior.
3. After discussing rule-governed versus contingency-shaped behaviors, write down at least three examples of each behavior. Can you think of any of your behaviors that may have been shaped through both processes?

EXERCISES

1. Select some instances of specific behaviors and identify the antecedent events and consequent events surrounding them. Make sure that the examples include both small or trivial responses as well as more obvious

or important responses. In what ways are these responses affected by their relationship with antecedent and consequent events?

2. Select an experimental study from a scientific journal and identify the independent variable, dependent variable, and possible extraneous variables. Does the study have more than one independent variable? What did the investigator(s) do to minimize the influence of extraneous factors?

3. The text discusses the importance of what behavior(s) should be measured and how to measure it. Ask students to identify additional examples where identifying and measuring a target behavior using one definition or dimension may impact how the effects of the intervention are interpreted.

4. After discussing rule-governed versus contingency-shaped behaviors, have students write down at least three examples of each behavior. Can they think of any of their behaviors that may have been shaped through both processes?

CHAPTER TWO

Behavior as a Scientific and Practical Subject Matter

WHAT IS BEHAVIOR?

It may seem obvious that behavior is the subject matter for all behavior analysts, whether we are conducting research or delivering services. Unless we agree on what behavior is and is not, however, it is difficult to maintain a unified discipline and to identify exactly what it is that we need to know. It is especially important that researchers and practitioners hold a shared understanding of the features and limitations of behavior as a natural phenomenon. That will help assure that research findings continue to guide the development and practice of ABA and lessen the risk that the delivery of services will morph into an increasingly different field over time, unconstrained by a proper research foundation.

Coming to a shared definition of behavior is easier said than done for many reasons. We learn to identify behavior just as we learn to label everything else: through countless interactions with our verbal community. Although the results vary from one person to another, our ability to distinguish behavior from everything else seems pretty serviceable as long as we keep it simple. If we observe an organism doing something, we say it is behaving. Most people seem comfortable with that kind of assessment, and the language resulting from our shared verbal history usually works well enough for everyday purposes. True, things get more complicated when we go beyond the reaches of direct observation. For instance, describing covert activity as behavior even though others cannot see it raises questions about whether such activity should be lumped together with overt behavior. If behavior is everything we do, then it seems to follow that covert activity should be included in our definition. On the other hand, there have to be some limits. Maybe behavior that can only be observed by the behaving individual is not the same as "regular" behavior. And what about our physical machinery – all the physiological processes that are part of being alive? Calling all of those processes behavior would seem a step too far. Are there reasons to make distinctions here?

We should certainly have an understanding about the nature and limits of behavior that clearly distinguishes between what is real and what is fictional. Unfortunately, our colloquial history does not help with that at all. We are taught to label apparent features of human activity without regard for their physical underpinnings or lack thereof. For instance, most people talk about "expecting a letter" and "walking to the mailbox" as if expecting and walking are pretty much the same kind of phenomena. But unlike "walking," "expecting" does not have any physical components; it is merely an invented term. Fortunately, a good dose of **radical behaviorism** can help by providing a conceptually sound alternative to mentalistic inventions that masquerade as real (for example, see Baum, 2005; Johnston, 2015; or Moore, 2008).

Cleaning up the rampant **mentalism** embedded in our vernacular dialect still leaves genuine questions about the nature of behavior as a distinct phenomenon. The most persistent of those involves the line that might be drawn between behavior and its biological underpinnings. Those questions may be more tactical than fundamental, however. Both behavior and physiology are real, so they may be best differentiated by figuring out the most useful approach to studying their features and interactions. How might we define behavioral and physiological phenomena in ways that enable us to learn what we need to know in order to design good studies and interventions?

Radical behaviorism. The philosophy of science of behavior analysis, which focuses on behavior as a physical phenomenon and avoids mentalism in all forms.

> **Mentalism.** Attributing the causes of behavior to events and processes said to occur in a mind or inner world that lacks physical dimensions.

These definitional issues might seem somewhat esoteric to practitioners. After all, there would seem to be little debate about whether "pestering other students" or "sassing the teacher" on the part of a 10-year-old boy are really behaviors. If they were intervention targets, the practitioner would need to carefully consider how to define them, but anyone would agree that the boy's actions constitute behavior. The targets of ABA interventions are not always so obvious, however. Is "trying to do X" a behavior? How about "not doing X?" How would you define "choosing" or "making a choice?" Is "sharing" a behavior? How about "getting angry?" Considering the variety of behavioral challenges practitioners are called on to resolve, there are many targets whose behavioral status might be questioned. Sometimes the issue may be more about how the behavior should be defined or labeled than whether actual behavior is involved, but matters of definition and labeling cannot be properly understood without a clear conception of the nature of behavior as a physical phenomenon.

TOWARD A USEFUL DEFINITION OF BEHAVIOR

Defining Natural Phenomena

In considering the characteristics of behavior that differentiate it from other phenomena, it is important to remember the distinction is ours, not nature's. As scientists and practitioners, we create distinctions among natural phenomenon because they help us ask good questions, do good experiments, develop effective treatments, and make sense of the outcomes. For instance, although volcanic eruptions and geysers involve some of the same geologic processes, earth scientists find it useful to approach them as different kinds of natural phenomena. As we learn more about various aspects of nature, we revise our conceptions in whatever ways seem appropriate.

In thinking about how we might define behavior, it is helpful to remember that we are simply trying to identify and understand phenomena that share certain characteristics. We are trying to figure out what events might be usefully thought of as belonging in the same category and why other events, though somewhat similar, should not be placed in that category. Any definition is just our best guess at the time about the most useful way to organize our understanding of the world. A definition's usefulness is often a better criterion for evaluating it than its correctness. After all, it is hard to assess whether a definition is correct because we cannot know what we have not yet discovered about the defined phenomenon.

BOX 2.1

Inner "Causes"

B. F. Skinner (1953, Chapter 3) pointed out that in their early histories all sciences looked for causes of action inside the things they studied. The problem is not that inner causes cannot be true but that they are likely to be difficult to observe and study. That difficulty may encourage us to be casual in assigning properties to inner causes because it is easy to assume we are right, if only because it is difficult for someone to prove us wrong.

Skinner classified the most common inner "causes" of behavior into three categories. *Neural inner causes* use the nervous system as a convenient explanation without clear evidence of its actual role. Our colloquial language offers many such possibilities. We speak of a nervous breakdown or that our nerves are on edge as explanations for behaviors, but those are merely convenient, invented descriptions. Researchers and practitioners in the social sciences often show the same tendency to rely on neural causes that may be described with technical terminology but are nonetheless hypothetical.

Psychic inner causes lack the physical dimensions of neural causes, instead referencing features of the "mind" or an inner "personality." From that perspective, an inner person (sometimes called a homunculus) is often seen as initiating the action; the outer person executes it. The psychic agents might be called processes, faculties, traits, wills, impulses, wishes, instincts, emotions, and so forth. The trap lies in the ease with which they are assumed falsely to have the properties necessary to account for the behavior of interest.

The most common inner causes Skinner called *conceptual inner causes*, and they have neither neurological nor psychic dimensions. These include general qualities such as intelligence, abilities, talents, habits, and so on. Explanations in these terms do not really describe cause-effect relations but are just redundant descriptions of the same observed facts. If someone is often seen fighting, saying that he does so because he is aggressive does not explain why he often fights; it only restates that fact in other terms.

Behavior as Part of Biology

Distinguishing Behavior from Biology. Although it is important to focus on behavior as a subject matter in its own right, we must acknowledge that behavior is fundamentally a biological phenomenon. Behavior analysis is concerned with how behavior changes as a result of interactions between an organism and its environmental circumstances, but such changes unavoidably also involve changes in the organism's biology. Biological processes are the subject matter of other scientific specialties; nonetheless, they have important implications for behavior analysts.

Although behavior is part of biology, it has been useful for researchers to distinguish between those two aspects of living organisms. The challenge is determining where to draw the dividing line. It might seem easiest to stipulate that events that occur inside the skin should be designated as physiological and events that occur outside the skin should be called behavioral. However, that has long been recognized as an arbitrary and even misleading demarcation. It is particularly challenging to differentiate some physiological activities from some movements that go on inside the skin. Even though such movements may be very small and very brief, that does not mean that they should not be considered behavior. For example, Hefferline and Keenan (1963) showed operant control over invisibly small thumb twitch responses that were measured in microvolts of muscle contraction. Should they be considered behavior? What about the movement of various valves inside the body or the beating of the heart? What about the time required for a movement to occur? Although the duration of most overt responses can be measured in seconds or even minutes, some movements can occur in fractions of a second. Should they be considered instances of behavior?

And what about phenomena that seem to be behavioral in nature but involve no apparent movement? For example, our reactions to environmental stimuli such as visual or auditory events involve not only our sensory equipment but also behavioral components. In seeing a familiar stimulus such as a friend, we not only see with our eyes, we also learn the behavior of seeing. In fact, we get so good at this skill that we can "see" things such as our friend's face even when it is not present as an external stimulus. We may say that we are imagining our friend's face. Similarly, we learn to "hear" a tune in our head or "taste" a favorite food that we plan to have for dinner. There is no evident movement with behaviors like these, but they seem to be learned skills that are merely covert versions of what we do when the stimuli are public. Of course, there are neurological activities associated with sensory behaviors like seeing and hearing, but it may not be useful to talk about the underlying physiological processes as behavior. (See Johnston, 2014, Chapter 4 for further explanation of sensory behavior.)

The fact that we engage in **covert behavior** that involves no obvious movement suggests that the boundary between behavioral and biological events remains uncertain. Perhaps the best we can do is acknowledge that scientific definitions of a phenomenon are limited by what we do not know and are therefore always works in progress. Fortunately, questions like these do not arise very often among behavior analytic researchers and practitioners. The movements they typically label as behavior are easily identified and measured by relatively simple, noninvasive methods that often involve no more than visual observation.

> **Covert behavior.** Behavior that is similar to overt or public behavior but occurs at a reduced magnitude and is often detectable only by the behaving individual.

An Intraorganism Phenomenon. Another implication of the fact that behavior is a biological phenomenon is that it occurs only at the level of individual organisms – that is, behavior is an **intraorganism** phenomenon. Put another way, since behavior is a feature of an organism's biology, it can only be found by observing single organisms. That may seem obvious, but it conflicts with some popular cultural preconceptions. For instance, when two people interact in some way, the only behavior involved occurs separately for each person. If two people are playing a game of tennis, for example, there is nothing going on "between" them; the only behavioral events that can be detected are the separate actions of each person. Although each person's behavior is influenced by the actions of the other, that does not add any behavioral phenomenon to the situation. Each person's behavior is merely part of the other person's environment.

This point might be more difficult to accept in the case of two people having a conversation. Our everyday dialect implies that something emerges from two people talking with each other that is more than the sum of their individual behaviors. What is said to emerge is sometimes called "communication," as if there are not just two people saying things but an additional behavioral phenomenon that is the result of their interactions. That implication is easily evaluated by looking for the physical characteristics of the presumed emergent phenomenon of "communication." There are none to be found beyond the verbal behavior of each person, so there is no justification for referring to any additional phenomenon (see Johnston, 2014, Sept. 22 for more discussion of this point).

> **Intraorganism.** A reference to the individual organism as the level at which behavior occurs and can be studied, due to the fact that behavior depends on relations between the individual organism and its environment.

The fact that behavior can only occur separately for each individual means that references to **group behavior** are misleading. A group is not a biological organism and therefore cannot behave. When we talk about a group of individuals responding to some environmental event, it is the individuals in the group who are behaving, not the group as a whole. That is true even when the individuals are responding in a coordinated way, such as "doing the wave" at a football game. The intraorganism nature of behavior does not imply that individuals might not behave differently under social circumstances than they would if alone, however. For instance, people might do things as part of a mob they would not do if they were by themselves, but even in a mob it is still individuals who are doing the behaving. To put it simply, there is no physical phenomenon that should be described as group behavior.

> **Group behavior.** Often inferred from the result of combining the data from multiple individuals who may be related in some way (e.g., sharing exposure to an experimental condition or applied intervention or interacting in some way). Does not refer to a natural phenomenon distinct from the behavior of individual organisms.

It follows that if we wish to identify the effects of an experimental variable or clinical intervention on behavior, we must examine the behavior of individuals. Even though an intervention may have been implemented with all children in a classroom, for example, the intervention affects the behavior of each individual child. An important implication is that if individual data are summarized in a group average, the combined data will necessarily obscure the actual effects of the intervention for the different children. Those can only be seen by looking at the data for each child separately. Some children's data may show a substantial effect and others no effect at all. Figure 12.1 provides one illustration of how grouped data can hide differences in responding across individuals. This point will be discussed further in other chapters.

Relations with the Environment

Meaning of Environment. In behavior analysis, the term "environment" is defined in a specific but comprehensive way. **Environment** in this context refers to the totality of physical circumstances in which any behavior occurs. The term is comprehensive in that any physical events may be considered for their contribution to behavior. It is specific in that for any particular behavior, the focus is usually on only those environmental events that are functionally related to individual responses. That is, the environmental events that are usually most important are antecedent or consequent events related to a specific behavior in some way. In any case, the environment for any particular behavior is everything that is not part of the behavior itself.

> **Environment.** The physical circumstances in which the organism or referenced part of the organism exists. This includes any physical event or set of events that is not part of a behavior and may include other parts of the organism.

It is important to understand that the relevant environment is not restricted to events outside the skin. It may include any aspects of the organism that are not part of the behavior of interest. In fact, physiological events going on inside the skin are often related to particular behaviors in important ways. For instance, if you go out for a run on a hot summer afternoon, some of the stimuli related to how far and how fast you run involve your physiology. You may be aware of some of these stimuli (increasing discomfort in your leg muscles) while you may not be able to sense others (various changes in your biochemistry). As another example, when you scratch an itch, the stimulation from your skin is likely an establishing operation that increases the effectiveness of relief from the itching as a negative reinforcer and makes the behavior of scratching more likely. Our bodies are an ongoing source of antecedent and consequent environmental events related to responding. That fact again suggests that the skin is not an especially important boundary in defining and understanding behavior.

Functional Relations. In general, behavior has a hand-in-glove relationship with the environment and cannot occur without impacting it in some way. Sometimes these influences are obvious, but they are often subtle and easily missed. We have no problem recognizing behavior-environment interactions that are physically apparent or culturally important, such as making a pot of coffee or answering a phone call. We are less likely to notice that the act of reaching for our coffee cup involves both visual and proprioceptive consequences, or that when we stop reaching and start grasping it is influenced by both visual and tactile stimuli.

Of course, we understand quite a lot about the other side of the equation: how changes in the environment that result from responding in turn affect behavior. The scientific literature describing that relationship is extensive and well established (see Catania, 2013 for a comprehensive summary). It describes the reciprocal effects of interactions among behavioral and environmental events in impressive detail and is the foundation for ABA technology.

The relationships that are the key to understanding behavior as a phenomenon are functional or causal in nature. That is, behavior is a phenomenon that changes and is changed by interactions between organism and environment. Not all interactions between organism and environment affect behavior, however. For example, if an action can be fully explained by the laws of physics – in other words, if it does not require a live organism – it does not make sense to call it behavior. The **Dead Man's Test** (see Box 2.2) helps explain this point. For example, imagine an admittedly gruesome situation in which a person is killed and their dead body is then thrown down a flight of stairs. We might agree that the fact that the person was dead means that the movements involved in reaching the bottom of the stairs would not be considered behavior. Those movements are accounted for by gravity and the biomechanics of the human body. On the other hand, if you were to accidentally fall down some stairs, an observer might see you grab for the railing or raise your arms to protect your head. A dead person could not perform those actions, so by grabbing for the railing or raising your arms, you passed the Dead Man's Test.

> **Dead Man's Test.** An informal test of whether a particular event is a behavior. The test is that if a dead man can do it, it is not behavior.

The focus on functional relations between the behavior of living organisms and environment accommodates both behaviors that consist of easily discernable movement and behaviors for which no movement is apparent. It is easy to propose that clearly observable actions – even small ones – are behaviors. The challenge for a definition of behavior is how it handles things organism do that are not readily observable. We refer to these behaviors as covert, and they seem like private versions of otherwise public behavior. We have already mentioned the sensory behavior of "seeing" or "hearing" events that are not present. Thinking also seems to fall in this category (see Box 2.3). Although it may be argued that thinking involves a continuum of actions that range from more or

---

BOX 2.2

The Dead Man's Test

Ogden Lindsley was a behavior analyst – one of Skinner's students – at the University of Kansas who devoted much of his career to helping teachers use behavioral principles in the classroom. He developed an approach that he called **Precision Teaching** because of the central role it gives to precisely measuring student behavior and displaying the data on standardized graphs. Among the many ideas he developed to help teachers learn this technology is the Dead Man's Test, which is a rule for making sure that teachers target only actual behavior. The rule is quite simple: *If a dead man can do it, it isn't behavior.*

---

less public to fully private, at the covert extreme no movements are evident, even to the person doing the thinking. Otherwise thinking seems just like more physically obvious behavior. B. F. Skinner was always clear in his position that thinking should be considered behavior (see Moore, 2008, Chapter 10). The environmental events that might be functionally related to that behavior can be public or private. For example, others may say something to us, or we may "talk" with ourselves covertly and thereby generate both responses and consequences. In that case, we are functioning as both speaker and listener in Skinner's analysis. It is thus a key feature of radical behaviorism, the field's philosophy of science, that our definition of behavior is not limited to publicly accessible movements.

Fortunately, the behaviors of interest to researchers and practitioners are usually easily observable, at least in principle. Behavior analysts are accustomed to measuring a wide variety of behaviors that can be described in terms of specific or general actions. The responses of interest may involve gross motor activity (a study participant touching a stimulus on a computer screen; an individual with an intellectual disability doing his laundry in a group home) or more subtle actions (a study participant looking at an array of stimuli; a child sitting quietly at a desk in a classroom). Under such conditions, it is possible to engage in activities that allow us to identify functional relations between behavior and environment.

Behavior as Interface. The distinction between passing or failing the Dead Man's Test hinges on the fact that behavior involves some form of interaction between the organism and the environment. Consider the recently deceased person thrown down a flight of stairs. On the way down, the environment will affect the movement of arms and legs. It would go too far, however, to describe that movement as an interaction between organism and environment because in this case the relationship is strictly one-sided. The environment has its effects, but what is missing is any contribution from the individual. The point is not just that behavior requires a live organism. The two-way relationship – the impact of behavior on environment and the reciprocal impact of the changed

---

BOX 2.3

Thinking Is Behaving Too

Although behavior analysts are usually interested in behavior that involves easily detectable actions, the definition of behavior does not require explicit movement. It accommodates any muscular or neural features of the organism that are functionally related to the environment. An important example of behavior that does not involve apparent movement is thinking. Led by Skinner's arguments (see Moore, 2008, Chapter 10), behavior analysts have always viewed thinking as behaving. In fact, the inclusion of thinking and other private events in the definition of behavior distinguishes Skinner's radical behaviorism from earlier forms of behaviorism.

Accommodating various forms of thinking into our conception of behavior gets a bit complicated. Moore (2008, Chapters 4 and 10) does a good job of presenting the issues. It helps to appreciate that thinking involves more behavioral variety than might be suspected. Putting everyday dialect aside, it may be best considered as lying on an overt-covert continuum, ranging from thinking out loud to thinking privately – a perspective that has been borne out by research (Schlinger, 2008). At its most private, thinking presents obvious problems of measurement, but the fact that it occurs inside the skin is not a barrier to including it with more easily detected aspects of behavior. The key is that such behaviors participate in functional relations with the environment.

Defining behavior in a way that does not require movement leads us to the ragged edges of our understanding of behavior distinct from physiological processes. After all, research has shown that many aspects of physiological functioning are functionally related to features of the environment. Any movement involved in physiological processes may be trivial, but does that mean all such events could be considered behavioral in some sense? The location of the boundary between behavior and other aspects of biology is a fascinating topic, but the inevitable uncertainties need not restrain the interests of most behavior analytic researchers, and certainly not practitioners.

Perhaps the most important guidance offered by a definition of behavior lies in helping us avoid accepting invented or fictional possibilities as behavior. That is an especially risky trap because everyday dialect is full of references to qualities of human (and nonhuman) nature that are assumed to be somewhat like behavior. Although these supposed qualities lack obvious physical dimensions and are typically said to "exist" somewhere inside (for example, in the mind), it is tempting to assign them some sort of behavioral status. The behavioral character of thinking, on the other hand, is relatively obvious because of its continuity with overt verbal behavior.

---

environment on behavior – means that behavior is the biological result of the interaction between an organism and its environment. Another way to put it is that behavior is not a part of the organism; it is part of the interface between the organism and its environment.

One of the implications of this perspective is that it is not useful to think of behavior as a property or attribute of the organism. Behavior is not something an organism possesses. A particular behavior is not stored somewhere waiting to be called forth; rather, it exists only when there is a certain interactive condition between an organism and its surroundings. This conceptualization suggests that physiological "states" of the organism should not be viewed as behavior. It means, for example, that "being hungry" is not behavior, because it does not involve meaningful interactions between the organism and the environment. Hunger and other physiological states are real biological conditions, but they involve no active relationship between the organism and the environment. Although the physiological events we label as hunger depend on environmental factors (a period of food deprivation), the physiological condition itself is not a behavior, because it is not an action that changes the environment and is in turn changed by the environment – an interaction. Most behavior-environment interactions produce physiological changes, but it is not helpful to routinely refer to those changes as behavior.

In a similar sense, conditions or changes in the environment that do not involve interactions with behavior are not occurrences of behavior. For example, someone walking in the rain gets wet, but "getting wet" is not a behavior. A child may receive tokens for correctly working out math problems, but "receiving tokens" is not a behavior. Both examples fail the Dead Man's Test because there is no interaction between actions and the environment. This distinction is more than just a matter of how we label and measure behaviors. It is essential for selecting targets that enable us to design interventions to produce meaningful effects. For instance, it would not be too difficult to measure "getting wet," but if the practical objective were to change "getting wet," what would you do? The intervention contingencies would have to focus on actions like reading the weather forecast or carrying an umbrella rather than on "getting wet," which does not involve a specific action.

Impact on the Environment. Another implication of defining behavior in terms of interactions with the environment is that it is impossible for a behavior not to influence the environment in some way. In fact, behavior analysts typically measure behavior by measuring its effects on the environment. That is, when a researcher or practitioner measures responses, they are actually measuring some environmental effects of those responses. Often the impact of a response is easy to detect. For instance, a laboratory researcher measures a pigeon's key pecking by recording the displacement of the key. A practitioner measures an individual's progress in learning to make change by counting the coins a learner hands to the trainer on each trial following the trainer's instruction.

In many applied settings, the environmental impacts of a behavior are often inferred from the effect it produces on the behavior of other people who record something about what they observe (see Chapter 6). That is a perfectly acceptable approach to measurement as long as two conditions are met. First, changes in the measuring "instrument" – the observer – must not be the only evidence of the existence of the behavior. If there is truly no evidence that the behavior exists apart from the measurement process, it is probably not really a behavior. Consider this example: Is "expecting" to do well on a test a behavior?

BOX 2.4

Traits and Colloquial Language

Thousands of terms in the English language refer to enduring or temporary qualities of human behavior. In discussing the issues they raise for a science of behavior, B. F. Skinner (1953) provided an example of familiar traits using just those starting with the letter "h."

> There was a remarkable change in his behavior. Where he had been *happy-go-lucky*, he grew *hesitant* and *heavy-handed*. His natural *humility* gave way to a sustained *haughtiness*. Once the most *helpful* of men, he became *heedless* and *hard-hearted*. A sort of *histrionic horseplay* was all that remained of his fine sense of *humor*. (pp. 194–195)

In everyday dialect, we use traits as summary references to an individual's behavioral tendencies or characteristics. It would be awkward and time-consuming to describe the behavioral details of many different samples of a person's behavior, so we just summarize our observations. These summaries usually work fairly well for conversational purposes, but they fall well short of the precision required by scientists and practitioners.

A more serious problem lies in our tendency to go further than referencing traits as summaries of behavior by implying that they are causes of the same behavior we are summarizing. We do this, for example, when explaining Jennifer's sunny disposition by saying it's because she is a happy person. As Skinner observed, there is only one set of behavioral facts involved (observations of the person smiling, laughing, etc.). If we are going to summarize those facts about Jennifer in terms of a trait, using the same facts to explain the trait contributes nothing to our understanding of why she behaves in this manner. In order to understand the causes of Jennifer's behavior, we would have to know about the environmental factors in her history that made such behavior likely and the environmental conditions under which the behavior occurs now. The colloquial conception of behavior, however, assumes that traits are somehow inherent qualities of each individual's personality. (See Johnston, 2015, Chapter 3 for additional discussion.)

What is the evidence for the existence of a behavior we might call "expecting?" Because there is no evident movement involved, the evidence that might be offered would be some kind of verbal report, such as the person's responses on a set of questionnaire items combined into a "measure of expectation." In this case, the only basis for talking about "expecting" as a behavior would be the score on the questionnaire, which partly represents the behavior of the person who designed the instrument. It would be more accurate to refer to the behavior of the individual who responded to the questions as "filling out the questionnaire." It is certainly not useful to call such behavior "expecting."

Second, it is important that all behaviors are described or labeled in terms of the organism-environment interaction. To illustrate, consider describing the act of helping someone pick up a heavy object as "cooperativeness" or "being

---

BOX 2.5

Parsimony

Even though it is not often discussed, *parsimony* is one of the most respected attitudes of science. In a word, it means to be stingy. Scientists are parsimonious in their preference for exhausting simple and well-established explanations of phenomena before turning to complex and less well-understood explanations. A parsimonious perspective urges us to explain the observable facts of behavior with reference to physical variables, which the natural sciences understand pretty well, before inventing a nonphysical world of the psyche, which certainly goes beyond the laws of nature.

Scientists follow this strategy because they have learned over the years that it makes science more efficient. It helps them avoid wild goose chases and blind alleys, which are always a risk in scientific research. Instead of offering fanciful explanations of some event, scientists cautiously insist on trying to explain the event in terms of research findings that they already understand fairly well because the odds of successful resolution are usually better than with more "far out" notions.

A parsimonious attitude may be even more important for ABA practitioners (who work at the interface between the science and the culture) than it is for researchers. Practitioners are on the front lines every day trying to sell the fruits of scientific discovery in the form of problem-solving behavioral technology. They must confront the full range of non-scientific conceptions of behavior as well as countless explanations that lack even a shred of scientific support. Grounded by their professional training, practitioners can benefit society by encouraging others to share their parsimonious perspective on answering questions about behavior.

---

cooperative." Is "being cooperative" a behavior? If it is, what are the actions and their effects on the environment? If the latter question is answered by referring to the act of "picking up a box," it could be argued that "picking up a box" would be a more descriptive label than "being cooperative." "Cooperating" might be adequate as an informal label, but it is not useful for investigating or intervening. After all, in everyday language, a wide variety of behaviors occurring under a wide variety of circumstances might be described as "being cooperative." If all such instances were described with that single label, however, it would be difficult to learn about the different behaviors and environmental events involved in each circumstance. That problem is avoided when we relate particular types of actions to specific environmental circumstances.

A WORKING DEFINITION OF BEHAVIOR

An Interim Guide

As we noted earlier, in drafting a definition of behavior we are guessing about the fundamental nature and extent of a natural phenomenon. It is necessarily a guess because we can never be certain about any characteristics and limits that may lie beyond our present understanding. Furthermore, a definition of behavior is itself only a bit of verbal behavior, and the phenomenon might not exactly match the knowledge and assumptions reflected in the definition. It is important to remember that the task of behavioral scientists is to discover through experimentation the features of behavior and how they relate to other natural phenomena, not to try to force nature to fit our preconceptions.

This perspective suggests that any definition is only an interim guide to help researchers and practitioners do their jobs. The value of a definition of behavior lies in the extent to which it helps researchers ask good experimental questions, design measurement procedures, and evaluate the impact of experimental variables. For practitioners, a definition of behavior is especially important for deciding how to select, define, and measure target behaviors that affect the everyday lives of their clients. As upcoming chapters will show, how we define behavior also directs us toward or away from certain methodological practices.

A Definition of Behavior

The following definition of behavior identifies the features that are essential for behavior analytic researchers and practitioners:

Behavior is an organism's interaction with its environment that involves functional relations between biological features of the organism and the environment.

Consider the parts of this definition in light of the issues discussed in the previous section. First, the wording makes clear that behavior is biological in nature by limiting it to the biological features of organisms. So, for example, references to the "behavior" of the stock market clearly do not meet the requirements of this definition. Any implication that the aggregate buying and selling of stocks involves something more than the behavior of individual investors or fund managers misunderstands the nature of behavior as a biological phenomenon.

Second, the definition identifies behavior as an interaction between organism and environment. This focus avoids implying that behavior is a possession of the organism and highlights the requirement for an interactive condition. In other words, the definition identifies behavior as the result of an interactive condition between organism and environment. It is part of the interface between organism and environment.

Third, the definition specifies that behavior involves causal relations between the biological elements of the organism – muscular or neural – and the environment. The requirement for functional relations means that the definition includes actions that others can see as well as covert responses that are directly observable only by the behaving individual.

Finally, it is important to understand that this definition of behavior does no more than circumscribe the limits of behavior as a natural phenomenon for the purpose of scientific study and delivery of behavior analytic services. In other words, this is a "working" definition. It should serve as background for decisions that are called for in planning research projects or clinical interventions. Researchers must decide what aspects of behavior are appropriate for different experimental questions, for example. Why would one behavior be more likely to reveal the effects of experimental variables than another? The interests of practitioners in one behavior or another may sometimes be forced on them by the presenting problem, but there are still choices that must be made about how to define particular behaviors and why some ways of conceptualizing a target behavior may be more useful than others. For instance, imagine that a second-grade teacher asks a behavior analyst to develop an intervention for a student whom the teacher describes as being "off task" too often when he is supposed to be doing seat work. To even begin to assess the problem, the behavior analyst must choose the actions and environmental circumstances on which to focus. Among other questions, she should ask whether better targets for intervention are likely to be behaviors that the teacher characterizes as "off task" or the behaviors required to perform the tasks the student is being assigned. The behavior analyst must also ask what effects the student's behavior has on the environment. Chapter 4 addresses ways of crafting specific definitions that will be used to measure target behavior.

A FEW IMPLICATIONS

Inclusions and Exclusions

The task for any definition is distinguishing what belongs inside its boundaries from what belongs outside of them. Although at first our definition of behavior might seem narrow, it is actually broadly inclusive. Any biological features of an organism that are functionally related to the environment fit its basic requirements. That includes a truly infinite array of behaviors, both overt and covert. In fact, making up a comprehensive list of behaviors would be impossible if only because we could not come up with enough different labels to accommodate all of the different behaviors we could identify.

Although discussing the inclusiveness of the definition is almost pointless, perhaps examining its exclusions will help clarify its usefulness. The definition denies behavioral status to all of the following:

1. Events that do not involve a live organism.
2. Events that do not involve the physical environment.
3. Events that do not involve an interactive condition between organism and environment.
4. Events for which the sole evidence is their effect on a measuring instrument.

These exclusions suggest that anything that does not involve functional relations between a live organism's interactions with the physical environment is probably not usefully called behavior. If this is a good definition for guiding scientific research and clinical practice, its requirements should exclude only events that are more usefully described in other ways, as well as "events" that are fictional and do not exist.

It is worth noting that the list does not exclude events for which there is no discernible movement. This is an important refinement of the definition proposed in the previous edition of this text (Johnston & Pennypacker, 2009, Chapter 2). Although behavior analytic researchers and practitioners are usually interested in behavior that involves obvious movement, we do not want to imply that phenomena that seem similar to other behavior but can only be detected by the behaving individual are fundamentally different from publicly accessible behavior. Recall that the previous discussion of this issue used thinking and sensory behavior like seeing and hearing as examples of covert human activity that seem to share all of the definition's features.

BOX 2.6

Where Should We Draw the Line?

The inclusiveness of this definition requires a cautionary question: Where should the line between behavior and physiology be drawn? Defining behavior to include not just biological features that involve movement but also those for which movement is not evident leaves that question unanswered. As the text notes, however, that approach is valuable because it accommodates covert behavior (such as thinking) and sensory behavior (such as seeing and hearing) that seem to share the same general features as overt behavior. That breadth must be considered in light of the fact that modern technology enables researchers to measure changes in almost any facet of physiology, including biochemical and electrical activity in the brain. If it can be shown that some of those phenomena are functionally related to environmental stimuli, does it mean that all such brain activity should be considered behavior?

We have to be especially careful of our technical dialect in answering this question. For example, researchers who use brain imaging technologies often propose that what those technologies measure reflects or even constitutes mental qualities, which are often labeled with everyday terms such as anticipating, wanting, remembering, and so on. Those measures, however, do no more than quantify biochemical or electrical features of brain activity, so they may not satisfy the requirement that changes in the measuring instrument must not be the only evidence of the existence of the "behavior." Merely labeling a physiological process with a term that suggests that it represents or constitutes a mental quality does not make it so. We must ask about the independent evidence for such qualities. Theories and interpretations of measures of brain activity that rely on the vagaries of everyday dialect fall short of supplying that evidence.

This inclusive approach to a definition of behavior is not without its risks, however. For example, in considering whether cognitive "activities" meet the requirements of our definition, it is important to ask whether such activities have physical features, regardless of how difficult they might be to observe and measure. If it is said that a person is "anticipating" a road trip with friends, for instance, it is fair to ask if "anticipating" is a physical event. Just because we have learned to talk about anticipating does not mean there is such a real phenomenon. Failure to meet the terms of our definition certainly does not mean that there is no physical phenomenon to be referenced, but how are we to know if it exists? How can we know what anticipating is and how it is different from physiological events in the brain?

Although neuroscientists can now directly measure some types of brain activity when a person is engaging in some task, it is dangerous to assume that electrical or biochemical activities reflect specific cognitive qualities or processes (Faux, 2002; Uttal, 2011). Without physical evidence apart from measures produced by neuroimaging technologies, researchers who study phenomena that might be called cognitive or mental face the most difficult of scientific challenges: studying events whose very existence is unclear. In addition to the problem of measurement, practitioners who focus on such activities face challenges in arranging environmental contingencies that might change them. Proposing that an observable behavior can serve as a substitute for a mental event might seem to be a solution, but it raises the question of how one can know that the behavior is perfectly correlated with events that cannot be directly detected (Johnston, 2015, Jan. 12).

Challenges like these result from the fact that the dialect of psychology and the other social sciences is burdened with cultural preconceptions about human nature. Perhaps not surprisingly, a conception of behavior based on sound scientific findings fails to accommodate many of them. As a result, some readers may feel that the working definition proposed here leaves no place for cherished human qualities. It may help to consider that those omissions are only a matter of the difference between how we have learned to talk about behavior and what is really there.

For instance, when we speak of someone as having a particular attitude, the unspoken implication is that attitudes exist as physical things. The fallacy in that assumption can be uncovered by considering what leads us to describe someone as having a certain attitude. In fact, it is observing the person emitting certain behaviors under certain conditions that encourages us to use the attitudinal terms we have been taught by our verbal community. At best, descriptors of attitudes are only crude ways of summarizing many instances of behavior. They may be convenient for everyday conversation, but they are not useful for researchers or practitioners, because they lead to scientific and practical dead ends.

The problem, then, is not that the definition of behavior leaves out real aspects of human nature but that the culture has invented so many fictional qualities in the first place. It is only the everyday language we use to talk about behavior that implies that these qualities actually exist inside of us, if only in a

BOX 2.7

Theory, Concepts, and Observability

It is important to understand that the main problem faced by cognitive and social scientists is not that the focus of their interests seems to be unobservable. Many phenomena of scientific interest are not directly observable but that has not proven to be a serious stumbling block in the development of the natural sciences. The problem, at least in part, is with explanatory concepts that are based on unobservables located inside the organism (Lee, 1981). To understand this problem, it is necessary to consider the nature of scientific theory.

Skinner (1961) identified three stages of theory building. The first stage involves identifying the basic data. That has proven a considerable challenge for psychology, while behavior analysts long ago decided that behavior would be a sufficient source. The second stage focuses on expressing relations among the data. That effort culminates in well-established laws or summaries of consistent relations. The science of behavior analysis has made considerable headway on this task due to its focus on interactions among behavior and environmental events. The third stage goes beyond observable relations to unobservable concepts. For instance, Galileo studied the relation between the position of a ball on an inclined plane and the elapsed time since its release and developed the unobservable concept of acceleration. He did not, however, attribute acceleration to a force inherent in the ball. Skinner (1961) emphasized the importance of this stage by pointing out that terms like wants, faculties, attitudes, drives, ideas, interests and capacities should be developed as proper scientific concepts at this level.

In other words, theories are built on concepts that refer to unobservable features of the observable subject matter. Those unobservable concepts must not be simply invented, however. In order for a theory to work, it must emerge from a sound database describing functional relations in the subject matter. Ultimately, explanation in the natural sciences is made in terms of such theories (Lee, 1981).

mental sense. In fact, researchers who attempt to study mental activity measure either behavior (including responding to tests of some kind) or physiological events because that is all there is to measure. They are then forced to infer some relationship between their measures of these physical phenomena and the mental "events" of interest. The resulting subject matter is therefore a collection of these kinds of culturally based assumptions. That sets psychology and the other social sciences apart from natural sciences that investigate phenomena whose existence is the basis for, rather than the result of, experimental inquiry. (See Johnston, 2014, Sept. 22.)

Learning to talk about behavior, especially human behavior, without using familiar everyday terms is difficult at first. The correct terms seem awkward and insufficient, and something often seems left out. The richness with which we talk about behavior in ordinary language is clearly missing. Learning a science-based technical dialect about behavior is unavoidably difficult, given that we have had a lifetime of instruction from our verbal community that is

BOX 2.8

Pure versus Quasi-behavioral Research

The ways investigators approach behavior as a scientific subject matter allow a distinction between pure behavioral research and quasi-behavioral research (Johnston & Pennypacker, 1993b). **Pure behavioral research** uses methodological practices that preserve the fundamental qualities of behavior in undisturbed and uncontaminated form. Studies are designed to learn about the effects of environmental variables on behavior at the level of the individual. **Quasi-behavioral research** is based on data that originated with observations of behavior but whose methods prevent the data from representing the fundamental qualities of behavior fully and without distortion or contamination. Studies may permit data from multiple individuals to be aggregated and used to learn about behavior in a more superficial or informal sense.

For example, in a study analyzing the behavioral effects of a classroom management procedure, interest may lie not just in identifying the main effects but in understanding the reasons those effects occur. Such corollary questions might concern the role of different components of the intervention, whether student characteristics are relevant to the effects, and the key factors that will ensure that the procedure yields consistent effects. Addressing those questions would require measuring and analyzing the behavior of individual students, which is where the intervention's effects actually occur.

On the other hand, the interests of investigators or practitioners might be limited to a statistical description of the average outcomes of the classroom procedure. In that case, collating data across students might be quite permissible. That would, however, prevent discovery of a clear answer to analytical questions about what is happening at the level of the individual student. Using behavioral data to answer questions about aggregate outcomes can be quite legitimate, but it is not appropriate to suggest that the grouped data represent the effects on each individual or to argue that the study identified the reasons for the overall outcome.

Choosing one kind of behavioral interest over the other should be done at the outset based on the focus of the question. However, the distinction between pure and quasi-behavioral approaches often results unintentionally from the experimenter's methodological decisions. A study aimed at discovering behavior-environment relations can be made quasi-behavioral by incorporating methodological practices that prevent a clear picture of the fundamental qualities of behavior.

The challenges lie in figuring out when each type of question about behavior is appropriate and being willing to live within the interpretive constraints required by the way the project is conducted. This text focuses on pure behavioral research interests, whether the study is basic or applied in focus. In doing so, it highlights the limitations of some tactics (such as aggregating data across individuals) that might be acceptable in studies aimed at quasi-behavioral interests.

The distinction between pure and quasi-behavioral research is especially important for practitioners who are consumers of the applied research literature. They must understand what methodological practices allow what kinds of conclusions. For example, a study that presents only grouped data does not permit conclusions about the effects of an intervention on individual participants. The overall outcomes could represent especially strong effects for a few individuals but much weaker effects – or no effects at all – for most participants.

chock-full of prescientific conceptions. Unfortunately, the colloquial parlance that seems to work reasonably well on an everyday basis conflicts with the need for a precise scientific vocabulary that is limited to real events and devoid of surplus meaning. With a scientific language that follows rather than leads discovery, behavior analysts are uncovering the kind of richness and complexity that scientists long ago revealed in other natural phenomena.

Methodological Consequences

As the chapters in this book unfold, it will become clear that the primary importance of the definition of behavior lies in how it guides the work of researchers and practitioners. Almost every facet of the methods described in this book is partly based on the implications of the definition. Its suggestions emerge from what our science has already learned about behavior. We know, for example, that behavior occurs only at the level of individuals, that it has effects on the environment and is in turn affected by the environment, that it is a continuous process, and that what has happened with a particular behavior in the past continues to influence it in the present. Of course, these are only a few basic facts about behavior. Over the years, the accumulating research literature has revealed a wealth of general principles and complex details (see Catania, 2013).

When we look to our understanding of behavior for guidance about the best ways to study and manage it, a number of methodological practices seem important. For instance, in order to capture all of the fundamental qualities of behavior, we need to measure the behavior of each individual separately. Furthermore, we need to keep each individual's data separate as we analyze them. As we have already suggested, combining observations of different participants into group averages makes it difficult to see any differences in how experimental variables or interventions affected the behavior of each individual – the actual behavioral outcomes.

What we know about behavior also suggests that it is important to measure a target behavior a number of times under each phase of an experiment or practical intervention. Any behavior is influenced by its continuously evolving history, and the more recent the history, the greater its impact. This means that we can get a clear picture of the effects of any particular environmental condition only if we give each participant enough exposure to that condition to be sure that the changes in the target behavior are due primarily to that condition and not to prior experiences.

The following chapters will explain these and many other methodological practices that have proven to be highly effective for behavior analytic researchers and practitioners. For researchers, the "bottom line" is that nature's secrets will be revealed only when we ask the right questions in the right way. For practitioners, the "bottom line" is that a clear picture of the outcomes of intervention procedures will only emerge when we measure and evaluate behavior change with the right procedures. We cannot force nature to fit our preconceptions and methods. Those who work with behavior – whether their interests lie in experimental discovery or practical management – must adapt the general principles of scientific method that have worked so well with other sciences and their technologies to suit the features of behavior as a subject matter.

CHAPTER SUMMARY

1. As the field continues to evolve, it is essential that behavior analytic researchers and applied behavior analysis practitioners hold a shared understanding of the features and limitations of behavior as a natural phenomenon. This may be easier said than done.

2. In thinking about how we might define behavior, it is helpful to remember that we are simply trying to identify and understand phenomena that share certain behaviors. Any definition is just our best guess at the time about the most useful way to organize our understanding of the world.

3. Behavior is fundamentally a biological phenomenon. Although behavior is part of biology, it has been useful for researchers to distinguish between those two aspects of living organisms.

4. Behavior is an intraorganism phenomenon and therefore must be studied at the level of the individual. One implication of this involves examining individual data that are summarized in a group average – the combined data will necessarily obscure the actual effects of the intervention for the different individuals in the group.

5. The environment for any particular behavior is everything that is not part of the behavior itself and is not restricted to events outside of the skin.

6. The relationships that are key to understanding behavior as a phenomenon are functional in nature. Behavior is a phenomenon that changes and is changed by interactions between an organism and its environment. The environmental events that might be functionally related to that behavior can be overt or covert.

7. Behavior is the biological result of the interaction between an organism and its environment, and therefore is not something an organism possesses. The behavior exists only when there is a specific interactive condition between an organism and its surroundings.

8. The value of a definition of behavior lies in the extent to which it helps guide the work of researchers and practitioners.

9. A good brief definition of behavior is an organism's interaction with its environment that involves functional relations between biological features of the organism and the environment.

10. Anything that does not involve functional relations between a live organism's interactions with the physical environment is probably not usefully called behavior.

11. Those who work with behavior – whether a researcher or a practitioner – must adapt the general principles of the scientific method that have worked so well with other sciences and their technologies to suit the features of behavior as a subject matter.

HIGHLIGHTED TERMS

Covert behavior. Behavior that is similar to overt or public behavior but occurs at a reduced magnitude and is often detectable only by the behaving individual.

Dead Man's Test. An informal test of whether a particular event is a behavior. The test is that if a dead man can do it, it is not behavior.

Environment. The physical circumstances in which the organism or referenced part of the organism exists. This includes any physical event or set of events that is not part of a behavior and may include other parts of the organism.

Group behavior. Often inferred from the result of combining the data from multiple individuals who may be related in some way (e.g., sharing exposure to an experimental condition or applied intervention or interacting in some way). Does not refer to a natural phenomenon distinct from the behavior of individual organisms.

Intraorganism. A reference to the individual organism as the level at which behavior occurs and can be studied, due to the fact that behavior depends on relations between the individual organism and its environment.

Mentalism. Attributing the causes of behavior to events and processes said to occur in a mind or inner world that lacks physical dimensions.

Radical behaviorism. The philosophy of science of behavior analysis, which focuses on behavior as a physical phenomenon and avoids mentalism in all forms.

TEXT STUDY GUIDE

1. Why is it important that researchers and practitioners hold a shared understanding of the features and limitations of behavior as a natural phenomenon?
2. Why may it be difficult to agree on a shared definition of behavior?
3. According to the authors, what determines a definition's usefulness?
4. Why is the skin not a good basis for distinguishing between biology and behavior?
5. What is a covert behavior? Provide an example.
6. What does it mean to say that behavior is an intraorganism phenomenon?
7. What is group behavior?

8. Describe what it means when there is a functional relationship between the behavior of a living organism and its environment.

9. Describe the Dead Man's Test.

10. What are some examples of "behaviors" that do not pass the Dead Man's Test?

11. "Behavior is the biological result of the interaction between an organism and its environment." Why does this suggest that behavior is not a property, attribute or possession of the organism?

12. Why is it that real or hypothetical states cannot be behavior?

13. Why is "waiting for someone" not a behavior?

14. Can you think of an example of a behavior that does not affect the environment in some way? If you can, are you sure it meets the requirements of the definition of behavior?

15. What would be the problem if the only evidence for the existence of a supposed behavior was the product of the measurement process?

16. What does it mean to say that there must be some independent evidence of the existence of a behavior?

17. Why is "aggression" or "being aggressive" not usefully referred to as a behavior?

18. Explain how an individual can be part of the environment for his or her own behavior.

19. What is the value of having a definition of behavior?

20. What are three key implications of the definition of behavior provided by the authors?

21. Why could researchers not develop a comprehensive catalog of all human behaviors?

22. Write a good one-sentence summary of the exclusions implied by the definition of behavior.

23. How does the authors' definition of behavior address events for which there is no discernible movement?

24. Describe the influence of cultural language on how we talk about and explain behavior.

25. What is the "bottom line" for researchers and practitioners? How are they impacted by how we define behavior?

BOX STUDY GUIDE

1. Describe the three categories of "inner causes" discussed by Skinner and what is wrong with referring to them when attempting to explain behavior.

2. What is the Dead Man's Test?

3. How do behavior analysts address "thinking"?

4. Describe two reasons traits are not useful concepts for a science of behavior.
5. Describe the scientific attitude of parsimony and why it is important for ABA practitioners.
6. What are the three stages of theory building Skinner described?
7. Distinguish between pure and quasi-behavioral research.
8. What are the limitations of quasi-behavioral research?

SUGGESTED READINGS

Johnston, J. M. (2014). *Radical behaviorism for ABA practitioners*. Cornwall-on-Hudson, NY: Sloan Publishing. Chapter 1. An unavoidable (but reasonable) assumption.
Moore, J. (2008). *Conceptual foundations of radical behaviorism*. Cornwall-on-Hudson, NY: Sloan Publishing. Chapter 4. Behavior as a subject matter in its own right.

DISCUSSION TOPICS

1. Consider phenomena at the boundary between behavior and biology, such as heart beating, burping, etc. Discuss the pros and cons of considering these as behavioral or biological events.
2. Discuss how to study the actual behaviors involved in what might generally be talked about as group phenomena, such as doing the wave at a football game, three friends loading a sofa onto a pickup truck, a riot, etc.
3. Discuss the list of exclusions resulting from the definition of behavior. Is there anything else the definition seems to exclude? If so, consider why these exclusions might not actually be behavioral events.

EXERCISES

1. Come up with examples of what might usually be referred to as behavior but would not pass the Dead Man's Test.
2. Choose some examples of everyday behaviors that we do not pay much attention to and figure out their specific effects on the environment.
3. Are the results of an fMRI indicative of specific covert behaviors? Form two groups of students for a brief debate. One group of students must argue that the results are representative of covert behavior(s); the second group must argue that the results do not represent behavior.

CHAPTER THREE

Asking Questions: What Do You Want To Know?

LEADING QUESTIONS

First Horse, Then Cart

The process of discovering things you want to know begins with figuring out exactly what questions you are trying to answer. That might seem obvious, but working out the details of the questions motivating a project often seems to be given short shrift compared to the effort put into developing measurement procedures or planning a sequence of intervention phases. The fact that a researcher or practitioner is contemplating a project of some sort means that he or she is already curious about something, or is faced with helping a client solve a problem. It is easy to assume that the "something" is sufficiently clear to turn to the meat and potatoes of methods – measurement and designing the conditions that will be compared. But compared to what end? What conclusions will satisfy the curiosity or the practical demand that is driving the effort? Will the methods and the data that are generated justify those conclusions? If they do not, will the mismatch between questions, methods, data, and interpretations be identified? After all, just because a project has taken a lot of time and effort does not automatically legitimize the conclusions that might have been preferred at the outset. As discussed in other chapters, convincing nature to share its secrets is an uncompromising game. If you fail to play by the rules, your convictions about what you think you have learned may not match nature's reality – and it is nature's reality that counts.

As this chapter will show, understanding where you want to wind up is a prerequisite to making the decisions that will get you there. The curiosity or practical need that gets you started is just as much a key feature of methods as measurement or experimental design or data analysis. Basing decisions about methodological details on a question that has not been thought through can make it difficult to collect meaningful data or be confident about whether those data answer the question. For example, choosing inappropriate measurement procedures can result in data that fail to reveal what you need to know about how a target behavior changes from one condition to another. Similarly, comparing responding under an initial baseline condition to a subsequent treatment condition may tell you something, but by itself that one comparison should not be enough to make you confident that you understand why responding changed or whether you can depend on getting that outcome every time.

Figuring out the right question or questions that should guide methodological decisions requires a careful consideration of possible options. In this process, it helps to understand the circumstances that might be encouraging possible questions, in part because those circumstances may also encourage certain conclusions once all is done. In fact, it can be useful to begin thinking about questions by working backwards: What kind of conclusions would you like to draw when you are analyzing the data? This "starting from where you want to wind up" approach does not mean that you should set up a project to "prove" what you think you already know. The reason for conducting a research or clinical project is to discover things that you may or may not know, even if some of them are surprising or even contrary to your suspicions or preferences. Figuring out what you want to learn by working backwards is a way to make sure you design measurement procedures and arrange baseline treatment comparisons that will not leave you frustrated when the project is done because the outcomes are not clear and convincing.

Consider the following: Wanting to know whether an intervention package is effective in meeting clinical objectives is quite different from wanting to know the relative contribution of the components of the package (some may have been necessary while others had no benefits). Being interested in documenting a reduction in tantrumming behavior is different from wanting to know to what extent the decrease was the result of fewer tantrums or shorter episodes. An interest in whether the effectiveness of an intervention procedure depends on client characteristics such as the level of verbal skills is different from wanting to evaluate the way intervention procedures were implemented. These are only a few of the kinds of conclusions that might be of interest to researchers and practitioners. Each should lead back to how particular questions might best be expressed to guide wise decisions about how behavior is measured, what conditions should be evaluated and compared, and how the data should be analyzed.

Questions as Verbal Behavior

Before considering where questions might come from and what functions they might serve, it is important to understand that research questions are verbal behavior. This means that investigators do not "create" experimental or clinical questions any more than they "create" other behavior such as eating, driving a car, or watching a football game. Questions are emitted under the influence of our verbal history and current circumstances, and it is useful to analyze them in that general context.

Framing research or clinical questions is not the only behavior of interest, however. Our extended professional repertoire also involves such activities as reading research literature, talking with colleagues, accumulating practical experience, and writing and thinking about topics of interest. Of course, we are quite aware of our own professional behavior, but that familiarity may make it difficult to appreciate how our colleagues see it. That may be why we are sometimes surprised by feedback on a journal submission, the reactions of co-workers when we present a case at a monthly peer review meeting, or the observations of colleagues when we present at a professional convention. Those varied opinions should remind us that there is more than one way to approach a topic or set up measurement procedures or compare conditions or analyze data. The reactions of colleagues to your decisions may or may not suggest better methodological options, but at the very least they make the point that each of the various means of accomplishing each task in a project has strengths and weaknesses that should be considered. The following chapters will detail those options and their consequences.

WHERE DO QUESTIONS COME FROM?

There Are Always Questions

Asking good questions is a challenge for both researchers and practitioners. Although it might be tempting to assume that researchers are more likely than practitioners to ask explicit questions about behavior, practitioners almost certainly win this competition. It is true that researchers often invest a lot of time developing and conducting an experiment that is focused on a single question or closely related set of questions. A research project might take many months to plan and complete. Even a relatively uncomplicated clinical case is likely to raise multiple and varied questions about an individual's behavior and methodological options through assessment and treatment stages, and practitioners typically manage a number of cases over the course of a year.

Of course, this disparity has some important side effects. A behavior analytic researcher who is focused on a single project with limited questions has the advantage of being able to carefully select from among methodological options at every stage of the effort. Initial decisions must be made about what behavior will serve as the dependent variable and how it will be defined and measured and about the nature and sequence of control and experimental conditions, but the researcher can second-guess those choices. If the way the target behavior is defined seems not quite right, it can be modified. If data suggest that observer performance is problematic, improvements can be made. If the measurement procedures are not revealing important changes in target behaviors, they can be revised. If extraneous factors seem to be interfering with seeing the effects of the experimental condition clearly, they can be controlled or eliminated. If comparisons between experimental and control conditions fail to show the anticipated outcomes, the conditions or how they are compared can be changed.

True, these "do-overs" often come at a price. They are the reason that research projects sometimes take longer than originally anticipated. On the other hand, that price buys a level of clarity and confidence in the results that is one of the defining features of science. If investigators take care to make the best decisions, it may increase the likelihood that their published findings will hold up when other researchers use them in their own projects and when practitioners depend on them to yield predictable clinical results. (Later chapters will help make this point.) In fact, second-guessing methodological choices as a project moves along (and even after it is finished) is a key feature of scientific method. Given that the objective is to discover answers to research questions that accurately reflect the true state of nature, this cautious approach is worth whatever time it takes.

Aside from their use of the research literature, practitioners approach their daily curiosities about behavior in a very different context. Their job is to determine an individual's behavioral needs and then find a way to achieve them. Their interests are often determined by factors beyond their control. There are usually limited options for the selection of target behaviors, the relevance of particular environments, and the desired outcomes. Furthermore, the explicit agenda to change behavior for practical ends precludes some of the second-guessing that researchers can consider. Not only that, practitioners are often under some pressure to make progress without undue delay. After all, they are being paid to resolve behavioral issues that are problematic not just for the direct recipient of services but for others as well.

This does not mean that practitioners should ignore the many questions about behavior that arise in the course of planning and conducting interventions. Such questions typically emerge from assessing the nature of the presenting behavioral issues and designing interventions that are intended to achieve specific behavioral outcomes. (Chapter 7 discusses assessment issues in detail.) For example, assessment procedures usually involve collecting behavioral data under specific conditions in order to determine the nature of the target behaviors and the variables influencing them. Sometimes the assessment procedures are quasi-experimental in style (Iwata, Vollmer, & Zarcone, 1990). Interventions aimed at establishing or changing target behaviors often take on an informal experimental style. Most interventions involve a series of phases in which specific environmental factors are manipulated in order to produce particular changes in a target behavior. Ongoing measurement allows practitioners to evaluate the effects of each intervention procedure as well as adjustments to those procedures. Sometimes the adjustments are planned, but when expected outcomes are not obtained, the clinician must then try out options that may be more effective. In this process, practitioners ask the same question researchers might entertain: What are the effects of this condition?

What the practitioner can do about questions that arise in the course of providing services will be the focus of upcoming chapters. At the very least, such questions should not be ignored. Even though the priorities are practical rather than scientific, answering the questions is often necessary to provide the most effective and timely resolution of the problem. In addressing such questions, matters of methodology are almost always front and center. Consideration of the characteristics of a target behavior, for example, raises questions about how it might be defined, how observers are trained, what features should be the focus of observation, when observation should occur and for how long, what observation procedures should be used, and how the resulting data should be managed and analyzed. Questions about why an intervention procedure is not working as intended or what alternatives might be more effective should lead to consideration of how different conditions might be evaluated or compared, as well as how the data might be displayed to encourage good answers. Although practitioners may not plan to publish their projects in professional journals, the ways they pose and answer questions have very important implications for the individuals they serve.

From Graduate Training

Graduate training is certainly one of the most powerful influences on our curiosities. It is in graduate school that we are metaphorically conceived as

researchers or practitioners – or both! Through the miscegenation of our professors, we gestate as fetal behavior analysts. We are finally thrust out of the
ivy-covered womb wearing only a scanty thesis or dissertation, still very much
neonatal in a field that is itself still young in some ways.

We come to graduate school knowing relatively little about this field and
leave with at least a rudimentary professional repertoire. Along the way, we
learn to restrict much of our pre-professional repertoire about behavior to
everyday discourse. A specialized, scientific verbal repertoire about behavior
gradually replaces that colloquial repertoire in a growing range of professional
circumstances.

The academic experience also brings our behavior into contact with a variety
of powerful reinforcers that influence our professional behavior throughout
our careers. For example, we may find laboratory research more reinforcing
than clinical practice or *vice versa*. Working with individuals diagnosed with
intellectual disabilities who live in group homes may be more enjoyable than
working with children with autism spectrum disorders in home and school
settings – or not. Certain issues in the research literature are likely to be much
more interesting than others. Preferences developed in graduate school may
stay with us throughout our careers and nudge our curiosities in one direction
or another as researchers or practitioners.

From Published Literature

One of the effects of graduate school is to make the field's research literature –
whether basic or applied – a powerful influence on our professional interests
and activities. Of course, an individual can be familiar with only some areas
of the field's literature, so it is not unusual for students to specialize in a few
topics. Although this unavoidable specialization is a blessed relief to the over-
achievers among us, it also means that we might not be aware of studies that
could be relevant to our interests.

Given a particular interest, the published literature on the topic naturally
guides us toward certain kinds of questions. So if a basic researcher is interested
in learning more about delay discounting (Madden & Bickel, 2010), for example,
it is natural that the existing literature on that topic would be the best place to
look for guidance about what has already been accomplished and what questions remain to be addressed. A practitioner who is developing interventions to
improve clients' health decision-making might look for research on how delay
discounting influences behaviors like smoking, eating, and exercising.

The existing literature may also raise questions because of what it does not
reveal. That might be especially important to practitioners, who must provide
services in spite of insufficient evidence about the appropriateness, format,
or effects of a procedure. For instance, research may not have established any
specific procedure as the most effective for reducing elopement (wander-
ing) in people with autism and other developmental disabilities (Lang et al.,
2009). Because that behavior can result in injury and even death, however, a

practitioner working with a client who elopes has no choice but to develop an intervention. Even though existing research may not provide a complete blueprint, the practitioner would be wise to use that research to guide the development of an intervention plan for her client.

It can also be helpful to examine the literature in other disciplines that might suggest useful ways of approaching an issue. Although some areas might represent conceptual perspectives and methodological practices that are not well suited to the study of behavior, behavior analysts can often find ideas that merit experimental attention. Descriptive studies from developmental psychology, for example, identified several behaviors that typically emerge very early in childhood, starting with shifting eye gaze between an environmental event and a familiar person and progressing to include gesturing toward the event and vocalizing. Cognitive and developmental psychologists label such behaviors "joint attention," which they view as coordinating attention in order to share interesting experiences with others. Other descriptive studies revealed that joint attention behaviors correlated positively with the development of language and social skills and that many young children with autism did not engage in joint attention interactions. Behavior analysts broke those interactions down into component skills and contingencies in order to foster development of behavior analytic procedures for assessing and building joint attention skills in children with autism (e.g., Dube, MacDonald, Mansfield, Holcomb, & Ahearn, 1994; MacDonald et al., 2006).

Finally, familiarity with our field's literature contributes to an overall perspective about its general directions and needs. This sense of where the field is going and where it needs to go influences how researchers and practitioners react to particular studies. A newly published study does not lead all readers in the same direction, and some directions will probably be more productive than others. The best research questions lead to answers that are not only useful for a specific topic but also serve the larger interests of the field.

From Experimental and Extra-experimental Contingencies

For many investigators, research questions flow from an ongoing program of investigation. In one way or another, each study may provide the foundation for another. One study often generates findings that suggest new questions. Sometimes the next questions might have been anticipated from the outset, but it is not unusual for a study to produce unexpected evidence. (If researchers could accurately predict their results, there would be no reason to do experiments.) Results may also be unclear or confusing. For example, some participants may have reacted to a condition in one way and others in a different way. That kind of result begs for resolution, which is usually achieved by trying to determine what factors underlie the different patterns of responding. Finally, conducting a study may reveal problems with measurement procedures or how control and treatment conditions were designed or implemented. In such cases, the problems will have to be corrected and the study repeated.

BOX 3.1

Research Styles

Scientific research has little in common with the fashion industry, but there are different styles of investigation. Instead of changing seasonally, these styles can be observed year after year in all scientific disciplines. The style of a research project refers to the function that it serves for the experimenter and the effect that it has on the field. A study's style is largely determined by its question and the question's impact on how the researcher designs, conducts, and interprets the experiment.

Research styles sometimes come in complementary pairs. For instance, a **thematic** style can be contrasted with an **independent** style (see Box 3.2). A thematic study is designed to fit into a predetermined position in a larger research program or area of literature, whereas an independent experiment is not conceived of in the context of any ongoing program or research area. These differences have important consequences for the field (see Box 3.2).

Another contrasting pair of research styles may be labeled **demonstration** versus **explanatory**. Demonstration research focuses on showing that a certain result is possible, which can be a very important achievement. In contrast, explanatory research strives for an understanding of how and why certain relations work. Although they can be valuable, demonstration studies leave important questions unanswered because they fail to follow up and show why their results occurred. That is why it is important for each area of literature to have many explanatory studies for each demonstration study.

Pilot and **in-house** research styles often involve methodological short cuts. Pilot research is conducted as a preliminary effort to learn things that will guide a more substantial experimental project. A risk is that the preparatory nature of the effort will justify weak or sloppy methods, which will be an unsound basis for making decisions about how to conduct the planned research project. Research that is only designed for local or in-house use carries the same risk. Sidman (1960) offered a simple rule for avoiding such problems: If the methods are sound, then conclusions are justified; if not, then conclusions may be inappropriate.

A research style that raises a similar concern results from a researcher using experiments to advocate for a particular result. **Advocacy** research may involve decisions about what to do and how to do it that are biased toward the investigator's interests in getting certain results (see Box 3.3). Such studies can often be identified by examining the focus of the question and the related methodological decisions. Those choices by the investigator may facilitate obtaining a certain result instead of evaluating the impact of experimental conditions in a neutral manner. The risk is that the findings may differ from those that would have been obtained from a less biased approach.

Finally, although the research styles just described represent important aspects of how scientists approach their work, the distinctions are not "official" in any way, and you can look for other styles as you learn more about research literatures. Each research style will be discussed further as it appears in different chapters.

The investigator's behavior in planning and conducting a study and analyzing the outcomes constitute research contingencies. They exert influence on how questions are framed that is valuable because it encourages thematic research efforts. In contrast to experiments conceived independently of other studies, projects conducted in a thematic research style fit more or less systematically into the literature on a topic and are designed to serve particular functions for that literature. Although experiments developed independently of the literature may be quite sound in every respect, studies designed to play a specific role in relation to past and future research are likely to be especially valuable for the field (see Box 3.1).

In contrast, contingencies that do not directly affect the details of a study or its role in the literature might be described as extra-experimental and may have somewhat different effects. Those contingencies involve the relation between how the investigator designs and conducts a study and the consequences of its results that go well beyond scientific considerations to include professional reputation, grants, patents, consulting contracts, books, tenure and promotion, access to a setting or population, and so forth. When those issues intrude on the process of developing research questions, the result may be studies that serve personal interests more than the needs of the field. For instance, a study may be set up so that it will produce only what the investigator or a funding

---

BOX 3.2

Thematic versus Independent Research Styles

Investigators who design experiments that are related to other studies in specific ways are using a **thematic research style**. Any experimental question can lead to thematic research. The key is that the study is part of a coherent program or aims at filling in gaps in the literature. With this approach, the resulting picture is likely to be complete and easily interpretable. The value of thematic research lies in the integration of the resulting data. Thematic findings are likely to have collectively greater utility than the results from the same number of independent experiments addressing the same topic because they were designed to fit together, like pieces of a jigsaw puzzle.

An **independent research style** results from a researcher conceiving of a study independently of any coordinated research program or even the existing literature. In other words, such studies are not designed to precede or follow other studies in a predetermined way. They often originate from opportunistic situations having to do with the availability of subjects or a setting. Experiments conducted in an independent style may be perfectly worthy studies in every way, and their results may be quite useful. Sometimes their importance may only become clear at a later point in a literature's development. This style becomes a problem, however, when it tends to dominate a literature or field. It can lead to a lack of cohesiveness among studies and contribute to a lack of direction in the literature.

source wants to find. More extreme examples can even involve fudging the data in some way – a serious ethical violation.

From Observing Behavior

The field of behavior analysis has accumulated large basic and applied research literatures offering a wealth of diverse research themes showcasing countless studies. That body of research is a rich source of ideas for what remains to be learned about behavior. Studies with weak or unclear findings need to be replicated. Solid studies suggest gaps that need to be filled in or new directions that might be fruitful. Important themes that have not yet been adequately pursued beg for attention.

Relying too heavily on the archival literature as a source of research questions carries risks, however. Questions that emerge from published studies naturally tend to pursue the themes already established in the literature. That is not always a problem, but it can lead to questions in an area gradually becoming more about the literature than about the phenomenon of interest.

An especially worrisome risk of relying on the existing literature for research questions is that the literature may not adequately represent all of the research

---

BOX 3.3

Advocacy Research

When an experiment's question, procedures, and write up suggest that the investigator's primary goal was to generate support for a predetermined conclusion, it can be called **advocacy research**. Just because an investigator has preconceptions about the topic of a study and an interest in how the data turn out, however, does not mean the experimental procedures and interpretations will be inappropriately biased. But when the extra-experimental contingencies are powerful, there is naturally a good chance that the way an experiment is conceived, conducted, and interpreted will be biased in favor of the preferred outcome, even if the researcher is unaware of this impact.

The ways a study can be improperly prejudiced are endless, ranging from asking a question that looks only for a desired outcome to making measurement and design decisions that facilitate preferred results and discourage contrary data. Sometimes the most obvious evidence of an advocacy posture is the tone of the published report.

We all have our prejudices, and it is the rare investigator who can scrupulously ignore all of them. But when the influence of such partialities begins to interfere with conducting a fair experiment, the result can be promoting results that are less than fully true or do not hold up well when others use them. Under those conditions, the investigator has taken on the role of an advocate who defends a cause, not a scientist who searches for understanding.

directions needed by the field. For example, although the applied behavior analytic literature has many strengths, it falls short of addressing a number of research themes that are important for both researchers and practitioners. Relatively few replications are published, for instance, despite the critical importance of replication for both advancing scientific knowledge and providing practitioners, consumers, and funders with assurance that a study that produced promising results was not a fluke. Similarly, although many (perhaps most) of the interventions used by practitioners are "packages" comprising multiple components, studies to determine which components are essential for producing desired effects are relatively scarce.

It is a matter of balance. How researchers and practitioners develop questions should be influenced not only by the existing literature but also by experiences with the subject matter itself. Behavior is a phenomenon that is always present in accessible and relevant forms. Well-trained behavior analysts are skilled in observing behavior in everyday life, and the questions that emerge from their observations can lead to fruitful research. The importance of simple observation has long been respected in other fields, and in his autobiographical volumes (1976, 1979, 1983) B. F. Skinner revealed that his contributions to the study of behavior typically had such mundane origins. Many examples of his lifelong observations of behavior in daily life are captured in a sampling of entries from his notebooks (Epstein, 1980).

From Providing Services

In the course of their work, practitioners focus on the everyday behavior of individuals with widely varying repertoires in diverse settings for the purpose of changing behavior in targeted ways. Those experiences are ideal for prompting questions about behavior. Some questions may be casual and not warrant a serious effort to answer them; thoughtful speculation within the bounds of established operant learning processes may be sufficient to satisfy a momentary curiosity. That does not mean such questions are trivial, merely that the circumstances are not right for giving them the attention that would be required for an experimental analysis. For instance, a practitioner might wonder if she could use systematic desensitization procedures to train a student with autism to tolerate environmental sounds like school bells and fire alarms instead of covering his ears with his hands whenever he encounters them or wearing noise-canceling headphones constantly, but she may lack the time and the support from the rest of the treatment team to try systematic desensitization.

On the other hand, some questions may be more pressing. In the course of assessing influences on possible target behaviors, designing intervention procedures, implementing those procedures, and analyzing changes in behavior, practitioners cannot help but encounter many questions that need to be addressed in order to make good decisions about how to proceed. By its very nature, the assessment process is filled with such questions. What are the influences on this behavior? Are different forms of responding part of the same behavior or are they different behaviors? What will happen if a particular environmental variable is changed in some way? Does the client have the pre-requisite or component skills for a particular performance in her repertoire?

The list of potentially important questions grows longer as measurement procedures are selected. Practitioners consider many options in deciding on a measurement protocol, and as data accumulate, it is hard not to wonder if options that were not chosen might have revealed more informative aspects of responding than the selected protocol. How might changes in the defini-tion of the target behavior affect the data? How would the data look if duration of responding was measured instead of frequency or rate? What if different observation procedures were used? These kinds of questions are important because their answers can change the data that will be the basis for drawing conclusions about what is going on.

Perhaps the most tempting questions facing practitioners concern inter-vention procedures and their effects on target behaviors. The array of possible procedures and their details assures almost endless options for engineering behavior change. Choosing among them can bring up many questions, some of which may warrant formal investigation to find at least tentative answers. Will it be more efficient to manipulate antecedent environmental variables or focus on arranging consequences? Which of the two contingencies will be most effective? What consequences are maintaining maladaptive behav-iors? Are there consequences for alternative behaviors that will compete effectively with those? Should error correction procedures be used, or would errorless training procedures be better? What about prompting and prompt-fading?

A particular intervention protocol may seem to work well, producing rea-sonable progress toward treatment goals. As target behaviors change, however, procedures are likely to need adjusting. At some point, procedures will even need to be faded and eventually discontinued. That happy outcome brings its own set of questions. Consider a teenager with an intellectual disability who has learned to bus tables in the school cafeteria by following a photo activity schedule on an iPad. A goal is for him to get a job bussing tables in a local res-taurant where he will not be able to use an iPad. To prepare him for that, should intervention shift to gradually replacing the photos in the activity schedule with printed words that can then be transformed into a written checklist on an index card that the young man can carry with him on the job? Or would it be better to start fading the activity schedule by removing photos one at a time until he is performing the task with no visual prompts at all?

Given the complexity of behavior, the variations among environmental contexts, and the many intervention options in ABA technology, it is often the case that an initial intervention protocol invites ongoing reconsideration of some decisions. There are always operational details that might be corrected or improved. Personnel may need better training, prompting procedures may need to be revised, reinforcement procedures may need to be strengthened, and so on. The need to fine-tune intervention details is a given. Sometimes the data do not show satisfactory progress at all, however. Questions may then focus less on minor details and more on the original assessment information, the influence of existing environmental factors, the correctness of implementation, and the appropriateness of different intervention options.

In sum, in providing services practitioners run into countless questions. Many require attention because their answers are necessary to assure effective interventions in a reasonable period of time. Although it might seem that addressing questions about methods in the course of service delivery is a distraction, practical questions like those are an integral part of the job of providing good services.

WHAT MAKES A GOOD QUESTION?

Good, Better, or Best

The preceding section suggests that it should not be difficult to come up with questions worthy of investigation. Whether the planned outcome is a study that warrants publication in a peer reviewed journal or conclusions that guide services to clients, the question should at least be sufficiently important to justify the effort to answer it. The challenge for investigators – both researchers and practitioners – is to pose questions that will generate data that are more revealing and useful than might be produced by any other approach to the topic. Some questions are simply better than others. The best question results from a process of comparing and refining possible variations of a core question, often in the context of the pertinent literature. That will produce one way of asking the question that seems better than the others. Of course, different investigators focusing on the same issue will come up with different "best" ways of framing their interest. Within limits, that is good for the field because we cannot always know which ways of approaching an issue will turn out to be the most profitable.

Worrying about the best way to frame a question for a particular investigation is always a productive activity. Sifting through existing studies, considering different facets of an issue, thinking through what will be required to answer the question, and comparing alternative variations can only lead to a more informative outcome. For instance, if a researcher is interested in further examining a question that has already been addressed, poring over published findings in order to figure out what remains to be clarified is likely to lead to a new question that generates more useful information than merely repeating someone else's study. To return to a previous example, a practitioner searching the literature on interventions for elopement might find that instead of just using a procedure described in a published study with her client she can address a question whose answer will help fill in one of the gaps in that literature. As another illustration, a practitioner may need to think through whether a particular question can be properly addressed under the limitations of a service setting. There is no point in selecting a question when the resources required to answer it are not available or methods will have to be compromised too

---

BOX 3.4

Questions versus Hypotheses

Although this chapter is about questions, you may be surprised that we hardly mention hypotheses. In a way, a hypothesis is the opposite of an experimental question. Instead of asking a question, a **hypothesis** states a conjecture or prediction about the outcome of an experiment, which is a fancy way of referring to an educated guess. In this sense, all investigators have hypotheses or make speculations about the outcomes of their experiments. If an investigator had absolutely no suspicions about how a study might turn out, he or she could probably be accused of not knowing the relevant literature very well. Furthermore, even though scientists are supposed to be fairly neutral or at least open to any and all results, it is the rare investigator who does not have some preference for one outcome over another.

Any speculation can be dressed up and called a hypothesis as long as you understand the risks of doing so. Because even the best investigators do not approach their studies in a completely neutral manner, there is a real possibility that biases will have an impact on how experiments are designed, conducted, and interpreted. When the investigator replaces the question with a public commitment in the form of a hypothesis, the prediction only increases this risk. Having forecast the experiment's outcome, it is understandably tempting to design and conduct the study in a way that confirms the prediction. This certainly does not mean that investigators who state formal hypotheses intentionally bias their experimental decisions, but there are many ways of increasing the chances of getting the "right" results that have become an accepted part of that tradition. One such tactic is to increase the number of participants in each group to help "reach" statistical significance.

Actually, investigators do not need to state hypotheses if they are asking questions about nature. When the experimental question simply asks about the relation between independent and dependent variables, there is no scientific reason to make a prediction about what will be learned from the data. Whatever is learned will describe something about that relation that was presumably not known before. Whether it matches anyone's expectations has nothing to do with its truth or importance (Sidman, 1960). It is only when the question is about a formal theory or when statistical procedures will be the basis for inferences that a formal hypothesis becomes part of the exercise (for reasons having to do with experimental logic). Otherwise, heed B. F. Skinner's warning quoted at the beginning of this chapter. Ask yourself whether you are more interested in learning about nature or the accuracy of your guesses.

---

much. What if a teacher is interested in evaluating the effects of the frequency and duration of recreational breaks on the academic work of students in a special education classroom, for instance, but has no means of observing and recording changes in the behaviors of interest? That constraint will require revising the question to be consistent with the resources or putting it aside for the time being.

Considering different ways of wording a question may result in more than one possibility that seems viable. But what makes one question better than another? When an investigator intends to contribute to a particular literature, the best questions are those that overcome weaknesses in other studies, correct misunderstandings, or clarify ambiguous findings. Results of investigations to address such questions help fill in gaps in existing knowledge or show new possibilities and directions that turn out to be valuable. Great questions go to the heart of an issue and lead to findings that help resolve it. In other words, really valuable questions lead to results that are importantly useful to other researchers or to practitioners.

When the focus is more practical in nature, perhaps aimed at modifying treatment for a single individual, the question may focus on information that may prove most valuable clinically and on the resources necessary to come up with the answer. For instance, the issue may concern ways of defining the target behavior, features of the behavior to be measured, or observation procedures that will generate the data. If the primary interest lies in the intervention protocol, questions may focus not only on different procedural options but also on adjusting their features to improve effectiveness.

Although there are many considerations for developing and evaluating questions, there is no simple criterion for assuring that a question will be the best, or better than another. There is, however, a tactic that is likely to get you there: approaching the process of coming up with a good question as a distinct and important step. Instead of pushing ahead with an initial curiosity, considering alternative possibilities encourages reflection about why each variation might be better or worse than others and is likely to suggest criteria for evaluating each possibility. The result may not always be the best question from someone else's perspective, but it will usually be better than the one you started with.

Write it Down

We began this chapter by pointing out that research and clinical questions are verbal behavior, so let us consider this verbal behavior in more detail. The best way to do that is to actually write down candidate questions, and it is often an informative and revealing exercise. It may become evident that there really is no question as such. That is, the central interest may lie in demonstrating an outcome that is already known, strongly suspected, or even preferred. As Box 3.4 notes, there is not necessarily anything wrong with such a focus. Demonstration studies certainly have their place in science, but their emphasis is often more a prediction than a question. For instance, contingencies that have proved effective for increasing paper recycling by workers in an office might reasonably be predicted to also increase plastic recycling by those same workers.

Another revelation may be that the questions being considered are not actually asking about behavior. They may instead focus on a point of theory or a method of controlling behavior. For example, applied studies are often aimed at assessing whether a certain procedure changes behavior in particular ways. Although such questions are clearly about behavior, they focus primarily on procedures. That is not improper in any way, but such questions may reveal less about behavior than those that ask directly about behavior, such as its nature and the factors that influence its development and maintenance.

Worrying about the precise wording of a question helps clarify the focus of the intended project. That interest needs to be plainly stated so that neither the investigator nor others will be unclear about the project's objectives. For researchers, this clarity helps guide the decision-making that transforms a question into an experiment. It also helps readers of the published study evaluate the investigator's methodological choices in light of the conclusions he offers. Clarity is no less important when the question is intended to guide clinical decisions. Practitioners must make the same methodological decisions as researchers in order to get useful answers.

Even when the focus of a question is clear, there may still be issues about how it is phrased. Consider the following examples:

1. Will delivery of reinforcers on a response-independent, fixed-time schedule (often termed "noncontingent reinforcement") reduce rates of aggressive behavior?
2. What are the relations between noncontingent delivery of reinforcers and rates of aggressive behavior?

At first glance, both questions may appear to pose the same query, and in a general sense they do. However, the differences in phrasing suggest that the authors of these questions may set up their projects somewhat differently. If so, there is a good chance that one study might be more fruitful than the other. The first question appears to be fairly narrow in its focus. It asks if delivery of reinforcers on a fixed-time schedule will produce a certain pattern of responding. The answer will likely be equally narrow: yes or no. When questions are asked in a way that allows them to be answered in such a simple and narrow manner, it suggests that the investigator has limited curiosity or is more interested in one outcome than the other, which can lead to designing the study so as to make the desired results more likely than might be the case with different procedures. Sometimes the way the investigator interprets the data confirms that prior interest.

In contrast, the second question is open-ended; it does not hint at a specific outcome. It simply asks what will happen to response rates (frequencies) when reinforcer delivery is not contingent on responding, which might imply that the investigator is interested in whatever results might be obtained. That possibility is further implied by the fact that "relations" is plural, suggesting that the results could be complex rather than black and white. An investigator who phrases the question this way might design procedures that probe for the fullest possible description of those relations.

In general, it may be wise to phrase questions in ways that do not explicitly anticipate experimental results. "What are the relations between ..." or "What are the effects of ..." are good representatives of a neutral posture. When a question's wording leans toward a particular outcome, that bias, even if innocent, may affect how the study is designed, conducted, and interpreted. Moreover, answering a yes-no question may add little to the literature, even if the study is otherwise excellent in design and execution. The recommendation to use neutral phrasing is based on the likelihood that efforts to develop open and searching wording will alert the investigator to possible biases and their consequences.

In sum, the importance of committing to a particular wording lies in encouraging a thoughtful examination of exactly what is being asked and why. As the following section shows, the question should be the touchstone for the subsequent methodological decisions, which will have a pervasive impact on the data and their analysis. If an investigator cannot state precisely at the outset what answers the project is designed to find and why they are being pursued in a particular way as opposed to alternative possibilities, perhaps he or she is not ready to proceed.

WHAT ARE QUESTIONS FOR?

Guiding Research Procedures

General Strategy. A good question about behavior is a carefully worded expression of an investigator's best judgments about the direction and focus of his or her interests. As such, it should serve as a guide for the many decisions that must be made to create and manage a project that will satisfy those interests. The choices may be obvious or subtle, but almost every methodological decision can be directly related to the question.

The reason for making sure the question serves as a touchstone is that we expect the resulting procedures to yield data that answer the question. When the design and conduct of a study fail to properly reflect the interests of the question, there is a risk that the results will not provide a clear answer. The problem arises when the investigator fails to recognize that risk and proceeds to answer the question based on procedures and data that do not fully suit the question. As a result, the conclusions may not be entirely correct and therefore may not hold up when others use them.

Consider a question that asks about the effectiveness of procedures for training students to use good study skills. If the investigator chooses to measure only student test performances, the data may not clearly answer the question. Although we might expect changes in study skills to result in changes in test performance, test scores may not provide evidence that the trained study skills were actually used as designed. Furthermore, test performance is likely to reflect the influence of factors other than study practices, such as existing knowledge of the tested material and test-taking skills. Keep in mind that the question was about the effectiveness of procedures for training students to study in particular ways, not the effects of study practices on test performance.

Measures of test performance would not reflect the impact of the training procedures alone. Although they might partly represent the effects of the training procedures, they would also reflect the influence of other factors and therefore limit the accuracy and generality of conclusions.

Selecting Participants. One of the first challenges an investigator faces is selecting participants whose behavior will serve as the dependent variable in the investigation. The criteria for choosing some individuals over others emerge from examining the needs of the question. The question should suggest certain participant characteristics that will help reveal how participants' behavior is affected by treatment variables as well as other factors that might interfere with seeing those effects.

For many questions, the need to select participants with specific characteristics is obvious. Species, gender, age, history, and repertoire are almost always important considerations. The focus of the question, the nature of the conditions that are being investigated, and the setting in which the project is conducted will usually dictate some of the selection criteria. For instance, a study investigating procedures for increasing compliance with exercise regimens by arthritis patients will presumably require participants who have that disorder, perhaps even a particular type of arthritis. An investigator who wants to study the effects of error correction procedures on the acquisition of skills by individuals with intellectual disabilities will need to select individuals with similar levels of functioning and existing skills so that observed effects can appropriately be attributed to the error correction procedures.

Each research question will also require participants who can contact experimental conditions in a particular way. Even simple availability can be an issue. For instance, a study designed to measure the effects of psychotropic drugs on the behavior of individuals with diagnoses of depression might require selecting participants who are in an in-patient program rather than outpatients, who might be less likely to show up for daily testing sessions.

It is also important to select participants whose behaviors have the characteristics needed to serve as the dependent variable. By directing how the treatment and control conditions are designed, the question will suggest how participants will need to behave in order to react meaningfully to those conditions. For example, a study of how the stimuli used in a matching-to-sample procedure affect conditional discrimination learning in typical young children would probably require that the children share a certain level of development and the skill to perform match-to-sample tasks presented on a computer with a touchscreen.

TABLE 3.1
Participant characteristics that may be important

• Species	• Accessibility
• Gender	• Repertoire
• Age	• Environmental history

Another way to think of needed behavioral characteristics is in terms of an environmental history that participants must share. The focus of the question, together with the planned treatment and control conditions and the behavior that will serve as the dependent variable, sometimes dictates that participants will need to respond on the basis of a particular history. That history may be one of the selection criteria, although it can instead be established by a pre-training regimen or even a control or baseline condition. To continue the preceding example, before they begin the conditional discrimination study, children could be pre-trained to perform match-to-sample tasks on a touchscreen-equipped computer using stimuli that will not be used in the study proper.

Choosing a Target Behavior. The question is also an important consideration in figuring out the characteristics of the behavior the investigator chooses as the dependent variable. (Chapter 4 will address this topic in detail.) In some investigations, particularly those guided by applied interests, the target behavior may be largely specified by the focus of the question. If a project is going to examine procedures for reducing self-injurious behavior, for instance, the investigator will only have to determine whether there are any particular features of that category of behavior that might be important to include or exclude. If the question does not dictate a specific kind of behavior, the selection of a target behavior may be more open.

The way to figure out what behavior might help answer the question is to focus on the features that a behavior should or should not exhibit. With such a list, the investigator is then ready to either identify a behavior already in the participant's repertoire that has those characteristics, or determine how to create the desired behavior by arranging pre-training conditions. There are a number of key features that might be of interest.

One consideration noted in the previous section is that participants must already exhibit, or can be taught, the kind of behavior that will be required. For example, in a project focusing on procedures for teaching new skills to children with autism spectrum disorder, participants may need to have certain prerequisite skills like orienting toward an adult, sitting at a table, and perhaps following basic instructions. The control and treatment conditions will also require participants to behave in certain ways. Changes in such behavior will represent the effects of the compared conditions. So if the study involves evaluating interventions for stereotypic behavior, for instance, the target behavior must be a certain form of such behavior.

Perhaps the most important role for any behavior that might serve as the dependent variable is to be sensitive to the independent variable. Sensitivity does not mean that it must be clear before the project starts that the candidate behavior is strongly affected by the treatment condition. If this were true, there might be little reason to conduct an experiment. In this context, sensitivity means that the behavior will change in ways that reflect a relation between a treatment condition and the behavior, if there is one. An appropriately sensitive target behavior would be able to vary over an adequate range of values, for example. That would not be possible if the chosen behavior occurred very infrequently (or very often), because it might then be difficult to detect decreases (or increases).

One of the most common constraints on the sensitivity of a behavior comes from powerful extraneous variables, which are often not under the investigator's control. If measures of participant behavior reflect not just the impact of carefully managed treatment and control conditions but also the uncontrolled effects of factors that are not of interest, it will be difficult to draw conclusions about the effects of treatment conditions alone.

Selecting behaviors that are not overly susceptible to extraneous factors is a frequent challenge in applied work because non-laboratory settings typically involve many influences that are not the focus of the study but can be quite powerful. Although one of the reasons for choosing applied research settings is to assess interventions under real-world conditions, the influence of powerful extraneous factors can make it difficult to see the effects of treatment variables. (Later chapters will consider extraneous variables in greater detail.)

Another characteristic of a target behavior that can have a big impact on what the data reveal is its relevant dimensions. (Chapter 5 will address this topic in detail.) By dimensions we mean the different aspects of responding that might vary over time or across conditions. They include the number of responses (count), their duration, and the rate or frequency of responding (how often the behavior occurs), among others. Each dimension reflects a different aspect of a behavior, much as describing an object in terms of its weight, height, or length reveals different characteristics. The question, together with the nature of the treatment and control conditions, may suggest that some dimensions of the behavior may reflect changes in responding across conditions better than others. For instance, if a treatment procedure is likely to produce important variations in the rate of responding, it may be necessary to choose a behavior that can easily vary in that dimension, such as spontaneously requesting a preferred toy. On the other hand, if the study will use a procedure in which the participant must wait for each trial to start (e.g., presentation of a picture by a computer or investigator), measuring the participant's behavior in terms of rate of responding is likely to be misleading. With such a procedure, the pace of the participant's responding will partly depend on the computer software or the investigator and therefore will not clearly show the impact of the treatment condition.

Finally, because the target behavior will serve as the dependent variable, it is important that it can be accurately measured. This means that the selected features of each response must be observed and recorded. This is usually not difficult in more controlled research settings, but it can be challenging in some field settings, especially when human observers are used. Chapter 6 considers these issues.

Designing Measurement Procedures. Many of the considerations involved in setting up measurement procedures are fundamental and do not vary much from one study to another. For instance, obtaining accurate measures of responding is always important. However, the issue of how long and how

TABLE 3.2
Considerations in choosing a target behavior

• Compatibility with procedures	• Relevant dimensions
• Sensitivity to independent variable	• Measurability
• Influence by extraneous variables	

often periods of measurement should occur depends in part on what information the question requires about how the treatment condition influences responding. Sometimes relatively brief daily sessions may provide adequate information, but under other circumstances measurement sessions may need to continue for extended periods.

Consider an investigation of the effects of diet on hyperactivity in young children. One project might compare the effects of a restricted diet versus a typical diet, with each type of diet being followed for a few weeks at a time in turn. In this situation, it may be necessary to obtain samples of behavior throughout each day in varied settings, probably involving parents, teachers, and others as observers. In contrast, a different approach might ask about the effects of a particular substance by preparing a series of dietary challenges. Under this procedure, the effect of consuming any substance would last only a few hours, and measurement would therefore need to occur continuously during specified periods of time following each challenge in order to capture any effects.

Selecting Independent Variables. The independent variable is the centerpiece of investigations, and the question's most important role is to guide its selection. The question is only the investigator's verbal behavior and is not worth much until it leads to action. The independent variables that are embedded in a project's procedures are the means by which we translate the question into environmental events the participants will experience. The correspondence between the question and its treatment conditions must therefore be very close in order for the data to clearly answer the question.

Unfortunately, there are no simple rules for how the question should lead to selecting independent variables. One way to approach the problem, however, is to ask what kind of data will be required to answer the question. That is, given the question, imagine the ideal kind of data that would clearly answer it. Working backwards, then consider what particular features of a treatment condition might generate such data.

For instance, what if a question asks about the effects of quantity of food consumed on the behavior of post-meal ruminating in individuals diagnosed as severely or profoundly intellectually disabled (Rast, Johnston, Drum, & Conrin, 1981)? If we ask what kind of data would answer this question, we might find that we would need to be able to compare the effects of eating different amounts of food on ruminating. Although we could certainly select three or four different amounts of food for comparison, if there is no evidence from prior studies about whether food quantity has any effects on ruminating, an initial study might focus on merely seeing if there is any such relation.

BOX 3.5

The Null Hypothesis Game

For historical reasons that are beyond the scope of this book, a tradition has evolved in psychology and other social sciences (in marked contrast to the natural sciences) that has a powerful influence on how research questions are conceived and phrased. When inferential statistics are used to interpret experimental data, the investigator must usually identify both a null hypothesis and an alternative hypothesis. The **null hypothesis** is a routine statement that there is no difference between the performance of the experimental group and that of the control group. The **alternative hypothesis** states that there is a difference and that it is due to the only thing that distinguished the two groups: exposure to the independent variable.

If a statistical test of the data shows that there is indeed no substantial difference, then the null hypothesis must be accepted, and the investigator can only argue that there would have been a difference if things had been different. If the test shows that there is a difference, the investigator happily rejects the null hypothesis and turns to the alternative hypothesis as the best explanation of the difference between the groups (given a small likelihood that the difference occurred by chance).

There are a number of problems with this approach to asking experimental questions that will be examined in other chapters. For now, you should understand that it restricts the type of question asked to the general form, "Is there a difference (between experimental and control groups)?" The sole permissible answers are inevitably "Yes" or "No," which is both inefficient and a distortion of customary scientific curiosity. The tradition of statistical hypothesis testing requires investigators to play science by the rules of the Twenty Questions Game, in which queries must be phrased in ways that can be answered by yes or no.

In fact, if we look closely enough, there will almost always be a difference. What we really want to know, however, is the nature of the difference and the reasons for it. Instead, the statistical hypothesis-testing approach encourages the investigator to focus on detecting a particular predicted difference between two groups rather than on capturing any features of the relationship between independent and dependent variables. Worse still, wording questions this way encourages investigators to design and conduct the experiment in whatever ways are necessary to get an affirmative conclusion, regardless of its truth in nature.

In that case, it would be important to be able to compare rates of ruminating under a typical diet with rates under a diet that showed a clear impact on ruminating. A typical diet might mean single portions of foods that would normally be served to individuals living in a group home. It would not be permissible to serve less food than that, so in order to assess the effects of food quantity, the comparison condition would need to involve larger amounts of food. Because we would not know how much extra food might be required to see an effect on ruminating, we would want to choose a sufficiently large amount of food to be sure to see an effect, if there is such a relation. Assuming no associated health risks, we could encourage participants to eat until they were satiated. Of course, we would need to insure that the satiation-size meals otherwise had the same characteristics as the single-portion diet. In sum, a question focusing on the effects of food quantity on ruminating might be answered with an independent variable defined as satiation quantities of the same foods served in a typical single-portion diet (the control condition). Developing the full details of both control and experimental conditions would require additional decisions about how the food was presented and consumed, how satiation was defined in terms of participant behavior, and so forth.

Selecting an independent variable defines all other variables as extraneous to the current interests. The unfortunate function of extraneous variables is to supply alternative explanations for what might otherwise appear to be the effects of the treatment condition. Sometimes extraneous factors come attached to the independent variable. For example, it would unavoidably take longer to eat a satiation meal than a single-portion meal, and it is possible that the extra time has its own effects on ruminating, unrelated to how much food is consumed. Extraneous factors can also accompany features of control conditions, the general experimental setting, the behavior serving as the dependent variable, or other characteristics of participants. In fact, extraneous variables can intrude on the effects of treatment conditions in endless ways, and they are a major challenge to drawing clear and sound conclusions about the contribution of the independent variable alone. Discussion of extraneous variables will occur through the book.

Creating Comparisons. Designing an investigation involves arranging control and treatment conditions in ways that allow meaningful comparisons of responding under each type of condition. These two types of conditions are usually designed to be the same except for the presence of the independent variable in the treatment condition. If responding is found to be consistently different under control and treatment conditions, the investigator reasons that those differences are likely due to the only thing that differed between them: the independent variable. Such a conclusion should help answer the research question. By guiding the selection of the independent variable embedded in a treatment condition and a control condition in which the independent variable is not present, the question indirectly suggests such meaningful comparisons.

The key word here is "meaningful." When questions ask about the effects of environmental variables on behavior, meaningful comparisons between responding under control versus treatment conditions entail at least two requirements. First, each participant must be exposed to both control and treatment conditions in turn. Second, the data for each participant must be measured and analyzed separately, as we pointed out in Chapter 2. This approach is called a within-subject (or within-participant) research design. "Within-subject" refers to the fact that comparisons are made between data obtained from individual participants who experienced both the control and the treatment conditions. That is, the key comparisons of responding under the two kinds of conditions are made "within" each participant. The term also implies that control-treatment comparisons are made separately for each participant. The chapters in Part 3 will explain why this approach is essential for studying behavior and will go into more detail about other aspects of research design. For now, the remaining decisions concern how to arrange the sequence and timing of control and treatment conditions throughout the course of the investigation. The question is unlikely to suggest particular arrangements, but it is important to keep in mind exactly what comparisons will be needed to answer the question.

Analyzing Data. The data in a study result from measuring the behavior serving as the dependent variable as each participant experiences treatment conditions containing the independent variable as well as control conditions lacking the independent variable. Given the key role of the question in selecting independent and dependent variables, it should come as no surprise that the question should also influence how the investigator analyzes the data.

Data analysis procedures serve three functions: (a) modifying initial decisions about how the study will be conducted as the study moves along, (b) identifying and describing data that may answer the question, and (c) discovering relations in the data that were not anticipated and that may be interesting. The first two objectives should be guided by the research question, which tells the investigator what to look for. The third objective must not be ignored in trying to answer the original question, however. It is important that the question not limit the investigator's general curiosity. It is this open search for any potentially interesting findings that leads to serendipitous discoveries, which are neither rare nor trivial in science.

Guiding Research Conclusions

All of the functions of the research question involved in designing and conducting a study support the final step in the process: drawing conclusions that may answer the question. The conclusions are inevitably important to the researcher, who has gone to quite a lot of trouble to get to that point. The motivation to find certain results is understandable but risky. Although it is appropriate that the data will have a big impact on the investigator's conclusions, the conditions under which the data were obtained must be given a major role as well.

It is easy to appreciate this caution in the case of measurement procedures. For instance, without considering the details of measurement operations that

---

TABLE 3.3
Objectives of data analysis procedures

- Modifying initial decisions as experiment proceeds
- Identifying and describing data that answer the question
- Discovering unanticipated relationships

BOX 3.6

Serendipity

The term **serendipity** generally refers to unplanned or chance occurrences that are beneficial. It comes from an old Persian fairy tale titled *The Three Princes of Serendip.* The princes had a knack for finding valuable or agreeable things they were not looking for. In science, serendipitous discoveries are actually fairly common. That should not be surprising, because the openly inquisitive nature of science encourages investigators to be on the lookout for unexpected features of their data. Such unanticipated discoveries are sufficiently frequent that most investigators can point to examples in their own careers. Although serendipitous findings are not typically so important or unusual that they resolve major problems or redirect entire fields of study, they can be very useful.

Behavioral investigators can increase the chances of making important serendipitous discoveries by using experimental methods that capture the essential qualities of behavior and making sure the data are free of contaminating and misleading influences. The investigator's attitude toward the experimental process is no less important, however. Investigators who approach experiments as opportunities to learn whatever their procedures might reveal are more likely to make serendipitous observations than those who see experiments as occasions for showing things they already assume are true.

---

changed behavioral facts (what actually happened) into behavioral data (the quantitative picture of what happened), it is impossible to know exactly what each data point represents. The same issue exists for how the target behavior was defined, how independent variable conditions were designed and implemented, how extraneous variables were controlled, and so forth. In other words, the task of interpreting the data is really a much broader challenge of interpreting the entire study. The impact of each of the methodological features of the study on the data must be considered in figuring out what the data do and do not reveal.

Guiding the Science and the Culture

You can tell a lot about a science from its research questions. They reveal where the field has been and where it is going in learning about its subject matter. Research questions are more than merely revealing about a field's evolution, however. Because of their influence on methods on discovery, they guide the style and direction of the development of a science – and in fields like behavior analysis, applications of the science.

This suggests that when we develop our questions we should consider not only their role in guiding a particular project but their impact on the development of our science and practice. This requires some awareness of where the field is at any point and where it needs to go. Are the questions already established in the literature good for the field's development? Are there more profitable directions in which to invest the field's resources? Are there unexplored areas that should be pursued? Are there particular themes that should be avoided? What effects might each study have on the field as a whole?

Finally, researchers and practitioners should also examine the larger impact of their questions on society. This is not an uncommon consideration in scientific fields. After all, researchers and practitioners are members of the culture so are understandably influenced by it. In addition, funding sources encourage researchers to be aware of the potential impact of research on everyday life. Science has for many years now been an indispensable part of the culture. We need it just to survive the complexities and problems that it has, in part, allowed us to create. The culture has increasingly come to appreciate the contributions of science to explaining human behavior and addressing behavioral problems in everyday life. As behavior analysts shoulder their share of that burden, we must compose our questions with the care that befits its importance in the culture.

CHAPTER SUMMARY

1. The process of discovering things you want to know begins with figuring out exactly what questions you are trying to answer. Figuring out the right question or questions that should guide methodological decisions requires a careful consideration of possible options.

2. Whether developed by a researcher or a practitioner, perhaps the most important fact about experimental questions is that they are verbal behavior. Being aware of the behavioral status of experimental questions helps us to consider both the factors that influence question-asking behavior and how these questions affect the way we design, conduct, and interpret experiments.

3. Faced with different objectives, interests, resources, and extra-experimental contingencies, behavior analytic researchers and practitioners often vary in the types of questions they ask and their associated methodological decision-making.

4. One of the effects of graduate school is to make the field's research literature a powerful influence on our professional interests and activities. It can also be helpful to examine broader areas of literature outside the field. This approach may provide us with a better overall perspective about the general direction of our field and areas in need of additional development.

5. How researchers and practitioners develop questions should be influenced not only by the existing literature but also by experiences with the subject matter itself.

6. For both researchers and practitioners, the challenge is to pose questions that will generate data that are more revealing and useful than might be produced by any other approach to the topic.

7. A good question about behavior is a carefully worded expression of an investigator's best judgments about the direction and focus of his or her interests. It should serve as a guide for the many decisions that must be made to create and manage a project that will satisfy those interests.

8. The experimental question should serve as a guide in selecting participants with specific characteristics that will help to reveal how their behavior is affected by the independent variable, as well as any extraneous variables that might interfere with seeing these effects.

9. When selecting a response class to serve as the dependent variable, the investigator must choose a behavior that will be sensitive to the independent variable. The investigator must also be sure that the dependent variable(s) can be accurately measured and will not be overly susceptible to extraneous factors.

10. The experimental question's most important role is guiding the selection of the independent variable(s). To accomplish this task, the investigator must determine what kind of data will be required to answer the question.

11. To create meaningful comparisons between responding under control versus treatment conditions, each participant must be exposed to both conditions, and the data must be measured and analyzed separately.

12. The analysis of the data allows the investigator to modify the experimental design as the study proceeds and to identify and describe the data that may answer the experimental question. Data analysis also allows the investigator to discover relationships in the data that were not anticipated but are of interest, even if it was not part of the original question.

13. All of the functions of the research question involved in designing and conducting a study support the final step in the process: drawing conclusions that may answer the question. Although it is appropriate that the data will have a big impact on the investigator's conclusions, the conditions under which the data were obtained must be given a major role as well.

14. Research questions are informative not only because they address a particular need in the field but because they can reveal how a science has developed and identify where it is going.

TEXT STUDY GUIDE

1. Why might it be beneficial to begin thinking about questions by working backwards?

2. Why is it important to acknowledge that questions are verbal behavior?

3. Briefly discuss some of the similarities and differences in the types of question asking and the corresponding methodological decision-making that occur between researchers and practitioners.

4. What does reinforcement have to do with how graduate training affects our professional interests?
5. How can studies outside of the primary literature of interest be useful to investigators?
6. What are experimental contingencies, and how do they influence the way we might ask questions?
7. What are extra-experimental contingencies?
8. What is a risk of using only the research literature as a basis for developing questions?
9. Describe how practitioners' daily experiences prompt the type of questions they ask.
10. Why is it useful to focus on developing the best question for a topic?
11. Describe what makes one question better than another.
12. Why is it valuable to actually write down questions under consideration?
13. Why might it be wise to phrase questions so they do not anticipate or forecast results?
14. What is the general strategy for how questions should guide development of procedures?
15. How can the question guide selection of participants?
16. What are some of the considerations in choosing a target behavior that might stem from the question?
17. What are two key requirements for creating meaningful comparisons between the effects of control and experimental conditions?
18. What are three objectives data analysis should meet?

BOX STUDY GUIDE

1. What are research styles?
2. Contrast thematic versus independent research styles.
3. How are explanatory and demonstration styles of research different?
4. How might you recognize research that advocated a particular outcome?
5. What is a hypothesis? What are the risks of using hypotheses to guide experimentation?
6. What is a null hypothesis? What are possible problems with this approach to asking questions?
7. What is the scientific attitude of serendipity?
8. How can investigators maximize their chances of making serendipitous discoveries?

SUGGESTED READINGS

Epstein, R. (Ed.). (1980). *Notebooks, B. F. Skinner.* Englewood Cliffs, NJ: Prentice-Hall.

DISCUSSION TOPICS

1. Select two observations about everyday behavior that you have made recently and consider the experimental questions that they might generate.
2. Select a specific research issue (e.g., effects of video modeling on social initiations by children diagnosed with autism spectrum disorder) that can generate different experimental questions. Break into small groups and develop one question addressing this issue. Afterwards, have a class discussion of the pros and cons of the resulting questions that are developed.

EXERCISES

1. Select a research article from a behavior analytic journal and identify the experimental question. Practice writing different ways of phrasing the experimental question.
2. Using the same research article, evaluate how the question might have guided the investigator's decisions about the study's methodological features, including participant characteristics, target behavior, measurement procedures, and independent variable.
3. Select a research article from a behavior analytic journal and identify the independent and dependent variable(s) in the study. Describe at least two additional independent and dependent variables that the investigator(s) could have considered utilizing as part of the study. Why do you think they did not include these variables?

PART TWO

MEASUREMENT

CHAPTER FOUR

Selecting and Defining Target Behaviors

STRATEGIC ISSUES

Unit of Analysis

In Chapter 2, we considered the general characteristics of behavior as a natural phenomenon and identified key features that are especially important to researchers and practitioners. In any single investigation, however, we do not study behavior in general. We approach each question by focusing on only a small piece of each participant's repertoire. Whether the purpose is to design an experiment or an intervention, the investigator must determine the specific kinds of behavior that will suit the needs of the project and how to go about distinguishing those behaviors from the rest of the repertoire.

As in other natural sciences, the part of the phenomenon that serves as a basis for study in behavior analysis is called the **unit of analysis**. Any phenomenon may have different units of analysis, depending on the focus of the project. The cell, for example, is an important unit of analysis in the study of biological systems, even though cells are composed of even smaller components that can also serve as units of analysis.

> **Unit of analysis.** A constituent part of a whole phenomenon that serves as a basis for experimental study. In the study of behavior, the unit of analysis is the response class.

The early scientific study of behavior was hindered by the lack of a clear understanding of an appropriate unit of analysis. Investigators tended to define environmental stimuli and behavior in purely physical terms and independently of any relation between environment and behavior. One of B. F. Skinner's earliest and most important contributions was the development of a different approach (1935). He argued that stimuli and responses should be defined not in terms of their physical structure or form but in terms of their function or relation with each other. For example, instead of defining the behavior of "making a bed" by describing the movements that are typically involved in that act, one would define it to include any movements that produce beds that are "made up." In other words, the individual responses that result in made-up beds form a class defined by their shared effects, just as those effects (neatly made beds and possibly the accompanying social reinforcers) function as a class of stimuli because they presumably serve as reinforcers for the responses. This approach to defining classes of responses and environmental stimuli is important because it accommodates the way behavior and environment actually work together.

Natural Response Classes

Chapter 2 defined behavior in terms of certain kinds of interactions between organisms and their environments. The details of those interactions have been thoroughly documented in the scientific literature. Our understanding of how behavior works provides a way of organizing the countless instances of behavior that make up repertoires into meaningful groupings or classes – behaviors – in a way that respects natural processes. In the case of operant behavior, this approach involves identifying responses that have the same kind of environmental consequences, which in turn have a common influence on those responses. The shared outcomes or functions of responses and

---

BOX 4.1

Units of Analysis versus Units of Measurement

Because units of analysis and units of measurement share a reference to units, it is easy to confuse them. As defined in this chapter, a **unit of analysis** is that part of a larger phenomenon that serves as a basis for study. The atom, the cell, and the response class are units of analysis. In contrast, a **unit of measurement** refers to a specific amount of some dimension of the thing being measured. For example, the meter is a unit of measurement for measuring length, just as the kilogram serves the same function for measuring weight. A unit of measurement is therefore a particular amount by which we quantify dimensions such as weight and length. A unit of measurement tells how much of a dimension was observed.

You can keep these two types of units straight by remembering that a unit of measurement describes how much of some dimension of a unit of analysis is observed. For example, an observer might report that a school child sat at her desk for a duration of 37 minutes. The unit of analysis is the response class of "sitting at desk." The unit of measurement is the minute, in this case used to describe how much duration was observed.

---

the reciprocal effects of outcomes on behavior point to responses that should be grouped together and defined as instances of a particular behavior. It is important to remember that no matter how we choose to define a particular behavior for a research project or practical intervention, functional relations between responding and its consequences are always at work.

The challenge for investigators is to define target behaviors in ways that suit the interests of the project while taking into account how individual responses come together in natural classes. This objective helps minimize the chances of defining a behavior in a way that comingles responses that have different ties with the environment and therefore actually belong in different natural classes. That in turn minimizes variability in the data by ensuring that the responses that are observed and recorded share similar environmental influences and are therefore likely to change in similar ways when exposed to baseline and treatment conditions.

Consider the example of a child diagnosed with autism spectrum disorder who engages in what are loosely called "stereotyped behaviors." Such behavior might include hand flapping, playing with string in a repetitive manner, and face slapping, among other possibilities. In trying to come up with a definition of one or more target behaviors, the investigator must ask whether those different forms of responding belong in the same class or in separate classes. The fact that the form or appearance of the responses varies does not mean that they are functionally different. If responses that look different produce the same consequences, they may belong in the same class. Similarly, just because responses look alike does not necessarily mean they serve the same function and are instances of the same behavior.

BOX 4.2

Behavior, Response Classes, and Responses

It is tempting to use these three terms interchangeably, but to well-trained behavior analysts they are not the same thing. We have already defined the term **behavior** when used in the general manner described in Chapter 2. When reference is made to a *specific* behavior, the term refers to a single class of responses, such as reading, dressing, walking, and so forth. (Branch and Vollmer [2004] argue that there are some technical problems with this usage, but it is widespread in the applied community.) In other words, **a (particular) behavior** is the same thing as **a response class**. As this chapter explains, a behavior or response class is a grouping of individual responses that share the commonalities specified in the definition of the class. **Responses**, then, are the individual instances of a behavior that make up that class.

Given these distinctions, it would be incorrect to say that "Betty did 15 behaviors today" if you mean that she emitted 15 instances (responses) of a particular target behavior or response class. Similarly, saying that a study focused on three responses would be misleading if what was meant was that three different response classes served as target behaviors.

Functional versus Topographical Definitions

In spite of the endless variety in an organism's repertoire, there are only two basic ways of defining any particular behavior: in terms of its topographical characteristics (form or appearance) or in terms of the functional relations between the behavior and certain features of the environment. There are no other ways of defining a behavior. All definitions of a target behavior are based on either its form or its function, although definitions can also combine those two aspects in various ways.

If a behavior is defined to include only those responses whose occurrence depends on (is a function of) particular environmental stimuli that precede or follow individual responses, it is termed a **functional definition**. The alternative approach involves specifying particular requirements of form or topography. This is called a **topographical definition** because it requires deciding on the three-dimensional form each response must exhibit to be included.

The everyday behavior of opening doors provides a good illustration of these two kinds of definitions. We have a history of engaging in certain actions in the presence of doors so that someone or something can pass through them, which is usually a reinforcing change in the environment. Those contingencies have the effect of making the actions occur in a coordinated way when doors are encountered under conditions that make opening them reinforcing. (It is no accident that we do not walk up to blank walls and behave in the same way we do in front of doors.) Although all of the pieces of the behavior required to open doors may be in our repertoire, our reinforcement history with such

BOX 4.3

But What about Operational Definitions?

At this point, you may be wondering about operational definitions. Where do they come in? References to operational definitions appear routinely in ABA literature and textbooks (e.g., Cooper, Heron, & Heward, 2013). The general idea is to come up with a definition of a target behavior that will guide measurement decisions. If an intervention targets "tantrumming," for example, observers need to know exactly what behavior should be recorded or ignored.

What seems to justify calling the resulting definition "operational" is that it specifies the criteria that observers are supposed to use. The same summary label for the behavior (e.g., tantrumming) might be applied in many circumstances, so it needs to be "operationalized" for each particular case. An operational definition specifies at least part of the observing and recording operations involved in measuring a target behavior. This reasoning makes sense, of course. A simple label for a behavior is almost always an inadequate basis for guiding observing and recording procedures. There are good reasons why a detailed definition of any one behavioral label will need to vary from one case to another.

But when is a definition of a target behavior *not* operational? Can you have one definition of a particular behavior that is operational and another definition of the same behavior that is not operational? Answering this question requires a clear understanding of what we are defining. We are not defining the label we are using to identify the behavior but the actual behavior itself. Given its features, what do we want to record? Any behavior will have far more characteristics than we are interested in, and a definition specifies which ones we want to capture and which ones we want to ignore. If we do not specify those choices in advance, they will be made anyway as measurement proceeds, though by criteria that are unspecified and that are likely to be inconsistent.

So it is impossible to define a behavior for purposes of measurement in a way that does not require decisions about the features that are or are not of interest. *This means that all definitions are operational.* We cannot usefully talk about a particular behavior unless we are clear about the key features of interest. If we're talking about tantrumming, we need to know the key topographical and functional elements that warrant that label. We always have to talk in operational terms because behavior is complex and varied, and summary labels just don't give us the information we need for measurement procedures.

This means that there is no reason to specify definitions of behavior as operational. They are all operational, so the adjective is unnecessary and useless. In other words, *there is no reason to refer to definitions of target behaviors as "operational definitions."* It is not merely a matter of terminological niceties. The apparent challenge of developing operational definitions may distract us from thinking about details of topography and function that are often important for different reasons in different circumstances. That is a serious side effect. Crafting the right definition of a target behavior in terms of function and form is critical because different definitions of the same behavior are likely to reveal different effects of an intervention. We always have to ask how the data might be different if we had defined the behavior differently.

stimuli pulls them together into an organized and functional form only under relatively specific conditions. It is only the kinds of actions that have produced open doors in the past that are likely to occur under those conditions.

How would functional versus topographical definitions of door-opening behavior differ? A functional definition of opening doors would capture all responses occurring in the presence of doors that result in them opening enough to pass something through, which we will assume to be a reinforcing consequence. Using this criterion, the form or topography of included responses may vary a good bit. Depending on the door, functional responses might include reaching for a doorknob with either hand, pushing a bar, pulling a handle, pushing with a foot or another body part, and so on. However, all qualifying responses would open the door.

In contrast, a topographical definition of door-opening behavior might specify that responses must involve twisting a doorknob with the right hand and pushing the door open at least 12 inches, or some other equally specific set of physical requirements. Although the included responses would look very similar, it is quite possible that they would not all serve the same function. For instance, it might be that opening a door only 12 inches would not always be enough to allow a reinforcing outcome, such as someone walking through.

> **Functional definition.** A definition of a behavior based on the functional relations between its responses and classes of antecedent and consequent environmental events.
>
> **Topographical definition.** A definition of a behavior based on the form of responses in three-dimensional space.

You can see that applying these two types of definitions to the same behavior results in somewhat different rules for which responses are included. After all, each type of definition specifically ignores the criteria of the other. A functional definition means responses may be included even though they may look quite different from others, and a topographical definition may include responses that do not share the same functional relations with environmental events.

As an example of what these differences might mean, suppose we are studying self-injurious behavior in individuals diagnosed as intellectually disabled who attend a developmental center. Our task is to define and measure such behavior as part of an effort to treat it. A functional definition would focus on determining the antecedent and consequent stimuli related to the self-injurious behavior. For instance, if Mariel hits her head with her hands, we might look for the stimuli that serve as important consequences for such responses because different responses that involve touching her head may serve different functions. Some responses may leave a red mark or make a sound, both of which will generate certain sensory consequences as well as possible attention from staff members. Other responses may involve scratching an itch, playing with her hair, or putting on a hat, which presumably involve different consequences. We would want our definition to capture only those responses that shared the self-injurious consequences of the behavior. In this example, those effects may be staff attention paired with sensory consequences. Staff members are likely to intervene only when Mariel hits her head hard enough to be heard or leave a mark and are less likely to react when she touches her head in other ways.

In contrast, a topographical definition would specify the physical details individual responses must show to be considered occurrences of self-injury. Criteria would specify exactly what constituted a "head hit," such as what area of the head was hit, how hard the blow was, whether it involved Mariel's hand or an object, and so forth. A purely topographical definition would not include criteria related to the consequences of the responses, such as whether they left a mark or made a sound or led to staff attention. With this approach, we would have to be careful to word the definition so that other ways of touching her head that did not involve risk of injury were not counted as occurrences of "head hitting."

Movement Cycle

Whether a target behavior is defined in terms of its environmental functions or topography, it is either occurring or not occurring at any point in time. One of the reasons for developing a definition is to remove any ambiguity about the momentary status of the behavior by clearly describing the rule that determines whether any responses in an individual's ongoing flow of behavior qualify for membership in the defined response class.

In developing behavioral definitions, it may help to understand the idea of a **movement cycle** (Lindsley, 1966). The movement cycle for a single response simply includes its beginning, middle, and end. The beginning is the point at which the behavior changes from not occurring to occurring. Whatever its characteristics, an instance of the behavior has been initiated in a way that should be captured by the definition. The beginning may not exhibit all of the characteristics of the behavior, but it at least reveals its front end. There is also a middle – identified as whatever goes on between the beginning and the end – which may show additional features, depending on the behavior. The end of the behavior is especially important. This is the point at which the response is completed and another instance of the behavior could therefore occur.

Some behaviors take only a moment or two to complete this cycle, and others can go on for seconds or even minutes. Snapping your fingers has a limited range of topographical elements, and it takes only a fraction of a second to complete a single response. In contrast, opening the locked door to your car involves a heterogeneous chain of actions that consistently occur in a particular sequence. They are presumably maintained as a coherent behavior by the reinforcing consequence of making other responses possible, such as getting in, starting the car, and driving away. A longer-duration behavior can also be made up of a single temporally extended action, such as TV-watching behavior.

The underlying assumption of a movement cycle is that a behavior cannot occur when it is already occurring. It might seem easy to think of apparent contradictions to this point, but they may misrepresent the nature of natural

---

BOX 4.4

The Earlier Life of Operational Definitions

The phrase "operational definition" had a life before ABA came along – and still does. There was a time when talking about operational definitions involved a discussion of mentalism, operationism, and Skinner's famous 1945 paper. As explained in detail by Moore (2008), the principle of operationism came from a physicist named P. W. Bridgeman. He argued that "we mean by any concept nothing more than a set of operations: the concept is synonymous with the corresponding set of operations" (Bridgman, 1927: 5).

Psychology found that approach appealing because it offered a way to deal with mental events without worrying too much about their existence. One thing led to another, and what evolved was the view that language is a symbolic activity in which private subjective meanings have a mentalistic existence. That is, words supposedly have meaning in a private mental lexicon.

Not surprisingly, Skinner had serious problems with that approach to operationism, and he delivered a paper explaining his contrary views at a conference on that topic (Skinner, 1945). He proposed that the meaning of a word lies not in a mental dictionary but in an analysis of the environmental factors that determine the emission of the word as a verbal response. In other words, he did not treat verbal behavior any differently from other behavior. The contrast with psychology's approach to operationism was stark.

Skinner's 1945 paper is famous among behavior analysts because his argument was immediately accepted as an important element of the conceptual foundation of the field. As a result, the phrase "operational definition" was widely understood in the context of Skinner's paper as referring to a tactic for understanding everyday terms through a search for their sources of control as verbal responses. In other words, the only occasion for behavior analysts to talk about operational definitions was when the task was understanding the "meaning" of terms referencing personal qualities that were unclear and often fictional. For behavior analysts, the phrase referred to operationism as a topic or, perhaps, to the tactic Skinner gave us for understanding the "meaning" of verbal behavior in a way that avoided mentalism.

So there was a time when the foregoing is all that "operational definitions" meant. Because many of today's ABA practitioners have been taught to refer to all definitions of target behaviors as operational definitions (but see Box 4.3), it is now necessary to be clear which sense of the phrase is pertinent to any discussion.

---

response classes. Although it may seem that two responses in the same class can occur at the same time, the two responses are likely to represent two different, albeit quite similar, behaviors. For example, if you are exceptionally talented, you may be able to write your name with each hand at the same time. That may seem like two instances of the same behavior, but it is actually two different behaviors with different histories and characteristics. For some purposes the differences may be trivial, but they are there nevertheless. To the extent that the assumption is valid, the end of a movement cycle is the point at which the behavior can occur again.

The concept of a movement cycle is useful in defining a target behavior. It encourages distinct and detailed consideration of what actions constitute the beginning, middle, and end of a single instance of the behavior, which in turn encourages a clear specification of how to distinguish between successive responses. This line of reasoning helps supplement the everyday preconceptions we usually bring to this task. Ordinary assumptions about the makeup of a certain behavior are important as a starting point because they are usually closely tied to the question, but they must then be broken down into the more technical aspects required to investigate the behavior in relation to environmental events.

> **Movement cycle.** The beginning, middle, and end of a single response such that the organism is in a position to emit another instance of that behavior.

The Role of Target Behaviors

Given all of these basic issues, what are the objectives that should guide how researchers and practitioners select and define target behaviors? First, as Chapter 3 points out, the behavior must suit the needs of the question. Both researchers and practitioners typically ask how features of the environment influence the behavior of interest. The characteristics included in the definition of the behavior therefore provide one set of limits on what the data will reveal about that relation.

For instance, if a question asks about the effects of a certain psychotropic drug on the behavior of an elementary school student, the investigator must be confident that the target behavior will reveal the effects of the drug, if there are any. There might be a number of possible target behaviors, including performing selected tasks in a classroom, engaging in disruptive behavior during recess, and so forth. If it were feasible to measure a number of different behaviors, it would likely be found that they differ in how clearly each changes when the drug is being administered compared to when it is not being used. Of course, that luxury is not often available, so it is critical that the selected behavior be well suited to the question.

Second, the characteristics of the target behavior must also suit the general needs of the investigation. Each investigation is made up of specific procedures involving measurement, treatment and control conditions, the way those conditions are compared, and so forth. The target behavior must meet the requirements of all of the investigation's features. For instance, if the behavior occurs very infrequently, it might not clearly reflect the influence of treatment variables, because it does not contact them often enough. Another kind of problem that can limit the sensitivity of the target behavior is excessive influence by extraneous factors. That might be the case if a study measured some form of acting-out behavior in school children that was so heavily influenced by peers that it did not show the effects of the treatment condition. Still another

TABLE 4.1
Objectives of selecting target behaviors

- Suit the needs of the question
- Suit the general needs of the investigation
- Suit the requirements for measurement

---

example involves the way treatment and control conditions are compared. If the research design requires that those conditions alternate every other day, it will be critical for the selected behavior to change rapidly from one condition to the other in order to clearly reflect any differences in their effects.

Third, the characteristics of the target behavior and how it is defined may affect decisions about measurement procedures. A behavior that is otherwise suitable may be difficult to observe, for example. Although automated observing and recording equipment may be available in some settings, in many situations human observers are required. The definition must enable observers to consistently distinguish between responses that are supposed to be measured and the rest of the participant's ongoing behavior. The target behavior must also be easy for them to see and accessible for adequate periods of time. If the target behavior for an elementary school student only occurs during recess, for example, it may be difficult for observers to always be in the right place to see if it is occurring, and recess periods may provide too brief a sample to provide a meaningful picture of responding.

Finally, when it comes to selecting target behaviors, practitioners may often be in a different situation than researchers. Practitioners might justifiably argue that they do not always have a choice about what behaviors are used to evaluate the effects of interventions. When the overriding objective is to modify behavior for practical purposes, it may be necessary to focus on specific behaviors. If the challenge is to teach communication skills to a child with autism or to improve math skills of a sixth grader, for example, the practitioner will have limited options for selecting target behaviors. Nevertheless, some of the issues discussed previously are just as important for practitioners as for researchers. The selected target behavior must facilitate sound measurement procedures and clearly reflect the influence of intervention protocols, whether the project is intended for publication as a research study or to address purely practical issues.

TURNING ISSUES INTO ACTIONS

Developing Functional Definitions

The first step in developing a functional definition is to consider the everyday context of the behavior of interest. For example, if we wish to study the behavior of stealing by adolescent boys in a residential facility, we can start by considering the cultural learning history we all share that broadly defines that behavior. That is too loose a conception for research or professional purposes, but it is important that our focus be socially valid. We can eliminate at least some informality by narrowing our interest to behavior that leads to possessing something that belongs to someone else without first getting permission.

Next, we may speculate on the events that might precede and follow acts of stealing, and we could test our guesses by informally observing that kind of behavior among the boys in the facility. In doing so, we are using both our personal and professional histories as a kind of crude screening device to see what we might find out about possible functional relations between the environment and the behavior. For instance, what we usually call stealing is a response that involves taking or possessing things that belong to other people without getting the owner's approval. In fact, the owner is usually either absent or the item is taken by force. We might also suspect that possession of the stolen item is usually strongly reinforcing.

If our informal assessment seems sound, we are ready to try out possible definitions and see how they work. Trying out a definition means writing it down, using it to guide measurement procedures, and evaluating what is observed and recorded. In this example, suppose that we begin with a definition of responses that produce the consequence of possessing an object that belongs to someone else. We ask staff members to observe and record behaviors that meet that definition.

Right away, staff will probably call to our attention the fact that the definition includes responses that are preceded by the owner of the "stolen" object giving permission for its use. That is probably an important basis for differentiating between stealing something and borrowing it, so we might modify our definition accordingly. Unfortunately, it is likely to be difficult for observers to know if a boy they see with an item that belongs to someone else got permission from the owner. One solution is to ease the observers' task by modifying the environment. We might institute a policy that no boy may possess or use anything belonging to others without first getting a staff member to witness the owner giving permission and signing a "borrowing card" that the borrower must keep until the item is returned. The card is a permanent product of the interchange that allows observers to distinguish between stealing and legitimate borrowing.

We can now revise our definition to include responses that involve possessing an item that belongs to someone else in the absence of the owner's approval, as evidenced by the lack of a borrowing card. As we continue trying out measurement procedures using this new definition, we may see the need for further revisions. For example, staff members may report that they are recording responses that involve both surreptitious taking and taking by force or threat of force. That distinction certainly reflects different antecedent conditions, not to mention different legal contingencies. Although we could certainly define both types of responses as a single behavior for purposes of the project, the different circumstances might represent different sources of environmental control. That suggests that the two variants of the behavior of stealing might be affected differently by our treatment conditions. Including both in the definition might increase variability in the data and make it more difficult to evaluate the effects of treatment. To avoid that risk, we could add to our definition a proviso that the owner must not have been present when the item was taken, which means that actions that involve taking by force or threat would not be measured. Of course, we could always use two definitions – one for each type of stealing – which might be even more informative.

This example should make clear that developing a functional definition is not just a literary exercise. Neither does it necessarily require a lengthy trial-and-error process. It is often easy to develop a sound functional definition by simply observing the behavior of interest under typical environmental conditions and making reasoned guesses about the antecedent and consequent events to which responses are related. The key is that the definitional criteria should make it clear that qualifying responses share the same relations with environmental events.

Developing Topographical Definitions

Because topographical definitions specifically avoid considering functional relations between target responses and the surrounding environment, they are relatively easy to develop. The researcher or practitioner begins by identifying the reason for defining the behavior in terms of the form of individual responses. For instance, if an investigator is working with physical therapists to develop more effective rehabilitation methods for patients with a certain type of injury, it may make sense to define specific therapeutic exercises strictly in terms of their form. A definition might specify bending an arm in a certain way or reaching a certain distance. Although eventually those movements may need to accomplish practical functions, it is understandable if the therapist's initial focus is on topography alone. As a different example, a project might focus on the form of responses on a particular task with office employees. It may be that particular forms of a target behavior are known to yield good productivity, low rates of errors, or proper use of office equipment.

Developing a topographical definition involves carefully describing the limits of form that individual responses must show in order to be considered occurrences of the target behavior. The written definition should detail rules for observers to use in identifying which responses meet those limits and which fall outside the class. Definitions of target behaviors often focus on the form of individual responses because target behaviors must be performed in a specific way. For example, if a trainer is teaching individuals with intellectual disabilities how to make Jell-O, the definition of the target behavior will have to specify the form of each component of that complex skill and the sequence in which the components must occur. Successful performance of the target behavior may allow almost no variation in the form of some component responses.

Choosing Functional and Topographical Features

Depending on the needs of a project and the characteristics of the behavior of interest, both functional and topographical definitions have their place. In fact, if you were not aware of the distinction, the definitions you developed based on your general experience would often include both functional and topographical elements. Combining functional and topographical features in the definition of a target behavior can work well as long as there are good reasons for including responses that may differ in form and function. For example, an investigation of procedures for training athletic behaviors might require definitions that include both topographical and functional features. A definition of the behavior of hitting a baseball might include a particular stance in the batter's box as well as topographical features of swinging the bat but with the added functional element of hitting the ball so that it lands in play.

In considering whether to craft a definition that separates or combines functional and topographical features, remember to select only responses that are targeted for specific reasons and avoid those that might seem similar but are actually different in some important way. Responses that meet the terms of the definition will be represented in the data describing what happened from one session to another under control and treatment conditions. The key is that the data must reflect the impact of the conditions on a homogeneous collection of responses that provide a meaningful basis for drawing conclusions.

What makes a definition meaningful? It depends on the focus of the question, the natural features of the target behavior, and the nature of the treatment and control conditions. For instance, in an evaluation of procedures for teaching sharing behavior to children diagnosed with autism spectrum disorder, it will be important to develop a definition that captures the same key features for each child from one occasion to another and across all children who participate. If the project will involve more or less naturally occurring instances of sharing as opposed to a highly structured protocol in which sharing can only occur in programmed ways, it will be difficult to define the behavior in terms of the form of individual sharing responses. After all, what we usually think of as sharing can involve responses that vary widely in form but have a common social context. This suggests that a functional definition would be required to ensure that all of the measured responses involve the same kind of social interactions. That approach would mean that the data would not only represent the same kind of responses, they would likely be affected in the same way by the intervention procedures. Such an outcome would help the investigator draw sound conclusions about the effects of the intervention.

In contrast, a topographical definition would require specifying in advance the actions that constitute sharing. Some actions might involve the same social functions that would meet the requirements of a functional definition, but others might not. Differences in the measured responses might lead to variability in the data, which would make them somewhat less meaningful than data generated by a functional definition.

On the other hand, consider a project evaluating different ways of completing a production task using a piece of equipment in a manufacturing plant. The investigator is not concerned about the quality of the final products (the equipment may ensure that they are always acceptable) but wants to identify behavior that is optimally efficient and safe. In this case it may be more useful

BOX 4.5

Parent: "What Did You Do Today?" Child: "Nothing."

As parents have always suspected, because behavior is one of the characteristics of living (as opposed to dead) organisms, someone cannot ever be "doing nothing." A person can, however, not do a particular thing at a certain time. When a particular behavior is of research or practical interest, it is occasionally tempting to define a behavior in terms of "not doing _____." Of course, when a person is "not doing _____," he or she is actually doing something else.

Defining a target behavior in this negative form is problematic, to say the least. For instance, how will an observer know when to record each non-response, given that the individual will be "not doing _____" most of the time? One solution is to define a specific class of environmental events that function as occasions or opportunities for the behavior of interest and then count the occasions on which responses do not occur. There are problems with that approach, however. The events that seem to serve as opportunities must first be empirically determined to actually have that discriminative function. Second, those events must not also set the occasion for other behaviors that might interfere with the target behavior. Third, interventions are likely to change the discriminative relations – that is, the opportunities to respond. Because measurement of the non-behavior is tied to those opportunities, this would require changing the definition, perhaps repeatedly. Such changes would make it difficult to know what the data actually represent.

In practical situations, it would also be difficult to arrange contingencies involving non-behaviors. When a defining opportunity occurs and a response is not emitted, what should a consequence be contingent on? It cannot follow the behavior of interest because it did not occur. A consequence must follow whatever behavior did occur, and it might be those behaviors that change as a result, rather than the non-behavior.

The message is this: If you are tempted to focus your interest on a non-behavior, keep thinking about the situation until you figure out another way to define your interest. For example, if you are concerned about "not getting out of bed in the morning," it would be better to define the behavior of "getting out of bed" and measure its latency from when the alarm clock goes off.

for the investigator to define target behaviors in terms of their form rather than their function. Certain ways of using the equipment might be specified under different test conditions. That would ensure that conclusions about different ways of using the equipment were based on responses that were alike in their key features.

Variations and Refinements

Adding Temporal Dimensions. It is impossible to define a target behavior solely in terms of a temporal (time) dimension, but it may sometimes be useful

TABLE 4.2
Adding temporal dimensions to target behavior definitions

Temporal dimension	Example
• Interresponse time	Pacing of rowing responses
• Response latency	Response to emergency alarm
• Duration	Tying a bleeding artery

to add a temporal requirement to a functional or topographical definition. If that is done, responses that satisfy the basic definition but fail to meet the temporal requirement would not be recorded. There are three basic circumstances in which addition of a temporal requirement might be important.

When the frequency or pacing of individual responses is of interest, the definition should specify the amount of time that can or must occur between successive responses. In sculling, for example, the time between successive responses of pulling oars, regulated by the rhythmic chanting of the coxswain, is a major determinant of the boat's speed. With that temporal requirement included in the definition, observers would only measure responses that met both a core requirement (such as a particular form of a rowing response) and the temporal feature (such as a minimum time between successive rowing responses). As another example, consider a young child who does not chew and swallow each bite of food completely before taking the next bite, which puts her at risk of choking. If an intervention goal is to slow down the pace of eating, the definition of the target behavior should include a minimum amount of time between swallowing one bite and putting the next bite in her mouth.

Sometimes it is important to ensure that a response is counted only if there is some minimum or maximum latency between an environmental event and responding. For example, when a safety engineer is concerned about how quickly employees initiate corrective action following a signal of an unsafe condition, the definition of the target behavior should include not only the form of the action employees should take, but also the maximum amount of time between the onset of an alarm and occurrence of the target behavior. For an adolescent with Down syndrome who is training for a job with a landscaping crew, target behavior definitions might need to include minimum latencies between instructions from his supervisor and his initiation of tasks in addition to topographical descriptions of the tasks to be performed.

The time required to complete a response may be an important dimension to add to some definitions. For instance, the time it takes a surgeon to tie off a bleeding artery during an operation is obviously important. The young man from the example above might need to complete some landscaping tasks within certain time limits to meet job requirements. In such instances, the definition of the target behavior may need to include a minimum or maximum response duration.

Response Product Definitions. The effects of behavior on the environment are often transient. If you say "Hello" as you pass a friend on your way to class and she answers by saying "Hi," there is no trace of your behavior once she walks on. However, it is not uncommon for some effects of a behavior to leave some relatively durable changes in the environment. Changes that last for at least a while are called **response products**. These products are sometimes tangible, such as a completed test paper or litter in a city park. Response products may also be intangible, such as a light left on in a room indicating that someone was there.

> **Response products.** The tangible or intangible environmental effects of responding that are more than transitory in duration.

Defining a target behavior in terms of its environmental products is a way of implementing a functional definition. What is observed is one of the effects or functions of responding, rather than the responses themselves. Response product definitions can be especially useful when real-time observation would be difficult. That might be the case when the target behavior occurs infrequently over extended periods of time. The National Park Service uses this approach when it estimates usage of a remote hiking trail with a logbook at the trailhead that hikers are asked to sign. Sometimes it might be useful to define a behavior in terms of its products to avoid having to maintain contemporaneous observation procedures. For example, in a manufacturing facility where employees' work results in completed steps in a manufacturing process, it could be more efficient to observe the completed products than to observe each employee's behavior.

The physical products of responding can be a useful way of specifying a target behavior, but three possible problems can complicate interpreting the resulting data. First, the owner of two puppies who comes home to find a single pile of excrement on the living room rug will recognize the problem of *determining authorship* of the response that created the product. A park ranger may likewise question the existence of a group of hikers that included George Washington, Carl Sagan, and Lady Gaga.

A second challenge in drawing conclusions from response product data may be illustrated by considering whether counting pieces of litter could be used to measure the littering behavior of people using a city park. Because there is no real-time direct observation of the behavior, *assuming one-to-one correspondence* between response products and actual responses may be unwise. It is conceivable, for example, that most of the littering was done by a small number of park users.

A third possible limitation of this approach to a functional definition arises from the investigator's *lack of contact with the actual topographical variations* that make up the target behavior. Observing the response product may reveal little about the form of the different responses involved. Sometimes variations in the form of responses may be unimportant, of course, particularly in situations in which topography may be narrowly constrained by the situation. For example, the form of a nurse's behavior of taking a blood sample

TABLE 4.3
Risks in interpreting response product data

Interpretive risk	Example
• Determining authorship	Puppy mess
• Assuring 1:1 correspondence	Litter in a park
• Lack of contact with topography	Golf swing

may be partially dictated by the equipment being used and the necessity of getting a sample of blood. However, subtle variations in the form of responses can influence their effectiveness. This is often true of athletic behavior, such as swinging a golf club. Investigators may learn useful things from observing those variations. A researcher studying worker performance may find it valuable to observe responding as it is happening in order to see differences from one response to another that might affect errors and productivity.

Group Definitions. So far, we have considered ways of defining target behaviors for individuals. That is appropriate because behavior is a phenomenon that occurs only between individuals and their environments (see Chapter 2). There may be times, however, when interest lies in the aggregate performance of a number of people. Box 2.4 notes that the collected behavior of individuals who behave in a related way is often referred to as group behavior.

Be careful to avoid misunderstanding that phrase. Although we often refer to the "behavior" of groups in everyday discourse (e.g., "The class was making lots of noise when the teacher was out of the room"), groups do not behave. Behavior is a biological function of organisms, and a group is not an organism. It is certainly true that individuals often behave differently when they are with others than when they are alone, but their behavior in social environments is still just individual behavior. There is no new, fundamentally different phenomenon that emerges when individuals behave in group situations. The differences in a person's behavior under social versus solitary conditions are due to the different contingencies often operating in social environments.

Sometimes, however, there is a legitimate interest in the collective output of the behavior of multiple individuals. There are three basic ways the behavior of individuals can contribute to some group outcome. First, the behavior of different individuals may make collective and equivalent contributions to some result through their interactions. For example, consider using the noise made by a class of fourth graders as the dependent variable in a study of classroom management procedures. If a device is used to record sound levels in the classroom, the noise-making behavior of any or all of the children will contribute in an equivalent way to the collective effect. Additionally, this functional definition of the group's "responding" takes into account the possibility that each child's behavior may be influenced by the behavior of others.

Second, interest may center on an arbitrarily defined collection of individuals who do not interact in the usual sense of a group but may all respond in the same way in the same setting. That is illustrated by shoppers who engage in

TABLE 4.4
Types of group response class definitions

Type of group contribution	Example
• Collective, equivalent, interactive	Measuring effects of noise-making behavior
• Collective, equivalent, non-interactive	Measuring store purchases of shoppers
• Collective, non-equivalent	Measuring work products

purchasing behavior in a store. Using sales receipts, we could measure purchasing responses by the number of people who buy something in a store, though they do not interact or influence each other's behavior.

Third, the behavior of individuals may contribute to some collective outcome, though their behavioral contributions may differ and the individuals may not interact. In many work scenarios, for example, some product (such as assembled automobiles) results from the varied efforts of different workers.

Measuring the collective behavioral contributions of different individuals may sometimes be useful. However, it is important to recognize how these ways of defining "group behavior" restrict interpretations of the data. Although the data take the behavior of different individuals into account, their separate contributions to the collective outcome are not typically recorded. Measures of behavior are usually expressed only in some aggregate form. That means we cannot make statements about the effects of treatment conditions on the behavior of individuals. For instance, if a teacher's implementation of a classroom management plan is followed by a decrease in sound level data from that fourth-grade class, we know only that the sum of all noise-making behavior decreased. We do not know whether that decrease occurred for each child or only some. Indeed, some children may have gotten noisier. In other words, we do not know from the data how the effect on the group "response" was produced. Even though the data represent effects for at least some of the children, we do not have any evidence about effects on the behavior of individual children. Therefore, we do not actually know the effect of the intervention on behavior. (Remember, there is no such phenomenon as group behavior.)

This interpretive limitation applies not only to the participants in the study but also to individuals in general. If group data show that an intervention resulted in a substantial increase in responding, for instance, it might seem legitimate to conclude that the same outcome should be expected if the protocol is used with other participants, even though we may know that responding did not increase for all participants. It is important to remember that although group data reflect individual behavioral effects, it hides the effects of the intervention on the behavior of individuals in the group. That is, the group "effect" is not a simple and direct reflection of the actual behavioral effects. This can be a difficult limitation to grasp.

As we will learn in later chapters, this limitation applies whenever the data from different individuals are grouped by any method of defining, collecting, displaying, or analyzing behavioral data. Drawing conclusions based on any type of grouped data must be limited to statements about the effects of treatment conditions only as aggregate outcomes. As a result, how well the effects hold for individuals will be less clear than if the data showed the effects for each individual. In the example of the fourth-grade class, individual data might have shown that although a majority of the children got quieter when the intervention was initiated, a number of them made as much or even more noise. With only grouped data, we might properly conclude that the collective effect of the intervention was to produce a decrease in noise-making behavior. However, collecting data separately for each child would allow us to describe more specific effects, such as less noise-making behavior, no change, or even an increase. Such data might encourage researchers to conduct further studies to determine what factors predict those different outcomes, which would allow teachers to decide whether the intervention is appropriate in different situations or how to optimize its effectiveness.

Is it always important to be able to identify the effects of interventions on the behavior of each individual? Not necessarily, but more often than you might suspect. If the objective is to learn something about behavior, the answer is almost always "yes." If a company hires you to study why worker performance in one section of an electronics factory has deteriorated and how to improve it, a group definition of the target behavior will probably not be sufficient. As you implement changes and look at their effects on performance, you may need to know what those effects are for each worker. For example, if you compare the effects of two different types of equipment on performance, you will want to know if the effects depend on whether workers are right- or left-handed or wear glasses. Grouping the data across workers will usually hide such variations.

On the other hand, if you only need to measure behavior in aggregate form, you might be able to get away with a group definition of target behavior. For example, if you address a company's absenteeism problem by implementing a well-established program for dealing with that issue, it might be sufficient to show an improvement in aggregate data. If you did not get the planned improvements, however, you might need to learn why. That would probably require looking at individual patterns of absenteeism.

In sum, the decision to define target behaviors in terms of the collected contributions of individuals depends on the kinds of conclusions required to answer the guiding question. If the goal is to understand behavior-environment interactions, target behaviors must be defined, measured, and analyzed for individuals. That is also preferable when the goal is to apply established procedures to achieve a practical outcome, even if the interventions involve multiple participants. (Analysis of the effects for each individual can always be supplemented with grouped summaries of individual data.) In some instances, however, it may be sufficient to define a target behavior as a combination of that behavior in different individuals. The choice should be based on an understanding that the focus of the question allows the limited conclusions that will be possible if target behaviors are defined in terms of group performance.

Selecting Target Behaviors

Specificity. Defining a target behavior involves developing a rule for separating selected responses from the rest of an individual's repertoire. The major features of the target behavior will be determined by the focus of the question, the characteristics of participants, the opportunities for measurement, and the needs of treatment conditions. In accommodating these interests, the investigator also has the opportunity to choose the breadth or specificity of the definition.

The "size" of the target behavior can be important. If too small a piece of behavior is specified by the definition, it may not be sufficiently relevant for the investigation. For example, pushing a button in a laboratory task may not adequately represent more complex behaviors in everyday life. On the other hand, selecting too large a piece of behavior may prevent discovery of important sources of variability. For instance, if a practitioner is interested in a child's social behavior, defining a target behavior as "interacting with other children" will make it difficult to identify strengths and weaknesses in the child's social repertoire or discover exactly how various interventions affect social interactions.

Aside from defining a target behavior with a level of specificity that is meaningful for the issues of interest, the frequency with which the behavior occurs can also be an important consideration. If the target behavior occurs very often or with very little time between successive occurrences, the specificity or breadth of the definition may need to be adjusted. Consider the example of a child who gets in fights with peers. If the target behavior is fighting, the definition may need to include several topographically different responses that are intermingled and occur rapidly, one after the other. It may be difficult, however, for observers to accurately count separate occurrences of each of those responses. That may also be the case even if the target behavior is defined more narrowly as hitting others if the child tends to hit repeatedly with little time elapsing between each strike.

One solution to this problem is to define and measure **bouts** or **episodes** of responding. Such episodes may constitute functional classes; for instance, an episode of fighting might include any or all of the topographically different behaviors of hitting, kicking, and cursing, all of which have the same environmental effect. Defining and measuring episodes requires giving observers clear rules for identifying the onset and offset of an episode. Although it may be clear when fighting or hitting is occurring, it must also be clear when each episode starts and ends. One risk of using this approach with target behaviors that encompass more than one response is that changes in the number of episodes may mask what is happening with the smaller response classes. For example, a decrease in the number of fighting episodes each day may hide the fact that the number of cursing responses in each episode is increasing. A related risk is that measuring just the number of episodes may not fully reveal the effects of treatment, which might include changing the duration of episodes as well or instead. A straightforward solution is to have observers record the duration of each episode (the time from onset to offset), which will also yield a count of the number of episodes that occur during each observation period.

Episode (or bout). A relatively brief period of responding defined by the relatively frequent occurrence of one or more specific response classes and distinguished from other such episodes by relatively extended periods in which the target responses do not occur.

A different problem can occur when the behavior of interest happens very infrequently. One such example might involve customers who make purchases in a shopping mall. An individual customer may buy something only occasionally, perhaps two or three times per month. That rate or frequency of responding is so low that it would be difficult and time-consuming to detect whether it decreased. A tactic to address that problem is to look for components of purchasing behavior that might occur with a more useful frequency. These might include going into different stores, handling merchandise, or asking questions of sales personnel in addition to actually purchasing items. This approach can be particularly useful in addressing problem behaviors that have serious consequences but occur too infrequently to be suitable targets for interventions. For example, an individual with intellectual disabilities living in a group home may break a window with his fist only a couple of times a year. Each occurrence obviously has medical risks that warrant efforts to reduce the behavior, but the fact that it occurs so infrequently means that it will not contact intervention contingencies often enough for them to have an effect. It may be, however, that precursor behaviors that often precede punching windows and similar responses occur much more often and therefore make a better target for intervention than punching windows.

Sensitivity. Finally, one of the most important considerations in selecting a target behavior lies in its potential to be influenced by treatment variables. In both research and practical scenarios, it is important that the behavioral features of interest are free to vary so that any effects of interventions can be detected through those changes. One kind of limit to sensitivity occurs when the behavior being measured has lower or upper limits on variability for some reason. Under such circumstances, measures of responding may not reveal the effects of interventions that would otherwise be found. For instance, the behavior of initiating conversations is clearly limited by the number of opportunities available to a client. If she is already initiating conversations on almost every opportunity, it might be difficult for an intervention to produce an increase in responding unless the number of opportunities also increases.

A similar limitation may occur for different reasons when the target behavior occurs very infrequently. If a behavior does not occur very often, it may receive so little exposure to a treatment that it does not show any effects, even though effects might be clear if the behavior had greater contact with the treatment contingencies.

Perhaps the most common risk to the sensitivity of a target behavior results when it is so heavily influenced by extraneous factors that it is not very

TABLE 4.5
Limitations on sensitivity

Type of limitation	Problem	Example
• Upper limit on variability	Increases in responding may not be detected	Limited opportunity for behavior to occur
• Lower limit on variability	Inadequate contact with treatment conditions	Behavior occurs very infrequently
• Excessive extraneous influences	Treatment effects not found	Behavior heavily influenced by non-treatment factors

susceptible to the treatment. This preemptive control by extraneous variables can result from a single, powerful source or from a collection of weaker influences. In educational settings, for example, it is not unusual for academic behavior to be so heavily influenced by social factors associated with peers and teachers that the impact of teaching procedures can be difficult to evaluate. Although it is easy to understand this type of limitation on the sensitivity of a target behavior, the impact of extraneous factors will not necessarily be evident in the data, which is a bit late to be addressing that problem. The only recourse is for investigators to wonder about the susceptibility to significant extraneous factors when they are considering possible target behaviors.

Defining Target Behaviors

Assuming that the general nature of the behavior of interest is already clear, let us summarize the steps in defining a target behavior. First, consider the characteristics of the behavior. What are its functional relations with environmental events, if those are known? What are its topographical features? How might the behavior be affected by treatment variables? What challenges are likely to be involved in observing and recording the behavior?

Second, decide whether the definition will be functional or topographical or if both kinds of elements should be taken into account. In making that decision, consider differences in the composition of the target behavior that would result from one approach versus another. How important might those differences be? How might they affect the data and conclusions?

Third, write out a draft definition that includes all of the features and criteria you think will be necessary. Compose the definition like a lawyer writing a contract. Make sure that every important detail is present and that nothing unnecessary is included. The definition should be a plain statement that unambiguously specifies whether candidate responses should be recorded or ignored. If measurement will be conducted by observers, the definition should be seen as a rule telling them what to observe and record. It should not usually include any reference to the reason the behavior is being measured, performance criteria related to the intervention, or the outcomes that might be anticipated (see Chapter 6).

TABLE 4.6
Steps in defining a target behavior

- Consider the characteristics of the behavior
- Decide on the type of definition needed
- Compose a written draft definition
- Try out the draft definition by using it to measure responding. Modify as necessary and try out the modified definition
- Determine how the definition will guide measurement procedures
- Start the investigation, but be ready to modify the definition further if necessary

Fourth, put the draft definition into practice by using it to obtain some informal information through still careful measurements. Use that experience and the resulting data to modify the definition in whatever ways seem appropriate. Continue collecting data using the now improved definition. Evaluate the effects of any modifications by comparing new data to data obtained under earlier versions. What do the data tell you about your decisions?

Fifth, once you are satisfied with the definition, determine how it will guide measurement procedures. If observation and measurement will be automated, insure that the equipment performs in exactly the way required by the definition. If human observers will be used to collect data, what does the definition suggest about how they will need to be trained and monitored (see Chapters 6 and 8)? Collect the evidence you feel you need to convince yourself and others that the definition you have written is exactly the same as the one being used to measure the behavior.

Sixth, start the investigation using your measurement system. Be ready to modify it continuously if problems emerge while you gain experience with it. Although that may require throwing out the data collected to that point, it may be worth it to avoid burdening the data with unnecessary limitations.

In sum, developing a definition of a target behavior is not difficult, but it takes thoughtful consideration of the behavior and what definitional criteria will best guide measurement procedures. Beyond the intellectual effort, it involves putting draft definitions to the test by using them to generate some data, learning from the experience, and trying again. Coming up with the right definition is not a mundane exercise. After all, it specifies the dependent variable in research or practical interventions, which will be the basis for drawing conclusions about treatment effects.

LABELING TARGET BEHAVIORS

One of the biggest challenges in defining a target behavior has to do with helping others properly interpret research or clinical findings. Whatever its features, each definition is typically described with a brief label that serves the same everyday communication functions as do other labels for objects and events. The problem is that any particular summary label may be interpreted differently by different people. "Disruptive behavior," for example, could certainly mean very different things to a researcher or a parent or teacher, regardless of how that behavior is defined for a specific investigation.

Other sciences minimize this problem by using a technical vocabulary in place of colloquial terms. Instead of referring to "vultures," for instance, biologists refer to a specific grouping of birds, such as the families Aegypiidae and Cathartidae, or even to a specific genus and species. Among biologists, technical labels like those have very narrow definitions, so there is little chance of misunderstanding what kinds of birds are being referenced.

The science of behavior has no such taxonomic vocabulary of behavior, nor is it even possible to come up with a technical label for every behavior. This limitation stems from the fact that what might seem to be the same behavior from one person to another is actually unique for each individual. Furthermore, because behavior continuously adapts to changing environmental circumstances, any particular behavior is always changing, even if only in subtle ways. Together, these characteristics mean that there are probably an infinite number of behaviors in a person's repertoire.

When a researcher attaches a shorthand label to a carefully defined target behavior in a published study, others can check the definition and be pretty clear about what the label refers to. However, when the label is used by others under different circumstances, it will be attached to different definitions for different participants in research and service settings. In spite of that variability, such labels are often used to refer to entire large categories of responding (for example, self-injurious behavior).

The unavoidable variations in how particular labels are used raise an important question: How well do the findings of different studies focusing on the same labeled behavior hold across all such studies, and in everyday practice? If a published study shows that certain intervention procedures increased cooperative play behavior in preschool children, for example, how can other researchers or practitioners know if they will get the same results if they use similar procedures in their own situations? Differences between the definition of cooperative play used in the published study and the cooperative play behavior of other preschool children may be important, even to the extent that the published findings do not hold for children who seem very similar to the study participants. These are questions about the generality of research findings, and they have no easy answers. Each chapter of this book identifies some factors that bear on the answers, and Chapter 16 addresses the issue of generality in detail.

Nevertheless, the summary label we attach to the particular definition of a target behavior in a study or practical intervention can make a difference in how we interpret the results. What can researchers and practitioners do to communicate clearly about the kind of behavior under investigation? First, using clearly stated definitions of each target behavior probably helps more than anything else. Whether a definition is functional, topographical, or a combination of both, it is essential that the characteristics shared by all measured responses result in data that reveal treatment effects and enable sound conclusions. Second, when deciding what to call a target behavior, it can help to be aware of how others may interpret or use the label. "Hitting others" is less likely to be misinterpreted than the more ambiguous label "aggression," which suggests a vague trait rather than a behavior. Similarly, "calling clients" or "analyzing spreadsheets" would probably be better labels than "working." Third, choosing labels that describe the relation of the behavior to the environment may also encourage precise interpretations. For example, the term "playing" covers an endless variety of behavior-environment possibilities. In contrast, "playing with blocks" or "playing house with peers" narrows possible interpretations.

Although these suggestions may aid clear communication about target behaviors, there is no perfect solution to this challenge. The nature of behavior guarantees endless variety in its forms and relations with the environment, and everyday language cannot meet the requirements for scientific specificity. Nevertheless, it is our task as researchers and practitioners to describe our work for colleagues and to translate it into the language of the culture. As we come to better understand the factors that determine the generality of our research and clinical findings, we will be better prepared to refine the way we describe target behaviors.

CHAPTER SUMMARY

1. B. F. Skinner's approach helped shift the focus from defining stimuli and responses in purely physical terms to include a description about their function and relationship with each other.

2. Functional definitions include only those responses whose occurrence is dependent upon a specific class of stimuli that either precede or follow the response. In contrast, topographical definitions may include responses that do not share the same functional relations with environmental stimuli, even though they are topographically the same.

3. The concept of a movement cycle is useful in defining a target behavior, as it encourages a clear specification of how to distinguish between successive responses.

4. The selection and definition of target behaviors should be guided by a number of objectives, including: (a) that the behavior suit the needs of the question, (b) that the characteristics of the target behavior suit the general needs of the investigation, (c) the type of measurement procedures utilized, (d) the goals of the practitioner or researcher.

5. The first step in developing a functional definition is to consider the everyday context of the target behavior, including possible antecedents and consequences. Following this assessment, the investigator can write a preliminary definition and use it to guide measurement activities and evaluate what is recorded.

6. The first step in developing a topographical definition is to identify why it is necessary to define the behavior in terms of the form that each individual

response takes. The experimenter should then carefully describe the limits of form that responses must show in order to be measured.

7. Target behavior definitions may include temporal requirements. Requirements may be added that address: (a) the time between the presentation of a stimulus and the occurrence of the target behavior, (b) the time required to complete a response, or (c) the amount of time that must occur between successive responses.

8. Response product definitions may be useful when real time observation may not be feasible. However, these definitions are limited due to the fact that: (a) you may not always be able to determine who produced the product, (b) you cannot assume a 1:1 correspondence between the response product and occurrence of the behavior, and (c) the response product may not tell the researcher anything about the topography of the response.

9. Recall that behavior exists only at the level of the individual. When speaking about group behavior and drawing conclusions based on any type of grouped data, our conclusions must be limited only to statements about the effects of treatment conditions as an aggregate outcome.

10. When selecting a target behavior, the investigator must be sure that the response class is neither too small (may not be relevant to the study) nor too large (may inhibit the identification of important sources of variability). Investigators must also consider how frequently the target behavior occurs when deciding what behaviors to include.

11. One of the most important considerations in selecting a target behavior lies in its potential to be influenced by treatment variables. It is important that the target behavior not be too restricted, otherwise it will not be able to display all of the effects that the intervention may produce. The investigator must also make sure that the selected target behavior is not so heavily influenced by extraneous factors that it is not very susceptible to the impact of the treatment condition.

12. Developing a definition of a target behavior is not difficult, but it takes thoughtful consideration of the behavior and what definitional criteria will best guide measurement procedures.

13. When labeling target behaviors, researchers and practitioners must be sure to communicate clearly about the behavior under investigation. This may be accomplished by clearly stating the definition of each target behavior, being aware of how others may interpret or use the label that has been selected, and using behavior-specific labels when possible.

HIGHLIGHTED TERMS

Episode (or bout). A relatively brief period of responding defined by the relatively frequent occurrence of one or more specific response classes and distinguished from other such episodes by relatively extended periods in which the target responses do not occur.

Functional definition. A definition of a behavior based on the functional relations between its responses and classes of antecedent and consequent environmental events.

Movement cycle. The beginning, middle, and end of a single response such that the organism is in a position to emit another instance of that behavior.

Response products. The tangible or intangible environmental effects of responding that are more than transitory in duration.

Topographical definition. A definition of a behavior based on the form of responses in three-dimensional space.

Unit of analysis. A constituent part of a whole phenomenon that serves as a basis for experimental study. In the study of behavior, the unit of analysis is the response class.

TEXT STUDY GUIDE

1. What is a unit of analysis?
2. What is a response class?
3. Distinguish between functional and topographical response class definitions.
4. What is a movement cycle and why is it useful in defining a target behavior?
5. List the objectives that should guide an investigator's selection and definition of target behaviors.
6. How do you go about developing a functional definition?
7. What is required to develop a topographical response definition?
8. What makes a definition meaningful?
9. Describe three ways of adding a temporal requirement to a behavioral definition.
10. Explain each of the following issues associated with defining a behavior in terms of its products: (a) determining authorship, (b) assuring one-to-one correspondence between responses and products, and (c) lack of contact with topographical variations.
11. Defend the statement that there is no such phenomenon as group behavior.
12. What are three ways of defining a response class that involve the behavior of different individuals in some combined form?
13. What are the interpretive restrictions required by using group behavior definitions?
14. Explain the problems that can result from a target behavior definition being too large or too small.
15. What is a bout or episode of a behavior? Provide an original example.

16. What is meant by the "sensitivity" of a target behavior?
17. List the steps in defining a target behavior.
18. Describe the problems with attaching everyday labels to target behaviors.

BOX STUDY GUIDE

1. Distinguish between units of analysis and units of measurement.
2. Explain the proper use of the following terms: behavior, response class, and responses.
3. What is an operational definition? What did Skinner have to say about them?
4. Explain the complications of defining a non-behavior.

SUGGESTED READINGS

Moore, J. (2008). *Conceptual foundations of radical behaviorism*. Cornwall-on-Hudson, NY: Sloan Publishing. Chapter 5: Categories of behavior.
Skinner, B. F. (1945). Operational analysis of psychological terms. *Psychological Review, 52*, 270–281.

DISCUSSION TOPICS

1. Select some everyday references to behavior and discuss how to translate them into response classes.
2. Start with a general description of a behavior and then discuss how to develop a functional versus topographical definition.
3. Using some target behaviors defined in journal articles, discuss the implications of different kinds of summary labels that might be used.

EXERCISES

1. Without prior discussion, write a definition for a generally described behavior. Then, analyze other students' definitions, focusing on how these differences would generate variances in observations, data collection, and the resulting data.
2. Outline two original examples of when it might be useful to add temporal requirements to a target behavior definition.
3. Develop two target behavior definitions that utilize response products. Identify for each definition whether any of the three problems described in the chapter might apply.

CHAPTER FIVE

Dimensions of Behavior and Units of Measurement

MEASUREMENT OF BEHAVIOR
    Dimensional Measurement
    Dimensions of Individual Responses
        Event-Response Latency
        Duration
        Count
        Topographical Dimensions
    Dimensions of Multiple Responses
        Interresponse Time
        Rate or Frequency
        Celeration
LIMITATIONS OF RATIOS
    Loss of Component Information
    Dimensionless Ratios
SELECTING BEHAVIORAL DIMENSIONS
DESCRIBING DIMENSIONAL DATA

MEASUREMENT OF BEHAVIOR

Dimensional Measurement

To this point, we have considered the nature of behavior as a scientific subject matter (Chapter 2) and how to select and define particular pieces of behavior for investigation or practical management (Chapter 4). We now turn to the next step in measuring behavior: deciding what aspects of the target behavior we might be interested in and how to describe what we observe.

When we observe a target behavior and make a quantitative record of our observations, the numbers we record represent how much of a particular dimension we observed. A **dimension** is simply a quantifiable aspect of a natural phenomenon, so the process just described is called **dimensional measurement**. For example, if we use a timer to measure the amount of time that a student spends working on an assignment during a class period, we are measuring duration – one of the dimensions by which behavior can be described.

Dimensional measurement requires specifying exactly how much of a dimension is observed. That function is served by **units of measurement** (see Box 4.1). For the dimension of duration, for example, those are units of time, such as seconds, minutes, and hours. Units of measurement refer to a fixed amount of a dimension, and it is important that they are defined independently of what is being measured and in a standard way across scientific disciplines. The units of time fit those requirements.

> **Dimension.** A quantifiable aspect of a natural phenomenon.
>
> **Dimensional measurement.** An approach to measurement that involves attaching a number representing the observed extent of a dimension to an appropriate unit of measurement.
>
> **Unit of measurement.** A determinate amount of a dimension of the phenomenon being measured.

Dimensions of Individual Responses

Event-Response Latency. Consider the dimensions that may be used to characterize individual responses. As a physical phenomenon, behavior can be described in terms of some of the same dimensions as other natural phenomena. For example, interactions between organisms and their environments occur in time, so we can locate individual responses in time with reference to other events. That information is reflected in the temporal dimension of **latency**. Figure 5.1 shows an **event-response latency**. This dimension describes how much time elapses following an environmental event before a response occurs. We can record the event-response latency for each individual response and also sum the latencies across all responses in a session, or even calculate a mean or median latency. The standard units of time specify exactly how much latency is observed.

To illustrate, a teacher might be interested in how quickly a student begins working each of five rows of math problems on a worksheet after the teacher gives an instruction to start a row. To measure event-response latencies, the teacher would have to first select a timing instrument (such as a wristwatch with a stopwatch function or an app on an electronic device) and decide exactly when the observer is to start and stop timing. For example, timing might start when the spoken instruction ends and stop as soon as the response

---

BOX 5.1

The United States and the Metric System

If a friend asked you how your diet was going and you said you had lost 20 kilograms, your answer might seem out of place only in the United States, where the US Customary System of measurement predominates. The rest of the industrialized world has long used the decimal-based metric system of units of measurement. Although the US government has supported the metric system since 1866, even to the extent of statutes requiring certain uses of the metric system, many people in the United States are still not comfortable with metric units. Familiarity with metric units in daily life is growing, however, and they will eventually be routine in everyday conversation.

It should not be surprising that all fields of science the world over use metric units. Should ABA practitioners in the United States follow suit? After all, ABA technology is rooted in the science of behavior analysis, and both basic and applied research journals in our field use metric units. The answer lies with the need for practitioners to communicate clearly. ABA practitioners in the United States are likely to find that clients, families, teachers, and others with whom they work are not conversant with metric units. Overcoming this shortfall may not be a high priority for practitioners, however. It is more important for them to help people understand what is happening with target behaviors and what the data mean for ongoing management of interventions. Pushing others to deal with metric units may interfere with good communication.

---

begins, defined as the moment the student orients her face toward the worksheet. The event-response latency in each instance is the observed elapsed time, recorded as seconds or minutes (the unit of measurement). Depending on the question that interests him, the teacher might compare the latencies for responding to the first rows of problems with those for the middle or final rows, or sum the latencies for all rows and calculate the mean.

> **Latency.** A dimension that refers to the time between two events. In the study of behavior, the first event may be a response or an environmental event, and the second event is usually a response.
>
> **Event-response latency.** In the study of behavior, a type of latency representing the time between an environmental event and a response.

Duration. Another temporal dimension that is often useful in describing behavior is **duration**. The duration of a response is defined as the time from when it starts until it is completed. The durations of individual responses may be quite brief, as might be the case with a stereotypic behavior such as hand

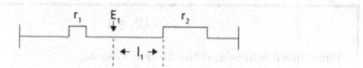

FIG. 5.1. Schematic representation of event-response latencies.

flapping or body rocking. On the other hand, durations may extend to minutes or even hours. Longer durations might be especially likely when a target behavior is defined in terms of bouts or episodes (see Chapter 4). For example, playing with peers might include varied activities that can occur for minutes at a time without a break.

The diagram in Figure 5.2 represents the durations of two responses. The definition of the target behavior should enable observers to determine when target responses are or are not occurring. That makes it possible to measure when each response starts and stops and record the time each response takes from beginning to end. If the diagram in Figure 5.2 represented total responding during a session, we could sum the duration of the two responses (r_1 and r_2) to get the total duration of the behavior during the session. As with latencies, the units of measurement for duration are the units of time.

As mentioned in Chapter 4, duration can be a useful dimension for describing behaviors that occur in rapid succession, making it difficult for observers to determine when each response begins and ends. Repetitive and stereotypic behaviors like those exhibited by some people with developmental disorders are a case in point. Observers usually can be trained to detect when a bout or episode of such behavior begins and ends and to record the duration of each episode. That was done in a study to evaluate the effects of response interruption and redirection on the vocal stereotypy of four children diagnosed with autism spectrum disorder. Vocal stereotypy was defined as noncontextual or nonfunctional vocalizations (e.g., singing, babbling, grunting, squealing, and uttering words or phrases unrelated to current circumstances). The duration of each episode of vocal stereotypy occurring during each 5-minute session was measured in seconds. Those recorded durations were summed, divided by 300 (the total number of seconds in a session), and multiplied by 100% to yield the proportion of each session during which the child engaged in vocal stereotypy. For all four children, the intervention reduced those proportions substantially in comparison to baseline (Ahearn, Clark, MacDonald, & Chung, 2007).

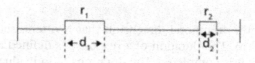

FIG. 5.2. Schematic representation of the duration of two responses.

> **Duration.** A dimension that refers to the elapsed time between the beginning and ending of an event. In the study of behavior, the event may be a single response or a bout or episode of responding.

Count. Another aspect of behavior that is particularly revealing has nothing to do with time. Individual instances of a target behavior (responses) can occur repeatedly, regardless of how often. The dimension reflecting the recurrence of a behavior is called **countability** or **count**. The unit of measurement that specifies how much countability is observed is the **cycle**, which is used in the natural sciences to specify how many instances of an event are observed. That term is not widely used in behavior analytic research and practice, however. For example, it is commonly reported that a participant emitted 32 target responses during a session or that the target behavior occurred 32 times. It is technically more correct, however, to refer to 32 cycles of the target behavior in order to maintain the distinction between the unit of analysis (the target behavior or response class) and units of measurement (see Box 4.1). Behavior analysts tend to substitute "responses" for a distinct reference to cycles as the unit of measurement that specifies how much count was observed.

Figure 5.3 diagrams the countability of three responses. Even though the figure suggests some temporal information (for example, we can see that r_2 has a longer duration than the other two responses), if we were measuring only count for this "session" we would know only that three cycles occurred. We would not know anything about their durations or how much time elapsed between responses. What we would make of the fact that three responses occurred might depend partly on having some temporal information as well, however. For example, in addition to knowing that a student solved 25 math problems correctly during a study period, we would also probably like to know how long it took. Similarly, in addition to the total duration of the behavior of working math problems during the period, we would probably want to know how many responses (cycles) contributed to that duration. Although it might be useful to know that a student spent 30 minutes working math problems, it would be even more informative to also know that she solved 25 problems correctly during that time.

> **Countability or count.** A dimension reflecting the occurrence of the event being measured, independent of any temporal features.
>
> **Cycle.** A unit of measurement for the dimension of countability or count. In the study of behavior, "responses" is often used as a substitute label.

This example makes the point that although each of these three dimensions by which we can describe individual instances of a target behavior tells

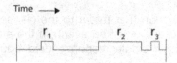

FIG. 5.3. Schematic representation of the countability of three responses.

us something important, each fails to describe other aspects of responding that might also be important. For example, latency does not tell us anything about how long each response lasts, duration does not reveal anything about the number of times the behavior occurred, and number of cycles provides no temporal information at all. Each dimension tells us about only one aspect of behavior. As we will see, that limitation often encourages us to get a more comprehensive picture.

Topographical Dimensions. Latency, duration, and count are not the only dimensions that reflect aspects of individual responses. Because behavior can be described in terms of its form, there are a number of other dimensions that can be useful, depending on the nature of the target behavior and the goals of a project. For example, a focus on athletic performances may make dimensions such as distance, angle, and force useful. Each of those dimensions might be relevant in teaching someone to swing a golf club, serve a tennis ball, or hit a baseball. Target behaviors that are important in work settings may also suggest measuring topographical dimensions. For instance, it may be important to measure variations in the placement of material in a machine or the torque used to tighten a nut. In Chapter 4, we mentioned the need for physical therapists to measure topographical dimensions in their focus on restoring physical capabilities. Interests in the spatial dimensions of behavior are quantified in terms of the same units of measurement used by other sciences.

Dimensions of Multiple Responses

Interresponse Time. Countability, duration, and event-response latency are dimensions that describe aspects of single instances of a behavior. However, researchers and practitioners usually observe a particular behavior throughout a session during which it may occur multiple times. The availability of multiple responses allows the use of other dimensions to describe different aspects of responding.

For example, one characteristic of repeated responses involves a second type of latency called **interresponse time** or IRT. Interresponse time refers to the time elapsing between two successive responses. It is measured from the end of one response to the beginning of the next, which is the latency between successive responses. In Figure 5.4, the interresponse time for the second response (r_2) is l_1, which is the latency from the end of the

---

BOX 5.2

Using a Rubber Ruler

Dimensional measurement depends on using units of measurement that are defined in a fixed or unvarying manner independently of the event being measured. They are called **absolute units**. The reason that a description such as "68 kilograms" is unambiguous, for example, is that a kilogram is defined in terms of the mass of a platinum-iridium cylinder kept at the International Bureau of Weights and Measures near Paris. If different researchers had different ways of defining a kilogram, or if that unit of measurement could vary from one application to another, descriptions of weight would lead to endless confusion. When absolute units are accepted and used in the same way by all scientists, they may be described as standard. All of the natural sciences long ago accepted the need for absolute and standard units of measurement.

Dimensional measurement is a routine feature of daily life, but it is not always the way that behavior is measured. Sometimes behavior is measured in ways that violate principles of dimensional measurement. For example, consider measuring a student's performance on an achievement test in terms of grade levels, such as 5.2 years. The unit of "years" in this application is not an absolute and standard unit of time but is defined in terms of variability in the performance of students making up the population used to compile scoring tables for the test. The meaning of "years" varies from one achievement test to another and one standardization population to another. Behavioral rating scales have a similar problem. When observers assign a value from 1 to 5 to some aspect of behavior, there is no standard and absolute meaning to the value. A "3" on a 1 to 10 scale does not mean the same as a "3" on a 1 to 7 scale. Neither is there any identification of the unit (1 to 5 what?). These shortcomings contribute to a well-documented problem with rater reliability in the assignment of scale values. Failing to follow dimensional measurement practices is like trying to measure length with a rubber ruler, where the outcomes vary with how much the ruler is stretched in each application. See Reading 3 in Johnston and Pennypacker (1993b) for a detailed discussion of various traditions of behavioral measurement.

---

first response (r_1). The unit of measurement for interresponse time is **time per cycle**. Interresponse time can be an important aspect of responding, especially when the pace of responding is of interest. Many skills require short IRTs to be effective, which is a technical way of saying that responding must occur rapidly. For instance, the IRTs associated with reading words must be fairly short in order for the skill to be useful in certain contexts. Long IRTs between reading words may suggest that other behavior, such as struggling to decode a word, is intervening. In other instances, however, short IRTs may not be desirable – for example, in the case of a student who reads aloud so rapidly that the words run together, or a young child who does not take enough time between bites of food to chew and swallow each bite.

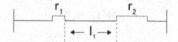

FIG. 5.4.   Schematic representation of interresponse latencies.

Interresponse time (IRT). A dimension referring to the elapsed time between two successive responses.

Time per cycle. The unit of measurement for interresponse time.

Rate or Frequency. One of the most broadly useful dimensions that describe multiple occurrences of a behavior is **rate** or **frequency** of responding. (As explained in Box 5.3, we use those two terms interchangeably.) In the study of behavior, measures of rate or frequency take the form of a ratio of the number of times a behavior occurs over some period of time. Skinner (1938) regarded this dimension as the fundamental datum in the study of operant behavior, and it has proven to be a very useful characteristic. The unit of measurement for rate or frequency is **cycles per unit time**, although in the field of behavior analysis that is most often expressed as responses per minute. Loosely put, rate or frequency describes how often a behavior occurs averaged over a period of observation. For instance, we might say that a behavior occurred once every 30 seconds or two times a minute.

A study to evaluate the effects of an intervention on the vocalizations of three children with autism and severely limited vocal speech provides an illustration. Pre-experimental assessments identified a vocalized speech syllable that was designated a treatment target (S+) and one that was designated a non-target (S−) for each child. In baseline sessions lasting 10–15 minutes, an experimenter simply vocalized the S+ and the S− on 10 trials each, mixed in random order. During the first intervention phase, sessions again consisted of mixed S+ and S− trials. Immediately after presenting each S+, the experimenter delivered a preferred stimulus to the child – a procedure called stimulus-stimulus pairing, which may increase the conditioned reinforcing value of speech sounds and make production of those sounds automatically reinforcing. No preferred stimulus was delivered to the child following presentations of the S− vocalizations. In a programmed reinforcement phase, the experimenter delivered a reinforcer every time the child vocalized a target sound (S+) during each 5-minute session. That was followed by a noncontingent reinforcement phase consisting of 5-minute sessions during which the experimenter delivered reinforcers to the child on a fixed-time 30-second schedule. The investigators reasoned that if target vocalizations occurred in the absence of contingent reinforcement, it would suggest that those responses were maintained by automatic reinforcement resulting from the stimulus-stimulus pairing procedure. They recorded every child-produced target and non-target vocalization that occurred during intertrial intervals in baseline and stimulus-stimulus pairing sessions and during the programmed and noncontingent reinforcement sessions. Data were reported in terms of the rate of responding – i.e., the number of responses per minute. Results indicated that rates increased moderately during the pairing phase in comparison to baseline and increased further with programmed reinforcement but were not maintained during the noncontingent reinforcement phase for two of the three children (Esch, Carr, & Grow, 2009).

> **Rate or frequency.** A dimension describing the average number of events per unit of time. In the study of behavior, rate or frequency is calculated by dividing total count by either total IRT or the total time during which responses occurred.
>
> **Cycles per unit time.** The unit of measurement for the dimension of rate or frequency. In the study of behavior, minutes are most often the time unit used (e.g., 1.5 cycles per minute).

Determining the rate or frequency of responding requires a simple calculation: dividing a measure of count by a measure of time. There are two ways investigators calculate rates of responding. The most common approach is to divide the total count of responses by the total time behavior was observed. That is straightforward and may be fine in many situations, but sometimes an alternative calculation may be preferred. It involves dividing the total count of responses by the total amount of time responses were not occurring, rather than by the total session time. This measure of time is the same as the total observation time minus the duration of all responses. The same result can be obtained by summing the total time between responses (total interresponse time). These alternative ways of determining the amount of time by which total count is divided can be confusing, so it will help to understand when the difference between them can be important.

Remember that when we look at rates of responding, we are looking at how often a behavior occurred. That involves an important assumption – that responding could have occurred at any point. Let us examine this assumption more closely. Imagine, for example, that we are calculating rates of taking bites of food in an individual with Prader-Willi syndrome during one-hour sessions. Assume that the behavior cannot occur as often in some sessions as in others because a caregiver sometimes moves the food out of reach until the individual has finished chewing and swallowing the last bite taken to reduce the likelihood of choking. If the individual was prevented from taking bites of food for a significant portion of some sessions, rates of responding might be lower in those sessions just because there were fewer opportunities for the behavior to occur. The lower rates in those sessions would be misleading when compared to the rates obtained in sessions when responding was possible throughout the full 60-minute period. The way to avoid this problem is to divide the total count for each session by the number of minutes in each session during which the individual could reach the food and therefore had

BOX 5.3

Frequency versus Rate

In the natural sciences, frequency usually refers to cyclic features of natural phenomena such as sound and light over time. The typical unit of measurement is cycles per second or minute. Dictionary entries are consistent with that approach, defining frequency as the number of times something happens during a period of time. To confuse matters, however, frequency is used in descriptive statistics to refer to count, as in a frequency distribution (for example, the number of kindergarten teachers who are male). The distinction between those two uses of the term is important. One refers to a ratio of count over time, and the other is just count, so they are completely different definitions of frequency.

The term rate has its own issues, with an even greater number of meanings. For example, a common meaning is speed, as in miles per hour, which is a measure of count (number of miles) over time (hours). The numerator is not a recurring process but a unit of distance. This meaning of rate (velocity) is not relevant to our need to describe how often a target behavior occurs in terms of responses (cycles) per minute. Other meanings of rate are more colloquial and equally unhelpful. References to the rate for a hotel room, the interest rate on a loan, or how you would rate the service in a restaurant do not suggest ratios of count and time. In spite of these other meanings of rate, the term is widely used in behavior analysis to refer to ratios of count and time.

References in the field of behavior analysis to measures of the number of responses over some period of time have long involved both terms, with attendant confusions (Merbitz, Merbitz, & Pennypacker, 2016). A paper by Carr, Nosik, and Luke (2018) clarified the contemporary usage of "frequency" by surveying both widely cited textbooks in the field and the 2016 volumes of the *Journal of the Experimental Analysis of Behavior* and the *Journal of Applied Behavior Analysis*, focusing on how the term was defined. Among the textbooks, six used frequency to mean count, four used the term to mean rate, and three did not use the term. The survey of journal usage showed somewhat greater consistency, with 81.8% of references in the *Journal of the Experimental Analysis of Behavior* (JEAB) and 84.8% of references in the *Journal of Applied Behavior Analysis* (JABA) using frequency to mean count. Nevertheless, the remaining references to frequency in JEAB were synonymous with rate, and other JABA references to frequency were inconsistent or unclear. The authors recommended following the mainstream though still unreliable practice of defining frequency in terms of count, leaving rate as the default reference to counts of responses over a specified period of time.

Previous editions of *Strategies and Tactics of Behavioral Research* have reflected this inconsistency, with the first two editions defining frequency as count but the third edition defaulting to the natural science practice of defining frequency as a reference to a ratio of cyclic features of natural phenomena, leaving rate as a somewhat less technical synonym. In spite of the evidence accumulated by Carr et al. (2018) suggesting that in contemporary behavior analysis frequency is more often than not taken to mean count, we continue to recommend frequency and rate as synonymous references to measures of count over time, as argued by Merbitz et al. (2016). Although it might be easier to give in to the modal tendencies revealed by Carr et al. (2018), it remains appealing to define frequency in a manner consistent with practices in other natural sciences. In any event, it is at least clear that you should be careful when discussing or reading about measures of the number of responses over periods of time.

the opportunity to respond. (Box 5.4 provides an example of this issue using quantitative values.)

This example makes clear that when we look at a series of values describing the rate of a behavior, it may be important for those values to reflect how often the behavior occurred *when responding was possible*. That is important because of the fact that all of the time during a session that the target behavior is occurring is time during which there is no further opportunity to respond. In other words, a behavior cannot usually occur when it is already occurring,

---

BOX 5.4

A Tale of Two Rates (or Frequencies)

In order to show the differences that can result from the two basic ways of calculating rate or frequency, imagine a study in which responding was measured during 20-minute sessions. Let us suppose that in the first session there were 4 responses and that their total duration was 16 minutes. If we calculated rate by dividing the number of responses by the total session time, the result would be 0.2 responses per minute (4 responses divided by 20 minutes). If we calculated rate by dividing total count by total IRT (in other words, by subtracting the total duration of responding – 16 minutes – from the 20-minute session time), however, the rate would be 1.0 response per minute (4 responses divided by 4 minutes).

Suppose that in a second session 4 responses also occurred but their total duration was only 8 minutes. If we calculated rate by dividing total count by total session time, the rate would still be 0.2 responses per minute (4 responses divided by 20 minutes). If the rate for the second session were calculated by dividing the number of responses by the total IRT (in other words, by subtracting the total duration of 8 minutes), however, the result would be 0.33 responses per minute (4 responses divided by 12 minutes).

In sum, if we compared response rates in the two sessions, depending on which calculation we used we would either find that the rates were the same (0.2 responses per minute) or different (1 response per minute versus 0.33 responses per minute). Which calculation would provide us with the most useful information? Even though the same number of responses occurred in each 20-minute session, the "total session time" approach that gives us the same rates for both sessions would be misleading if we knew that the time available to respond was different in the two sessions. What we expect rate or frequency to tell us is how often responding occurred, given that responding was possible in the first place.

a point also discussed in Chapter 4 in the section on movement cycles. For responses that are typically very brief in duration (self-injurious behavior in the form of hand-to-head hitting, for example), this limitation may not matter much. For responses that have longer durations, however, it can greatly restrict how much time is available for responses to occur. For example, if the behavior was hand mouthing, a few responses could take up most of a session, with the result that there would be little time available for additional hand-mouthing responses to occur.

One solution to this problem is to measure duration when responses are likely to vary significantly in that dimension. If rate is being calculated, it may be necessary to divide the number of responses in a session by the amount of time responses were not occurring – that is, to subtract total duration of responding from total session time before dividing. Human observers can often record the onset and offset of each response quite easily using a computer, tablet, or smart phone so that the total duration of responding can be calculated readily. That calculation becomes especially important when response durations are relatively long, which is not uncommon in applied settings. When response durations are consistently brief, on the other hand, there is probably little error involved in dividing total count by total session time.

TABLE 5.1
Methods of calculating frequency or rate

Method	Application
• Total count/total IRT	Variable and/or long response durations
• Total count/total observation time	Consistently brief response durations

Celeration. Let us now turn to a dimension closely related to rate – **celeration**. Rate or frequency of responding represents the number of responses observed divided by time. To calculate celeration, you then divide rate by time. In other words, rate reflects change in responding over time, but celeration represents change in rate over time. This distinction can be observed when you are driving a car. If you drive down the road at 45 miles per hour, that is your rate – the number of miles you would travel if you maintained that speed for one hour. If you accelerate to pass another car, the pace at which your rate or speed increases from moment to moment is a measure of your acceleration. That is what you feel in a powerful car when you seem to be pushed back against the seat.

Of course, we could talk about deceleration in the same way, which we feel when we push hard on the brakes and are pressed forward against our seat belts. The term "celeration" drops the prefixes and becomes a general reference to a change in rate over time. The unit of measurement for celeration is **cycles per unit time per unit time** (cycles per unit time squared), except that behavior analysts often substitute responses for cycles.

TABLE 5.2
Dimensions of behavior and units of measurement

Dimension	Unit
• Latency	Time units
• Duration	Time units
• Countability	Cycle
• Rate or frequency	Cycles/Unit time
• Celeration	Cycles/Unit time/Unit time
• IRT	Time/Cycle

Celeration. A dimension that describes change in the rate or frequency of responding over time.

Time per cycle per cycle. The unit of measurement for celeration.

LIMITATIONS OF RATIOS

Loss of Component Information

Ratios are valuable ways of looking at data because they highlight the relationship between two different dimensions. Rate or frequency of responding, for example, averages count over time and makes it easy to see an aspect of behavior that would otherwise not be obvious. Ratios have two features that can sometimes be limiting, however. First, when we combine two dimensions in a ratio, we necessarily lose sight of the component values. This characteristic of ratios is both an advantage and a disadvantage. The reason for calculating a ratio is to see the relationship between the two dimensions more easily. The other side of the coin, however, is that you cannot then see the different count and time values that contributed to the rates. If all you know about a behavior during a session is that the rate was 0.5 responses (cycles) per minute, you do not know how many responses there were or how long the session was.

Figure 5.5 illustrates this situation graphically. Try covering up the bottom panel and looking just at the ratio values in the top panel. Describe the patterns of responding that you see. When is responding relatively stable and when is it changing? Now, uncover the bottom panel. The ratios in the top panel were calculated by dividing the Q1 data set (the solid triangles) by the Q2 data set (the solid squares). Suppose the Q1 values represent total counts over a series of sessions and the Q2 values represent time values, which would make the data in the top panel represent rates of responding. By comparing the three data sets, we can see that the rate values in the top panel do not reflect what is happening with either count or time values. For example, during sessions 9 through 19 rates of responding look fairly stable, but you can see that the count and time data are both increasing during this period. The last dozen rate values are also relatively stable, but the component count and time data are both decreasing.

122 MEASUREMENT

The fact that calculating ratios hides their contributing values and limits the information available is neither inherently good nor bad. It just means we need to take that limitation into account when we interpret the ratio values. For instance, we may need to examine the component values to see whether the ratios are changing because of changes in one, the other, or both. Again assuming that the top panel in Figure 5.5 shows rates of responding, it could be that rates are changing not because count measures are changing but because of changes in time measures. These are behaviorally very different situations.

Dimensionless Ratios

When we divide total count by some measure of time such as minutes, we express the result in terms of the units of measurement for both contributing dimensions – responses (cycles) per minute. If we are dividing two like dimensions, however — such as duration of talking divided by duration of eating

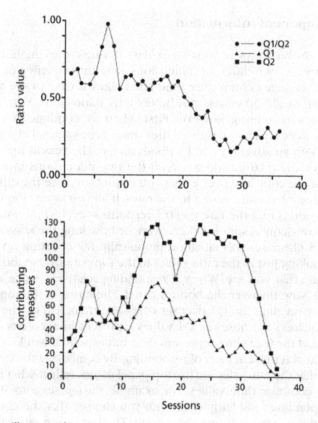

FIG. 5.5. Data illustrating how ratio values (top panel) can misrepresent their contributing component values (bottom panel).

during meals – the time units cancel and we are left with a ratio that has no dimensions. That is, 15 minutes of talking divided by 20 minutes of eating is 0.75. There is no reference to the contributing temporal dimensions in terms of a unit of measurement. In some scientific usages (for example, describing variability in a set of measures), this can be an advantage. In other cases, it can be a problem.

For instance, it is common to divide two counts, which does not allow for a reference to units of measurement. If we then multiply the result by 100, the outcome is referred to as a percentage. So if we divided number of test items answered correctly by the number of items attempted and then multiplied by 100, we would call the result "percent correct." However, neither percent nor percent correct is a dimension of behavior. **Dimensionless ratios** may describe useful information about responding, but it is important to be aware that they take us one step away from reference to actual behavioral dimensions.

> **Dimensionless ratio.** A ratio of like dimensional measures that results in a unitless or scalar number.

SELECTING BEHAVIORAL DIMENSIONS

How does an investigator know which of the common dimensions describing some aspect of behavior should be measured? The short answer is that there is no way to be sure in advance which dimensions will reveal important information about the target behavior. The solution to this dilemma lies in thinking through considerations that might guide the decision about which dimension – or dimensions – to measure. First, the research or clinical question may suggest specific dimensions. For example, if the question asks how some variable affects duration of responding, it is obvious that at least duration should be measured.

Second, the research literature may provide specific information. Other researchers who have studied the same issue will have selected certain dimensions and generated some evidence regarding their usefulness. In planning a project intended to contribute to the literature, it makes sense to measure at least the same dimensions represented in the existing literature so that findings can be compared.

Third, it may be obvious that certain features of the target behavior must be measured. For example, consider an intervention aimed at reducing a student's off-task behavior in a classroom by improving academic performance. Academic performance might improve without yielding any reduction in off-task activities, so in addition to measuring dimensions reflecting academic performance, it would be important to see what is happening with off-task behavior as well. Depending on how they are defined, such activities could be measured in terms of dimensions of different kinds of off-task behavior, or the total duration of such activities.

Fourth, in most applied work the objectives of a study or intervention make certain dimensions important. For example, if a practitioner is interested in encouraging physical activity in a consumer with intellectual disabilities in a group home by changing the individual's daily schedule, duration of playing basketball would probably provide a more meaningful picture than the count of shots attempted. On the other hand, the latter dimension would be a better choice if the objective were to improve the consumer's basketball skills.

Fifth, the nature of intervention procedures can direct the choice of dimensions. The question that should be considered is what changes in the target behavior might be anticipated given the characteristics of the planned intervention. Sometimes a procedure may directly involve a particular dimension. For example, if reinforcers are earned by engaging in a behavior for extended periods of time, it might be important to capture changes in duration. On the other hand, a procedure may suggest avoiding certain dimensions. If a discrete-trial procedure is to be used to teach a skill, measuring frequency (rate) of responding would be unwise because both the pace and the number of opportunities to respond will be determined by the trainer, not the learner, so frequency of responding would be misleading.

Perhaps the best option is to measure multiple dimensions in order to capture whatever kind of changes in the target behavior might turn out to be interesting or important. That avoids having to guess what aspects of behavior might change from one condition to another and may not be as challenging as it might seem. After all, the definition of a target behavior should allow clear identification of when the behavior is or is not occurring. In other words, the definition should make it easy to determine the beginning and ending of individual responses (movement cycles). Recording the occurrence of each response in terms of those two points in time affords the option of examining count, duration, interresponse time, rate, and more. That may not be practical when individual responses are consistently brief, which leaves recording count and calculating rate in terms of count divided by total session time. However, when individual responses are longer or variable in duration, this more comprehensive approach means that the data can be analyzed to reveal whatever dimensional changes might have occurred in and across conditions.

Observing and recording the onset and offset of each instance of a target behavior can be difficult or easy depending on the details, such as the demands placed on observers. For instance, if observers are tasked with managing participant behavior, dealing with materials, following treatment protocols, and observing and recording multiple target behaviors, asking them to record the duration of individual responses can be too much, especially when the responses are relatively brief and frequent. On the other hand, with technology the job can be

TABLE 5.3
Factors that guide selection of behavioral dimensions

- Research or practical question
- Research literature
- Target behavior
- Investigation objectives
- Intervention procedures

BOX 5.5

Is Probability a Dimension of Behavior?

The concept of probability has a long history in science, and philosophers and mathematicians have been arguing about its meaning since the 17th century (Durbin, 1968). The three most common approaches include: (a) the *classical* or *a priori* definition, which defines probability as the ratio of favorable to total, equally possible cases; (b) the *frequency* or *a posteriori* interpretation, which defines probability in terms of the limit of the relative frequency of an attribute in an infinite sequence of events, and (c) the *subjective* interpretation, which says that probability is simply a measure of a degree of belief (Salmon, 1966).

To further complicate matters, scientists seem to use the term in rather informal and varied ways. A survey of behavior analysts, for example, showed that all of the above usages were common, and almost a quarter of the respondents reported still other usages (Johnson & Morris, 1987). Interestingly, more than 25% questioned the usefulness of the concept, which seems to serve more colloquial than technical functions in the language of science. In sum, however the term is used it does not refer to a quantifiable dimension of behavior or any other phenomenon (Johnston & Pennypacker, 1993b, Reading 5).

---

as simple as tapping a touchscreen when a response starts and stops, with the software calculating all of the dimensions and even producing graphs.

In sum, although there are no firm rules for selecting dimensions for measurement, it is not usually difficult to figure out why some dimensions would be more useful than others for each target behavior. In selecting dimensions, it is important to remember that the goal is to measure all dimensions that will yield data to answer the guiding question. Another way of saying this is that the conclusions that can be drawn from the data are necessarily limited by the dimensions that were measured. If you do not measure it, you should not talk about it.

DESCRIBING DIMENSIONAL DATA

Having selected and measured certain dimensions of behavior, it is important to carefully describe what the data reveal. As a rule, we should always describe changes in responding specifically in terms of the dimensions that were actually measured. It is often tempting, however, to express outcomes in a more general way than the data directly support. For example, if the rate of a target behavior is measured, the data should only be described in terms of changes in the rate (or frequency) of responding, rather than referring generally to changes in "responding." The data in Figure 5.5 illustrate how this can be a problem because the changes in rate values across sessions in the top panel do not necessarily reflect what is going on with count and time dimensions.

The rule about describing the data only in terms of the dimensions that were measured also applies to any descriptions of responding based on a single dimension. Data on the measured dimension provide no information on what other dimensions might have revealed if they had been measured. If the data describe the number of times the target behavior occurred (count), we do not know what happened with duration or interresponse time, for instance. That is why we must limit our descriptions of responding to the dimensions that were measured. It is not appropriate to make general statements like "responding increased under the treatment condition" because it implies that the statement is true for any or all dimensions, but we cannot know how dimensions that were not measured might have changed. Instead, we should report that "rate of responding changed," "the total number of responses increased," "aggregate duration decreased," and so forth. In sum, general references to what the data show about "responding" are usually not appropriate.

CHAPTER SUMMARY

1. Dimensional measurement requires specifying exactly how much of a dimension is observed. That function is served by units of measurement.

2. In order to be scientifically useful, a unit of measurement must have a standard definition within and across scientific disciplines. Additionally, the unit of measurement must refer to a fixed amount of a dimensional quantity.

3. Since the interaction of the environment and behavior occurs in time, an individual's behavior has several temporal properties that can be examined. Latency measures the amount of time that passes between the onset of an environmental event and the occurrence of the target behavior (event-response latency).

4. Investigators may also record duration. The duration of a response is defined as the amount of time from when it starts until it is completed. Duration can be a useful dimension for describing behaviors that occur in rapid succession, making it difficult to determine when each response begins and ends.

5. Individual instances of a target behavior (responses) can occur repeatedly. The dimension reflecting the recurrence of a behavior is called countability or count. The unit of measurement that specifies how much countability is observed is called the cycle.

6. Because behavior can be described in terms of its form (topography), there are a number of other dimensions that may be useful depending on the nature of the target behavior and the goals of a project.

7. One characteristic of repeated responses involves a second type of latency called interresponse time or IRT. Interresponse time refers to the time elapsing between two successive responses. The unit of measurement for IRT is time per cycle. Interresponse time can be an important aspect of responding when the pace of responding is of interest.

8. One of the most useful dimensions that describes multiple occurrences of a behavior is rate or frequency of responding. Essentially, rate or frequency describes how often a behavior occurs averaged over a period of observation.

9. Rate of responding is calculated in one of two ways. The most common approach is to divide the total count of responses by the total time behavior was observed. A second approach requires dividing the total count of responses by the total interresponse time (or total observation time minus the duration of all responses). Although more difficult to measure in applied settings, this approach is useful for behaviors that are often relatively extended in duration, as this can greatly restrict how much time is available for additional responses to occur.

10. Ratios are valuable and common ways of looking at data, but they can limit our interpretations. When we combine two dimensional quantities (e.g., count divided by duration), we lose the ability to examine the component values. In order to interpret any changes in our ratio value we must examine both contributing measures to determine why the change has occurred.

11. Dimensionless ratios (e.g., percent correct) may describe useful information about responding, but it is important to be aware that they take us one step away from reference to actual behavioral dimensions.

12. When selecting dimensional quantities to measure, our goal is to measure all the quantities that will yield data to answer the guiding question. Selection of these measures should be guided by the research or clinical question, research literature, target behavior, objective of the study/intervention, and the nature of the intervention procedure(s).

HIGHLIGHTED TERMS

Celeration. A dimension that describes change in the rate or frequency of responding over time.

Countability or count. A dimension reflecting the occurrence of the event being measured, independent of any temporal features.

Cycle. A unit of measurement for the dimension of countability or count. In the study of behavior, "responses" is often used as a substitute label.

Cycles per unit time. The unit of measurement for the dimension of rate or frequency. In the study of behavior, minutes are most often the time unit used (e.g., 1.5 cycles per minute).

Dimension. A quantifiable aspect of a natural phenomenon.

Dimensional measurement. An approach to measurement that involves attaching a number representing the observed extent of a dimension to an appropriate unit of measurement.

Dimensionless ratio. A ratio of like dimensional measures that results in a unitless or scalar number.

Duration. A dimension that refers to the elapsed time between the beginning and ending of an event. In the study of behavior, the event may be a single response or a bout or episode of responding.

Event-response latency. In the study of behavior, a type of latency representing the time between an environmental event and a response.

Interresponse time (IRT). A dimension referring to the elapsed time between two successive responses.

Latency. A dimension that refers to the time between two events. In the study of behavior, the first event may be a response or an environmental event, and the second event is usually a response.

Rate or frequency. A dimension describing the average number of events per unit of time. In the study of behavior, rate or frequency is calculated by dividing total count by either total IRT or the total time during which responses occurred.

Time per cycle. The unit of measurement for interresponse time.

Time per cycle per cycle. The unit of measurement for celeration.

Unit of measurement. A determinate amount of a dimension of the phenomenon being measured.

TEXT STUDY GUIDE

1. What is dimensional measurement, and how is it related to units of measurement?
2. Describe event-response latencies and how they differ from duration.
3. Provide an example of when the use of duration would be more beneficial than latency.
4. Describe at least two topographical dimensions that behavior analysts might be interested in recording.
5. What is the unit of measurement for countability?
6. Define IRT. What is its unit of measurement?
7. Define rate/frequency. What is its unit of measurement?
8. Distinguish between two ways of calculating rate. Explain why response duration can make a difference in which approach is most useful.
9. Define celeration. What is its unit of measurement?
10. How is celeration related to rate?
11. How do ratios limit the information about responding that can easily be seen?
12. What is a dimensionless ratio?
13. List the factors that might guide selection of dimensions for measurement.
14. Describe what the authors mean when they state that we should always describe changes in responding specifically in terms of the dimensions that were measured.

BOX STUDY GUIDE

1. What are absolute units?
2. Why are rate and frequency likely to be confused?
3. Is probability a behavioral dimension?

SUGGESTED READINGS

Johnston, J. M., & Pennypacker, H. S. (1993b). *Readings for strategies and tactics of behavioral research*. Hillsdale, NJ: Erlbaum Associates. Reading 3: Traditions of behavioral measurement.

Johnston, J. M., & Pennypacker, H. S. (1993b). *Readings for strategies and tactics of behavioral research*. Hillsdale, NJ: Erlbaum Associates. Reading 4: Describing behavior with ratios of count and time.

Johnston, J. M., & Pennypacker, H. S. (1993b). *Readings for strategies and tactics of behavioral research*. Hillsdale, NJ: Erlbaum Associates. Reading 5: Probability as a scientific concept.

DISCUSSION TOPICS

1. Discuss examples in which particular dimensions would be more appropriate than others.
2. Discuss situations in which it might be important to calculate frequency by dividing total count by total IRT.

EXERCISES

1. Find examples in the research literature in which more than one dimension was measured for a particular target behavior. How do the data from each dimension provide different information about the effects of the treatment condition?
2. Start with a data set that includes both number of responses and number of opportunities to respond, measured across multiple sessions. Divide the former by the latter and multiply by 100 to calculate the percent of responses. Plot these values on a graph across sessions and describe the data. Then plot the number of responses and the number of opportunities separately and contrast these two functions with the percent function.

CHAPTER SIX

Observing and Recording

APPROACHES TO OBSERVATION
   Goal of Observing and Recording
   Direct versus Indirect Measurement
   Automated versus Human Observation
   Complete versus Incomplete Observation and Recording
   Continuous versus Discontinuous Observation and Recording
PROCEDURAL DECISIONS
   Making Observations
     With Equipment
     With Human Observers
     With Participants as Observers
   Scheduling Observation Periods
   Recording Observations

APPROACHES TO OBSERVATION

Goal of Observing and Recording

Although we may not often think about behavioral measurement in formal terms, it involves the following steps: (a) identifying responses that meet the requirements of the target behavior's definition, (b) determining the amount of the selected dimension observed for each response, (c) deciding how long observation sessions will be and when they will take place, and (d) in each session, making some kind of record of the amount of behavior using an appropriate unit of measurement (see Box 4.1). This is what we are doing when we observe target behaviors and record the results. It is through observing and recording that the facts of what happened during a session get transformed into data.

TABLE 6.1
Components of behavioral measurement

- Identify responses meeting the requirements of the target behavior definition
- Determine the amount of the selected dimension(s) for each target behavior
- Make a record of this amount in terms of the appropriate unit of measurement

Behavioral measurement is also a way of systematically ignoring – at least for purposes of formal measurement – those aspects of a participant's behavior that are not targeted for study. In other words, observing and recording filters everything going on with a participant's behavior during a session through a set of measurement procedures. This filtering process leaves behind everything the researcher or practitioner has decided is not important in favor of a record of only the kind of information desired. The session-by-session record is actually nothing more than a series of numbers and units of measurement, such as 1.4 responses (cycles) per minute attached to a defined behavior. Because this is all that remains, it is important that observation procedures capture everything that the researcher or practitioner might wish to see later on.

The overarching goal of observing and recording is to produce data that will guide correct and meaningful interpretations. That makes it imperative for both researchers and practitioners to ensure that the record of participant behavior is a complete and accurate representation of what happens to the target behavior over the course of an investigation. Otherwise, researchers risk disseminating information that is misleading, and practitioners risk making decisions that do not serve their clients well.

As data are analyzed, investigators may transform them into tables, graphs, or statistical outcomes (see Chapters 14 and 15). As they work with the data, they try to produce stimuli that help them and others make the right kinds of interpretations. Both researchers and practitioners should study the data as they accumulate throughout each condition and from one phase of a project to another. What the data reveal is often useful in guiding ongoing decisions about how to manage a study and is essential for making decisions about practical interventions. For example, the accumulating data may suggest that the definition of the target behavior needs to be revised, intervention procedures need to be adjusted, or observers need to be given more training. As we will see, there are many ways data can guide the management of a study or intervention.

Direct versus Indirect Measurement

When what you are measuring is exactly the same as what you are drawing conclusions about, measurement is **direct**. In contrast, when what you actually measure is different in some way from what you are drawing conclusions about, measurement is **indirect**.

> **Direct measurement.** Measurement practices in which the events that are measured are exactly the same as those about which conclusions are drawn.
>
> **Indirect measurement.** Measurement practices in which the events that are measured are not the same as those about which conclusions will be drawn.

For example, suppose that you have been hired by a company to evaluate the effects on work performance of installing a new lighting system in a manufacturing facility. You decide to compare the performance of employees under the old lighting system versus the new lighting system. If you observe and measure particular work behaviors under the old lighting system and then under the new lighting system in order to draw conclusions about the relative effects of the two lighting systems on job performance, it would be considered direct measurement.

If instead you ask employees to complete a questionnaire asking how they thought their performance was affected by the change in lighting systems, it would be indirect measurement. Many - perhaps most - indirect measures take the form of verbal reports. What makes measurement indirect in this case is that what is being measured (responses to a questionnaire) is not the same as what conclusions will be about (actual work performance). There are a variety of reasons why the questionnaire data might not provide an accurate picture of actual work performance. For instance, the employees might answer the questions in such a way as to lead management to think that their work had improved because of the new lighting.

Many researchers and practitioners prefer direct measurement over indirect measurement. The reason is that verbal reports about events often do not correspond closely to the actual events and are prone to influence by many factors. Indirect measurement therefore requires making assumptions about the relationship between the indirect measures (the questionnaire data in our example) and what those measures are supposed to represent (actual job performance). When there is good evidence that the indirect measures reflect the events of primary interest, indirect measurement can be acceptable. For example, before using a questionnaire like the one just described, you could do a study examining the correspondence between questionnaire responses and direct measures of actual work performance. If the relationship was quite close, you might then be justified in accepting questionnaire data as a good measure of job performance.

It can be tempting, however, to use indirect measurement when there is no evidence of close correspondence between the indirect measures and what they are actually supposed to reflect. Social scientists often fall into this trap by defining their interests in terms of mental rather than physical processes. If a researcher is interested in frustration, for instance, it is likely that some kind of questionnaire will be used as an indirect measure. Because there is no direct evidence that frustration is a distinct physical phenomenon, there is no way to assess what particular behaviors the questionnaire responses actually represent. Another common trap is assuming incorrectly that verbal responses match the other responses they describe.

Automated versus Human Observation

In designing observing and recording procedures, researchers and practitioners must first decide how observation and measurement is going to be done. There are two basic choices. Target behaviors may be detected by some automated means using equipment, or human observers may be used.

In laboratory research, target behaviors are often defined in terms of the participant's interaction with equipment of some sort. For instance, the target behavior may be pushing a lever, pressing a panel, hitting a key on a keyboard, or touching a computer screen. Laboratory settings make it relatively easy to use commercially available devices, including computers, to detect and record such behaviors. Depending on the nature of the target behavior, this approach may be used in applied settings as well. For example, a student's academic work may be measured through an electronic interface, with the student responding with a pointing device such as a mouse or directly on a touch-sensitive screen.

In projects that take place in field settings, however, it is more typical to have human observers detect and record target behaviors. In those settings, target behaviors are likely to be selected for their relevance to a practical issue, and the features of target behaviors often vary widely. Although it is sometimes feasible to measure everyday behavior automatically, that may require some investment in time and money. Practitioners often find that using human observers is the best – or the only – option.

The decision to use a device or a person to detect and record behavior involves more than the issue of feasibility, however. We might also ask which approach is more likely to produce accurate observations. Are there any general advantages to using automated versus human observers? In answering this question, remember that the essential goal of observation is to accurately detect the occurrence of target behaviors. Accurate data result from detecting and recording every response that fits the definition – no more and no less. In other words, the only influence on what is observed and recorded should be the target responses themselves.

Measurement must often take place while all kinds of other things are happening, especially in field settings. The researcher or practitioner may be interested in many of those things, such as the behavior of other individuals in the setting (for example, family members in the home or teachers in a classroom) or whether a procedure is being implemented properly. Although such factors may be important, they should not influence whether target behaviors are detected. And then there are all the events that may be irrelevant to the project, such as people coming and going, a television blaring in the background, and so forth.

BOX 6.1

How Do You Measure Slouching?

Sometimes it may take some thought to figure out how automatic observation and recording might work in a particular situation. For example, it might not be obvious how slouching behavior, which can occur in any circumstances at any time, could be detected automatically. A group of researchers not only figured out how to do that in the 1960s, they used what we would describe today as crude technology. Azrin, Rubin, O'Brien, Ayllon, & Roll (1968) were interested in developing a means of controlling the posture of typical participants in a variety of natural environments. Instead of employing platoons of trained observers, they chose to develop a simple apparatus that continuously detected the key features of postural behavior under almost all daily circumstances.

The apparatus defined slouching as a specific distance between two points on a participant's back. That was detected with a snap-action switch taped on a particular spot on the participant's back. The switch was attached to an elastic cord so that rounding the back caused the switch contacts to close. In order to eliminate switch closures due to normal activities, a mercury tilt switch was adapted to block posture switch output when the torso was tilted forward more than 10 degrees. The definition of slouching required an uninterrupted switch closure for at least 3 seconds. The cumulative duration of slouching was recorded by a miniature elapsed time meter. Calibration (a procedure for checking the device's functioning) showed that measurement error was only about 30 seconds at the 4-hour time range used for most participants. The apparatus also contained a small speaker and a transistor circuit that could be programmed by the experimenter to sound a 500-hertz tone at 55 decibels, which played a role in modifying the behavior. The apparatus was worn under regular clothing. Of course, today there are more sophisticated devices for measuring posture, such as wearable accelerometers (e.g., Bussman et al., 2001) and microswitches (e.g., Lancioni et al., 2013).

Under such "messy" conditions, using devices to detect and record behavior may have an advantage over using human observers. Equipment generally has the characteristic of doing what it is designed to do and nothing else. As long as they operate as designed, for example, devices like those described in Box 6.1 measure slouching and other postural responses consistently and without influence from other factors. In contrast, faced with the challenge of doing the same thing in exactly the same way over and over, human observers are, to put it gracefully, human. They get bored, pay attention to the wrong things, get distracted by other tasks, fail to follow definitional or observational rules, become confused, make idiosyncratic judgments, fail to show up, and so on. In other words, for tasks where we need a high degree of accuracy and consistency, human beings may come in second to machines.

On the other hand, human observers are very good at doing things that can be difficult to design equipment to do. Most hardware is unresponsive to events that fall outside of its design parameters, but humans can be trained to be quite sensitive to novel or emergent features of a situation. For instance, they can be taught to notice when the characteristics of a target behavior are changing or a protocol is not being followed or unexpected events occur that might influence responding.

These contrasts suggest there may be complementary roles for automated and human observers. Automated observation may be most effective in detecting and recording target behaviors in a consistent and accurate manner. Human observers may be ideal for providing supplementary monitoring to ensure that everything is going according to plan and to look for unexpected events during sessions that might be important in managing a study or intervention. Choosing between these alternatives may be a luxury that is often not available, especially in-service settings. Using human observers is typically the default choice in everyday environments, although we will see that it comes with a number of challenges.

Complete versus Incomplete Observation and Recording

We have already indicated that the goal of behavioral measurement should be to produce a record of participant behavior that is both complete and accurate. That has implications for how much of the target behavior should be measured. The issue here is whether measurement is designed to detect and record all instances of the target behavior or to merely sample from all possible occurrences.

If observation and recording are ongoing whenever target responses occur – that is, during virtually all of a participant's waking moments throughout every day – it is possible to produce a complete record of the behavior. This is called **complete observation** (not to be confused with *continuous* observation and recording, defined later). In this case, there are no concerns about sampling from among all occurrences of the target behavior, because all responses matching the definition can potentially be detected. When observation is scheduled in a way that may not detect all target responses, it is said to be **incomplete**. This involves scheduling observation periods (or sessions) so that they only sample from among all possible target responses. Figure 6.1 shows the distinction between complete and incomplete observation and recording.

> **Complete observation.** A schedule of observation that allows detection of all occurrences of the target behavior.
>
> **Incomplete observation.** A schedule of observation that samples from all occurrences of the target behavior and may therefore fail to detect some responses.

Let us examine the effects of these two approaches on the resulting data. First consider the accuracy of the data they yield. Although complete

FIG. 6.1. Illustration of complete and incomplete observation.

observation and recording is ideal, it does not guarantee that the resulting data will be accurate. For example, even though all occurrences of the target behavior can be detected, it does not mean they will be. Furthermore, responses that should not be recorded may be included erroneously. Incomplete observation and recording entails those same risks, which are amplified by the fact that there are fewer opportunities to observe the target behavior. In other words, regardless of whether an observation schedule is designed to capture all occurrences of the target behavior or merely sample them by observing for limited periods of time, the data may be inaccurate because they involve some error.

Second, consider the matter of how well the resulting data represent what they are supposed to represent. A schedule of observation that captures all occurrences of the target behavior (putting aside the possibility of error) yields data that represent a complete picture of what is happening with that behavior. A schedule of incomplete observation, on the other hand, raises the possibility that the data may not fully represent what is going on with the target behavior. After all, there were periods of time when the behavior could have occurred but observation and recording did not occur. The seriousness of this risk depends on how the observation periods are scheduled, how long they last, and what the researcher or practitioner wants to learn.

For example, suppose that an investigator is measuring coffee drinking in individuals whose doctors have told them to cut back on their consumption of caffeine. If the researcher chooses to schedule observation sessions only in the morning between 7:00 and 10:00, the resulting data (we will assume they are accurate) may not represent the participant's coffee drinking practices very well. The data will likely underestimate the total daily amount of coffee drinking because the investigator failed to measure the behavior during the rest of the day. The data may also overestimate the amount of coffee drinking in the afternoon and evening, when most people drink less coffee than in the morning.

Although complete observation is clearly ideal, incomplete observation is not necessarily a poor choice. Both approaches can yield accurate measures of responding during observation periods. In order for incomplete observation to yield data that represent responding that was not measured, however, it is necessary to arrange observation periods so that they provide evidence of the amount and distribution of responding that the project requires. So, if the investigator needs the data to show the total amount of coffee consumed each day, a schedule of complete observation will have to be arranged. However, if the investigator only needs to evaluate the effects of an intervention on coffee drinking, it may be sufficient to sample the behavior during a morning session. Considerations in scheduling observation periods are discussed further in the Procedural Decisions section of this chapter.

Continuous versus Discontinuous Observation and Recording

Let us now turn to the procedures operating during observation periods themselves, regardless of whether observation is scheduled to be complete or incomplete. When observation procedures are designed to detect and record every occurrence of the target behavior during an observation period, it is called **continuous observation**. Because complete observation involves detecting all target responses whenever they occur, it is necessarily continuous, but the two terms are not synonymous. Observation can be continuous when it is incomplete – that is, when observation periods only sample from all the times during which the behavior can occur. For example, staff members in a group home for individuals with intellectual disabilities may be charged with observing and recording certain social interactions for a particular individual from the time she returns from a day program until dinner is ready each weekday. Although the target behaviors could occur at other times (such as at the day program, in the evenings after dinner, or on weekends), it may not be feasible or necessary for staff to observe at all or most of those times. They can, however, observe and record continuously throughout the designated periods before dinner each weekday. Although continuous observation has the potential to be accurate, errors can always occur. There is also the question of whether data recorded during designated observation periods properly represent responding that occurred when observation was not going on.

When observation procedures are designed so that observers cannot detect and record all occurrences of target responses during observation periods, it is called **discontinuous observation**. Discontinuous observation and recording procedures only sample from among the target responses that occur during an observation period. This makes it likely that some responses will be missed, which in turn means that data resulting from discontinuous observation and recording are not likely to accurately reflect behavioral dimensions such as count, duration, or rate (frequency). Those procedures can yield only estimates of actual behavioral dimensions. The only way to evaluate the degree of error in those estimates is to compare data resulting from discontinuous and continuous observations from the same sessions. If continuous records are not available, there is no way to determine how accurately the data produced by discontinuous observation and recording reflect the actual occurrences of the target behavior.

> **Continuous observation.** Observation and recording procedures in which all occurrences of the target behavior can be detected during observation periods.

> **Discontinuous observation.** Observation and recording pro-
> cedures in which all occurrences of the target behavior are not
> necessarily detected and recorded during observation sessions.

In spite of this problem, discontinuous observation and recording procedures are often used in applied behavior analytic research and practice. They take many forms, the most common of which is called **interval-based recording**. In a typical application, the observation period is divided into equal intervals, which might range in length from a few seconds to a number of minutes. Some means of signaling the observer when each interval begins and ends must be arranged, such as an auditory cue provided through ear buds. The observer must also have a means of recording observed responses, such as making pencil marks on a paper data sheet or touching keys on an electronic device. These procedures are commonly used to obtain information about multiple responses that may occur in the same observation session, e.g., several target behaviors for one participant or the behavior(s) of a group of participants. They apply to free operants – responses that can occur at nearly any time.

In **partial interval recording (PIR)**, the observer is charged with observing during each interval and recording an occurrence if the target behavior occurs at least once at any time during the interval, even if it is not started or completed during the interval. Only one occurrence is recorded regardless of how many responses were observed during the interval. In **whole interval recording (WIR)**, the observer must observe throughout each interval and record an occurrence only if the target behavior occurs without ceasing throughout the interval. With either procedure, the total number of intervals in which a response was recorded (often called scored intervals) is typically divided by the total number of intervals in the observation period, and the result is then multiplied by 100% to yield the percentage of intervals that were scored. So, if a 30-minute session were divided into 15-second intervals, there would be a total of 120 intervals. If an occurrence of the target behavior was recorded in 73 of the intervals, 61% percent of the intervals were scored. Often, however, such data are described as representing the percentage of the observation period during which the target response occurred, or simply percent occurrence. As we shall see shortly, that is misleading.

Another common form of interval-based recording is called **momentary time sampling (MTS)**. Again, observation periods are typically divided into equal intervals, but the observer does not need to observe during the intervals. Instead he observes only briefly when each interval ends and scores the interval only if the target response is occurring at that moment. This procedure obviously eases the burden on observers in comparison to PIR and WIR, although the price can be high. The sample of responding is limited to a series of brief observations, with no observations occurring most of the time that responding could occur. As with PIR and WIR procedures, the data resulting from MTS are often expressed in terms of percentage of occurrences, even though occurrences during intervals are not measured.

Interval-based recording. A category of discontinuous observation and recording procedures in which observation periods are divided into equal intervals, and occurrences of the target response are recorded by interval according to some rule.

Partial interval recording (PIR). A form of interval-based recording in which an occurrence is recorded if the target response (or even part of a response) is observed at any time during the interval. Only one occurrence is recorded, even if multiple responses occurred during the interval.

Whole interval recording (WIR). A form of interval-based recording in which an occurrence is recorded if the target response occurs without ceasing throughout the entire interval.

Momentary time sampling (MTS). A form of interval-based recording in which observation periods are divided into equal intervals, but the observer only records whether the target response is occurring at the end of each interval.

Interval-based recording procedures seem straightforward, but they have several potentially serious problems. Figure 6.2 illustrates records produced by each of the interval-based procedures during an observation period consisting of 8 equal intervals (indicated by hash marks and the numbers at the bottom of the figure). Actual occurrences of the target response are represented on the top line, where vertical lines indicate the onset and offset of each response and the horizontal lines that connect them indicate the duration of the response. Looking at the record resulting from PIR, you can see that an occurrence was recorded in 7 intervals even though there were multiple occurrences in some intervals and the durations of responses varied. For example, the response occurred once in interval 1 and 3 times in interval 3, but only a single occurrence was scored in both intervals. An occurrence was recorded in each of intervals 4, 5, and 6 because a single response that started in interval 4 ended in interval 6. Intervals 7 and 8 were also scored because one relatively long response overlapped those two intervals. In contrast, WIR resulted in only

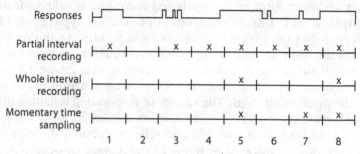

FIG. 6.2.   Illustration of interval recording procedures.

intervals 5 and 8 being scored because they were the only instances where responses occurred throughout the entire interval. In the MTS record, only intervals 5 and 7 were scored because those were the only instances when the target response happened to be occurring at the moment the interval ended. In short, none of the interval-based recording procedures captured any dimension of the target response (count, rate, or duration) with a reasonable degree of accuracy.

Comparing the actual responses represented in the top line in Figure 6.2 with the records produced by each of the interval-based recording procedures shows why those procedures typically produce data that cannot be clearly related to actual dimensions of target behaviors (i.e., count, duration, rate or frequency). In PIR, for example, when the first response occurs during an interval, that interval is scored. Additional responses occurring in the same interval are ignored. In other words, a scored interval may contain only one response or many, which means that scored intervals may differ from each other in terms of the responses that occurred. That cannot be discerned, however, from the recorded data. In MTS, an interval is scored if the target response is observed at the end of the interval, but responses occurring during the interval are missed. Because the number of responses in each interval is not recorded with either PIR or MTS, the resulting "percent of scored intervals" data cannot produce an accurate estimate of count or rate. Similarly, because response durations are not recorded, "percent of scored intervals" data cannot accurately estimate duration. Parallel limitations apply to data recorded using WIR procedures. Although the target response may occur continuously throughout an interval, when it starts and ends is not recorded, so the resulting data do not represent the actual or estimated duration of responding. And as Figure 6.2 shows, responses that do not occur throughout an interval are not recorded at all, so WIR data cannot be used to represent or estimate count or rate.

The correspondence between actual behavioral dimensions and data produced by interval-based observation and recording methods is also influenced by the length of the intervals used. Additionally, given a certain distribution of responding throughout any particular session, different size intervals will usually yield different percent scored interval values for the session. Figure 6.3 illustrates this point by showing that for the sample of responding shown, two different interval durations produce different pictures of responding. Line A shows a hypothetical session with 8 responses occurring in an 80-second period. Line B shows that when the session is divided into 10-second intervals and scored according to the partial-interval rule, 62.5% of the intervals

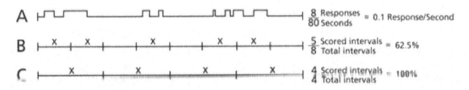

FIG. 6.3.   Illustration of the effect of interval size on percent of scored interval calculations.

BOX 6.2

Counting within Intervals

Intervals are occasionally used in an observation procedure that differs from typical interval-based recordings. In this variation, a session is divided into equal intervals, but instead of scoring intervals, observers record the actual number of responses in each interval. This approach might be taken if dividing sessions into intervals somehow makes the measurement of count or frequency easier for observers, or if the investigator wants other information than just the total number of occurrences in each session. For instance, the fact that each target response is counted in each interval allows the behavior to be summarized for each session in terms of total count or rate (total count divided by time). It also makes it possible to show the distribution of responding throughout a session by graphing the number of responses in successive intervals throughout the session. This graphical result is sometimes called a "scatterplot," although that use of the term is different from long-established practice in descriptive statistics. Otherwise, if the investigator's question requires only the total number of responses in each session, there is no reason to divide sessions into intervals.

---

are scored. Line C shows the session instead divided into 20-second intervals, with the result that 100% are scored. These differences (62.5% versus 100%) are problematic because they do not reflect differences in the participant's behavior. This means that graphed data showing percent of scored interval data across a series of sessions would likely look different had the intervals been shorter or longer. That problem would be magnified if the distribution of responding within sessions varied from session to session. Unfortunately, there is no way to determine how the data for any given session would have been affected by different interval lengths without carefully measuring the occurrences and distribution of responses continuously for the same session and making the comparison shown in this example.

Numerous studies have investigated discrepancies between the information provided by interval-based recording procedures and continuous observation and recording of count, duration, and rate or frequency (e.g., Devine et al., 2011; Gardenier, MacDonald, & Green, 2004; Hanley et al., 2007; Ledford et al., 2015; McNamee & Van der Mars, 2005; Meany-Daboul et al., 2007; Radley et al., 2015; Rapp, Carr et al., 2001; Rapp, Colby et al., 2007; Rapp, Colby-Dirksen et al., 2008; Schmidt et al., 2013; Sharp, Mudford, & Elliffe, 2015; Wirth, Slaven, & Taylor, 2014; Zakszeski, Hojnoski, & Wood, 2017). As might be expected, the studies show that the direction (over- or underestimate) and size of the measurement errors produced by each of the interval-based observation and recording procedures vary with the number of behaviors observed, characteristics of the behaviors (e.g., duration of each response or bout, interresponse times, rate), the amount and direction of behavior change over successive observation periods, length of observation periods, and length of intervals. Because so many factors can influence the resulting data, it is difficult to draw broad conclusions or recommendations regarding these procedures from the research that has been conducted to date. It does appear, however, that (a) WIR often produces unacceptably large measurement errors; (b) PIR can yield reasonably good estimates of rate (but not duration) when intervals are no longer than 10 seconds; and (c) the magnitude of error in MTS estimates tends to correlate with interval length, generally being smaller when intervals are shorter (i.e., 30 seconds and under). The latter two findings make sense when you consider that the shorter the intervals, the larger the number of observations that can potentially occur during a session. For example, dividing a 30-minute session into 10-second intervals means that there will be 180 opportunities to observe, whereas using 2-minute intervals only provides 15 observation opportunities. Regardless of interval length, however, research shows that it is difficult to predict in advance which interval-based observation procedure will detect (be sensitive to) intervention effects and what types of errors each will produce (Devine et al., 2011; McNamee & Van der Mars, 2005; Rapp, Colby-Dirksen et al., 2008; Wirth, Slaven, & Taylor, 2014). Additionally, data produced by those procedures (especially WIR and PIR) have been shown to lead investigators to draw erroneous conclusions about functional relations and the effects of interventions (e.g., Bartlett, Rapp, & Henrickson, 2011; Devine et al., 2011; Meany-Daboul et al., 2007; Rapp, Colby-Dirksen et al., 2008).

Another form of discontinuous observation and recording applies to restricted operants, which are responses that occur only when specific opportunities arise – typically when environmental events occur (a sound indicating arrival of a text message; a spoken greeting from someone nearby; an instruction delivered by a trainer; etc.). Many ABA interventions target restricted operants, and opportunities for those responses to occur must be explicitly planned and arranged. For instance, many skill-building interactions involve a series of trials, each consisting of a specific antecedent stimulus presented by a trainer, an opportunity for the learner to emit a specific response, and a consequence delivered to the learner by the trainer, depending on the response. These discrete trial procedures have a long history in experimental psychology and behavior analysis and are used by ABA practitioners to develop many important skills in many types of clients, such as learners with autism. Some proponents of one model of autism intervention encourage practitioners to record responses discontinuously (e.g., on just the first trial or first and last trials of a series, or on weekly one-trial "cold probes") rather than continuously on all trials (Dollins & Carbone, 2003; Sundberg & Hale, 2003). That has led several researchers to compare conclusions about learner performances based on data produced by those and other forms of discontinuous observation (e.g., recording data on subsets of all trials or sessions) with conclusions based on data resulting from continuous observation and recording. The studies published so far show that although the data from these forms of discontinuous observation and recording sometimes seemed to indicate that learners' performances had met mastery criteria, those conclusions tended to be inaccurate and premature. Maintenance was much better for skills on which data were recorded continuously (Cummings & Carr, 2009), and continuous recording was more sensitive to changes in performance, especially when the type and level of prompt provided on each trial was also recorded (Carey & Bourret, 2014; Giunta-Fede et al., 2016; Lerman et al., 2011).

Aside from discontinuous observation and recording, there are a variety of other ways by which observation can result in a picture of responding that is limited in some way. For example, conducting observation sessions by alternating intervals of observing (whether continuous or discontinuous) with brief periods during which observation does not occur creates an incomplete record. This is easy to see in a measurement procedure in which each ten seconds of observing is followed by five seconds allowed for recording, which means that observing only occurs during two-thirds of a session and is going on only during intermittent 10-second intervals. Another approach to observation involves rotating brief periods of observation across different participants. For instance, each child in a classroom might be observed for 15 seconds before switching to the next child for 15 seconds and then to the next in a fixed sequence. The data from this procedure would then typically be collated for all children, which adds the limitations of grouped data (see Chapter 4) to those of interval-based recording.

In sum, continuous observation and recording is inherently superior to discontinuous measurement because it allows measurement to be complete, accurate, and dimensional – the holy grail of scientific measurement. Discontinuous observation and recording procedures meet none of those important criteria. The resulting data can only be interpreted in terms of the observational protocols themselves (e.g., percent of intervals scored in designated ways or responses on a small, non-representative sample of trials or opportunities), not as representations of actual behavioral dimensions.

The use of discontinuous observation and recording procedures is often justified on the grounds that they are easier and more convenient to use than continuous observation and recording (e.g., Fiske & Delmolino, 2012). That may be true for MTS when multiple behaviors are being observed or intervals are long enough to permit the data collector to do something else (such as implement intervention protocols) during intervals, but not when intervals are short enough to produce highly accurate estimates of behavioral dimensions. It is certainly not true for WIR or for PIR with very short intervals, because those procedures require the observer's undivided attention to the client or study participant and frequent recording, so the observer might as well do continuous observation and recording. Recording responses on only small subsets of trials or opportunities for restricted operants would seem to save time and effort; however, Carey and Bourret (2014) found that the savings were minimal, and other research has shown that any benefits are more than offset by the problems that occur when investigators have incomplete, inaccurate data.

Most importantly, research has shown that conclusions based on data produced by discontinuous observation and recording are often wrong. When such conclusions are published in professional journals, they can misinform the entire field. When they are made by practitioners, they can harm vulnerable

BOX 6.3

Two Birds, One Stone?

Interval-based recording procedures suggest the possibility of trying to kill two birds with one stone. If a practitioner is interested in making the target behavior occur more or less often, it may be tempting to use recording intervals as part of reinforcement contingencies for treatment purposes. For example, the partial-interval procedure can be used to support a contingency in which reinforcers are delivered at the end of intervals during which the target response did not occur. Depending on baseline levels of responding, this contingency would encourage a decrease in responding. Conversely, the whole-interval procedure can be used to encourage an increase in responding if reinforcers are only delivered following intervals in which the behavior occurs continuously throughout the interval.

There is nothing necessarily wrong with these behavior change contingencies, but rolling them into observation procedures confuses measurement and intervention objectives, with the result that measurement interests may be short-changed. The sole purpose of behavioral measurement is to capture a record of selected features of the target behavior in order to evaluate changes that might result from intervention procedures or other variables. It is important to design measurement procedures to produce the best possible picture of what is happening with the participant's behavior. When intervention procedures force the selection of measurement procedures, there is a risk that this priority will result in inferior measurement.

If the intervention objective is to increase responding, for instance, and it seems appropriate to use an interval contingency as described above, that decision should not encourage selection of a whole-interval observation and recording procedure. The whole-interval observing rule brings with it a number of problems described in the text, as do the partial-interval and momentary time sampling rules. Selecting continuous observation procedures will create a better picture of the effects of interval-based reinforcement contingencies than will discontinuous measurement.

---

clients. If continuous observation and recording cannot be done in real time – or even if it can – the ready availability of easy-to-use video recording devices with time-stamping features makes it feasible to record sessions (with appropriate consent and privacy protections, of course) so that actual frequency, duration, and count data can be produced using continuous observation procedures.

PROCEDURAL DECISIONS

Making Observations

With Equipment. Most of the target behaviors that interest behavior analytic researchers and practitioners involve movement of some sort, and those movements change the environment, even if only momentarily. Those changes may be relatively obvious and permanent (as in the work products of an employee) or more transient and subtle (as in a child's social interactions during recess). It is sometimes feasible to measure such movements or their associated environmental changes using some type of device or equipment, a possibility we noted above. This option can be easy to arrange in many situations, though more challenging in others. Depending on hardware to detect and record target behaviors can help achieve good accuracy and reliability, but the main benefit it offers is avoiding the issues associated with human observers.

The first step in deciding whether to use equipment is identifying the key features of the target behavior. It is important to be sure that the responses or the associated environmental changes are a reliable characteristic of the behavior. Although the target behavior may often generate reactions by other individuals, for instance, such reactions are not usually consistent and should not serve as the basis for measurement using equipment.

Once you have identified the features of the target behavior, the next step is to consider whether one or more of them can be detected by a sensor or device. In some cases, the target behavior may involve interacting with a device such as a computer or tablet via a touchscreen, touchpad, keyboard, or mouse. Detecting and recording such responses with existing or proprietary software is straightforward. More creativity may be required to figure out how to detect target behaviors that do not naturally involve a built-in sensor. There is no catalog of equipment for such applications, but there is an almost limitless array of sensors and devices than can detect anything about behavior we might want to capture. Some engineering may be required to create a suitable behavioral measurement tool using devices that were designed for other purposes. For example, accelerometers (electromechanical sensors that measure acceleration forces) have been adapted for measuring posture and a wide range of movements in typically developing individuals (e.g., Bussman et al., 2001) as well as stereotypic motor movements (e.g., Goodwin et al., 2010) and several topographies of problem behavior (e.g., Plotz et al., 2012) in people with autism and other developmental disorders.

Once a suitable device has been adapted for behavioral measurement, the third step is to set up procedures for making sure it is working as intended. This process is called calibration and is covered in Chapter 8. It involves ensuring that the equipment is functioning properly and will accurately detect all instances of the target behavior but nothing else. If its output is not within acceptable limits, the equipment must be adjusted or modified until it performs as needed. Scientists and others routinely calibrate their equipment in this manner.

One approach to automated observation is widely used and merits special mention. As noted earlier, it is often feasible to make a video recording of a participant's behavior throughout each observation period. This can create a useful two-dimensional record of the target behavior, though mixed with other behaviors and events that are not of interest. The price of this approach is that

TABLE 6.2
Requirements for setting up equipment observation

- Identify features consistently associated with the target behavior
- Determine how features can be detected by equipment
- Establish procedures to be sure equipment is working as intended

someone must watch the videos later to detect and record target behaviors. In doing so, they have an important advantage over observers who must do the job in real time: they can replay the video repeatedly to be sure to record all occurrences of target behaviors. The disadvantage of this approach is that more time is required to observe the video and generate a record of responding than is typically required when observations are made in real time. Ethical standards also require that specific written consent for video recording be obtained in advance and that procedures are in place for using and storing videos so as to protect participants' privacy.

With Human Observers. Measuring behavior with the aid of equipment is often feasible for behavior studied under laboratory conditions, but human observers are used to detect and record behavior in most field situations. Although the use of human observers is a common feature of applied research and practice, it is a fairly complex and time-consuming enterprise.

The first step is determining task requirements observers will have to meet. That is, given the target behavior and its environmental circumstances, exactly what will observers be asked to do? Will participants be in one place or moving around? Will it be easy for the observer to see the target behavior whenever it might occur? Will participants be alone or interacting with others? How many target behaviors will need to be observed concurrently? What type of behavioral definition – functional or topographical – will be used? What behavioral dimensions will be measured? What will observers have to do to make a record of their observations? What will they be asked to do in addition to observing and recording?

The answers to these and similar questions can result in a considerable list of performance demands on observers. It is generally the case that the longer the list, the greater the risk that some aspects of observer performance might fall short. The second step, then, is to consider how the demands on observers can be minimized. For instance, is there a means of recording observations that will make that part of the job easier? For example, recording responses with mechanical or electronic counters can be less demanding than marking a paper recording form. Timers and other devices can provide visual, auditory, or even tactile signals to observers if needed. Laptop computers, tablets, and smartphones can be used to record observer inputs in real time and create records of when responses occurred or even how long they lasted.

With a clear picture of what observers will be asked to do, the third step is recruiting and selecting the individuals who will serve in this role. Although all observers will require training, it can be helpful to select individuals who have had experiences that might give them advantages over others. For example, psychiatric nurses might be a better choice than undergraduate students if the task involves observing patients in a mental hospital. Of course, it is always important to select individuals who are likely to respond well to training, show up when scheduled, and try to comply with the measurement protocol.

Whatever the background and motivation of the individuals selected to be observers, the fourth step is to design and implement a training program that will enable them to accurately detect and record target responses. More behaviorally, the objective of observer training is to bring their behavior under precise control of the defined features of the target behavior and the rules for observing and recording. Achieving this objective will require not only detailed written and oral instructions but also modeling and repeated practice with feedback, perhaps using videotapes of participant behavior or even practice under field conditions. Observer training usually involves multiple sessions, and observers should be required to demonstrate that they can observe and record target behavior accurately and consistently before they are allowed to collect the data that the investigator will use to make decisions.

Even when observers meet training standards initially, their performance may deteriorate over the course of a project. The fifth step is, therefore, to set up procedures for evaluating their performance on an ongoing basis. (Chapter 8 will consider these procedures in detail.) There are many reasons why observer performance may vary over the course of a study, a phenomenon called **observer drift**. Observers may gradually change the criteria they use for detecting and recording target responses or even the response definitions. Their judgments may be influenced by differences in procedures or circumstances from one phase to another. For instance, baseline conditions may present different challenges to observation than treatment phases. Some conditions may change the behavior of participants in ways that make it more difficult to identify responses. For example, improvements in the target behavior may make responses less obvious or more difficult to detect. In projects conducted in everyday settings like classrooms, homes, or treatment centers, any number of events can occur during observation sessions that make it difficult for observers to see, hear, or remain focused on target behaviors. Mechanical or electronic devices used for recording can malfunction, or observers might forget how to use them. Fatigue may affect observations in the latter parts of long sessions. Observers' performance may also be affected by what is going on in the rest of their lives. For instance, on some days they may be tired, preoccupied, or not feeling well. Since the data recorded by human observers will be the basis for important decisions, the foregoing should make it clear that it is essential to check their performance frequently and carefully and retrain them when necessary.

Depending on the nature of the study, investigators may choose to limit observers' access to information about the study as a way of minimizing the chance that it might influence their judgments. When this is done, observers may be described as **blind**, though the procedure is not as cruel as it sounds. Blind observers are prevented from having information like why the study

TABLE 6.3
Requirements for setting up human observation

- Determine task requirements observers will have to meet
- Consider how observer demands can be minimized
- Select observers
- Design and implement observer training program
- Establish procedures for evaluating observer performance

is being conducted, the features of or rationale for treatment conditions, any expectations the investigator may have about outcomes, or the nature of the accumulating data. Studies in which neither researchers nor participants know key features of experimental and control conditions are called double-blind studies. This technique is commonly used in investigating the effects of drugs, for example: Neither physician nor patient knows whether the patient is receiving the experimental drug or a placebo.

Because most behavior analytic studies involve direct observation of target behaviors and environmental events, it can be difficult to keep observers blind to certain aspects of an investigation. They can hardly help learning some things about the project, such as whether baseline or treatment conditions are in effect. Nevertheless, investigators should do all they can to minimize the risk that observers' records will be biased (discussed further in Chapter 8).

> **Observer drift.** A change in an observer's performance, often gradual and for reasons that may not be obvious to the investigator.
>
> **Blind.** A reference to being unaware of the goals of an experiment, the nature of experimental or control conditions, or the outcomes of each condition. May apply to the investigator, observers, or participants. If both investigator and participants are blind, it is called a *double-blind* experiment.

Finally, just as with any desirable behavior, an observer's showing up as scheduled and performing well should generate sufficient reinforcement to be maintained at acceptable levels. Observers are sometimes paid, but they are often employees of a research or service delivery organization and do not receive extra pay for this duty. It is still important to ensure that observers earn positive reinforcement contingent on faithfully following measurement protocols, even if the reinforcers are only social in nature. As Chapter 8 will show, the data from formal evaluation of measurement procedures can provide opportunities to differentially reinforce each observer's performance.

With Participants as Observers. It might seem that the individuals who are the least appropriate candidates for serving as observers are participants themselves. After all, they are not exactly disinterested in what is going on, and their involvement may ensure that they are difficult to train, motivated to detect

---

BOX 6.4

A Special Case?

Using participants as observers is not so difficult when the target behavior is publically observable, as is often the case. But what about when the definition of a target behavior means it can be detected only by the participant and no one else? For example, what if the target behavior is "urges to smoke a cigarette?" Such behaviors fall in the category of private events. B. F. Skinner has extensively discussed the issues associated with private events (see Chapter 17 in Skinner, 1953, for example), and their treatment in the field of behavior analysis is fundamental to its philosophy of science, radical behaviorism (Calkin, 2009; Johnston, 2014; Moore, 2008).

In brief, behavior analysts acknowledge that the fact that a behavior is not publically observable does not mean it is different in any way from public behaviors and merely raises issues of accessibility. In fact, it is helpful to consider accessibility as a continuum. At one end, the behavior is publically observable in principle though difficult to get at on each and every occasion. For instance, swallowing can be observed by others, though it would be challenging for an external observer to detect each such behavior in someone else. At the other end, the behavior is fully private in that it cannot be detected by anyone other than the behaving individual, such as thinking negative self-thoughts.

Although fully private behavioral events are not a special or different kind of phenomenon than public behaviors, they do provide some special challenges to investigators. For instance, in training an individual to observe a particular behavior that only he or she can detect, how can the investigator make sure that detected responses meet the agreed upon definition and that they are being captured exactly as the investigator intends? These questions are not usually too difficult to satisfy when the behavior is public, even though the investigator may have to take some special steps. However, determining whether the data resulting from private observations are accurate when there is no way to collect alternative measures means that evaluating the private observations is unavoidably difficult, if not ultimately impossible. A discussion of the methodological issues associated with private events may be found in "Reading 6: The problem of limited accessibility" in Johnston and Pennypacker (1993b).

Accepting the methodological challenges that come with measuring private events may sometimes be worth it. Both research and practical questions may require access to private behaviors. If the question concerns whether chewing nicotine gum affects the frequency of urges to smoke compared to the frequency of lighting a cigarette, there is no choice but to train the participant to measure this target. What other private target behaviors might be useful in research or clinical projects?

---

either more or fewer target responses than actually occurred, likely to be influenced by the data they are collecting, and sometimes not inclined to cooperate. With these potential problems, why would anyone ever want to use participants as observers of their own behavior? The answer is that participants have one notable advantage over other observers: They are always around. Using participants to observe and record their own behavior solves one of the most difficult challenges of using human observers – gaining complete access to the target behavior. Participants are always present when the behavior occurs.

In fact, participant observers present investigators with problems that are similar to those faced with other observers. Both participant and non-participant observers have histories that may not encourage good observing, and both may be influenced by events going on in and outside of the study as well as the emerging data. As with other observers, participant observers must be selected, trained, evaluated, and retrained with care, and their data must meet customary measurement standards. When all that is done, participants have the distinct advantage of potentially being able to produce complete records of behavior. Indeed, using participant observers may sometimes be the only

---

BOX 6.5

The Problem of Measurement Reactivity

When a participant's behavior is influenced by measurement procedures, it is called **measurement reactivity**. If the procedures used to observe and record behavior are detectable by the participant, it is possible that the participant may behave differently than when he or she is not being observed. Although we might assume that knowing that we are being observed will always have some impact on our behavior, investigators usually find either that there is no apparent effect or that any effect dissipates quickly. Nevertheless, the risk of measurement reactivity must always be considered until it is clear that it is not a problem.

It is sometimes easy to minimize reactivity by taking care with how equipment or observers are used. For example, a video camera might be left in place all the time rather than just being set up just for observation sessions, so that participants learn to ignore it. Observers might be stationed unobtrusively rather than placed in an obvious location. If the risk of measurement reactivity seems especially great, it may be necessary to design observation procedures that are not detectable by participants.

Whatever preparations are taken to minimize measurement reactivity, there remains the question of whether they are successful. That question can only be answered by devoting some experimental comparisons specifically to this issue. Such manipulations would have to compare responding under routine observation procedures to responding under somewhat different (perhaps unobtrusive) observation procedures. Of course, it is not possible to compare responding in the presence versus the total absence of measurement; without measurement, there would be no data at all.

Again, although measurement reactivity is certainly possible, the effect is usually small and transient, if it occurs at all. Because behavioral measurement continues throughout an investigation, any durable effects of measurement may at least be constant, so may not complicate comparisons of treatment and non-treatment conditions.

feasible way to collect the data that are needed. If the target behavior can occur during all waking hours under varying environments, for instance, using others as observers usually requires restricting the times and situations under which observations take place. That can limit the representativeness of the data and the generality of the findings. Using participants as observers can avoid those constraints. A major disadvantage, however, is that even the best-trained participant is likely to be biased in recording data about her own behavior. That increases the burden on the investigator to evaluate the measurement procedures by checking the correspondence between data recorded by participants and independent observers on the same samples of behavior frequently over the course of the project.

Scheduling Observation Periods

We have already considered the basic issues underlying decisions about how observation is scheduled. The ideal is that observation should be ongoing whenever target behaviors might occur. For behaviors that can – or typically do – occur only under limited conditions, such as in a classroom or during a training session, that may be an easy standard to meet. Some behaviors can occur during all waking hours and in multiple settings, however, and it can sometimes be challenging to arrange for complete observation under those conditions. For example, stereotypic and other repetitive behaviors in individuals with autism are likely to occur under varied circumstances throughout the day.

If complete observation is not feasible, observation periods must be scheduled so that they sample adequately from all the times and circumstances under which the behavior could occur. In making these decisions, the key questions are "How often should observation periods be scheduled?" and "How long should each observation period last?" The answers are straightforward: "As often as possible and as long as possible." In other words, the objective is to arrange observation periods that come as close as is reasonably possible to complete observation.

The reason for this approach is to minimize the risk that incomplete observational data fail to adequately represent what is going on with the target behavior while it is not being observed. How important it is for the data from limited sessions to represent a complete picture of the target behavior depends on the nature of the question. When the data are used to make decisions about intervention effects that can affect a client's welfare or the relations between the independent and dependent variables in a study, those data must reflect the occurrence of the behavior throughout the times when it is not being recorded. It would be a problem, for example, if the data from limited observation periods showed that a problem behavior was decreasing to low levels as a result of an intervention but staff or family members could clearly see that it was continuing to occur as much as ever during other times.

On the other hand, for many research projects it may only be necessary for the data to show how a target behavior is affected by experimental variables.

For example, an initial comparison of two intervention procedures may only need to evaluate effects on target behaviors during research sessions, as in a study evaluating two differential reinforcement procedures for reducing rates of motor and vocal tics by Capriotti and colleagues (2017).

The characteristics of the target behavior must also be considered when deciding how often observations should be scheduled. Free operants that tend to occur at comparable rates across most times and situations could be observed at almost any time of day, with several observation sessions conducted each week. Many repetitive and stereotypic behaviors exhibited by people with developmental disabilities, for example, have those characteristics. It would be ideal if the observations could be scheduled so that they occurred at different times over the course of a week – say, three times each in the morning, around midday, and in the afternoon. For free operants that occur only a few times each day (e.g., eloping, destroying property) it may be necessary to observe multiple times throughout every day in order to get an adequate sample. Alternatively, if there is evidence that such behaviors tend to occur at certain times or in specific contexts, observations should be scheduled accordingly. Examples are disruptive behaviors by a young student (making noises, poking other students) that occur mostly during math instruction in the classroom; bolting or flopping (falling to the ground) by an adult with intellectual disabilities that occurs only during transitions between areas at his day program; and hand flapping by a child with autism that tends to occur during unstructured activities like free play. Observations conducted under those conditions are more likely to yield meaningful data than observations scheduled at other times.

By definition, restricted operants can occur only when they are specifically occasioned. For many of those target behaviors, then, observations must coincide with sessions during which interventionists are implementing procedures designed to strengthen the behaviors or bring them under stimulus control. Research cited in the preceding section on discontinuous observation points up the importance of using continuously recorded data rather than relying on samples from subsets of instructional trials (e.g., Carey & Bourret, 2014). Of course, some restricted operants must be measured outside of planned intervention sessions. Examples include an adult with a traumatic brain injury returning greetings from co-workers in their break room at work, or a preschooler with autism responding to play bids from other children on the playground. Again, it makes sense to schedule observations of such target behaviors during times when antecedents for them are most likely to occur rather than at other times.

Research shows that in general, the longer the observation period, the more likely the data will be representative of a target behavior's overall occurrence. That varies, however, with the duration of each response or bout of responding, the relative duration of the response (i.e., the proportion of the total observation period it consumes), the distribution of responding within each observation period, and other characteristics of the target behavior (Ferguson, Briesch, Volpe, & Daniels, 2012; Mudford, Beale, & Singh, 1990; Tiger et al., 2013). For instance, one set of investigators found that when behavior was fairly stable, data from 10-minute observations provided a representative picture, but when variability was high, extending observation periods to 60 minutes failed to result in data that represented the actual overall occurrences (Tiger et al., 2013). The most prudent approach might be to record data continuously throughout a couple of fairly lengthy observation periods – say, 2 hours or more – using procedures that capture characteristics of the target behavior like those just described and analyze the resulting records to determine how long observation periods need to be.

In many service delivery settings, practical constraints make it difficult to conduct the optimal number of observation periods. Behavior analysts who are responsible for services to clients might be tempted to ask the interventionists and caregivers who interact with the clients to record something about every occurrence of a target behavior that those individuals observe (or hear about) throughout all or most of the clients' waking moments. That might seem like a good way to supplement the data from the formal observations, but it is important to realize that unless all of those additional observers are trained and their ongoing performance checked frequently as described earlier and in Chapter 8, the "data" they record will reflect only their subjective personal impressions. It will not be comparable to the data that results from properly conducted observation and recording and therefore cannot be interpreted as representing actual behavioral dimensions. A better tactic is to train a small number of those individuals on the behavioral definitions and observation and recording rules and have them conduct a few brief observations throughout the day. That will be a better use of their time than recording lots of anecdotal information and will give the investigator some additional sound data on which to base important decisions.

Recording Observations

The effort put into defining and observing a target behavior only matters when observations are recorded. The goal of recording observations is to preserve the observed facts regarding the target behavior in a manner that accurately reflects the observations. It is through recording that facts become data. Once a session is over, the data are all that remain.

When the target behavior and other events are detected automatically by equipment of some sort, the resulting record is usually also created automatically in the form of an electronic file. More often, especially in applied settings, human observers serve both observing and recording functions. When that is the case, the distinction between observing and recording can be especially important. Sometimes the behavioral requirements of these tasks are incompatible, which creates the risk that the requirements of recording will interfere with the job of observing and result in inaccurate data. Of course, it is also possible for observational obligations to interfere with making an accurate record.

The demands of recording start with the nature of the information that has to be preserved. At a minimum, recording may only require noting something simple about the target response, such as the fact of its occurrence or the moment it starts or ends. With an electronic device and the proper software, all the observer should have to do is touch a preprogrammed button or two on a screen or keyboard. If the information to be recorded is numerical, it is only slightly more demanding to input a value. The key is to use software that accommodates the particular observational data to be recorded, preferably in a custom format, so that it minimizes the time required to record something. The most common conflict between observing and recording comes from requiring the observer to break visual contact with the participant's behavior in order to record information. Even a few seconds spent getting and marking a recording form, whether digital or paper, can cause the observer to miss seeing responses.

These are simple situations, however. It is not uncommon for observers to be asked to monitor multiple behaviors – possibly for multiple individuals – as well as various environmental events that are important, such as features of intervention procedures. The workload is even worse when information must be transcribed onto a paper form. Recording in this format usually requires more time than making a digital record – time that cannot be devoted to observing responsibilities. It is therefore especially important that paper recording forms be carefully designed to minimize the time required to enter information. That can be done by using single letters or abbreviations as codes for target behaviors and environmental events so that the observer only has to circle or make a hash mark through a code to record an observation. Recording forms can also include behavioral definitions and brief descriptions of observation and recording rules to help ensure that observers follow protocols.

The greater the demands of observing and recording, the greater the risk that one or both assignments will be compromised so that the final record falls short in terms of what was observed or how well it was recorded. That is why it is so important to think through the details of observing and recording tasks with the same care that is given to planning intervention procedures and other features of a project. The challenge for the investigator is figuring out how the tasks of observing and recording can be minimized or simplified and how to design their behavioral details.

This raises the issue of when observational information should be recorded. Should observations be recorded immediately after an event has occurred or might recording take place only periodically? Some kinds of observations require recording events as soon as they occur. For example, if temporal information such as the distribution of responding throughout sessions, the duration of responses, or interresponse times is being measured, it will be necessary to in some way note the exact moment responses occurred or the time each response started and ended.

When only the occurrence of a target behavior is being counted, each response does not have to be recorded as soon as it occurs, but how often is sufficient? The answer depends on the details of each project, the requirements of the observation protocol, and how frequently there is something to be recorded. The more often observing is interrupted to record something, the more likely the observer may miss something else that may be important. On the other hand, the longer the delay between observation and recording, the greater the chance of error. If the target behavior does not occur too often and observers are not burdened with too many other duties, it is best to record each response as soon as it occurs. Under less favorable conditions, observers are sometimes permitted to record their observations well after they occur – not just minutes but even hours later. This is not uncommon in service delivery situations and can easily result in discrepancies between what occurred and what is recorded. The best approach to any conflicts between observing and recording is to first identify the conflicts and then work toward minimizing if not removing them. In the end, it is important that observational requirements be met and the recorded data accurately reflect what was observed.

In sum, recording is the terminal step in a complex sequence that begins with defining the target behavior of interest and selecting relevant dimensions, proceeds through observing and recording, and culminates in a permanent record of the target behavior. All of these steps must result in a record that accurately preserves targeted features of the participant's behavior.

CHAPTER SUMMARY

1. Behavioral measurement involves the following steps: (a) identifying responses that meet the requirements of the target behavior's definition, (b) determining the amount of the selected dimension observed for each response, (c) deciding how long observation sessions will be and when they will take place, and (d) in each session, making some kind of record of the amount of behavior using an appropriate unit of measurement.

2. The overarching goal of behavioral measurement is to produce data that will guide correct and meaningful interpretations by the investigator. To accomplish this, our observations and recording of the target behavior(s) must be complete and accurate.

3. When what you are measuring is exactly the same as what you are drawing conclusions about, measurement is direct. In contrast, when what you actually measure is different in some way from what you are drawing conclusions about, measurement is indirect.

4. Many researchers and practitioners prefer direct measurement over indirect measurement. The reason is that indirect measurement requires making assumptions about the relationship between indirect measures and what those measures are supposed to represent.

5. Automated observation may be most effective in detecting and recording target behaviors in a consistent and accurate manner. Human observers may be ideal for providing supplementary monitoring and to look for unexpected events during sessions that might be important in managing a study or intervention.

6. Although complete observation is an ideal approach, it does not guarantee that the resulting data will be accurate. Incomplete observation is not necessarily a poor alternative as long as the investigator is able to arrange

observation periods so that they provide evidence of the amount and distribution of responding that the project requires.

7. Continuous observation and recording is inherently superior to discontinuous measurement because it allows measurement to be complete, accurate, and dimensional.

8. Discontinuous observation and recording procedures only sample from among the target responses that occur during an observation period. This makes it likely that some responses will be missed, which in turn means that data resulting from discontinuous observation and recording are not likely to accurately reflect behavioral dimensions such as count, duration, or rate (frequency).

9. In partial interval recording (PIR) the observer is charged with observing during each interval and recording an occurrence if the target behavior occurs at least once at any time during the interval. In whole interval recording (WIR), the observer must observe throughout each interval and record an occurrence only if the target behavior occurs without ceasing throughout the interval.

10. In momentary time sampling (MTS), the individual observes only briefly when each interval ends and scores the interval only if the target response is occurring at that moment.

11. Because so many factors can influence the resulting data, it is difficult to draw broad conclusions or recommendations regarding discontinuous procedures. However, it does appear that: (a) WIR often produces unacceptably large measurement errors; (b) PIR can yield reasonable estimates of frequency when intervals are less than 10 seconds; and (c) the magnitude of error in MTS is generally smaller when intervals are shorter (i.e., 30 seconds or less).

12. In determining whether to observe and record behavior with a device, the first step is to identify those changes associated with the target behavior and determine how they could be detected with a particular device. Once a device is selected, the investigator must be sure that it is working properly and will accurately detect and record all of the target responses.

13. When human observers are used, the first step is to determine what exactly they will be required to do. Once these specific requirements have been determined, it is often beneficial to consider how the demands on the observer can be minimized. The observers are then selected and trained on how to observe and record the target behavior. The investigator should also be sure to monitor their observers and evaluate their performance on an ongoing basis.

14. If complete observation is not feasible, observation periods must be arranged so that they come as close as is reasonably possible to complete observation. This will help to minimize the risk that incomplete observational data do not adequately represent what was occurring with the target behavior when it was not being observed.

15. The goal of recording observations is to preserve the observed facts regarding the target behavior in a manner that accurately reflects the observations.

HIGHLIGHTED TERMS

Blind. A reference to being unaware of the goals of an experiment, the nature of experimental or control conditions, or the outcomes of each condition. May apply to the investigator, observers, or participants. If both investigator and participants are blind, it is called a *double-blind* experiment.

Complete observation. A schedule of observation that allows detection of all occurrences of the target behavior.

Continuous observation. Observation and recording procedures in which all occurrences of the target behavior can be detected during observation periods.

Direct measurement. Measurement practices in which the events that are measured are exactly the same as those about which conclusions are drawn.

Discontinuous observation. Observation and recording procedures in which all occurrences of the target behavior are not necessarily detected and recorded during observation sessions.

Incomplete observation. A schedule of observation that samples from all occurrences of the target behavior and may therefore fail to detect some responses.

Indirect measurement. Measurement practices in which the events that are measured are not the same as those about which conclusions will be drawn.

Interval-based recording. A category of discontinuous observation and recording procedures in which observation periods are divided into equal intervals, and occurrences of the target response are recorded by interval according to some rule.

Momentary time sampling (MTS). A form of interval-based recording in which observation periods are divided into equal intervals, but the observer only records whether the target response is occurring at the end of each interval.

Observer drift. A change in an observer's performance, often gradual and for reasons that may not be obvious to the investigator.

Partial interval recording (PIR). A form of interval-based recording in which an occurrence is recorded if the target response (or even part of a response) is observed at any time during the interval. Only one occurrence is recorded, even if multiple responses occurred during the interval.

Whole interval recording (WIR). A form of interval-based recording in which an occurrence is recorded if the target response occurs without ceasing throughout the entire interval.

TEXT STUDY GUIDE

1. Describe the steps of behavioral measurement.
2. Explain how behavioral measurement is a filtering process.
3. What is the goal of behavioral measurement?
4. Explain the difference between direct and indirect measurement.
5. Why is direct measurement preferred over indirect measurement?
6. What advantage does automated observation have over human observation?
7. How can human observation supplement automated observation?
8. What is the difference between complete and incomplete observation?
9. Compare complete and incomplete observation with regard to the accuracy of data.
10. What issue does incomplete observation raise?
11. Explain the difference between continuous and discontinuous observation and recording.
12. What is the primary weakness of discontinuous observation and recording?
13. Explain partial and whole interval recording procedures.
14. Describe how partial interval recording may misrepresent actual responding.
15. Describe how whole interval recording may misrepresent actual responding.
16. Explain the momentary time sampling procedure.
17. Describe how momentary time sampling may misrepresent actual responding.
18. Explain how interval size affects percent of scored interval data.
19. What is the consequence of the fact that percent of scored intervals is a dimensionless quantity?
20. What are restricted operants? Describe how these behaviors may be recorded.
21. What is the best way to minimize the disadvantages of discontinuous observation procedures such as interval-based recording?
22. List the steps involved in designing an observation procedure that utilizes equipment.
23. List the steps in designing an observation procedure with human observers.
24. What is observer drift?
25. What are blind observers?
26. Explain how participants can be considered as suitable observers of their own behavior. What could be a disadvantage of using this approach?
27. Describe how the characteristics of the target behavior can impact how often observations should be scheduled.
28. What is the goal of recording observations?

BOX STUDY GUIDE

1. What is the benefit of recording count within an interval?
2. Describe the risk(s) investigators encounter when intervention procedures force the selection of measurement procedures.
3. What challenges do fully private behavioral events present to investigators?
4. What is measurement reactivity?

SUGGESTED READINGS

Barrett, B. H. (1962). Reduction in rate of multiple tics by free operant conditioning methods. *Journal of Nervous and Mental Disease, 135*, 187–195.
Gardenier, N. C., MacDonald, R., & Green, G. (2004). Comparison of direct observational methods for measuring stereotypic behavior in children with autism spectrum disorders. *Research in Developmental Disabilities, 25*, 99–118.

DISCUSSION TOPICS

1. Select a target behavior and discuss how direct versus indirect measurement might be used.
2. Identify three examples of target behaviors and discuss how automated measurement procedures might be developed.
3. Select some "real world" examples of specific behaviors and discuss how the frequency and duration of incomplete observation sessions should be scheduled.
4. Identify and discuss any behavior analytic examples of when using a blind procedure might be useful.

EXERCISES

1. Have one student engage in the behavior of finger snapping for 5 minutes. Have a second student serve as an observer who will record the exact time of each response. After these data are available, divide the 5-minute session into intervals. In one case, use 10-second intervals. In a second case, use 30-second intervals. In a third case, use 1-minute intervals. Then score each set of intervals based on the continuous record of responding using the partial-interval rule and calculate the percent of scored intervals. Discuss the results in terms of the issues raised in the chapter.

CHAPTER SEVEN

Behavior Analytic Assessment

BEHAVIORAL ASSESSMENT

Many articles, chapters, and textbooks have been written about behavioral assessment. That term often encompasses strategies and tactics used in clinical psychology, school psychology, behavior therapy, and other disciplines in addition to behavior analysis. This chapter provides an overview of the large array of assessment approaches, types of instruments, and procedures that behavior analytic researchers and practitioners are likely to encounter or use.

GOALS OF ASSESSMENT

Research Projects

The behavior analyst who is preparing to conduct a research project with human participants must select or design assessment procedures that will serve the overarching goal of answering the research question. That may entail conducting – or having others conduct – assessments to identify individuals with characteristics that would make them appropriate study participants. For instance, the research question may require that participants have a diagnosed disorder or condition (e.g., Tourette's syndrome, bulimia, autism spectrum disorder), a prespecified level of skill or performance in one or more domains (e.g., a receptive vocabulary of no more than 200 nouns; grade-level reading skills; adaptive skills that are at least 50% below those of same-age peers), or a prespecified level or rate of a problem behavior (e.g., smoking at least 5 cigarettes a day; consuming foods in only one of the major food groups; exhibiting aggressive behavior toward peers 3-6 times per day). If the research is funded, the funding source may prescribe the use of specific assessments for this purpose. Otherwise, the research literature or colleagues with expertise in these types of assessments are good sources of guidance.

The researcher must also decide how to assess the effects of the independent variable – i.e., how to measure the dependent variable – to best serve the goal of answering the research question. A related goal is communicating the study results to the relevant research community via publications or presentations at professional meetings. The funding source and the conventions followed by others who conduct and publish research in the subject matter may influence decisions about dependent measures.

Practical Projects

For most ABA practitioners, the main goal of assessment with a new client is to identify one or more socially important behaviors to be targeted for treatment and the environmental events that influence them. A closely related goal is to develop a written treatment plan that specifies the information shown in Table 7.1. Implicit in the treatment plan are the additional goals of measuring the client's baseline levels and progress on each target behavior and reporting those data to caregivers, other treatment team members, and funding sources. Decisions about assessment procedures for achieving those goals may be influenced by input from those stakeholders as well as regulatory requirements, such as laws and policies governing healthcare, educational, or rehabilitation services.

TABLE 7.1

Components of a behavior analytic treatment plan

For each target behavior:
- Definition written in observable, measurable terms
- Measurement procedures
- Current or baseline level
- Short- and long-term objectives for changing the behavior
- Criteria for determining if the objectives are met
- Procedures for bringing about the changes
- Setting(s) in which treatment will be delivered
- Procedures for ensuring that behavior change generalizes across people, settings, stimuli, time, etc.
- Personnel who will implement the treatment plan (including caregivers where applicable)
- Estimated amount of treatment (in terms of hours per week, total number of weeks or months, and the like) required to achieve the objectives

ASSESSMENT TOOLS AND PROCEDURES

Standardized Instruments

Definition and Importance. In Chapter 6 we drew a distinction between **direct measurement**, where what is measured is the same as what one is drawing conclusions about, and **indirect measurement**, where those two are not the same. Many assessment instruments fall into the second category, in that responses to a fixed set of items – either by the individual of interest or by an examiner or informant – are used to draw inferences about the existence or proficiency levels of certain behavioral repertoires (such as skills in an area of academics or work performance) or of unobservable constructs (such as personality traits, aptitudes, or intelligence). With some instruments that are completed by informants, the informant is to observe the individual of interest in real time while completing the assessment, but in many cases the informants' responses are based on their recollections of previous observations or other sources of information. Many assessment instruments that are used in the social sciences and education are designed to compare the individual's results to those produced by large numbers of other people. Instruments developed by behavior analysts, on the other hand, tend to focus on the individual's behavior and environmental events that influence it. The primary focus is on changes in the individual's behavior over time, though results may also be used for comparisons with other individuals.

Regardless of the conceptual framework in which an assessment instrument is couched or the comparisons that are to be made, it is essential for the instrument to be **standardized** to ensure that comparisons reflect actual differences in the behavior of the individual(s) of interest instead of differences in assessment procedures, including the behavior of those who complete and score the assessment. That requires the assessment items, materials, time limits, administration procedures, and scoring procedures and criteria to be the same

---

BOX 7.1

Idiographic and Nomothetic Assessment

The terms *idiographic* and *nomothetic* are sometimes used to describe the approaches to research and assessment that are contrasted at several points in this book. Generally speaking, idiographic strategies focus on the individual, while nomothetic strategies are concerned with groups. Idiographic assessment procedures and the criteria by which the resulting data are evaluated are designed specifically for each individual client or study participant. That approach characterizes the behavior analytic methods that are described in this chapter and in Chapters 6 and 8. Nomothetic assessment procedures are identical for all individuals to whom they are administered – that is, the administration and scoring procedures are standardized, and the resulting data for an individual are compared with results obtained with large numbers of other people. They are used widely in the social sciences, education, and other fields.

Much has been written about the pros and cons of idiographic and nomothetic assessment strategies. Some authors have argued that they are entirely dichotomous, while others have pointed out that some of the distinctions between the two are blurry and that it is often advantageous to integrate the two approaches. For example, idiographic assessment procedures can be standardized so that results can be compared across clients or study participants, and many nomothetic assessments yield a "big picture" that can be helpful for making judgments about treatment targets and the effects of treatments on individuals. This chapter takes the tack that both approaches can produce information that can be useful to behavior analysts depending on the specific practical or research questions they are trying to answer.

---

every time the instrument is administered. Standardization lends objectivity to an assessment by minimizing the extent to which the results are affected by biases and errors on the part of those who administer and score it. In short, standardization is essential for comparing assessment results within and across individuals of interest as well as administrations of the instrument by different people and by the same person at different points in time. Otherwise the reported results constitute nothing more than the subjective impressions of the person who administered and scored the assessment at a particular point in time.

> **Standardized assessment.** An assessment instrument or procedure on which all components (contents, timing, administration and scoring procedures, etc.) are the same every time the assessment is administered.

Specific procedures are required to standardize an assessment instrument. The items must be selected and sequenced carefully. That is often done by searching the relevant research literature, studying well-researched instruments that purport to assess the same behaviors, having multiple experts in the subject matter review the items, and conducting systematic pilot testing with carefully selected and well-characterized samples of participants. Instructions for administering each item must be developed, tried out, evaluated, and revised until typical examiners can carry them out accurately and consistently. The same goes for procedures for scoring each item and the assessment as a whole. It is not sufficient for the developer of the instrument to assert that the necessary development and evaluation has been done; rather, that work should be subjected to peer review by knowledgeable professionals such as journal reviewers and editors or individuals who are employed by publishers of assessment instruments. The end result should be a clearly written protocol and a manual with detailed instructions for administering and scoring it.

A good description of the kind of research that is required to standardize an assessment instrument is provided in a report about the development of the Communication Complexity Scale by Brady, Fleming, Thiemann-Bourque, Olswang, Dowden, and Saunders (2012). The authors set out to develop an assessment of the communication status of individuals with severe intellectual and developmental disabilities. First, they conducted a comprehensive analysis of research on the development of early communication skills in typically developing children and those with several types of disabilities and disorders. They examined existing measures of what they termed "presymbolic" communication skills and noted the limitations of those measures. From those sources, they developed scripts for assessment sessions in which examiners presented specified items or activities designed to evoke communication responses to participants who were diagnosed with intellectual or developmental disabilities and assessed to have expressive communication vocabularies of no more than 20 words (speech, signs, or symbols). Multiple examiners at three different sites conducted sessions that were videotaped, coded by the developers, and discussed. The content and scoring of the scale were further developed and refined. A manual was developed, tried out systematically, and revised. Inter-rater agreement was evaluated across several dimensions, and scores for a subset of participants were compared with their scores on two well-established standardized assessments as well as the results of two informant (caregiver) questionnaires. Four experts in early communication development also reviewed and evaluated the scale. Results showed that the Communication Complexity Scale accurately captured the communication skills of the study participants.

Norm- and Criterion-Referenced Assessments. A common misconception is that all standardized assessment instruments are **norm-referenced**, meaning that an individual's score is interpreted relative to the scores of other individuals in a defined group (e.g., typically developing individuals of the same chronological age, or individuals with the same diagnosis). In fact, many standardized instruments are **criterion-referenced**, in that an individual's score is compared to a prespecified performance standard. Development of a good norm-referenced assessment involves first developing and validating the protocol as described previously, then administering the instrument to one or more large samples of individuals who represent a well-defined population. The results are used to create a table of norms by converting the sample's raw scores into percentile ranks. The table shows the percentage of individuals in the norming sample who received a particular raw score. For some instruments, the table also includes age or grade equivalents. An individual's score on the instrument can be looked up in the table to determine how her performance compared to the performances of the norming sample. Many standardized instruments for assessing intellectual, communication, social, adaptive, and other skills are norm-referenced, as are many instruments for diagnosing disorders and assessing "personality" types and aptitudes. For a standardized criterion-referenced assessment, research must be done to establish a score that represents mastery or some other level of proficiency in the skill domain assessed. Common examples are academic achievement tests and exams for getting into college, graduate, or professional schools or for obtaining a credential to practice a profession or trade. An individual's score is compared to a prespecified mastery, cutoff, or passing score. Some assessment instruments are both norm- and criterion-referenced.

> **Norm-referenced assessment.** An assessment on which an individual's score is interpreted relative to the scores of other individuals in a defined group.
>
> **Criterion-referenced assessment.** An assessment on which an individual's score is compared to a prespecified performance standard.

Checklists, rating scales, and curriculum-referenced assessments should also be standardized so that they are administered in uniform ways and their results can be compared across examiners and participants. Even then, however, the results should be interpreted cautiously in light of the problems with such instruments that are discussed in Box 6.5.

Psychometric Properties. Chapter 8 addresses approaches to assessing the quality of data produced by the direct observation and measurement procedures that are used most often by behavior analysts. Different strategies and tactics are used to evaluate the quality of the results produced by the indirect measurement procedures that characterize many assessment instruments used in the social sciences and education. Most of those evaluation methods have been drawn from classical test theory, which is part of the subject matter of the field of study known as **psychometrics**, or psychological measurement. They are described in detail in *The Standards for Educational and Psychological Testing*, which are developed jointly by the American Educational Research Association, American Psychological Association, and National Council on Measurement in Education and updated periodically, as well as numerous textbooks. Some of the basic concepts and methods are described next.

> **Psychometrics.** The field of study whose subject matter is psychological testing and measurement.

In psychometric assessment, **validity** refers to the appropriateness and usefulness of inferences that are drawn from assessment results. There are several types of evidence about the validity of such inferences. **Construct validity** is the extent to which an instrument is shown to assess the construct that it purports to measure, such as intelligence in the case of IQ tests. Developers of an IQ test might hypothesize that individuals who "have" different degrees of intelligence will acquire new skills at different rates when training is directed by another person than when learning is self-managed. The test developer might conduct a study in which one group of participants experiences each of those training conditions, and the rates with which they acquire the target skills are measured. All participants would also be administered the IQ test. If the test scores differentiate the two groups, the developer would take that as some evidence that the test measures the construct of intelligence, but evidence from results of studies to evaluate other types of validity would be required to establish construct validity. **Content validity** refers to the extent to which scores on an assessment represent the content that the instrument purports to measure. It is determined by subject matter experts, who define very precisely the complete universe (or domain) of content that the assessment is assumed to measure and then determine how well the assessment items sample that universe. For example, the developers of the Communication Complexity Scale discussed earlier had subject matter experts select items to include on the initial version of the scale, and then had other experts test to see if those items constituted an adequate, representative sample of the full range of presymbolic communication skills that might be exhibited by individuals with severe intellectual and developmental disabilities.

   Predictive or criterion-related validity is the degree to which predictions based on assessment results are confirmed by measures of the later behavior of the individuals who were administered the assessment. The measure of the later behavior constitutes the criterion against which predictions are validated. Studies to evaluate that type of evidence often involve calculating correlation coefficients using group mean scores on the initial and later measures — for instance, scores for a group of students on a college entrance exam and their grade point averages at the end of their first year of college. A statistically significant correlation is usually considered acceptable evidence regardless of the value of the actual coefficient. **Concurrent validity** is a type of criterion-related validity, defined as the extent to which results produced by a new assessment correspond with results of a well-established assessment of the same construct or domain. It is usually evaluated by administering both assessments to a well defined sample of individuals within a short period of time and calculating correlation coefficients between the mean scores on the two assessments. The established assessment is the criterion against which

168 MEASUREMENT

the new assessment is validated. In the Brady et al. (2012) study discussed earlier, for example, scores on the new Communication Complexity Scale were compared with scores on two well-established instruments: the Mullen Scales of Early Learning and the Preschool Language Scale. Both sets of correlations were found to be statistically significant.

> **Validity.** In psychometric assessment, the appropriateness and usefulness of inferences that are drawn from assessment results.
>
> **Construct validity.** The extent to which an instrument is shown to assess the construct that it purports to measure.
>
> **Content validity.** The extent to which items on an assessment represent the content that the instrument purports to measure.
>
> **Predictive or criterion-related validity.** The degree to which predictions about the behavior of individuals that are based on the results of an assessment conducted at one point in time are confirmed by measures of the later behavior of the same individuals.
>
> **Concurrent validity.** The extent to which results produced by a new assessment correspond with results of a well-established assessment of the same construct or domain.

In psychometric terms, **reliability** of an assessment refers to how much measurement error is present in the results yielded by the assessment. Assumptions are made that each individual has a true score on the assessment, that the obtained score has a certain amount of measurement error (i.e., deviation from the true score), and that errors of measurement are random. True score and measurement error in this context are hypothetical constructs, so they cannot be measured directly, only estimated. Several strategies are used to estimate the reliability of assessment results by calculating correlation coefficients. **Alternate-form reliability**, as the name suggests, involves correlating the results of two different forms of the same assessment administered to the same group of individuals. Each of the forms has a different set of items that are meant to measure the same construct or domain. **Test-retest reliability** is evaluated by administering the same assessment to a sample of individuals at two different points in time. Determining the test-retest interval can be tricky because if it is too short participants might remember how they responded on the first assessment, and if it is too long they might change in ways that affect their scores. **Inter-tester (or inter-rater) reliability** is evaluated by having several examiners administer the assessment to a sample of individuals and then correlating their obtained scores with each other. Low correlation coefficients suggest that there were errors in administering and/or scoring the assessment, but further investigation is required to determine the source(s) of the errors (e.g., inadequate standardization of administration and scoring procedures, unclear protocol instructions, examiners who are poorly trained or do not follow the protocol).

Reliability. In psychometrics, the degree of measurement error in the results yielded by an assessment.

Alternate-form reliability. The extent to which the results of two different forms of the same assessment administered to the same group of individuals correlate.

Test-retest reliability. The extent to which the scores from two administrations of the same test correlate.

Inter-tester (or inter-rater) reliability. The extent to which the scores recorded by several examiners on an assessment administered to a sample of individuals correlate with each other.

Uses and Limitations. Well-researched, valid, and reliable standardized assessments are essential when measures are to be compared across individuals of interest, examiners, settings, and other dimensions. That is why they are often used to identify appropriate participants and to measure the effects of independent variables in research projects. Many third-party funders of ABA services require practitioners to use standardized assessments to help determine if a client is eligible for services, to identify treatment targets, and/or to measure client outcomes. Such requirements may be imposed by government regulators or agency administrators to control the allocation of funds or to evaluate the costs and benefits of funded services.

Many standardized assessments can be viewed as a means of sampling socially important behaviors in the domains assessed. They may also have items sequenced in the order in which skills emerge during typical development, or from simple to complex. Practitioners can therefore use information from standardized assessments to identify a client's overall strengths and needs as well as caregiver priorities in order to develop additional assessment procedures (e.g., direct observation and measurement), with the ultimate goal of pinpointing age-appropriate treatment targets and setting treatment goals. Additionally, standardized norm-referenced assessments repeated over time are necessary to address questions as to whether treatment changes participants' rates (or trajectories) of development. Those questions are often central to research and practical projects involving participants whose acquisition of socially important skills lags behind that of their typically developing peers, such as children who are diagnosed with autism and other developmental disorders. Similarly, repeated administrations of standardized criterion-referenced assessments are useful for evaluating whether an intervention is effective for moving participants' performances towards a prespecified standard, such as a passing score on an academic achievement test or functional proficiency on a set of communication skills.

Some of the limitations of standardized assessments should be obvious from the preceding descriptions. For instance, they necessarily sample only a subset of all possible content or skills in a domain, or all possible questions that might be asked of a caregiver or other informant. The validity of inferences as to how well the responses on the assessment items represent an individual's performance on the domain as a whole depends critically on how carefully the items were selected and sequenced and the administration and scoring procedures developed and evaluated. Additionally, because many standardized assessments involve indirect measurement, they entail all the limitations of indirect measurement that are discussed in Chapter 6. In particular, results of assessments completed by third-party informants should be interpreted cautiously unless they are corroborated by data from careful direct measurement. As noted previously, however, they can provide useful information about such things as caregivers' views of the importance of certain behaviors and the effects of treatment (i.e., indices of social validity). For behavior analysts, the main limitation of most standardized tests is that they do not by themselves yield sufficient information to address many research and practical questions in our field. Other assessments are needed.

Behavior Analytic Assessment Procedures

Importance. Given the subject matter of behavior analysis, it follows that the main aims of behavior analytic assessment are to identify and define behaviors of interest, the environmental events that influence them, and the conditions under which they do and do not occur. The importance of conducting direct observation and recording so as to obtain a complete picture of behavior and environmental events as well as the procedures for doing so are described in Chapter 6. Chapter 8 details rationale and strategies for ensuring that direct measurement procedures yield values that are accurate, reliable, valid, and believable. Of course, the most common assessment strategies used by behavior analysts are the direct observation and recording procedures described in Chapters 6 and 8. Some specialized variations of those procedures are described here.

Antecedent-behavior-consequence (ABC) recording, sometimes called anecdotal or narrative recording, is typically used to try to record all of an individual's behaviors and the conditions under which they occurred during a specified (usually fairly brief) period of time. The observer may not record any quantifications of behaviors or environmental events but may simply write down descriptions of everything they see the individual do and what happens just before and just after occurrences of behaviors that may be of interest. A variation involves checking off observed behaviors, antecedents, and consequences in lists that are prepared in advance. The original purpose of this procedure was to collect information that could be used to identify potential target behaviors for subsequent definition and measurement (Bijou, Peterson, & Ault, 1968). A related method results in what is called a **scatter plot** (that term is used somewhat differently in statistical contexts). Usually the observer records occurrences of a behavior in a series of time intervals (e.g., 30 minutes) during a lengthy observation period (e.g., a day) over multiple days. The recorded information is analyzed visually to determine if the behavior tends to occur more often at certain times than others. If it does, the activities in which the individual was engaged at those times can be scrutinized for events that might have influenced the behavior. In the seminal study of this method, the self-injurious behaviors (SIB) of two of the three participants with intellectual disabilities were found to cluster around certain times. Changes in some of the conditions occurring at those times were reported to result in decreases in SIB (Touchette, MacDonald, & Langer, 1985).

Antecedent-behavior-consequence (ABC) recording. A procedure in which an observer records descriptions of all of an individual's behaviors and the conditions under which they occurred during a specified period of time.

Scatter plot. A record of observed occurrences of a behavior in a series of time intervals during a lengthy observation period over multiple days. The record is analyzed to determine if the behavior tends to occur more often at certain times than others. The term is used somewhat differently in statistical contexts.

Extensive behavior analytic research has been conducted to develop and evaluate procedures for conducting **preference assessments**, mainly with individuals who have limited communication skills. They aim to identify stimuli that are highly preferred by an individual and so may function as reinforcers in behavior change contingencies. Indirect procedures involve asking caregivers to identify objects (edibles, toys, leisure items) or activities that an individual might like by having them complete an interview, checklist, or rating scale. Direct measurement procedures involve setting up a situation in which the individual is given opportunities to approach or select among items. In one format, the individual is brought into a small room in which several items have been placed. The amount of time (duration) the individual spends approaching or engaging with each item during an observation period is recorded. Other formats involve a series of trials on which an examiner presents one, two, or several items to the individual on each trial (termed single-stimulus, paired-stimulus, or multiple-stimulus preference assessments) and records the individual's response (i.e., whether they approached, engaged with, or consumed the item in the single-stimulus procedure; which item they picked up, pointed to, consumed, or manipulated in the paired- or multiple-stimulus formats). Variations include presenting pictures instead of actual objects or activities and asking individuals to name their selection on each trial, among others. Depending on the format used, the durations of time the individual spent engaged with each item or the number or percentage of trials for which they selected each item during a session are calculated and used to rank the stimuli from most to least preferred or to categorize them as high, moderate, or low preference (Canella, O'Reilly, & Lancioni, 2005; Tullis et al., 2011; Virues-Ortega et al., 2014).

Preference assessments. A category of procedures for identifying stimuli that are preferred by an individual and so may function as reinforcers in behavior change contingencies.

In behavior analysis, **functional behavior assessment** refers to a category of procedures for assessing relations between environmental events and behaviors. Some use the term to encompass procedures that simply describe behaviors, environmental events that immediately precede and follow their occurrences, and other contextual variables (e.g, motivating operations) as well as procedures in which environmental events that may influence a behavior are systematically and repeatedly presented and withdrawn one at a time while the behavior is observed and recorded. The resulting data are graphed and analyzed to see if the behavior occurred more often in the presence of some events than others. The latter subset of procedures is referred to as **functional analysis** (sometimes *experimental functional analysis* or *analogue functional analysis*). Some behavior analysts use functional behavior assessment to refer only to descriptive procedures in order to differentiate those from experimental functional analysis procedures. Although Skinner (1953) used "functional analysis" to mean experimental demonstrations of cause-effect relations between environmental events and *any* class of behaviors (recall our discussion of functional relations in Chapter 2), in applied behavior analysis the term has come to refer mainly to experimental analyses of relations involving behaviors that are characterized as maladaptive or problematic. The notion is that if the assessment procedures yield clear evidence that certain environmental variables control a problem behavior, that information can be used to develop effective procedures to change the behavior.

> **Functional behavior assessment.** A category of procedures for assessing relations between environmental events and behaviors.
>
> **Functional analysis** (experimental functional analysis, analogue functional analysis). An assessment procedure in which environmental events that may influence a behavior are systematically and repeatedly presented and withdrawn one at a time while the behavior is observed and recorded.

There has been a tremendous amount of research on both descriptive and experimental functional behavior assessment and analysis procedures since the early 1980s. Descriptive procedures include direct observation methods like the ABC and scatter plot described earlier, and indirect methods such as interviewing caregivers or having informants complete checklists, rating scales, or questionnaires. Experimental functional analyses typically involve direct observation and recording as described in Chapter 6. They are often conducted in rooms or areas designed for that purpose, though they may be conducted in classrooms and other settings. Many variations of experimental functional analysis procedures have been developed and studied. A review of the large body of literature on these topics is beyond the scope of this chapter. Interested readers are referred to a special issue of the *Journal of Applied Behavior Analysis*

(1994, Volume 27, Issue 2); Beavers, Iwata, and Lerman (2013); Hanley (2012); Hanley, Iwata, and McCord (2003); and Neef and Peterson (2007). Suffice it to say that functional behavior assessment and analysis procedures are widely used by ABA researchers and practitioners.

Measurement Properties. Because ABC and scatter plot assessment procedures involve direct observation and recording, their accuracy, reliability, and believability could be evaluated using the methods described in Chapter 8. Unfortunately, that has rarely been done, so little is known about the quality of the data they produce.

A key question about indirect preference assessment procedures is the extent to which the list or hierarchy of preferred stimuli identified by caregivers corresponds to the results of direct preference assessments – a type of concurrent or predictive validity. Although studies addressing that question have produced mixed results, overall the correlations between the two sets of data have been fairly low. Many of the published reports of studies to develop and evaluate direct stimulus preference assessment procedures include indices of interobserver agreement (IOA), a measure of the degree of correspondence between the participant responses recorded by two observers. As we discuss in Chapter 8, if IOA indices are reasonably high, they lend believability to data recorded by human observers, but they provide no information about the accuracy of the data recorded by either observer – that is, the extent to which the recorded values reflect true values, or what actually happened with the behavior – or the reliability of the observers' recording. Some investigators have evaluated the test-retest reliability of direct preference assessment procedures and reported satisfactory correlations. The most important question about preference assessment procedures is whether stimuli identified as preferred actually function as reinforcers. To answer that question, several investigators have correlated data from preference assessments with data from tests of reinforcer effectiveness – again, a type of predictive validity. Results varied somewhat across preference assessment formats and participant characteristics, but in general correlations were reasonably high, suggesting that direct preference assessments can identify effective reinforcers (Canella, O'Reilly, & Lancioni, 2005; Kang et al., 2013; Tullis et al., 2011; Virues-Ortega et al., 2014).

Relatively little research has evaluated the quality of data produced by indirect functional behavior assessment procedures (interviews, checklists, rating scales). The available evidence shows that inter-rater agreement and predictive validity (as evidenced by correlations with results of direct functional analyses) tend to be low (Floyd, Phaneuf, & Wilczynski, 2005; Kelley, LaRue, Roane, & Gadaire, 2011; Neef & Peterson, 2007). It appears that authors of most studies of functional analysis procedures reported sufficiently high IOA indices to meet journal publication requirements, but little attention has been paid to evaluating the accuracy or reliability of the direct observation and recording procedures used in those studies. Neither IOA nor other procedures for evaluating the quality of the recorded data were mentioned in two comprehensive reviews of research on functional analysis procedures (Beavers, Iwata, & Lerman, 2013; Hanley, Iwata, & McCord, 2003).

Uses and Limitations. Both ABC and scatter plot recording have come to be used widely, not just to obtain informal samples of behavior but also as a basis for inferring the existence of functional relations between problem behaviors and environmental events. Because the methods are strictly descriptive, however, no such inferences are warranted. Additionally, neither has been shown to produce objective, accurate, reliable data on occurrences of target behaviors or their controlling variables. An analysis of scatter plot data recorded on 20 participants exhibiting various problem behaviors for 30 days failed to replicate the original study's finding of temporal patterns of behavior (Kahng et al., 1998). The best use of ABC and scatter plot recording procedures is to collect information about problem behaviors, the situations in which they occur, and environmental events that can then be used to design functional analysis procedures. There is also some evidence that interviews in which caregivers are asked to describe problem behaviors and the antecedents and consequences that might influence them can yield information to guide the development of efficient functional analysis procedures (e.g., Jessel, Hanley, & Ghaemmaghami, 2016).

As noted above, indirect preference assessment measures do not reliably identify stimuli that turn out to be highly preferred in direct preference assessments. They are best used to identify stimuli to present to an individual in a direct preference assessment. Several direct preference assessment procedures have proved useful for identifying stimuli that may function as reinforcers. The operative word is "may." It is not safe to assume that any stimulus that appears to be highly preferred on the basis of a preference assessment will strengthen responses when delivered contingently on their occurrence; that must be tested directly. Additionally, results of preference assessments vary depending on the stimuli and format used, participant characteristics, presence or absence of certain motivating operations, and other factors.

Functional analyses have generally proved useful for identifying environmental events that influence problem behaviors, though results are not always crystal clear (Beavers, Iwata, & Lerman, 2013; Hanley, Iwata, & McCord, 2003). Substantial research shows that interventions tend to be more effective and reinforcement-based when they are guided by the results of functional analyses than when they are not (Ervin et al., 2001; Pelios, Morren, Tesch, & Axelrod, 1999). There have been extensive discussions and debates, however, about functional analysis procedures, including the risks and benefits of conducting experiments that are explicitly designed to evoke behaviors that can be harmful to participants and others, the practicalities of carrying out such experiments in many everyday settings (such as homes and schools), the expertise required, the conditions that should be tested, how long sessions should be, how many sessions should be conducted, how the data should be analyzed, and the generality of findings from contrived to everyday situations.

PROCEDURAL DECISIONS

Selecting Assessment Instruments or Procedures

Research Projects. For behavior analytic researchers, decisions about assessments to identify or ascertain study participants are often influenced by such factors as the research question, the nature of the behavior(s) to be assessed, requirements imposed by those who are funding the study (if applicable), and the interests and practices of the principal consumers of the study findings. To illustrate, if the aim of the study is to evaluate the effects of an intervention on people who meet diagnostic criteria for a particular condition, the investigator would be wise – or might be required by a funding source – to ensure that all participants have been assessed by a qualified evaluator using a widely accepted, valid, and reliable diagnostic instrument. For a study evaluating the effect of an intervention on certain communication or reading skills, the initial assessment to identify participants might be conducted using direct behavioral observation and recording methods or a standardized test. That choice is likely to be based in part on the research question and in part on the practices and preferences of the research community to whom the study findings are to be reported.

Some of the factors just discussed must also be considered when researchers are deciding how to assess the effects of independent variables. Of course, most behavior analytic studies ask questions about behavior interacting with environmental events, so assessment involves observing and measuring the defined responses of individual participants repeatedly under control and experimental conditions as described in this book. To answer certain questions or to satisfy funders or journal reviewers, however, a researcher might need to use other types of assessment methods. As an example, a common and important question about comprehensive, intensive intervention for young children with autism spectrum disorder is whether it changes the rate at which children develop skills over the course of the year(s) the intervention is in place, often referred to as the "developmental trajectory." That question can only be addressed by assessing each child's skills periodically (e.g., every 6–12 months) using standardized tests that allow the child's performances to be compared to the performances of typically developing children of the same age (e.g., see Green, Brennan, & Fein, 2002; Howard et al., 2014; Klintwall, Eldevik, & Eikeseth, 2015). Therefore, reviewers of grant proposals or research articles submitted to certain journals may only consider studies of comprehensive interventions for young children with autism that include standardized, norm-referenced outcome assessments. Similar considerations apply to studies that address other "actuarial" questions, such as how exposure to a particular curriculum affects the reading performances of groups of third-grade students, on average.

Practical Projects. Practitioners who must make complex and important decisions about what to include in clients' treatment plans (see Table 7.1) are wise to consider assessment information from multiple sources. Many clients will have been evaluated by other professionals, so the behavior analyst's assessment might begin (after appropriate consents and clearances have been obtained) with a review of medical records, diagnostic evaluations, assessments of skills in various domains, and evaluations of family functioning. Records of prior treatment, if applicable, should also be reviewed. In the course of reviewing records, the behavior analyst might determine that some additional assessments are needed – for instance, to evaluate whether a medical condition might be contributing to a behavioral difficulty or to obtain an overview of the client's current communication skills in comparison to other individuals of the same age. If so, referrals to the appropriate professionals are in order. Because it is important to include clients and their caregivers in the selection of treatment targets and procedures, the behavior analyst might have those individuals complete indirect assessments such as behavior rating scales, adaptive behavior inventories, or social validity questionnaires as well as interviews.

Reviewing results of assessments like those just described often gives the practitioner a general picture of the client's current level of functioning, their living and other circumstances, and treatment targets that might be high priorities for the client and caregivers. The client's or caregiver's responses to specific items on an assessment instrument are likely to be more informative than the overall score. For instance, items on tests of intellectual or academic skills can be viewed as samples of how a client responds to certain types of problems or instructions. A parent's responses to items on assessments of adaptive behaviors can point to important skills that could be strengthened or challenging behaviors that could be reduced. The behavior analyst can use information from those types of global assessments to select behaviors to assess further using direct observation and recording procedures. That might be accomplished by observing and recording samples of each behavior in everyday situations where it is likely to occur or arranging conditions that might evoke the behavior. For example, a client's communication skills might be observed and recorded in several different situations where opportunities for the client to communicate are likely to occur naturally, but it may also be helpful for the practitioner to set up situations where the client must communicate with another person in order to obtain a preferred item or has questions or comments directed to him by a peer. For a problem behavior, a functional analysis might be necessary to identify environmental events that set the occasion for and reinforce the behavior.

Data from directly observed and measured samples are used to verify or refine the results of global assessments. They help the behavior analyst and the other members of the client's treatment team winnow a large set of potential target behaviors down to a set of high-priority targets that is manageable for an initial treatment period. For the selected treatment targets in an ABA treatment plan, frequent and repeated direct observation and recording is the principal approach for measuring the client's progress toward the goals and objectives laid out in the treatment plan. Other types of assessments, however, might also be necessary to address certain practical questions, communicate with other professionals, or fulfill regulatory or funding requirements.

Conducting, Scoring, and Interpreting Assessments

When a research or practical project calls for assessments involving direct observation and recording of behaviors and environmental events, those can and should be conducted and interpreted by professional behavior analysts or individuals they train and supervise using procedures described in Chapters 6 and 8. In designing protocols for conducting and interpreting preference assessments and functional analyses, several important variables should be considered in addition to those discussed in this book. For guidance on preference assessments, see Virues-Ortega et al. (2014). A thorough analysis of common obstacles to conducting functional analyses and suggestions for overcoming them can be found in an article by Hanley (2012).

Some indirect assessments, such as interviews and certain checklists and rating scales, can also be administered, scored, and interpreted by behavior analysts. For other indirect assessment instruments, however, it is essential to know and comply with laws, regulations, publishers' policies, and test developers' requirements. Most licensure laws, for example, include a definition of the regulated practice that is often referred to as the profession's scope of practice. The definition is usually a fairly brief summary of the range of activities in which licensees may engage, and it reflects the content to which members of the profession are typically exposed during their pre-professional training and on which they are tested in certification and/or licensure exams. Licensure laws, the rules for implementing them, and the profession's code of ethics also typically state that each professional must practice within the boundaries of their education and training, known as the individual's scope of competence. Although licensure laws vary across jurisdictions and there are overlaps in the scopes of practice of many professions, conducting certain types of assessments is generally not in behavior analysts' scope of practice or scope of competence but is in the scope of other licensed professions. Prominent examples include assessments for diagnosing conditions or disorders and certain psychological tests (e.g., intelligence, personality, and aptitude tests). Most professional behavior analysts who are certified by the Behavior Analyst Certification Board, which is also a qualification for obtaining a license in most jurisdictions that have adopted behavior analyst licensure laws, will not have received the training in standardized testing and statistics that is required to administer, score, and interpret the results of those kinds of assessment instruments. They may not even be able to purchase such instruments because many publishers will sell them only to individuals who meet qualifications specified in the *Standards for Educational and Psychological Testing*, mentioned previously. That said, many publishers have requirements (called qualification levels) for purchasing other kinds of assessment instruments that many behavior analysts meet by virtue of holding a valid professional certification or license and having had some training or experience in the relevant area of clinical assessment. There are no special requirements for administering and scoring some published assessment instruments.

Some gray areas complicate decision-making about which assessments to conduct and who can conduct them. For instance, behavior analysts who have been trained to administer a diagnostic instrument may be allowed to do that provided they refrain from interpreting the results and rendering a diagnosis. Similarly, it may be acceptable for behavior analysts to administer and score (or have a computer score) certain standardized, norm-referenced assessments as long as they do not try to interpret the resulting statistics (such as z, standard, or age-equivalent scores or standard deviations) for caregivers and others unless they have been trained to do so. In fact, some behavior analysts might be required to administer standardized assessments and report the scores to funders who are using such data to evaluate treatment outcomes. Additionally, as discussed previously, behavior analysts can glean information from actual responses to items on standardized assessments that can be very useful for planning additional assessments to identify treatment targets.

Whether for a research or a practical project, it is wise for the behavior analyst to consult several sources when making decisions about the use of assessment procedures other than direct behavioral observation and recording: (a) the publisher of the assessment instrument (where applicable); (b) the manual for administering, scoring, and interpreting the assessment; (c) applicable licensure and other laws and regulations; (d) funders' policies; (e) published research on the instrument's standardization and measurement properties; (f) colleagues who are qualified to administer, score, and interpret the assessment. If it is necessary or desirable to use assessment procedures on which the behavior analyst is not trained and competent or that he may not be allowed to administer by laws or other policies, the help of qualified professionals must be enlisted.

CHAPTER SUMMARY

1. The behavior analyst who is preparing to conduct a research project with human participants must select or design assessment procedures that will serve the overarching goal of answering the research question. That may entail conducting or having others conduct assessments to identify individuals with characteristics that would make them appropriate study participants.

2. For most ABA practitioners, the main goal of assessment with a new client is to identify one or more socially important behaviors to be targeted for treatment and the environmental events that influence them.

3. Many assessment instruments that are used in the social sciences and education are designed to compare the individual's results to those produced by large numbers of other people. Instruments developed by behavior analysts, on the other hand, tend to focus on the individual's behavior and environmental events that influence it.

4. Regardless of the conceptual framework in which an assessment instrument is couched or the comparisons are to be made, it is essential for the

instrument to be standardized to ensure that comparisons reflect actual differences in the behavior of the individual(s) of interest instead of differences in assessment procedures, including the behavior of those who complete and score the assessment.

5. A common misconception is that all standardized assessment instruments are norm-referenced, meaning that an individual's score is interpreted relative to scores of other individuals in a defined group. In fact, many standardized assessments are criterion-referenced, in that an individual's score is compared to a prespecified performance standard.

6. Construct validity is the extent to which an instrument is shown to assess the construct that it purports to measure. Content validity refers to the extent to which scores on an assessment represent the content that the instrument purports to measure. Predictive or criterion-related validity is the degree to which predictions based on assessment results are confirmed by measures of the later behavior of the individuals who were administered the assessment. Concurrent validity is a type of criterion-related validity, defined as the extent to which results produced by a new assessment correspond with results of a well-established assessment of the same construct or domain.

7. In psychometric terms, reliability of an assessment refers to how much measurement error is present in the results yielded by the assessment. Assumptions are made that each individual has a true score on the assessment, that the obtained score has a certain amount of measurement error, and the errors of measurement are random. Several strategies are used to estimate the reliability of assessment results by calculating correlation coefficients.

8. Well-researched, valid, and reliable standardized assessments are essential when measures are to be compared across individuals of interest, examiners, settings, and other dimensions. Many third-party funders of ABA services require practitioners to use standardized assessments to help determine if a client is eligible for services, to identify treatment targets, and/or to measure client outcomes.

9. Many standardized assessments can be viewed as a means of sampling socially important behaviors in the domains assessed. They may also have items sequenced in the order in which skills emerge during typical development, or from simple to complex. Practitioners can therefore use information from standardized assessments to identify a client's overall strengths and needs as well as caregiver priorities in order to develop additional assessment procedures, with the goal of pinpointing age-appropriate treatment targets and setting treatment goals.

10. For behavior analysts, the main limitation of most standardized tests is that they do not by themselves yield sufficient information to address many research and practical questions in our field.

11. Antecedent-behavior-consequence (ABC) recording, sometimes called anecdotal or narrative recording, is typically used to try to record all of

an individual's behaviors and the conditions under which they occurred during a specified period of time.

12. The scatter plot method requires the observer to record occurrences of a behavior in a series of time intervals (e.g., 30 minutes) during a longer observation period (e.g., a day) over multiple days. The recorded information is analyzed visually to determine if the behavior tends to occur more often at certain times than others.

13. Extensive behavior analytic research has been conducted to develop and evaluate procedures for conducting preference assessments, mainly with individuals who have limited communication skills. They aim to identify stimuli that are highly preferred by an individual and so may function as reinforcers in behavior change contingencies.

14. There has been a tremendous amount of research on both descriptive and experimental functional behavior assessment and analysis procedures. Descriptive procedures include direct observation methods like ABC recording and scatter plots, and indirect methods such as interviewing caregivers or having informants complete checklists, rating scales, or questionnaires. Experimental functional analyses typically involve procedures in which environmental events that may influence a behavior are systematically and repeatedly presented and withdrawn one at a time while the behavior is observed and recorded.

15. A key question about indirect preference assessment procedures is the extent to which the list or hierarchy of preferred stimuli identified by caregivers corresponds to the results of direct preference assessments. Although studies addressing that question have produced mixed results, overall the correlations between the two sets of data have been fairly low.

16. The most important question about preference assessment procedures is whether stimuli identified as preferred actually function as reinforcers. Research has shown that results vary somewhat across preference assessment formats and participant characteristics, but in general correlations were reasonably high, suggesting that direct preference assessments can identify effective reinforcers.

17. Functional analyses have generally proved useful for identifying environmental events that influence problem behaviors, though results are not always crystal clear. Substantial research shows that interventions tend to be more effective and reinforcement-based when they are guided by the results of functional analyses than when they are not.

18. For behavior analytic researchers, decisions about assessments to identify or ascertain study participants are often influenced by such factors as the research question, the nature of the behavior(s) to be assessed, requirements imposed by those who are funding the study (if applicable), and the interests and practices of the principal consumers of the study findings.

19. Practitioners who must make complex and important decisions about what to include in clients' treatment plans are wise to consider assessment

information from multiple sources. Many clients will have been evaluated by other professionals, so the behavior analyst's assessment might begin (after appropriate consents and clearances have been obtained) with a review of medical records, diagnostic evaluations, assessment of skills in various domains, and evaluations of family functioning.

20. Licensure laws, the rules for implementing them, and the profession's code of ethics typically state that each professional must practice within the boundaries of their education and training, known as an individual's scope of competence. Although licensure laws vary across jurisdictions and there are overlaps in the scopes of practice of many professions, conducting certain types of assessments is generally not in behavior analysts' scope of practice or scope of competence, but it is in the scope of other licensed professions.

21. Whether for a research or a practical project, it is wise for the behavior analyst to consult several sources when making decisions about the use of assessment procedures other than direct behavioral observation and recording: (a) the publisher of the assessment instrument (where applicable); (b) the manual for administering, scoring, and interpreting the assessment; (c) applicable licensure and other laws and regulations; (d) funders' policies; (e) published research on the instrument's standardization and measurement properties; (f) colleagues who are qualified to administer, score, and interpret the assessment.

HIGHLIGHTED TERMS

Alternate-form reliability. The extent to which the results of two different forms of the same assessment administered to the same group of individuals correlate.

Antecedent-behavior-consequence (ABC) recording. A procedure in which an observer records descriptions of all of an individual's behaviors and the conditions under which they occurred during a specified period of time.

Concurrent validity. The extent to which results produced by a new assessment correspond with results of a well-established assessment of the same construct or domain.

Construct validity. The extent to which an instrument is shown to assess the construct that it purports to measure.

Content validity. The extent to which items on an assessment represent the content that the instrument purports to measure.

Criterion-referenced assessment. An assessment on which an individual's score is compared to a prespecified performance standard.

Functional analysis (experimental functional analysis, analogue functional analysis). An assessment procedure in which environmental events that may influence a behavior are systematically and repeatedly presented and withdrawn one at a time while the behavior is observed and recorded.

Functional behavior assessment. A category of procedures for assessing relations between environmental events and behaviors.

Inter-tester (or inter-rater) reliability. The extent to which the scores recorded by several examiners on an assessment administered to a sample of individuals correlate with each other.

Norm-referenced assessment. An assessment on which an individual's score is interpreted relative to the scores of other individuals in a defined group.

Predictive or criterion-related validity. The degree to which predictions about the behavior of individuals that are based on the results of an assessment conducted at one point in time are confirmed by measures of the later behavior of the same individuals.

Preference assessments. A category of procedures for identifying stimuli that are preferred by an individual and so may function as reinforcers in behavior change contingencies.

Psychometrics. The field of study whose subject matter is psychological testing and measurement.

Reliability. In psychometrics, the degree of measurement error in the results yielded by an assessment.

Scatter plot. A record of observed occurrences of a behavior in a series of time intervals during a lengthy observation period over multiple days. The record is analyzed to determine if the behavior tends to occur more often at certain times than others. The term is used somewhat differently in statistical contexts.

Standardized assessment. An assessment instrument or procedure on which all components (contents, timing, administration and scoring procedures, etc.) are the same every time the assessment is administered.

Validity. In psychometric assessment, the appropriateness and usefulness of inferences that are draw from assessment results.

TEXT STUDY GUIDE

1. Describe the role that participant characteristics may play when selecting and conducting an assessment as part of a research project.
2. What is the main goal of assessment for most ABA practitioners?
3. Describe the difference between direct and indirect measurement as it relates to assessment instruments.
4. How do many of the instruments developed by behavior analysts differ from those used by investigators in the social sciences and education?
5. What does it mean when an instrument is referred to as "standardized?"
6. Identify and describe the benefits of using a standardized assessment instrument.

7. Briefly describe the procedures that are necessary to standardize an assessment instrument.

8. What is the difference between norm-referenced and criterion-referenced assessment instruments?

9. Describe construct validity, and discuss why it is important for assessment instruments.

10. What is content validity? Provide an example.

11. Describe criterion-related validity. How does it differ from concurrent validity?

12. In psychometric terms, what does the reliability of an assessment tell an investigator?

13. What is alternate-form reliability?

14. How is test-retest reliability evaluated?

15. Describe how inter-tester reliability is assessed.

16. Describe the various benefits for practitioners and/or researchers of using a standardized assessment.

17. What are some of the limitations of standardized assessments?

18. Outline the main aims of behavior analytic assessment, and provide an example of each.

19. Describe ABC recording.

20. As it relates to behavior analysis, what is a scatter plot, and what kind of information can it provide?

21. What is a preference assessment? Describe examples of both indirect and direct procedures to measure an individual's preferences.

22. Describe functional behavior assessment and how it differs from functional analysis.

23. Briefly discuss the extent to which results from indirect preference assessment procedures correspond to the results of direct preference assessments.

24. According to the text, what is the most important question about preference assessment procedures? What does research suggest about this issue?

25. Describe the uses and limitations of indirect and direct behavior analytic assessment procedures described in this chapter.

26. Briefly describe the various factors behavior analytic researchers may consider when making decisions about assessment instruments or procedures.

27. Why should practitioners consider assessment information from multiple sources?

28. What role does an individual's scope of competence play in conducting and/or interpreting assessments? What other factors are involved in this decision-making process?

29. Identify and describe at least five different sources behavior analysts should consult when making decisions about the use of assessment procedures other than direct behavioral observation and recording.

BOX STUDY GUIDE

1. Compare and contrast idiographic and nomothetic assessment.

SUGGESTED READINGS

Gall, M.D., Gall, J. P., & Borg, W. R. (2006). *Educational research: An introduction* (8th ed). Upper Saddle River, NJ: Pearson.

Haynes, S. N., O'Brien, W. H., & Kaholokula, J. K. (2011). *Behavioral assessment and case formulation*. Hoboken, NJ: John Wiley & Sons.

DISCUSSION TOPICS

1. After reviewing Chapter 6, elaborate on the advantages and disadvantages of using assessments that use direct versus indirect measurements.

2. Chapter 8 discusses interobserver agreement (IOA) procedures. After reviewing the section on IOA, discuss how inter-rater reliability differs from interobserver agreement.

3. Chapter 7 briefly mentions curriculum-referenced assessments. Review additional information about curriculum-based assessments/measurement, and discuss how they may be incorporated in behavior analytic interventions.

EXERCISES

1. Identify a minimum of two standardized assessments used by behavior analysts that are not described in the chapter. Describe whether each assessment (a) utilizes indirect and/or direct measurement, (b) is norm-referenced and/or criterion-referenced, (c) any data related to the assessment's validity and reliability, and (d) any necessary qualifications (e.g., licensure) required to provide or interpret the results of the assessment.

2. Read the article by Wolf (1978) that introduces the idea of social validity. Describe how social validity corresponds to the other forms of validity discussed in the chapter. Select a recent research article from a behavior analytic journal that did not assess social validity, and describe how the researchers could have assessed this kind of validity.

3. Select a target behavior of your own (or ask for permission to record a friend's/family member's behavior), and conduct an ABC assessment.

Record this same behavior using a scatter plot. Describe any issues you can identify related to the validity and reliability of your findings.

4. To learn more about functional behavior assessments, functional analyses, and stimulus preference assessments, review the videos on these topics posted on Western Michigan University's Autism Center of Excellence (http://wmuace.com/videos). After viewing the respective videos, describe the limitations of these assessments and possible ways to address their shortcomings.

CHAPTER EIGHT

Evaluating Measurement

STRATEGIC ISSUES

Rationale

It is not enough to set up procedures for measuring target behaviors and then collect data, confident about the outcome of this process. Even well designed and carefully implemented measurement procedures may result in data that have shortcomings. The problems may concern any of the topics addressed in the previous chapters in this section: how the target behavior is defined, what features of the behavior are selected for measurement, and how observing and recording are designed and carried out. Regardless of the particulars, the data may not faithfully reflect what actually happened. Whether the discrepancy is minor or serious, the risk is that those who use the data to guide their interpretations and decisions may not be aware of any problems or appreciate their consequences. This means that flawed data could encourage conclusions about a research project or clinical decisions about a client's progress that are not sound.

The quality of behavioral data is so important to both ongoing management of a project and final conclusions about what happened that researchers and practitioners must routinely take steps to evaluate measurement procedures and the resulting data. That has long been a standard feature of scientific method because it has proved valuable for uncovering problems and convincing colleagues that the data properly support research findings. Professionals who work with science-based technologies usually adopt the same procedures and criteria for evaluating measurement. Research and practice in behavior analysis should follow those traditions.

Estimation

The goal of measurement in science and science-based practice is to arrive at the best possible estimate of the true value of events that have occurred. The products of measurement are considered to be only an estimate of what really happened because there is always the possibility that data include some error – discrepancies between what measurement reveals and what actually occurred. Most of the time, these differences are so small that they do not prevent investigators and practitioners from understanding what the data show. On the other hand, the discrepancies – and their consequences – can be more substantial, even to the point of invalidating otherwise obvious conclusions.

One of the advantages of conceding that the data are only estimates of the actual facts is that it encourages efforts to obtain the best estimates possible. (Chapter 6 considers some ways to avoid measurement error, for example.) This cautious approach sets up the obligation of determining the extent to which error is present in the data and helps minimize the risk of basing conclusions on data that are substantially tainted. This chapter focuses on ways of evaluating data and, by extension, the measurement procedures that produced them.

Observed Values versus True Values

Let us begin by making a distinction between observed values and true values. **Observed values** are simply the values that result from the observation and recording procedures set up for a particular research project or practical application. Observed values are usually in the form of numbers representing some amount of a behavioral dimension – for instance, a duration of 2.6 minutes or 0.75 responses (cycles) per minute (rate or frequency). It is observed values that will, if they pass muster, serve as the data that will be used by the researcher, practitioner, and others to make various decisions.

True values (sometimes called *criterion* values) are also obtained through observation and recording; after all, there is no other way to find out what happened. In order to say that recorded observations result in true values, however, the investigator must take special precautions to ensure that possible sources of error have been avoided or minimized. The special steps that might be taken depend on the nature of the target behavior and how it is being observed. At the least, the procedures that are used to obtain true values must be somewhat different from those used to obtain the observed values being evaluated.

> **Observed values.** Values resulting from observation and recording procedures used to collect the data for a study.
>
> **True (criterion) values.** Values resulting from special observation and recording procedures that are somewhat different from those used to collect the data being evaluated and that involve special efforts to minimize error.

For example, researchers studying the performance of employees cleaning donated items in a salvage business set up procedures by which the employees would measure their own work behavior throughout the day. In an effort to evaluate these data, the researchers set up special procedures to obtain true values. Members of the research team periodically took boxes of cleaned items leaving the work area and compared the employees' counts with their own counts. However, the availability of permanent behavioral products (cleaned items) gave the researchers the luxury of counting the contents of each box being sampled multiple times using counting procedures that minimized error (Stoerzinger, Johnston, Pisor, & Monroe, 1978).

Of course, just because special efforts are made to avoid or remove possible sources of error in obtaining true values does not guarantee that such data are error-free. In fact, there is no way to be absolutely sure that any set of data is accurate. Someone can always argue that the true values being used to evaluate observed values might themselves contain some error. That is why scientists are always looking for more accurate measurement procedures.

Accuracy

Accuracy is the term used to describe the extent to which observed values approximate what actually happened. (In metrology – the science of measurement – accuracy is defined as the absence of consistent over- or under-estimates of true values. The term *precision* is used to refer to the absence of random measurement errors). There are two requirements for evaluating the accuracy of a set of observations. First, the data must represent real (physical) events. This means that the data must not be the only evidence that what is supposedly being measured actually exists. Second, it must be possible to measure the events directly. Behavior certainly qualifies on both counts, so evaluating the accuracy of behavioral measurement is feasible in principle. In contrast, although we speak of intelligence as if it is a physical phenomenon, the only evidence of its existence is in the form of measures of behavior sampled by intelligence tests. It is from those data that we infer that some amount of "intelligence" is present. Neither of the two requirements can be met in the case of intelligence.

Reliability

If the data are found to be less than fully accurate, the next question concerns the nature of the error. Is the error consistent in some way (as in when a

---

BOX 8.1

Reliability in the Social Sciences

The conception of reliability offered here is consistent with well-established usage in the natural sciences. However, certain applications in the social sciences have led to an alternate perspective. These applications typically involve some kind of psychometric test or instrument administered by researchers or clinicians as a way of making statements about general features of behavior or about mental qualities.

This approach to measurement is quite different from direct measurement of a specific target behavior, and different procedures have been developed for assessing what is described as the reliability of such tests. For example, the *split-half method* involves dividing the items on the test into two halves, such as odd versus even numbered items, and using the correlation between the two versions as an estimate of the whole test's reliability. Another method is said to estimate *test-retest reliability* because it uses correlations between scores from two administrations of the same test.

It should be clear that these procedures represent a fundamentally different conception of reliability from that used in the natural sciences. They do not involve assessing the relationship between directly observed measures and the events they actually represent.

bathroom scale is always high by three kilograms), or does the size or direction of the error vary? When we are talking about the nature of the error, we are talking about reliability. **Reliability** refers to the consistency of the relationship between observed values and the events that actually occurred. For example, measurement would be considered highly reliable if a scale always gave measures of the weight of an object that were high by three kilograms. On the other hand, we might consider measurement unreliable if an observer viewing a videotaped sample of a participant's behavior during a session reported values that varied considerably when she recorded data on the same sample a second or third time.

Validity

When it is not clear that the data represent what they are supposed to represent, the issue of **validity** arises. This is typically a problem when indirect measurement is used. Recall the example in Chapter 6 about evaluating employee performance under an old versus a new lighting system by having employees complete a questionnaire about how their work was affected by the change. The validity of the questionnaire data is inherently suspect because it would not be clear whether responses on the questionnaire represented employees' actual work performance. In this example, it would at least be possible to evaluate validity by collecting direct measures of work performance and comparing them to the questionnaire data. In many cases, however, that option is not available. There is often no evidence that whatever is indirectly measured actually exists independently of the measurement operation, as in the example of intelligence. Measures of hypothetical qualities produced by

---

BOX 8.2

The Relationship between Accuracy and Reliability

It can be easy to get confused about accuracy and reliability. If a set of observations are determined to be completely accurate, they are also completely reliable. In fact, if the data are fully accurate, there is no reason to even raise the issue of reliability. After all, reliability is only an issue if there is some error. Only then can we ask whether the error is small or large, high or low, or consistent or variable.

Let us assume the data are not completely accurate, however, and we are evaluating the reliability (consistency) of the error. If our assessment shows that the observed values are very reliable (for example, always low by the same amount), we might describe the data as very reliable. As we can see from the example, this does not mean that the data are also accurate. Accuracy and reliability are very different aspects of the relationship between what was measured and what really happened. If data are reliable, it says nothing at all about their accuracy. The error might be very consistent but quite large, for example.

instruments like many psychological tests, inventories, and rating scales often leave researchers and clinicians unable to evaluate whether such data are valid because there is usually no way to measure such qualities directly.

Believability

Accuracy, reliability, and validity all involve some evaluation of the relationship between recorded observations and the actual events they are intended to represent. Sometimes the outcome of this evaluation is not satisfactory. For instance, the accuracy of the data may prove to be less than desirable, reliability may be poor, or the evidence for validity may be weak. Such circumstances constitute a real problem for the investigator and for others who might be interested in the project. They cannot be sure that the data properly represent what actually happened, so conclusions based on the data could be misleading. In fact, in mature natural sciences, the lack of evidence of

---

BOX 8.3

Validity in the Social Sciences

Questions about the validity of data are unusual in behavior analytic research because investigators are usually able to find a way to measure the behavior of interest directly. Much research in the social sciences, however, involves indirect measurement. That means the behavior that is actually measured (for instance, completing a questionnaire) is only used to make inferences about other behaviors or unobservable mental qualities or processes.

Assessing the validity of an indirect measurement procedure is therefore a common challenge in social science fields such as psychology, and a number of techniques have been developed. Chapter 7 briefly explains the various types. For instance, *criterion validity (also called predictive validity)* refers to comparing the results of the procedure under examination to those produced by the later administration of an existing instrument that is accepted as an adequate indicator of the characteristics of interest (called the criterion measure). The validity of an aptitude test might be evaluated by seeing how well it predicts job performance as defined by some objective measure. One weakness of that approach lies in how the validity of the criterion measure is established. It may simply be that it is popular or has been around for some time.

Another approach concerns *content validity*. Here the validity of a measurement instrument is assessed by inspecting its content, rather than by using an empirical method. The usefulness of that technique clearly depends on who is doing the assessment, and the process is subjective by definition. *Construct validity* addresses the question of how well a test measures the underlying construct it is intended to measure, such as aptitude. That approach is also quite subjective because the construct the measurement procedure is supposed to illuminate is hypothetical so is not observable.

acceptable accuracy, reliability, and validity would probably prevent a study from being published.

This situation does not necessarily mean the data are worthless, but it does mean that their worth cannot be clearly established. That leaves the investigator in the unfavorable position of trying to enhance the **believability** of the data. Unlike accuracy, reliability, and validity, believability does not refer to the relationship between the data and the events they are supposed to represent. The term indicates that this approach focuses on persuading others that the data are "good enough" for interpretation, even though there is no direct evidence that would clearly support such a belief.

> **Accuracy.** The extent to which observed values approximate the events that actually occurred. In metrology, the absence of consistent over- or underestimation of true values.
>
> **Reliability.** The stability of the relationship between observed values and the events that actually occurred.
>
> **Validity.** The extent to which observed values represent the events they are supposed to represent and that will be the focus of interpretation.
>
> **Believability.** The extent to which the investigator can, in the absence of direct evidence, convince others to believe that the data are good enough for interpretation. Does not involve direct evidence about the relationship between data and the events they are intended to represent.

TACTICAL OPTIONS

Evaluating Validity

It is most often the case in both behavioral research and in the delivery of behavioral services that target behaviors can be directly measured. When this is done, the data are valid by definition because they represent exactly what investigators or clinicians will be drawing conclusions about. The use of indirect measurement procedures raises the question of whether the data are valid reflections of the real focus of interest. It is important to find an acceptable answer to this question. If there is no evidence that indirect measures of behavior are valid, it forces those using the data to make an uninformed assumption one way or the other.

The ideal approach to evaluating the validity of indirect measures involves finding a way to collect evidence about the correspondence between the indirect measures and what they are intended to represent. For example, it can be difficult to directly measure the exercise behavior of individuals whose medical conditions require that they exercise regularly. This might lead a researcher or practitioner to ask participants to complete a weekly questionnaire as a way of measuring certain features of their exercise behavior. It remains possible to periodically measure exercising directly, however, even though that option may present some challenges. For instance, direct measures might be obtained from family members, health club computers, or even sensors worn by participants that could then be compared to the questionnaire data.

Even if direct measurement of the behavior of actual interest is not feasible, it may be possible to collect data that would at least bear on the question of the validity of the indirect measures. For example, if an individual reports completing certain exercise routines on a questionnaire, it might be reasonable to expect that there would be some correspondence between questionnaire data and certain physical functioning and capability that could be measured directly. For example, regular aerobic exercise should be reflected in lower blood pressure readings.

There are, then, two approaches to evaluating the validity of indirectly measured data. One option is to arrange for direct measurement of the target behavior on a periodic basis. That will usually require special arrangements – after all, if it were easy to measure the behavior directly there would be no reason to resort to indirect measurement in the first place. It may be sufficient to show close correspondence between the results of indirect and direct measures for only a portion of the total number of sessions. A second option provides more ambiguous evidence but can be convincing. It involves collecting corroborative data that, although not direct measures of the behavior, are at least consistent with the assumption that the indirect measures are valid.

Evaluating Accuracy and Reliability

Sequence of Evaluation Efforts. The overriding interest in evaluating behavioral data lies in their accuracy. If the data (for example, the results of measuring responding during a single session) can be shown to be completely accurate, there are no further questions about their suitability for research or clinical purposes. If the evidence shows that the data are less than fully accurate, it raises the question of what kind of error is acceptable. That issue is discussed in a later section.

When the degree of error is within acceptable limits, interest turns to the stability of the error. That is, is the error relatively consistent from measurement to measurement, as when a kitchen thermometer is always high by five degrees? Or is the error unstable, varying substantially from occasion to occasion? The concern here is about the reliability (consistency) of the data. When the data

---

TABLE 8.1
Procedures for assessing validity

- Directly measure target behavior on a periodic basis
- Collect corroborative evidence supporting the assumption of validity

are inaccurate to some degree, the researcher or practitioner must determine the characteristics of the error, including how large the errors are and how consistent they are. Those characteristics must then be evaluated in terms of the field's standards and the needs of the particular investigation.

For example, if the data are only somewhat inaccurate but fairly reliable, they might be usable. If the data are unacceptably inaccurate but highly reliable, it may be possible to correct the data by adding or subtracting the consistent error. (A better approach would be to fix the problem that is leading to inaccurate data.) If the data are both moderately inaccurate and unreliable, they may not be usable. There is no clear standard for judging the balance between accuracy and reliability, however. In addition to the considerations discussed in an upcoming section, decisions partly depend on the practices of colleagues working in the same area.

In sum, in evaluating measurement procedures and the resulting data, the first priority is to determine the accuracy of the data. If they are accurate, the question of reliability does not arise because accurate data are reliable by definition (see Box 8.3). All that is left to do is to periodically evaluate the accuracy of data from future sessions. However, if the data are not fully accurate, the nature of the error must then be considered. If it is minor, it may be acceptable to proceed, though with caution. If the error is more substantial, there are two alternatives. The best option is to identify the problem that is causing the data to be inaccurate and fix it. The other option is to determine the extent of the error and how consistent (reliable) it is. With this information in hand, it is sometimes feasible to correct the data as necessary. If the error is relatively inconsistent – that is, if reliability is poor – the data may not be usable, which means measurement procedures will have to be reconsidered and improved. Table 8.2 summarizes these evaluation priorities.

Procedures for Evaluating Accuracy. The procedure for evaluating accuracy is straightforward: The observed values being assessed must be compared to true values. In practice, this involves first determining a procedure for obtaining true values. There is no single best way to do that. There are only the requirements that (a) the procedure must be at least somewhat different from that used to collect the data being evaluated, and (b) the procedure must incorporate rigorous steps to avoid or remove possible sources of error. For example, a practitioner interested in measuring the compliance of arthritis patients with physician recommendations for walking exercise could use pedometers to

TABLE 8.2

Priorities for assessing measurement

- Determine accuracy of the data
- If error is found, determine its size and direction
- If error is minor, proceed with caution
- If error is substantial, improve measurement procedures
- If feasible, correct error as necessary
- If error is substantial and cannot be corrected, improve measurement procedures

---

measure the distance walked each day. If the patients wear their pedometers as instructed, the accuracy of the instruments can be measured by comparing their output to a course of a known distance (for example, a running track) or to measures obtained by another device, such as a distance measuring wheel. Procedures for checking data produced by measurement instruments against well-established standard measures are often referred to as *calibration*. When behavior is measured by instruments that are functioning properly and calibrated periodically, the investigator can generally be confident that the observed values are accurate. If such data are available, they can serve as true values for the purpose of evaluating the accuracy of values produced by human observers, such as practitioner-recorded counts of steps taken by an arthritis patient.

Of course, automated measurement of target behaviors is not feasible for most projects that take place in field settings, so investigators must find other means of evaluating the accuracy of data recorded by human observers. One common approach involves making videos of samples of the target behavior. The recorded samples can then be viewed by a well-trained independent observer – multiple times if necessary and perhaps even in slow motion – whose objective is to record the relevant dimension (frequency, duration, etc.) of every instance of the behavior with as little error as possible. The resulting data can then be considered true values to be compared with the values recorded by other observers. Another procedure is possible when a target behavior results in products that can be measured later. For example, a client's performance in a supported employment setting might result in measurable physical products, such as the proportion of recycling items sorted correctly, or the number of restaurant tables cleared of dishes. Those data could be treated as true values to be compared with data on the client's performance that were recorded by an observer in real time.

In evaluating accuracy, the investigator must decide how to compare true and observed values and how to quantify the degree of accuracy. Comparisons between true and observed values can involve individual responses or summaries of responding. Measures of individual responses during an observation period are often summarized in a session total. Those totals might be used to compare observed and true values and calculate an index of accuracy (agreement) by dividing the smaller total by the larger total, for instance. Conclusions about accuracy that only consider session totals can be misleading, however, because high agreement between those totals does not mean that they represent measures of the exact same responses. There could be discrepancies in which responses were observed and recorded by the two observers over the course of the session. In order to state that data are accurate at the level of individual responses, it is necessary to show agreement between observed and true values for each response.

Three methods are commonly used by behavior analysts to compare two sets of data produced by continuous observation and recording methods and calculate the extent to which they agree. When a set of true values is compared to a set of observed values mathematically, the resulting index of agreement represents an index of the accuracy of the observed values. The *exact agreement* method involves imposing brief intervals (e.g., 10 seconds) on both data records. Intervals for which both records are completely identical – showing the exact same number of responses if the dimension is frequency, the same number of seconds for duration, or no occurrences – are scored as agreements. Intervals for which there are any discrepancies between the two records are scored as disagreements. The total number of agreements is divided by the total number of agreements plus disagreements, and the result is multiplied by 100% to obtain an index of agreement (accuracy). The *block-by-block* method also requires imposing brief intervals on both data sets. For each interval (block), the smaller number is typically divided by the larger number to yield a score between 0 and 1. Intervals for which both records show no occurrences are scored 1. The scores are summed across all intervals, that sum is divided by the total number of intervals, and the result is multiplied by 100%. In the *time-window analysis* method, the two records are compared second by second. For each second when both records have a response (or 1 second of occurrence for duration) or no occurrence recorded, an agreement is scored. Any second in which there is a discrepancy between the two records is scored as a disagreement. The window can be expanded so that observations recorded within a prespecified interval around each second are included. The total number of agreements is divided by the total number of agreements plus disagreements and the result is multiplied by 100% (Mudford, Martin, Hui, & Taylor, 2009; Mudford, Taylor, & Martin, 2009; Phillips, Mudford, Zeleny, & Elliffe, 2014). One set of investigators found that all of those methods produced biased estimates of accuracy. The block-by-block and exact agreement methods inflated the accuracy of observed values for responses with low rates and durations, while the exact agreement method underestimated accuracy for higher rates and relative durations and the time-window analysis overestimated accuracy at relatively high but not low response rates and durations (Mudford, Martin, Hui, & Taylor, 2009). More research is clearly needed to evaluate and refine methods for evaluating the accuracy of behavioral data.

Procedures for Evaluating Reliability. There are two ways to evaluate reliability. One way is a byproduct of evaluating accuracy. That is, when comparing observed and true values to determine accuracy, it may be easy to also track the nature of any error. If error is found and is fairly consistent from one data set to another, the data might be described as fairly reliable. Of course, this would have nothing to do with how accurate the data were (see Box 8.3). The size of the error might be large, but if observed and true values always differed by the same large amount, the data would be considered reliable – very inaccurate, but reliably so.

A second way of evaluating the reliability of observed values does not require true values. In this approach, a sample of the target behavior must be preserved in some way, such as in a video format. An observer records data on that recorded sample at two or more different points in time. Those data sets are compared, and the extent of agreement is calculated as described previously to evaluate the consistency of that observer's measurement. If the

TABLE 8.3
Procedures for assessing accuracy and reliability

- Accuracy: Obtain true values and compare to observed values
- Reliability: (1) Obtain true values and compare to observed values
  (2) Present observer with same sample multiple times

agreement indices are reasonably high, the observer's measurements would be considered reliable, even though their accuracy is still unknown. This is often referred to as intraobserver agreement or reliability.

Calibration. Another approach is to identify problems with measurement procedures early and again periodically over the course of a project and fix them so that the project does not have to be abandoned. That approach is called **calibration**. It involves evaluating the data from a measurement procedure and using the findings to adjust the procedure so that its output meets desired standards. Scientists, engineers, manufacturers, and others in fields whose work depends on sound measurement routinely calibrate measurement systems to insure that they produce accurate and reliable data.

Calibration. Evaluating the accuracy and reliability of data produced by a measurement procedure and, if necessary, using these findings to improve the procedure so that it meets desired standards.

In behavioral research and practice, calibration means using the results of measurement evaluation to guide decisions about how to improve the quality of behavioral data. It may be necessary to adjust the definition of the target behavior, change the behavioral dimension being measured, change the way that observations are made, or retrain observers. In fact, it is unlikely that the investigator's initial decisions about measurement procedures will result in acceptably accurate and reliable data. There are so many facets of behavioral measurement, especially under field conditions, that something usually needs rethinking or adjusting after data collection is underway. It is not uncommon to have to discard early data because it falls short of accepted standards. Even if initial data are usable, improvements in measurement procedures may mean early data cannot be viewed in the same way as subsequent data.

One measurement evaluation method that is akin to the calibration of instruments in the natural sciences involves comparing observed values with true values for the same samples of behavior using linear regression analysis. For a given sample of behavior, the true values are plotted on a line graph with reference to the x axis and the observed values are plotted with reference to the y axis. A regression line (line of best fit) is plotted through the data points by the least squares method. The accuracy of the observed values is indicated by the closeness of the slope of the regression line to the diagonal (the closer, the more accurate), and precision is indicated by the closeness of the data points to the regression line (the closer, the more precise). Applications of this method to behavioral data recorded by humans were described and evaluated in two studies. The investigators demonstrated that the calibration method enables a more thorough evaluation of measurement by human observers than the methods described above, thereby increasing opportunities to detect and correct problems. That in turn increases confidence that the values recorded by observers represent what actually happens with target behaviors over the course of a study or clinical intervention (Mudford, Zeleny, Fisher, Klum, & Owen, 2011; Phillips, Mudford, Zeleny, & Elliffe, 2014).

Building Believability

Interobserver Agreement. In applied behavior analytic research and practice, the most common approach to evaluating measurement procedures and their data does not involve evaluating accuracy and reliability. Instead, it is typical to arrange for simultaneous but independent observation by two or more observers for some sessions. One is usually designated the primary observer; the other the secondary observer. This procedure allows calculation of the degree of agreement between observers.

This outcome of that calculation is called the **interobserver agreement** (IOA) index or coefficient. It is important to be clear that IOA data provide no information about either the accuracy or reliability of the measures of the target behavior. Evaluating accuracy unavoidably requires access to true values so they can be compared to observed values. Reliability is usually evaluated in the same way, although it can also be determined by repeated observation of the same sample of behavior by the same observer. A second or third observer used in the same way as the primary observer cannot be assumed to create true values just because they are being used to evaluate the primary observer's performance. When two observers are used, there is usually no information available regarding the accuracy of the data recorded by either. After all, if one of the two observers were shown by some evaluation procedure to consistently produce accurate data, there would be no reason to use a second observer.

The fact that two observers obtained the same or highly similar measures of the target behavior for a session provides no information about the accuracy or reliability of either result. Perfect agreement between observers watching the same participant during a session might be comforting, but it only allows the conclusion that their observations agreed. When that agreement is based on the totals recorded by the two observers, it does not even mean that they detected the same responses. Each observer may have failed to detect or may have erroneously detected different responses, while the two still arrived at the same total measures.

In other words, just because two observers report the same or similar total measures of responding for a session does not mean that either report accurately reflects what happened with the target behavior. In fact, IOA data provide no information at all about the participant's behavior. At most, then, reasonably high IOA levels might encourage the investigator and others to accept the data on the participant's behavior as believable or "good enough." That might seem reasonable based on our shared experiences that independently veri-fied reports often appear to be true, but such conclusions should be made cautiously. There is nothing about IOA *per se* that assures that the reports of either observer are true. Additionally, research has shown that IOA indices can be influenced by many variables and are easily inflated (e.g., Rapp, Carroll, Stangeland, Swanson, & Higgins, 2011). That is why the natural sciences and their associated technologies require the higher standards of accuracy and reliability described previously. In spite of their serious limitations, however, IOA procedures are widely used in applied behavior analytic research and prac-tice. In fact, they are the only procedures that have been reported in most of the approximately one-third of published studies in applied behavior analysis that involved efforts to evaluate measurement procedures (Kostewicz, King, Datchuk, Brennan, & Casey, 2016).

The soundest interpretation of IOA data is as a measure of the behavior of the observers involved. Substantial differences in the data recorded by two observers as reflected in relatively low IOA indices should serve as red flags to investigators. They could indicate that the target behavior definition is not suf-ficiently clear and complete, or that one or both observers need more training or is not adhering to the definition or the rules for observing and recording. Periodic IOA checks enable the investigator to identify and correct such prob-lems so that data do not have to be discarded, or worse (Cooper, Heron, & Heward, 2007; Rapp et al., 2011).

Determining Interobserver Agreement. The following steps are typically followed to determine IOA. First, the individuals who will serve as the primary and secondary observers must be selected and trained. The sole distinction between them is that the primary observer's data will serve as the project's results, and the secondary observer's data will be used only for comparison. Although it might be tempting to suppose that the best performing trainee should be selected as the primary observer, it is important that the secondary observer be no less skilled. Remember, when comparisons of their data do not agree, it will not be known which is correct or if either of them are.

Second, during sessions when both are scheduled to observe, each must be positioned so that neither is at a disadvantage in viewing the participant's target behavior. This can be challenging in some field settings. Additionally, each must also not be able to tell when the other is detecting and recording

TABLE 8.4
Procedures for determining interobserver agreement

- Select and train primary and secondary observers
- Set up independent observation procedure
- Select agreement formula and calculate agreement

a response. That is, their judgments and recordings must be independent of each other. If either can tell when the other is recording a response, it could influence their behavior.

Third, the two sets of observations must be compared in some manner. There are a number of ways of doing this, depending on what about the target behavior is being observed and recorded, and how. Here are four common procedures for calculating IOA.

The **total agreement procedure** is typically used when observers are recording behavioral dimensions such as count, duration, or latency using continuous observation and recording methods. When the number of responses is being recorded, the investigator sums the total count recorded by each of the two observers for a session, divides the smaller total by the larger total, and multiples the result by 100% to arrive at the percent IOA. The formula for this calculation is

$$\text{smaller total} \div \text{larger total} \times 100\% = \% \text{ agreement}$$

This formula can also be used to calculate IOA for duration or latency data. For example, if the total duration of responding recorded by the primary observer during a session was 180 seconds and the total duration recorded by the secondary observer was 200 seconds, there would be 90 percent agreement (180 seconds divided by 200 seconds times 100%).

A more demanding variation of the total agreement procedure for continuously recorded data, called **exact agreement**, has already been described. With this approach, either the observers record the number or duration of responses in each of a series of pre-determined intervals, or brief intervals are imposed on the records of the two observers after the fact. Only intervals in which the two observers agreed on the exact count are considered agreements; others are scored as disagreements. When the intervals are very short – for instance, a few seconds – this procedure can come very close to assuring that the observers are recording the same responses. Percent agreement is calculated as described in the preceding section on accuracy (Mudford, Martin, Hui, & Taylor, 2009; Mudford, Taylor, & Martin, 2009; Phillips, Mudford, Zeleny, & Elliffe, 2014).

A procedure called **interval agreement** is used when observers are using interval-based recording procedures (partial-interval, whole-interval, or momentary time sampling). Each interval in which both observers recorded an occurrence or no occurrences is counted as an agreement. Intervals for which only one observer recorded an occurrence are counted as disagreements. In order to obtain the percent agreement, the total agreements are divided by the total number of intervals (total agreements plus total disagreements), and the result is multiplied by 100%. That is, the formula is

$$\text{total agreements} \div \text{total number of intervals} \times 100\% = \% \text{ agreement}$$

This calculation is widely used, but the procedure has an important limitation. If the participant's responding occurs very frequently or very infrequently, the number of agreements can be misleading. For instance, suppose that responses occurred in only five out of 180 intervals. Even if the two observers disagreed on the five intervals when responses occurred, they would probably agree on most of the many intervals when the behavior did not occur. As a result, the IOA index would be very high, which would imply incorrectly that the two observers usually agreed on scored intervals (Bijou, Peterson, Harris, Allen, & Johnston, 1969). That problem is compounded by the finding that IOA indices for data recorded with partial-interval and momentary time sampling procedures were higher than the IOA indices for continuously recorded data on the same samples of behavior (Rapp et al., 2011).

The solution to this problem is to use a fourth procedure called **occurrence/nonoccurrence agreement**. This is a more conservative approach because it involves calculating and reporting agreement separately for both occurrences (scored intervals) and nonoccurrences (unscored intervals). That prevents IOA from being inflated by especially frequent or infrequent responding (Bijou, Peterson, Harris, Allen, & Johnston, 1969; Hawkins & Dotson, 1975). Agreements are counted when both observers score an interval or when both fail to score an interval. Disagreements occur when one scores an interval and the other does not. The formula for calculating occurrence and nonoccurrence percent agreement is the same as for interval agreement, except that occurrence agreements and nonoccurrence agreements are calculated separately. In other words, to calculate occurrence agreement, the number of intervals for which the two observers agreed that the behavior occurred is divided by the number of occurrence agreements plus the number of intervals that only one observer scored. To calculate nonoccurrence agreement, the number of intervals for which the two observers agreed that the behavior did not occur is divided by the number of nonoccurrence agreements plus the number of intervals that only one observer scored.

Interobserver agreement. A procedure for enhancing the believ-ability of data that involves comparing simultaneous but independent observations from two or more observers. Provides no information about accuracy or reliability.

Total agreement procedure. A procedure for calculating interobserver agreement typically used with dimensions such as count, duration, and latency that involves summing the total count for each of the two observers, dividing the smaller total by the larger total, and multiplying the result by 100 to arrive at the percent agreement.

Exact agreement procedure. A procedure for calculating interobserver agreement that involves dividing the observation period into intervals in which observers record the actual number of responses. In order to obtain percent agreement, only intervals in which the two observers agreed on the exact count are considered agreements.

> **Interval agreement procedure.** A procedure for calculating inter-observer agreement when interval recording or time sampling is used. Each interval scored by both observers is counted as an agreement, and each interval that is scored by neither observer is also called an agreement. Intervals for which only one observer scored the behavior are counted as disagreements.
>
> **Occurrence/nonoccurrence agreement.** A conservative approach to calculating interobserver agreement when interval recording or time sampling is used that involves calculating and reporting agreement separately for both occurrences (scored intervals) and nonoccurrences (unscored intervals).

TABLE 8.5
Formulas for calculating interobserver agreement

Procedure	Formula
• Total agreement	smaller total ÷ larger total × 100
• Exact agreement	total agreements ÷ total number of intervals × 100
• Interval agreement	total agreements ÷ total number of intervals × 100
• Occurrence/nonoccurrence Agreement	total agreements ÷ total number of intervals × 100

Procedural Issues

Implementing Evaluation Procedures. In order to assess accuracy, reliability, and interobserver agreement, an investigator must make a number of procedural decisions. One concerns *when evaluation efforts should be made*. As a general rule, it is important to start evaluating measurement procedures as soon as a project begins. If problems are discovered, they can be fixed right away, which will minimize the amount of data that might have to be discarded if the problems are serious. Furthermore, because problems with measurement procedures can occur at any point, evaluation efforts should continue throughout all phases of a study or treatment program.

Although evaluation efforts should be ongoing, investigators still need to decide *how often measurement procedures should be evaluated*. If observation sessions occur every weekday, for example, should evaluation efforts be scheduled multiple times each week, only once per week, or even less often? There is no rule to guide this decision. Although some authors suggest that about one third of all sessions is appropriate (e.g., Bailey & Burch, 2002; Kennedy, 2005), that standard is arbitrary. The decision should partly depend on the complexity of the measurement procedures. If measurement involves observing only a single behavior that is clearly defined and easily detected, the procedures may not need to be evaluated very often. On the other hand, if observers must detect multiple behaviors in multiple participants in a busy setting, it may be wise to evaluate the procedures fairly often. More frequent assessment may also be necessary when observers are assigned additional duties, such as recording the status of treatment conditions or the behavior of key individuals other than participants. The frequency with which measurement evaluation is conducted also depends on what the evaluations reveal. That is, the better the evaluation outcomes, the less often such evaluations may need to be made. On the other hand, if evaluations reveal certain kinds of problems, it is best to be cautious and conduct an evaluation frequently.

Another factor to consider when scheduling evaluations of measurement procedures concerns *sampling different circumstances throughout a study*. There are many factors in a study that might affect how well measurement procedures work and the quality of the resulting data. In scheduling evaluation, it is important to make sure that measurement procedures are evaluated under each of these different circumstances. For example, different experimental or treatment phases may affect not only participant behavior but measurement operations; that is, the behavior of observers. The nature of certain conditions can make observation more difficult or even affect how observers make judgments. Different conditions may change the participant's behavior in ways that affect observer performance. Measurement evaluation should therefore be conducted during each phase of a study or intervention. The individuals serving as observers may also change during a study or intervention, so it is essential to make sure that the performance of each observer is evaluated as well. That is especially important with regard to the primary observer, whose recorded data will be used to make critical decisions about the results of a study or the treatment of a client.

Standards for Evaluation Results: Origins. The reason for evaluating the quality of the data is to allow an informed decision about whether they fully represent what they are supposed to and are therefore acceptable for interpretation. Researchers and practitioners who are responsible for a project are naturally interested in taking any necessary actions along the way to ensure that the accumulating data meet their standards. As findings are shared with colleagues, those individuals will use the evaluation information to make their own decisions about the quality of the data.

Standards for the quality of experimental or clinical data vary from one field to another. The nature of the phenomenon being investigated, how well it is understood, the measurement technology available, and the data quality typically achieved by established investigators and practitioners all contribute to the criteria used to evaluate measurement outcomes for particular areas of investigation. Considerable variation may be found within the field of behavior analysis. Measurement of behavior under highly controlled conditions like laboratories is usually conducted with equipment and is evaluated by insuring proper operation and regular calibration of equipment components. Behavioral measurement under field conditions, whether in a research project or in the context of providing services, more often involves human observers. As noted previously, their performance is most often evaluated by determining agreement among multiple observers, which leaves much to be desired from a scientific standpoint.

Sometimes standards for evaluating data depend on certain strengths and weaknesses in a project's methods. For example, consider two clinical interventions whose effects were measured using partial interval recording procedures. Assume that interobserver agreement findings were weak in both cases but that one study used 2-minute intervals and the other used 10-second intervals. Would the disadvantage of weak evaluation data be overcome by the advantage of the shorter interval length? Consider a second example. Would weak accuracy data be more acceptable if the measurement procedures involved continuous observation and recording than if they involved momentary time sampling? The answers should depend on the details in each case, but it is sometimes reasonable to balance strengths and weaknesses of the particular measurement procedures used. That is a risky practice, however, and can easily tempt sliding down a slippery slope. When measurement procedures or the evaluation of those procedures are seriously flawed, no compromises are appropriate.

Standards may even depend on how conclusions may be used. That is also risky because the truth of a project's conclusions does not depend on how they will be applied. Nevertheless, it may be reasonable to consider the consequences of accepting data as credible when setting a standard for their credibility. For example, when the findings of a project might lead an agency to initiate an expensive but badly-needed intervention program for an at-risk population, it is certainly important that the quality of the data fully justify the study's conclusions.

Standards for Evaluation Results: Interpretation. Even though there may be no general standard in behavior analytic research and practice for accuracy, reliability, or interobserver agreement outcomes, it is important to understand what a particular criterion might mean. For instance, it is not uncommon for authors of applied behavioral research published in peer-reviewed journals to report interobserver agreement values as low as 80% (Bailey & Burch, 2002; Cooper, Heron, & Heward, 2007; Kennedy, 2005). Does this mean that if a researcher obtains about 80% IOA – or even 80% accuracy – from measurement evaluation procedures throughout a study it is appropriate to continue the study and confidently draw conclusions when it is completed? Is this standard appropriate for practitioners evaluating treatment effects?

One way to think through what a standard such as 80% means is to figure out the worst impact it could have on how the data are interpreted. That is fairly straightforward in the case of accuracy and reliability. If we know that the data are 80% accurate, we can determine not only the exact amount of the error but also its direction. That is, because true values are available to evaluate observed values – the only way to assess accuracy – we can see which observed values are incorrect, by how much, and whether they are higher or lower than the true values. In fact, if we have this information for each observation, we can simply correct the errors. Even if we have accuracy data for only 30% of the values, we can plot both the observed and true values on a graph. That would show not only the extent of the error but also how it is distributed (its

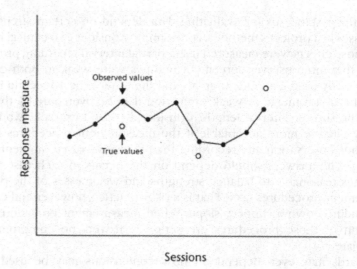

FIG. 8.1. Graphical display of primary data and associated true values.

reliability) and allow us to evaluate how it might influence our interpretation of the observed data (see Figure 8.1). If the error was systematically different from one condition to another, it might change our conclusions.

If the measurement evaluation information were in the form of interobserver agreement indices, the meaning of 80% would be more complicated and uncertain. Take the relatively simple case in which two observers independently count responses using continuous observation. Here, 80% agreement simply means that one observer's total count for a single session was 20% higher or lower than the total obtained by the other. Over a series of such 80% agreement values, either observer might have the higher or lower value, although only the data from the primary observer would constitute the study's database. It would not matter if we knew which observer provided the high or low value, however, because we would not know if either count was accurate in the first place. In fact, we would not even know if 80% agreement represented agreement on the same responses. All we would know is that two observers watching the same participant came up with total counts that differed by 20%.

One way of considering these outcomes is to construct a graph of the study's data that displays the full data set from both the primary and secondary observer, as shown in Figure 8.1. Unlike in the previous example, however, we do not know if either value of each pair of data points is accurate. That means we have no guidance about which of the two sets of observations should be used as the basis for drawing conclusions about the study or intervention (putting aside the problem that in Figure 8.1 one data set is less complete than the other).

Another possibility is to display the data from the primary observer surrounded by data sets displaced by 20% in either direction, as shown in Figure 8.2. This display helps us consider what the findings would look like if the differences in interobserver agreement of 20% were interpreted in the most

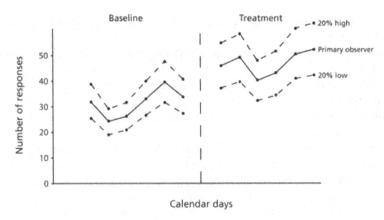

FIG. 8.2. Graphical display of primary observer data and data sets representing 20% disagreement in both directions.

conservative manner. For instance, what if the differences in agreement varied systematically from one phase to another? Using the data in Figure 8.2, what if the upper dotted line represented responding under baseline conditions but the bottom dotted line represented responding during treatment? How much might this interpretation change the meaning of the results? Would a marked increase in responding in one phase be reduced to a slight increase or none at all? Would a moderate decrease in a treatment phase compared to a preceding baseline disappear entirely?

Finally, if the interobserver data being considered were based on interval recording procedures, their interpretation would require a slightly different interpretation. When two observers are simply counting a participant's responses, 80% agreement means one count was 20% higher or lower than the other. However, when two observers are scoring intervals following the rules of partial interval recording, for example, 80% agreement means that they disagreed on whether the behavior occurred at all in 20% of the intervals. In the case of whole interval recording, it would mean that they disagreed about whether the behavior occurred continuously during 20% of the intervals. We cannot know how much disagreement 20% might represent in terms of behavioral dimensions such as count, duration, or latency.

Standards for Evaluation Results: Failing to Meet Standards. What if the evaluation process shows that the data fall short of the field's standards? This question is first addressed by the researcher or practitioner in charge of the project. That person has the advantage of monitoring measurement procedures and seeing the data as they accumulate session by session. That affords opportunities to fix problems and improve the measurement procedures on an ongoing basis. Sometimes corrective actions will involve only minor effort, such as giving observers refresher training. However, it may be that more significant improvements in measurement procedures are necessary, such as revising definitions of the target behavior or modifying measurement procedures.

If data collected following any improvements in measurement procedures cannot be interpreted in the same way as those collected previously, it may be necessary to discard the old data. That might be the case, for instance, if the definition of the target behavior was revised, which would mean that new data and the old data do not represent exactly the same behavior. The risk of having to discard observations underscores the importance of identifying and resolving problems with the quality of the data as soon as possible. The sooner problems are discovered, the fewer observations may have to be thrown out. (Chapter 14 will consider the issue of discarding data in more detail.)

If accuracy or interobserver agreement data are available weekly, for example, an unacceptable evaluation made on a Friday casts doubt on all of the data collected since the last assessment, so an entire week's data might have to be discarded. That is certainly less painful, however, than what would happen if measurement procedures were evaluated only once in each phase. Then it might be necessary to throw out the data for the entire phase, fix the measurement problems, and run that phase again.

Unlike the researcher or practitioner in charge of the project, others who look at the data can only passively evaluate decisions about measurement procedures and the resulting evaluation evidence. When a colleague is interested in a project's findings but has concerns about its measurement procedures or the quality of the data, this can be a frustrating limitation. In the case of published research, others have no choice but to make their own judgments about the quality of the data and whether they allow defensible conclusions. The findings from service delivery projects are not usually published in any form, though they may be confidentially shared with clients, their families, colleagues, or other professionals who are involved with an individual's care. Given the potential impact of decisions on the lives of clients, careful evaluation of measurement procedures is at least as important as it is for research.

Reporting Evaluation Results. The fact that a researcher or practitioner continues a project to its conclusion means that he or she is satisfied with the quality of the data generated by measurement procedures. In disseminating the results of the project, whether at a treatment team meeting, at a conference, or in a research report submitted to a professional journal, the task is to report evidence about the quality of the data in such a way that others can make their own evaluations. There is no standard way of reporting data evaluation findings in the field of behavior analysis. How such evidence is reported – or whether it is reported at all – most often depends on the requirements of the recipients (such as journal editors), the measurement procedures that were evaluated, and the nature of the evaluation outcomes.

For many published research reports, the methods section must at least describe the measurement evaluation procedures. When true values are used to evaluate accuracy and reliability, it is necessary to describe how those special observations were made. When interobserver agreement procedures are used, it is important to describe how secondary observers were trained and deployed. When evaluation procedures are not conducted for each observation period but on a periodic or intermittent schedule, their frequency and distribution must be described. It can be especially important to be clear about how evaluations were scheduled across different conditions and observers, and whether any important changes occurred over the course of a study. It is also important to clarify the formulae used to calculate evaluation results.

This information is usually described in a published report and sometimes in conference presentations. Sometimes the results of evaluation procedures may be summarized in a short statement as well. For example, if the accuracy and reliability of data were evaluated and consistently found to be very good, it might be sufficient to simply describe the evaluation procedure and state the results. On the other hand, it is usually necessary to provide more detail, including separate evaluation outcomes for each phase of a study. That is especially important when the evaluation findings vary substantially, particularly from one phase to another or across observers.

It is often easier for readers to understand measurement evaluation data presented in a table or graph than in text. Again, there is no set way of reporting evaluation results quantitatively. Tabular presentations are typically straightforward organizations of evaluation results distributed across conditions, as represented in Table 8.6. Graphical descriptions of evaluation findings vary widely. One option is to add evaluation outcomes to graphs showing the study's primary data. That approach has the advantage of showing exactly when evaluation data were collected. Figure 8.1 shows an example of this type of display.

Regardless of whether evaluation outcomes are reported in text, tables, or graphs, the investigator must decide how much detail to report. When evaluation findings are consistently strong, it may not be necessary to report each assessment value. However, it is not uncommon for investigators to summarize evaluation data for each phase or observer using a single value, such as a mean or median. Of course, it is not appropriate to summarize multiple evaluation values if that hides significant variations. One way to reassure readers about what might be hidden in a summary value is to also report a quantitative measure of the variability represented by such values. Range, variance, and standard deviation are typical measures of variability.

The guiding interest in collecting and reporting evaluations of the quality of data is to ensure that they closely approximate what really happened with the target behavior and are therefore worthy of interpretation. It is the

TABLE 8.6
Example of tabular presentation of interobserver assessment results

	Control Condition 1	Intervention Condition 1	Control Condition 2	Intervention Condition 2
Initiating social interactions	83%	85%	92%	80%
Complying with requests	89%	93%	86%	94%
Classroom	87%	92%	85%	95%
Playground	79%	77%	85%	81%

responsibility of the researcher or practitioner leading the project to make sure that the credibility of the data is established from the outset. Others then have the responsibility to make that judgment for themselves. If data fail to properly reflect participant behavior, they cannot be interpreted as evidence of what actually happened in the project.

CHAPTER SUMMARY

1. The goal of scientific measurement is to arrive at the best possible estimate of the true value of some event that has occurred. Acknowledging that data are often only estimates of the facts may encourage researchers and practitioners to try to obtain the best possible estimates and to minimize measurement errors.

2. Observed values are the values that are recorded from simple observation. True values are obtained from observations in which special procedures were followed to detect every occurrence of the target behavior and to minimize or avoid error.

3. There are two requirements for evaluating the accuracy of a set of observations. First, the data must represent real events. Second, it must be possible to measure the events directly.

4. If the data are not accurate, we must consider the nature of the error that is contributing to the inaccuracy. Reliability measures address that issue by evaluating the consistency of the relationship between observed values and the events that actually occurred. A measurement procedure is reliable if it yields the same result every time it is used to measure the same responses.

5. Validity addresses whether the data represent what they are actually supposed to represent. Validity is usually of concern when indirect evaluation procedures are used because there is often no evidence that the focus of the indirect measures actually exists independently of the measurement operation.

6. The ideal approach to evaluating the validity of indirect measures involves finding a way to collect evidence about the relationship between the indirect measures (e.g., survey, questionnaire) and what they are intended to represent (physical behavior).

7. In order to evaluate the accuracy of a data set, observed values must be compared to true values. True values must be collected using a procedure that is different than what was used to collect the observed values, and the procedure must incorporate very specific steps to capture every instance of responding and to avoid or remove any possible source of error (e.g., in repeated viewings of video recordings).

8. The reliability of a measurement procedure may be evaluated in conjunction with measuring accuracy. When comparing observed and true values, the investigator can examine the nature of any error. If the pattern of the

errors is consistent, the data may still be described as reliable even though they are inaccurate.

9. Investigators in the natural sciences and engineering often evaluate measurement instruments or procedures against accepted standard measures or other instruments and use their findings to adjust instruments or procedures until the output meets standards. This process is known as calibration. It is especially important when accuracy and reliability are both unacceptable.

10. Applied investigators often evaluate their measurement procedures by occasionally using two observers. In an interobserver agreement procedure, the observers record their observations of participant behavior independently of one another during a session. The investigator compares the two resulting data sets to determine the extent to which the observers' records agreed on the dimensions of the target behavior. This procedure provides no information at all about the accuracy or reliability of the data recorded by either observer. It only informs the investigator whether both observers recorded similar measures of responding.

11. There are several ways of calculating interobserver agreement. They vary somewhat with the dimension of the target behavior that is being recorded and the observation and recording methods that are being used (continuous or discontinuous).

12. The evaluation of measurement procedures should begin immediately and continue throughout all phases of a study or intervention project. That will allow the researcher to identify and remedy any problems with the procedures and minimize the amount of data that must be discarded.

13. The reason for evaluating the quality of the data is to allow the investigator and others to make informed decisions about whether the data are valid and acceptable for interpretation.

14. Most disciplines have certain general standards that data must meet in order to be viable for interpretations. If the data do not meet those standards, the researcher must alter the measurement procedures in an attempt to improve the study and the data collected.

15. When an investigator is satisfied with the quality of the data generated by the measurement procedures, the results may be disseminated. There is no standard way of reporting measurement evaluation findings, but at the very least, the researcher must be sure to fully and accurately describe the evaluation procedures.

HIGHLIGHTED TERMS

Accuracy. The extent to which observed values approximate the events that actually occurred. In metrology, the absence of consistent over- or underestimation of true values.

Believability. The extent to which the investigator can, in the absence of direct evidence, convince others to believe that the data are good enough for interpretation. Does not involve direct evidence about the relationship between data and the events they are intended to represent.

Calibration. Evaluating the accuracy and reliability of data produced by a measurement procedure and, if necessary, using these findings to improve the procedure so that it meets desired standards.

Exact agreement procedure. A procedure for calculating interobserver agreement that involves dividing the observation period into intervals in which observers record the actual number of responses. In order to obtain percent agreement, only intervals in which the two observers agreed on the exact count are considered agreements.

Interobserver agreement. A procedure for enhancing the believability of data that involves comparing simultaneous but independent observations from two or more observers. Provides no information about accuracy or reliability.

Interval agreement procedure. A procedure for calculating interobserver agreement when interval recording or time sampling is used. Each interval scored by both observers is counted as an agreement, and each interval that is scored by neither observer is also called an agreement. Intervals for which only one observer scored the behavior are counted as disagreements.

Observed values. Values resulting from observation and recording procedures used to collect the data for a study.

Occurrence/nonoccurrence agreement. A conservative approach to calculating interobserver agreement when interval recording or time sampling is used that involves calculating and reporting agreement separately for both occurrences (scored intervals) and nonoccurrences (unscored intervals).

Reliability. The stability of the relationship between observed values and the events that actually occurred.

Total agreement procedure. A procedure for calculating interobserver agreement typically used with dimensions such as count, duration, and latency that involves summing the total count for each of the two observers, dividing the smaller total by the larger total, and multiplying the result by 100 to arrive at the percent agreement.

True (criterion) values. Values resulting from special observation and recording procedures that are somewhat different from those used to collect the data being evaluated and that involve special efforts to minimize error.

Validity. The extent to which observed values represent the events they are supposed to represent and that will be the focus of interpretation.

TEXT STUDY GUIDE

1. What risks are involved when the measurement procedures that are utilized result in flawed data?

2. Why is the concept of estimation a useful way to approach behavioral measurement?

3. What is the distinction between observed and true values? Given that true values must be created through some form of observation, why might they be considered "true" values?

4. Describe the two requirements for evaluating the accuracy of a set of observations.

5. What is the difference between accuracy and reliability?

6. What is validity? Why is validity not usually a concern in behavior analytic research and practice?

7. How is believability fundamentally different from accuracy, reliability, and validity?

8. What are two approaches to evaluating the validity of indirectly measured data?

9. With directly measured data, what should be the sequence of evaluation questions?

10. What are the two requirements for obtaining true values?

11. If observed and true values agree at the level of session totals, what can you say – and what can you not say – about accuracy?

12. Describe the three commonly used methods to compare two sets of data produced by continuous observation and recording methods to determine the extent to which they agree.

13. What are two basic ways of evaluating the reliability of data?

14. Explain the concept of calibration as it applies to behavioral measurement.

15. What is the basic procedure for obtaining interobserver agreement?

16. What does interobserver agreement tell you and not tell you?

17. What is the formula for calculating total interobserver agreement?

18. What is the rationale and formula for calculating exact interobserver agreement?

19. What is the formula for calculating interobserver agreement for data recorded with interval-based methods?

20. What is the rationale and formula for calculating occurrence/nonoccurrence interobserver agreement?

21. When should evaluation efforts begin?

22. What factors influence the decision about how frequently to evaluate measurement procedures?

23. Describe what should occur if the evaluation process shows that the data fall short of the field's standards.

24. Discuss the issues related to how behavior analysts report their findings. Are there any field standards?

BOX STUDY GUIDE

1. How is reliability interpreted in psychometric assessment?
2. Distinguish between split-half and test-retest reliability.
3. Complete the following sentence using the terms "accurate" and "reliable." If data are _____, they must be _____. Why is the converse not true?
4. Distinguish between criterion, content, and construct validity in psychometric measurement.

SUGGESTED READINGS

Kostewicz, D. E., King, S. A., Datchuk, S. M., Brennan, K. M., & Casey, S. D. (2016). Data collection and measurement assessment in behavioral research: 1958-2013. *Behavior Analysis: Research and Practice, 16,* 19-33.
Lerman, D. C., Tetreault, A., Hovanetz, A., Bellaci, E., Miller, J., Karp, H., Mahmood, A., Strobel, M., Mullen, S., Keyl, A., & Toupard, A. (2010). Applying signal-detection theory to the study of observer accuracy and bias in behavioral assessment. *Journal of Applied Behavior Analysis, 43,* 195-213.
Mudford, O. C., Zeleny, J. R., Fisher, W. W., Klum, M. E., & Owen, T. M. (2011). Calibration of observational measurement of rate of responding. *Journal of Applied Behavior Analysis, 44,* 571-586.

DISCUSSION TOPICS

1. Discuss ways of obtaining true values in field research.
2. Discuss the limitations of interobserver agreement.
3. Select a published study and discuss the options for evaluating measurement procedures and data.
4. Using Figures 8.1 and 8.2, discuss the implications of 80% as a standard for accuracy and for interobserver agreement.

EXERCISES

1. Provide observed and true value data sets and use the (a) exact agreement, (b) block-by-block, and (c) time-window analysis method to calculate an index of the accuracy of the observed values.
2. Provide interobserver data sets and calculate the different types of interobserver agreement discussed in the chapter.

PART THREE

DESIGN

CHAPTER NINE

Behavioral Variability

IMPORTANCE OF BEHAVIORAL VARIABILITY

What Is Behavioral Variability?

It seems that no two phenomena are ever exactly alike. Scientists have learned that if we measure carefully enough, differences can almost always be found. It may be especially easy to agree with this assumption when behavior is the subject matter. Even when we study very simple behaviors such as a pigeon's key pecking under restricted laboratory conditions, responses that at first seem very similar can be shown to be at least a little bit different from one another (Schwartz & Gamzu, 1977).

It is the differences among individual instances of a behavior or response class that are at the root of what we refer to as **behavioral variability**. If an investigator is measuring self-injurious behavior in a child with autism, for example, each response will be a bit different from the next in topography, duration, interresponse time, force, velocity, or other features. From session to session, these differences will add up to variation in whatever dimension the researcher or practitioner is measuring. In fact, it is relatively uncommon for measures of responding to be the same from one session to another. Each data point is often different from the next.

> **Behavioral variability.** Variations in features of responding within a single response class, as well as variations in summary measures of that class.

Levels of Behavioral Variability

Although variability in a behavior always comes down to differences among its individual responses, there are many ways of looking for and describing it. Behavioral researchers and practitioners look at variability in their data much as other investigators use a microscope. By switching lenses, different degrees of magnification become available. This means viewers can make choices about what level of "magnification" might be revealing in each case.

For behavioral researchers and practitioners, magnification takes the form of summarizing data in some way, and there are at least three levels of summarization that are usually of interest. The greatest detail can be found by looking at the distribution of individual responses over time during an observation period. There are a number of ways of doing this. One way is to construct a cumulative graph in which each response adds to the existing total number of responses, usually displayed over time (see Chapter 14). B. F. Skinner developed a device called a cumulative recorder just for this purpose, and laboratory investigators routinely examined behavioral data in this format (Skinner, 1956). Panel A in Figure 9.1 shows an example of a cumulative record. These data show key-pressing responses of a nonverbal individual diagnosed as profoundly

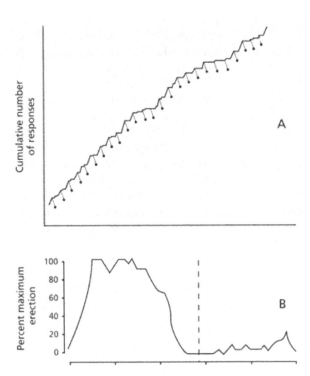

FIG. 9.1. Examples of data displays showing the distribution of individual responses during observation periods. Panel B is adapted from Henson, D. E. & Rubin, H. B. (1971). Voluntary control of eroticism. *Journal of Applied Behavior Analysis, 4*, 37–44, p. 42. Copyright 1971 by the Society of the Experimental Analysis of Behavior, Inc. Used by permission.

intellectually disabled working under a fixed interval 40-second reinforcement schedule. The graph shows that responding was characteristically infrequent immediately following reinforcement (indicated by the downward slashes) but increased considerably toward the end of the intervals.

Panel B of Figure 9.1 illustrates a non-cumulative display of responding during a session. This graph shows continuous variation in penile erection responding (Henson & Rubin, 1971). The participant was watching an erotic film during both phases. He was instructed not to inhibit responding during the first phase but to inhibit responding during the second phase. The data shows moment-by-moment variability in responding.

Another level of summarization results from combining measures of responding during each session into a single value. Variability at this level is evident in the differences among these summary values across a series of sessions. Although this approach prevents seeing variability among individual responses, it has the advantage of revealing variability that would be difficult to see by looking only at individual responses.

Researchers and practitioners typically find this view of variability very informative, and it is the most common way of looking at behavioral variability.

It does not allow the investigator to see what is going on within each session, but this perspective helps highlight changes in behavior from one session to another under the same condition, which can reveal the overall impact of that condition. It also helps the investigator make comparisons of changes in the target behavior under two or more different conditions. Chapter 10 will show that this view of variability is especially important for making decisions about when to terminate one phase and initiate the next phase.

Figure 9.2 shows two examples of this way of looking at behavioral variability. Panel A shows the rates of public speaking habits (filled pauses, tongue clicks, and inappropriate use of "like") in baseline conditions and following awareness training for each of four college students (Spieler & Miltenberger, 2017). Panel B shows the performance of a child diagnosed with autism and profound intellectual disability on simple visual discrimination tasks (Graff & Green, 2004). The graph shows the percentage of trials on which responses

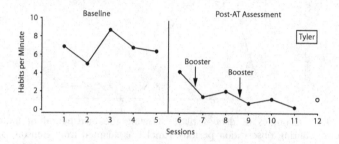

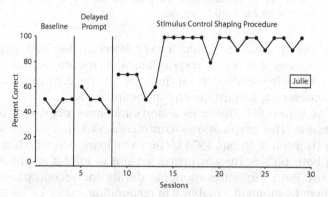

FIG. 9.2. Examples of data displays showing responding in the form of session summary values within and across conditions. Panel A is adapted from Spieler, C. & Miltenberger, R. (2017). Using awareness training to decrease nervous habits during public speaking. *Journal of Applied Behavior Analysis, 50,* 38–47, p. 45. Copyright 2016 Society for the Experimental Analysis of Behavior. Used by permission. Panel B is adapted from Graff, R. B. & Green, G. (2004). Two methods for teaching simple visual discriminations to learners with severe disabilities. *Research in Developmental Disabilities, 25,* 295–307, p. 301. Copyright 2004 Elsevier Ltd. Used by permission.

were correct during baseline, with a delayed prompting procedure, and with a stimulus control shaping procedure across three pairs of stimuli. Both graphs make it easy to see changes in responding within each phase and from one phase to the next.

A third view of behavioral variability involves summarizing measures of responding across sessions. The resulting values represent measures of responding for a number of sessions, such as all of the sessions under a particular condition. This view prevents seeing changes in response measures from one session to another but helps highlight differences between conditions. A practitioner may want to compare responding under baseline and treatment phases, for example, or between the same treatment condition implemented at two different points in time.

The two panels in Figure 9.3 show examples of this view of variability. Panel A shows the average number of cigarettes smoked per day for 14 participants. Their self-reported data were averaged across days for each of four conditions (Glenn & Dallery, 2007). This bar graph or histogram also shows data points representing the means (averages) for individual participants for each phase.

Panel B shows data from a project evaluating the use of computer-based instruction for teaching young children pre-reading skills (Connell & Witt, 2004). The graph summarizes performance over multiple sessions for a series of tasks under various conditions (before training, after training Task 1, and so forth). This view makes it easy to compare each participant's performance across the important features of the study.

The degree of summarization represented in these graphs is substantial, so there is a real risk that interesting features of responding are being missed. Behavior analytic researchers and practitioners therefore tend to use this view of variability to summarize their data only after they have examined more detailed pictures of responding.

Where Does Variability Come From?

There are two conflicting perspectives about the nature of behavioral variability. The traditional assumption is that variability in behavior is **intrinsic**. This point of view holds that behavioral variability is in one way or another inherent in the nature of humans and other animals. It implies that the origins of variability are somehow simply part of what it means to be a living organism. If variability is inherent, the further implication is that the causes of human behavior are built into our nature and therefore are not influenced by other factors.

TABLE 9.1
Levels of behavioral variability

- Displaying distribution of individual responses over time
- Displaying summaries of response measures for each observation period
- Displaying summaries of response measures across multiple observation periods

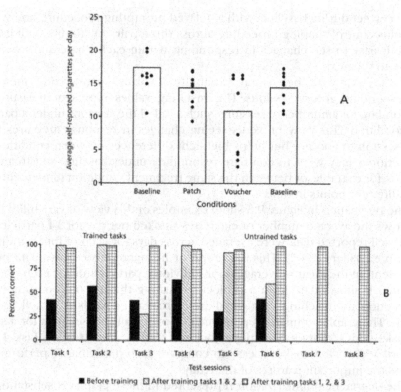

FIG. 9.3. Examples of data displays showing responding summarized across conditions or phases. Panel A is adapted from Glenn, I. M. & Dallery, J. (2007). Effects of internet-based voucher reinforcement and a transdermal nicotine patch on cigarette smoking. *Journal of Applied Behavior Analysis, 40,* 1–13, p. 8. Copyright 2007 by the Society of the Experimental Analysis of Behavior, Inc. Used by permission. Panel B is adapted from Connell, J. E., & Witt, J. C. (2004). Applications of computer-based instruction: Using specialized software to aid letter-name and letter-sound recognition. *Journal of Applied Behavior Analysis, 37,* 67–71, p. 70. Copyright 2004 by the Society of the Experimental Analysis of Behavior, Inc. Used by permission.

Although most people acknowledge that behavior is at least partly influenced by experiences, it is also common to hear assertions that people may do things for no reason, that they can make free choices, or that some aspects of behavior are beyond scientific explanation. Such comments all suggest an underlying assumption that variability in behavior is intrinsic.

In fact, most philosophical, religious, and cultural explanations of behavior rest on an implicit assumption of intrinsic variability. It is easy to see why this perspective is so comfortable. Variation in human behavior is obvious, and its causes are often subtle and difficult to identify. In lieu of trying to understand what influences are actually at work, it is convenient to invent causes such as the mind ("I just made up my mind to quit smoking") or to assume that behavior has no causes ("I'm free to choose any item on the menu").

The contrasting position – one taken by behavior analysts – is that the variability we observe in behavior is **extrinsic**. To say that behavioral variability is extrinsic means it is not part of the essential nature of behavior but is describable, explainable, and predictable with reference to other natural phenomena. Scientists long ago learned that an organism's behavior is the result of its biology and its environmental experiences. This position therefore holds that the variations we see in a particular behavior from moment to moment or day to day are the result of both biological and environmental influences. Contrary to the intrinsic assumption, variation in responding is not assumed to be the result of a fundamental quality that is supposedly an inherent property of all organisms.

Of course, in practice we often have to admit we do not know why a particular behavior occurs, especially under specific circumstances. The extrinsic position at least allows us to optimistically argue that its causes are within the realm of science and can, in principle, be found. It also enables us to continue to improve our understanding about the causes of behavior and our ability to resolve behavioral challenges in daily life.

> **Intrinsic variability.** The assumption that variability in behavior is in one way or another inherent or built into the nature of organisms. See *Extrinsic variability*.
>
> **Extrinsic variability.** The assumption that variability in behavior is describable, explainable, and predictable in terms of variation in other physical phenomena, whether biological or environmental. See *Intrinsic variability*.

It is important to remember that the intrinsic and extrinsic positions about the nature of behavioral variability are only assumptions. We cannot decide between these two points of view by proving that one is correct and the other is wrong. Proving the extrinsic argument, for example, would require finding causes for every instance of behavior in order to show that such causes exist. Not only would that be impossible, the attempt would also be an unwise use of scientific resources.

From a practical perspective, it may be sufficient to consider the consequences of taking the intrinsic versus the extrinsic view. For instance, if an operating assumption is that variability is intrinsic, it follows that identifying the determinants of a target behavior and controlling them is ultimately impossible. That conclusion might encourage researchers and practitioners to view variability in their data as an unavoidable aspect of behavior. That might in turn lead to accepting excessive variability in behavioral data rather than taking steps to improve control over extraneous influences.

In contrast, the extrinsic assumption tends to encourage investigators to design studies that minimize the contribution of extraneous factors so that the impact of treatment conditions can be more clearly identified. With this point of view, practitioners might be inclined to look for medical or environmental factors unrelated to intervention procedures that could affect how clients react to those procedures. As we have already seen, the choices involved in designing measurement procedures provide many opportunities for minimizing extraneous influences. Later chapters will show many more such opportunities associated with creating comparisons between conditions and analyzing data.

BOX 9.1

Free Will versus Determinism

The argument about whether variability in behavior is intrinsic or extrinsic is just another way of talking about free will versus determinism. As human culture and language evolved, people tended to invent explanations for the events in their daily lives for which they had not yet discovered explanations. Of course, these invented explanations were usually false. Scientific discoveries of the last century or two have greatly reduced the popularity of invented causes for most physical phenomena. (We no longer believe that life generates spontaneously or that the earth is flat.) It has been more difficult to overcome the endless assumptions about the nature of human nature.

One of the most persistent convictions people often share is that each person is free to make decisions and take actions that are not influenced by outside events. In other words, many assume that human behavior is often free in the sense that it is not caused by any specific factors. It is easy to appreciate why this seems so obvious. Most people do not understand the real causes of human behavior, which are complex and sometimes poorly understood even by scientists. As a result, we are usually unaware of the factors that actually influence our actions. Our language encourages us to assign causation to our "selves" rather than to influences in the physical world. So we say that we did something because we "wanted to" or that we "changed our mind."

In his book *Beyond Freedom and Dignity* (1971), B. F. Skinner tried to show that such assumptions about human nature are actually quite troublesome. They get in the way of understanding how our behavior is affected by our experiences. In turn, this limits our ability to grow personally or to learn to be more successful in our daily lives. In fact, if it were really true that some aspects of human nature were without natural causes, it would be very discouraging. Assuming that certain aspects of behavior are "free" means they are without causes, which is the same thing as saying they are random or capricious. If this were so, it would be pointless for scientists to study behavior because it would be impossible to find consistent relations between behavior and environmental variables.

It should not be surprising, therefore, to learn that when scientists go to work every morning, they assume that the events they are studying are not free but are determined by other events. This simply means that scientists assume that all events have causes, even though they do not know what all of the causes are in each case.

What Can We Learn from Behavioral Variability?

In the most general sense, variability is the subject matter of all sciences and at the heart of their technologies. It is the task of behavioral scientists to describe variability in behavior through measurement procedures and to discover exactly why behavior changes as conditions change. Such discoveries are the foundation of the basic and applied behavior analytic research literatures. Although practitioners may not routinely arrange formal comparisons that enable them to explain why target behaviors change like researchers do, they too describe changes in behavior with great care and are similarly interested in learning from what they observe.

There are three general functions that variability in behavior serves. First, variation in responding motivates and guides investigators' curiosities. Such curiosities tend to be directed by questions about a particular aspect of variability. One project might ask why different individuals respond differently to the same set of conditions. For example, why might some children have no difficulty learning to read when a particular teaching procedure is used while others fail to progress? The objective might be to develop procedures for reducing that kind of variability so that the procedure will be effective with more children. Another project might investigate what it would take to induce changes in behavior. For instance, an investigator might be interested in discovering the kinds of compounds in explosives to which detector dogs are alert. If researchers can learn about those compounds, handlers can train dogs to be more effective in detecting explosive materials. Still another project might focus on ways of increasing variability. For example, what procedures can be effective in training people to be more creative?

Second, variability in behavior guides decision-making as a study or clinical intervention proceeds. Both researchers and practitioners make many decisions suggested by the patterns of responding they observe during the course of a study or practical intervention. Designing and modifying measurement procedures, selecting and adjusting intervention conditions, identifying and controlling extraneous variables, beginning and ending phases, and selecting data analysis techniques all involve choices that depend on how responding varies across time and conditions.

For example, we saw in the discussion about defining target behaviors (Chapter 4) that when a definition of a behavior is first used for observation, the data may suggest the need for some adjustments. If the data are highly variable, it could be the result of problems with the definition. It might be too broad, encompassing two or more behaviors that have different sources of influence. That might result in variation in the data from session to session as the included behaviors change in different ways. The definition might also present problems for observers, who might therefore make incorrect decisions about what responses should be recorded. The variability that results from such problems is an indication that the definition may need to be modified.

Third, variability in responding provides the foundation for how we interpret the outcomes of experiments and practical interventions. Here, graphical

226

226
TABLE 9.2
Functions of behavioral variability

- Motivates and guides researcher or practitioner curiosities
- Guides decision-making as a study or clinical intervention proceeds
- Provides the foundation for interpreting experiments and practical interventions

displays of measures of the target behavior within each phase of a project and from one condition to another are especially important. They prompt researchers and practitioners to draw certain conclusions about the role of treatment variables as well as the influence of extraneous factors that might complicate the picture of what happened with the behavior over the course of the project.

To illustrate, let us suppose that responding following a baseline condition decreased when an intervention was initiated but then gradually increased to baseline levels as the intervention phase continued. This change in responding during the intervention phase, when the intervention procedures were presumably the same from day to day, might suggest that it would not be appropriate to conclude that the primary effect of the intervention was to decrease responding from the baseline. It would also be important to note the gradual recovery of responding to baseline levels, which might suggest that the effects of the intervention were not very long lasting. The remaining chapters in the book describe ways of using variability to draw conclusions that reflect what really happens in a project.

Managing Variability

Variability Due to Independent Variables. Investigators pursue these three ways of using behavioral variability in a two-part approach: (a) increasing variability in responding by manipulating independent or treatment variables whose influence is in question and (b) reducing variability in responding by identifying and controlling extraneous factors. The first part is the primary focus of both experimentation and service delivery: to see if a certain condition will affect behavior and, if so, what kind of effects it will have. Often a particular intervention condition is selected because it seems likely it will produce a change in the target behavior. Researchers hope the change, which represents a particular form of variability in the target behavior, will help answer the experimental question. Practitioners similarly hope to learn whether an intervention will produce desired changes in the target behavior.

As an example of this approach, consider applied research questions, which often concern the impact of a procedure on a behavior having some practical importance. The tactical interest is learning whether responding observed under control or baseline conditions will change in particular ways when the treatment condition is present. If so, the changes in responding may allow conclusions about the practical effects of the intervention. The more substantial and distinctive the intervention's impact on responding compared to baseline, the more confident the researcher or practitioner might be about the role of the treatment condition. The objective is therefore to maximize the impact of the treatment condition on the target behavior that is serving as the dependent variable.

This is a good occasion to more fully define what we mean by an independent variable condition (also called a treatment, intervention, or experimental condition). In some projects a single, narrowly defined change in the environment may serve as the independent variable. This might be the case in a laboratory project that varied the dosage of a drug or a parameter of a reinforcement schedule, for instance. In most projects, however, the independent variable condition is made up of a coordinated set of environmental changes. This is typical in most applied research. When an intervention involves even a relatively simple procedure such as differential reinforcement, for example, what is introduced is actually an array of factors, including a particular reinforcer in a particular amount, a reinforcement contingency, a schedule of reinforcer delivery, and an extinction contingency, among others. We will see later that clearly defining each independent variable condition is especially important in deciding what might have caused any changes in the dependent variable.

Variability Due to Extraneous Variables. The second part of this approach – reducing behavioral variability by controlling extraneous factors – is necessary in order to be sure that the treatment condition is the only factor responsible for observed changes in the target behavior. It might be that other factors unrelated to researcher or practitioner interests also contributed to observed changes in responding, perhaps even substantially. If the introduction of an intervention condition is accompanied by changes in other variables, it will not be clear what is responsible for any observed changes in responding.

As an example of this risk, suppose that an investigator is interested in learning about the effects of a new, behaviorally active drug on the aggressive behavior of a dually diagnosed client (an individual diagnosed as both intellectually disabled and mentally ill) living in a residential facility. The project might start with a baseline or control condition so that the pattern of responding characteristic of this condition can be examined. Next, the investigator would introduce the treatment condition – a particular dosage of the new drug – and watch for any changes in the target behavior. Suppose, however, that at about the same time the drug condition started the client was relocated to a new residential facility. This change by itself might be expected to have an impact on the client's behavior, possibly including the target aggressive behavior. Because the initiation of the drug regimen and the facility relocation occurred together, it would not be clear which factor contributed to any observed changes in the target behavior.

There are two ways of managing the role played by extraneous variables. One involves holding the extraneous factors constant across all conditions in a study. If that is feasible, it will mean that their effects may still be present but they will at least be the same across baseline and treatment phases. In the above example, the investigator would make sure that the client's living arrangements did not change during the study. Although what is happening every day on the residential unit might well influence the client's behavior, those influences would be more or less the same throughout all phases of the study. They would therefore be unlikely to be responsible for changes in behavior observed only when the drug condition was present.

This tactic of holding extraneous variables constant may not help if the effects of extraneous factors are so powerful that they obscure the effects of the treatment variables. If it turns out that staff members are unwittingly reinforcing aggressive behavior in the residence, for instance, such behavior may remain quite frequent, making it difficult to see any decrease that might otherwise result from the new drug.

Another way to manage extraneous variables is to completely eliminate the problematic factors from the situation so they cannot have any influence. For example, consider the challenge for an investigator interested in studying how social factors influence alcohol consumption. Even though it might be preferable to measure drinking patterns under everyday conditions, there are so many factors in daily life (for example, money and opportunity) that can affect drinking besides the social variables of interest that it would be difficult to get a clear picture of the effects of social variables by themselves. The solution might be to conduct studies in a residential treatment setting, where those other factors can be largely (if not entirely) eliminated.

These two tactics – holding extraneous variables constant or eliminating them – can be implemented to varying degrees. At a minimum, the investigator can either control or eliminate extraneous sources of variability one by one until the desired degree of control over responding is achieved. This approach may be time-consuming, but it has the advantage of managing only those extraneous factors that are significant, leaving more trivial variables free to vary. This option is therefore economical in terms of the investigator's time and effort.

At the other extreme, the investigator can attempt to control or eliminate all possible sources of extraneous variability from the outset, regardless of their potential impact. Although this approach can be quite effective, it may be challenging to accomplish and comes at a price. The more experimental conditions differ from the situations of ultimate interest, the more difficult it is to know whether the same results would be obtained under more realistic situations. This is a particularly important concern for applied research. The goal of studies conducted under applied circumstances is to find results that will hold for particular real world situations. For a project investigating staff training procedures, for instance, it is important that practitioners who apply its procedures and findings can reasonably expect to get similar results. If the research was conducted under special or artificial circumstances, the results might depend on those circumstances and not be obtainable under common everyday conditions.

Although dealing with extraneous factors might seem a distraction from the investigator's primary interest, it is not unusual for this effort to require more attention than arranging the desired control and experimental conditions. Researchers have learned, however, that reducing the effects of unwanted

TABLE 9.3
Managing the role of extraneous variables

Tactic	Limitation
• Hold extraneous variables constant across conditions	Effects still present and can mask treatment effects
• Eliminate extraneous variables as necessary	Creates unrepresentative circumstances

factors is worth the time and trouble in order to increase the chances that their conclusions about the effects of treatment conditions will be true and can be depended upon by others.

Extraneous factors are even more problematic for practitioners, who are usually focused on obtaining outcomes that benefit their clients rather than results that have scientific value. Practical services are usually delivered under everyday circumstances, and it is often not realistic to manage factors that might interfere with seeing the effects of treatment protocols uncontaminated by other factors. This is one of the most important differences between research and practice.

SOURCES OF BEHAVIORAL VARIABILITY

Organism

It is easy to get the impression that an organism's environmental experiences have a greater influence on its behavior than its biology. It might seem this way because we can usually get at environmental variables more easily than biological factors. Although environmental factors are undeniably potent, however, it would be a mistake to fail to acknowledge the pervasive influence of an organism's biology.

We often think of an organism's genetic endowment and physiological functioning in terms of limits they place on behavior. What we can sense about the world we live in and how we can react to everyday events is indeed limited by our physical features and capabilities. No matter how fast we might flap our arms, we can't fly, and although we have good eyesight compared to many species, we still can't see in the dark as well as a cat.

In contrast, many features of our biology provide not so much limits as a powerful array of ongoing influences. Some are relatively stable, such as the physiological processes that maintain various life functions. For instance, the behavior of breathing is controlled by the body's need to maintain homeostasis in oxygen levels in the blood, and the behavior of eating is partly controlled by the need to balance energy consumption and expenditure.

A different set of organismic variables is developmental in nature and therefore changes over time. Some changes in behavior are influenced by physiological factors that change over time because of genetic influences on the way the body ages. For example, changes in infant brains in the early months of life have subtle but significant effects on behavior. Puberty is defined by hormonal changes that have broad and noticeable effects on behavior. As we age further, cellular changes in the body contribute to changes in behavior in obvious (posture) and subtler (memory) ways.

Biological processes do not go in just one direction, however. Like behavior, they are influenced by the organism's interactions with the environment. There are many environmental events that lead to changes in biology, which in turn lead to behavioral changes. For example, drugs and other environmental chemicals (for example, toxic substances) can contribute to behavioral variability by how they affect the organism's physiology. Even food can be thought about in this way. Geophysical variables affect behavior in ways we are still learning about. Jet lag, which results from rapidly moving across time zones and abruptly modifying sleep cycles, is a good example of this kind of phenomenon. Physical injuries and some diseases might also be thought of as the result of environmental influences on the organism's biology that often have behavioral effects. Conversely, as Skinner noted long ago, changes in behavior are necessarily accompanied by changes in physiology. In recent years, research has confirmed that experiences with the environment – including those that are specifically arranged to change behavior – also affect biological factors, often in profound ways. Those factors include brain structures and physiology throughout all phases of development and even the way genes are activated and deactivated (Schneider, 2012). This should make it clear that arbitrarily categorizing influences on behavior as either environmental or biological is inaccurate and unhelpful and that factors in both of those categories can affect behavioral variability.

Finally, although behavior analysts think about an organism's history as largely the result of environmental factors, those influences are mediated by the organism's biology. For example, we often speak as if the environment is changed by learning processes ("the neutral stimulus has now become a conditioned reinforcer"), but it is the organism that has changed at a cellular level in ways we do not yet fully understand.

Each participant in a study and each individual receiving behavioral services brings their unique learning history with them, of course, and it can be a potent source of behavioral variability. Sometimes those historical influences are more powerful than experimental or treatment variables. For example, human participants with well-developed verbal repertoires are likely to talk to themselves about what is going on during experimental sessions (Catania, Shimoff, & Mathews, 1989). Studies have shown that this kind of talk can have a substantial influence on how they react to experimental procedures. Participants who do not have such repertoires (including babies, individuals with severe communication difficulties, and nonhuman species) may respond differently than participants who can talk to themselves when exposed to the same procedures (Lowe, 1979). Because the effects of learning histories are often unrelated to research interests, selecting participants whose behavioral characteristics suit the particular needs of the study is a key feature of research methods.

BOX 9.2

What is Inside the Organism?

Our language makes it easy to talk about what seems to be going on inside the organism. As we learn to talk in childhood, we learn to explain behavior by using words like memory, intelligence, abilities, ego, mind, compassion, wants, impulses, images, information, attitudes, inhibitions, virtues, habits, intentions, beliefs, knowledge, and so forth. Instead of replacing colloquial language, psychology and other social sciences have tended to incorporate and elaborate such terms, and to add many of their own.

As nouns, these words almost seem to refer to things, even though no one has actually seen them because they have no physical existence. Our language needs agents for verbs that express action, so these kinds of terms are often given the function of causing behavioral actions. For instance, we may say "He does well in school because he is smart," "She has a big ego, so she is always talking about herself," or "If you think about what you were doing, it will help jog your memory."

Of course, all anyone can actually find inside the organism is the physical equipment of its biological functioning. This does not mean, however, that all inner "causes" of behavior to which such words seem to refer have nothing to do with behavior. To propose that the qualities such words suggest do not exist in some sense might be as naïve as arguing that they refer to real, physical events. Instead, the critical issue is what is *really* there and how we should talk about it. When scientists are not completely sure about the physical status of some supposed phenomena, they pay special respect to the notion of parsimony (see Box 2.5). The scientific attitude of parsimony means we should be careful to try to explain aspects of the behavior of human and nonhuman animals in terms of principles or laws that are already well established scientifically before turning to less understood or more troublesome causes. Inventing a nonphysical or mental universe of causes for behavior certainly leads to endless problematic explanations.

Being careful about how we talk about the causes of behavior is also critical to avoiding scientific dead ends. Although it might seem harmless to say that expectations influence behavior, for example, if it encourages some researchers to spend the field's resources trying to study expectations, considerable harm may be done. Refining our professional language to avoid this kind of trap is difficult, but it can be done. It involves making sure we only assign causal roles to phenomena we are reasonably certain physically exist, although it is more complicated than this. For an introduction to how to talk about behavior in a scientifically cautious manner, read B. F. Skinner's books *Science and Human Behavior* (1953) and *About Behaviorism* (1974). He spent much of his career trying to improve our scientific vocabulary about human affairs. *Radical Behaviorism for ABA Practitioners* (Johnston, 2014) is a good treatment of these issues in the context of practitioner interests.

Practitioners do not have that luxury, of course, and can only take into account the effects of prior environmental influences on the current behavior of their client in developing and implementing intervention plans. As Chapter 7 describes, they start by learning about historical factors as best they can and by explicitly assessing the role of existing influences. This information helps guide decisions about what procedures will be most effective in supporting or supplanting the effects of prior experiences.

Research or Service Setting

In any research project or practical application, the behavior of interest occurs in a setting composed of many potential sources of variability. One or more of those variables will be considered independent or treatment variables because they are the primary focus of the investigator's attention. The remainder are considered extraneous variables, signifying that they are not the primary interest.

Consider the kinds of extraneous variables that might be present. First, some extraneous factors may have nothing to do with the setting itself, such as when a research participant or a client gets sick or is under stress for reasons unrelated to the project. Second, some extraneous variables are part of the general physical space in which research is conducted or services are delivered. The lighting or ventilation in a room or noises coming from outside the room are common examples. Third, still other extraneous influences are associated with the general procedures in which the independent or treatment variable is embedded. These might include the nature of the task, instructions from the investigator, or the nature of reinforcers used. Fourth, sometimes extraneous factors can be associated with the treatment condition even though they are not formally defined as part of it. For instance, in a study examining a teaching technique, the social interactions between a teacher and students might not be considered part of the procedure being evaluated even though they are intermingled with the teaching procedures.

Although investigators distinguish between independent or treatment variables that are the primary interest and extraneous variables, which might be considered "nuisance" factors, *all* environmental variables have the potential to affect behavior. Of course, it is tempting to ignore extraneous factors or at

TABLE 9.4
Types of extraneous variables

Category	Example
• Unrelated to the research or applied setting	Sickness, stress
• Part of the research or clinical setting	Lighting, ventilation
• Associated with general procedures	Task features, instructions
• Associated with the independent variable though not defined as part of it	Social interactions tied to non-social independent variable

least suppose they will have little or no effect on the target behavior. Once those influences have occurred, however, they cannot be disentangled from the impact of independent or treatment variables by argument or speculation. In other words, the best time to address the role of extraneous factors is when the project is being planned.

It is particularly important for practitioners to try to minimize the effects of extraneous variables. Many – perhaps most – clients who receive ABA services are likely to come into contact with multiple extraneous variables that could affect behaviors that are targeted in their ABA treatment plans. For instance, it is common for people with autism and related disorders to receive many different types of interventions and services concurrently (Green et al., 2006; Schreck, Karunaratne, Zane, & Wilford, 2016; Smith & Antolovich, 2000). Studies have shown that some of those interventions can undermine or negate the effects of ABA interventions. Examples include "sensory" techniques that maintain or strengthen stereotypic, self-injurious, and other maladaptive behaviors (e.g., Devlin, Healy, Leader, & Hughes, 2011; Kay & Vyse, 2005; Peterson, Piazza, & Volkert, 2016); psychotropic drugs that can produce various side effects and interact with ABA interventions in other ways (Weeden, Erhardt, & Poling, 2010); and eclectic, mixed-method programming for youngsters with autism that limits the possibilities for them to benefit from effective intervention (Eikeseth, Smith, Jahr, & Eldevik, 2007; Howard, Stanislaw, Green, Sparkman, & Cohen, 2014). Even when a client receives comprehensive ABA services within a single agency or program, interventionists may introduce variables in one context (e.g., by delivering the client's preferred edibles as consequences during communication training) that can interfere with interventions delivered by others in other contexts (e.g., to get the client to eat a wider range of foods at mealtime). Failing to eliminate – or at least carefully monitor the effects of – such extraneous factors can create many problems for ABA practitioners. First and foremost, their clients may suffer because interventions are not as effective as they could have been. That may lead family members and funders to decide that ABA does not "work" and to put their time and resources elsewhere.

Measurement

Defining Target Behaviors. Sometimes variability in the data can be traced to how the target behavior is defined. Definitions may unintentionally capture responses other than target behaviors. (Chapter 4 discussed this possibility in some detail in considering functional versus topographical response classes.) When this is the case, the resulting data may show more variability than would be found if the target behavior were more narrowly defined.

To understand how this possibility might arise, consider a project focusing on the potentially self-injurious behavior of head hitting in an individual diagnosed as profoundly intellectually disabled. Suppose the definition of the behavior includes all actions that involve contact between her head and her hands or any object. Even though the definition might exclude responses associated with putting a hat on her head or combing her hair, there would still be a good chance that the remaining responses covered by the definition do not all share the same influences. For instance, the definition may include responses that could be subdivided among two or three somewhat different topographies, such as hitting her head with her hands versus hitting her head against objects. Such differences might in turn yield differences in sensory or even social consequences. Those differences in consequences might mean that the responses could represent different classes. In addition, some responses may occur only when staff are present; others when the client is alone. Those may also represent different response classes, even if the responses have the same general topography.

Variations in the form or environmental circumstances of individual responses can mean that the definition of the target behavior actually encompasses multiple behaviors. Because the factors that influence each behavior are likely to vary from one moment or session to another, the occurrence of one or another of the included behaviors would be higher at some times and lower at others. This can result in more variability than would be detected if the target behavior were defined in a way that involved only a single functional response class.

Selecting Behavioral Dimensions. Chapter 5 explained that any behavior may be described in terms of different dimensions. Both researchers and practitioners are naturally interested in selecting those dimensions that are likely to reveal changes in responding generated by intervention conditions. If a dimension chosen for measurement does not capture meaningful changes in the target behavior, the data may encourage misleading conclusions about the effects of an intervention.

For example, if a therapist uses discrete-trials procedures to teach a skill, measuring progress in terms of frequency or rate of responding is likely to be misleading. This type of procedure usually involves conducting a series of trials within a session, each of which is initiated by the trainer. Therefore, the pace of responding is at least partly determined by the trainer because the learner cannot respond until the trainer presents an antecedent stimulus to start a trial. Measures of the learner's performance in terms of rate of responding would therefore produce misleading data because that dimension would partly reflect the behavior of the trainer, not the learner.

Observing and Recording. As Chapter 6 explains, decisions about observing and recording procedures can have a major impact on variability in the data. For instance, decisions about when and where observations take place and how long sessions last influence the picture of variability in the same way a film maker making a movie about a foreign country determines the impression viewers will get by how scenes are selected. Researchers and practitioners can easily test the impact of their choices on the data by trying out alternative observation procedures. Conducting observation sessions several times a day, in several different settings, or for varying periods of time is a good way to test whether different sampling procedures might show different patterns of responding.

The choice of continuous versus discontinuous observing procedures is especially likely to have a substantial impact on the nature of the data collected. One limitation of discontinuous procedures such as interval-based recording is that they fail to provide a picture of what is happening with behavioral dimensions because the data reflect only the number or percent of scored intervals. Another problem is that the number of intervals scored unavoidably depends on the length of the intervals. These and other problems described in Chapter 6 make it difficult to compare the picture of responding obtained by discontinuous observation procedures with data resulting from continuous observation procedures, such as counting the number of times the target behavior occurs during an observation period. Even if discontinuous observation and recording procedures yield data that show the same general increases or decreases from one condition to another as data recorded continuously during the same sessions, the data points in the two kinds of samples represent fundamentally different information. Because they are incomplete, records produced by discontinuous procedures cannot provide a clear picture of variability within or across observation periods.

Experimental Design

Approaches. The phrase **experimental design** refers to how investigators arrange comparisons between control and experimental (treatment) conditions so as to permit inferences about any effects independent variables may have on responding. Decisions about how these comparisons will be made can have a profound impact on the variability the data reveal. Perhaps the most fundamental decision concerns how comparisons will be made. There are two distinct alternatives. One approach is to measure each participant's behavior as he is exposed to control and experimental conditions in sequence. That is, the investigator looks at the data from each participant separately and compares responding under a control condition with responding under an experimental condition. This approach is called **within-subject design** because comparisons between control and experimental conditions are made "within" each subject (they are now called participants). A fundamentally different approach involves dividing the participants into two groups, one of which is exposed to a control condition and the other to the experimental condition. Each participant is assigned to a group by the investigator, perhaps using some algorithm or procedure to try to ensure that the two groups are similar with respect to certain key variables. The performances of all participants are measured once at the beginning of the study and often just once more, at the end of the study. The data from each set of participants are grouped into a collective outcome, such as the group average or mean score. Those outcomes for the control and experimental groups are compared statistically, usually to confirm that the average performances of the two groups were similar when the study began and to see if their average scores differed after one group experienced the experimental condition (treatment) for a certain period of time while the other group experienced the control condition. This approach is called **between-groups design**.

> **Experimental design.** Arrangement of control and experimental (treatment) conditions that permits comparisons that help identify the effects of the independent variable on the dependent variable.
>
> **Within-subject design.** A method of arranging comparisons between control and experimental (treatment) conditions in which each subject is exposed to both control and experimental conditions in sequence and the data represent the performance of individual participants under both conditions.
>
> **Between-groups design.** A method of arranging comparisons between control and experimental (treatment) conditions in which different groups of subjects are exposed to control and experimental conditions. Data from the individual participants in each group are combined so that the data that are analyzed represent the combined performance of individual participants who have experienced only one of the conditions.

Behavioral Requirements for Experimental Design. These two approaches to experimental design result in very different pictures of participant behavior. To understand the differences, consider the following points. First, recall that behavior is a biological phenomenon and is therefore a characteristic of individual organisms. It is a result of interactions between individuals and their environments. Only by understanding this relationship can we understand behavior and how it is influenced by particular environmental factors.

Second, it follows that no two individuals behave exactly alike. Even identical twins raised in the same family do not share exactly the same histories. If they did, twins would behave identically from moment to moment, just as a shadow follows its owner. Each person has a unique history and is likely to respond to similar events at least a little bit differently – and perhaps very differently.

Third, a description of a single individual's behavior represents something very different than a description of the combined behavior of two or more individuals. Suppose, for example, that we have measured the performances of two participants – Harry and Sally – on a problem-solving task. If we look at the data for each, we will know exactly how each person performed. However, if we combine their individual performances in some way (for instance, by averaging their responses), we will not know the performance of either Harry or Sally. They may well have performed differently, which means that the average will not correctly represent the performance of either person.

Let us add some detail to this example by stipulating that Harry solved 10 problems correctly and Sally solved 16 correctly. These are measures of each one's behavior. It is clear that the average (13 correct responses) is not an accurate measure of either individual's behavior. Hidden in this average is the difference (6) between the two individuals' performances. This difference is not a measure of either individual's behavior, which is why it is misleading to describe the difference between the performances as "6 correct responses." If 6 correct responses were a measure of behavior, whose behavior would it represent? Neither Harry's nor Sally's, because we know they got 10 and 16 problems correct, respectively. Instead, this difference is an artifact of combining data this way. This artifact is called **intersubject variability**, which here refers to the differences between the behaviors of two or more participants.

> **Intersubject variability.** Differences in responding among participants.

Fourth, because intersubject variability has nothing to do with the description of behavior (an intraorganism phenomenon), it is not helpful in explaining the behavior of a single organism. Knowing the difference between Harry's and Sally's performances tells us nothing about why either behaved as they did. On the other hand, an adequate account of why each behaved as they did will explain any differences between their performances. This certainly does not mean that the differences among individuals are unimportant. However, if researchers want to explain those differences, their data must reflect pure measures of behavior, undiluted by intersubject variability.

Fifth, the reactions of each participant to a condition are the actual effects of the condition. Combining Harry's and Sally's data will hide the true effects of the condition, which may partly depend on certain factors unique to each individual. Any condition or intervention produces individual effects, not average effects. The usefulness of studies reporting average effects will therefore be limited because those outcomes do not necessarily reflect the actual effects of either the treatment or the control condition on participants' behavior.

Although this discussion is couched in the language of experimental research, the points apply fully to the interests of practitioners as well. Of course, practitioners are often interested in only a single individual at a time,

TABLE 9.5
Argument for analyzing individual data

- Behavior is a characteristic of individual organisms
- No two individuals behave exactly alike
- A description of one individual's behavior is fundamentally different from a measure of the behavior of multiple individuals, which creates intersubject variability
- Intersubject variability has nothing to do with the description of behavior
- The effects of a variable are on the behavior of individuals, not on aggregate measures across individuals

so there may be less temptation to combine one client's data with those of another. The interpretations that are most important are about the effects of each successive treatment phase on the target behavior(s) of the individual who is the focus of ABA services.

Sequence Effects. One of the differences in within-subject and between-groups approaches to experimental design concerns the experiences of participants. In a typical group-design study, participants are often assigned to either a control or an experimental condition and therefore do not have contact with both. In contrast, each participant in a study using a within-subject design experiences both types of conditions. They may respond under a sequence of conditions throughout a study, such as an initial control condition (baseline), a subsequent treatment condition, a return to the control condition, and then a return to the treatment condition. Many different sequences of this sort can be arranged.

As we will learn in upcoming chapters, there are important advantages to measuring the behavior of each participant under each of the conditions to be compared. For now, it is sufficient to understand that moving from one condition to another creates the possibility that the experience of a prior condition may influence a participant's reaction to a subsequent condition. This kind of variability is called a **sequence effect**, and the possibility of such an effect is inherent in within-subject designs. It is an unavoidable fact that responding can be influenced by an individual's prior experiences, and the more recent the experiences, the greater the chance they may have a lingering effect.

> **Sequence effect.** The effect of exposure to one condition on responding in a subsequent condition.

Sequence effects may be useful or problematic. For example, an investigator may be interested in studying how prior contact with one condition will affect performance under a subsequent condition. A study may require that participants first undergo a training regimen (phase 1) in order to acquire a new skill that is necessary for evaluating the impact of the independent variable or treatment condition (phase 2). For example, a learner with autism may need to be taught how to perform the chain of responses involved in match-to-sample procedures before those procedures can be used to assess his skills in matching various types of stimuli (e.g., Kelly, Green, & Sidman, 1998). In that case, a sequence effect would be useful.

On the other hand, it is often important that performance under a treatment condition reflects only the effects of that condition, uncontaminated by the participant's experience under a prior condition. For instance, an investigator may want to evaluate the effects of an initial match-to-sample training condition and a variation of that condition. If the way the participant responds in the second treatment phase is affected by having previously experienced the initial version of the condition, this sequence effect may prevent seeing a clear picture of the effects of the second condition alone. In this situation, the investigator must find ways to minimize the sequence effect and to evaluate the extent of its impact on responding.

Fortunately, the likelihood of obtaining sequence effects can be either enhanced or minimized, depending on the investigator's interests. For instance, giving participants a long history with one condition and then switching to a different condition increases the chances that experience with the first condition will affect responding under the second condition. However, any influence of the first condition will usually weaken as an individual gains exposure to the second condition. One way to separate sequence effects from treatment effects is to use this gradually shifting impact to separate the effects of one condition from those of the next. Making sure participants are exposed to a second condition long enough for any impact of a prior condition to fully dissipate often leaves a clear picture of the effects of the second condition alone. This common tactic will be discussed in detail in the next chapter. Later chapters will also discuss ways of assessing the extent of possible sequence effects.

Finally, practitioners are no more likely to run into sequence effects than researchers, but they may be less inclined to work around them. After all, their primary interest lies in making good progress toward service delivery goals, not cleanly disentangling primary treatment effects from possible sequence effects. As we will see in upcoming chapters, this practical agenda comes with limitations with which practitioners often have to live in interpreting clinical data.

Data Analysis

As the raw data in a research project or practical intervention accumulate, the investigator must choose how to display and analyze the data so she can evaluate how the effort is progressing and what the data have to say about its outcomes. Chapter 14 considers this topic in detail, but it is important to recognize that different pictures of variability can result from different analytical techniques. Some views of variability can be valuable in highlighting what the data reveal, but other ways of looking at variability can obscure important information or even be misleading.

For example, Figure 9.4 shows hypothetical data from control and experimental conditions displayed in terms of individual sessions (Panel A) and as means across all sessions within each condition (Panel B). Both displays show correct and potentially useful information, depending on what the investigator or others need to know. The two pictures of variability in the data differ markedly, however. Summarizing the daily session data into a single mean value for each phase hides the fact that responding gradually increased throughout the control condition and continued increasing throughout the experimental condition, as Panel A makes clear. As the next chapter will show, knowing that

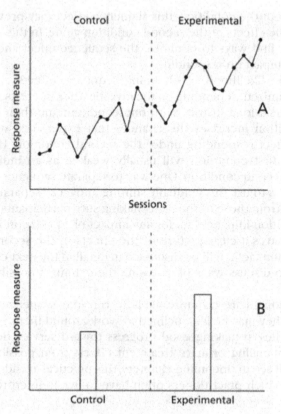

FIG. 9.4. An example of data from control and experimental conditions displayed across sessions (Panel A) and summarized by conditions (Panel B).

responding gradually increased across both control and experimental phases is important in evaluating the role of extraneous factors. These data suggest that something may have been producing an increase in responding throughout both phases that had nothing to do with the effects of each phase by itself. That possibility is hidden by the display in Panel B.

Independent Variable

Finally, the independent variable is an obvious source of behavioral variability. In fact, it is the only source of variability whose impact is intentional and the primary focus of interpretation. All other features of a study are arranged just to clarify the effects of the independent variable or treatment condition on the target behavior. The goal of experimentation is to measure responding accurately while minimizing all other influences on variability. Upcoming chapters will consider how to arrange experimental comparisons so that the role of the independent variable is clearly revealed.

Unfortunately, researchers cannot assume that an independent variable condition will remain consistent in its features throughout an entire phase, which may last for some time. Any of its characteristics may vary in unplanned ways over time, which might result in variability in the data. This means that researchers must take steps to ensure that the independent variable and circumstances in which it is embedded operate exactly as planned throughout the entire treatment phase. This can be a considerable challenge, especially in applied research, and this goal often conflicts with the realities of service delivery. In applied settings, treatment conditions are often complex arrangements involving the behavior of others such as parents, teachers, or staff members. For example, an intervention condition may require a teacher not only to respond in a specific way each time a child emits the target behavior but also behave in a different way toward the child the rest of the time. Merely training the teacher to respond appropriately may not be sufficient to insure consistent reactions over a period of weeks. That is why it is necessary to collect and report evidence that experimental and control conditions actually operated as designed (Fryling, Wallace, & Yassine, 2012; Peterson, Homer, & Wonderlick, 1982). More on this point later.

CHAPTER SUMMARY

1. There are many ways of looking for and describing behavioral variability. There are at least three levels of summarization in which researchers and practitioners are often interested. The greatest detail can be found by examining individual responses over time.

2. Another level of summarization requires the investigator to combine measures of responding during each session into a single value. While this approach prevents seeing variability among individual responses, it can reveal variability that might have been difficult to see by only looking at single responses. This approach is informative because it highlights changes in behavior from one session to another session in the same phase.

3. A third view of variability requires the researcher to summarize measures of responding across individual sessions. This view prevents seeing changes in responding from one session to another, but it helps to highlight differences between conditions.

4. The traditional assumption is that variability is intrinsic or inherent in the nature of organisms. If this logic is used, it implies that the causes of behavior are built into our nature and cannot be influenced by the environment.

5. The contrasting position is that variability is extrinsic and may be described and explained with reference to environmental and biological events. This approach encourages investigators to minimize the contribution of extraneous factors to reduce variability, rather than just accept variability as an unavoidable aspect of behavior.

6. There are three general functions that variability in behavior serves. The first is that variation in behavior may guide and motivate an investigator's curiosities. Second, variability in behavior guides the investigator's decision-making throughout the study or clinical intervention. Lastly, variability provides a foundation for how we interpret the outcomes of experiments and practical interventions.

7. Investigators pursue these three ways of using behavioral variability by producing variability in responding by manipulating independent variables, and by reducing variability in responding by identifying and controlling extraneous factors. The first part of this approach is the primary focus of experimentation – to see if a specific variable will affect behavior and, if so, what kind of effects it will produce.

8. Reducing behavioral variability by controlling extraneous factors is necessary in order to be sure that the treatment condition is the only factor responsible for observed changes in the target behavior.

9. Extraneous variables may be managed by either holding extraneous factors constant across all conditions of a study or by completely eliminating the problematic variables. At a minimum, the investigator should control or eliminate extraneous sources of variability one by one until the desired degree of control over responding is achieved.

10. Extraneous factors are even more problematic for practitioners. Practical services are usually delivered under everyday circumstances, and it is often not realistic to manage factors that might interfere with seeing the effects of treatment protocols uncontaminated by other factors. However, it is important that practitioners try to minimize the effects of extraneous variables.

11. Behavioral variability may occur for a number of reasons, including: (a) biological factors, (b) the research or service setting, (c) the general experimental procedure, (d) environmental variables, or (e) the treatment condition.

12. Variability in the data can also be traced to how the target behavior is defined. Definitions may unintentionally capture responses other than target behaviors.

13. The experimental design may also influence how the investigator views variability. The use of a within-subject design or a between-subject design will present a very different representation of a participant's behavior.

14. Moving from one condition to another creates the possibility that the experience of a prior condition may influence a participant's reaction to a subsequent condition. This kind of variability is called a sequence effect. Sequence effects are inherent in within-subject designs and may be useful or problematic.

15. The most obvious source of behavioral variability is the independent variable. This is the only variable whose impact is intentional and the primary focus of interpretation.

HIGHLIGHTED TERMS

Behavioral variability. Variations in features of responding within a single response class, as well as variations in summary measures of that class.

Between-groups design. A method of arranging comparisons between different groups of subjects exposed to control and experimental conditions. Data from the individual participants in each group are combined so that the data that are analyzed represent the combined performance of individual participants who have experienced only one of the conditions.

Experimental design. Arrangement of control and experimental (treatment) conditions that permits comparisons that help identify the effects of the independent variable on the dependent variable.

Extrinsic variability. The assumption that variability in behavior is describable, explainable, and predictable in terms of variation in other physical phenomena, whether biological or environmental. See *Intrinsic variability*.

Intersubject variability. Differences in responding among participants.

Intrinsic variability. The assumption that variability in behavior is in one way or another inherent or built into the nature of organisms. See *Extrinsic variability*.

Sequence effect. The effect of exposure to one condition on responding in a subsequent condition.

Within-subject design. A method of arranging comparisons between control and experimental (treatment) conditions in which each subject is exposed to both control and experimental conditions in sequence and the data represent the performance of individual participants under both conditions.

TEXT STUDY GUIDE

1. What is behavioral variability?
2. Distinguish among three levels of behavioral variability.
3. What does it mean to propose that variability in behavior is intrinsic?
4. Describe the position that variability in behavior is extrinsic in nature.
5. What are the practical outcomes of assuming that behavioral variability is intrinsic?
6. What are the practical outcomes of assuming that behavioral variability is extrinsic?
7. Describe the three general functions of variability for investigators.
8. Describe the two-part approach investigators utilize to deal with variability.
9. Explain how it can be experimentally useful to increase variability.
10. What are synonyms for the independent variable condition?
11. Describe two ways of managing extraneous sources of variability and the limitations of each.

12. Explain why extraneous factors that contribute to variability are more problematic for practitioners than researchers.

13. Describe three types of biological influences on behavioral variability.

14. Why is it appropriate to view an organism's environmental history as a biological influence?

15. Discuss some of the extraneous variables that may be associated with a research or service setting.

16. How can behavioral variability be influenced by the target behavior's definition?

17. How can behavioral variability be influenced by the selection of dimensions?

18. How can behavioral variability be influenced by observing and recording procedures?

19. What is experimental design? Describe the two distinct alternatives to how comparisons can be made.

20. Describe the argument that the study of behavior must be based on comparisons of the behavior of individual participants under control and experimental conditions.

21. What is intersubject variability?

22. What is a sequence effect? Are they useful or problematic?

23. Describe how an investigator could enhance or minimize the likelihood of obtaining sequence effects.

24. Discuss how different pictures of variability can result from different analytical techniques.

BOX STUDY GUIDE

1. What are the implications for a science of behavior of saying that people are "free" in the sense that their behavior does not have causes?

2. Why do we tend to explain behavior by referring to causes inside the organism?

SUGGESTED READINGS

Sidman, M. (1960). *Tactics of scientific research*. New York: Basic Books. Chapter 5: Intrinsic vs. imposed variability.

Skinner, B. F. (1971). *Beyond freedom and dignity*. New York: Alfred A. Knopf.

DISCUSSION TOPICS

1. Discuss ways in which colloquial language suggests that variability is intrinsic to human behavior.

2. Discuss everyday observations about behavioral variability that might suggest experimental studies. What kind of extraneous variables would you anticipate having to manage?

EXERCISES

1. Write a definition for aggression. Compare your definition with other students, and discuss how each definition may unintentionally capture responses other than the target behavior.

2. Find or create a data set with values in at least two phases. Analyze the data graphically at each of the three levels of summarization.

3. Select three published behavior analytic studies. For each study, identify the independent variable(s). Additionally, identify those factors in the independent variable condition that are not part of the independent variable itself.

4. For each of the studies selected above, identify at least two extraneous variables. Did the investigator(s) attempt to manage these extraneous factors? If so, describe their approach.

5. Have three people independently create a data set with 12 values in each of two phases, and graph each data set. Do not let others see these graphs. Calculate a mean for each of the 24 sets of "observations", and graph the mean data. Discuss what the mean data set shows across the two phases, and compare the mean graph to the individual graphs.

CHAPTER TEN

Steady States and Transitions

STEADY STATE STRATEGY

Collecting Repeated Measures

Let us suppose that we are trying to address some of the behavioral needs of a child diagnosed with autism spectrum disorder who has been newly placed in a special education classroom. One of the target behaviors we have defined is stereotypic hand flapping. Occurrences of the behavior occur in such rapid succession that it is difficult to count each hand flap, so we have decided to measure the duration of each episode or burst of hand flapping and sum the durations of all episodes to get the total duration of hand flapping for each observation session. We have set up observation procedures and are ready to start collecting data under baseline conditions. The first graphed data point summarizing responding during an observation session will tell us something we never knew before, but it will only make it obvious that one data point does not tell us very much about what responding looks like under this condition. In particular, we will not know whether that value is typical of what we should expect in these circumstances or is misleading in some way. Perhaps it is higher or lower than we might usually find if we had a fuller picture.

The only way to begin to get a more complete picture is to measure for another session. What we will likely learn is that our second data point is not the same as the first. Our question then becomes, "Which of these two values is more representative of the duration of hand flapping in the classroom under baseline conditions?" There is no way to settle this issue except to observe and measure for still another session.

We should not be surprised if the third value is at least somewhat different from the other two. However, if the three values are not wildly different, they may begin to tell us something about responding in this situation. Still, it would be easy to admit that we do not yet have a very complete picture of the typical duration of hand flapping. After all, the child has had only limited exposure to the classroom, and we know it can take a bit of time for a behavior to adapt to a new set of influences. In other words, there is good reason to anticipate that the initial impact of our baseline conditions may not be a very good predictor of how responding might change with increasing experience in this situation.

As we keep collecting data from one session to the next, our graph will gradually draw an increasingly comprehensive picture of the duration of the child's hand flapping. With luck, we may find that these measures of responding under this condition are relatively stable. This means that the total duration of hand flapping per session is neither generally increasing nor decreasing and that the variability from one value to another is not excessive and is fairly consistent. We may even begin to feel some confidence in answering the original question of what durations of hand flapping are typical for the child under baseline conditions in the classroom.

BOX 10.1

Measuring One Participant Many Times versus Many Participants a Few Times

There are two different approaches to obtaining a picture of the effects of baseline (control) and intervention (experimental) conditions on responding. You can measure the behavior of one individual many times under both control and treatment conditions or measure the behavior of many individuals who experience just one of those conditions a few times (often just once at the beginning of an investigation and once at the end). Although you can wind up with lots of data either way, there is a big difference between these alternatives for our ability to discover things about behavior.

To understand the distinction, remember the discussion in Chapter 2 about the fact that behavior is a biological phenomenon. This means that behavior can be clearly observed only at the level of the individual organism. In other words, the influence of any variables on behavior can be clearly seen only as they impact the behavior of each individual. Although we might wish that treatment variables would affect different individuals in exactly the same way, we cannot assume that will be the case. In fact, part of what we are trying to learn is how treatment affects individuals, and using grouped data from many different individuals makes it difficult to answer that question.

As this chapter shows, observing the behavior of a single individual repeatedly under a condition gives investigators the opportunity to obtain a complete and clear picture of the effects of that condition on a target behavior. It should be easy to appreciate that observing the behavior of an individual only once cannot provide the same information. It may not be so obvious that measuring the target behavior in a number of different individuals, averaging the results, and comparing the group averages statistically before and after one group experiences the treatment does not provide a clear or complete picture of the effects of either the control or the treatment condition on the behavior. Although that tactic would provide many observations, we would know no more about the effects of either condition on the behavior of each individual – effects that might vary depending on each person's unique histories and characteristics – than we would if we measured a single individual once under each condition. In other words, the point is not merely to get a lot of data but to get enough of the right kind of data. What we need are data that reveal exactly how each participant's behavior is influenced by a condition because that is how behavioral effects can be detected.

Comparing States of Responding

With this answer, we may decide we are ready to see how responding changes when the behavior encounters an intervention condition. This unavoidably involves a comparison between hand flapping under baseline and intervention conditions. In order to make this comparison, we must determine how hand-flapping behavior is affected by this new condition. As we accumulate data points across repeated sessions in the intervention phase, the graph will gradually reveal a new picture of responding. We might find that responding is initially like that observed in the baseline phase but that it gradually transitions to a different level. On the other hand, it might be that responding changes in some way as soon as the intervention phase starts. Whatever the initial changes, we should not be surprised to learn that they do not necessarily predict the changes that we eventually find. In other words, the more sessions we observe, the better we understand the full effects of the intervention condition.

By measuring hand flapping repeatedly under the baseline condition and then under the intervention condition, we are trying to get a graphical picture of that behavior under each condition that is *complete* and *representative*. That is, we want to make sure that we collect enough data to be confident that we have learned what the durations look like under each condition after its effects on the target behavior are fully developed and no longer changing. This will allow us to compare responding under the two conditions and be sure we are comparing data that fully represent the impact of each condition.

Getting sufficient data to show the impact of each condition is also important because we want to be sure that the differences we see are typical of the two conditions and do not represent the effects of anything else that might be going on. If the initial reactions of peers to the hand-flapping behavior or the intervention procedure cause hand flapping to increase, for instance, a comparison of data from the two conditions might be contaminated by that factor.

The Risk of Extraneous Variables

What may complicate our conclusion is the risk that responding under either condition might be influenced not just by the condition itself but also by extraneous factors – a topic introduced in Chapter 9. Making repeated measurements of responding under each condition provides one way of assessing this risk, and upcoming chapters consider additional ways of managing or evaluating the role of extraneous influences. The usefulness of repeated measures depends on the investigator's success in minimizing session-to-session variations in key features of the baseline or control condition and the treatment or experimental condition. This certainly does not mean that a participant's experiences are identical across sessions within each of the two phases. However, it does mean the key factors that define each condition are relatively consistent across the participant's experiences.

Given this consistency, if the data show that our measures of the target behavior are unstable in certain ways under either condition, we should assume there are factors responsible for these variations in responding. We should reason that if the variations are not due to changes in the condition, which is being held constant across sessions, they must instead be due to extraneous factors. More optimistically, if the data are relatively stable during a condition we might assume that either extraneous factors are not having noticeable effects or that any extraneous effects are consistent.

In other words, when the data within a phase are relatively stable it might suggest that extraneous influences are relatively minor. As we shall see, however, that conclusion is not necessarily true, though it is at least reassuring that the data are not markedly or systematically variable. Whenever there is variability, we have no choice but to worry that extraneous factors may be causing it. In particular, marked changes in measures of the target behavior from session to session in a phase require us to acknowledge that the data represent not just the effects of the condition but the effects of the extraneous factors as well. If that is the case, we are not in a good position to compare responding under that condition with responding under another condition. Such a comparison would not allow us to conclude that differences in responding were due only to differences in the conditions themselves. We would have to admit that the differences could be due to those other factors.

In short, a graphical picture of stable responding across sessions under a baseline or a treatment condition provides some encouragement that the data represent the effects of that condition and that the contribution of extraneous factors is minimal or at least constant. Stable responding – a steady state – is therefore a marker for two important characteristics of the data. First, as just discussed, stable responding suggests that extraneous influences are minimal, though they could merely be consistent throughout the condition. Second, stable responding suggests that any transition from the initial effects of the condition to its more enduring effects is complete.

As an example of this approach, consider the data shown in Figure 10.1. They depict results of an evaluation of the effects of an intervention on the performance of six fire safety skills by three young boys with autism in educational settings (Garcia, Dukes, Brady, Scott, & Wilson, 2016). The investigators used a research design called a multiple baseline across participants. In baseline probe sessions, a fire alarm was sounded for 30 seconds. The investigator merely observed and recorded the boy's performance of the six skills; no instructions or feedback were provided. The baseline data (to the left of the vertical phase change line in each of the graphs) showed that there was some variability in Aaron's responding (top graph). Notice, however, that his baseline phase continued until the data indicated that responding did not change much; it stayed within a narrow range. Baseline responding for the other two boys was stable. The baseline data suggest that any extraneous factors that may have been present – such as opportunities for the boys to practice the skills and observe other children performing them during regular fire drills – had little or no effect on the responding of any of the boys. Intervention, which was delivered in 1-to-1 sessions, consisted of an instructor providing the boy with spoken instructions, modeling, opportunities to demonstrate the skills, correction and prompting if needed, and brief praise following correct performances. The data points in the intervention phases (to the right of the vertical phase change line) represent performances on probe trials (no instructions, prompts, or feedback) conducted at least 5 minutes before each intervention

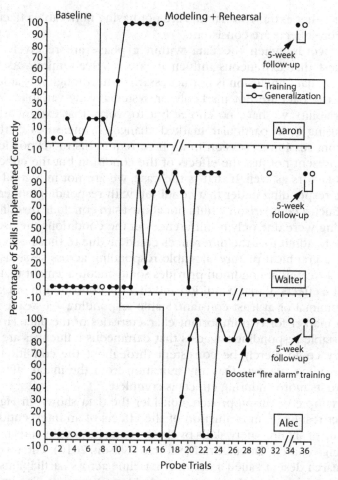

FIG. 10.1. Example of using the steady state strategy to determine typical responding under comparison conditions. From Garcia, Dukes, Brady, Scott, & Wilson (2016). Using modeling and rehearsal to teach fire safety to children with autism. *Journal of Applied Behavior Analysis, 49(3)*, 699–704. Used by permission.

session. Note that for all three boys, performances in the first two intervention sessions were like those in the baseline phase. Aaron's data then show a rapid transition to correct performance of all six skills by the fourth intervention session, which remained very stable for five more intervention sessions. For both Walter (middle graph) and Alec (bottom graph), the transitions were gradual and marked by considerable variability across several sessions until their performances too became highly accurate and unchanging. That is, it took some time for the full effects of the intervention to be seen. Had the investigators stopped before the data were stable, they would have drawn faulty conclusions about the effectiveness of the intervention for Walter and Alec.

Summary

The **steady state strategy** is an approach to making comparisons between the effects of conditions on a target behavior. It involves repeatedly measuring responding for an individual under each condition in an effort to assess and manage extraneous influences so as to obtain stable patterns of responding that represent the full effects of each condition. This strategy evolved in the work of B. F. Skinner and his students (Skinner, 1956) and was first described in detail by Sidman (1960). It is a powerful and effective way of identifying and managing extraneous influences and obtaining a clear picture of the effects of each condition. That allows comparisons of responding under control and intervention conditions that focus on actual differences resulting from treatment variables, which helps investigators draw conclusions that are likely to hold up when tested or used by others.

> **Steady state strategy.** An approach to making comparisons between the effects of two conditions on a target behavior that involves repeatedly measuring an individual's responding under each condition. It is essential for assessing and managing extraneous influences in order to get stable patterns of responding that represent the full effects of each condition.

The steady state strategy is equally important and usable in basic and applied research projects as well as practice settings. Generally speaking, the simpler and more controlled the environment, the easier it is to find stable responding because there are fewer troublesome extraneous factors that might influence the target behavior. Investigators face more challenges in dealing with extraneous factors when projects take place in relatively uncontrolled, everyday settings. Regardless of the setting, however, if investigators collect only a few measures under a condition, the data cannot help the investigator identify extraneous influences and may not provide a full picture of the effects of that condition. Such limitations increase the risk that comparisons of responding under control and treatment conditions will be misleading. As a result, when others use this information in their own situations, there is a greater chance they will not get the same results.

Practitioners often have the opportunity to measure a client's behavior repeatedly over extended periods as the impact of an intervention is allowed to develop. A baseline or pretreatment phase is typically followed by an initial intervention designed to change responding in some desirable way. The first treatment procedure is often followed by variations required to make the procedure more effective or to accommodate changes in the behavior or surrounding circumstances. Each phase is often long enough to allow practitioners to examine the ebb and flow of the target behavior across many sessions.

Of course, the primary interest of practitioners is delivering effective services, not arranging comparisons for the purpose of publishing research findings.

Clinical considerations might seem to take precedent over steady state criteria in making decisions about when to change conditions. If they do, however, the practitioner will not be in a strong position to assert that the client's behavior changes were due to the treatment procedures rather than other events. That could make it difficult to persuade others to continue investing time, labor, and other resources in the treatment. If that is important, or just to enhance their confidence about the effects of their treatment procedures, practitioners would be wise to continue each phase until responding is relatively stable and to chase down possible extraneous factors whenever feasible.

STEADY STATES

Definition

A **steady** or stable **state** of responding may be defined as a pattern of responding that shows relatively little variation in the dimension(s) of interest over some period of time. In behavior analytic research and practice, steady states are typically evaluated over a series of sessions and days. Let us examine some implications of this definition.

> **Steady state.** A pattern of responding that shows relatively little variation in the dimension(s) of interest over some period of time.

First, it is important to understand that the meaning of the term "steady" is relative. Exactly how much variability or what patterns of variability are required to describe responding as stable or unstable will vary from one research project or practical intervention to another. Such factors as the characteristics of the target behavior, the features of the general environment, the details of intervention procedures, and the focus of the research or practical question may influence the investigator's judgment. For example, an investigator conducting a laboratory study of the effects of toxic chemicals on the behavior of rats may expect a very low level of variability, given testing conditions and the findings of similar studies already published. On the other hand, a practitioner conducting a project in a group home for individuals with intellectual disabilities may need to accommodate the effects of day-to-day variations in extraneous variables that cannot be easily managed, such as changes in scheduled activities or staff member assignments from one day to another. The research literature also provides investigators with a guide of sorts by showing the kind of stability colleagues were able to achieve in similar projects. All of these considerations mean that it is not feasible to define steady state responding with any kind of quantitative formula.

Second, even though the behavioral dimension being measured might be stable, it does not mean that other dimensions not being measured are also stable. For example, although the number of responses (count) might show good stability across successive sessions, the duration of responses could be changing in some way. In fact, when two or more dimensions are being measured, it is not uncommon for them to vary in different ways. Of course, there is no way to know about the stability of behavioral dimensions that are not being measured. That is why evidence of stability in a particular dimension should not prompt a general statement that responding is stable. Instead, it is more appropriate to say that a particular feature of responding is stable.

Third, just because some aspect of responding is stable, it may not be correct to conclude that the environment is also stable. A relatively consistent pattern of responding can result from a mix of changing variables whose net effect on the target behavior appears stable. Some environmental factors may even change in obvious ways but not influence the target behavior. For example, a substitute teacher would seem to be an important change in a classroom environment, but that change may not be evident in the target behavior. All we can say about the environment from observing stable responding is that any environmental changes affecting responding are either very weak or have effects that are balanced by other environmental factors.

Uses

Evaluates Measurement Decisions.

Evaluates Measurement Decisions. The steady state strategy is valuable because of how it guides decision-making as a project progresses. This benefit begins by helping the investigator evaluate prior decisions about how the target behavior is defined and measured. Collecting data for a number of sessions as originally planned provides a picture of responding that may prompt rethinking how the behavior is defined, which of its dimensions are measured, and how and when observation is conducted.

For example, the pattern of variability across sessions might suggest that the definition of the target behavior should be reconsidered. If the data tend to show distinct differences from one session to another (such as higher versus lower values), it could mean the definition has combined different functional classes. For instance, a definition of "aggressive" behavior may include both hitting and cursing. In some sessions, the target responses may be largely in the form of hitting, and on other days the measured responses may be mainly cursing. If cursing tends to occur at higher frequencies than hitting, sessions in which responding was mainly in the form of cursing would have higher values than sessions in which responding was mostly hitting. This pattern of variability might raise the question of whether there is a problem with how the target behavior is defined. Perhaps it would be more useful to define and measure hitting and cursing separately.

Collecting repeated measures under each successive condition may also encourage curiosity about other measurement decisions. For example, if the data showed very little change from one session to another, it might be tempting to conclude that responding was stable. We have already pointed out, however, that stable data only provide assurance that the dimension being measured is stable. Informal observation of what is happening during sessions might show that other dimensions of the target behavior vary a good bit from session to session. Together with the stable data, these observations could suggest that measuring other dimensions might provide a more informative picture of what is happening with the behavior.

As an example of this situation, consider data collected by partial interval recording using 2-minute intervals that showed consistently high percentages of scored intervals. It could be that the relatively long intervals result in most being scored as containing at least one instance of the target behavior. Interval recording procedures do not measure specific behavioral dimensions, however, so the investigator might worry that important variation in quantities such as count, duration, or rate is being missed. Again, steady state data does not always mean that all aspects of responding are stable. Such data must be examined in light of what is being measured and how it is being observed and recorded.

Reveals the Effects of Conditions. The steady state strategy is particularly useful for understanding what is going on with the target behavior as it accumulates increasing contact with a condition. When a behavior is exposed to a new condition, it typically changes in some way. Although the new condition may have some immediate impact, responding may also continue to be influenced by its recent history for at least a little while. In other words, the data often show a mixture of influences at the beginning of a phase that reflects a transition in control from the previous condition to the new condition. Although this transition is sometimes a particular interest, more often it is merely a nuisance because it makes it difficult for the investigator to see a clear picture of the effects of the new condition alone.

When the data suggest that a transition in responding that started when conditions changed is coming to an end, it is tempting to assume that the effects of the new condition are finally evident. The data may now represent a level of responding that is clearly higher or lower than in the previous phase. Although this change in level of responding may reveal the impact of the current condition, the steady state strategy asks for evidence that the new level of responding is durable. That is, the investigator needs to be sure that the apparently stable responding will continue as long as the condition is in effect. If the target behavior eventually changed in some way, it would be important to take that change into account in describing the effects of the condition. For instance, responding might gradually decrease when a condition is started. With continued exposure, however, the level of responding might gradually climb back to the higher level observed in the previous condition. By encouraging the investigator to repeatedly measure the target behavior across a number of sessions, the steady state strategy helps to capture all of the changes that might be characteristic of the condition.

Evaluates Extraneous Influences. Measuring a behavior repeatedly under baseline and treatment conditions can also alert the investigator to the role of extraneous variables. Remember that any factors that are not explicitly part of the independent variable are extraneous to the researcher's or practitioner's interests. As Chapter 9 described, extraneous factors may be unrelated to the treatment procedures and may occur unsystematically (for instance, a fire drill in a preschool). However, they may also be attached to the general circumstances of an investigation and may therefore have continuing or systematic effects (such as influence from co-workers in a project conducted in the workplace). They can even be attached to the independent variable itself and therefore come and go as it is presented and withdrawn (for example, instructions associated with treatment procedures).

The steady state strategy creates a good opportunity to detect the influence of unsystematic extraneous influences. As we will see, merely identifying instability in the data is not usually difficult, although its origins must usually be guessed from observing what is going on during sessions. If the impact of extraneous factors comes and goes from session to session, variability in responding may hint at their presence under an otherwise stable condition. It is more challenging to identify the influence of extraneous factors that are consistent throughout a condition, however, and it is easy to miss their contribution.

So, the steady state strategy can help identify unstable responding, but the real question is what needs to be done about excessive variability once it is detected. The objectives of each project guide this decision. Some research questions and procedures require a high level of control, perhaps even a laboratory setting. However, even applied studies conducted in messy, real-world settings often require some management of extraneous influences. Practical objectives may accommodate greater variability than basic research interests, but this leniency comes with limitations on the conclusions that can be defended. For instance, if data show clear changes in measures of the target behavior in an intervention phase but variability in the data suggest that non-treatment factors had a significant contribution, conclusions about the effects of the intervention may have to be very tentative. Whatever the requirements of a particular project, the level of stability in responding reflected in the data is a measure of the level of control the investigator has achieved.

Facilitates Comparisons. As we will see in more detail in upcoming chapters on research design, the steady state strategy provides the foundation for making comparisons between the effects of control and intervention conditions. Drawing conclusions about the effects of an intervention condition that have a good chance of being true depends on how well the effects of both control and intervention conditions can be described and understood.

Efforts to establish stable responding under each of the conditions being compared help the investigator do this in two key ways. First, repeatedly measuring the target behavior under each condition helps identify both the initial and ongoing patterns of responding in each phase. Second, these data encourage efforts to manage extraneous variables, which helps minimize their influence and thereby clarify the effects of the primary features of each condition. Because each condition is defined by the investigator's effort to hold a set of key variables relatively constant, variations in responding during a phase may represent the effects of extraneous factors that are not being managed. This may prompt the investigator to intervene in some way that reduces the role of extraneous variables.

These two outcomes of the steady state strategy help the investigator distinguish between effects of the conditions themselves and the effects of other factors. With this advantage, the resulting comparison is more likely to be an accurate description of the effects of the intervention alone. This means that the reported findings have a good chance of holding up when colleagues use them for their own purposes.

As an example, let us suppose a researcher is conducting a study to evaluate the effects of a certain special diet on the acquisition of new social skills by children with autism. Each child's performance measured repeatedly under control and dietary intervention conditions will be partly a function of the basic measurement procedures used throughout both conditions. Of course, performance under the diet condition may reflect the influence of the diet. But what if there are events in the children's daily lives that vary from one day to another and that might affect the target behaviors in daily sessions? One child may be moved from home- to center-based services, a change that could have broad effects on behavior. Another may spend weekends with grandparents and behave differently on Mondays as a result. Still another has sleep problems that affect his social interactions some days.

Effects of these extraneous factors may show up as variations in acquisition of the target social skills from one session to another. If the researcher ignores those variations and concludes that the differences in skill development under the two conditions are due solely to the diet, the finding may not hold up very well for other researchers or for practitioners. It may be that the diet actually did not impede learning new skills but extraneous factors made it seem like that was the case. Using the variability in responding within each condition to identify extraneous influences and minimize their contribution could minimize this risk. This approach would make it possible to identify the influence of the diet.

Identification

Trends. One of the challenges of the steady state strategy is recognizing when the data show stable responding and when they do not. There are particular features of variability in a series of data points that often bear on this

---

TABLE 10.1
Uses of the steady state strategy

- Evaluates measurement decisions
- Reveals the effects of conditions
- Evaluates extraneous influences
- Facilitates comparisons

---

decision. One pattern of variability is called a trend. A **trend** may be defined as a relatively consistent change in a series of data points in a single direction, either increasing or decreasing. Although there are some exceptions, steady state data do not show strong or consistent trends in either direction.

It is not always obvious that the data in a phase are generally trending upward or downward because there are many ways a sequence of data points can show trends. The graphed data sets in Figure 10.2 show some possibilities. The data in both Panels A and B show a slight but consistent increasing trend. However, the greater range of the values in Panel B might mask the fact that the slope of the trend in these two data sets is actually the same.

Panel C shows a decreasing trend that might also be easy to miss because most of the data points fall in the middle range on the vertical axis. The existence of a downward trend results from the fact that there are four high values in the first half of the data set and four low values in the second half. This type of trend is also shown in Panel D. Here, although most points fall in the middle of the vertical axis, a number of lower values appear in the latter half of the data set. In both of these graphs, the trends result from the values of only a few of the data points in the set.

Panels E and F show what are called "local" trends because they are embedded in otherwise relatively stable patterns of responding. In Panel E, the values

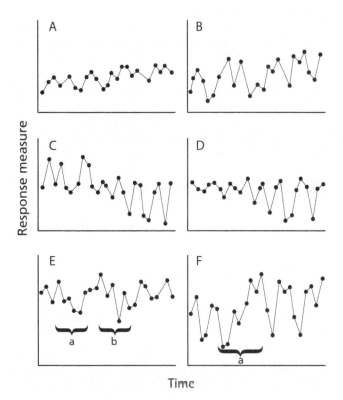

FIG. 10.2. Graphed data sets showing different trend patterns.

marked *a* and *b* reveal brief decreasing trends, and the values marked *a* in Panel F show a sharp increasing trend. It is tempting to ignore such local trends because they are temporary and are surrounded by more stable data. That might not be a problem, but if such changes happened to occur at the beginning of a new condition, it would be easy to mistake them for the effects of the new condition.

The deterministic assumption that there are always reasons for changes in behavior (see Chapter 9 and Box 9.1) means that a trend should encourage us to wonder what factors might be having that effect on a target behavior. When trends follow the start of a new phase, perhaps even persisting for a while, we are not likely to be surprised because we know that the environment has changed. But when the trend occurs beyond the expected transition under conditions that are supposed to be consistent from session to session, it is important to worry about what factors are producing the change in responding. If the investigator is successfully managing the environmental conditions defining a control or intervention phase, the participant's experiences should be very similar from session to session and so should responding. If a relatively consistent increase or decrease in responding occurs without any obvious reason, we should assume that something is producing the change.

There are at least three reasons to worry about trends that have no obvious explanation. First, a trend means that something is influencing behavior in significant ways, and its effects might interfere with getting a clear picture of the impact of the conditions of primary interest. Second, when we are unaware of what is causing a trend, it is not clear how we might more effectively control the environment so as to eliminate its influence. Third, trends make it difficult to determine the effects of an intervention. If the effects of either a baseline condition or a treatment condition are unclear, this distorts their comparison. The result can be that the impact of the intervention condition is seen as greater or smaller than it really is. This topic is discussed later in this chapter.

Finally, there are circumstances in which trends may be considered stable patterns of responding. That might be the case when procedures produce a repeating pattern of brief trends throughout both control and intervention conditions. The data in Figure 10.3 illustrate this kind of pattern. Each brief

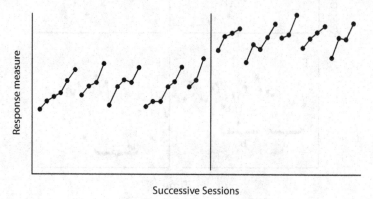

FIG. 10.3.   Data showing trends as a pattern of stable responding.

increasing trend shows the improving performance of a student working on a series of math problems involving multiplication facts. Performance is typically poor when the student is first challenged with each new multiplication task but improves over a series of sessions with instructions and practice. After a certain level of performance is achieved, the teacher provides the next set of multiplication exercises. Performance again starts out weak but gradually improves. This pattern runs throughout both a control condition and the following intervention condition, which adds a particular error correction procedure. A stable pattern of repeated trends with each new multiplication task under each condition allows a clear comparison of the two conditions and determination of the effects of the intervention.

Range. Another feature of variability that is important in identifying steady states is range. The highest and lowest values in a data set define its **range**. It is particularly easy to determine the range of a set of values when data are plotted on a graph. Figure 10.4 shows some different patterns of variation in range that can influence decisions about steady states.

The data sets in Panels A and B each show a fairly consistent range from beginning to end. Whether the range of either data set would be acceptable for an investigator would depend on the actual values the data points represent,

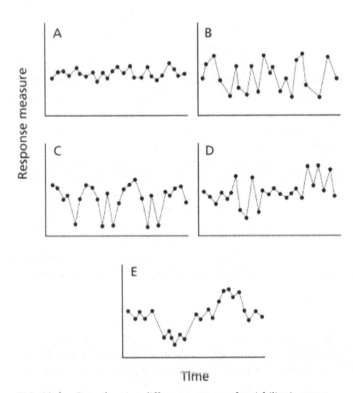

FIG. 10.4. Data showing different patterns of variability in range.

given the features of the study. For example, the nature of the research question, the relevant literature, the target behavior being measured, the general preparation under which responding occurs, and the independent variable all may suggest how much variability is acceptable. For these reasons, a laboratory study of the effects of a drug on the schedule performance of rats might require less variability in the data than a field study of the effects of an intervention on the behavior of children with learning disabilities in a classroom setting.

Although most of the data points in Panel C fall in the same range, five values are markedly lower. Those lower values seem consistent and do not apparently occur more often than others throughout the data set. Nevertheless, they suggest that some influence may be at work in some sessions that is different from most other sessions. If the investigator knows why responding is lower on some days, it might be acceptable to ignore those values. However, if they have no obvious explanation, it should be worrisome that they might become more frequent, possibly making it more difficult to see the effects of an intervention condition alone.

Panel D presents a similar problem. In this case, most of the values in the set fall within a relatively narrow central range. However, more than a few data points are either markedly higher or lower and fall outside of that range. This kind of variation in range from one group of values to the next does not seem like a very good basis for predicting the outcome of future measurements. In other words, if the next phase was started at this point, it would not be clear whether any changes in responding represented the factors that are already contributing to variations in the range or to the new condition.

The data points in Panel E represent a particularly troubling situation. Although we could determine the range of the entire data set, doing so would ignore the fact that the data points fall into groups of values that have a similar, relatively small "local" range. The local range is initially at the midpoint on the vertical axis and then moves lower, back to the mid level, higher, and then back again to the mid level of the scale. Whether encountered in a baseline or a treatment phase, this moving pattern of local range values would be a problem. As a baseline, this pattern of variability would make it unclear what level of responding should represent the effects of the control condition to be compared with the data from an intervention condition. If this kind of variability represented a treatment condition, it would not be clear how the level of responding should be described. In either case, if a baseline or treatment condition was supposed to represent a consistent set of procedures from session to session, this pattern of variability suggests that uncontrolled extraneous factors are at work.

Cyclic Variability. A cyclic pattern of variability is a locally complex pattern of change that, like trends, can sometimes be considered a stable pattern of responding. A cycle is a repeating pattern of local variability that often involves sequences of increasing and decreasing trends (in either order). The highest and lowest values in each cycle define its range, and the time taken from beginning to end is called its period. The periodicity of the cycles may be either regular or unpredictable. Furthermore, the cycles themselves may appear consistently or on an irregular basis. Cycles may be considered stable or unstable in their features, including their form, the level of responding involved, and their frequency of occurrence.

> **Trend.** A relatively consistent change in the data in a single direction.
>
> **Range.** A measure of variability defined by the highest and lowest values in a data set.
>
> **Cyclic variability.** A repeating pattern of local variability, often involving sequences of increasing and decreasing trends.

Cyclic patterns of variation in behavior are not uncommon. Identifying them requires careful measurement and good environmental control, which suggests that they are more likely to be clearly detected under laboratory conditions than field conditions. However, patterns of cyclic responding are sometimes found in applied research and practice. For instance, regularities in environments and activities from one week to another may show up in fairly consistent changes in target behaviors throughout each week. An individual living in a group home who goes home to visit her family each weekend may behave differently on Mondays or Fridays, for example.

Figure 10.5 shows three stylized examples of cyclic patterns of variability. In Panel A, the cycles are regular in their form and frequency of occurrence within each phase. The fact that a number of cycles occur under each condition helps provide a good basis for comparing differences in responding under the two conditions. Panel B shows cyclic variations that are less regular. They still show the same general level of responding throughout the first phase and then a different but consistent level of responding in the second phase. Therefore, the investigator is in a good position to compare responding under the two conditions.

The data in Panel C show the greatest risk associated with cyclic data. In this case, the cyclic character of the data is not recognized, and phase changes happen to correspond to the increasing and decreasing trends defining the cycle. With the advantage of hindsight, it is easy to see that the decrease in responding under the treatment condition might be at least partly due to the factors causing the cycle, rather than the treatment condition alone. This risk is another reason to avoid changing conditions when the data show a clear trend, especially when the expected change in responding is in the opposite direction.

TABLE 10.2
Features of variability

- Trends
- Range
- Cycles

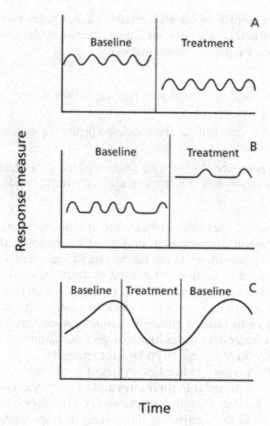

FIG. 10.5. Stylized data showing various cyclic patterns of data.

Criteria

Uses. Deciding when steady state responding has been attained is such a frequent challenge that a variety of informal criteria or rules has evolved to help investigators. There is certainly no denying the importance of the decision because it is not just about whether responding is stable. It is also about whether to continue the present condition unchanged, modify the environment by managing more variables to improve stability, or end the condition and begin the next phase. Furthermore, it is an assessment about whether the effects of each condition have been fully determined and represent its typical influence on the target behavior. The decision is therefore about whether there is a sound basis for comparing that condition to a different condition. Of course, the nature and importance of that judgment are the same for both baseline and treatment conditions.

The function of a decision rule is not necessarily to force identification of steady states as much as it is to help the researcher or practitioner focus on some important considerations. Remember that the decision about when stable responding has been achieved should be guided by the nature of the question, the procedures used in the investigation, and the standards evident in the literature. Sidman (1960) summarized the task nicely:

> The utility of data will depend not on whether ultimate stability has been achieved, but rather on the reliability and validity of the criterion. That is to say, does the criterion select a reproducible and generalizable state of behavior? If it does, experimental manipulation of steady states, as defined by the criterion, will yield data that are orderly and generalizable to other situations. If the steady-state criterion is inadequate, failures to reproduce and to replicate systematically the experimental findings will reveal this fact. (pp. 257–258)

Statistical. One kind of criterion involves a statistical description of variability. This approach usually specifies a limited amount of variability that will be permitted over a certain number of data points. For example, such rules might describe the maximum range for some number of sessions: "No data point may deviate by more than 5% from the median of the last five sessions." Alternatively, they might impose a limit on the difference between the means or ranges of two successive series of sessions: "The means of two consecutive sets of 10 data points may differ by less than 10% of the total range." The possible specifications of this type of rule are nearly endless.

Although the mathematical precision of this type of criterion might seem reassuring, it has some risks. Consider that the degree of variability in the data may well change from one condition to the next. For instance, it is not uncommon for an intervention condition to produce less variability than what was observed under a prior control condition. In that case, it is possible that a fixed criterion would select good stability in one phase but would be too easily met in another phase. That might not allow for sufficient exposure to the second set of conditions.

For example, consider an intervention procedure designed to build particular verbal skills in a child diagnosed with autism spectrum disorder. Suppose that a baseline condition with fairly variable data was followed by a training condition that generated much less variable responding. A stability rule that ended each phase after a period of reasonably stable responding might lead to a decision to terminate the training condition before its effects on responding are fully developed. That suggests that investigators who decide to use a statistical criterion of stability should not do so blindly. They will need to remain alert to the need to adjust the criterion if the circumstances warrant.

Graphical. The most popular approach to stability criteria is based on ongoing visual inspection of graphically displayed data. This preference avoids the risky commitments of statistical rules in favor of thoughtful judgments. These intentionally subjective judgments involve carefully studying the evolving graphical picture of variability in a phase as each new data point is added. Researchers and practitioners look at the characteristics of variability in their data and wait until their professional history tells them when stability has been attained. We might call this type of criterion the Supreme

Court standard: "I can't tell you in advance what it is, but I'll know it when I see it."[1]

It would be a mistake to view this kind of criterion as less demanding than the statistical approach just because it does not involve an *a priori* mathematical statement. For well-trained investigators, this graphical approach is more sophisticated than a quantitative rule, and it may yield a more meaningful picture of stable responding. Researchers and practitioners using a graphical standard should be able to specify each aspect of the data they are considering and why those features might be important.

Figure 10.6 shows data in baseline and intervention phases that illustrate this approach to steady state criteria. It may again be helpful to put a piece of paper over the graph and uncover the data points from left to right (in chronological sequence) one at a time. The early data points labeled *a* in the baseline phase show a sharp decreasing trend, so there should be no temptation to describe them as stable. As the data labeled *b* are fully revealed, we see that was a wise decision because an increasing trend becomes unmistakable. Additional data points (labeled *c*) tend to fall mostly in the upper end of the overall range. However, we keep finding an occasional low value, which should make us a bit concerned about the influence of extraneous factors. That might even prompt an effort to identify and control the suspected factors. Finally, we see more data points (labeled *d*) in the upper part of the range, though with no lower values intruding. Perhaps most importantly, those values show no further evidence of the increasing trend. We might find the data labeled *d* indicative of an adequate steady state of responding.

The intervention phase begins with a relatively rapid decreasing trend (labeled *e*), which "bottoms out" at a lower level than was seen under the stable portion of the baseline phase *(d)*. If we had reason to expect that the intervention would produce a decrease in responding, we might be tempted to assume that these data represent the effects of the intervention. However, by continuing to collect data we see that the data labeled *f* show an increasing trend. As we see the data points labeled *g*, however, it becomes clear that the trend has "topped out" and responding has become relatively stable. In sum, the successive values in each phase show some local trends that eventually end in a series of relatively stable values. In hindsight, it is easy to see that neither phase provided a picture of stable responding until the last ten or so values were obtained. Even without the benefit of hindsight, the data in each phase show enough evidence of a trend or outlying values to encourage the investigator to continue the phase a bit longer and look for – or even work toward – a clearer picture of stability.

Non-data. Investigators often face limits on the amount of time available to complete a project. The limiting factors might be participants who will only be available for a certain time, restrictions on access to a setting, pressure to

[1] Based on the well-known statement of Justice Potter Stewart in his concurring opinion in the Supreme Court's pornography decision in Jacobellis v. Ohio, 1964.

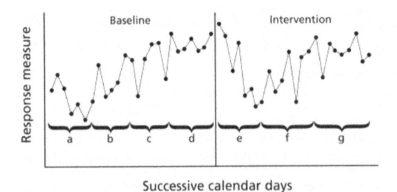

FIG. 10.6. Data illustrating the complexity of decisions required by graphical steady state criteria.

move quickly to a treatment condition that will resolve clinical problems, or financial constraints, among others. In such situations, it may be necessary to set advance restrictions on the number of sessions for each of the planned phases of a study. For instance, this might mean allotting ten days for a control or baseline phase, three weeks for an intervention phase, and so on.

In such circumstances, each phase lasts a pre-determined number of sessions. We can call this a non-data criterion because it is based on considerations that have nothing to do with the nature of the data obtained under each condition: each phase is terminated without regard for what the data reveal about responding. Even though responding might be unstable in some way throughout a phase, the next condition would be implemented because the schedule requires it. That often results in a weak basis for comparing the effects of control and intervention conditions.

Although using non-data criteria to decide when to change phases is risky, there is no denying that investigators might sometimes find it necessary to keep phases brief. That may be particularly true for practitioners, given that clinical outcomes may often be a higher priority than methodological niceties. The ideal solution is to try to resist the factors that encourage compromising sound methodological standards. If it is not feasible to resolve those pressures, the investigator may need to consider whether the planned investigation can be conducted successfully under the circumstances. At the least, it is important to be especially cautious in drawing conclusions about the effects of treatment procedures. Without a reasonably clear picture of stable responding that represents the full effects of each condition, it may be better

TABLE 10.3
Types of steady state criteria

- Statistical
- Graphical
- Non-data

---

to only describe the evident changes than to confidently conclude what caused them.

Establishing Stable Responding

It is easy for discussions of the steady state strategy to create the impression that obtaining stable responding is largely a matter of being patient. It might seem that all an investigator has to do is continue a phase long enough and eventually acceptably stable data will accumulate. Sometimes that passive approach does indeed work. For example, unwanted variability may be due to the effects of the previous condition "wearing off" or the effects of the present condition becoming fully established. In those situations, simply continuing a phase until the transitions are complete may yield satisfactory stability.

On the other hand, excessive variability may result from poor control over the procedures defining a condition or from uncontrolled extraneous factors. Merely continuing the phase will not usually resolve such problems. Specific efforts to strengthen or stabilize the effects of the factors that are supposed to be operating or to control the effects of extraneous influences will probably be required. Ongoing data collection will then reveal whether those efforts were successful in producing a clearer picture of responding.

Establishing stable responding can sometimes be challenging and time-consuming. When that is the case, it is important to avoid the temptation to manipulate data in ways that imply a level of stability that has not actually been achieved. As an illustration, the three panels in Figure 10.7 show how combining data over different units of time affects the resulting picture of variability. All three graphs are based on the same values collected over a two-month period. When the values are combined into monthly averages (Panel A), the two data points are similar, suggesting good stability. When the same data are averaged on a weekly basis (Panel B), we can see that they indicate an upward trend followed by a downward trend. When the data are displayed on a daily scale (Panel C), the weekly trends are again evident. However, the daily time unit also reveals a weekly cycle in which Monday and Friday values tend to be higher than the other days of the week. These three displays show very different pictures of the variability in the same data set. It is easy to appreciate that the display in Panel A would be misleading as a description of stability, given the information revealed by the same data when displayed over smaller units of time as in Panels B and C.

TRANSITIONS

Transition States

Any sequence of data points representing a target behavior that we accept as indicating a steady state is necessarily preceded or followed by a series of

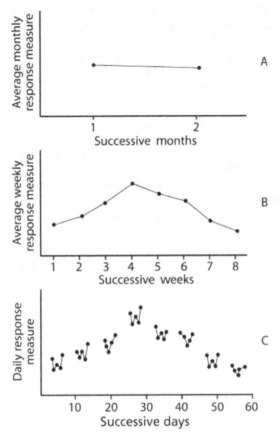

FIG. 10.7. Graphs showing the effects of combining data over different units of time on displayed variability.

values that are unstable in some way. In order to identify when responding is stable, we must therefore be able to identify when it is not stable. When responding is changing in ways that do not represent a steady state, it may be described as being in transition. One kind of transition is called a **transition state**. In transition states, responding is changing from one steady state to a different steady state. We are especially familiar with transition states because they often result from giving an individual experience with one condition for a number of sessions and then switching to a different condition. Measures of a target behavior that settle into a relatively stable pattern under the first condition are typically disturbed by the change in circumstances, though they often stabilize in a different steady state that presumably represents the influence of the new condition.

Given an emphasis on steady states that represent the impact of prevailing conditions, it might seem that investigators might not be especially interested in transition states. When they follow a change from one condition to the next, transition states reflect an expected mixture of influences from the old and new conditions. Because the investigator is typically interested in identifying the effects of each condition alone, the transitional interlude would seem to be a distraction.

In fact, understanding what makes behavior change and what these changes look like is a central focus of behavior analytic research and important to practical interests as well. After all, the overarching agenda for both researchers and practitioners is to create predictable changes in target behaviors. Identifying changes is a matter of understanding when behavior is in transition. When stable responding is disturbed following a switch from one condition to another and then a new kind of steady state is eventually reestablished, we may have a picture of the behavioral changes associated with the switch. Although the before and after steady states are important indicators of the effects of the two conditions, we should be no less interested in the kind of changes in responding that were produced by switching conditions. In other words, the steady states preceding and following the switch are not the only effects of changing conditions. The effects of following one condition with a new condition include the transition just as much as the steady state that eventually emerges.

Figure 10.8 shows a schematic representation of different kinds of transitions that might result from changing from one condition to another. In each

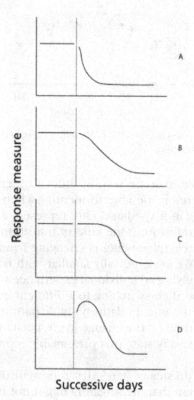

FIG. 10.8. Schematic representation showing different types of transitions resulting from introducing a new condition.

example, the level of steady state responding in the first and second conditions is the same, thereby highlighting differences in transitional responding at the beginning of the second phase. In Panel A, the transition between the two steady states begins as soon as the second condition starts and quickly terminates in the new steady state. In contrast, Panel B shows a transitional pattern between the two steady states that is slower or more gradual. Panel C shows a transition that does not start for some time after the second condition begins. The transition in Panel D is unlike the others in that a temporary increase in responding occurs before the decrease that ends in a lower steady state. Depending on the features of the investigation, including the nature of target behaviors and the details of the two conditions, such differences in transitional responding may be no less important than the fact that changing from the first to the second condition eventually resulted in a decrease in responding.

Transition states do not only follow changes in the environment initiated by the investigator. Extraneous variables can lead to behavioral changes at any time during a phase that terminates in a different level of responding. Such transitions can be mistaken for the effects of treatment conditions, so it is important to describe them fully. If an unanticipated transition state appears well after an existing condition has begun, for example, it may be wise to suspect an extraneous influence. For example, if a provider agency assigned a therapist to work with a child diagnosed with autism spectrum disorder who was unfamiliar to the child, the change would be considered an extraneous variable. Even if the new therapist followed the same treatment protocol as the previous therapist, it would not be surprising if the switch resulted in systematic changes in target behaviors and a new level of stable responding.

Figure 10.9 shows an example of this situation. Responding increases immediately following the start of the second phase, suggesting that in this instance

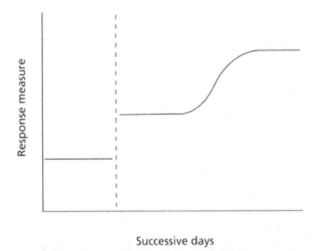

FIG. 10.9.   Data showing a transition state occurring well after the implementation of a new condition.

there may not be a gradual transition following the change in conditions. However, well after the new phase is underway, responding abruptly increases further and eventually levels off. The transition state is a problem because it is now unclear whether it is a delayed effect of the new condition or the result of some extraneous factor that happened to occur at that point. Because the data provide no basis for answering that question, we do not know whether the real effect of the new condition is reflected by the level of responding at the beginning or at the end of the second phase. One way to resolve this dilemma is to identify and eliminate the suspected extraneous factor and see what happens to responding. It may even be necessary to rerun the two phases again.

Transitory States

We have so far considered transitions from steady state responding that eventually result in a different steady state. Transitional patterns may instead end in a return to the original level or pattern of responding, however. These are called **transitory states**. Such temporary deviations from stable responding are common in research projects, despite efforts to hold conditions constant, and they are routine in intervention projects conducted in everyday settings where it may be very difficult to avoid or control extraneous events.

> **Transition state.** A pattern of responding involving change from one steady state to a different steady state.
>
> **Transitory state.** A pattern of responding involving a deviation from a steady state that ends in a return to the same steady state.

Distinguishing between transition states and transitory states is very important. In one case (transition states), changes in responding result in a different level of responding than before. In the other case (transitory states), changes in responding return to the original level of responding. If one was mistaken for the other, it might lead to misunderstanding the effects of an intervention.

Here is one way that can happen. Although transitory states often result from extraneous factors that occur during a phase, they can also be the outcome of treatment conditions. An investigator may expect an intervention not only to change an individual's behavior but also to maintain that new level of responding as long as the condition is present. However, it may be that the impact of the intervention is only temporary. An initial change in responding may dissipate, eventually leaving responding at the level that existed before the condition was introduced. That kind of change in responding is temporary – a transitory state.

In such situations, it is critical to determine whether the initial change in responding was going to lead to a new steady state or back to the one that was observed before the condition was implemented. If measurement for some reason only captured the initial change, we would not know whether

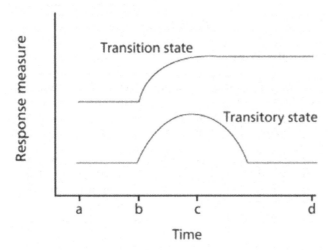

FIG. 10.10. Schematic representation of transition and transitory states.

the effect of the intervention was durable or temporary – a very important distinction. Figure 10.10 shows a schematic representation of this scenario as well as what can be done to avoid confusion. The initial steady states (between *a* and *b*) and transitions (between *b* and *c*) are the same for both functions. At Point *c*, the investigator cannot tell which type of transition is happening. In order to find out, the phase must be continued until at least Point *d*, at which time we can see that stable responding has developed in both cases, though at different levels. If the condition that started at Point *b* was terminated at Point *c* – for instance, if that is where the investigation ended – we would not know whether the transition presumably induced by the new condition resulted in a durable change in the target behavior or only a temporary change. In other words, any conclusion about the effect of that condition might be wrong and the investigator would not know it. That is one reason it is so important to obtain stable responding under each of the conditions being compared.

Identification

Identifying transition and transitory states is a matter of identifying the steady states immediately prior to and following the transition. The frequency with which measurement occurs can affect how well an investigator is able to describe the transition and distinguish it from the surrounding steady states. The more often responding is measured during a transition, the more precisely the transition's boundaries can be described.

Figure 10.11 illustrates this point. The three panels show the same hypothetical transition, but the features of the transition depend on how often measurements were made. The infrequent measurement shown in Panel A suggests that responding simply jumped to a higher level of responding by the second data point in the new condition. The increased frequency of measurement in Panel B begins to capture the true form of the transition. However, that picture fails to locate the point at which stable responding reappears because the last two data points indicate an ongoing downward trend. The data in Panel C remedy that shortcoming because the frequency of measurement is sufficient to provide a full picture of the transition and to identify its end points.

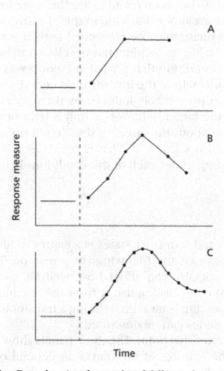

FIG. 10.11. Data showing the results of different frequencies of measurement during a transition state.

Making Phase Change Decisions

We have already emphasized the general risks in deciding to change from one condition to another when responding is unstable. There are some special cases of this scenario that warrant discussion. The examples in Figure 10.12 represent situations in which it may be tempting to change phases even though stable responding has not been obtained. It may again be useful to look at these graphs by covering the graph with a piece of paper and gradually sliding it from left to right, uncovering new data points one at a time.

Panel A shows an increasing trend in the first phase followed by a continuation of this trend in the second phase. If there was some reason to expect that the second condition would lead to an increase in responding, it might be tempting to conclude that this new condition produced an increase in responding. Although a new condition might initially produce a transition like this, we should be concerned that the trend actually started during the first condition. Because the investigator is trying to hold the features of each condition constant throughout each phase, it is reasonable to guess that the initial trend is the result of uncontrolled extraneous factors. Those factors are likely to be unknown; otherwise the investigator would presumably have tried to minimize their influence. If they are unknown, there would be no basis for assuming that their influences ceased when the second phase was started. That means they could be responsible for the continuing trend in the second phase, which would raise doubts about the contribution of the condition itself. In other words, the data in Panel A cannot support a conclusion that the increased responding in the second phase is due to the variables defining that condition.

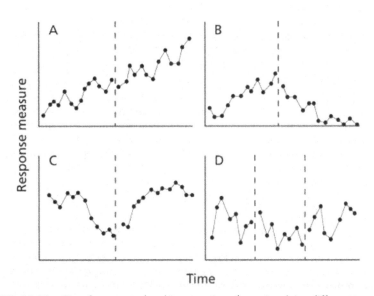

FIG. 10.12.   Data from control and intervention phases involving different types of instability.

Panel B shows a similar increasing trend in the first phase and a contrasting downward trend in the second phase. That change in responding associated with the second condition might seem to allow a clear basis for attributing the change to the new condition. Although that might seem a reasonable assumption, it is not exactly what the investigator should be trying to learn. The real question is not whether an intervention can change behavior but what kind of effects the condition produces *by itself*. The problem here is actually the same as in Panel A. Because the investigator does not know what extraneous factors are operating in the first condition, there is no reason to assume that they suddenly disappeared in the second condition. The proper interpretation of the data in the second phase is that they may represent the effects of the condition plus the extraneous variables that produced the trend in the first phase. That is, the investigator does not know what responding in the second phase would have looked like without the contribution of the extraneous factors.

In the first phase of Panel C, a higher cluster of values is followed by a lower cluster. Responding then increases in the second phase, terminating at about the same level as the higher cluster of values in the first phase. As in Panels A and B, this increase in the second phase could reflect (a) the influence of the unknown variables that produced the changes in responding in the first phase, (b) the impact of the new condition by itself, or (c) an interaction of those two influences. The data do not support one alternative over the other.

BOX 10.3

How Long Should Each Phase Last?

By now you should realize this is not the right question. You should also know that no general answer in terms of a certain number of sessions can be correct. If there is any rule, it is only that phases should last until satisfactory stability has been obtained. The level of stability that is necessary depends on the unique features of each project. For each investigation, the standards in the existing literature, the nature of the question, the features of the response class, the details of measurement procedures selected, and the characteristics of control and intervention conditions are all factors that should be considered.

Notice that this list does not include the difficulty of obtaining stable responding. It is certainly true that some projects provide insurmountable limitations on the investigator's ability to engineer stable responding. However, those challenges do not lessen the value of the steady state strategy. Neither do they reduce the risks of proceeding without them.

Finally, it is important to understand that obtaining stable responding is not merely a "ticket" to the next phase, like touching each of the bases on your way to home plate in order to get a home run. Getting stable responding is part of the larger strategy of obtaining in an effort to get a sample of responding that fully represents the effects of each condition. That information allows comparisons between conditions that have a good chance of being both reliable and general.

Finally, Panel D shows three phases containing relatively variable data that overlap a good bit across conditions. Although the values in the second phase are lower overall than in the other two conditions, the decrease is modest. The level of variability across the three phases begs for not only a greater number of observations under each condition, but also for efforts to either reduce variability or strengthen the effects of the intervention, if not both. Efforts to reduce variability in the target behavior need not focus only on controlling extraneous factors. Sometimes the best solution is to reconsider the general conditions under which the project is being conducted that affect responding throughout control and intervention phases. It may be that those circumstances involve too many extraneous influences or one powerful extraneous factor that is not easily managed. Such factors may be part of the setting itself, which is not uncommon in applied research or clinical practice. For example, there may be too many things going on in a preschool playroom to provide a stable picture of a target behavior. Sometimes extraneous factors are even associated with the procedures that are set up to evaluate changes in the target behavior. For example, if the preparation requires child peers to behave in particular ways in the playroom and it is not possible to ensure that their behavior is consistent within or across phases, there may be so much variability in the target behavior that the effects of the treatment procedure cannot be clearly seen. Finally, another option for reducing excessive variability is to reconsider the full array of measurement decisions that reflect changes in the target behavior. Adjusting how the behavior is defined, which dimensions are selected, and how observation and recording are conducted can have a big influence on variability in the data.

Upcoming chapters will more fully explain why the steady state strategy is the heart of within-subject, single-subject, or small-N research designs. It is the foundation for drawing conclusions about whether and why a target behavior changed when conditions changed over the course of a research or clinical project. Conclusions about what might be responsible for changes in the target behavior when baseline and treatment conditions switch are weakened to the extent that stable responding is not achieved under each of the conditions.

CHAPTER SUMMARY

1. The steady state strategy involves measuring responding for each participant repeatedly under both control and intervention conditions, with the objective of obtaining a stable pattern of responding that represents the full effects of each condition.

2. By providing repeated exposure to the baseline and then treatment condition, we are attempting to get a graphical picture of that behavior under each condition that is complete and representative.

3. Stable responding across sessions is a strong indication that the data fully represent the effects of that condition and that the contribution of extraneous variables is minimal or at least constant.

4. Clinical considerations might seem to take precedent over steady state criteria in making decisions about when to change conditions. If they do, however, the practitioner will not be in a strong position to assert that the client's behavior changes were due to the treatment procedures rather than other events.

5. A steady or stable state of responding may be defined as a pattern of responding that shows relatively little variation in the dimension(s) of interest over some period of time. Exactly how much variability or what patterns of variability are required to describe responding as stable or unstable will vary from one research project or practical intervention to another.

6. The steady state strategy is valuable because of how it guides decision-making as a project progresses. This benefit begins by helping the investigator evaluate prior decisions about how the target behavior is defined and measured.

7. It is important to remember that even though the behavioral dimension being measured may be stable, it does not mean that the other dimensions that are not being measured are also stable. Likewise, just because some aspect of responding is stable, one should not conclude that the environment is also stable. A relatively consistent pattern of responding can result from a mix of changing variables whose net effect is stable responding.

8. The steady state strategy is also valuable because it encourages the investigator to repeatedly measure the target behavior across a number of sessions, which helps to capture all of the changes that might be characteristic of the condition.

9. The steady state strategy creates a good opportunity to detect the influence of unsystematic extraneous influences. If the impact of extraneous factors comes and goes from session to session, variability in responding may hint at their presence under an otherwise stable condition.

10. Drawing conclusions about the effects of an intervention condition that have a good chance of being true depends on how well the effects of both control and intervention conditions can be described and understood. By repeatedly measuring the target behavior under each condition, it helps identify both the initial and ongoing patterns of responding in each phase. These data encourage efforts to manage extraneous variables, which helps minimize their influence and clarify the effects of the primary features of each condition.

11. There are at least three reasons to worry about trends that have no obvious explanation. First, a trend means that something is influencing behavior in significant ways, and its effects might interfere with getting a clear picture of the impact of the conditions of primary interest. Second, when we are unaware of what is causing a trend, it is not clear how we might more effectively control the environment so as to eliminate its influence. Third, trends make it difficult to determine the effects of an intervention.

12. Deciding when steady state responding has been attained is not just about whether responding is stable; it is about whether to continue the present condition unchanged, modify the environment to improve stability, or end the condition and begin the next phase. Ultimately, it is a decision about whether there is a sound basis for comparing one condition to another condition.

13. There are several ways to aid determining if stability has been met. Statistical criteria usually specify a limited amount of variability that will be permitted over a certain number of data points. Although the mathematical precision of this type of criterion might seem reassuring, investigators need to remain alert to the need to adjust the criterion if the circumstances warrant.

14. The most popular approach to stability criteria is based on ongoing visual inspection of graphically displayed data. This approach requires the investigator to be able to specify each aspect of the data they are considering and why those features might be important.

15. It might seem that all an investigator has to do is continue a phase long enough so that eventually stable responding will occur. This approach may be sufficient; however, excessive variability may result from poor control over the procedures in a phase or extraneous variables. Simply continuing the phase will not usually resolve such problems.

16. Distinguishing between transition states and transitory states is important. In one case (transition states), changes in responding result in a different level of responding than before. In the other case (transitory states), changes in responding return to the original level of responding. If one was mistaken for the other, it might lead to misunderstanding the effects of an intervention.

17. Identifying transition and transitory states is a matter of identifying the steady states immediately prior to and following the transition. The frequency with which measurement occurs can affect how well an investigator is able to describe the transition and distinguish it from the surrounding steady states. The more often responding is measured during a transition, the more precisely the transition's boundaries can be described.

HIGHLIGHTED TERMS

Cyclic variability. A repeating pattern of local variability, often involving sequences of increasing and decreasing trends.

Range. A measure of variability defined by the highest and lowest values in a data set.

Steady state. A pattern of responding that shows relatively little variation in the dimension(s) of interest over some period of time.

Steady state strategy. An approach to making comparisons between the effects of two conditions on a target behavior that involves repeatedly measuring an individual's responding under each condition. It is essential for assessing and managing extraneous influences in order to get stable patterns of responding that represent the full effects of each condition.

Transition state. A pattern of responding involving change from one steady state to a different steady state.

Transitory state. A pattern of responding involving a deviation from a steady state that ends in a return to the same steady state.

Trend. A relatively consistent change in the data in a single direction.

TEXT STUDY GUIDE

1. Why should an investigator collect repeated measures of responding under a condition?
2. What do you need to know about responding under each of two conditions in order to compare their effects?
3. What do unstable data say about the role of extraneous variables?
4. What do stable data generally say about the role of extraneous variables?
5. What are two particular conclusions that stable responding allows?
6. Explain the steady state strategy.
7. How do the circumstances of researchers and practitioners compare in regards to the steady state strategy?
8. What is a steady state?
9. What does it mean to say that the meaning of the term "steady" in the phrase steady state is relative?
10. What can you not say about responding when the data show a steady state?
11. What does stable responding say about the environmental conditions under which it occurred?
12. Explain how stable data allow the investigator to evaluate measurement decisions.
13. How does the steady state strategy reveal the effects of a condition?
14. How does the effort to obtain stable responding under each phase help the investigator evaluate extraneous influences?
15. Explain how the steady state strategy facilitates comparisons.
16. What is a trend?
17. What are three reasons why an investigator should be concerned about trends in the data that have no obvious explanation?
18. Under what conditions can trends be considered stable responding?
19. Define range. How is it relevant to steady state decisions?

20. What is a cycle? Under what conditions might cycles be considered steady states?
21. Explain the following statement: The usefulness of a data set depends on the reliability and validity of the criterion that defines its stability.
22. What are the pros and cons of statistical steady state criteria?
23. Why can it be said that graphic steady state criteria are more complex and potentially more useful than statistical criteria?
24. What are the risks of using non-data steady state criteria?
25. What does it mean to say that obtaining stable responding is an active rather than a passive process?
26. Distinguish between transition and transitory states.
27. How do you identify transition states?
28. Why is it important to distinguish between transition and transitory states?
29. What are the consequences of introducing a new condition when responding is unstable?

BOX STUDY GUIDE

1. What are the differences in the resulting data of measuring one participant many times versus many participants a few times?
2. How does choice between measuring one participant many times versus many participants a few times relate to the fundamental nature of behavior?
3. Why can it help to look at a series of data points one at a time in sequence?
4. How long should each phase last?

SUGGESTED READINGS

Sidman, M. (1960). *Tactics of scientific research*. New York: Basic Books. Chapter 8: Steady states.
Sidman, M. (1960). *Tactics of scientific research*. New York: Basic Books. Chapter 9: Steady states (continued).
Sidman, M. (1960). *Tactics of scientific research*. New York: Basic Books. Chapter 10: Transition states.

DISCUSSION TOPICS

1. Discuss why practitioners should be cautious about drawing conclusions about why their treatment procedures were effective in changing a client's behavior.

2. Using articles published in behavioral journals, select a graphed data set representing a single phase that contains at least 20 values. Present the data points one at a time and have others decide exactly when they believe stable responding has been displayed. Discuss the factors they considered in reaching their decisions.

EXERCISES

1. Using articles published in behavioral journals, find examples of graphed data sets for individual phases in which the data suggest the presence of uncontrolled extraneous influences.

2. Using articles published in behavioral journals, find graphed data sets from individual phases that exemplify different patterns of values across sessions that reveal trends.

3. Using articles published in behavioral journals, find graphed data sets from individual phases that exemplify different patterns of variability in range.

4. Using articles published in behavioral journals, find graphed data sets from individual phases that exemplify cyclic variability.

5. Using articles published in behavioral journals focusing on basic research (e.g., *Journal of the Experimental Analysis of Behavior*), find examples of statistical rules used to define stable responding. See if you can find similar examples in more applied focused journals.

CHAPTER ELEVEN

Designing Behavioral Comparisons

HOW COMPARISONS WORK

Control and Experimental Conditions

The previous chapter explained how the steady state strategy provides a representative picture of an individual's behavior under each phase or condition. Ongoing measurement can be made into a formal experiment by arranging two different types of phases so their effects on a target behavior can be compared. When the factors that make up a phase are not the specific focus of the researcher's interest, it is called a **control** or **baseline condition**. In other words, in this type of condition the independent variable is not present.

Baseline or control conditions serve as background or context for looking at the effects of another type of condition or phase called an **experimental**, **treatment**, or **independent variable condition**. In this type of condition, the independent variable is present. The **independent variable** is made up of environmental events the investigator has arranged in order to see how they might affect the target behavior. The particular target behavior being measured serves as the **dependent variable**. It is called the dependent variable because what happens with it depends on the independent variable controlled by the investigator.

> **Control or baseline condition.** A condition or phase of an experiment in which the independent variable is not present.
>
> **Experimental, treatment, intervention, or independent variable condition.** A condition or phase in which the independent variable is present.
>
> **Independent variable.** An environmental event whose presence or absence is manipulated by the investigator in order to determine its effects on the dependent variable.
>
> **Dependent variable.** In behavior analytic research, usually a response class, at least one dimension of which is measured throughout all phases of a study.
>
> **Experimental (research) design.** Arrangements of control and experimental conditions that permit comparisons that help identify the effects of the independent variable on the dependent variable.

In other words, the objective in an experiment is to determine the effects on the target behavior of an experimental or treatment condition containing the independent variable compared to the effects of a control condition that is otherwise the same but does not include the independent variable. The reason for making this comparison is to be sure that the changes in responding observed when the treatment condition is present are solely the result of the variables of interest in the treatment phase. **Experimental** or **research designs** are ways of arranging control and treatment conditions to permit comparisons that help isolate the effects of the independent variable on the dependent variable. Because the research or practical question typically asks about the effects of the independent variable, this information should help answer the question.

Experimental Reasoning

Identifying the effects of the independent variable in a research study or a practical project requires making sure that the only thing that differs between a treatment or intervention condition and its matching control condition is the independent variable itself. In other words, the treatment and control conditions should be as similar as possible, except that the independent variable is present only during the treatment condition. When that is the case, the only way to explain differences in the target behavior under the two conditions is in terms of the presence or absence of the independent variable.

As an example, consider a project focusing on the impact of a procedure intended to decrease the occurrence of hand mouthing by Ella, a child with Down syndrome, in a preschool setting. The basic preparation involves measuring the occurrence of hand mouthing during group free play sessions, which are scheduled two or three times each day. The free play sessions involve the same basic features from one day to another. Because the investigator is not asking about the impact of any specific feature of these free play sessions, they serve as a control or baseline condition. After measuring the occurrence of Ella's mouthing during a number of these sessions, the investigator has a good picture of what the behavior looks like under those circumstances. The investigator then initiates an intervention or treatment phase in which an aide prompts Ella to play with a toy that requires both hands to operate and produces brief musical tones that Ella enjoys (differential reinforcement of incompatible behavior). This phase continues the same general free play preparation but includes a new feature relating to the target behavior. As measurement continues from session to session under these modified conditions, a picture emerges of any changes in Ella's hand mouthing. Finally, as a further step in comparing responding under these two conditions, the investigator repeats both the initial control phase and then the intervention phase as well. These additional comparisons help answer the question of whether any changes in hand mouthing following the shift from the baseline to the treatment condition the first time would be found if the comparison was repeated.

Figure 11.1 shows measures of the target behavior across these four phases. We can see that the target behavior consistently occurred less often when the intervention condition was in effect. The figure also describes the conditions present in each phase. Because the free play circumstances were the same across all four phases, the only apparent explanation for the changes in the target behavior is the treatment procedure implemented during each session in the intervention phases. This interpretation is defensible only if the free play sessions are essentially the same throughout both control and

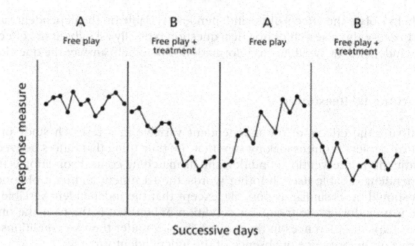

FIG. 11.1. Data showing responding under successive control and treatment conditions.

intervention phases. In other words, the treatment procedure should be the only significant change in the environment that could explain changes in the target behavior.

If free play sessions had systematically changed in some other way during the intervention phases (such as more teacher aides being present), it would be possible that this extraneous factor could have contributed to changes in Ella's hand mouthing. The problem is that we would not know if the decreases in responding in the treatment phases were due to the treatment procedure, the fact that more adults were present, or both. If we concluded that the changes were the result of the treatment procedure, we might be right, but we might also be partly or even entirely wrong. This risk is why it is important that control and intervention conditions differ only in the presence of the independent variable. This basic reasoning underlies all experimentation in science.

PLANNING RESEARCH AND PRACTICAL INVESTIGATIONS

Elements of Behavioral Comparisons

Independent Variable Condition. We often discuss the independent variable as if it is a single, narrow feature of the environment. In some laboratory studies, that may be the case. For instance, an investigator may be interested in the effects of changing the schedule of reinforcement. Under the control condition, an animal might be receiving reinforcers on a fixed ratio 3 schedule (reinforcer delivered after every 3 responses), and implementing the treatment condition might then involve nothing more than changing the schedule (e.g., to variable ratio 3). The independent variable is simply the new reinforcement schedule.

In most behavior analytic studies, however, the independent variable is a mix of different features. That is especially likely to be the case in applied research and practice. For example, in a project looking at methods of training staff members, the independent variable presented in the intervention phase may incorporate verbal instruction of skills to be learned, modeling of those skills, role-playing, and video feedback – all delivered as a coordinated intervention package. When the investigator's interest lies in the collective effects of multiple variables, it is still appropriate to refer to them collectively as the independent variable.

It may seem that the independent variable is usually something that is added to the baseline preparation of the control condition. Instead, the independent variable may involve merely changing some factor in the baseline procedures. In the earlier example of a laboratory study of the effects of different reinforcement schedules, the new schedule used in the experimental condition is not so much a matter of adding something to the baseline procedures as changing one of the baseline variables. Similarly, the independent variable may involve removing a variable in the baseline preparation. That might be the case when an investigator is interested in evaluating the effects on the target behavior of eliminating a particular feature of a procedure.

For example, consider a study examining various features of a group contingency designed to minimize disruptive behavior of students in an elementary classroom setting. The procedure may involve a number of elements, including announcement of the contingencies, dividing the class into teams, a point system with certain values, and the consequences associated with various point outcomes. The study may begin with the group contingency procedure in place, and experimental phases may systematically manipulate some of those components. Working with the teacher, the investigator may revise the point system, drop the team component, or change the consequences. Any such changes constitute an independent variable.

The matter of how the independent variable is defined is more important than it might seem. After all, its effects are what the investigator will be drawing conclusions about. Especially in applied projects, it is easiest to say that the independent variable consists of everything that is going on during sessions throughout the treatment condition. That means that the independent variable includes not only the actual protocol implemented during the phase but also any associated factors that might accompany it, as well as any unrelated or unplanned influences that happen to occur. As long as those factors are identified and fully included along with the treatment protocol as possible explanations for changes in responding, such a broad definition is perfectly reasonable. The key is that the investigator and anyone else who uses the study's findings must be fully aware of the variables that were responsible for the effects observed under the treatment condition. Obviously it would be misleading if the investigator attributed the results to the treatment protocol but failed to acknowledge the contribution of other factors.

What other factors might be important? Remember that any features of the intervention condition that are not included in the description of the independent variable are, by definition, extraneous to the investigator's primary interests. Extraneous factors include not only all of the features of the control condition that continue throughout the treatment phase but also any other influences that occur during the treatment condition. In principle, we can put aside those factors that are merely a continuation of the baseline condition. Many features of the control or baseline condition influence responding, but they continue unchanged throughout the treatment condition and presumably have no differential influence between conditions. In the study on staff training, for example, the baseline procedures might include the staff members themselves, their training curricula, the training targets they are working on, the consumers they are training, the setting in which training takes place, and the procedures used to measure the behaviors of staff members and consumers. All of those variables operate throughout both baseline and intervention phases and provide the context for implementing the package of factors making up the independent variable.

The real challenge is to identify variables that are present only during the treatment phase but that the investigator might not wish to consider as part of the treatment protocol itself. One category of such variables includes what might be described as side effects or extensions of the protocol. For instance, a protocol that involved getting parents to use specific instructional procedures with their child with autism might lead them to interact with the child differently outside of training sessions, which in turn might improve the effectiveness of the instructional protocol. That would probably be considered a bonus clinically, but it would be important to acknowledge its possible contribution, which might not occur for every family. A second category includes factors that are unrelated to the treatment protocol, such as significant changes in the treatment setting, a participant's health, or the performance of project personnel.

Identifying and weighing the contribution of these two kinds of extraneous influences is especially difficult for investigators because of the understandable focus on the protocol at the heart of the independent variable. The problem with failing to recognize such influences is that their role is by default unknowingly allocated to the independent variable, which may then misrepresent its importance in explaining the data. As a result, the investigator and others may be disappointed when they use the findings under other circumstances and fail to get the expected outcomes. In sum, deciding exactly what is included in the definition of the independent variable is important because of how it guides interpretation of the data (see Chapter 16). Simply accepting everything that goes on during treatment phase sessions as equally relevant and important in explaining the data – especially without distinguishing between the independent variable and extraneous variables that are along for the ride – is a convenient but risky option.

Control Condition. There are two jobs a control or baseline condition must do. First, it must establish the conditions under which participants will behave. The control condition defines the basic preparation for a study or a practical intervention. In the earlier example concerning staff training, it includes the participants, target behaviors, the general setting, the features of the environment that make up the circumstances of the project and provide a context for identifying any effects of the independent variable, and the measurement procedures required to collect data. The investigator either selects such features or is willing to accept those about which there is no choice. The objective guiding decisions about what will make up a control condition is to help identify the effects of the independent variable. All of the decisions involved in determining the characteristics of the control condition must result in a preparation that generates responding by participants that will be sensitive to any effects of the independent variable when it is introduced.

The risk is that some decisions about the control condition might actually make it difficult to detect effects of the independent variable. For example, in a project aimed at evaluating a classroom intervention procedure, targeting out-of-seat behavior could be a poor choice because powerful reinforcement of the behavior by peers might exert strong control and make it difficult to detect the effects of an academic intervention. In that case, the target behavior might not be sensitive to the intervention procedure serving as the independent variable. Selecting a different behavior might be more likely to reveal the effects of the intervention procedure. As a further example, the decision to measure out-of-seat behavior at a particular time of day (for instance, before recess) might lead to data that do not represent intervention effects that would be observed at other times (such as after lunch). These examples suggest that the control condition, which serves as the context for studying the influence of the independent variable, should be constructed with great care.

As we have emphasized, the control or baseline condition should run throughout its associated experimental or treatment condition. Because it is the foundation for the procedural changes required by the independent variable and detecting the resulting changes in the target behavior, the investigator should design the control condition and its associated treatment condition as a matched pair. This leads to an important question about the second task that a control condition must accomplish: What does it control for? The control condition controls for all of those factors in the intervention condition that are *not* part of the independent variable. This means that in evaluating the effects of the independent variable all of the background factors included in the control condition are eliminated from consideration. If the factors making up the control condition continue unchanged throughout the treatment condition, they cannot explain any changes in the target behavior that occur during the treatment condition. That is, they are controlled for.

TABLE 11.1
Functions of the control condition

- Establish general circumstances under which participants will behave
- Control for factors in the experimental condition that are not part of the independent variable

---

This is why each different experimental or treatment condition should be matched to its own control condition. In a study that includes two different independent variable or treatment conditions, each must be uniquely matched to its own baseline condition that serves the necessary control function. For example, consider a project examining the effects of reinforcement contingencies on the behavior of patients recovering from cardiac surgery who are supposed to comply with exercise routines as part of a hospital rehabilitation program. Aside from other general factors, the initial baseline condition may involve no explicit reinforcement contingencies for complying with the required exercise program. That condition might provide a good basis for comparing exercise compliance without reinforcement (the control condition) to compliance under an intervention condition in which participants are praised by rehabilitation personnel when their performance meets certain standards. That pair of conditions will allow conclusions about the effects of a praise contingency compared to a no reinforcement condition.

Following the praise phase, the investigator might then wish to see what effects would result from adding a points contingency (points earned might be exchanged for backup reinforcers) to the praise contingency. Answering the new question about the effects of praise plus points compared to praise alone will require a different control condition than the one used in the first comparison. Now the praise contingency that served as the intervention condition in the first comparison will serve as a good control condition for comparison to a praise-plus-points condition. Table 11.2 summarizes these two pairs of control and experimental phases.

Arranging Appropriate Comparisons. The last example provides another opportunity to emphasize that the difference between experimental or independent variable conditions and control or baseline conditions lies with the investigator's interests. If the investigator is interested in drawing conclusions about the effects of certain factors associated with a condition, that interest makes those factors the independent variable. If the investigator is not interested in drawing conclusions about the variables making up a condition, that lack of interest makes that phase a control condition. However, a control condition should be more than just a baseline during which the independent variable is not present. Remember that it should also be constructed so it serves as a control for a particular treatment condition by including everything going on in that condition except the factors defined as the independent variable.

TABLE 11.2
Control and experimental comparisons

Question	Control condition	Experimental condition
• Effects of praise?	No reinforcement	Praise
• Effects of adding points?	Praise alone	Praise + points

In arranging pairs of control and experimental conditions, it is important to avoid comparing data from two conditions in which the variables operating in one condition are discontinued and largely replaced by a different set of variables in the other. For example, consider a study of reinforcement contingencies used in backward chaining procedures with children diagnosed with autism spectrum disorder. Suppose that during an initial phase trainers used food reinforcers and in the next phase they switched to social reinforcers. If the investigator were interested in drawing conclusions about the effects of each type of reinforcer, comparing the data from the two phases would present a problem. Because the investigator's interest defines each type of reinforcer as an independent variable, we must ask what the matching control condition is for each of the two phases. Neither condition can serve as a proper control for the other. The problem is that when the first phase ends, the food reinforcer procedures stop and are replaced by the social reinforcer procedures. That means that when the first phase ends and the second phase starts, two changes occur at the same time. Assuming that the children's performances change in the second phase, we do not know whether they behaved differently because the food reinforcers were no longer present or the social reinforcers were now being used – or perhaps both influences were operating. Although the way responding changes might give us a hint, there would be no way to be sure with this single comparison.

Of course, there is nothing wrong with the investigator being interested in the effects of both types of reinforcers. One way to ask about the effects of each type of reinforcer is to arrange comparisons in which each of the two conditions is matched with a control condition in which no reinforcement contingency is used. The baseline procedures would continue unchanged throughout the following reinforcement phase so that the food or the social reinforcers would be the only change in procedures that could explain any changes in responding. With this type of comparison, the investigator would learn about the effects of each type of reinforcer, as well as whether one was more effective than another. Table 11.3 illustrates this approach.

Sequence of Conditions: Rationale. It is customary for the control condition to precede its matched experimental or treatment condition. That often makes practical sense because the control condition embodies all of the

TABLE 11.3
Alternative control and experimental conditions for evaluating the effects of social reinforcers

Design alternatives	Conditions			
	First	Second	Third	Fourth
• Original design	Food	Social		
• Better design	Food	Food + social		
• Best design	No reinforcers	Food	No reinforcers	Social

variables that will be operating in the treatment condition except for the independent variable itself. The control condition is therefore often used to fine-tune the general preparation by allowing needed adjustments to be made early on.

For example, it may be that some features of the procedures need to be changed so they generate better responding. The investigator may learn that the definition of the target behavior can be improved, or that a different behavioral dimension should be measured. The data may suggest that observational procedures should be revised. It is also not uncommon for the data to reveal unstable patterns of responding that will make it difficult to identify the effects of the treatment condition. The investigator may then need to identify and better control extraneous factors.

As any adjustments are made, the investigator can continue the control phase until it is clear that everything is working as intended. This flexible, repeated measures approach is one of the major advantages of the steady state strategy. Because control conditions establish baseline responding that will be used to assess any effects of the independent variable, they are often called baseline conditions or just "baselines."

Another reason for the control condition to come first is that it is sometimes designed to give participants a particular kind of history they must have in order to be ready for the treatment condition. For example, a control condition is often used to generate a certain kind of performance because that performance is necessary to later reveal the effects of the independent variable. In other words, an initial control phase may be used to give participants a certain training experience.

Sometimes the desired training is somewhat indirect, as when participants simply adjust to the baseline procedures. This might be the case in a study in which individuals diagnosed with intellectual disabilities are serving in a study of prompting procedures. Among other things, each participant must learn to cooperate with the training procedure before the baseline phase goes very far. On the other hand, sometimes the training objective within a baseline phase is a key element of the project. That might be the case in a study of two staff management procedures. Paraprofessional staff might be trained during an initial phase to use certain prompt and prompt-fading procedures to teach adults with intellectual disabilities to set the table for meals. The frequency with which they implemented those procedures at dinner time in the clients' group home would then serve as the dependent variable in assessing the effects of the two types of staff management procedures – say, verbal reminders from their supervisor before dinner versus feedback from the supervisor afterwards.

Baseline phases are especially likely to precede intervention phases in service delivery scenarios. In addressing the challenges of a new case, ABA practitioners are often faced with an existing set of circumstances surrounding the occurrence or nonoccurrence of target behaviors. The practitioner may see the need to modify those circumstances somewhat before turning to treatment options, but some variation of the presenting circumstances often serves as a good control condition for comparison to a planned treatment condition. For example, consider a young boy with autism who can say the names of his preferred foods but rarely does so to request items during mealtimes. Initial observations by the practitioner reveal that the boy's parent puts all food items so close to him throughout most meals that he can easily get them himself. The practitioner might instruct the parent to instead place preferred foods within the boy's line of sight but just out of his reach during a series of mealtime sessions. By measuring the rate of the boy's unprompted vocalized requesting in those sessions, the practitioner can see if that modification of the mealtime conditions has an effect on the behavior. If it does and the effect is sufficiently large, no other intervention might be needed. If there is no or only a small effect, that condition can serve as a control for comparison to a treatment condition in which preferred foods are arranged so that they are visible to the boy but beyond arm's length, and when he reaches toward an item his parent waits for him to vocalize the name of the food or an approximation, prompts if no vocalization occurs within a few seconds, and gives the boy the item contingent on occurrences of target vocalizations (incidental teaching procedures; Fenske, Krantz, & McClannahan, 2001; Hart & Risley, 1982).

Although there are advantages to having the control condition come first, it is not required. It can sometimes work just as well for the treatment condition to come first. When steady state responding under a matching pair of control and treatment conditions is compared, the sequence of the conditions does not change the experimental reasoning. Either way, the investigator winds up comparing responding in the absence versus the presence of the independent variable with all other variables held reasonably constant. In fact, experimental designs often involve comparisons between an experimental phase and a following control phase. Consider a design consisting of a baseline phase like the modified mealtime condition in the preceding example, followed by an incidental teaching treatment phase, which is then followed by a return to the previous baseline conditions. Those three phases will permit two comparisons of the rate of the boy's vocalizing under control and treatment conditions. One comparison comes from the first two phases (control-treatment), and the other comes from the second and third phases (treatment-control).

Sequence of Conditions: Sequence Effects. We indicated previously that one condition can be used to make it more likely that a target behavior will be useful in identifying the effects of the next condition. That relationship is called a sequence effect. As we described in Chapter 9, sequence effects are a common aspect of within-subject designs because each participant experiences both the control and the intervention conditions. An example of a useful sequence effect might be when exposure to a baseline condition establishes a form of responding that is needed for a following intervention phase, such as when a participant is trained to perform match-to-sample tasks so that match-to-sample procedures can be in a subsequent treatment condition.

Although sequence effects can be beneficial, they can also be problematic. In general, they are undesirable when the effects of one condition interfere with seeing a clear picture of the effects of a following condition. It is not unusual for investigators to run into this situation when trying to evaluate whether a treatment condition is actually responsible for changes in the target behavior that occurred during that phase. One way to make this assessment is to start out with a baseline phase, follow it by a treatment phase, then terminate the treatment phase and return to the original baseline condition to see if responding returns to baseline levels. If the treatment condition leads to changes in the target behavior that are supported by the non-treatment environment, however, those changes may continue even when the treatment condition is terminated. That might occur, for instance, when treatment results in acquisition of a skill that is evoked and reinforced frequently in an individual's everyday learning or living environments. Although that might be a desirable outcome in clinical situations, it does not help clarify the impact of the treatment condition.

It is important to understand that just because one condition immediately follows another does not mean that exposure to the first condition will necessarily affect responding in the second condition. There may be no sequence effect at all, or any effect may be negligible or short-lived. Although operant behavior is a function of both past experience and current conditions, the effects of historical influences tend to give way to the impact of current contingencies – often fairly quickly.

Given the uncertainties surrounding sequence effects, researchers and practitioners need to address two questions when they design projects. First, are there reasons to arrange for sequence effects so they will help highlight the effects of treatment conditions? That is, does an intervention phase require participants to behave in particular ways that will need to be established by their experience in a prior condition? If so, the investigator will need to figure out how the prior condition must be designed to produce the desired impact on responding. To expand on a previous example, match-to-sample procedures are often used to evaluate interventions to establish conditional discrimination performances. Investigators would be wise to use procedures in the condition preceding the intervention phase that have proved effective and efficient for training similar participants to perform match-to-sample tasks like those that will be used in the intervention phase, and to make sure each participant is performing those tasks with a high degree of accuracy before they proceed to the intervention phase.

Second, how might sequence effects occur that could interfere with identifying treatment effects? It may be more difficult to answer this second question because it requires guessing how a prior condition may influence responding in a way that can interact with the effects of the treatment condition. The challenge is that sequence effects do not announce themselves in any way. The changes in the target behavior in the treatment phase may be orderly and expected, but that does not mean they would have looked the same without the contribution of variables in the baseline condition. The task is to recognize the changes in responding that could have depended on features of the control condition and ask whether this dependency should be more clearly identified and acknowledged – or even eliminated. Again expanding on the preceding example, if the stimuli used in a match-to-sample pretraining condition are physically similar to stimuli used in a subsequent conditional discrimination intervention condition, that could affect participants' responding during intervention. That is, their performances during the intervention phase could look different – maybe better, maybe worse – than they would if similarities among the stimuli to which they were exposed in the two phases were minimized or eliminated.

Sequence of Conditions: Letter Designations. Finally, describing sequences with words can sometimes get a bit awkward if all we want to do is get across the order of different conditions. To avoid this problem, researchers long ago started using the letters of the alphabet as a kind of shorthand. The rule is simple: Each different phase in temporal sequence is assigned successive letters of the alphabet. In other words, the first phase is labeled A and the second phase is labeled B. The label for the third phase will depend on whether it is a repeat of the first phase (A) or a new phase (C). Because a control or baseline condition is often the first phase in a study, it is common for baseline conditions to be labeled A. This can get awkward when a study starts with a treatment condition instead of a control condition. In that case, the treatment condition would be labeled A because it is the first phase. In other words, the letters merely indicate a sequence, not the nature of the condition in each phase. In experimental designs that include multiple phases with two or more pairs of control and treatment conditions, although the initial control phase would be labeled A, a different control phase later in the study might be labeled C or even some subsequent letter.

For example, consider the sequence of phases in Table 11.4 describing a study of contingencies designed to reduce absenteeism among employees. The A-B-A-B-C-B sequence of letters represents a study with two different independent variable or treatment conditions: B (public posting of absenteeism data) and C (public posting plus a lottery in which all employees whose absenteeism falls below a specified level are eligible for prizes). The public posting condition is compared with a control condition involving no particular attention to employee absenteeism (A), and the public posting plus lottery condition is compared with the public posting phase (B). The phase descriptions below the letters clarify that the A-B-A sequence of phases allows two comparisons of treatment 1 with its matching control condition (A-B and B-A), and the following B-C-B sequence allows two comparisons of treatment 2 with its control condition (B-C and C-B). As you can imagine, this lettering system of summarizing sequences of phases in a study works well only for relatively simple experimental designs.

TABLE 11.4
Illustration of ABABCB design

Sequence of conditions

A	B	A	B	C	B
Control (1)	Treatment 1	Control (1)	Control (2)	Treatment 2	Control (2)
Standard	Public posting	Standard	Public posting	Posting+lottery	Public posting

Functional Relations

The reason for comparing measures of a target behavior (the dependent variable) under paired control and treatment conditions is to learn enough about the effects of the independent variable to be able to show that particular changes in responding are a function of the independent variable *and nothing else*. This result is called a **functional relation**.

> **Functional relation.** An experimentally determined relation that shows that the dependent variable depends on or is a function of particular variables, ideally the independent variable and nothing else.

This goal is more demanding than it might seem. It is not necessarily difficult to show that a target behavior changes in a particular way whenever an intervention condition is ongoing compared to its control condition. However, to say that those changes in responding are a function of the independent variable operating only during the intervention phase depends on how the independent variable is defined and requires confidence that other factors are not contributing to the observed changes. As we discussed in the section on the independent variable, those other factors are extraneous to the investigator's primary interests. Investigators can always argue that no such factors are operating, but if circumstances suggest otherwise, the only way investigators can convince themselves and others that likely extraneous variables are not playing a role is to control or eliminate them.

Suppose, for example, that an investigator is evaluating self-monitoring procedures for increasing social initiations to co-workers for Sam, a young man with autism who has started a job entering data into spreadsheets for a recycling company. Measurement during baseline showed that Sam did not initiate more than one verbal interaction with a co-worker per 15-minute break period at work; in most observations, he had no initiations. During intervention, each workday just before the morning break Sam and his job coach review an index card on which is printed "On break, talk to 3 friends" followed by a comment or question that Sam is to address to each of the three co-workers (e.g., "Joe, did your son's soccer team win its game?" "Siobhan, I like your glasses." "Marv, what are you having for lunch today?") The job coach instructs Sam to put the index card in his pocket and to take it out when the break ends and write a check mark next to each question or comment he made. After the break, Sam brings the index card to his job coach, who was observing him unobtrusively during the break and recorded his initiations to co-workers. On a separate index card, the job coach records one point for each comment or question that Sam accurately reports having made during the break, accompanied by brief praise statements. She also records two bonus points for each additional comment or question initiated by Sam that was not written on the card, again accompanied by praise. The points card is

---

BOX 11.1

Levels of Empirical Elegance

A functional relation may be viewed as one end of a continuum of the elegance or completeness of empirical explanations. At the other end are investigations that take the form of *demonstrations*. A demonstration simply shows that something is possible. It can reveal the operation and effects of a process or procedure that has not yet been fully defined and explained. Demonstrating a relation does not require experimentally manipulating an independent variable or explaining why something works. However, a well-designed demonstration can eliminate arguments that a certain outcome is not possible. For that reason, demonstration studies occupy an important position in the history of science. Nevertheless, they are limited in that they only permit an empirical statement in the form of "if...then" (If you do this, then you will get that outcome). Furthermore, a single demonstration only shows a relation for the variables operating in that one case.

Correlations are in the middle of the continuum between demonstrations and functional relations. This form of investigation requires identifying and measuring multiple values of the variables in question, such as annual sales of single malt scotch in the United States and annual professors' salaries. The resulting statements take the form "When X1 occurs, Y1 occurs." Because correlational studies do not involve manipulating variables, no statements should be made about the reasons for the correlation. In this way, they share the explanatory limitations of demonstration studies. Correlations merely show that two variables show some association, not that one variable causes or is functionally related to the other.

Only the pursuit of *functional relations* involves actual experiments in which independent variables are manipulated in order to determine their effects on dependent variables. This leads to a kind of "co-relation" expressed as $y=f(x)$, where x is the independent variable of the function and y is the dependent variable. Although it is often useful to show that x is *sufficient* to produce y, it is more informative to show that x is *necessary* to produce y. Showing that y occurs *only if x* occurs is the most complete and elegant form of empirical inquiry in science.

---

given to Sam. When he returns to his supported living apartment after work, he exchanges the points for time on his choice of electronic devices. Those procedures are repeated every work day for two weeks. If the data show that Sam's initiations to co-workers are higher during the self-monitoring phase than they were in baseline, can we be confident that the increase is solely due to the program?

As we look more closely at what actually happened, we might be able to identify other factors that could have contributed to the increase in Sam's verbal initiations to co-workers. For instance, it might be that that category of behavior was also being targeted in a social skills group in which Sam participated on the weekends. Let us assume the investigator went beyond the initial baseline and intervention phases to implement an A-B-A-B design, stopping and later restarting the self-monitoring program a second time. Let us also assume that the data showed the same changes from low rates of initiations in baseline phases to higher rates under intervention conditions.

Would these data allow the investigator to argue that they showed a functional relation between the self-monitoring program and social initiations? The problem with drawing that conclusion is that as long as Sam was participating in the weekend social skills group, the self-monitoring intervention at work could be confounded by the extra practice on the target skill. In order to look at the effects of the self-monitoring intervention alone, the investigator would have to convince Sam to stop attending the social skills group, or conduct the evaluation with a different participant who was not receiving any other intervention designed to increase social initiations. It would take multiple phases, if not additional investigations, to determine if the self-monitoring procedures were consistently responsible for increasing initiations to co-workers by themselves.

Of course, from a practical point of view, it might be useful if the group social skills instruction supplemented the effect of the self-monitoring intervention. From a research or practical perspective, however, it is important to learn whether the self-monitoring procedures are effective by themselves, and it may also be valuable to assess the separate contribution of the social skills group. As the results of the investigation are used with different participants or by other researchers or practitioners, it is important to know which factors have what effects. Agencies offering services to similar young adults with autism need to know if self-monitoring procedures are functionally related to increased interactions with co-workers or if they must be supplemented with a group social skills program in order to obtain the desired outcome.

This example suggests that showing that a particular behavioral outcome is solely the result of a certain independent variable – demonstrating a functional relation – will often require more than a single investigation. It is not enough to show that a certain outcome is reliably associated with an intervention. Most intervention conditions, particularly in applied research and practice, are confounded with a variety of extraneous factors. It is risky to merely assume that those extraneous factors have no effect and conclude that the designated independent variable is solely responsible for changes in responding. Proposing that an independent variable is functionally related to a particular behavioral outcome requires convincing evidence that the relation does not depend on other factors. (See Box 12.1 for more discussion of the risks of extraneous variables.)

There is no clear standard for when it is appropriate to conclude that changes in a target behavior accompanying changes in conditions constitute a functional relation. The more inclusive the definition of the independent variable, the easier it would seem to be to argue that the independent variable is mainly responsible for observed changes in responding. What limits our certainty about making this kind of statement is the possibility that extraneous variables are significantly contributing to the observed outcome. Although investigators may learn more about the relation between the independent and dependent variables with each new project, they must still acknowledge the possibility that someone will

---

BOX 11.2

Why Scientists Don't Talk About Causes

Media reporters often seem frustrated when interviewing scientists. When reporters ask about some discovery, scientists tend to hedge their bets. They seem to qualify everything using phrases such as "As far as we know…," "Under such-and-such conditions…," "There seems to be a relation…," "We're still not sure why…," and so forth.

The reason for their caution is more than wanting to avoid embarrassment by being wrong. Scientists learn that the world is a complex place and things are often not as simple as they seem. They learn to talk in conservative terms in order to avoid implying more than they know because they have learned that every research literature is a story of revisions of what we once thought was correct. That is why scientists tend to avoid saying that one thing "causes" another. The notion of "cause" suggests we know everything about the relation between the "things" of interest, which is almost always untrue. For the same reason, scientists don't talk about "proving" something. Instead of talking about causation, scientists may say one variable is "related to" another. They may talk about a correlation or an association between two variables. In fact, all we ever really know is that two variables are "co-related" in some way. It is difficult to show that no other factors are playing a contributing role in a relation because that requires identifying all possible extraneous variables and then showing they are not relevant. That is why science is better at disproving than proving.

---

discover conditions under which the relation does not hold, either because of factors yet to be identified or because additional factors are partly responsible for the relation. It may be helpful to be cautious about concluding that we have shown a functional relation, especially on the basis of a single study.

Experimental Control

Rationale. We have established that investigators should design and conduct evaluations in which (a) the independent variable is the only thing that can explain changes in the dependent variable and (b) those effects are clear and consistent. **Experimental control** refers to how successful the investigator is in this effort. Although the phrase might imply that this objective is mainly a priority for formal research projects, practitioners interested in drawing conclusions about the reasons for changes in target behaviors share this interest with researchers.

> **Experimental control.** The management or control of different variables in a study, including the independent variable and extraneous variables.

The pursuit of experimental control is one of the hallmarks of both basic and applied behavior analysis research and is one of the main factors underlying the achievements of this science. The obligation to demonstrate experimental control pervades the investigator's decision-making from the outset. Decisions about the setting and the general procedures for an investigation that will serve as the context for responding, the desired characteristics of participants, the nature and dimensions of the target behavior that will be measured, and the measurement procedures themselves all affect how clearly the influence of the independent variable is revealed.

In addition, the details of the independent variable can have a substantial impact on how easy it is to identify its effects on responding. Designing an intervention that does not properly represent the variables of interest may fail to provide a good test of their potential impact. That might be the case, for example, if a study of a training procedure incorporated weak reinforcers as part of an otherwise sound procedure. In addition, selecting an intervention that is difficult to implement properly from session to session may fail to provide a good test of its potential. Consistency in control and treatment conditions can sometimes be especially difficult to achieve in field settings, such as an elementary school classroom or a home.

Implementation. Concern with issues of control only starts with how a study is designed. Once the effort is underway, the investigator must closely monitor the general circumstances of the study, measurement procedures, the independent variable, and the resulting data to evaluate those initial decisions. As we have already seen, one of the strengths of the steady state strategy is that it allows ongoing opportunities to assess earlier decisions and adjust certain features to improve experimental control as an investigation proceeds. Collecting repeated measures of an individual's behavior under both control and treatment conditions also provides the opportunity to react to unanticipated and emergent factors that might interfere with seeing treatment effects clearly.

This ongoing monitoring often leads investigators to find things that require their attention as the project moves along. Sometimes they discover problems from simply observing what is going on. They also find it useful to talk with individuals who are involved in the project in some way, including participants, those who are implementing procedures, and observers who are collecting data. Finally, the data will sometimes suggest issues that need attention. Responding might be highly variable, for instance, or fail to change in ways that might be anticipated.

The problems investigators might identify are likely to fall into three general categories. First, it may be necessary to modify how the target behavior is defined and measured so that the data will be more useful. Altering the definition may be necessary to better reflect research interests or to improve observer accuracy. For instance, it is often difficult for observers to count responses that occur repeatedly in rapid succession, as is the case with many stereotypic behaviors. Having observers record the duration of each episode or bout of responses instead is likely to produce more accurate and useful data. Changing observation times and durations may allow better sampling of the behavior. If a child with a language delay tends to talk less in large-group than small-group situations, for example, observing and recording her utterances just once or twice a day in the latter will probably yield a more representative picture of her vocal repertoire than doing so several times each day in both large- and small-group settings.

Second, it may be necessary to modify some features of the control and treatment conditions. Sometimes it may become evident that procedures should be adjusted to better represent key variables. For instance, it might be that the stimuli presented in a match-to-sample procedure need to be changed, enlarged, or rearranged to have the intended effect. More often, it is discovered that a procedure is not operating as intended. That is frequently the case when individuals who are implementing the procedure are required to behave in specific ways. To return to an earlier example, an intervention to help adults with intellectual disabilities learn to set the table may require trainers to implement a prompt and prompt-fading protocol, and it may become clear that they need additional training and monitoring to do so correctly. It is often the independent variable itself that is not working as expected and needs to be adjusted.

Making sure key features of the control and treatment conditions are operating as designed is critically important, so investigators should take care to measure those features so they can verify and report that the procedures were implemented as designed – a process described as evaluating **procedural integrity**, **independent variable integrity**, or **treatment integrity**. Without objective evidence that procedures were implemented correctly and consistently throughout all control and treatment phases, an investigator is on shaky ground when it comes to drawing conclusions about experimental control, which is all about relations between independent and dependent variables. In other words, unless we can be reasonably confident that the independent variable operated as it was meant to, we cannot be certain that it was responsible for any observed changes in the dependent variable. When procedures are implemented by automated devices, as in many laboratory studies, ensuring their integrity is usually just a matter of verifying that the devices worked properly throughout the study. In most applied research and practice, of course, it is humans who carry out procedures. Measuring procedural or treatment integrity in applied investigations therefore involves observing and recording the behavior of implementers. The target responses are typically selected by the investigator and specified in written protocols and/or spoken instructions. Decisions about the dimension(s) of those responses to measure and the observation and recording methods should be guided by the same considerations as decisions about measuring participants' behavior that were discussed in Chapters 5 and 6, and those measurement procedures should be evaluated as described in Chapter 8. The resulting data – such as a summary of the accuracy with which procedures were implemented in each phase – should be reported alongside data on the behavior of participants when the project is reported to others. Despite the fact that the importance of ensuring the integrity of procedures in applied behavior analysis has been recognized for decades, however (e.g., Peterson, Homer,

& Wonderlick, 1982), it appears that measurement of procedural or treatment integrity has not received the attention it warrants from applied researchers (e.g., Fryling, Wallace, & Yassine, 2012).

> **Treatment integrity (procedural integrity, independent variable integrity).** The extent to which the independent variable or other key features of a condition are consistently implemented as designed.

Third, investigators may find that unanticipated extraneous factors are intruding on control or treatment conditions. As we have suggested, applied researchers and practitioners are particularly likely to encounter problems with extraneous influences. The challenge is to determine which factors should be managed in some way and which can safely be allowed to vary. As we indicated in the discussion of steady state issues in Chapter 10, just because an extraneous variable is obvious does not mean it is having a substantial impact on responding. For instance, in an investigation conducted in an elementary school classroom, it might seem that a substitute teacher would have a major effect on target behaviors, but that is not necessarily true. On the other hand, less obvious factors such as unscheduled events happening outside of the classroom setting (a fight between two students during recess, for instance) can have substantial effects on responding.

In sum, the interest of researchers and practitioners in seeing clear effects of the treatment condition requires considerable effort throughout a project to optimize experimental control. Only those involved with a project will see those efforts, however. They are considered a routine part of the job of obtaining clear and meaningful findings and are not necessarily reported in journal publications or convention presentations. It is actually not unusual for early data to be thrown out as improvements are made in how an investigation is being implemented. In fact, sometimes a first attempt is scrapped entirely and replaced with an improved second try. The only thing that counts in the end is getting data that justify meaningful conclusions that will hold up for others.

How Much Control? We have seen that achieving sufficient experimental control involves attention to (a) designing and implementing sound measurement procedures, (b) selecting and managing control and independent variable conditions, and (c) minimizing the contribution of extraneous variables. Our discussion also suggests we can group those responsibilities into two categories: (a) those that can be anticipated from the outset and accommodated in how the investigation is designed and (b) those that might not be expected and will have to be dealt with as the project progresses.

Let us take a closer look at these two options. Designing an investigation from the outset to minimize unwanted intrusions is relatively easy to do if the question can be addressed under the relatively controlled conditions of a laboratory. For example, using laboratory animals such as rats means that genetic and environmental histories can be fairly tightly specified. The researcher does not have to worry about how rats spend their time between sessions or even what they eat, and experimental chambers provide a consistent and controlled experimental setting. Treatment variables can usually be arranged with computer precision, and data collection is comprehensive and automatic.

This approach to experimental control works well for the most basic research questions, but many research and practical issues involve human participants behaving under more or less everyday circumstances. In fact, part of the point of applied projects is to evaluate intervention effects under real-world circumstances. The challenge for applied researchers and practitioners is deciding just how much control is necessary. The general answer involves a balance between two interests. On the one hand, there must be enough control to allow sound conclusions about the role of the independent variable. On the other hand, there must not be so much control that the preparation does not reflect the circumstances needed to get a meaningful answer to the question.

For instance, if an investigator wants to learn about procedures for building social skills in small group settings with young children with autism, it may be necessary to tolerate some extraneous factors associated with small groups of children in a preschool setting. As long as such factors have only minor effects on responding, that may not be a problem. It might be that the number of times typically developing children serving as peer partners provide appropriate prompts and consequences for the social responses of the children with autism varies a good bit from session to session. In other words, the number of training trials or opportunities might not occur equally often from day to day. That would presumably result in variations in the performance of the children with autism. In addition, the typically developing peers might sometimes interact with the children with autism in ways that are inconsistent with the intervention protocol. Addressing those problems by redesigning the study so that sessions are conducted in a training room with a single peer interacting with a single child with autism might help mitigate them and result in better experimental control. That might create another problem, however: The conditions would no longer represent the circumstances required by the research question about small group settings.

As we will see in later discussions, the extent to which experimental control is optimized without limiting the relevance of the investigation often determines whether clear and accurate conclusions are justified. When designing a project, investigators understandably tend to accommodate the focus of the research question or clinical interest guiding the project (see Chapter 3). As their methodological decisions accumulate, it can be difficult to pull back from the circumstances of interest and tighten requirements for the individuals who will participate, or to modify problematic features of the setting to avoid the possible complications of extraneous influences. It is easier to move ahead as planned and worry about the impact of those factors when the time comes for drawing conclusions. At that late stage, however, it is difficult for investigators to resist drawing conclusions about why the target behavior changed from one condition to another even when the data reveal significant problems with experimental control.

The way to avoid this situation is to address issues of experimental control from the outset as a routine cost of doing business. Along the way, it may become apparent that conducting a good investigation is going to require a workable compromise between the characteristics of a preferred setting and preparation and what is needed to achieve a satisfactory level of experimental control. The investigator may have to accept that getting good data is going to require making adjustments in the setting, participants, and procedures. Sometimes it may even be necessary to concede that a proper investigation cannot be conducted under the desired conditions. It is certainly better to recognize that limitation than to go ahead with an investigation that yields findings that cannot be defended.

Managing and Evaluating Extraneous Variables. As we have pointed out, achieving sufficient experimental control requires attending to measurement issues, features of control and treatment conditions, and extraneous factors. Because investigators create the conditions of a study, including its measurement procedures, making sure everything is working as intended is usually a reasonable challenge. Managing extraneous factors can be more problematic. Although some extraneous influences may be identifiable from the outset, others may have nothing to do with the investigator's plans. There are three ways to manage extraneous variables. They can be (a) eliminated entirely, (b) held constant across conditions, or (c) investigated directly.

By definition, eliminating an extraneous factor is an effective tactic for insuring that it has no effect on responding. That is often not feasible, and even when it is, it can have undesirable side effects. As we have already discussed, eliminating extraneous influences can change features and circumstances of an investigation so that it does not adequately reflect the intended state of affairs. That can be especially burdensome for applied projects when the extraneous factors are part of the applied situation itself. In other words, eliminating extraneous variables can make an investigation more contrived and less characteristic of the circumstances to which its findings are intended to apply than leaving the extraneous factors in place. The price of this approach is that it will be unclear how well the findings apply to less contrived (more real-world) situations. For instance, consider a project to evaluate the effects of ABA interventions to build peer social skills in children with autism in an integrated public school classroom. Although the effects of those interventions would be easier to see if the typically developing peers always responded to social bids from the children with autism in ways that were scripted by the investigators, the results would not be applicable to situations in which peers respond as they would to other typically developing youngsters.

The gap between the features of the study and those typical of everyday circumstances to which the findings should apply must be bridged by additional investigations. Achieving experimental control by eliminating certain extraneous factors may require further research to evaluate the generality of the findings to the circumstances of interest. If that requirement seems to discourage the option of eliminating extraneous variables, remember that the price for failing to deal with them can be misleading results with poor generality.

The second tactic for managing extraneous factors is to hold them constant from one phase to another. If that can be done, the extraneous influences of concern will be the same across phases. In an investigation focusing on dietary compliance in diabetic children, for example, it might be important to hold attention from medical personnel constant across both control and intervention conditions. That would address any argument that dietary compliance under the intervention phase was partly or even entirely due to extra attention from medical staff. The potential problem with this tactic is that the extraneous influences are still operating under both conditions. That is not always a serious issue, but it can be. For instance, consider a study of the effects of ABA procedures for reducing problem behaviors in individuals diagnosed with intellectual disabilities. If individuals were receiving drugs that influenced those behaviors, holding the drugs and dosages constant throughout the phases of a study would not mean they had no effects on responding. Indeed, the drug effects would make it impossible to determine what impact the ABA procedures would have had if the individuals had not been receiving drugs.

A third tactic for managing extraneous variables is investigating them directly in order to evaluate their contribution. That can be done as part of the current investigation or in a subsequent effort. It usually involves comparing data from phases in which the presence or absence of the extraneous factor in question is the only difference in order to see if it has an effect. For example, a study using a computer-based program for teaching basic academic skills to learners with autism may raise the question of whether extra attention from a teacher in the form of helping participants respond to stimuli on a touchscreen contributes to their performance. That is, does the mere fact that teachers interact with participants a lot have a significant influence on acquisition of the target skills? That question could be answered by arranging control and intervention conditions in which teacher attention is systematically separated from teacher assistance and varied as the independent variable.

Although directly investigating an extraneous variable can be a distraction from the primary research agenda, it can lead to learning useful things about its impact. It might reveal that the variable is not influencing the target behavior, in which case it would not need to be controlled and could not explain any treatment effects. On the other hand, if the investigation shows that the extraneous

TABLE 11.5
Managing extraneous variables

Tactic	Advantage	Disadvantage
• Eliminate	Effective	Limits generality of results
• Hold constant	Same for all phases	Influence still present
• Evaluate	Learn about variable	More time and resources

variable does have a significant effect, the investigator can then decide what to do about it. Such an investigation might also identify a potent influence on the target behavior that could have practical value. For instance, learning that the actions of peers in a classroom (laughing when a target student makes rude noises) affects the target behavior might suggest an intervention procedure (having the teacher's aide praise responses that are incompatible with laughing at the target student, such as remaining quiet or answering questions from the teacher).

Finally, let us consider the possibility that we are being overly conservative in our assessment of the risk that the effects of extraneous variables may invalidate otherwise appealing conclusions about the impact of the independent variable. After all, if we could assume that the changes in responding associated with a treatment condition were due solely to the independent variable, it would be much easier to defend straightforward conclusions about its impact. Is our caution about the role of extraneous factors selectively associated with the treatment condition warranted? In answering this question, it is important to admit that we cannot be sure that a treatment condition is free of contamination by associated extraneous factors merely by inspection, which for interested parties can come uncomfortably close to wishful thinking. Additionally, whether we suspect particular extraneous factors may not be a good guide to their impact. As we have suggested, an obvious extraneous variable may have little influence on the target behavior, and unrecognized factors can have substantial effects.

What are the consequences of guessing wrong? The conclusion we presumably want to draw from control/treatment comparisons is that the changes in responding observed during the treatment condition are due entirely to the features that distinguish that condition from its control condition. To the extent that such a conclusion is mistaken, researchers and practitioners who accept it will find that they have difficulty reproducing the outcome when they implement what seems to be the same treatment condition subsequently. If a report of a study in which the investigator failed to identify the contribution of extraneous variables is published in a journal and becomes part of the field's research literature, it will stand as a misleading guide to users – both researchers and practitioners. If such reports were infrequent, this might not be a serious problem. However, if publication of misleading findings were common, it would greatly depreciate the value of the field's research literature and the credibility of the entire field. Comprehensive reviews of research might survey many studies, but the size of the literature would not overcome weak or misleading methods and outcomes in the reviewed studies. That would be a serious threat to the viability of our evidence-based discipline.

What about practitioners who are just interested in learning from their own clinical experience? As we have acknowledged, they may often find it difficult to adhere to the niceties of research designs, especially when it comes to evaluating the influence of extraneous variables. It is also understandably difficult to resist the temptation to conclude that a treatment protocol was responsible for observed changes in a target behavior, especially when that is what the treatment was intended to do. If such conclusions are mistaken, however, it depreciates the value of the practitioner's accumulating experience. Convictions about the appropriateness and effectiveness of particular procedures may become an unreliable guide to decision-making about treatment plans. Of course, it may be easy to adjust a procedure when it does not work as past clinical experience suggests, but if that experience rests on faulty conclusions, interventions are likely to be less effective and efficient than they would be otherwise.

Replication

Types. Replication means repetition, and repetition pervades every nook and cranny of scientific method. (In order to be clear about what is being repeated, it is helpful to use **replication** to refer to repeating procedures and **reproduction** to refer to repeating results.) Repeating things helps researchers discover and correct their mistakes. There is a lot of repetition in any single study, but repetition also occurs over time within an area of investigation as different investigators replicate parts of their colleagues' projects in order to learn more about a topic or hone treatment protocols.

> **Replication.** Repetition of any parts of an experiment.
>
> **Reproduction.** Repetition of results, usually as an outcome of repeating procedures.

One of the strengths of making comparisons between control and treatment conditions using within-subject or repeated-measures designs is that they ensure a lot of repetition of important parts of a study. Distinguishing among the following types of replication will help make this point. In some studies, the basic procedure may be repeated a number of times in each session. This is called **replication across trials**, or whatever serves as the key element of the procedure representing the independent variable. A study of prompts used in a training procedure with children with autism might involve repeating the prompting procedures on each of a series of trials during each of a series of sessions. In order for those repetitions to provide useful information about the consistency of responding across repetitions, the investigator must measure responding continuously throughout each session. Furthermore, the data must be displayed trial by trial so the reproducibility of the performance can be examined at that level. The basic research literature has many examples of this approach, in part because laboratory equipment makes it relatively easy to create moment-by-moment records of repeated cycles of procedures and their effects on responding. For many years, standardized cumulative records were used to display the outcomes of within-session replications (see Figure 9.1, Panel A).

A second type of replication stems from the steady state strategy. Obtaining repeated measures of responding under each condition means that each participant will be presented with the same condition a number of times, such as once each day for a number of days in succession. This is called **replication across sessions**. Seeing its effects requires graphing the data session by session within and across each phase. Chapter 10 described the value of data showing the consistency of each individual's performance as the same conditions are repeated session after session within each phase.

A third type of replication repeats an even larger portion of the study. When the investigator repeats an entire phase, it is called **replication of a condition or phase**. That is, within the span of a study, a condition or phase may be repeated in order to evaluate the reliability of a comparison between that phase and another just like it. For example, in an A-B-A design where A represents the control condition and B the treatment condition, the first phase is repeated following the treatment phase. That adds a second comparison (B-A) of the two conditions to the initial comparison (A-B). In an A-B-A-B sequence, both conditions are repeated once, which allows three comparisons of the two conditions (A-B, B-A, and A-B). This form of repetition is a key strength of within-subject research design because it allows investigators to assess the reproducibility of an effect. To evaluate such comparisons properly, data must be displayed session by session for each phase.

A fourth type of replication occurs within an area of research as different investigators repeat whole studies. This may be called **replication of entire studies**. Regardless of the care with which a study was done, the credibility of its findings remains uncertain until other investigators repeat the study and are able to reproduce the original results. Researchers have learned that this is an important step because there are often unidentified factors unique to a particular investigation that sometimes turn out to be crucial to obtaining the results. When other investigators replicate the original study but fail to reproduce the finding, it prompts a search for the variables that may be the key to getting the effect.

Finally, **replication across research literatures** or even different fields of science is the zenith of replication. When different fields of inquiry discover the same phenomena at work in similar ways under different conditions, those discoveries help integrate our knowledge of how the world works. For example, Skinner (1975) suggested that the migratory patterns of certain species may involve replications of the basic process of shaping by gradually adjusting contingencies of reinforcement. This process is well understood at the level of individual organisms, but Skinner saw that the same process might operate across successive generations of a species. Given the now well-established understanding of how the location of continents drifts over very long periods of time, the migratory behavior of a species would have to gradually change accordingly. Data provided by Carr (1966) concerning sea turtles confirmed Skinner's predictions and helped draw the fields of zoology and geophysics closer to the science of behavior.

TABLE 11.6
Types of replication

- Replication across trials
- Replication across sessions
- Replication of a condition or phase
- Replication of entire studies
- Replication across literatures

Replication across trials. Repetition of a basic element of procedure throughout each session. Requires trial-by-trial display of data.

Replication across sessions. Repetition of the same condition many times in succession throughout a phase. Requires session-by-session display of data.

Replication across a condition or phase. Repetition of an entire phase during the course of an experiment. Requires session-by-session display of data for each phase.

Replication of entire studies. Repetition of an earlier study, usually by other researchers.

Replication across research literatures. Repetition of phenomena under different conditions across different fields of science.

Functions. Whatever form replication takes, it serves one of two general kinds of functions. It either assesses the reliability of the original findings or the extent to which the findings might be obtained under somewhat different conditions (their generality). Although each type of replication can be used to ask about either reliability or generality, investigators are probably most often interested in learning more about reproducing the effects of a treatment condition on responding. That is, they are primarily interested in replication of a condition or phase.

Information about the reliability of treatment effects answers the question of whether they will occur under highly similar conditions if the same independent variable condition is presented again. Researchers and practitioners do not want to report findings to colleagues that cannot be consistently reproduced under the same conditions. In order to assess reliability, replications should be designed to repeat the original condition as closely as possible. Sidman (1960) called this direct replication.

Of course, it is impossible to make a replication truly identical to the original version, but it is important to come reasonably close. Trying to establish the reliability of treatment effects when the replication involves a number of differences from the original conditions is a bit risky. If the effects are not reproduced, the investigator may not know where to start looking for the reasons, especially if the changes that occurred were not planned or are unknown. If the replicated conditions are highly similar to the original versions, failing to reproduce the same effects directs the investigator to look for reasons why the same intervention does not consistently result in the same kind of change in responding. (It might be, for example, that the original effects were actually due to extraneous factors, not the independent variable.) However, if the replication differed from the original investigation in a number of ways, failure to reproduce the original findings could be due to the investigator having tampered with some factors that were critical to the original effect. In other words, if the replication involves a number of changes from the original – whether large or small – the investigator will not know if a failure to reproduce the original findings indicates that the effect is inconsistent or that the changed variables are essential to the effect.

A good illustration can be found in the research literature on intensive, comprehensive ABA intervention for preschool-aged children with autism and related disorders. In the initial between-groups study of one model of that intervention, just under half (47%) of the children who received ABA intervention for at least 40 hours per week for at least two years were reported to move from the delayed range into the normal range in multiple areas of functioning (Lovaas, 1987). Several studies that were published over the next few years also showed that most young children with autism and related disorders who received intensive ABA intervention improved, though not as many had changes as large as those reported by Lovaas (1987). Some of those studies were described as replications of the original (e.g., Birnbrauer & Leach, 1993; Eldevik et al., 2006; Smith, Groen, & Wynn, 2000); however, the ABA intervention was delivered at lower intensities and/or for shorter durations than in the Lovaas (1987) study, so in Sidman's (1960) terms they were only partial replications. In subsequent studies where the dosage and duration of ABA intervention more closely approximated the original (at least 30 hours per week for at least two years), the sizes of change scores and the proportions of children who moved from the delayed into the typical range on one or more measures also closely approximated those in the Lovaas study (e.g., Howard et al., 2014; Sallows & Graupner, 2005; also see Eldevik et al., 2010).

It is important to understand the limitations of arranging highly similar replications in order to assess the reliability of an effect. Even if they show that repeating an intervention condition results in the same outcomes, such data do not confirm that those effects were actually due to the independent variable. Reproducing an effect only shows it was at least not due to extraneous factors uniquely operating during the original phase or study. It still might be the case that extraneous factors, especially ones specifically associated with the intervention condition, are contributing to the effects.

For example, recall the earlier example of a study using a computer-based program for teaching basic academic skills to learners with autism. In discussing that example, we noted that attention from a teacher helping participants is an extraneous factor that happens to be selectively associated with the intervention condition. If one or more other investigators repeated the original study and showed that the effects of the intervention could be obtained reliably, it would not mean that the effects are due solely to the computer-based program. They could depend partly on the extra teacher attention. In other words, evidence that a finding is reproducible is primarily valuable in building confidence that the impact of a treatment condition on responding is worth further experimental attention.

Using replications to pursue the generality of treatment effects addresses the question of whether the same effects will be obtained even if some features of the preparation are intentionally changed in some way. When replication is aimed at providing information about the generality of effects, it does not help to try to repeat the original procedures exactly. If the repetition involved nearly the same conditions as originally used, reproducing the original findings would not provide any information about whether the effects would still be found if certain features were different. Answering the question about generality requires making limited changes in the original conditions in order to assess whether those particular changes were important to the original findings. Sidman (1960) called this systematic replication.

If the same findings are obtained even though certain features were changed, it suggests that those features may not be critical to getting the effects. Another way to say this is that the effects of the intervention condition on responding may be general to the extent of the changes. For example, when the same findings are obtained in a later study using different participants, it suggests that the effects did not depend on unique characteristics of the original participants. If one component of a procedure was dropped in a replication but the same findings were obtained, it would mean that component may not be necessary to getting the original outcome. As long as the same effects are found, the more changes incorporated in a replication, the broader the statement about generality that can be made.

This approach to learning about the generality of a finding involves some risk, however. If the replication has a number of features that differ from the original preparation and the original findings are not reproduced, it will probably be unclear which changes might be responsible for the shortfall. The investigator might then have to go back and separately investigate each changed feature to see what role each plays in the treatment outcomes. To illustrate, a replication of the original study on the computer-based academic skills program might involve learners with intellectual disabilities and no diagnosis of autism and have teachers provide only corrective feedback following incorrect responses instead of helping learners respond to each set of stimuli presented on the computer. If the results differed from the original study, the only way to know whether that was because of differences in the participants' or the teachers' behavior would be to repeat the original study using the exact same teaching procedures with learners with intellectual disabilities, and to conduct a separate study in which teachers provided corrective feedback only to participants who were very similar to those in the original study.

In sum, demonstrating the reliability of the effects of an intervention tells us about the certainty of our knowledge, whereas demonstrating generality

TABLE 11.7
Functions of replication

Function	Question	Procedure
• Reliability	If repeat procedure, get same effect?	Repeat exactly
• Generality	If change procedure, get same effect?	Repeat with changes

actually increases our knowledge by suggesting variables that may or may not be required to get the same effect. As we will see in Chapter 16, which addresses generality of findings more broadly, learning about factors that are and are not necessary to obtain a certain outcome is what enables us to predict the circumstances under which that outcome will or will not be found.

Issues. Replicating treatment conditions to see if their effects can be reproduced raises a number of questions. The first question concerns how to decide when an intervention should be replicated. In general, replications should be considered if (a) the existing literature on the topic is small or weak or has produced mixed results, (b) the findings contradict the existing literature, (c) the investigator has little experience with the procedure, (d) there are obvious alternative explanations for the effects, (e) failure to reproduce the same outcome under other conditions is likely to be costly in some way, and (f) the replication will be relatively easy to do.

If a finding is not reliable or general, others will eventually discover limitations as they attempt to use the results in some way. If the original investigator takes responsibility for reporting findings that are at least shown to be reliable, however, it improves the quality of the archival literature. If each researcher leaves this responsibility to others, published findings will sometimes be misleading, making it difficult for readers to distinguish between results that can be reproduced and those that cannot be depended on. For example, Sidman's first experiment on stimulus equivalence involved a boy with intellectual disabilities who could match spoken words to pictures and name pictures but did not name printed words or match them to corresponding pictures. After being trained to match spoken words to corresponding printed words, the boy then matched the printed words to pictures and named the printed

TABLE 11.8
When should replications be considered?

- When the existing literature on the topic is small, weak, or includes mixed results
- When the findings contradict the existing literature
- When the investigator has little experience with the procedure
- When there are obvious alternative explanations for the effects
- When failure to reproduce the same outcome under other conditions is likely to be costly in some way
- When the replication will be relatively easy to do

words accurately without any direct training. Although that initial experiment included replications of the training and testing procedures with multiple stimulus sets, Sidman immediately recognized the importance to both researchers and practitioners of evaluating whether the rather startling findings would hold up under other conditions. So he and a colleague repeated the first experiment with two different boys with intellectual disabilities, using some controls that were not used in the initial experiment (a systematic replication; see below). The main findings were similar to those of the first experiment, which gave Sidman and other investigators sufficient confidence in the reliability of the findings to go on to conduct many additional studies involving a wide range of human and nonhuman participants, stimuli, and procedural variations (Sidman, 1994).

A second question concerns whether to focus on establishing the reliability of the treatment effects or pursuing their generality. In other words, the researcher or practitioner must decide how similar the replication should be to the original condition. In addressing this question, remember that a result that is not reliable can have no useful generality, no matter how many attempts are made to reproduce it. If interest lies primarily in the generality of a reliable outcome, the investigator must decide which variables should be changed in the replication. The particular circumstances of each study guide these decisions. One approach is to vary or even eliminate factors the investigator suspects might not be critical to the effect. This might allow the intervention to be refined or reduced to a more efficient form. A contrasting approach would be to vary factors that are suspected of playing a critical role. Verifying their contribution would clarify the key features of a procedure. For their second experiment on stimulus equivalence, Sidman and his colleague could have elected to change any of several variables that were present in the original experiment. They decided that in order to convince others that the effect was reliable, it was most important to test the possibility that training the auditory-visual (spoken word-printed word) stimulus relations was necessary for the emergence of untrained relations among the visual stimuli (printed words and pictures). So instead of training all of the auditory-visual relations at once as in the original experiment, they trained the auditory-visual matching performances in a series of subsets, each followed by testing for untrained matching of visual stimuli. That systematic replication of the original experiment reproduced the main effect – emergence of untrained visual-visual stimulus relations – while also demonstrating that that effect occurred only after the prerequisite auditory-visual relations were established (Sidman, 1994).

A third question concerns the number of replications necessary to establish reliability or to at least suggest a certain extent of generality. Because replications that duplicate the original condition provide little information beyond the reliability of their effects, there is no point in continuing such replications once an effect has been shown to be reliable. On the other hand, each replication that changes some variables creates the possibility of learning something new about the role of those factors. This kind of replication can be endlessly useful. For example, scores of systematic replications of the early experiments on stimulus equivalence by Sidman and others have produced a wealth of knowledge that continues to prove very useful to basic and applied researchers as well as practitioners.

A fourth question asks how to determine when a replication is successful in reproducing the original results. That is, how close to the original findings do the reproduced results need to be? It is unlikely that the reproduced results will duplicate the quantitative details of the original data, of course. The objective is to instead reproduce the form of the original relationship between the intervention condition and responding. For example, each participant in a project may respond under control and intervention conditions in slightly different ways. One individual may respond more often than another under both conditions, or one may show a more rapid transition at the beginning of the intervention condition. These differences are usually unimportant, however, as long as responding is generally affected in the same way by the intervention condition. In other words, the standard for a successful reproduction of earlier results is obtaining the same form of the relationship. That is what occurred in the first systematic replication of Sidman's original stimulus equivalence study, discussed previously.

Finally, there is the question of what to do when the replication does not reproduce the original results. If the replication is highly similar to the original effort on key dimensions like participants and procedures, a failure suggests that the original findings might have been due to extraneous factors that were not present during the replication. For example, it might be that the results depended on the way a particular staff member administered an intervention procedure and that person was not involved in the replication. If the replication focused on generality by incorporating specific changes from the original effort, those changes must be examined more closely to assess their role in the original results. For instance, a practitioner might find that a procedure worked well with one individual but poorly when tried with another individual. That outcome would suggest that differences in participant characteristics could be important to the effectiveness of a procedure. Either way, the investigator obviously has more work to do.

Number of Participants

Rationale. As we emphasized in earlier chapters, the fact that behavior is a phenomenon that occurs only at the level of individual organisms means

TABLE 11.9
Questions guiding replication decisions

- When should replications be pursued?
- Should replications focus on reliability or generality?
- How many replications are necessary?
- How close to the original results should the reproduced results be?
- What should be done if the original results are not reproduced?

---

investigators must address each participant separately throughout all aspects of research projects or treatment programs. This means that decisions involved in conducting a study or providing services must be made separately for each individual, including measuring the target behavior, making steady state decisions, and analyzing data. It is almost as if each participant represents a separate study, even though it is usually practical to use multiple participants to get the most out of all the work involved in setting up a research project or treatment program.

In fact, as long as an investigation is well done, only a single individual's data are necessary to justify conclusions that have every bit as much chance of being true as when the data represent the behavior of a larger number of individuals. Although it could always be the case that any one individual is not typical of others with the same general characteristics (for example, first graders learning to read), each participant's data reflect a credible relation between the intervention condition and his or her behavior. Even if one individual's reaction to the intervention was unusual compared to how other individuals responded, it would still be a real effect and no less meaningful than others. Indeed, sometimes it is especially important to learn why one participant responded differently from others.

If only a single participant is required to draw sound conclusions about the effects of a treatment condition, how can the investigator know if those conclusions are typical of how others would respond under the same condition? This is an important question, and upcoming chapters will consider this topic further. However, we point out here that adding a second or even a third participant does little to answer the question. The investigator has no way of knowing the extent to which additional individuals are typical of the countless others who are not participating. Even if the second or third individual reacts similarly to the intervention, though differently from the first participant, it does not mean their results are "correct" and those of the first participant are "incorrect." Assuming accurate measurement, all three results are equally valid reflections of how individuals are affected by the intervention.

This point may be easier to grasp if we distinguish between the truthfulness of results and their generality to other individuals. The researcher's primary objective is to obtain data that truly represent the relation between the independent variable and the dependent variable. If that is not accomplished, nothing else matters. Only when the findings are "true" does the question of their meaningfulness under other circumstances become relevant.

As we will see in Chapter 16, the question about the generality of results to other individuals is not a matter of how many individuals participated in a study. Predictions about how well the findings will hold up with other individuals or under other circumstances depend instead on how well the investigator understands the factors that influence the effects of the intervention procedures. If the investigator knows, for example, that changing a particular component of the procedure will substantially change its effects or that a certain characteristic of participants is necessary to get the effects, he or she is in a better position to make predictions about the conditions under which the

findings will or will not hold. Learning these kinds of things does not depend
on how many participants are involved in a single study. Instead, it usually
requires a series of studies focused on identifying and evaluating key variables.
This is why statements about generality based on a single study should usually
be considered largely speculative.

Practical Issues. If the number of participants in a study has little to do
with the correctness or the generality of its results, how does the investigator

---

BOX 11.3

Why Psychology Likes Lots of Participants

In contrast with the requirements for good behavior analytic research, the style
of research that traditionally dominates psychology, education, and the social
sciences requires relatively large numbers of participants – the more the better.
That tradition is largely based on a view of generality that turns out to be inappropriate for the study of behavior.

The traditional approach to generality assumes that the purpose of behavioral
research is to allow comparisons between groups of participants. One group is
typically exposed to a control condition, and another group is assigned to an
experimental condition. That allows a comparison to be made by using inferential statistical tests to decide whether there is a significant difference between
some aggregate measures, such as the mean scores of the two groups on a test
or checklist completed when the study begins and again when it ends. The mathematical theory underlying such statistics requires a certain minimum number
of participants (usually comparatively large). The more participants used, the
smaller the relative differences between the group means that will qualify as
statistically significant.

This conception of experimentation has led many investigators to view generality as a sampling issue. The research question typically concerns whether,
given the size of the difference between the mean scores of the two groups,
the sizes of the control and experimental groups as samples of the population
of interest are sufficiently large to permit a speculation about the likelihood of
observing the effect in the population from which the samples were drawn. That
is a straightforward mathematical question, but it is not really pertinent to the
issue of generality in the study of behavior.

As Chapter 16 explains in greater detail, the main question about the generality of a study's findings is whether the effects of the experimental or treatment
condition will be obtained under conditions that differ somewhat from those
of the study. In order to know whether a particular result will be obtained for
a participant in a later study or under everyday circumstances, what we really
need to know is what variables are necessary to make the effect occur, what
variables will prevent it from occurring, and what variables will modulate the
effect. Merely increasing the size of the control and experimental groups cannot
provide that kind of information. It is necessary to conduct a series of studies that
identify and investigate such variables.

decide how many to involve? It usually comes down to some fairly common sense considerations. For example, it makes sense to take advantage of all the work of setting up a study by involving more than just one or two individuals. The more participants there are, the more data will be available for analysis. Even though each participant's data will usually be treated as equally credible, it is valuable to see if the findings are essentially the same for all participants or if some are noticeably different from others. It is reassuring, of course, when all participants react in the same way as the intervention condition is initiated or withdrawn. It may be no less useful, however, to learn that reactions tend to vary. Such an outcome might encourage the investigator to try to figure out why, which often leads to the discovery of ways of strengthening the treatment condition, controlling extraneous factors, or identifying key participant characteristics. In turn, those discoveries will lead to a clearer picture of the effects of the intervention condition, as well as possibly identifying some factors that improve predictions about the generality of the findings.

A second reason for involving multiple participants is to accommodate the possibility that things may not go as planned. The investigator may intend to expose all participants to the same sequence of conditions, but the emerging data may suggest other alternatives. For example, it might prove tempting to assess the impact of eliminating an extraneous factor on just a couple of individuals while others continue the planned sequence of phases. The investigator might also wish to adjust an intervention condition to see if its effects can be strengthened. Although this can be done with all participants, it might be sufficient to conduct that test with only two or three of them, again leaving the others to continue with the originally planned sequence of conditions.

A third advantage of starting with a sufficient number of participants is to allow for the likelihood that some individuals will not complete the study for various reasons. The reasons are all too familiar to investigators, especially those who work in applied settings. Participants sometimes get sick, have transportation problems, move away, or just quit. Regardless of the reasons, any time participants fail to get adequate exposure to a condition, their data may not fully reflect its effects. Sometimes that means the investigator must drop them from the study, or at least not include their data in the analysis. It is important to have enough participants to accommodate losses without having to start the project all over again.

A fourth possibility is that some participants may not meet various performance criteria under pretraining conditions. A study might require participants to reach a certain standard of performance in an initial phase that is necessary for evaluating the impact of a subsequent intervention condition. To return to a previous example, it might be necessary for participants to reach a certain level of competence in performing match-to-sample tasks presented on a computer with a touchscreen before they are exposed to intervention conditions. Failing to master that performance might mean that a participant's data would not be sensitive to the independent variable, so she should not continue in the study. That is another reason it may be wise to start a study with a few extra participants.

TABLE 11.10
Reasons for involving "additional" participants

- Take advantage of research preparations by assessing generality across participants
- Allow possibility of pursuing unplanned needs and opportunities with some participants
- Accommodate unplanned loss of participants
- Accommodate loss of participants who do not meet standards

All of these considerations might seem to suggest that more participants are better than fewer participants. However, each additional individual involves some extra effort. Each person must be recruited and permissions obtained. Depending on the nature of the project, each might need to be assessed or pretrained. The number of individuals involved also affects the logistics of actually running the study. All of the methodological issues discussed in previous chapters must be addressed for each participant, including measurement, experimental control, and data analysis. Finally, simply running each participant through the various control and intervention phases involves time and resources, which are inevitably limited.

After all is said and done, deciding on the number of participants needed comes down to making educated guesses and compromises. Starting with the minimum of one, the investigator adds up the number that might be needed to accommodate different considerations. That number is then balanced against the costs and limitations involved. Most within-subject design studies involve only a few participants, but more is not uncommon. On the other hand, it is fairly unusual for such a study to include more than a dozen participants if the data are being analyzed individually.

RESEARCH DESIGN AND PRACTICE

It might seem that a discussion of how to arrange comparisons of behavior under control and treatment conditions would be of more interest to researchers than practitioners. After all, practitioners are most often focused on providing services to individuals with unique behavioral needs, not on understanding how target behaviors are affected by independent variable conditions and sharing those outcomes with colleagues in journal publications and convention presentations. Besides, learning things about behavior that colleagues and others can depend on requires giving considerable priority to methodological standards, which often conflict with service delivery interests. In fact, although investigating research questions and providing practical services are certainly different agendas, they often demand the same competence in understanding how to answer questions about behavior.

There are at least two good reasons for practitioners to understand how to compare responding under control and treatment conditions. First, practitioners are key consumers of behavior analytic research, whether published or presented at professional meetings or in some other forum, such as a website or blog. In reading the literature and attending conventions and workshops, practitioners are often looking for ways to improve their clinical skills. They want to learn what investigators can tell them about how to apply research findings so as to better serve their clients. It would be easy to satisfy those interests if every published research report or presentation met the highest methodological standards so that users were assured of predictable results.

In reality, however, consumers of research – in all fields, not just behavior analysis – must be well informed and cautious. ABA practitioners must understand which studies warrant their attention and which should be passed by. Practitioners must understand the requirements for arranging comparisons among conditions just as well as researchers because they are responsible for judging what conclusions are credible. Simply accepting at face value the findings reported in a journal, at a convention, or on a website will too often lead to disappointment when the reported results are applied under local circumstances. There are particular reasons why some studies are stronger than others and some offer conclusions that are not adequately supported. As consumers of research, behavior analytic practitioners must be able to identify those factors and critically evaluate research findings.

Second, although most practitioners may not work in circumstances that allow them to conduct formal research projects, they often have the same kinds of questions about behavior that motivate researchers. Not all practitioners may be interested in conducting formal experiments, but all want to understand what is going on with their clients' target behaviors. Why is a behavior changing – or not – and what does that mean for the ongoing treatment plan? How can the treatment protocol be strengthened or streamlined without reducing its effectiveness? What can be learned from a particular case that may be useful in future cases?

Because applied behavior analysis evolved from the science of behavior analysis, ABA practice incorporates established research methods. Practitioners are therefore often in a good position to arrange sound comparisons between control and treatment conditions and, with the benefit of good behavioral measurement, draw at least tentative conclusions about the effects of intervention procedures. Although the challenge of managing extraneous variables and establishing good experimental control may often limit the clarity of those conclusions, by focusing on discovering why a target behavior is or is not changing, practitioners can learn a great deal from their experiences. The value of using practical experiences to augment professional expertise makes it important for practitioners to understand the prerequisites for drawing sound conclusions about their own interventions.

CHAPTER SUMMARY

1. The objective in an experiment is to determine the effects on the target behavior of an experimental or treatment condition containing the

independent variable compared to the effects of a control condition that is otherwise the same but does not include the independent variable. The reason for making this comparison is to be sure that the changes in responding observed when the treatment condition is present are solely the result of the variables of interest in the treatment phase.

2. Identifying the effects of the independent variable in a research study or a practical project requires making sure that the only thing that differs between a treatment or intervention condition and its matching control condition is the independent variable itself.

3. It may seem that the independent variable is usually something that is added to the baseline preparation of the control condition. Instead, the independent variable may involve merely changing some factor in the baseline procedures.

4. Any features of the intervention condition that are not included in the description of the independent variable are, by definition, extraneous to the investigator's primary interests. Extraneous factors include not only all of the features of the control condition that continue throughout the treatment phase but also any other influences that occur during the treatment condition.

5. The control or baseline condition must establish the conditions under which participants will behave. The objective guiding decisions about what will make up a control condition is to help identify the effects of the independent variable.

6. The control condition controls for all of those factors in the intervention condition that are not part of the independent variable. This means that in evaluating the effects of the independent variable, all of the background factors included in the control condition are eliminated from consideration. This is why each different experimental or treatment condition should be matched to its own control condition.

7. In arranging pairs of control and experimental conditions, it is important to avoid comparing data from two conditions in which the variables operating in one condition are discontinued and largely replaced by a different set of variables in the other.

8. It is customary for the control condition to precede its matched experimental or treatment condition. This allows the investigator to examine whether the procedures in place are working as intended. This sequence also allows the investigator to provide participants with a particular kind of history that may be required in order to prepare for the experimental condition.

9. Although there are advantages to having the control condition come first, it is not required. When steady state responding under a matching pair of control and treatment conditions is compared, the sequence of the conditions does not change the experimental reasoning.

10. The ordering of conditions may result in sequence effects, which may make responding more useful in identifying the effects of the next

condition. Although sequence effects can be beneficial, they can also be problematic. In general, they are undesirable when the effects of one condition interfere with seeing a clear picture of the effects of a following condition.

11. Given the uncertainties surrounding sequence effects, researchers and practitioners need to address two questions when they design projects. First, are there reasons to arrange for sequence effects so they will help highlight the effects of treatment conditions? Second, how might sequence effects occur that could interfere with identifying treatment effects?

12. When describing the sequence of conditions, each different phase in temporal sequence is assigned successive letters of the alphabet. The first phase is labeled A, and the second phase is labeled B. This lettering system of summarizing sequences of phases in a study works well only for relatively simple experimental designs.

13. The reason for comparing measures of a target behavior under paired control and treatment conditions is to learn enough about the effects of the independent variable to be able to show that changes in responding are a function of the independent variable and nothing else.

14. Concerns over experimental control and how investigators might identify and modify these problems are likely to fall into three general categories. First, it may be necessary to modify how the target behavior is defined and measured so that the data will be more useful. Second, it may be necessary to modify some features of the control and treatment conditions. Finally, investigators may find that unanticipated extraneous factors are intruding on control or treatment conditions.

15. A challenge for applied researchers and practitioners is deciding how much experimental control is necessary. The general answer involves a balance between two interests. There must be enough control to allow sound conclusions about the role of the independent variable. However, there must not be so much control that the preparation does not reflect the circumstances needed to get a meaningful answer to the question.

16. There are three ways of managing extraneous variables. They may be eliminated entirely, which is a good tactic but not always feasible and could result in creating conditions that are not characteristic of the circumstance. Extraneous variables could also be held constant across conditions, which assures us that they will be the same for each phase – but they will still have an impact. Finally, they may be directly examined to evaluate their contribution.

17. Replication is useful because it helps the investigator to assess the reliability of the original findings or the extent to which they might be obtained under somewhat different conditions (i.e., generality). However, even if the data show that repeating an intervention condition results in the same outcomes, such data do not confirm that those effects were actually due to the independent variable.

18. As long as an investigation is done well, only a single individual's data are necessary to justify conclusions that have as much chance of being true as when the data represent the behavior of a large number of individuals.

19. While the use of multiple participants has little to do with the correctness or generality of its results, there are advantages to using multiple participants, including the ability to analyze more data, which may lead to discovering new ways of strengthening treatment conditions and controlling extraneous factors. The use of additional participants is also helpful in case you have attrition or if your participants do not meet various performance criteria under pretraining conditions.

20. There are at least two good reasons for practitioners to understand how to compare responding under control and treatment conditions. First, practitioners are key consumers of behavior analytic research. Practitioners must understand the requirements for arranging comparisons among conditions just as well as researchers because they are responsible for judging what conclusions are credible. Second, practitioners often have the same kinds of questions about behavior that motivate researchers.

HIGHLIGHTED TERMS

Control or baseline condition. A condition or phase of an experiment in which the independent variable is not present.

Dependent variable. In behavior analytic research, usually a response class, at least one dimension of which is measured throughout all phases of a study.

Experimental control. The management or control of different variables in a study, including the independent variable and extraneous variables.

Experimental (research) design. Arrangements of control and experimental conditions that permit comparisons that help identify the effects of the independent variable on the dependent variable.

Experimental, treatment, intervention, or independent variable condition. A condition or phase in which the independent variable is present.

Functional relation. An experimentally determined relation that shows that the dependent variable depends on or is a function of particular variables, ideally the independent variable and nothing else.

Independent variable. An environmental event whose presence or absence is manipulated by the investigator in order to determine its effects on the dependent variable.

Replication. Repetition of any parts of an experiment.

Replication across a condition or phase. Repetition of an entire phase during the course of an experiment. Requires session-by-session display of data for each phase.

Replication across research literatures. Repetition of phenomena under different conditions across different fields of science.

Replication across sessions. Repetition of the same condition many times in succession throughout a phase. Requires session-by-session display of data.

Replication across trials. Repetition of a basic element of procedure throughout each session. Requires trial-by-trial display of data.

Replication of entire studies. Repetition of an earlier study, usually by other researchers.

Reproduction. Repetition of results, usually as an outcome of repeating procedures.

Treatment integrity (procedural integrity, independent variable integrity). The extent to which the independent variable or other key features of a condition are consistently implemented as designed.

TEXT STUDY GUIDE

1. What is the shared feature of experimental, treatment, or independent variable conditions that distinguishes them from control conditions?

2. Explain why it is important that the only thing that differs between an intervention condition and its matching control condition is the independent variable itself.

3. What is the problem when the changes associated with an intervention condition are confounded with other changes?

4. Describe the two jobs that a control condition must do.

5. What does the control condition control for?

6. Why must each experimental or treatment condition be compared to a matching control condition?

7. What problems would result if the features of a control condition were not continued throughout its matching intervention condition?

8. Describe reasons why it is often useful to start an investigation or clinical treatment with a control condition before introducing the treatment condition. Is this a requirement?

9. What is a sequence effect?

10. Describe how sequence effects can be beneficial. How can they be problematic?

11. What does the letter "A" represent in letter designations of conditions?

12. What is a functional relation?

13. Why might it often take multiple investigations to identify a functional relationship?

14. Explain the concept of experimental control.

15. Explain how collecting repeated measures of an individual's behavior provide opportunities to improve experimental control.

16. What is treatment or procedural integrity?

17. How much experimental control might be too much?

18. Describe the three ways of managing extraneous variables. What are the pros and cons of each approach?

19. What are the risks of concluding that changes in responding were due to the independent variable without identifying the possible contributions of extraneous variables?

20. How do the authors recommend distinguishing between the terms replication and reproduction?

21. List and describe five types of replication.

22. What are the two general kinds of functions that replication serves?

23. When replicating a condition to assess reliability, how closely should the replication match the original condition and why?

24. When replicating a condition to assess generality, how closely should the replication match the original condition and why?

25. At best, what is learned by replicating a condition exactly and reproducing the original results? What does this fail to show?

26. Describe what information might be used to decide when an intervention should be replicated.

27. What factors bear on the decision about whether to focus on establishing reliability or pursuing generality?

28. What considerations are relevant to evaluating whether a replication has been successful in reproducing the original effects?

29. How many participants are minimally required to make a defensible statement about the effects of the intervention on the target behavior?

30. Why does adding additional participants not help the investigator to understand whether the findings will hold for all similar individuals?

31. List the practical considerations for deciding on the number of participants needed in an investigation.

32. Describe two reasons why it would be beneficial for practitioners to understand how to compare responding under control and treatment conditions.

BOX STUDY GUIDE

1. Describe a demonstration study and the information it provides.

2. Describe a correlation study and the information it provides.

3. What is required to show a functional relation?

4. Why do scientists not talk about causes?

5. Contrast the approach to generality implicit in between-group designs using many participants and within-subject designs using a relatively small number of participants.

SUGGESTED READINGS

Johnston, J. M., & Pennypacker, H. S. (1993b). *Readings for Strategies and tactics of behavioral research* (2nd ed.). Hillsdale, NJ: Lawrence Erlbaum Associates. Reading 7: Traditions of experimental design.

Sidman, M. (1960). *Tactics of scientific research*. New York: Basic Books. Chapter 3: Direct replication.

Sidman, M. (1960). *Tactics of scientific research*. New York: Basic Books. Chapter 4: Systematic replication.

DISCUSSION TOPICS

1. Select a published study in a behavioral journal and determine the independent variable(s). Discuss the extent to which the presence of the independent variable(s) is the only thing that differed between control and treatment conditions.

2. Select a published study in a behavioral journal and determine the independent variable condition. Describe the control condition associated with this experimental condition. How well does it control for all variables in the experimental condition?

3. Provide the general outlines of a hypothetical study that might be conducted under field conditions. Designate the independent variable and then discuss possible extraneous variables to manage. Consider the pros and cons of managing these extraneous factors by eliminating them, holding them constant, or directly examining their influence.

EXERCISES

1. Select three published studies from behavioral journals. Identify the independent variable(s) and dependent variable(s).

2. Using a behavioral journal, find an example of a study in which one phase was intentionally used to create a sequence effect.

3. Using behavioral journals, find examples of the following types of replication: (a) across trials, (b) across sessions, (c) of a condition or phase, and (d) of entire studies.

4. Select a study from a behavioral journal that does not use a multiple baseline or multi-element design (see Chapters 12–13), and designate the sequence of phases using the letters of the alphabet.

CHAPTER TWELVE

Single Baseline Designs

INTRODUCTION

Designing Comparisons

There is no single term or phrase that universally refers to the behavior analytic approach to experimental design. One of the most common labels is "within-subject design." That term emphasizes the fact that each participant (replacing the older reference to "subject") serves as his or her own control by experiencing both the control condition and the independent variable or treatment condition in sequence. As we discussed in Chapter 11, the advantage of this approach is that the unique characteristics of each individual are shared

327

across both conditions. Whatever the influence of each person's features, they are at least held constant across both conditions being compared. The alternative is to expose each participant to only one of the two conditions and therefore compare the effects of each condition across different individuals, as is commonly done in studies using between-groups research designs. That means that the data from each condition would represent both the effects of that condition and the characteristics of the participants who experienced that condition. The comparison of data from control versus treatment conditions would therefore be confounded by the contributions of different participants.

To elaborate, although the participants for a study might be carefully selected to share a number of key features, each will unavoidably bring along many differences as well. The details of their histories and repertoires will certainly be different, and some of those characteristics may bear on how they respond to control and treatment conditions. To illustrate this important point, compare the performances of Jose and Maria under both control and treatment conditions shown in Figure 12.1. The data show that although Maria responded more frequently than Jose under both conditions, they both had a decrease in responding during the treatment phase compared to the baseline (control) phase. What if all we had to compare was Jose's performance under the baseline condition with Maria's performance under the treatment condition? We would likely conclude that the treatment condition had no effect, even though in fact it had the same effect for both individuals. We would be misled by the fact that this "between-subject" comparison confounded the effects of the treatment condition with the different characteristics of the two participants.

"Single subject research designs" or "single case research designs" is another common reference to the approach to research designs described in this book. It emphasizes that each participant constitutes a complete basis for legitimate conclusions, though without evidence of generality across other individuals. As we pointed out in Chapter 11, using more than one participant brings advantages and alternatives to a study. It is not the case, however, that each additional participant increases the correctness or credibility of any conclusions.

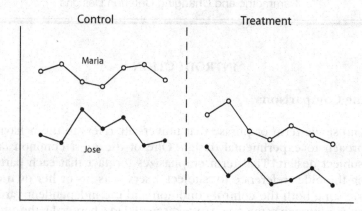

FIG. 12.1. Data illustrating the importance of making within-subject comparisons.

More participants only provide more of the same evidence available from a single participant. Multiple participants may provide some evidence about the reliability of a finding across different individuals, but a single participant is sufficient to draw credible conclusions about the effects of an intervention condition.

Other terms that provide the same emphasis as single subject designs are "N=1 designs" and "small N designs." Both are shorthand for indicating that only a single participant is necessary. Of course, the typical published study representing this type of design involves multiple participants, though rarely as many as in studies using between-groups designs. (Chapter 11 discussed how to decide how many participants might be needed.)

"Repeated measures designs" is still another way of labeling this approach to making comparisons between conditions. It emphasizes the steady state strategy described in Chapter 10 of measuring the target behavior for each participant repeatedly under each condition for a series of successive sessions before switching to the next condition. That design feature produces a picture of the effects of each condition that represents its fully developed influence on the target behavior. It allows more meaningful comparisons of control and treatment conditions than would be available if the data from either condition were atypical or misrepresentative in some way.

Working Assumptions

For purposes of discussion in this chapter and the next, it will helpful if we start out with a few general assumptions. First, unless otherwise specified, these two chapters addressing research designs assume that all variables are the same across the conditions being compared except that one condition includes the independent variable and the other does not. In other words, as explained in Chapter 11, we assume the control or baseline condition is constructed so it includes all of the factors operating in the treatment condition except for those variables that are defined by the investigator's interests as the independent variable. If the control condition were not matched in that way to the treatment condition, it would mean that factors besides the independent variable that differed between the two conditions could contribute to an explanation of any changes in responding.

A second assumption underlying these two chapters is that there are no problems with measurement procedures. That is, in order to focus on what different types of designs can reveal, it helps to assume the data sets being compared are fully accurate. Of course, that is often not the case in reality. When there are problems and weaknesses in measurement procedures, however, it means the comparisons available in the design must be tempered by that limitation. Sometimes measurement weaknesses are sufficiently serious that they do not allow defensible conclusions.

Third, it is also useful to assume the data show substantial and consistent differences in the target behavior between the two conditions being compared.

In other words, our discussion assumes stable responding in each phase and orderly transitions to different levels or patterns of responding when the conditions change. Again, if that is not the case, the data limit the conclusions that might otherwise be drawn.

In sum, this discussion of research designs assumes that all other aspects of a study are sound. That position allows us to discuss different comparisons of control and intervention conditions without any complications that might come from other features of an investigation. In any event, the interpretive options created by a research design cannot be improved by how other features of an investigation are treated. That is, the best-case conclusions that may be drawn are determined entirely by the nature of the comparisons that are arranged. Any shortcomings in measurement procedures, management of extraneous variables, or data weaken any conclusions the design would otherwise allow.

Types of Within-Subject Designs

The development of within-subject designs for the study of behavior began in B. F. Skinner's laboratory at Harvard University in the 1930s as a way of identifying functional relations between experimental variables and the behavior of pigeons. Skinner's description of his approach was notably informal: "So far as I can see, I simply began looking for lawful processes in the behavior of the intact organism" (Skinner, 1961, p. 80). Murray Sidman systematized and explained these experimental methods in his seminal volume *Tactics of Scientific Research* in 1960.

As the field has grown over the years, especially in applied directions, the basic approach to arranging comparisons between control and treatment conditions described by Sidman (1960) has remained largely unchanged. However, textbooks have increasingly distinguished variations in how within-subject comparisons can be arranged, and those variations are now often labeled as different types of designs. Although this chapter and Chapter 13 describe and explain those variations, it is important to understand that there are actually endless ways of arranging within-subject comparisons, all of which share the same core reasoning. Any single "type" of design can be implemented in different ways and even combined with other "types" to provide the basis for sound conclusions.

Although dividing various arrangements of control/treatment comparisons into formal types of designs may be useful for instructional purposes, such distinctions can blur the fact that they are all fundamentally the same kind of design. Once students understand the reasoning underlying all within-subject comparisons between control and treatment conditions, the different ways of creating those comparisons blossom into endless possibilities that can suit any situation. Our discussion of types of within-subject designs encourages that perspective by focusing on the shared features of what might seem to be distinct types of designs and the common reasoning on which they are all based. The key to that cohesive view lies in understanding how the different types of comparisons support conclusions about what is going on with behavior.

SINGLE BASELINE DESIGNS

AB Comparisons

AB arrangements are the core of all within-subject comparisons. Recall that "A" simply designates the first condition in a sequence and "B" identifies the second. Although the first condition is usually a control or baseline phase and the second is a treatment or intervention phase that includes the independent variable, the sequence can be the other way around. (In such a case, A would refer to the intervention condition and B to the control condition.) As Chapter 10 explains, there are often practical reasons for a baseline-treatment sequence, but the comparison is between the same two data sets, whichever the order. Figure 12.2 illustrates an AB comparison, with the passage of time reading from left to right.

> **AB comparison.** A within-subject sequence of phases composed of one control and one experimental condition.

A single AB comparison by itself has some merit, but it is important to recognize its limitations. A comparison of data from one sequence of matched control and intervention conditions provides evidence that in that one instance the two conditions revealed differences in responding. That is not trivial, of course. It shows that when the conditions changed, the target behavior changed as well.

If that is all there is, however, there are at least two important things we do not yet know. First, we do not know if the change in responding we observed is a typical or reliable outcome of terminating the control condition and implementing the treatment condition. What if we repeated the AB sequence of conditions or tried it with a different individual and did not get the same changes in behavior? What would we conclude then about the result of implementing the intervention condition?

Second, we also do not know if the change in responding was due to the independent variable associated with the intervention condition. It may seem very likely, but if we have only one baseline and one treatment data set we cannot be sure. That is often a difficult limitation to accept, especially for the investigator. After all, if everything was the same across the two conditions

A | B

FIG. 12.2. Notation of an "AB" design.

except for the independent variable, what else could explain why responding started changing when the intervention condition started and eventually stabilized at a different level of responding?

The answer is that extraneous factors selectively associated with the treatment condition could confound the effect of the independent variable. In other words, there is more than a fair risk that the independent variable

---

BOX 12.1

Are Extraneous Variables That Big a Deal?

The simple answer to this question is "Not necessarily, but…" First, we need to be honest and acknowledge that it is always possible that a treatment condition includes not only the independent variable but other factors that are just along for the ride. As we discussed in Chapter 11, they include variables that are related to the independent variable, though not explicitly a part of it, as well as unrelated variables that just happen. Any extraneous variable can be powerful or weak, overwhelming the effect of the independent variable or having little or no effect.

So what are the chances that they meaningfully influence responding, especially to the extent that they distort our interpretation of the role of the independent variable? The chances partly depend on how carefully the control and treatment conditions are designed and implemented. The tighter the degree of experimental control that is achieved, the lower the odds that extraneous variables will intrude, although there are no guarantees. However, the pursuit of experimental control is often challenging in applied behavioral research, not to mention practice. At best, it tends to conflict with the need to accommodate relatively messy applied circumstances and treatment protocols that are made up of lots of components.

As we note in Chapter 11, one way to deal with this challenge is to generously define the independent variable as "whatever goes on during the intervention phase." This can be a little bit fraudulent, however, because it simply defines the problem of extraneous influences away by rolling them unidentified into the definition of the independent variable. It also makes it easier to accept the changes in responding observed during the treatment phase as entirely due to its main feature, usually summarized with a simple label or phrase. In other words, an inclusive definition of the independent variable makes it easier to ignore the risks of extraneous variables complicating the picture otherwise evident in the data.

This is not to say that there is anything wrong with a simple conclusion that the changes in responding under the treatment condition are largely or even entirely due to the independent variable. They may well be. The origins of intervention effects are not always complicated. Extraneous influences are not always important, though if we look carefully enough they are probably always present. The problem is that we cannot know for sure whether extraneous factors contributed to the data in important ways without taking special steps. It is easiest to assume they did not, but if they did, concluding that the independent variable is fully responsible for the data will be misleading. So the bottom line question is, "How important is it that the conclusions be correct?"

built into the intervention condition was not the only difference between the two conditions. We have described a number of examples of this common problem. For instance, in Chapter 11 we explained how extra teacher attention (an extraneous variable) could influence the performance of a student using a computer program (the independent variable). In that example, the extra teacher attention was present in the intervention phase when the computer program was being used but was not available during the control phase. No matter how much the investigator might believe changes in academic performance were due to the computer program, it is certainly possible that the extra teacher attention contributed to those changes as well. It is even possible that the extra attention was entirely responsible for the changes in responding and that the computer program had no influence at all. The risk that the independent variable is confounded with extraneous factors specifically associated with the intervention condition is especially likely in applied studies, where there is usually a lot going on. A published study of such an intervention (Helton & Ivy, 2016) is discussed in the section on reversal designs that follows.

In sum, an AB comparison by itself provides a weak basis for drawing conclusions about the influence of the independent variable because it only shows a single instance of changes in behavior corresponding to changes in conditions and fails to evaluate the role of extraneous factors. It resembles an experiment because a dependent variable is measured under matched control and independent variable conditions, but it simply does not provide the kind of information necessary to conclude that the change in responding is functionally related to the independent variable. At best, the data from an AB comparison can be encouraging; it should not be convincing. It will be important to keep the limited value of a single AB comparison in mind as we consider ways of combining different types of comparisons in actual designs.

Reversal Designs

Basic Features. In contrast to a simple AB comparison, **reversal designs** come in many variations. A reversal design involves a pair of control and treatment conditions in which one or both conditions repeat at least once. The replication is often described as reversing or going back to a prior condition. The simplest form of a reversal design would be described in letters as an ABA sequence. That arrangement indicates that the first phase (for discussion purposes, we will assume it is a control or baseline condition) is followed by an intervention phase, which is in turn followed by a return to the original control condition (see Figure 12.3).

A | B | A

FIG. 12.3.   Notation of an "ABA" design.

Reversal design. A within-subject experimental design minimally involving a pair of control and experimental conditions in which one or both conditions repeat at least once.

What information might a reversal design reveal? A reversal design begins with an AB comparison and therefore shows that implementing a treatment condition is associated with changes in responding. Repeating the original control condition adds the advantage of a second comparison between control and intervention conditions. In other words, an AB design allows only one comparison between control and treatment conditions, while an ABA design allows two such comparisons (AB and BA). Although the second comparison is between the intervention condition followed, rather than preceded, by the control condition, it is still the same kind of comparison. Both AB and BA comparisons allow a conclusion about the correspondence between the presence and absence of the treatment condition containing the independent variable and any differences in responding.

This second comparison (BA) permits an evaluation of whether the changes that occurred during the intervention condition reverse to the kind of responding observed under the original control condition. That would provide some encouragement that the behavioral changes occurring during the intervention condition are indeed related to something about that condition because they go away when the intervention is discontinued. It would be premature to conclude that those changes are solely due to the independent variable, however. Repeating the control condition does not address the second concern associated with a simple AB comparison – that the changes in responding associated with the intervention condition might be influenced by related extraneous factors (see Chapter 11 and Box 12.1). In other words, showing that responding changes when the intervention starts, and continues while it is ongoing, then ends when the intervention terminates does not establish a functional relation between the independent variable and related changes in behavior. Although an ABA version of a reversal design is more informative than a single AB comparison, it does not provide a different kind of information.

What if we go further and replicate not just the control condition but the intervention condition as well – an ABAB design (see Figure 12.4)? What additional information does that repetition of the treatment condition provide? It offers another AB comparison for our conclusions. We can now consider three comparisons between the two conditions (AB, BA, and AB again). That provides at least preliminary evidence that the effect associated with the intervention condition is reliable. It comes and goes consistently with the presence and absence of the intervention.

A | B | A | B

FIG. 12.4. Notation of an "ABAB" design.

Unfortunately, the ABAB reversal design still does not eliminate a key alternative explanation for our findings. That design does not provide reassurance that the independent variable is solely responsible for the associated changes in responding. Someone could argue that the behavioral changes are due to extraneous factors associated only with the independent variable condition, and we would have no basis for a convincing rebuttal. Again, investigators may sometimes find that a difficult constraint to accept. When you have labored to plan and implement an investigation and have watched everything closely from day to day, it is tempting to believe that the features of interest in the intervention condition (the independent variable) are all that could affect responding. Colleagues reading a published report of the investigation might want to make the same assumption, especially if they are also interested in the suggested outcome. Nevertheless, the fact of the matter is that neither an ABA nor an ABAB design establishes a functional relation, because it does not address the role of extraneous factors selectively associated with the independent variable. That limitation does not mean that the independent variable is not fully responsible for the changes in responding, just that the reversal design does not tell us one way or the other.

Several of the issues just described are exemplified in an ABAB evaluation of the effects of a vocal generalized conditioned reinforcer (GCR) on completion of math problems by two elementary school students during one-to-one sessions with an experimenter (Helton & Ivy, 2016). Creation of a GCR was accomplished during a single session that started with the experimenter delivering four vocal utterances ("Step" plus a number name starting with "four" and proceeding in descending order to "Step one") one at a time every 30 seconds. After the fourth one was delivered, the student was given the opportunity to select one item from an array of four edibles identified via previous preference assessments. Then the student was presented with a letter identification task during which one vocal utterance was delivered following every five correct responses. After all four utterances were delivered, the student was again allowed to select one of the preferred edibles. Those pairings of the vocal utterances with presumed primary reinforcers were deemed to have established the utterances as GCRs.

During each session in the baseline phase (A), the student was given worksheets of single-digit addition problems and instructions to "do as much as you like but [you] do not have to do any if you do not want to. There will be no rewards in this session." There were no programmed consequences for correct responses. When a problem was answered incorrectly, the experimenter said "That one needs to be fixed" and asked the student to correct her answer. Intervention (B phase) sessions were identical to baseline except that the experimenter said "This session you can earn rewards" at the beginning and delivered the GCR following completion of a specified number of problems (a fixed-ratio schedule of 7 for one student, 10 for the other). After four GCRs were delivered, the student was allowed to select a preferred edible. For both students, the number of math problems completed correctly was substantially higher in both intervention phases than in both baseline phases. In their report, however, the authors noted correctly that because the intervention procedures included instructions, the behavior change could not be attributed to the vocal GCR by itself, and the effects of the instructions were unknown. Additionally, they noted that the two students discussed their experiences in the study with each other – another extraneous variable that could have affected the observed results.

Variations. Reversal designs can be arranged in seemingly endless ways. For example, it is not unusual for an investigator to start with a straightforward ABA design but then pursue a second treatment condition. Such an arrangement may be planned, but it often develops based on what is learned from the initial ABA phases. With the participants and procedures already in place, it can be easy to implement a variation of the original treatment condition (B) to ask what will happen if one of its components is removed or modified or if a new feature is added. In that situation, the B condition may be able to serve as an appropriate control for the new treatment condition (C) if the only thing that differs between them is the new independent variable. It is easy to then arrange a reversal comparison by following the C phase with a return to the B condition. Figure 12.5 shows the notation for this type of extended reversal design. For example, in the Helton and Ivy (2016) study that was just described, the investigators could have opted to follow the first intervention condition (B) with a new intervention condition that was identical to the first but without instructions from the experimenter (C). Reversing to the B condition and then back to the C condition would have enabled them to compare the effects of the GCR contingency alone against a baseline consisting of that contingency plus instructions.

The "build-a-design-as-you-go" approach has a long history in behavior analytic research, as investigators have used accumulating data to make decisions about what else they might learn by arranging new comparisons that were not planned at the outset. Done properly, that flexibility in arranging experimental comparisons is one of the strengths of this approach to research design. The option of arranging previously unplanned comparisons between control and treatment conditions may be especially appealing for practitioners who share the objective of improving a client's behavior, whatever it takes. Even the most careful assessment of an individual's behavioral needs leaves many uncertainties about what intervention procedures will be most effective, both initially and over time. For example, implementing an intervention following a baseline phase may reveal that a treatment protocol is not working as expected. The practitioner might repeat the original AB sequence to verify that result (ABAB) and then choose to introduce a revised form of the treatment protocol (C). If the practitioner is curious about whether the effects of the revised protocol are reliable, she might then repeat the B condition (now serving as a control for the C condition) and then the C condition. The design at that point would be

A | B | A | B | C | B

FIG. 12.5. Notation of an "ABABCB" design.

notated ABABCB. As treatment progresses, each change in the treatment protocol might constitute a new phase. Even significant changes in non-treatment
features of the environment (for instance, changes in family circumstances,
health, and so forth) could be treated as phases in a growing sequence.

Although it can be informative to view a series of evolving treatment decisions as building a research design, real-world considerations often force some
interpretive limitations. Recall that meaningful comparisons of successive
control and treatment conditions require that they be properly matched so
that the only difference between them is the independent variable. In addition,
remember that a single AB comparison provides no evidence that the effects are
reliable or for concluding that the observed changes in responding were due
to the independent variable itself. Addressing those issues can be challenging
in the context of providing services. Practitioners often do not have the luxury
of arranging proper control conditions or repeating phases to assess reliability,
much less pursuing the impact of extraneous factors. That shortfall is one of the
distinctions between research and practice, and the price is that practitioners
may not be able to defend the conclusions they might like to draw.

What if Responding Does Not Reverse? A reversal design allows us to
see whether the change in responding associated with the B condition of an
ABA sequence ends when the B condition ends and responding returns to
patterns observed during the original A phase when it is repeated. But what
if responding under the second baseline condition does not yield the same
kind of responding found in the original baseline phase? What if responding
does not change when the B condition is terminated? Or what if responding
changes when the A condition is repeated but looks quite different from what
was observed the first time? Such outcomes would be a problem because the
investigator would then have AB and BA comparisons that showed different
behavioral results.

This situation is depicted in Figure 12.6. Responding in the second baseline
phase continues more or less unchanged when the B treatment condition ends

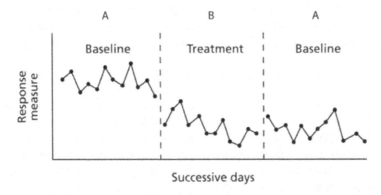

FIG. 12.6. Hypothetical data from an ABA sequence in which responding does not return
to original levels in the second baseline phase.

338   DESIGN

and fails to recover to the levels observed in the first baseline phase. The AB comparison shows responding is different under the two conditions, but the BA comparison shows it is the same. That conflict substantially weakens any argument that the treatment condition is responsible for the associated change in responding. If it were, terminating the treatment condition would presumably result in its effects going away as well.

In other words, the reversal design is informative only when responding reverts to the original baseline pattern after the intervention is removed. Unfortunately, there are some good reasons why baseline responding may not be recaptured when baseline conditions are repeated. First, it is in the fundamental nature of behavior that responding at any one point in time is likely to be influenced by recent history. Second, repeated measures designs optimize that historical influence by giving a participant repeated exposure to a condition before switching to the next phase. Third, designs that expose an individual to different conditions in sequence set up the possibility that the historical influence will be revealed as a sequence effect.

Investigators considering a reversal design should think about those factors in the context of each study. Sometimes it may be obvious that the changes induced by an intervention will have an enduring effect on responding. For instance, if an intervention trains a skill, particularly one supported by natural contingencies, it might be unlikely that discontinuing a training phase and reestablishing baseline conditions would result in the skill suddenly being lost. In other cases, it might be clear that it would be difficult to arrange the original baseline conditions a second time. For example, if an intervention changed a child's behavior in a classroom in ways that changed how other children interacted with her, it would not be feasible to reconstruct the original baseline conditions because it would require getting the other children to interact as they did before the intervention.

When responding under a replicated baseline does not recapture the kind of responding observed under the original phase (as in Figure 12.6), it may be tempting to argue that the intervention was responsible for the changes in responding and the effect was durable so did not dissipate when the intervention phase was terminated and baseline conditions were reinstituted. Although that may be true, supporting evidence is lacking. Situations in which recapturing baseline responding may be difficult should discourage the use of a reversal design.

Another explanation may also be viable. What if the change in responding during the treatment phase was influenced more by unidentified extraneous factors than the intervention protocol itself? If that were true, terminating the intervention and reverting to the original baseline condition might allow the unacknowledged extraneous influences to continue. Those extraneous variables might continue supporting the kind of responding observed during the intervention phase, thereby preventing baseline responding from being recaptured. For example, a treatment protocol might require teachers and other staff members in a preschool classroom to interact with Marla, a girl with autism, by giving her a sticker each time she responds correctly to an instruction directed to the entire class. When the treatment phase is terminated and baseline conditions are reinstituted, although the staff might properly stop implementing the protocol, the treatment may have established them as sources of reinforcement for Marla or increased the frequency of their interactions with her in ways that did not exist in the original baseline phase – changes perhaps not noticed by the investigator. That difference between the two baseline phases might mean that Marla's behavior in those phases would be different as well. In evaluating why Marla's responding to group instructions changed, the investigator would

---

BOX 12.2

Evidence over Preference

Graduate training and professional credentials in behavior analysis are supposed to instill a special set of values that benefit the field and those it serves. Paramount among those values is respect for objective evidence in our conception of behavior and in our efforts to understand how it works. For researchers, that means describing behavior as no more than a physical phenomenon and restricting conclusions to statements supported by quantitative measures and credible comparisons. For practitioners, it means focusing on objectively defined target behaviors, generating quantitative evidence of how they change, and proposing the reasons for the changes with appropriate deference to that evidence.

At least that is how it is supposed to work. In reality, it can be terribly hard to put aside one's biases, which are often already well established when a project is first conceived or a treatment plan is developed. Interest in a particular independent variable or treatment protocol tends to guide planning and methodological decisions as well as informal convictions about what is happening in the project. When it is time to draw more or less formal conclusions about why the target behavior changed as it did, it is understandable that those convictions provide the context for interpreting the data. Expected changes in responding associated with intervention conditions seem obviously caused by those conditions, and it may seem just as obvious that other factors did not play an important role. In other words, we may give too much weight to our preferences over the evidence.

The limit on that tendency is supposed to come from our peers. Whether through the formalities of journal peer review or informal feedback from colleagues, they remind us to be critical of our own work and cautious in our conclusions. Lacking our *a priori* convictions about the role of the independent variable or treatment procedures, peers find it easier to consider weaknesses in measurement and design as well as the possibility of alternative explanations for what might seem to us to be obvious findings.

Awkward questions from peers can be avoided by caring more about finding out what is true than about being right. That is easier to achieve with a thorough understanding of methods of discovery, not to mention respect for the larger interests of our field. If too many behavior analysts approach research and practice as opportunities to promote their convictions, programs, or products instead of occasions for discovery, the utility and credibility of our science will gradually diminish – a prospect from which recovery is unlikely.

need to consider not just the treatment protocol but also extraneous factors like associated changes in the stimulus value of the staff or in other aspects of their behavior. Failing to identify the role of such factors and instead arguing that the AB comparison is more meaningful than the conflicting BA comparison sets up the risk that others who use the findings in creating their own version of the protocol may fail to obtain the original results.

In sum, regardless of why responding does not revert to baseline levels in a reversal phase, it places the investigator in a weak position to draw conclusions about the influence of the treatment condition. It is not appropriate to discount the BA comparison because it failed to yield the same results as the AB comparison and instead accept the AB comparison as an adequate basis for concluding that the intervention was responsible for changes in responding. That amounts to accepting the AB comparison as legitimate but treating the BA comparison as invalid. Although that judgment might be true for some reason, it nevertheless reduces the investigation to a single AB comparison and ignores conflicting evidence. That unavoidably calls the impact of the intervention into question. The only recourse is to arrange other comparisons that will clarify the role of the intervention condition. Chapter 13 will describe a number of possibilities.

Multi-element Designs

Definition. A variation of a reversal design called a **multi-element design** exposes a participant to multiple conditions in some form of repeated alternation. This design involves at least two conditions – e.g., control and treatment – but may also involve comparisons of a control condition and two or more different treatment conditions, or even just different treatment conditions. Each contact with each condition is typically brief; usually a single session. The conditions may alternate in different ways, as described below. The two or more conditions are the "elements" in a multi-element design. This type of design is also called an alternating treatments design. It was first described by Sidman (1960) in the context of multiple schedules of reinforcement used in laboratory studies, but it has evolved considerably in applied research.

> **Multi-element design.** A variation of a reversal design that exposes a participant to two or more conditions in some form of brief, repeated alternation. Also called an *alternating treatments* design.

Multi-element or alternating treatments designs are generally used to evaluate control over responding by switching between the selected conditions repeatedly and relatively rapidly. As always, it is important that one condition be a control condition. When there is just one treatment condition, the control condition should be matched to it. If two or more treatment conditions are evaluated, they are often compared with a single control condition that is either alternated with the treatment conditions within the same phase or conducted as a baseline phase comprising repeated sessions of the control condition that is compared with a phase in which the treatment conditions are alternated. Showing that responding changes abruptly as soon as the conditions change can be a convincing demonstration of the power and reliability of any effect associated with the treatment condition(s). Of course, if an investigation using a multi-element design only allows comparisons between a single pair of control and experimental conditions, the data cannot provide convincing evidence about exactly why behavior changes. As we have seen, that kind of information usually requires pursuing the role of extraneous factors that may be embedded in the treatment condition.

There are different ways of arranging a multi-element design. As a general rule, it is advisable to ensure that each participant experiences each of the compared conditions equally often, and that the conditions alternate in unsystematic order rather than occurring in the same order every time. The latter is essential to reduce the likelihood that the effects of a condition will be influenced by the fact that it always precedes or follows another condition (usually called an order or sequence effect). For instance, the conditions could be alternated during each day, with each condition in effect in one session per day. Sometimes the alternation involves switching conditions during each session, perhaps multiple times. In either case, the investigator should arrange for the order of the conditions to vary unsystematically from day to day or session to session. The conditions should also be counterbalanced so that the participant experiences each condition equally often in each position in the order. For instance, consider an investigation comparing a baseline or control condition (A) and two treatment conditions (B and C). Only one condition is in effect in any session, and each participant experiences all three conditions each day. To minimize sequence effects, the investigator arranges the order of conditions as follows: Day 1 – BAC; Day 2 – ACB; Day 3 – CBA and so on for succeeding days, so that over the course of the investigation the conditions never occur in the same order on consecutive days and each condition occurs equally often in the first, second, and third position.

As noted earlier, with this type of design it is easiest to draw clear conclusions when responding changes as soon as a new condition starts. That is most likely to occur when differences in the conditions are readily discriminable to participants. Usually that is not an issue for comparisons between control and treatment conditions, but it can be when two or more treatment conditions are being compared in rapidly alternating fashion. In that case, unless the treatments are inherently quite different, the investigator is wise to arrange for distinctive stimuli to be associated with each condition, mimicking the origins of the design in multiple schedules of reinforcement. That reduces the risk that the effects of one condition will influence behavior in the other condition – a confound known as carryover or multiple treatment effects, which is of particular concern with these types of designs. Whatever the details, the repeated alternations should eventually accumulate an equal number of data points for each of the compared conditions.

A study by Petursdottir and Aguilar (2016) illustrates one variation of a multi-element or alternating treatments design.The authors evaluated the effects of two match-to-sample procedures – sample-first versus comparison-first – for training conditional relations among spoken word sample stimuli and picture comparison stimuli with three typically developing young boys. Sample stimuli were the spoken names of either four birds or four countries. Comparisons were color photographs of the corresponding birds or country flags. There were two sets of bird stimuli and two sets of flag stimuli for each participant. Each session consisted of sixteen match-to-sample trials presented via computer, and participants used the computer mouse to select a comparison stimulus on each trial.

In the sample-first procedure, each trial started with presentation of the auditory sample stimulus, followed by presentation of the visual comparison stimuli. That was flipped in the comparison-first procedure, where each trial started with presentation of the comparison stimuli, followed by presentation of the sample. Each participant was first exposed to a baseline phase in which he completed an equal number of unsystematically alternating sessions under the sample-first and comparison-first conditions with either the bird or the flag stimuli, with no programmed consequences for comparison selections. He then progressed to an intervention phase that also involved unsystematically alternating sessions between the two conditions except that there were differential consequences for selecting correct and incorrect comparisons (4 seconds of computer-produced animation and sound and a black screen, respectively). Each participant also completed baseline and intervention phases with the other stimuli (either flags or birds) – a multiple baseline design across stimulus sets (see Chapter 13). Results showed that both differential reinforcement procedures produced improvements over baseline and that the sample-first procedure yielded mastery-level performances more quickly than did the comparison-first procedure for all three participants (see Figure 12.7).

Risks. If an investigator is unsure about the effects that will be observed when switching between a control condition and an intervention condition or between two intervention conditions, the multi-element design can be a risky choice. The alternation feature of the multi-element design requires responding to change quickly in each session so that the data reflect the different effects specific to each condition. That makes it especially important for the investigator to already have a good idea as to how responding is likely to change when a treatment condition begins and how it is likely to continue to change with accumulating contact with the condition. As the discussion of steady states in Chapter 10 pointed out, it is often the case that responding changes only gradually as the features of an intervention condition begin to have their effect. It is typical for responding to take some time to reveal the full effects of the intervention – often a number of successive sessions, as can be seen in Figure 12.7. Furthermore, sometimes an initial transition to a different level of responding is only temporary and responding eventually returns to baseline levels. As Chapter 10 explained, distinguishing between transition states

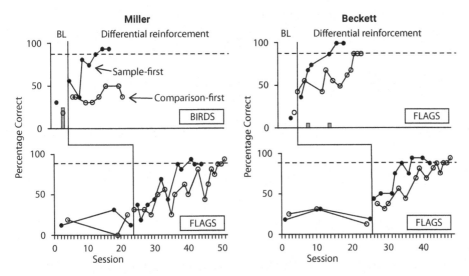

FIG. 12.7. Data from a study using a multi-element or alternating treatments design. From Petursdottir, A. I., & Aguilar, G. (2016). Order of stimulus presentation influences children's acquisition in receptive identification tasks. *Journal of Applied Behavior Analysis, 49,* 58–68. Copyright 2016 by the Society for the Experimental Analysis of Behavior, Inc. Used by permission.

and transitory states requires extending a phase long enough to be sure the changes initially observed are durable and represent the long-term or mature effects of each condition being compared.

In other words, selecting a multi-element design requires an investigator to already be reasonably confident about two things: (a) that the transition in responding between conditions will be immediate (occur in a single session) and (b) that the level of responding observed in a single session of exposure to each condition is typical of the level found with uninterrupted exposure over a series of sessions. If either of these is not true, the multi-element design may provide a misleading picture of the differences in responding between the conditions.

For example, although responding might consistently be higher in intervention sessions than in control sessions across repeated alternations, the increase could misrepresent the effects that might otherwise be expected if participants had contact with the intervention condition for an uninterrupted series of sessions. As illustrated in Figure 12.8, continued exposure to the intervention (the intervention only phase) might show that the initial increase becomes greater (a) or that it drops only temporarily and gradually, perhaps even to near baseline levels (b).

The risk just described can be minimized by obtaining stable responding over multiple successive sessions under each of the conditions being compared. Although that can be done after completing an alternation phase, it makes more sense to do it prior to implementing a rapid alternation phase. That

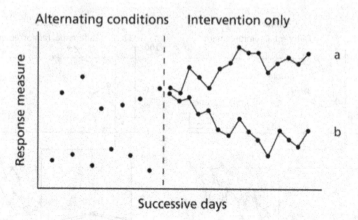

FIG. 12.8.   Data showing how multi-element design alternations can be misleading.

would allow the investigator to make a decision about using a multi-element design already knowing what the fully developed effects of the treatment condition(s) look like and what happens when treatment is terminated. Not only would the steady state data reveal the level of responding generated by both control and treatment conditions, it might also provide some guidance about how quickly responding would change upon initial exposure to a treatment condition as well as upon its withdrawal. If the effort to establish steady states showed a gradual change in responding when a treatment condition was implemented, it might suggest that the multi-element design would yield misrepresentative data. The data would be misleading if responding did not transition quickly enough in a single session for either control or treatment conditions and thereby failed to show responding representative of each condition. Comparisons of a series of such single-session values would encourage conclusions that would be different if the comparisons were based on steady state data.

The emphasis on obtaining steady state data for each of the conditions to be compared in a multi-element design suggests that the design's primary value is not so much to discover what the comparison has to offer as to highlight the control associated with presenting and withdrawing the treatment condition(s). Although this type of design could be used to help identify ways of facilitating a rapid change in responding when a treatment condition is implemented, it is more likely to serve as a way of demonstrating the effect of a treatment that is already understood. In applied research and practical situations, the design is often used to compare the effects of two or more treatments in a relatively short period of time without necessarily obtaining steady state data in each condition first. To avoid questions about what responding would look like if exposure to each condition continued for multiple successive sessions, however, rapid alternation data should be accompanied by steady state comparisons whenever feasible.

Parametric and Changing Criterion Designs

Parametric and **changing criterion designs** are single baseline designs that combine AB and reversal sequences to evaluate the effects of changing a specific feature of an intervention. A feature is typically narrowly defined as a single parameter of a procedure or as a particular criterion for the performance of participants. For example, a parametric design might manipulate the density of reinforcement from one phase to another in order to see if changes in that variable influence responding. A changing criterion design might systematically vary the minimum number of arithmetic problems that must be done correctly in order to earn reinforcement.

> **Changing criterion design.** A within-subject, single baseline design using AB and reversal sequences to identify effects of manipulating performance criteria.
>
> **Parametric design.** A within-subject, single baseline design using AB and reversal sequences to identify effects of manipulating a specific parameter of a variable or procedure.

There is no set sequence of control and intervention conditions that defines parametric and changing criterion designs. Their most typical feature is a sequence of phases in which a narrowly defined element of a more complex procedure is systematically changed from one value to another. In Figure 12.9, for example, a single parameter of a token reinforcement procedure (the value of a fixed ratio schedule of token delivery) is varied from FR1 to FR3, to FR10, to FR25, back to FR10, and back to FR1. As Figure 12.9 indicates, the letter notation for this sequence is ABCDCA. In this case, the parameter is a criterion for client performance that will determine when tokens are earned. However, the parameter could be any variable of interest in an investigation.

Let us deconstruct the example to illustrate the nature of the comparisons in this type of design. The initial phase is a control condition consisting of the token reinforcement contingency associated with the behavior of working math problems in a classroom setting. It is a good control condition because all features of the condition continue throughout the second phase, in which only a single variable (the schedule of token delivery) changes (from FR1 to FR3). That constitutes a straightforward AB comparison.

The same variable changes again in the third phase (from FR3 to FR10). If the FR10 phase is a new intervention condition, what is its control condition? Remember that a control condition controls for all of the factors in an intervention condition that are not the focus of interpretations. That is, all features

$$\text{A} \mid \text{B} \mid \text{C} \mid \text{D} \mid \text{C} \mid \text{A}$$

FIG. 12.9.   Notation of a parametric or changing criterion design.

of a control condition should continue throughout its matched intervention condition. Although the general token reinforcement procedure continues throughout all phases, the FR3 value in the second phase ends and is replaced with the FR10 value in the third phase. In other words, switching from the FR3 condition to the FR10 condition involves making two changes at the same time (terminating the FR3 value and starting the FR10 value). Therefore, the FR3 condition is not a proper control condition for the FR10 phase. That same limitation applies to comparing the FR10 and FR25 conditions, as well as the two reversal conditions.

As we have already pointed out, comparisons between conditions in which one condition largely ends and its features are replaced by a condition involving mostly different features are usually risky. That is because it is not clear whether any effects are due to terminating the first condition, starting the second condition, or a mixture of both. In the case of parametric and changing criterion designs, however, that kind of comparison can work because the changes are extremely narrow or specific variations in a single variable. In our example, the only thing that changes between the FR3 and FR10 conditions is the value of the token reinforcement schedule. If responding changes in predictable ways as that parameter is adjusted, there is often no question about why the change occurred. That specificity also eases the usual demand for replication to show that an effect is reproducible.

Parametric and changing criterion designs involve the same kind of control/ treatment comparisons and differ only in how they tend to be used. Researchers tend to focus on systematically varying a specific parameter to learn whether it influences the target behavior. A study of rumination of food by individuals with profound intellectual disabilities provides a good illustration (Rast, Johnston, & Drum, 1984). The project followed a previous study that showed that the quantity of food consumed at meals had a substantial effect on the frequency of ruminating after meals (Rast, Johnston, Drum, & Conrin, 1981). The original study only used single portion and satiation quantities of food served at meals and showed that satiation quantities produced large decreases in ruminating. The parametric follow-up study asked whether that reduction effect was proportional to the amount of food consumed. For two individuals, the amount of food fed and consumed at meals was increased over single portion baseline quantities in a series of 10-ounce increments from baseline plus 10 ounces to baseline plus 50 ounces before there was a return to baseline quantities. The data in Figure 12.10 shows that the amount of decrease in post-meal ruminating was indeed a step-wise function of food quantity. Other parametric sequences were conducted for additional participants.

Practitioners may be more likely to use variations of these types of designs to achieve desired treatment outcomes. As one example, Heffernan and Lyons (2016) used a changing criterion design to evaluate the effects of differential reinforcement of other behavior (DRO) procedures on the self-injurious nail biting of a preschool boy diagnosed with autism. As shown in Figure 12.11, baseline rates of nail biting were variable but high. The first treatment phase consisted of DRO 20-second reinforcement. During treatment sessions, at

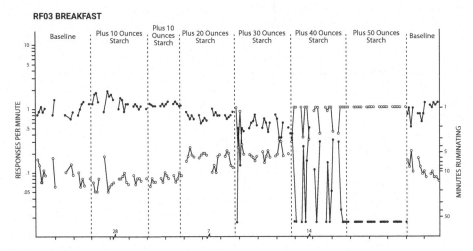

FIG. 12.10. Illustration of a parametric design. From Rast, J., Johnston, J. M., & Drum, C. (1984). A parametric analysis of the relationship between food quantity and rumination. *Journal of the Experimental Analysis of Behavior, 41(2)*, 125-134, p. 128. Copyright 1984 by the Society for the Experimental Analysis of Behavior, Inc. Used by permission.

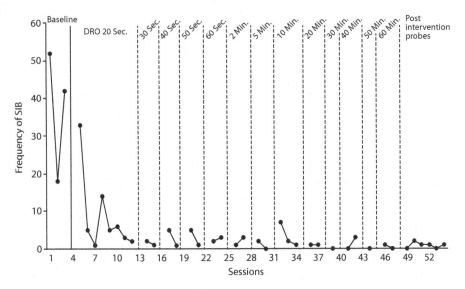

FIG. 12.11. Illustration of a changing criterion design. From Heffernan, L., & Lyons, D. (2016). Differential reinforcement of other behavior for the reduction of severe nail biting. *Behavior Analysis in Practice, 9*, 253-256, p. 255. Copyright 2016 by the Association for Behavior Analysis International. Used by permission.

the end of each 20-second interval during which no nail biting occurred, the boy's therapist delivered brief praise and gave the boy access to a highly preferred activity for 30 seconds. After two consecutive sessions in which nail biting occurred no more than five times, the DRO interval was increased to

30 seconds. When the behavioral criterion was again met for two consecutive sessions, the interval was increased to 40 seconds. Those procedures were repeated – that is, the criterion was changed by gradually increasing the DRO interval – over a series of ten additional intervention phases until the DRO interval was 60 minutes and nail biting was reliably occurring at very low levels during treatment sessions. At that point, the DRO procedures were introduced in other settings. Follow-up probes indicated that the treatment gains were maintained. Although the evaluation involved no reversals, a case can be made that experimental control was demonstrated nonetheless because the rate of responding decreased substantially within the first few sessions of the first DRO intervention phase and met or exceeded the criterion in each of the succeeding intervention phases.

As we have pointed out, all single baseline designs involve the same basic features and reasoning. They are easy to understand and usually straightforward to implement – the bread and butter of within-subject designs – especially for practitioners. Their relative simplicity can be seductive, however, leading researchers and practitioners to draw conclusions about the effects of a treatment condition with a degree of confidence that may not always be warranted. In fact, their simplicity hides some complexities that must be respected if those conclusions are to hold up when they are put to use.

CHAPTER SUMMARY

1. There is no single term or phrase that universally refers to the behavior analytic approach to experimental design. One of the most common labels is "within-subject design." That term emphasizes that each participant serves as his or her own control by experiencing both the control condition and the treatment condition in sequence.

2. AB arrangements are the core of all within-subject comparisons. In these comparisons, the investigator examines data from a sequence of phases representing matched control (often labeled "A") and experimental (e.g., "B") conditions to determine if there was a difference in responding between the conditions.

3. Although beneficial, an AB comparison fails to inform the investigator if the change in responding is a reliable outcome of switching between these two conditions, and it does not inform us if the change in responding was due to the independent variable.

4. A reversal design involves a pair of control and treatment conditions in which one or both conditions repeat at least once. Unlike a single AB comparison, repeating the original control condition adds the advantage of creating a second comparison between control and intervention conditions.

5. Neither an ABA nor an ABAB design establishes a functional relation, because it does not address the role of extraneous factors selectively associated with the independent variable. That limitation does not mean

that the independent variable is not fully responsible for the changes in responding, just that the reversal design does not tell us one way or the other.

6. Practitioners often do not have the luxury of arranging proper control conditions or repeating phases to assess reliability, much less pursuing the impact of extraneous factors. That shortfall is one of the distinctions between research and practice, and the price is that practitioners may not be able to defend the conclusions they might like to draw.

7. The reversal design is informative only when responding reverts to the original baseline pattern after the intervention is removed. Regardless of why responding does not revert to baseline levels in a reversal phase (e.g., sequence effects), it places the investigator in a weak position to draw conclusions about the influence of the treatment condition.

8. A multi-element or alternating treatments design is a variation of a reversal design that exposes a participant to multiple conditions in some form of repeated alternation. This design is generally used to evaluate control over responding by switching between the selected conditions repeatedly and relatively rapidly.

9. As a general rule, it is advisable to ensure that each participant experiences each of the compared conditions equally often and that the conditions alternate in unsystematic order to reduce the likelihood that the effects of a condition will be influenced by the fact that it always precedes or follows another condition.

10. Selecting a multi-element design requires an investigator to be confident about two things: (a) that the transition in responding between conditions will be immediate, and (b) that the level of responding observed in a single session of exposure to each condition is typical of the level found with uninterrupted exposure over a series of sessions.

11. Parametric and changing criterion designs are single baseline designs that combine AB and reversal sequences to evaluate the effects of changing a specific feature of an intervention. Their most typical feature is a sequence of phases in which a narrowly defined element of a more complex procedure is systematically changed from one value to another.

12. Parametric and changing criterion designs involve the same kind of control/treatment comparisons and differ only in how they tend to be used. Researchers tend to focus on systematically varying a specific parameter to learn whether it influences the target behavior. Practitioners may be more likely to use variations of these types of designs to achieve desired treatment outcomes.

HIGHLIGHTED TERMS

AB comparison. A within-subject sequence of phases composed of one control and one experimental condition.

Changing criterion design. A within-subject, single baseline design using AB and reversal sequences to identify effects of manipulating performance criteria.

Multi-element design. A variation of a reversal design that exposes a participant to two or more conditions in some form of brief, repeated alternation. Also called an *alternating treatments* design.

Parametric design. A within-subject, single baseline design using AB and reversal sequences to identify effects of manipulating a specific parameter of a variable or procedure.

Reversal design. A within-subject experimental design minimally involving a pair of control and experimental conditions in which one or both conditions repeat at least once.

TEXT STUDY GUIDE

1. Why is this approach to experimental design described as "within-subject"?
2. Describe the rationale for within-subject comparisons.
3. Name three additional terms for within-subject designs.
4. Where did the development of within-subject designs begin?
5. What do "A" and "B" refer to when discussing AB comparisons?
6. What two things do you not know when comparing responding under a control and an intervention condition?
7. Why is an AB design a weak basis for drawing conclusions about the effects of an independent variable?
8. Describe the general format of a reversal design and why it is better than an AB design.
9. What does a reversal design not tell you?
10. How is an ABAB design better than an ABA design?
11. What does an ABAB design not tell you?
12. Describe what the authors mean by a "build-a-design-as-you-go" approach in behavior analytic research.
13. Provide three reasons why baseline responding may not be recaptured when baseline conditions are repeated.
14. When responding does not reverse when a prior condition is reinstated, what can the investigator conclude about the effects of the intervention?
15. Describe a multi-element design. What is another name for this type of design?
16. What is the risk associated with a multi-element design? How can this risk be minimized?
17. Distinguish between parametric and changing criterion designs. Are there any differences between which type of design may typically be utilized by researchers as opposed to practitioners?

BOX STUDY GUIDE

1. What role does the level of experimental control play in the impact that extraneous variables may have?
2. What do the authors mean by the statement that "we may give too much weight to our preferences over the evidence"?

SUGGESTED READINGS

Johnston, J. M. (1988). Strategic and tactical limits of comparison studies. *The Behavior Analyst, 11*, 1–9.

Sidman, M. (1960). *Tactics of scientific research*. New York: Basic Books. Chapter 11: Selection of an appropriate baseline.

DISCUSSION TOPICS

1. Discuss why an AB arrangement does not provide information about what variables were responsible for any change in responding. Consider why an ABAB design involves the same limitation.
2. Select a published study in a behavioral journal that uses a single baseline design and shows a clear effect of the intervention condition. Discuss possible extraneous variables that could explain the results and different ways of addressing these alternative explanations.

EXERCISES

1. Identify a relatively simple target behavior of your own that you would like to modify (e.g., exercising, studying behavior) and record baseline data for one week. Develop and apply an intervention designed to improve the target behavior. If you recorded changes in responding what kind of conclusions can you draw? If you wanted to feel more confident that it was your intervention that had an impact than potential extraneous variables, what could you do?
2. Find a published study from a peer-reviewed behavioral journal that is an example of a "build-a-design-as-you-go" approach, and label each of the conditions using the letter sequencing protocol described in Chapter 11.
3. Describe an experiment or clinical treatment where the use of a reversal design would not be appropriate because responding would not be likely to revert back to baseline levels in a reversal phase.

CHAPTER THIRTEEN

Multiple Baseline Designs

MULTIPLE BASELINE DESIGNS

Rationale

Single baseline designs are limiting in that the investigator can only arrange different conditions one at a time in sequence. That is because AB, reversal, multi-element, and parametric or changing criterion designs require only a single participant, a single target behavior, and a single setting – in other words, a single baseline. As discussed in Chapter 12, comparisons between control and experimental conditions are therefore made using the same participant, which means that the unique characteristics of the individual are held constant across conditions. Although multiple participants are often used in a study or project, Chapter 10 explained that each participant is treated separately as if he or she were the only individual in the study. In other words, additional participants allow more comparisons of the same kind.

353

354   DESIGN

Multiple baseline designs involve the same fundamental comparisons between control and experimental conditions as single baseline designs, but the availability of additional baselines adds the opportunity for comparisons between control and intervention conditions within each of two or more baselines. (In this context, a baseline collectively refers to a single participant, the target behavior being measured, and the conditions under which it is measured.) The comparisons available in a basic multiple baseline design are illustrated in Figure 13.1. In this example, the first baseline involves a control condition (A) followed by a treatment condition (B). That allows a single comparison, indicated by curved arrow number 1 pointing to the two phases being compared. As we have seen, that simple AB arrangement provides potentially useful but limited information about the effects of the B condition.

The second baseline, represented beneath the first in Figure 13.1, sets up the same kind of comparison, putting aside the fact that the switch from control to treatment conditions occurs somewhat later than in the first baseline. The inclusion of the second baseline therefore adds a second AB comparison, indicated by curved arrow number 2. That replication makes the design twice as useful as a single AB arrangement. It would not matter if the two control-treatment sequences were not concurrent or coordinated in any way. One sequence could have been completed before the other was even started, and the same two AB comparisons would still be available.

Coordinating the two AB arrangements concurrently in time, however, provides a useful third comparison. By starting both baselines at about the same time and then staggering or delaying the introduction of the B condition in the second baseline compared to when it began in the first baseline, the investigator creates an opportunity to compare responding under the control condition in the second baseline with responding under the treatment condition in the first baseline. That third AB comparison is indicated in Figure 13.1 by a vertical arrow (number 3) pointing to those two phases. Although the third comparison is between a control condition from one baseline and a treatment condition from a different baseline, it is still a straightforward AB comparison.

One advantage of a *concurrent* multiple baseline design, then, is that two baselines each involving simple AB sequences can be used to create a third AB comparison. Just by coordinating the timing of the two AB baselines, a third comparison becomes available without the trouble of setting up a third baseline. If the two baselines do not start at about the same time and the

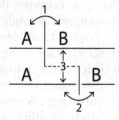

FIG. 13.1. Notation of a concurrent multiple baseline comparison using two baselines.

intervention condition in the second baseline is not staggered with reference to its introduction in the first baseline, that third comparison is not available. The arrangement would be reduced to two otherwise separate AB comparisons – an arrangement that is usually described as a *non-concurrent* multiple baseline design, which is discussed in a later section.

The bonus afforded by a concurrent multiple baseline arrangement provides a further benefit. The extra comparison helps to make up for the inherent weakness of an AB arrangement. Recall that although such an arrangement can provide useful information by showing that responding changes when conditions change, it does not tell us whether that relation is reliable. A reversal or ABA design begins to answer that question by adding a reversal back to the original condition. That allows the investigator to determine if responding changes only when the treatment phase starts and if that change lasts only as long as the treatment condition lasts. When the treatment phase ends and the original condition is reinstated, there is an opportunity to see if responding returns to the level or pattern observed under the original condition. Adding a reversal phase to an AB design is obviously a good idea in principle, but practical constraints sometimes get in the way. For instance, Chapter 12 pointed out that the nature of the treatment condition may produce changes in responding that might be expected to continue when that condition ends. Another practical problem is that it is sometimes inappropriate, unwise, or even unethical to discontinue a treatment condition when it produces valuable improvements in a clinically important target behavior. By providing not only a second AB comparison but also a third AB comparison, a concurrent multiple baseline design gets around those problems. Although none of the comparisons show what would happen if the treatment condition were terminated, if three AB comparisons show the same differences in responding under control versus treatment conditions, there is some reassurance that the change in responding is reliable.

The design features just described are illustrated in Figure 13.2, which shows results of a study by Roane, Kelly, and Fisher (2003). The authors evaluated the effect of access to preferred foods on rates of object mouthing by a boy diagnosed with autism, cerebral palsy, and intellectual disability. During baseline (control) sessions conducted in three different settings (a classroom, a playroom, and an outdoor area at the boy's school), a therapist was present but no intervention for object mouthing was implemented and no food items were available. In the treatment condition, the boy had continuous access to three preferred food items in a fanny pack that he wore throughout all sessions. No contingencies for object mouthing were arranged by the therapist. Treatment was implemented in the classroom while the baseline condition remained in effect in the playroom and outdoor area. Then treatment was introduced in the playroom and a little later in the outdoor area. The design allowed for three comparisons within baselines – that is, between the control (A) and treatment (B) conditions in each setting. It also provided three comparisons across baselines: the A condition in the playroom with the B condition in the classroom; the A condition in the outdoor area with the B condition in the classroom; and the A condition in the outdoor area with the B condition in the playroom.

356   DESIGN

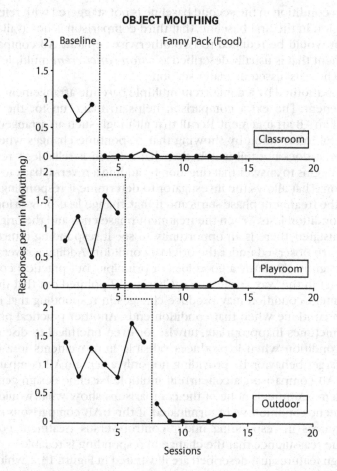

FIG. 13.2. Illustration of a concurrent multiple baseline design across settings. From Roane, Kelly, & Fisher (2003). The effects of noncontingent access to food on the rate of object mouthing across three settings. *Journal of Applied Behavior Analysis, 36,* 579–582. Copyright 2003 by the Society for the Experimental Analysis of Behavior, Inc. Used by permission.

Concurrent Multiple Baseline Designs

As noted above, a **concurrent multiple baseline design** uses two or more baselines in a coordinated way to allow control-treatment comparisons both within and across baselines. A concurrent multiple baseline design may involve baselines that vary across participants, behaviors, settings, stimulus materials, or some other dimension. In each variation, one component is different across the baselines and the others are the same. The Roane, Kelly, and Fisher (2003) study just described is an example of a multiple baseline design across settings.

> **Concurrent multiple baseline design.** A within-subject design that uses two or more concurrent baselines that are coordinated in time to allow control-treatment comparisons both within and across baselines.

In another common version of multiple baseline designs, each baseline involves a different participant, but the target behaviors and setting are the same for all participants. Figure 13.3 illustrates an example of this variation that involves three children in which the intervention targets the same behavior for each child (interacting with peers) in the same setting (a preschool classroom). Each child first experiences a control condition and then an intervention condition. Measurement of the target behavior begins at the same time for all three children, but when the intervention starts for Tina, the other two children continue in the control phase. Liz starts the intervention phase somewhat later than Tina, and Chrissy starts it sometime after Liz does. In other words, the introduction of the intervention phase is staggered in time across the three participants.

To further explain the reasoning associated with concurrent multiple baseline designs, Figure 13.4 adds numbered arrows to Figure 13.3 to identify the nature of the comparisons created by these three baselines. There is one AB comparison *within* each baseline (numbered 1, 2, and 3) and three more AB comparisons *across* the three baselines (numbered 4, 5, and 6). What if the three participants were exposed to the AB sequence independently? What if Tina completed her participation before Liz started hers and Chrissy did not start until Liz finished? Figure 13.5 shows that approach, which would create three temporally separate (non-concurrent) AB arrangements and allow only the associated AB comparison within each baseline. By conducting the three baselines in a concurrent and coordinated way, those three comparisons are joined by the three additional AB comparisons numbered 4, 5, and 6 in Figure 13.4.

Reasoning. We have already discussed the reasoning associated with comparisons between control and intervention conditions set up by single baseline designs. Each baseline in a multiple baseline design is made up of those AB arrangements, and the comparisons allow the same conclusions that would

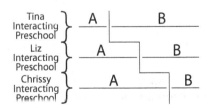

FIG. 13.3. Notation of a concurrent multiple baseline design across three participants.

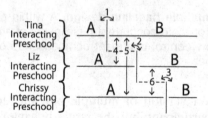

FIG. 13.4. Notation of a concurrent multiple baseline design across three participants with arrows indicating baseline-treatment comparisons.

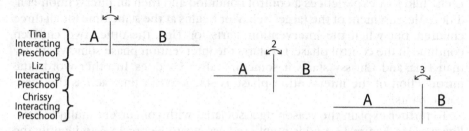

FIG. 13.5. Notation of multiple baselines across three participants implemented non-concurrently.

follow if each baseline were a separate study. (Remember that throughout this chapter we are assuming sound measurement procedures and strong and consistent changes in responding.)

As we have seen, multiple baseline designs also set up comparisons of responding between a control condition in one baseline and an intervention condition in another baseline. Drawing conclusions from such comparisons raises some special issues. Consider the two examples labeled X and Y of concurrent two-baseline designs in Figure 13.6 showing stylized data in successive control and treatment phases for each baseline. The pair of graphs labeled X shows responding in the second baseline did not change until the intervention started for that baseline. However, the two graphs labeled Y indicate that responding in the second baseline changed when the intervention started in the first baseline. That is, responding in the second baseline changed even though the control condition for that baseline was still operating. Furthermore, that change in responding occurred at about the time the intervention started in the first baseline.

For the results shown in the pair of Y graphs in Figure 13.6, how might we explain why responding changed when it did in the second baseline? The intervention procedure itself could not be responsible because it was not operating for the second baseline, which was still under the control condition. One possibility is that responding in the two baselines was tied together or dependent in some way. That is, for some unknown reason it might be that if one performance changed, the other performance would change as well.

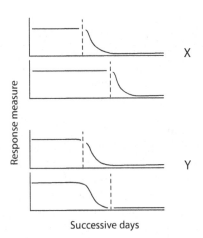

FIG. 13.6. Stylized data associated with two concurrent multiple baseline designs (Panel X and Panel Y) illustrating different outcomes associated with a staggered introduction of the intervention condition.

For example, if the two baselines involved two different target behaviors for the same participant (a student getting out of seat and talking during study period, for instance), it might not be surprising that one behavior would be likely to change when the other did, regardless of what else was going on. That kind of dependency could even occur with different participants who are concurrently in different phases. If the project was taking place in the same setting, such as a classroom, the students might interact in some way or at least see what was going on with classmates who were in a different condition. That could result in responding under the control condition being affected by what was going on in the concurrent intervention condition.

A second explanation might be that extraneous factors associated with the intervention in the first baseline influenced responding in the control condition of the second baseline. Although the intervention itself could not be responsible, it could be that extraneous factors occurring during that phase also influenced responding in the second baseline, which could explain why responding changed when it did. The extraneous factors could be related directly to the independent variable though not actually part of it. For example, the treatment protocol might require changes in the behavior of others in the setting, such as trainers or support staff. Some of the changes in their behavior could be unknowingly carried over to their interactions with participants during the control phase, thereby resulting in changes in participants' responding in that phase. Consider a project using a multiple baseline design across two academic tasks that requires a teacher to give a student instructions that differ from the teacher's customary directions. After making that change in the first baseline, the teacher might inadvertently also change his instructions for the second task while the control condition is supposed to be in effect.

Of course, an extraneous variable need not be associated with the independent variable to influence responding under a concurrent control condition in the second baseline. It could simply be a variable that happens to occur during the intervention phase and also directly affects a participant's responding in the concurrent control condition. For example, a project conducted in a school setting might run into events that affect participants under both conditions, such as an upcoming school holiday.

Whatever its origin, if an extraneous variable was responsible for a premature change in responding in one or more additional baselines, we would have to wonder if that same extraneous factor contributed to the change in responding in the first baseline that occurred when the intervention started. In other words, the data in the Y set of graphs in Figure 13.6 provide support for the possibility that the intervention in the first baseline might not have been responsible for the associated change in responding. Only one of the three control-treatment comparisons showed a decrease in responding associated with the treatment condition. If the multiple baseline design generated the data shown in the pair of Y graphs and that was the entire experiment, we would have to conclude that the data did not support a conclusion that the intervention condition was selectively associated with a decrease in responding. Instead, we would have to acknowledge that there was evidence that extraneous factors could be involved. In contrast, if the pair of X graphs represented the outcome of the study, we would be able to conclude that all three comparisons showed that the intervention corresponded with a decrease in responding.

Requirements. Merely replicating an AB arrangement across multiple participants, target behaviors, settings, or stimuli does not necessarily provide legitimate opportunities to make comparisons across baselines. There are five requirements that must be met to turn multiple baselines into a concurrent multiple baseline design.

First, each baseline must be independent of the other baseline(s). That is, responding in one baseline must not change just because responding in another baseline does. This risk might be especially likely when multiple baselines involve different behaviors in the same participant. For example, if one baseline targets Erika's behavior of responding to questions upon meeting a new adult and another baseline targets her social interactions with peers, both behaviors may increase when an intervention is implemented for only one of the targets.

Second, it is important to eventually demonstrate the sensitivity of the second and any additional baseline(s) to the intervention and associated variables. As we described above, our conclusions about the effects of the intervention condition depend partly on responding not changing in the control condition of a baseline until the intervention condition starts for that baseline. Any time conclusions are based on the fact that responding did not change, it is necessary to show that it did not fail to change merely because it was insensitive to the variables under investigation. (The design shown in Panel X in Figure 13.7 illustrates the problem.) That possibility can be tested by introducing the intervention condition for second and additional baselines at a later

---

BOX 13.1

Risks of Between-Subject Comparisons

Multiple baseline designs across participants raise a special issue. Comparing the performance of one individual in a control condition with that of a different individual in a treatment condition is not a within-subject comparison. The performance of the two individuals might differ not because they are experiencing different conditions but because their unique personal characteristics may influence responding in different ways. The inherent risk of that kind of between-subject comparison is eased by the fact that the behavior of each individual is independently measured under otherwise similar conditions for repeated sessions. Furthermore, the comparison usually involves only two or three individuals.

Between-groups research designs also involve comparisons across individuals, but in a far more problematic manner. Each participant is typically assigned to only one condition – either control or experimental. The behavior of each participant is measured (typically only once) before the investigation begins. Then she is exposed to the assigned condition for a specified period of time and her behavior is measured again at the end of that period. Each individual is given the same amount of exposure to the assigned condition because no evidence is collected that would suggest that some individuals need more or less exposure for the full effects of the experimental condition to be revealed. In this design approach, a relatively large number of participants is assigned to each condition, the data are combined across all participants in each group (e.g., into an average or mean), and the aggregate data from the two groups are compared statistically. In other words, the comparison is between the collective data of a control group and that of an experimental group.

The problems associated with the between-groups approach lie in what the investigator is not able to learn. Because there is no measurement of each participant's behavior repeatedly during exposure to the assigned condition, there is no way to use variability to identify extraneous factors that might be operating for any one individual or even for the group. It is also not possible to learn about different patterns of behavior among either group of participants because of the lack of repeated measures. Although that approach will tell us something about the difference between group means, it is individuals, not groups, that behave. In other words, it is not possible to learn how the experimental condition affected behavior.

---

point (as shown in Panel Y in Figure 13.7). That is typically done in concurrent multiple baseline designs, in part because it has the benefit of creating still another AB comparison.

Third, when the intervention is in place in one baseline, the control condition must be ongoing in the other baseline(s) used for comparison concurrently – that is, at the same time. That might seem obvious, given that one reason for staggering the introduction of an intervention across two or more baselines is to compare responding under the intervention and control phases across

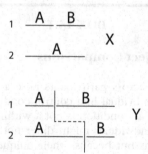

FIG. 13.7. Notation of a design that does not test the sensitivity of a baseline (Panel X) and a design that assesses sensitivity by introducing the intervention in both baselines (Panel Y).

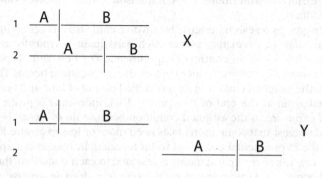

FIG. 13.8. Notation of comparisons showing the concurrent arrangement of control and experimental conditions in Panel X but not in Panel Y.

baselines. The two baselines shown in Panel X in Figure 13.8 show this arrangement, which allows the necessary comparisons. Panel Y shows the same AB sequence for two baselines, except that the second baseline is not operating concurrently with the first. That lack of overlap makes it impossible to see if responding changes under a control condition of one baseline when the intervention phase starts in the other baseline.

Fourth, not only must there be temporal overlap between control and intervention conditions in different baselines, the overlap must also be long enough to allow possible effects of extraneous variables associated with the intervention phase to emerge in the data from the control phase. If, for example, an AB sequence across each of two concurrent baselines were staggered by only one day, it would be fairly unlikely that any effects associated with initiating the intervention condition in one baseline would be evidenced by an immediate change in responding in the control phase of the other baseline on that one day. It is simply in the nature of operant behavior that environmentally induced changes often take some time to develop.

The fifth requirement concerns those extraneous factors that might be associated with, or at least present during, the intervention condition and that are not shared with the control condition. As we emphasized in Chapter 11, the control condition should include all variables present during the treatment condition except the independent variable itself. We have pointed out, however, that extraneous factors might be tied to the treatment condition in some way, whether directly associated with the treatment protocol or because they just happened to occur during the intervention phase. For example, in a project to evaluate the effects of specific types of instructions on a student's academic performances, a teacher might also provide response-contingent feedback to the student even though that is not a component of the intervention. That feedback is extraneous to the investigator's interest, which concerns only the instructions.

Here is the key point. In order to enhance the credibility of comparisons between control and intervention conditions across baselines, any extraneous factors associated with the intervention condition must have the opportunity of influencing responding under the control condition in the second baseline while the intervention is in place in the first baseline. Without that possibility, there is no reason to look for changes in responding in the control phase of the second baseline when the intervention is introduced in the first baseline. After all, we know that the treatment protocol itself cannot affect responding during the second baseline's control condition. So, for example, if different participants are used in the two baselines but the participant in the second baseline cannot possibly come into contact with these extraneous influences, there is no evaluation of their possible contribution. If daily intervention sessions for one participant are conducted at one school and control sessions for the other participant are conducted at another school, the second participant would have no opportunity to contact extraneous influences associated with the treatment condition. As a result, finding no change in the performance of the second participant under a control condition when the intervention started with the first participant would not tell us anything about the possible impact of extraneous factors tied to the treatment condition. Remember that finding such an impact on responding under a control condition raises a red flag about the possibility of those factors influencing responding under the treatment condition.

This fifth requirement can be difficult to grasp. As we have noted, there are only two reasons why responding under a control condition in one baseline would change when a treatment condition is concurrently initiated for a different baseline. First, responding in one baseline could for some reason be dependent on responding in the other. Second, responding in the second baseline could be influenced by extraneous factors associated with the intervention condition in first baseline. If those factors – which are often unidentified or not suspected of having any influence on responding – are operating and by some means affect responding under the control condition of the other baseline, they could also influence responding under the treatment condition. Failing to recognize that can result in misleading conclusions about the impact of the independent variable. Of course, there may be no extraneous factors of any importance, but that should not be assumed. Instead, an opportunity to see such influences should be set up. That is what the fifth requirement is about.

TABLE 13.1
Requirements for comparing responding across multiple baselines

- Each baseline must be independent of the others
- The sensitivity of each baseline to the intervention must be demonstrated at some point
- When the intervention is ongoing in one baseline, the control condition must be ongoing in the other baseline
- There must be sufficient temporal overlap between intervention and control conditions in different baselines to allow extraneous effects to develop
- Extraneous variables associated with the intervention condition must have the opportunity of influencing responding under the control condition

Collectively, these five requirements augment the credibility of comparisons of responding between an intervention condition in one baseline and a control condition in another baseline. If the requirements are not met, comparisons across baselines are weak and may be misleading. Consider that when the intervention is initiated in one baseline while the control condition is operating in another baseline, two possible outcomes will influence the investigator's conclusions: Responding will either change in the control condition baseline at that point or it will not. Meeting the five requirements means that if responding under the control condition does not change when the treatment condition is initiated for the other baseline there is reason to be encouraged that extraneous factors are not having a significant impact on responding in either baseline. If responding under the control condition does change at that point, the investigator should be worried about why it did because that fact raises the possibility of alternative explanations for what might otherwise be interpreted as treatment effects.

Non-concurrent Multiple Baseline Designs

Some years ago, Watson and Workman (1981) proposed a non-concurrent version of a multiple baseline design in which the control phase starts at different points in time and is a different length for each of two or more baselines (e.g., participants, responses, settings). Some of the requirements just discussed are explicitly not met, however. Panel Y in Figure 13.8 shows a non-concurrent comparison. In this arrangement, the treatment condition in one baseline typically does not overlap in time with the control condition in the other baseline. Therefore, the third requirement of allowing comparison of responding under concurrent treatment and control conditions cannot be met. Of course, the fourth requirement of allowing an adequate period of overlap cannot be met either. The lack of treatment/control overlap across baselines also means that extraneous factors that might be operating in the treatment condition would have no opportunity to influence responding under the control condition and thereby not allow the necessary check on their role.

Those shortcomings are often obscured by the common practices of stacking the graphed data from the AB arrangements in order of the length of the baselines and aligning the graphs vertically. Unless the author makes it clear that the baselines were not concurrent (e.g., by including the date of each session on the graph or plotting the data to show when sessions were conducted with respect to each other), that practice creates the misleading impression that baselines were concurrent. When the author also interprets the data by the same rules and logic that apply to concurrent multiple baseline designs, the possibilities for misleading conclusions are magnified (Carr, 2005). Nevertheless, the **non-concurrent multiple baseline design** is often used, and the authors of many published studies do not specify on graphs or in text whether baselines were concurrent (Carr, 2005; Coon & Rapp, 2017).

> **Non-concurrent multiple baseline design.** A within-subject design that uses two or more baselines in which matched control and treatment conditions are not operating concurrently and therefore do not permit control/treatment comparisons across baselines.

A study by Twohig and Woods (2001) illustrates this problem. The authors evaluated the effects of habit reversal treatment on the frequency of self-recorded skin-picking by two typically developing young men using a non-concurrent multiple baseline design across participants. Note that the reported results, shown in Figure 13.9, reflect the common practice of graphing data in a way that implies that the baselines were concurrent. The authors specified that they were not ongoing concurrently, however, and that the change from control to treatment conditions occurred when data from the control condition for each participant were stable. The graphed data suggested that the frequency of skin-picking decreased with treatment for both participants, but that inference was based on only two AB comparisons.

Compared to its concurrent multiple baseline design sibling, a non-concurrent arrangement is inherently weaker for two reasons. First, although setting up non-concurrent and concurrent arrangements takes about the same amount of work, assuming an equal number of treatment and control phases, a non-concurrent design provides fewer AB comparisons for the effort. As explained at the beginning of this chapter, two non-concurrent baselines each allowing an AB comparison provide two opportunities to compare responding under baseline and treatment conditions. However, if the two baselines are concurrent (as in Figure 13.1), a third AB comparison across the two baselines is created – a 50% gain in opportunities to compare baseline and treatment responding. So, in Panel X of Figure 13.8, there are three opportunities to compare responding under treatment and control conditions, whereas there are only two in Panel Y.

Second, because a non-concurrent design does not allow any AB comparisons across baselines, it omits the opportunity to see if responding under the control condition changes when the treatment condition is implemented in the other baseline, as already explained. That is arguably the more serious shortfall.

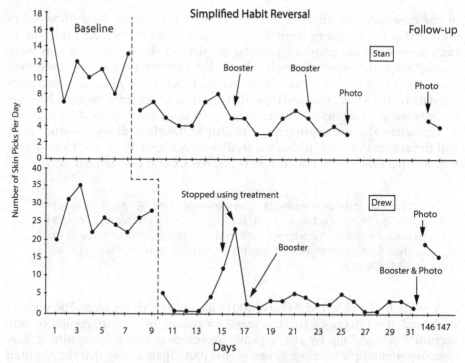

FIG. 13.9. Illustration of a non-concurrent multiple baseline design. From Twohig, M. P., & Woods, D. W. (2001). Habit reversal as a treatment for chronic skin picking in typically developing adult male siblings. *Journal of Applied Behavior Analysis, 34*, 217–220. Copyright 2003 by the Society for the Experimental Analysis of Behavior, Inc. Used by permission.

In Panel X in Figure 13.8, there is one opportunity to see if responding changes under the control condition when the treatment condition is implemented in the other baseline, but none in Panel Y. If there is no change in responding in the control condition, it provides some evidence that extraneous factors associated with the treatment phase were absent or not important. However, if responding in the control condition does change at that point, it signals not only the possibility that such factors are operating but also the possibility that they may contribute to responding under the treatment condition. It is important that investigators take every opportunity to evaluate those possibilities.

Watson and Workman (1981) argued that randomly assigning participants to each of several pre-determined baseline lengths allows investigators to rule out the contribution of extraneous events. Several authors have contended that non-concurrent multiple baseline designs can be useful for evaluating many educational and clinical interventions (e.g., Harris & Jenson, 1985; Harvey, May, & Kennedy, 2004), although others (e.g., Ledford & Gast, 2018) have noted various shortcomings. Importantly, Watson and Workman (1981) failed to acknowledge the inability of the non-concurrent arrangement to account for extraneous factors associated with treatment conditions, which is a particularly likely source, and that problem has not always been emphasized or appreciated fully.

To be clear, a non-concurrent multiple baseline design is otherwise a perfectly serviceable use of two or more baselines, each of which allows independent within-subject comparisons of responding under baseline and treatment conditions. It constitutes a simple AB arrangement (see Figure 12.1) replicated with additional participants, target behaviors, settings, or the like. The results of each control/treatment comparison within each different baseline can build support for a conclusion about the contribution of the treatment condition with its independent variable. Such comparisons can also provide reassuring evidence about the reliability of the effect associated with the treatment condition, although Chapter 11 pointed out that they do not provide a basis for evaluating the role of extraneous factors. Concurrent multiple baseline designs are simply a more useful and credible choice than non-concurrent designs for evaluating the impact of treatment conditions.

TURNING DESIGNS INTO EXPERIMENTS

Building an Experimental Design

We have already pointed out that comparisons of responding under control and intervention conditions are fundamentally the same for AB, reversal, parametric or changing criterion, multi-element, and multiple baseline designs. In fact, the distinctions among these types of designs may be more useful for training students than for guiding experimental design decisions, though the latter certainly require a good understanding of the types of questions that can be addressed by each design.

We also made it clear that in any single study an investigator may combine or intermingle different types of "designs" as needed. It would actually be difficult to describe the research design used in many studies as a single type. The AB comparison is obviously a component of all other types, for example. Reversal arrangements are often used as part of more complex designs. Although multiple baseline designs do not require reversal arrangements, the AB sequence in one or more of the baselines is often followed by a reversal to the original A condition. Many studies examine not just one, but two or three different treatment conditions.

This means that choosing a particular type of design is often only the first step in developing the comparisons that will be used throughout all stages of a research or practical investigation. One of the strengths of that approach to arranging control/treatment comparisons is that it is not necessary to commit to a specific design variation before the study starts that cannot be modified later if circumstances warrant. Although investigators should certainly begin with specific research objectives and a clear plan for attaining them, there are often good reasons for modifying both the objectives of the study and the nature of the required comparisons as the investigation progresses.

The most common reason for adjusting a research plan is to accommodate emerging data. That is particularly likely for practitioners, who must consider

---

BOX 13.2

Experimentum Crucis

There is a longstanding tendency in psychology and the other social sciences to try to learn too much from a single experiment, regardless of its complexity. An experiment offered as a grand and complete answer to a question is called an *experimentum crucis* or crucial experiment. Although it is tempting to imagine that one's study is grand and complete in some way, that almost always overstates its value – and a colleague will soon enough point that out, perhaps with some enthusiasm.

Perhaps we do not adequately appreciate that science works by taking very small steps. It is through the accumulation of little bits of very certain knowledge that science progresses. Science has been likened to creating a mosaic, with each tiny chip taking years to take shape. The natural sciences have built a clear record of that conservative style of experimentation. Perhaps the relative absence of such a track record in the social sciences prevents us from appreciating just how modest each experiment really is. This chapter and Chapters 11 and 12 show why it takes much more than a few comparisons between control and treatment conditions to answer the deceptively simple question of whether an independent variable is responsible for changes in a target behavior.

---

treatment objectives as well as their interests in understanding the best way to engineer intervention protocols and explain their effects on target behaviors. Suppose an investigator plans to start a study with an ABAB sequence of conditions to assess the impact of a treatment procedure. That design presupposes that the intervention will have a clear effect and that the effect will obediently come and go with reversal phases, showing it to be reliable. But what if the data from the first B phase fail to reveal a clear outcome? The investigator may then choose to modify the treatment procedure in some way to make it more effective. That change would establish a new condition (C), which might also be evaluated with a reversal sequence. Assuming that plan was carried through, the design would then involve an ABCACA sequence of conditions. Depending on the investigator's interests and emerging results, the evaluation could continue to evolve.

Having determined that the modified procedure has useful effects on responding, the investigator might wish to determine whether a particular feature of the procedure is playing a major role. That question might be pursued by dropping that feature and seeing if the procedure still produces the same effects. The revised procedure would be designated the D condition, and the C condition might serve as a good control condition against which to compare it. The sequence of comparisons would now be described as ABCACACD, although it would be a good idea to evaluate the reliability of the D condition's effects by reinstating it and the C condition at least once more each (ABACACADCDC). That illustrates how the behavior analytic approach to creating experimental designs provides investigators with flexibility to modify their plans as circumstances require. As long as investigators understand the requirements for sound control/treatment comparisons, the approach encourages powerful and efficient designs that can lead to clear and reliable results with good generality.

Evaluating Alternative Explanations

Another reason for modifying original experimental plans is to evaluate **alternative explanations** for the results. In order to appreciate alternative explanations, it helps to put yourself in the position of others in your field. It is perfectly appropriate for them to raise questions about your study's procedures and results. After all, one of the key features of science and science-based practice is that it is a public exercise. When investigators present or publish their findings, colleagues can independently evaluate the study and attempt to use its findings in their own research or practice. Such replication across investigators is routine in science. It helps uncover erroneous findings, which improves the accuracy and utility of the scientific literature.

> **Alternative explanation.** A way of explaining the results of a control/treatment comparison that takes into account factors other than the independent variable.

For a researcher, the process just described starts when she submits a research report for publication in a scientific journal. The editor handling the manuscript asks three or four researchers who are familiar with the topic to review the paper. In addition to evaluating the study's methods and results, those reviewers consider if and how the results might be explained by factors other than those proposed by the investigator. If an alternative explanation seems sufficiently credible but the study provides no contrary evidence, the paper may not be accepted for publication.

In anticipation of that assessment, researchers learn to design their studies in ways that avoid or at least minimize extraneous factors that could explain their results. When some alternative explanations still remain viable, it may be worth the trouble to evaluate their contribution to the results. That can be done by designing the study to include phases that test whether the extraneous factors are having any influence.

Consider a situation in which a medical researcher is studying the effects of a certain drug. The literature suggests that if patients take the drug as prescribed, particular changes will occur in their medical condition. The drug has certain unpleasant side effects, however, and the researcher is worried that some participants may not take the pills as directed (one pill four times a day). If the participants do not follow the protocol, it could be argued that the data describing their medical condition under the drug phase represent the effects of unknown dosages taken on an unknown schedule.

That extraneous factor could be eliminated by having participants take the pills in the presence of research staff, but the investigator might worry that requiring participants to come to the hospital four times a day to take a pill would make it difficult to recruit enough participants. Instead, the investigator might decide to take advantage of the fact that certain byproducts of the drug can be measured in serum, urine, and saliva for limited periods. Requiring participants to come by the hospital once every three days to provide biological samples will allow a test of whether compliance with the drug protocol could

---

BOX 13.3

Do Experimental Designs Have to Be Perfect?

It may seem that this chapter and Chapters 11 and 12 lay out some pretty tough standards for good research designs. Among other guidelines, for instance, those standards emphasize matching each treatment condition with a control condition that is the same except for the independent variable. They also encourage worrying incessantly about extraneous variables and all the ways they can confound and mislead. The risk of some shortfall between the ideals described here and the reality of actual projects, especially in applied settings, makes it reasonable to ask just how close to those standards investigators have to come in order to produce credible results.

In answering this question, keep in mind that in writing a textbook we must not compromise in describing the ideal relation between control and experimental conditions or the most effective way to handle extraneous variables. In fact, it is not necessarily difficult to achieve the standards described in this book, and even when there are practical limitations, good approximations are usually possible. Understanding what it takes to create sound control/treatment comparisons helps investigators appreciate the choices involved as well as the consequences when some standard cannot be met.

Fortunately, if a comparison is not based on perfectly matched control and experimental conditions, it does not mean that conclusions about treatment effects are necessarily invalid. The extent and nature of the mismatch might mean that the investigator and others need to qualify their conclusions, however. Furthermore, just because extraneous factors are unavoidable and can ruin an investigation, it does not mean failing to chase every one down will significantly depreciate the value of a project. Many extraneous variables have no ill effects, and powerful treatment effects can help justify unambiguous conclusions.

In other words, research designs certainly need not be perfect to lead to sound conclusions. On the other hand, weak designs can definitely result in misleading and incorrect interpretations. Furthermore, hoping that large treatment effects will rescue a weak design can lead to disappointment when strong effects fail to materialize. As Chapter 16 explains, there is no algorithm for weighing these and other methodological strengths and weaknesses in deciding what conclusions are legitimate. Therefore, in designing an experiment it is wise for researchers and practitioners to strive to meet the highest standards, compromise only when necessary, and then be willing to live with the interpretive consequences.

be a factor in interpreting the effects of the drug on the medical condition. If the data describing the drug byproducts in body fluids change appropriately when the drug regimen starts and remain stable throughout the drug phase, the investigator can argue that noncompliance with the protocol is not a credible explanation for the data concerning the participant's condition, leaving the drug as the most likely explanation.

The concern with evaluating alternative explanations extends to practitioners as well. As they share their experiences and data with colleagues, whether at a monthly agency meeting or through convention presentations, their peers are also alert to the possibility that factors other than the treatment protocol could explain the results. When a member of the audience at a convention asks about whether the presenter controlled for a certain extraneous variable, it is reassuring to be able to explain – and support with data – why that variable is not a consideration in evaluating the project's findings.

How Many Comparisons Are Enough?

As a study progresses and comparison phases accumulate, it is fair to ask how many comparisons are needed. In general, the answer is always, "As many as it takes to be reasonably confident about what the data have to say." It is easy to appreciate that no investigator wants to present or publish findings that later turn out to be misleading or even incorrect. The challenge is balancing the limitations of project resources with the ideal of continuing to refine results. An investigator might like to extend a project for an additional month or two, for instance, but limitations in funding, access to a research setting or participants, or clinical priorities may make that a luxury, if not an impossibility.

The "as many as it takes" rule is pretty vague, of course, so we need to be more specific about the decisions investigators face. Three tactics are especially important. First, it is essential to understand the general nature of the control/treatment comparisons and to keep interpretive statements within those limits. That is easier said than done. Investigators often find it difficult to be conservative about the conclusions their procedures and data might allow. For example, we have already pointed out that under ideal circumstances a single AB comparison only shows that responding changed when conditions changed. Such a comparison does not justify concluding that the change in conditions *caused* responding to change, no matter how likely it might be that that was the case. Although adding a reversal phase (making it an ABA design) generates a second comparison between control and treatment conditions, the constraint still applies. The fact that responding changed systematically as the treatment condition started and stopped only shows that the relation seems to be reliable. AB and reversal designs do not justify a conclusion that the independent variable, which is usually only part of what is going on in the treatment condition, was solely responsible for the changes in responding. (Remember that Chapter 11 discusses this point in some detail.) As we have seen, concluding that a functional relation has been established between the independent and dependent variables requires comparisons that show that extraneous factors are not meaningfully contributing to that relation.

Second, it is important to evaluate comparisons for each different treatment condition rather than for the investigation as a whole. That is, if an investigation has two kinds of intervention phases, the assessment of whether there are enough comparisons should be made separately for each different treatment condition. Consider the multiple baseline design represented in Figure 13.10. There are two treatment conditions, with the C condition being a variation of the B condition. The lower case letters indicate control-intervention comparisons for each of the two intervention conditions (Figure 13.1 shows a similar display). You can see that there are four comparisons of responding under the original baseline condition and the B condition. The B condition then serves as a control for the C condition, but there are only two BC comparisons. That means there is not as strong a basis for conclusions about the effects of the C condition as there are for the B condition. There is a third C comparison, however, but with the original baseline (rather than the B condition) as a control. Assuming that is a valid control condition, that comparison provides somewhat different information about the C condition.

Third, regardless of the number of comparisons available for each different intervention condition, it is important to consider any differences in the nature of the comparisons. In the example above, there are two types of comparisons involving the C condition. One involves the B condition as a control and the other uses the A condition as a control. Those different control conditions require different interpretations about any changes in responding under the C condition. Given that the C condition involves only a variation of the B condition, the two BC comparisons allow statements about the role of the variable that was changed. However, the AC comparison allows a statement about responding based on whatever the differences are between the A and C conditions. Note that there is only one of those comparisons, which provides no information about the reliability of any effects. So, although there are three comparisons involving the C condition, they reveal two different kinds of information about the intervention.

In sum, the approach to experimental design described in this chapter and Chapters 11 and 12 is powerful, efficient, flexible, and elegant. It is consistent with the characteristics of behavior as an intraorganism phenomenon, encourages a high level of experimental control, incorporates multiple levels

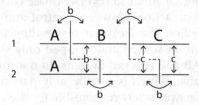

FIG. 13.10. Evaluation of comparisons for two conditions in a concurrent multiple baseline design.

of replication, and encourages investigators to identify the role of variables that enhance the generality of findings. Perhaps most importantly, it has proven highly effective over many decades in identifying lawful behavior-environment relations that support a powerful and practical technology.

CHAPTER SUMMARY

1. Multiple baseline designs involve the same fundamental comparisons between control and experimental conditions as single baseline designs, but the availability of additional baselines adds the opportunity for comparisons between control and intervention conditions within each of two or more baselines.

2. One advantage of a concurrent multiple baseline design is that two baselines each involving simple AB sequences can be used to create a third AB comparison. The extra comparison helps to make up for the inherent weakness of an AB arrangement.

3. A concurrent multiple baseline design may involve baselines that vary across participants, behaviors, settings, stimulus materials, or some other dimension. In each variation, one component is different across the baselines and the others are the same.

4. There are five requirements that must be met to turn multiple baselines into a current multiple baseline design. First, each baseline must be independent of the other baseline(s). That is, responding in one baseline must not change just because responding in another baseline does.

5. Second, it is important to demonstrate the sensitivity of the additional baseline(s) to the intervention and associated variables. Any time conclusions are based on the fact that responding did not change, it is necessary to show that it did not fail to change merely because it was insensitive to the variables under investigation.

6. The third requirement is that when the intervention is in place in one baseline, the control condition must be ongoing in the other baseline(s) used for comparison concurrently.

7. Fourth, not only must there be temporal overlap between control and intervention conditions in different baselines, the overlap must also be long enough to allow possible effects of extraneous variables associated with the intervention phase to emerge in the data from the control phase.

8. The last requirement is that extraneous factors associated with the intervention condition must have the opportunity of influencing responding under the control condition in the remaining baseline(s).

9. A non-concurrent multiple baseline design is inherently weaker than a concurrent arrangement for two reasons. First, although setting up non-concurrent and concurrent arrangements takes about the same amount of work, a non-concurrent design provides fewer AB comparisons.

10. The second weakness of a non-concurrent design is that it does not allow any AB comparisons across baselines; it omits the opportunity to see if responding under the control condition changes when the treatment condition is implemented in the other baseline.

11. Choosing a particular type of design is often only the first step in developing the comparisons that will be used throughout all stages of a study. One of the strengths of that approach to arranging control/treatment comparisons is that it is not necessary to commit to a specific design variation before the study starts that cannot be modified later if circumstances warrant.

12. The most common reason for adjusting a research plan is to accommodate emerging data. This is particularly likely for practitioners who must consider treatment objectives as well as their interests in understanding the best way to engineer intervention protocols and explain their effects on target behaviors. Another reason for modifying original experimental plans is to evaluate alternative explanations for the results.

13. As a study progresses and comparison phases accumulate, it is fair to ask how many comparisons are needed. In general, the answer is always, "As many as it takes to be reasonably confident about what the data have to say."

HIGHLIGHTED TERMS

Alternative explanation. A way of explaining the results of a control/treatment comparison that takes into account factors other than the independent variable.

Concurrent multiple baseline design. A within-subject design that uses two or more concurrent baselines that are coordinated in time to allow control-treatment comparisons both within and across baselines.

Non-concurrent multiple baseline design. A within-subject design that uses two or more baselines in which matched control and treatment conditions are not operating concurrently and therefore do not permit control/treatment comparisons across baselines.

TEXT STUDY GUIDE

1. Describe how single baseline designs limit the kinds of comparisons an investigator can make.

2. How are multiple baseline designs fundamentally similar to single baseline designs?

3. What is the benefit of staggering the introduction of the intervention condition in the second baseline relative to its introduction in the first baseline?

4. Describe how a concurrent multiple baseline design may help address some of the practical and/or ethical problems an investigator may experience when using the designs described in Chapter 12.

5. Describe three common variations in multiple baseline designs.

6. Provide two reasons why responding would change in the control phase of a second baseline at the point when the intervention condition starts in the first baseline.

7. List the five requirements for making comparisons across baselines in concurrent multiple baseline designs. Explain the rationale for each requirement.

8. Describe what concerns an investigator should have if the requirements listed above are not met.

9. What is a non-concurrent multiple baseline design?

10. Describe two reasons why a concurrent multiple baseline design is inherently stronger than a non-concurrent arrangement.

11. What is the most common reason for adjusting a research plan? Provide an example.

12. What is an alternative explanation?

13. List three factors that should be considered when deciding how many comparisons are needed in an investigation.

BOX STUDY GUIDE

1. Describe the problems associated with between-subject designs that assign each participant to one condition and analyze grouped data using inferential statistics.

2. What is the risk of designing experiments that try to do too much, or assuming that the results completely resolve a behavioral issue?

SUGGESTED READINGS

Sidman, M. (1960). *Tactics of scientific research*. New York: Basic Books. Chapter 12: Control techniques.

Sidman, M. (1960). *Tactics of scientific research*. New York: Basic Books. Chapter 13: Control techniques, continued.

DISCUSSION TOPICS

1. Discuss the requirements for comparing responding under control and experimental conditions across baselines in concurrent multiple baseline designs.

2. Select a published study in a behavioral journal that used a non-concurrent multiple baseline design. Discuss possible extraneous variables that could explain the results and different ways of addressing these alternative explanations.

EXERCISES

1. Select examples of multiple baseline designs from published studies and evaluate their adherence to the requirements for making comparisons across baselines.
2. Madison, Lena, and Makayla all engage in the same aberrant behavior (e.g., nail biting). Describe how you would structure a concurrent multiple baseline design across participants to assess the effects of a habit reversal intervention.
3. A behavior analyst is working with three clients, Christi, Mary, and Kylynn on abduction prevention skills. Describe how you would structure a concurrent multiple baseline design across settings for these individuals.

PART FOUR

INTERPRETATION

CHAPTER FOURTEEN

Graphical Analysis of Behavioral Data

DATA ANALYSIS STRATEGIES

Data Analysis as Stimulus Control

However a target behavior is observed and recorded, once each response has been measured, the resulting data are often the only source of information available about a participant's earlier actions. An individual's responses are present only momentarily, but the data permanently preserve the key features targeted by the investigator. These data, together with other aspects of the study, serve as stimuli that influence the investigator's reactions to what is going on during the project, as well as later interpretations about what the results mean.

In other words, analyzing behavioral data is a matter of arranging the data in ways that encourage researchers and practitioners to manage the project along the way and that then guide them toward conclusions that will hold up when others use them. From this perspective, data analysis is a matter of bringing the investigator's reactions under control of appropriate stimuli. Those stimuli result from different ways of manipulating the data describing each participant's behavior under each phase of the project.

Of course, there are endless ways to manipulate data, both mathematically and graphically. Viewing data analysis as a stimulus control problem means that the choice of data analysis techniques is not just a matter of whether a particular statistic or graph is done correctly. The more important issue is whether it encourages the researcher or practitioner, and eventually others, to make good decisions and draw sound conclusions. A graph may be constructed properly or a statistic calculated correctly but still prompt misleading interpretations.

For example, suppose an investigator plots an individual's performance using a histogram or bar graph in which a single column represents an average measure of responding for all sessions in each phase. That kind of graph does not show how responding changed from session to session throughout each phase. Displaying the same data using a line graph showing total responding for each session in each phase provides a very different picture. Those two displays might well prompt different interpretations.

Figure 14.1 shows such a case. The bar graph in Panel A shows that the average performance for all sessions was higher in the experimental condition than the control condition. That interpretation might encourage the conclusion that the experimental condition was responsible for the increase. However, the line graph in Panel B reveals that the difference resulted from an upward trend in the data in the control condition, which continued throughout the experimental condition. The pattern of increasing responding across both phases is troublesome because each condition represents a different set of factors, each of which were presumably constant throughout the respective phases. Those factors should have generated stable responding under each condition. The fact that responding instead increased throughout both conditions suggests that influences beyond the defining features of the two conditions were operating to produce the outcome. That likelihood prevents a credible comparison between the effects of the two conditions.

In other words, although both graphs are constructed correctly, they would likely evoke different reactions from viewers, even though they represent the same behavioral events. Choosing the best graphing format is a matter of figuring out what features of the data are most important and how to highlight those characteristics. The different pictures created by the two graphs should remind us why Chapter 10, as well as other chapters, emphasized the value of first examining the ebb and flow of responding in each phase in order to assess the stability of responding under each set of conditions. A bar graph might

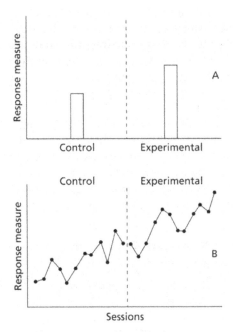

FIG. 14.1. Comparison of the same data set displayed as a histogram summarizing responding in each phase (Panel A) and as a line graph showing session-by-session responding throughout each phase (Panel B).

be a useful way of summarizing responding across different conditions once it is clear that the data from each phase are meaningful and warrant further attention in a summarized form.

Selecting Analytical Procedures

Exploring the Data. There are countless statistical and graphical ways of manipulating data, so how do researchers and practitioners choose the most illuminating approach for their data? Although it may be clear how a quantitative or graphical construction works and what it does to the data, knowing what impact it will have on someone interpreting the outcome is not always obvious. In fact, there is no way you can really know exactly what any particular calculation or graph will show without trying it out.

There are some useful guidelines for selecting analytical procedures, however. One concerns the idea of exploration. The goal of data analysis is to discover variability in the data that helps answer the question at issue. Each different way of looking at the data will reveal a somewhat different view of behavioral variability. Each will obscure other aspects of variability, as the two graphs in Figure 14.1 illustrate. The investigator needs to be aware of what each picture of responding may be hiding as it shows something else. The safest way to be sure about what might be missed is to look at alternative pictures of the same data. That tactic turns data analysis into an exploratory process in which the investigator looks into every promising nook and cranny.

Exploring what data have to say may sound straightforward, but preconceptions and biases can get in the way. Concerned that data analysis was too often approached as a matter of confirming *a priori* hypotheses instead of exploring broader possibilities in the data, Tukey described an analytical style he called **exploratory data analysis** or **EDA** (Tukey, 1977). That approach emphasizes largely graphical analytical techniques that focus on discovery of order and structure in data. Over the years, others have developed the approach further (Hoaglin, Mosteller, & Tukey, 1985; Velleman & Hoaglin, 1981), which is generally consistent with the analytical style long used in the study of operant behavior, as described by Sidman (1960) and in this volume.

> **Exploratory data analysis (EDA).** An approach to data analysis emphasizing largely graphical techniques focusing on discovering order and structure in the data. EDA may be contrasted with confirmatory data analysis or hypothesis testing.

In spite of the risk of allowing preconceptions to bias analytical procedures, researchers and practitioners can hardly help approaching this task with at least some idea of what the data might reveal. The job then becomes one of figuring out which calculations or kinds of graphs might highlight suspected findings. In the case of behavioral data, looking at the ebb and flow of responding as each phase unfolds is usually a good place to start. Although session-by-session graphical displays are excellent ways of seeing repeated measures of behavior change unfold, there are many choices about how data are organized and how graphs might be constructed. Once an investigator has identified a few graphical alternatives, it may just be a matter of trying them out. Fortunately, today's researchers and practitioners usually store data in digital form, so the cost of examining two or three different graphs of the same data is not much more than a few keystrokes

Simple to Complex. A second guideline concerns the sequence of analytical choices. In general, it is a good idea for data analysis to proceed from relatively simple techniques to more complex procedures. Collecting repeated measures of performance under each of several conditions in sequence makes it useful to begin data analysis as soon as there are data to analyze. Behavioral researchers typically add each day's data to relatively simple graphic displays that reveal an increasingly complete picture of responding as each phase evolves. Of course, that is done separately for each participant. As we pointed out in previous chapters, the primary benefit of analyzing data from the outset is that it helps the investigator manage the course of the project. Based on the emerging data, the investigator can then correct problems with measurement procedures, adjust control or treatment conditions, or even revise a planned sequence of phases.

BOX 14.1

How Science Deals with Subjectivity

Many people think of science as a highly objective enterprise. Scientists are seen as unusually impartial in their approach to their subject matter and able to put personal and even professional biases aside in the interest of scientific discovery. Scientists, and those who study how science really works, know better. In fact, scientists often have well-established prejudices about what they are looking for, and these biases can color their perception of what they find. Although it is true that science is a way of learning about the world that is demonstrably more effective than any alternatives, it is far from objective.

So why does science work so well? First, scientists are indeed trained to identify and acknowledge their biases. They are even encouraged to put them aside to some extent, or at least to limit their impact on experimental and interpretive decisions. This training helps, but it hardly produces neutral observers of nature. In fact, preconceptions about the topic of a project are not only inevitable, they are desirable. If a researcher does not understand what previous investigators have discovered well enough to develop some educated guesses about what to look for, he or she is probably not ready to conduct a study. These preconceptions are important in suggesting how to approach the topic and how to design and conduct the project. The "biases" (perhaps it would be better to just call them opinions) are also important when drawing conclusions. There are usually different ways of interpreting a study's outcomes, and it is not always certain which way is right.

In part, this subjectivity is permitted by the flexibility of research methods. It is also limited by another important characteristic of science – its public nature. Although experiments are relatively private exercises, their methods and results must be shared for all to see. Publication of procedures, data, and conclusions mean everyone else is welcome to assess the project and draw their own conclusions. Other investigators can even repeat the study and see if they obtain similar results. As Chapter 11 pointed out, replication is a key feature of scientific method. It helps to limit the impact of personal bias and corrects erroneous findings that do make it into the archival literature.

In summary, scientific methods accommodate subjectivity not only because it is unavoidable but because it is valuable. Research methods encourage creativity and original thinking while guarding against excessive ignorance and intentional dishonesty.

As control and intervention phases are completed and comparisons become possible, there may be a need for more complex analytical options. The investigator might wonder how the comparison would look if the same data were displayed in different ways so as to highlight different features. Figure 14.2 shows such an example using data from a research program concerning the behavior of ruminating (regurgitating and reswallowing food after meals) in individuals diagnosed as intellectually disabled (Rast, Johnston, Ellinger-Allen, & Lubin 1988). The study investigated whether getting participants to engage

384   INTERPRETATION

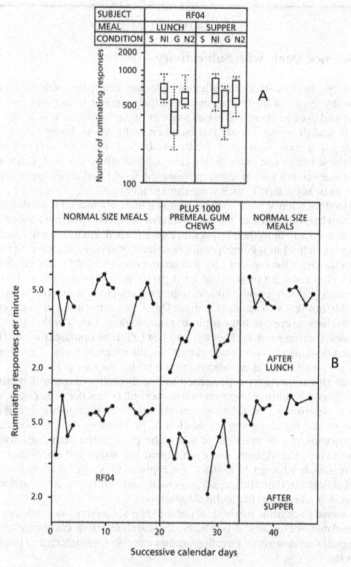

FIG. 14.2. Example of complex data analysis options. The data are adapted from Rast, J., Johnston, J. M., Ellinger-Allen, J., & Lubin, D. (1988). Effects of pre-meal chewing on ruminative behavior. *American Journal of Mental Retardation, 93(1)*, 67–74. Reproduced by permission of the American Association on Intellectual Developmental Disabilities.

in supplementary oral stimulation (chewing bubble gum) immediately prior to meals might decrease the amount of ruminating after meals.

Panel A shows the number of ruminating responses for one individual after eating regular lunch and supper meals. In the first phase, he did not chew gum before meals. In the second phase, however, he made a pre-determined number of gum-chewing responses immediately before meals. The third phase was a return to the original procedure not involving gum chewing. The graph uses box-and-whisker plots to summarize the number of responses in each phase (Tukey, 1977). In that type of display, a box encloses the middle 50% of the data in a phase, and the line inside the box represents the median. The distance between the ends of the box represents a measure of central variability. The dashed bars (whiskers) locate the data furthest away from the box (the range). Panel B shows the rate of responding of the same participant across the same phases. The top of the graph shows ruminating responses after lunches, and the bottom shows responses after suppers.

The graphs in Panel A and Panel B show different aspects of the participant's rumination behavior. In Panel A, the data show the number of responses in sessions as summarized in the box-and-whisker format. In Panel B, the data show the rate of responding session by session throughout each phase. In other words, the two graphs represent different dimensions (count versus rate), summarize the data across different time frames (phases versus sessions), and display that information in different formats (box-and-whisker plot versus line graph). Although both panels show a decrease in ruminating in the pre-meal chewing condition, their information is not redundant. Count and rate are different dimensions and could have been differently affected by the pre-meal chewing procedure, though they were not. Furthermore, Panel A reveals a number of facts about how many ruminating responses occurred during sessions, whereas Panel B shows how often those responses occurred. The two displays together, therefore, provide much more analytical detail to the researcher than either does alone. This is a good example of exploring a data set.

Risk of Intrusive Analytical Techniques. A third guideline is cautionary in nature. The more an analytical technique changes the picture of an individual's behavior as it actually happened, the greater the risk that interpretations are swayed more by the analytical technique than by what actually happened. For example, calculating a descriptive statistic such as a mean or a median for data describing a participant's behavior over a series of sessions reduces those values to a single number. Although the outcome may be what an investigator wants to learn, it nevertheless greatly changes the picture of how the individual responded over time.

We saw such a contrast in Figure 14.1, which suggested that calculating a measure of central tendency across all sessions in a phase prevents viewers from seeing the less processed picture of the participant's behavior session by session. Calculating a descriptive statistic such as the mean or median is the simplest of manipulations, however. Chapter 15 considers statistical techniques such as analyses of variance and other quantitative methods that involve processing data in ways that lose meaningful contact with more straightforward views of how a participant responded over time. Those techniques come with specific rules for how the outcomes must be interpreted, and the rules tend to have more impact on interpretations than what actually happened with the participant's behavior.

Summarizing Data

Within Participants. Exploring behavioral data often involves summarizing responding in different ways, as discussion and examples have illustrated. It is important to remember that summarizing data can simultaneously reveal and obscure important features of the data. When we summarize a set of data, we change its effects on those who view it, whether the resulting picture is graphical or numerical. Although we construct a summary because we want to see a different view, it is unavoidable that the summarized representation is quite different from unsummarized views of the same data. Of course, if we have already studied the unsummarized data, that may not be a problem.

One kind of summarization collates data separately for each participant. As we have emphasized all along, that can be important because the impact of variables on behavior occurs only at the level of the individual. The same treatment procedure may affect different participants in slightly or even substantially different ways. Summarizing within participants has the advantage of ensuring that the resulting picture represents real behavioral effects.

Summarizing data within participants may take two forms. The most familiar form involves summarizing over periods of time. In order to consider the possibilities, we must start with the only picture of responding that does not involve summarization: displays that show each response in a real time sequence. Figure 9.1 shows some examples. The most common level of summarization over time shows individual responses collated for each session, usually displayed in sequence within a phase. Figure 9.2 and Panel B of Figure 14.1 show that type of display.

A second way to summarize is across environmental variables rather than time. That is, a participant's performance might be collated across similar conditions, even though the resulting data are no longer in their original temporal order. For example, if the same condition is repeated multiple times, the data could be summarized across like phases. In an ABAB design, for instance, data from the two A phases might be combined and contrasted with data from the combined B phases. As a different example, an analysis might summarize data from only the days on which an extraneous factor was operating, such as looking at worker performance only when the temperature was above a certain level in a manufacturing plant.

Across Participants. Collating data across participants is not merely another approach to summarization. As we pointed out above (and emphasized in Chapter 2), because behavior is an intraorganism phenomenon, orderly relations between behavior and influencing variables can only be seen clearly by looking at the behavior of individuals. That does not mean investigators should not summarize data across participants. However, it sets up some limitations on the conditions under which they do so, as well as on what they can say based on group data. Certainly investigators should not group data across participants until they have already made a thorough analysis of the individual data. Any uses of group data should be only supplementary to analyses of individual data. One reason for this guideline is that group data obscures individual patterns of responding. Regardless of whether the collated data present an interesting picture, it does not necessarily represent what happened with each individual in the group. Remember, there is no such phenomenon as "group behavior" because there is no such organism as a "group" or an "average participant." If an effect appears in group data but not in individual records, the group "effect" should not be considered the straightforward result of a treatment condition. For example, calculating a group mean for all participants for each session may permit extreme values from some individuals to push means in a direction that suggests that a treatment condition had a certain effect for all participants. However, the individual data may show that the group "effect" is not apparent for any single individual or even the majority of all participants.

The stylized data in Figure 14.3 exemplify that kind of situation. The top graph displays data obtained by averaging the data from the four graphs below, representing the performance of four participants. The group data suggest that the responding in the first phase was followed by a gradually increasing and then stabilized performance in a second phase. Inspection of the individual

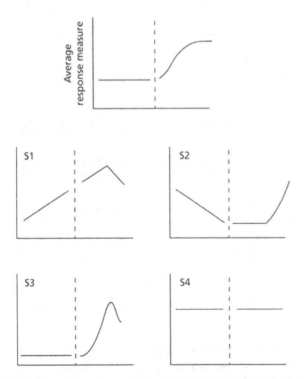

FIG. 14.3.   Schematic graphic representations of the individual performance of four individuals and the resulting average (top).

graphs, however, shows that that description does not describe the pattern of responding for any of the participants. The schematic displays have been created to show just how much individual data sets can vary from one another while still showing an average picture that represents none of the individual cases.

Discarding Data

Not all data are worthy of analysis. As the data from a project accumulate, investigators must decide if each value or series of values can be interpreted meaningfully. Data that do not qualify should be discarded or at least eliminated from future analysis. In other words, behavioral data should not be presented to others until the investigator decides that they warrant interpretation. Both researchers and practitioners have an obligation to their peers and the field to ensure that published or presented data are meaningful and important. When data are known to violate basic standards of measurement or represent circumstances other than those defining the project, the investigator should consider eliminating the offending data from analysis so they cannot mislead or confuse.

The reasons some data might be misleading or confusing are familiar to researchers and practitioners alike. A participant may have been ill or emotionally upset for some sessions. A particular extraneous factor may have had substantial effects, in spite of the investigator's best efforts. Observers may have had problems adhering to measurement procedures. Equipment may have malfunctioned. The procedures in control or treatment conditions may have deviated from the project's protocol for some reason. The list sometimes seems endless.

What qualifies data for being discarded is that some aspect of their measurement was unacceptable or that they were collected in the presence of unacceptable variables. In other words, in determining whether data should be discarded, only the circumstances surrounding the occurrence and measurement of the data should be considered. Whether the data are consistent with the investigator's preconceptions or interests is not legitimate criteria for keeping or throwing out data. If unacceptable circumstances arise concerning certain data, they must be set aside and not considered further, even if investigators like what they appear to show. If no disqualifying circumstances are evident, data must be considered in the analysis, even if they appear unusual or conflict with investigator preferences. In other words, whether the investigator likes the data should be irrelevant to the decision.

Consider a project involving some children in an elementary classroom. Assume the teacher's behavior is a key feature of the procedure and that he has been carefully trained to follow a specific protocol. What if the teacher is occasionally absent and is replaced on those days by a substitute teacher who is not trained on the protocol? Should the data (collected by research staff) be discarded for the days when there is a substitute teacher? What if the data show that the children's performance was not generally different when the substitute teacher was on duty compared to when the trained teacher was present?

Our guideline indicates that the data from substitute teacher days should be discarded, regardless of whether they suggested that the children's behavior was affected by that deviation from standard procedures. The data were collected under circumstances that were substantially different from those that were operating when other data were collected and should not be interpreted as reflecting the conditions in effect when the trained teacher was present. The fact that the data failed to suggest that the absence of the trained teacher had any effects should not encourage the investigator to use the data. Because the untrained substitute teacher could not have followed the project's protocol, the data collected on those days could not have reflected the effects of the protocol.

Selecting Representative Data

Within-subject experimental designs encourage repeated measurement of the behavior of each participant under each condition. As a result, those designs usually generate lots of data, even though there may be a relatively small number of participants. After examining the data to figure out what interpretations they support, the researcher or practitioner must decide how to communicate the findings with colleagues.

In considering how to describe a project's findings, experienced investigators know that scientific journals are interested in a report that describes the project as efficiently as possible. Journals struggle to balance their budgets, and editors have to make sure that every point of discussion and graph are necessary to communicate key findings. If an editor believes a point can be made with fewer graphs, the investigator will be asked to revise a submitted paper and make appropriate reductions. That pressure may be relieved by the trend for on-line journal publication, but even then economy of expression and data display will remain a priority.

Investigators are also aware that every data point from every participant is not equally important. For example, many data points represent transition states at the beginning of a phase and may not be important in describing the eventual impact of an intervention. As the discussion about discarding data suggested, some phases may include values that might be distracting to viewers because they represent measurement practices that were subsequently improved, extraneous influences that were later controlled, or deviations from protocol that were eventually corrected.

It is also the case that every data point from every participant is usually not necessary to describe the outcome of each comparison between control and intervention conditions. Because multiple participants are usually exposed to all conditions, there are often a number of comparable records for each interpretive point the investigator might wish to make. Although replications are valuable to the researcher, it may not be necessary to display all of the data when communicating findings to colleagues. The scientific and practitioner community needs to see only sufficient data to support the proposed findings.

A tactic that accommodates these points involves selecting records from individual participants that represent each interpretive issue the researcher wants to address. A record is some portion of the data from a participant. In showing the behavioral outcomes of a study, it is important to look for records – not participants – that represent what really happened. It is not often the case that the data from a single participant best represents each of the different findings supported by the data from other participants.

In order to appreciate this point, consider a project in which two different treatment conditions are investigated using five participants who experience both treatments and their associated control conditions. The investigator is interested in drawing conclusions about each of these two conditions. Let us assume that four of the participants responded to Treatment 1 in much the same way. It might be that data from any of the four participants would properly represent the performance of the other three. However, it might be a mistake to ignore the performance of the fifth participant. Even though we will assume that performance was markedly different from the others, it could be just as legitimate an outcome and should not be ignored (unless there is clear evidence the data are misleading for some reason). In that case, then, the researcher might need two records to represent the effects of Treatment 1 – one from any of the four who showed the same outcome and one from the participant who showed the different outcome.

For Treatment 2, however, assume that two participants showed one kind of effect, two showed a different effect, and the fifth was often absent and had insufficient contact with the condition. After deciding to discard the data from the fifth participant, the investigator will need to select one record from each pair to represent the two kinds of outcomes. Those records need not be from either participant whose data were used to represent Treatment 1 effects. The point is to select records, not participants, that represent the data not being presented, assuming that it is not feasible to present all pertinent data from all participants.

Finally, when selected records are used to represent data not presented, viewers are at a disadvantage in not being able to see how well the presented data reflect the data not made public. In order to provide at least a limited picture of the remaining data, it is customary to present some kind of summary of those other data. Figure 14.4 shows one example of how that might be done. It shows the last eight days of responding under each condition from one individual selected to represent the findings supported by the data from other participants. It also includes a summary of the other participants' data in the form of averages and ranges.

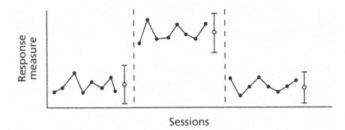

FIG. 14.4. Data showing a representative record from three phases, supplemented by the average and range for each phase of the data from other participants not shown.

BOX 14.2

Do We Need Data Analysis Police?

The preference for graphical analytical procedures as a way of deciding what behavioral data reveal sometimes bothers researchers in other fields who are more accustomed to analytical approaches based on inferential statistical models. In particular, they worry that the lack of clear interpretive rules that force or limit graphically based conclusions invites innocent or even malicious misinterpretation. They would rather have an unambiguous set of regulations that police this kind of interpretation. From this perspective, the outcome of data analysis procedures should be relatively inflexible, with conclusions required by rules that leave little room for the convictions of individual investigators. In effect, this view is that data analysis procedures should protect researchers from themselves.

The approach to data analysis described in this volume, as well as in many other sources, contrasts sharply with this perspective. The approach that has worked well in the natural sciences acknowledges that scientific investigation is an uncertain and necessarily idiosyncratic process. Ambiguity and bias are not only the norm; they are desirable within limits (see Box 12.1). Both formal research and clinical practice are journeys of discovery into unknown territory. There is no choice but to trust the motivations and actions of individual investigators. It is possible to create and enforce rigid interpretive rules, but it is not possible to guarantee the propriety of each investigator's actions throughout a project. In short, if an investigator really wants to cheat, it is easier to fake the data in the first place than to bias the analysis. And if an investigator is unaware of his or her prejudices, their impact will be embedded in how the study is conceived and implemented, not just at the stage of data analysis.

Finally, fixed interpretive rules would not guarantee accurate conclusions anyway. Because of their general and inflexible character, they would sometimes force acceptance of problematic data. Furthermore, as we emphasize in Chapter 16, good interpretation is not just about analyzing data. The meaningfulness of data cannot be understood without evaluating the entire context in which they were obtained.

GRAPHICAL ANALYTICAL TACTICS

Constructing Graphs

What Information Should Be Represented? Most graphs are constructed using the Cartesian convention of representing two dimensions with a pair of horizontal and vertical lines joined at one end to form a right angle.[1] The resulting lines are described as horizontal and vertical axes.

In behavior analytic research, the horizontal axis typically represents values of (a) a treatment variable (different intervention conditions), (b) units of time over which responding occurred (hours, days, or weeks), or (c) events corresponding to time (sessions). The vertical axis customarily represents measures of responding – the dependent variable. The vertical axis is usually labeled with a dimension such as number or count of responses, duration of responding in minutes, or rate of responding (responses per minute). The label may also indicate a dimensionless ratio such as percent.

When measures of responding are plotted across time or experimental conditions in a straightforward and uncomplicated manner, it is usually easy for viewers to understand the relationship between the two kinds of information represented on the two axes. As previous sections have emphasized, however, a single graph is unlikely to communicate everything the data might have to offer. One reason is that the same data may suggest different insights when displayed in different ways. Another is that most projects generate data describing multiple features of a procedure and different participant reactions that help the investigator and others understand what happened. Even simple projects often justify more than one graph to communicate outcomes.

What Measurement Scales Should Be Used? Once a decision is made about what features of the project will be displayed on each axis, numerical scales need to be selected that will allow specific values to be located on the axes. Although there are a number of possibilities (see Reading 10 in Johnston & Pennypacker, 1993b), the most common types of scales used in behavior analytic research are linear and logarithmic interval scales.

Linear interval scales allow descriptions of events that show how much they differ in terms of equal intervals between values. Most of the ways we are accustomed to measuring things in everyday life involve linear interval scales. When you weigh yourself, differences from one occasion to another are distinguished in terms of equal intervals. In other words, the difference between 300 kilograms and 301 kilograms is represented by the same distance on a linear interval scale as the difference between 301 and 302 kilograms.

---

[1] Although this type of graphical display is quite common, there are endless alternatives that may be more effective, as well as more efficient. Four volumes by Tufte (1983, 1990, 1997, and 2006) explore these possibilities and encourage investigators to think more creatively about ways of graphically displaying quantitative information.

Logarithmic interval scales allow descriptions of events that show how much they differ in terms of equal ratios between values. That kind of scale represents equal ratios by equal differences on the scale. For example, an increase in the rate of responding from 4 responses per minute to 12 responses per minute is proportionally equivalent to an increase from 40 responses per minute to 120 responses per minute. That is because the difference between two values on a logarithmic scale is equivalent to a ratio of the two values.

> **Linear interval scale.** A measurement scale that allows descriptions of events that show how much they differ in terms of equal intervals between values.
>
> **Logarithmic interval scale.** A measurement scale that allows descriptions of events that show how much they differ in terms of equal ratios between values.

These differences may be easier to appreciate by looking at the same data set plotted on both types of scales. Figure 14.5 shows two sets of values (a: 5, 3, 2, 1, 4 and b: 50, 30, 20, 10, and 40) representing responding in two phases. Panel A displays the values on a linear interval scale, and Panel B displays them on a logarithmic interval scale. The two scales obviously result in different pictures of the same data. Although the linear scale is probably more familiar to most people, the logarithmic scale highlights the fact that the values in the second data set are ten times as great as those in first data set by showing the same pattern of the values in each set. The contrast between the two graphs emphasizes how much different displays of the same data can have different effects on viewers. Figure 14.5 illustrates how different measurement scales may highlight different aspects of the data. Once again, it is not just a matter of whether a display is correct but whether it encourages sound interpretations.

How Should Scales Be Applied to Axes? In addition to selecting the type of measurement scale that will be applied to horizontal and vertical axes,

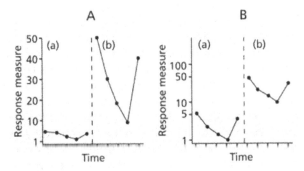

FIG. 14.5. Comparison of the same data sets on linear and logarithmic interval scales.

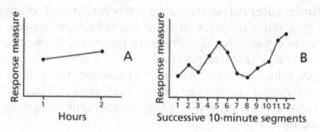

FIG. 14.6.   Graphs showing data displayed over longer (hours in Panel A) and shorter (10-minute periods in Panel B) intervals of time.

the investigator must choose the range of values that will be needed and how those ranges will be applied. That is usually a fairly straightforward decision. The lowest and highest values in the data set determine the minimum range each axis must display. Then it gets more complicated.

First, consider the horizontal axis. If it represents some measure of time, the investigator must decide what unit of time is most appropriate. That choice is something like selecting the lens on a microscope to produce different degrees of magnification. In general, the smaller the time unit, the more variability will be seen. Figure 14.6 makes this point by comparing the same data across hours versus successive 10-minute intervals. Using 10-minute blocks of time shows more information about responding than using hours. That advantage partly results from the fact that smaller time units simply show more values than larger time units.

A second issue in representing time on the horizontal axis concerns whether it is represented continuously or discontinuously. Of course, time is a continuous dimension, and a participant's behavior throughout a study can be located along that dimension. Any depiction of an individual's behavior that omits periods of time when behavior did not occur may make it more difficult for viewers to understand how responding was distributed over time. Figure 14.7 illustrates this point by showing the same data plotted on two graphs. Panel A shows a graph in which time is applied to the horizontal axis in terms of successive sessions. Any days on which there were no sessions are omitted on the axis. Although this approach saves space on the axis, it distorts the picture of responding as it actually occurred over time.

Panel B shows the correct temporal distribution for the data. By including on the horizontal axis times when sessions did not occur, the data in Panel B reveal a fairly regular pattern not evident in Panel A. In the first session following a day or two without sessions, responding was usually higher than in subsequent sessions. Knowing that encourages us to ask why. If the data came from an actual study, we would be able to consider possible explanations for that pattern. If sessions were not held on weekends, for instance, it could mean that something about weekend activities affected responding on Mondays. The point is that the behavior of participants during sessions can be influenced by events occurring between sessions. Displaying data across continuous representations of time allows discovery of such influences.

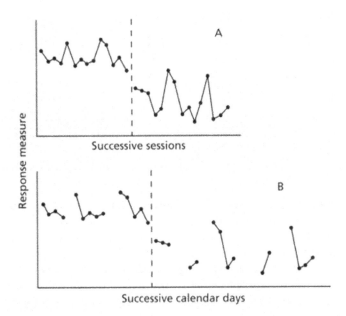

FIG. 14.7. Graphs showing data displayed across discontinuous (Panel A) and continuous (Panel B) representations of time on the horizontal axis.

A third aspect of how units of some dimension are mapped onto axes applies to both vertical and horizontal axes. Different ways of spacing intervals on the axis unavoidably affect the slopes of connecting lines. Figure 14.8 illustrates that impact by showing the same two values on two graphs in which time is mapped differently on the horizontal axis. In the graph on the left, a year's time is displayed in successive months, whereas in the graph on the right, the same year is divided into three 4-month seasons. The larger units of time are mapped onto the axis with shorter spaces between intervals. As a result, the slope of the line is steeper on the right graph than on the left. Both ways of constructing the axes are acceptable, but viewers might respond differently to each depending on what the data represent.

A fourth issue is most often relevant to the vertical axis. In selecting the range needed to display the data, it is important to create a display that suggests a fair

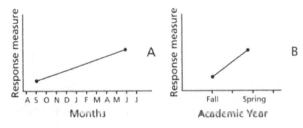

FIG. 14.8. Graphs illustrating the impact of interval spacing on the slopes of lines connecting data points.

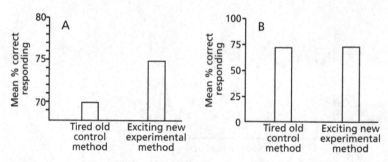

FIG. 14.9.   Graphs illustrating the impact of range on interpretations of data.

and meaningful interpretation. It is not appropriate to encourage conclusions that might be considered misleading. Figure 14.9 shows such an example. The range of values on the vertical axis in Panel A implies that there is an important difference in the outcomes of two procedures. Panel B shows the same data plotted against a different (larger) range, which might encourage a conclusion that the size of the difference between the two procedures is not important. Neither graph is necessarily incorrect, but which is more appropriate depends on what the difference in the data between the two conditions means in the context of the study's procedures and the literature.

Finally, it is generally improper to insert a break in the vertical axis, especially to accommodate outliers. (An outlier is a value that deviates substantially from other values.) When a data set includes one or more outliers, it can be tempting to apply scale values to the axis to highlight the majority of the values and locate the outliers on the other side of a break in the axis. Figure 14.10 shows that approach in Panel A. A break in the scale values above 45 allows plotting the two outliers in a way that does not require compressing the scale for the remaining values. The problem is that that treatment distorts the loca-

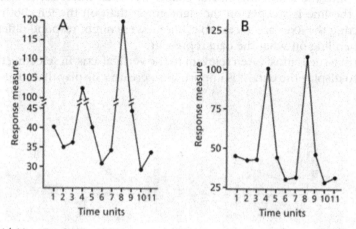

FIG. 14.10.   Graphs illustrating improper (Panel A) and correct (Panel B) displays of data sets containing outlier values.

tion of the outliers in relation to the other values. Panel B shows the same data without a break. Properly accommodating the outliers in a graph of the same size places the outliers in the correct spatial relation to the remaining values.

How Should Data Be Plotted? Even after the axes of a graph have been drawn, some issues remain before the investigator can plot data. One decision concerns how to represent each value, and computer graphing software usually provides a variety of options. The most common choices include representing each value with a symbol such as a dot (creating a line graph) or with a column or bar (creating a histogram). In general, line graphs will always work, but histograms are only useful when the data set does not include too many values. Plotting larger data sets in a bar graph format tends to require lots of relatively narrow bars. The key information communicated in a bar is its height relative to the vertical axis and other values, yet it requires tall vertical lines connecting that value to the horizontal axis. If one criterion for graphic efficiency is the ratio of amount of ink used to show the data to the total amount of ink used in the graph (Tufte, 1983), histograms are less efficient than line graphs. Busy histograms are more difficult to interpret than a line graph displaying the same data. Figure 14.11 illustrates the difference.

Ease of interpretation can also be an issue with line graphs. Problems arise when multiple data sets are displayed on the same graph, as illustrated in Figure 14.12. If the data sets do not overlap very much, it can be useful to contrast two or three different functions (lines) on the same graph. However,

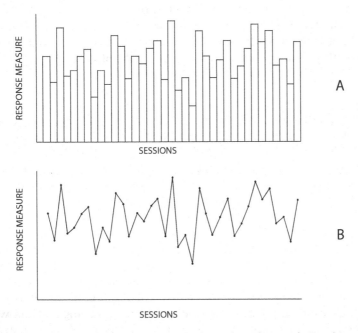

FIG. 14.11. Illustration of displaying many values using a bar graph (Panel A) versus a line graph (Panel B).

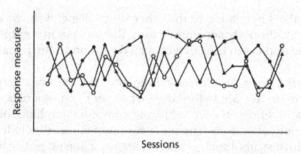

FIG. 14.12. Illustration of a line graph showing three overlapping functions.

as the number of data sets increases, particularly if they overlap somewhat, it can be difficult to follow individual functions. When that is the case, separate graphs are required.

A few plotting conventions have evolved in the behavior analytic research literature that concern when to connect or not connect data symbols. One rule is that data points should not be connected between phase changes. That is, the last data point in one phase should not be connected to the first data point in the next phase. That rule helps to highlight the breaks between phases.

Another plotting convention concerns whether to connect data points across intervening days when no data were collected, assuming the horizontal axis represents consecutive calendar days. The rule is as follows: If the target behavior could not possibly have occurred, the bracketing data points should not be connected. Those are called **no chance** days (Pennypacker, Gutierrez, & Lindsley, 2003). However, if the behavior could have occurred but measurement did not take place, the adjacent data points should be connected across the days with no values. Those are termed **ignored** days (Pennypacker et al., 2003). Figure 14.13 illustrates the two situations.

> **No chance day.** A plotting convention referring to days on which the target behavior could not have occurred. Data points bracketing such days should not be connected in line graphs.
>
> **Ignored day.** A plotting convention referring to days on which the target behavior could have occurred but was not measured. Data points bracketing such days should be connected in line graphs.

The reasoning underlying this convention is that if the target behavior could have occurred, it is reasonable to imply an estimate. The estimate is where the line connecting the adjacent values crosses the vertical line on which the missing value would have been placed. If the behavior could not have occurred, no such implication is appropriate. Therefore, the preceding and following data points should not be connected. This convention allows viewers to distinguish between those two types of situations.

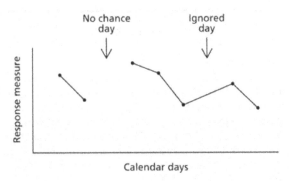

FIG. 14.13. Illustration of plotting conventions for no chance and ignored days.

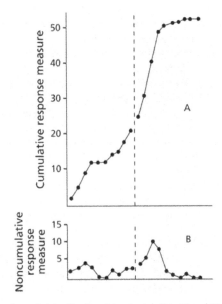

FIG. 14.14. Illustration of data displayed in cumulative (Panel A) and non-cumulative (Panel B) plots.

Finally, all of the examples thus far have plotted each value independently of previous values. There is another plotting rule that provides a very different picture by adding each new value to the previous total and plotting the new total value. The result is a cumulative picture of responding and is a type of display that has a long history in the study of behavior (Skinner, 1956). Using control and experimental data sets, Panel A in Figure 14.14 shows a cumulative plot across both phases, and Panel B shows a non-cumulative plot.

In a cumulative graph, successive data points can never go lower on the vertical axis, even if a new value is zero. In fact, if no responses are recorded for a series of days, the total response measure will not change and the same

---

BOX 14.3

The Cumulative Recorder

Plotting data cumulatively on the vertical axis has a special history in the study of behavior because, as Skinner (1956) described it, "Some people are lucky." (p. 224). In his earliest experimental efforts, he discovered that he could automatically draw a cumulative record of food deliveries using part of the food delivery apparatus. Further work led to the invention of the cumulative recorder. This device became a standard way of displaying operant behavior in laboratory settings, much as electrocardiograms (EKGs) use standard axes for displaying heart activity.

What makes the cumulative recorder valuable is not so much the cumulative picture it creates but the fact that it locates individual responses on a horizontal axis representing continuous time. In standard usage, one of the recorder's pens steps upward a small distance for each response. Because the paper rolls underneath the pen at a constant rate, the result is a graph of the cumulative number of responses over time, thereby showing the temporal distribution of individual responses (see Figure 9.1, Panel A).

This picture of responding provides the most basic level of analysis of a participant's behavior. Skinner and later generations of his students used this kind of display to reveal the intricate relations between behavior and environmental variables. Just as physicians learn to read the data from the standard EKG format, behavioral researchers learned to interpret this standard format showing variations in the slope of the line drawn by accumulating responses. These slopes are a graphic representation of the frequency of responding, so the cumulative record provides a moment-to-moment picture of changes in response frequency. This analytical technique is especially useful when brief experimental contingencies cycle repeatedly throughout a session, a common arrangement in much laboratory research.

The cumulative recorder is a laboratory device and has never been much used in applied settings. Today, data collection and display are computer-based in laboratory settings, and portable computers allow practitioners similar options. This makes cumulative graphs a convenient graphic option.

---

value will be plotted each day, resulting in a horizontal data line. As a result, interpreting cumulative graphs requires learning how to assess variations in the positive slope of a line. Nevertheless, that type of plotting can nicely highlight variability in some data sets. For example, it may be easier to see the ebb and flow of responding in Panel A in Figure 14.14 than in Panel B.

Analyzing Graphed Data

The previous section reviews some basic guidelines for selecting and constructing graphs of the sort most often used to display behavior analytic data.

It also explains some of the conventions and issues associated with how data may be plotted. Of course, a graphical approach to analyzing behavior analytic data offers many more options and complexities than those reviewed here – far more than a single chapter can cover. The fundamentals described here are the minimum necessary to explore the power of this analytical model.

In fact, graphical data analysis is remarkably intuitive, which may be why it is so widespread in the natural sciences. Analyzing properly graphed behavioral data should be straightforward for behavior analysts, who understand how each graph is designed and used and how its features influence their interpretations. Knowing how the components of graphic data displays affect interpretations helps users decide how to react. If the display enables the user to reach appropriate conclusions about what the data show, nothing further may need to be done. On the other hand, the features of the graph and how the data are plotted may make it difficult to identify the aspects of responding that might be important. If an investigator discovers that problem in working with their own data, it is easy to modify a graph so that it works as intended. When the

---

BOX 14.4

Does a Graphic Approach to Data Analysis Need Defending?

Psychology developed more as a social than a natural science. As a result, its methodological style was dominated by the development of inferential statistical procedures. These were first described by Fisher in 1935 and quickly adopted by a young discipline eager for the status associated by mathematical methods. Over the years, this quantitative approach to conceptualizing, conducting, and interpreting psychological data has come to so completely dominate social science research methods that alternative approaches are unavoidably in a defensive position.

From a broader scientific perspective, however, no such defense is required. With certain exceptions in the life sciences, the natural sciences were far less taken with a statistical approach to experimental design and analysis. Natural science researchers had a clearer, more thorough, and more certain understanding of their subject matters and methods than did their social science colleagues, which made them less inclined to use inferential statistics as a default approach to experimental design. As a result, today inferential statistics are used more narrowly and appropriately in the natural than in the social sciences.

Is graphic analysis an effective interpretive approach for behavioral research? The answer lies in its track record. These methods have consistently characterized the field of behavior analysis since its inception. The real test of a scientific literature is evidence that its findings are sufficiently complete and accurate descriptions of nature that they can be depended on in daily practice. The widespread application of applied behavior analysis procedures (e.g., Austin & Carr, 2000; Fisher, Piazza, & Roane, 2011), as well as comprehensive reviews of the effectiveness of those procedures (e.g., National Autism Center, 2015; Ontario Association for Behaviour Analysis, 2017; Wong et al., 2015), provides the reassuring answer to this question.

viewer does not have access to the raw data, however, it is not usually feasible for them to modify the display – for instance, when viewing someone else's graphed data in a treatment report, presentation, or publication. In that case, there may be no choice but to judge the graph fatally flawed and inappropriate for interpretation. That can be frustrating when you are interested in a project and its findings, but there is no point in drawing conclusions based on graphic displays that do not clearly reveal what happened.

As with other features of research methods, the greatest risk lies in not knowing what you do not know. If investigators or end users are not prepared to explain how various graphical options affect interpretations, they are also not likely to recognize the impact of those alternatives on their reactions to the data. That shortfall leaves the second-guessing to others – reviewers and colleagues who evaluate the study and make their own assessments of the investigator's graphical choices and conclusions.

In sum, although analyzing graphical data displays can be straightforward and productive, those benefits require both originators and end users to have technical knowledge about graphical displays and experience playing with graphical options using different data sets. That background encourages an appreciation for how powerfully various features of graphical data displays influence interpretive reactions. In turn, it provides the motivation to create – and demand from colleagues – displays that are optimally effective for each set of data.

CHAPTER SUMMARY

1. Analyzing behavioral data is a matter of arranging the data in ways that encourage investigators to manage the project effectively along the way and then to draw conclusions that are going to hold up when others use them.

2. The goal of data analysis is to discover variability in the data that helps answer the experimental question. Each of the multiple ways of collecting and viewing data will reveal a somewhat different view of variability. In doing so, each will obscure other aspects of variability that the investigator must be aware of. The safest way to be sure about what is being missed is to look at alternative viewpoints of the same data.

3. In spite of the risk of allowing preconceptions to bias selection of analytical procedures, investigators must approach this task with at least some idea of what the data might reveal. In selecting an analytical procedure, investigators should usually proceed from relatively simple techniques to more complex procedures. Collecting repeated measures of performance under several conditions in sequence makes it useful to begin data analysis as soon as there are data to analyze. As control and intervention phases are completed and comparisons become possible, there may be a need for more complex analytical options.

4. The more an analytical technique changes the picture of the participant's behavior as it actually happened, the greater the risk that interpretations may be swayed more by the technique than by what actually happened.

5. It is important to remember that summarizing data can simultaneously reveal and obscure important features of the data. Although we construct a summary because we want to see a different picture, it is unavoidable that the summarized representation prevents seeing unsummarized views of the same data.

6. Because behavior is an intraorganism phenomenon, orderly relationships between behavior and environmental variables can only be seen clearly by looking at the behavior of individuals. This does not mean investigators should not summarize data across participants. However, it sets up some limitations on the conditions under which they do so, as well as on what they can say based on grouped data.

7. Not all data are worthy of analysis. Investigators have an obligation to their discipline to insure that published data are meaningful and important. Whether the data are consistent with the investigator's preconceptions or interests is not legitimate criteria for keeping or throwing out data. If unacceptable circumstances arise concerning data from certain sessions, they should be set aside and not considered further, even if they appear acceptable. If no such circumstances are evident, data should be considered in the analysis, even if they appear unusual.

8. In behavior analytic research, the horizontal axis typically represents values of (a) a treatment variable (different intervention conditions), (b) units of time over which responding occurred (hours, days, or weeks), or (c) events corresponding to time (sessions). The vertical axis customarily represents measures of responding – the dependent variable. The vertical axis is usually labeled with a dimension such as number or count of responses, duration of responding in minutes, or rate of responding (responses per minute). The label may also indicate a dimensionless ratio such as percent.

9. The lowest and highest values in the data set determine the minimum range each axis must display. In determining how to examine data on the horizontal axis, the investigator first must decide what unit of time is most appropriate. In general, the smaller the time unit, the more variability will be seen.

10. In addition to determining the range, the investigator must decide how to space the intervals on the axis to allow the slopes of the data to be as representative and informative as possible. In addressing this issue, it is important to remember that it is generally improper to insert a break in the vertical axis, especially to accommodate outliers. The problem in doing so is that it distorts the location of the outliers in relation to the other values.

11. Graphical data analysis is remarkably intuitive, which may be why it is so widespread in the natural sciences. Analyzing properly graphed behavioral data should be straightforward for behavior analysts, who understand how each graph is designed and used and how its features influence their interpretations. Knowing how the components of graphic data displays affect interpretations helps users decide how to react.

HIGHLIGHTED TERMS

Exploratory data analysis (EDA). An approach to data analysis emphasizing largely graphical techniques focusing on discovering order and structure in the data. EDA may be contrasted with confirmatory data analysis or hypothesis testing.

Ignored day. A plotting convention referring to days on which the target behavior could have occurred but was not measured. Data points bracketing such days should be connected in line graphs.

Linear interval scale. A measurement scale that allows descriptions of events that show how much they differ in terms of equal intervals between values

Logarithmic interval scale. A measurement scale that allows descriptions of events that show how much they differ in terms of equal ratios between values

No chance day. A plotting convention referring to days on which the target behavior could not have occurred. Data points bracketing such days should not be connected in line graphs.

TEXT STUDY GUIDE

1. What is the benefit of viewing data analysis as a stimulus control problem?
2. What is the goal of data analysis?
3. Describe exploratory data analysis.
4. Explain the rationale for starting data analysis with simple options and gradually moving to more complex options.
5. What is the risk of using increasingly complex analytical procedures?
6. What is the basic effect of summarizing data?
7. Describe two general forms of summarizing data within participants.
8. How is summarizing data across participants fundamentally different than summarizing within participants?
9. What interpretive constraints apply when summarizing data across participants?
10. What are some reasons it might be appropriate to discard data?
11. What is the general guideline for when to discard or keep data?
12. Why can it be appropriate to select representative data?

13. What is the difference between selecting representative participants versus selecting representative records?
14. What information is usually represented on the horizontal and vertical axes in behavior analytic research?
15. What is the difference between linear and logarithmic interval scales?
16. What is the effect of representing different units of time on the horizontal axis?
17. Describe the consequences of representing time on the horizontal axis continuously versus discontinuously.
18. How can the spacing of time units on the horizontal axis affect the slope of the lines connecting data points?
19. Why is it improper to break the vertical axis in order to accommodate outlier values?
20. When are histograms a poor choice as a plotting format?
21. What is the convention for connecting data points across phase changes?
22. Explain the plotting conventions for no chance and ignored days.
23. Explain how data points are calculated in a cumulative graph.

BOX STUDY GUIDE

1. How can experimenter bias be useful? How is it limited by the scientific process?
2. Why would it not improve interpretive decisions to have rigid interpretive rules that all researchers had to follow?
3. What made the cumulative recorder a valuable recording format for early researchers?

SUGGESTED READINGS

Pennypacker, H. S., Gutierrez, A., Jr., & Lindsley, O. R. (2003). *Handbook of the standard celeration chart*. Gainesville, AL: Author.
Tufte, E. R. (2006). *Beautiful evidence*. Cheshire, CN: Graphics Press.

DISCUSSION TOPICS

1. Discuss the impact on interpretations for summarizing data within versus between participants.
2. Select a graph from a published study in a behavioral journal. Critique the graph using the standards discussed in this chapter. Consider how any shortcomings might affect interpretations.

EXERCISES

1. Select a graph from a published study in a behavioral journal. Estimate each of the values in each phase. Replot these values using a graphic format that differs in some way. Compare the picture presented by the two graphs, and consider how the differences might impact the interpretations.

2. Make up a data set of about twenty values or use a data set that is already available. Plot the data on a graph using a linear interval scale on the vertical axis and also on a graph using a logarithmic interval scale. Consider how the different displays might influence interpretations.

CHAPTER FIFTEEN

Group Research Designs and Statistical Analyses

COMPARING APPROACHES TO RESEARCH

Behavior Analysis

The approach to research described in this book is tailored to the subject matter of the science of behavior analysis: the behavior of organisms and its relation to the surrounding environment, past and present. That approach necessarily involves directly observing and measuring the behavior of individuals under specified conditions over time. It allows us to examine dynamic interactions among behaviors and environmental events. Behavior analytic researchers often focus on questions about relations between particular environmental variables and particular responses under control and experimental conditions, with the ultimate objective of establishing the reproducibility and generality of such functional relations. That can only be accomplished through repeated experimentation and measurement with many individual organisms. For practitioners, the approach enables precise, systematic evaluation of the effects of one or more environmental events (treatments or interventions) on the socially important behaviors of individual clients.

Other Disciplines

For much of psychology and other social sciences, the subject matter is not behavior; it is intelligence, aptitudes, attitudes, happiness, anxiety, satisfaction, political preferences, patriotism, and other hypothetical constructs. Behaviors like responses to items on tests or questionnaires are used to make inferences about the underlying construct. Research projects often address questions about how large groups of people compare on such constructs and other variables. Similarly, the aim of many research projects in medicine, epidemiology, education, and several other disciplines is to see how groups of people compare on certain variables, or to determine the effects of interventions on the symptoms or performances of groups. Generally speaking, the dominant research approach in those disciplines is to identify or assemble one or more large groups and measure each of the members once when a study begins and at least once again after some period of time. Those measurements are then aggregated for the group(s), and the aggregates (e.g., average or mean scores, standard deviations) are subjected to certain statistical tests. From the statistical analyses of the aggregated data, inferences are drawn about the associations (correlations) among variables, or the likelihood that some identifiable variable is responsible for any changes in those aggregates over the course of a study or any differences in the aggregated data of two or more groups.

WHY BEHAVIOR ANALYSTS NEED TO UNDERSTAND GROUP RESEARCH DESIGNS AND STATISTICAL ANALYSES

Being Informed Consumers

The majority of studies conducted by researchers in other disciplines involve group research designs and statistical analyses. Many institutions, payers, and governmental entities rely heavily on those kinds of studies to make decisions that have profound effects on behavior analysts. They include decisions about what types of research, services, and training programs will be funded and discontinued. For instance, policymakers have called for more studies comparing the effects of two or more treatments with large groups of people to guide decisions about how healthcare resources are allocated. Additionally, consumers of behavior analytic services are likely to be exposed to many reports about group-design studies on interventions that purport to change behavior via the popular press and social media. Behavior analytic practitioners are ethically obligated to help consumers make informed decisions about services and to use and recommend interventions that have proved most effective in scientific studies (Behavior Analyst Certification Board, 2016).

It should be clear from the foregoing that in order to communicate and collaborate with members of other professions, use the research findings of other disciplines, advocate for policies that support behavior analysis, and fulfill their ethical responsibilities, behavior analysts need to be informed consumers of research using group designs and statistical analyses. To accomplish that, they need to know at least (a) what types of research questions can or should be addressed in studies using group research designs and statistical analyses; (b) how to interpret the reported results of such studies; (c) the limitations of such studies, especially what can and cannot be inferred about the effects of interventions from statistical analyses of group means and other mathematical abstractions; and (d) how those research methods differ from behavior analytic research methods.

Addressing Questions that Require Group Comparisons

Some practical and research questions are best addressed in studies that focus on group measures rather than individual behavior. "Which science text should the school district adopt for its sixth graders?" is an example of such a question.

BOX 15.1

Comparing BSE Search Patterns

As part of a long-term project to develop improved methods for detecting breast cancer by manual palpation, two experiments were conducted to assess the relative thoroughness of three search patterns for breast self-examination (BSE). Experiment 1 compared the commonly taught concentric circle pattern to a new pattern composed of vertical strips. Experiment 2 compared a radial spoke pattern to the vertical strip pattern. Twenty-eight women participated in each experiment. Each was pretested, learned the elements of BSE, and was then posttested using the two patterns under investigation (order was counterbalanced). BSE thoroughness was measured by projecting a numbered grid on the participant's torso and having an observer mark each square of the grid palpated on a congruently gridded score sheet. A t-test analysis of percentages of area palpated favored the vertical strip method over the other two. Of the 112 intra-subject comparisons, the vertical strip pattern was superior in all but nine, of which four were ties (Saunders, Pilgrim, & Pennypacker, 1986). This simple use of statistical testing was appropriate to the experimental question and responsive to the interests of the funding agency and other user communities.

The conventional approach to answering that question might involve randomly dividing a large of group of sixth graders into as many subgroups as there are candidate textbooks, assigning one book at random to each of the subgroups at the beginning of the school year, then looking at the mean score of each of the groups on the science subtest of the state achievement exam given at the end of the year. Using analysis of variance (discussed later), one could determine which of the group mean scores was the highest and if that score was statistically different from the others. The school district might then decide to adopt the textbook that was associated with the highest test scores, on average.

Studies using group research designs and statistical analyses are also used to compare the effects of two or more medical or behavioral interventions, as described above. Behavior analytic researchers who want to address those kinds of questions therefore need to know how to design and conduct studies using those methods. Practitioners would do well to acquire skills in discriminating what types of questions can be addressed appropriately in group-design studies, how to interpret the reported results, and how to explain the relevance and limitations of such studies to audiences like third-party payers, consumers of ABA services, school or service agency administrators, and policymakers.

Responding to External Contingencies

Nancy Ator (1999) charmingly described some external pressures that may impinge upon the research behavior of behavior analysts. For example, many behavior analysts work in organizations that place a premium on publishing research. Some researchers work in areas in which the editorial boards of all or many of the principal professional journals favor or require group-design studies with statistical analyses. The academic behavior analyst who needs a certain number of publications to earn tenure, say, may have little choice but to use those methods. The same contingencies may apply to the behavior analyst who is part of a research team working on a problem in a field that requires statistical analyses for validation of results. Relatedly, many groups that review proposals for research grants are populated mostly or entirely by individuals who come from the group-design-with-statistical-analysis tradition. Some funding sources explicitly require the use of those methods. Behavior analysts who need grants to support their research may have to make their proposals conform to those requirements, even though they know that the research questions could be addressed as well or better using behavior analytic methods.

Summarizing Single-Subject Data

Last but not least, there are circumstances under which statistical analyses of data from studies using single-subject research designs can be informative. Indeed, the use of statistics to supplement visual analyses of individual behavioral data seems to be increasing. That includes analyses of data that are aggregated across multiple studies that involved single-subject research designs using meta-analytic methods. Behavior analytic practitioners and researchers therefore must be able to recognize when such analyses are appropriate, determine which statistical tools to use, and correctly interpret the results. For instance, before making a decision to change an independent variable, the behavior analyst needs to determine the typical or central value of the observations that have been conducted to that point and how stable those data are. She should also note any trend(s) in the data. Although that information can usually be gleaned from visual analyses of the graphed data, factors like extreme variability or changing trends within a data series or unexpected occurrences (e.g., illness or other events impinging on the participant; interruptions in data collection) can render those "eyeball" judgments very challenging. Alternatively, the behavior analyst might prefer to make more refined statements than "The data appear stable" or "There seems to be an increasing trend." If she aspires to share the results of the study with colleagues in a conference presentation or journal article, it might behoove her to include additional analyses.

COMMON TYPES OF GROUP RESEARCH DESIGNS

Randomized Controlled Trial (RCT)

As in Chapter 11, *design* refers to the arrangement of experimental (treatment) and control conditions that will allow for meaningful comparison of data sets.

Behavior analysts are likely to encounter a variety of group research designs. Some may be familiar from classes or journal articles in behavior analysis, psychology, or education. Others are used mainly in medical and epidemiological studies.

One type of group research design that is often used in studies of treatment effects is the randomized controlled or clinical trial (RCT). As with most group-design studies, large numbers (samples) of participants are typically involved in RCTs so that individual differences among participants average out; otherwise those differences might influence the outcomes of the study. Additionally, many statistical tests require large samples (commonly abbreviated as N or n). In an RCT, participants are randomly assigned to two groups (sometimes more). The experimental or treatment group is designated to receive a specific treatment while the other group (usually called the control or comparison group) receives no treatment, a placebo or sham treatment, "treatment as usual" (e.g., commonly available services), or a different specific treatment. The main purpose of random assignment is to ensure that investigator bias and other extraneous factors that could affect the outcome of the study are randomly distributed across the groups. It is presumed to result in groups that are equivalent in terms of key characteristics at the beginning of the study, leaving the independent variable (the treatment of interest) as the only difference between them. Put another way, random assignment is presumed to maximize the *internal validity* of group-design studies (see Box 16.2).

Once participants are assigned to groups, the dependent variable that could be affected by the treatment of interest is measured with all participants. The mean scores of the two groups – and perhaps other aggregated data – are compared statistically. At the beginning of the study, it is essential for there to be no significant difference between those groups' mean scores; otherwise the groups cannot be considered equivalent. The groups then experience their designated conditions for the same prespecified period of time. At the end of that time, the dependent measure is administered to all participants again, and again the group mean scores (and often other aggregates, such as standard deviations) are compared statistically. If there is a difference in the aggregated post-treatment scores in favor of one group and that difference meets standard criteria for statistical significance, the investigator is likely to conclude that the difference was due to the independent variable (treatment) rather than "chance" or some extraneous variable. The pre- and post-treatment mean scores of each group might also be compared statistically to evaluate change within the group over the course of the study. It is important to note, however, that findings of statistically significant differences in aggregate measures, whether between or within groups, provide no information about how the interventions affected any individuals, including whether any individuals improved and, if so, by how much. In other words, a finding of *statistical significance* does not indicate that an intervention produced *socially* or *clinically significant* improvements for any participants.

To illustrate, an investigator might be interested in comparing the effects of a developmental, play-based intervention and an ABA intervention on the social interactions of 5-year-olds with autism. He would need to find a sizeable sample of children who are similar not only in terms of their chronological age and diagnosis but also other key characteristics like gender, developmental level, extant language and social skills, and parents' socioeconomic status. Using a random number table, the investigator or an independent party would assign the children at random to either the developmental-play intervention group or the ABA intervention group, with half in each group. The social interactions of all children in both groups would be assessed with the same instrument or methods (the dependent measure) as when the study began and the mean scores of the two groups compared statistically. Both groups would then receive the designated intervention for the same prespecified period of time. At the end of that time, the dependent measure would be administered to all the children again, and again the mean scores of the two groups would be compared to see if there was a statistically significant difference favoring one intervention over the other.

Because random assignment of participants to treatment and control or comparison groups is assumed to eliminate biases and "wash out" any pre-treatment individual differences among participants, the RCT is considered by many to be the "gold standard" design for scientific studies of treatment effects. In point of fact, those assumptions are not always valid, and several sources of possible bias are inherent in RCTs. For example, random assignment does not guarantee that the groups will be equivalent. Even if they are equivalent at the beginning of the study, *attrition* may alter their composition over time. That occurs when participants drop out of the study because they find out they are in the control group, dislike the intervention, perceive that their condition has improved, have difficulty complying with the study requirements, or any number of other reasons. If there is more attrition in one group than the other, it can bias the study results. *Performance bias* occurs when participants in one group are treated differently by the researchers or others with whom they interact – especially those who deliver the intervention or administer the dependent measures – than participants in the other group, thereby influencing the study's outcome. That can be minimized by *blinding* those individuals – that is, keeping them unaware of the condition to which each participant has been assigned (see Chapter 6). That is often more difficult to accomplish with behavioral interventions, where the features of the interventions are easily observed, than it is in drug studies, where the placebo can be made to appear identical to the active drug. Finally, *assessment bias* occurs when there are differences in the way dependent measures are administered to the groups, such as the time of day or location in which the measures are conducted (Juni,

TABLE 15.1
Sources of possible bias in RTCs

- Attrition
- Performance bias
- Assessment bias

Altman, & Egger, 2001; Levin, 2007). In point of fact, all four of the concerns just described apply to all group-design studies, not just RCTs.

Some authors have called for more RCTs of ABA interventions, particularly "package" interventions comprising many procedures, interventions that have been or could be "manualized," and interventions on which sufficient development work has been completed to warrant evaluation of their effects when they are implemented on a large scale (e.g., T. Smith, 2013). Others, however, have pointed out the limitations of RCTs for evaluating the effects of behavioral interventions. They include ethical constraints on randomly assigning participants to control groups where they will receive no intervention, a placebo, or an intervention that is likely to be less effective than the one received by the treatment group. That is of particular concern when the behavior of interest puts potential study participants or those around them at risk of harm (e.g., smoking, overusing opioid drugs, self-injurious behavior, aggressive behavior). Indeed, it may be very difficult to secure informed consent for participation in studies like that. There are also several logistical challenges inherent in conducting RCTs and other group-design studies. For instance, it can be difficult for an investigator to assemble sufficiently large groups of participants who are similar on key dimensions and to keep those groups intact throughout the course of the study. That may be particularly problematic when the target population is very heterogeneous – that is, when there are substantial differences between or within individuals in the population, as is the case with those who are diagnosed with an autism spectrum disorder. That problem also applies to conditions and disorders that affect relatively small proportions of the population. A related challenge is ensuring that the treatment and control conditions remain exactly the same for all members of both of those groups for the entire duration of the study. For those and other reasons, RCTs are often resource- and labor-intensive and therefore costly and difficult to replicate. In addition to the limited information about the effects of the treatment and control or comparison conditions on individuals mentioned earlier, there are also limitations on the extent to which the results of RCTs can be applied to typical clients in everyday circumstances that bear little resemblance to the conditions of the RCT – a constraint on the *external validity* (see Box 16.2) of those types of research designs (Carey & Stiles, 2016; Keenan & Dillenburger, 2011; Stephenson & Imrie, 1998).

Non-Randomized Controlled Trial

As the name implies, this design (sometimes called a *quasi-experimental* design or *controlled clinical trial*) is like the randomized controlled trial except that participants are not randomly assigned to groups. Instead the groups might be assembled from two or more pools of similar individuals – say, one pool of adults diagnosed with a particular heart condition who are designated to receive a new drug (the experimental or treatment group) and another pool of adults with the same diagnosis who are designated to receive a placebo or a different drug (the control or comparison group). Investigators often take steps to ensure that the treatment and control or comparison groups are matched on key variables that could influence the study results. They might accomplish that by identifying pairs of similar individuals and assigning one member of each pair to the treatment group and the other to the control or comparison group. Alternatively, they could simply make sure that the overall makeup of the groups is comparable in terms of variables that are relevant to the research question, such as gender distributions, diagnosis, mean chronological age, mean level of education, and the like. Often investigators using this type of design conduct statistical comparisons to evaluate whether the method of assigning participants to groups had the same result as random assignment – that is, producing treatment and control or comparison groups that are equivalent when the study begins.

A study comparing intensive behavior analytic and eclectic (mixed-method) interventions for young children with autism illustrates some of the tactics just described. Random assignment to groups was deemed infeasible because of laws requiring parents and guardians, along with other members of treatment or education teams, to determine the services received by children with autism. The investigators identified a pool of children within a geographic region who had been diagnosed with autism or pervasive developmental disorder – not otherwise specified (PDD-NOS; an autism spectrum disorder) – had no other medical condition, had English as the family's primary language, had entered an intervention program prior to age 48 months, and had had no prior treatment of more than 100 hours. They then identified 29 children within that large pool whose treatment or education teams had selected behavior analytic intervention (the treatment group), 16 who received intervention involving a mixture of methods delivered in special education classrooms designed for children with autism spectrum disorders (comparison group 1), and 16 who participated in generic, mixed-method educational programming designed for children with various diagnoses (comparison group 2). The makeup of the three groups was shown to be very similar in terms of gender, ethnicity, diagnoses, parents' marital status, and severity of autism when the study began. Some between-groups differences in mean age at diagnosis, mean age at treatment entry, and parents' years of education were shown to be statistically significant when the study began but were controlled for in the statistical analyses of treatment effects (Howard, Sparkman, Cohen, Green, & Stanislaw, 2005).

Regression Discontinuity Design

This quasi-experimental design is identical to the non-randomized controlled trial with one major difference: study participants are assigned to groups based on whether their value on a specific variable (often termed the rating or assignment variable) falls above or below a cut point or threshold. For example, an investigator who wants to evaluate the effectiveness of a particular reading curriculum for third-grade students might assign students who scored 50% correct and below on a reading achievement test to the treatment group, and students who scored 51% and above to the control group. She would then use regression statistical analyses in which the value of the rating variable is controlled to evaluate differences between the mean reading achievement test scores of the treatment and control groups after the treatment group had been exposed to the curriculum (W. C. Smith, 2014).

Single-Group Pretest-Posttest or Posttest-Only Design

In studies using these designs, a group of participants who have certain characteristics is identified or selected. The dependent measure may be administered to all of them when the study begins and again after they have been exposed to a specified treatment for some period of time. The mean group pre- and post-treatment scores or other aggregate data are compared statistically to determine if change occurred over the course of treatment. In some studies, the dependent measure is administered only after the participants have experienced the treatment; there is no pretest. These designs avoid some of the problems inherent in between-groups comparisons, since each participant serves as his or her own control. Because the dependent variable is measured only once or twice with each participant and there is no control group, however, there is no basis for determining whether the effect (if any) was due to the treatment or to any number of extraneous variables.

Single-group designs are used fairly often in education research. For instance, an investigator who wants to evaluate a curriculum designed to teach beginning math skills might test a class of first graders on those skills at the beginning of a semester and again at the end of the semester. If the group mean posttest score is higher than the mean pretest score and that difference is statistically significant, the investigator might be tempted to conclude that the difference was due to the curriculum. He would be wise to note, however, that with that type of uncontrolled research design he cannot rule out the possibility that extraneous factors such as maturation, students leaving the class during the semester, or other experiences the students had (e.g., watching educational TV programs, getting homework help from parents) were responsible for the higher posttest score, in whole or in part. Their substantial limitations notwithstanding, single-group designs can be useful for conducting preliminary evaluations of educational, behavioral, or medical interventions to see if they warrant further research using experimental designs.

Cohort Studies

One subcategory of studies that are sometimes termed *observational* by medical and epidemiological researchers is the cohort study. In a *prospective* cohort study, a sample of people drawn from a specified population is identified and then followed for some period of time. For example, a cohort of children born into smoking households might be followed for several years to observe frequencies of asthma and other breathing disorders. Those data may be compared to data on occurrences of such disorders in a cohort of same-age children born into non-smoking households. In a *retrospective* cohort study, data are collected from historical records for one or multiple samples (cohorts) of people who have certain characteristics. As an analogy to the previous example, the past medical records of a cohort of children who lived in households with smokers might be examined for evidence of occurrences of asthma or other respiratory problems.

Although many cohort studies are purely descriptive rather than experimental, data from such studies are sometimes used to draw inferences about medical, educational, and behavioral treatments. For example, an investigator conducting a study with a cohort of adolescents diagnosed with Tourette syndrome might collect information, either prospectively or retrospectively, about any pharmacological or behavioral treatments the adolescents received during the study period. She might then calculate correlations between the occurrences of the treatments and the observed or reported frequencies of tics. If the correlations are positive and statistically significant, it might suggest that experimental (controlled) studies to evaluate the effects of those treatments are warranted. With either type of cohort study, however, it is important to recognize that various extraneous factors could explain any observed differences within or between cohorts, and of course even strong positive correlations between two variables do not indicate that one caused the other. Instead, one or both may be influenced by other as-yet unidentified factors.

Case Control Studies

Another subcategory of observational studies that is often used in medical and epidemiological research is the case control study. Typically, a group of individuals who exhibit a symptom, condition, or disorder is assembled. A second group is assembled that does not have the symptom, condition, or disorder but is matched to the first group as closely as possible on other relevant characteristics. Various possible causes of the condition of interest are identified and both groups are examined for their presence. Usually that search is conducted by taking careful medical histories. If a particular factor is found only in the affected group, it is implicated as a cause of the condition. Again, however, the actual cause cannot be determined with confidence from a case control study, because the influence of other factors cannot be ruled out.

STATISTICAL TOOLS

Concepts, Procedures, and Skills

The vast majority of group-design studies involve statistical data analysis, and some statistics can be useful for supplementing visual analyses of graphed data from studies using single-case research designs. Some of the most common statistical concepts and methods are described in this section, but only at an introductory level. Most computational formulae are excluded because they are easily obtained from textbooks or the internet, but basic applications and interpretations are discussed. Technical terms are identified but not explained in detail. Acquiring useful skills in conducting statistical analyses requires substantial training, typically including multiple graduate courses. Obviously, this section does not constitute or replace the necessary training. It is meant just to familiarize behavior analysts with some basic concepts and methods, and to point them to some sources of additional information.

Descriptive Statistics

Measures of Central Tendency. Whenever one has a collection of observations that have been quantified, it is possible to summarize that collection using descriptive statistics. Suppose, for example, we have obtained the heights and weights of every child in Mr. Ford's fourth grade class. Those data could be arrayed in a table with two columns, one labeled height and the other labeled weight. If the entries in each row of the table were accompanied by the student's name, we could look for any relation between the two measures. First, however, we would probably want to summarize the data in each column in order to make a rough comparison to similar data from another class. To do that, we would need to calculate a measure of central value or tendency and a measure of variability for the data in each column.

The three most commonly used measures of central tendency are the mean, median, and mode. The *arithmetic mean*, or average, is calculated by summing the values and dividing the result by the count (i.e., the total number of values). The mean may or may not correspond to any value in the set, but it has the advantage that the sum of the deviations of each score from the mean will always be zero. It is therefore a kind of balancing point. The *median* is the middle value. To determine its value, one must order the values from smallest to largest then count up from the smallest to the value that is midway up the column. If there are an odd number of values in the column, the median is easy to find. It will be the value that has an equal number of values on either side of it. If there is an even number of values, the median will be between the first half and the second half values. The *mode* is the value that occurs most often. If no two values are equal, there will be no mode.

All of the measures of central tendency are single-value summaries of individual measurements and therefore do not represent any one of those measurements. In data sets where there is considerable skew or where extreme values are present, measures of central tendency will obscure individual data and may be misleading. Put another way, these summary measures are easily distorted by very large or very small values, especially when the total number of values is relatively small.

Measures of Variability. In describing a collection of data, one may also wish to describe the variability around the measure of central tendency. The two most commonly used measures are the *range* and *standard deviation*.The range is simply the largest value minus the smallest value in the collection. Its advantage is that it describes the entire collection. In some graphic displays of data, a measure like the mean or median has a vertical line drawn through it with a little horizontal dash on each end. Those lines are called range bars, and they depict the range of the entire set (see Figure 14.4).

The *standard deviation* is more complex than the range. It is derived from a measure called the *variance*, which is the average squared deviation of each value from the mean.The standard deviation is the square root of the variance and figures prominently in statistical inference procedures (discussed later). From the point of view of simple description, the standard deviation (from the mean) is a minimum. If any value other than the mean was used to compute deviations, the resulting value would be larger than the standard deviation. Another measure of variability is the *semi-interquartile range*, which is the value that encompasses the middle half of the values in the collection. It is often used to describe distributions of educational measures, such as test scores. It has the advantage of removing from consideration extreme values at either end of the distribution.

All measures of variability serve essentially the same purpose: to indicate how well the chosen measure of central tendency represents the entire collection of values. It is important to note that statistical variability is not the same as behavioral variability.As we discuss in Chapter 9, the latter is a biological phenomenon that forms the basis of our science, whereas the former is a mathematical abstraction that can be derived from any set of numbers or measures that differ from each other. Behavioral variability can be described statistically but is not explained by that process.

Standardized Values (Z-Scores). For any data set, it is possible to convert each value into a standardized value known as a z-score. That is done by subtracting the mean from the value and dividing the result by the standard deviation. The resulting distribution of z-scores will have 0 as its mean and 1.0 as its standard deviation.That provides a convenient means of comparing individuals within or across different measures, such as test scores.

Association. There are several statistical tools for determining if multiple measures of the same or different behavior are associated, or correlated. For example, suppose Joe's caregiver records the latency from the ringing of the alarm to Joe's appearance at the breakfast table each morning. She also records the number of clothing items Joe puts on correctly. For each morning, then, there are two observations.An investigator might ask if they are related and, if so, how and how strongly. Those questions can be answered by calculating a *correlation coefficient* (r), which can range from -1 to $+1$. A value of $+1$ means the relation is perfect and positive – that is, the more items of clothing Joe dons, the longer it takes him to get to breakfast. If it is negative, it means that Joe shows up to breakfast faster if he has put on more clothes. The closer r is to 0, the greater the degree of independence between the two measures. Information like that can be helpful for developing treatment procedures. If there is a strong correlation between measures of two behaviors, for instance, it may be the case that applying contingencies to one will impact the other as well.

As always, it is important to analyze data in ways that allow you to learn as much as possible about the behavior of interest and variables that may influence it. To that end, it is a good idea to plot data to see if correlations are evident. To produce a *scatter plot*, use a simple linear scale for each variable and plot the pairs as dots. If the correlation is positive, the pattern of dots will go upward from left to right; if it is negative, the pattern will go downward. If there is little or no correlation, the scatter plot will just look like someone threw dots on the paper at random. Plotting data in this manner may reveal properties or patterns that are not obvious from the value of r alone. For example, suppose the data bunch up in one corner or the other. Why might that be? Or suppose the trend is not linear but curves one way or the other. That would tell you that the relation between the two variables is more complex than you might otherwise have thought.

Another way to examine association is through the use of *contingency tables*. Suppose you are teaching a 5th grade math class and want to see if there is a relation between the performances of girls and boys. You could assemble the scores from the latest math test, sort them by gender, and perform a t-test (see below), or simply arrange the scores in order and find the median. Then you could make a 2 × 2 table with Boy and Girl heading the columns and Above and Below labeling the rows. Each score would get a tally mark in one of the four boxes in the table. When you have finished entering those tallies, the row totals will be the numbers of scores above and below the median, and the column totals will be the number of each gender. The numbers of tally marks could be entered into a formula for computing the *chi square* ($\dot{X}^2$) statistic. If there is no association, the result should be close to 1.0. The larger the value of $\dot{X}^2$, the greater the likelihood that an association exists. In this example, that value would indicate whether scores on the latest math test were related in part to gender. These procedures are very useful for data snooping. Whenever data points can be tallied into one of four boxes as in the example, you can check for association in the manner described here.

Behavior analysts working in or interpreting research results from certain medical fields are apt to encounter a procedure known as *logistical regression analysis*. This is a correlation procedure in which the dependent variable is binary: dead or alive, pass or fail, positive or negative, etc. The independent variable(s) must be on an interval or ratio scale, not nominal or ordinal. A good example is breast cancer survival as predicted by age, size of tumor at time of detection, family history, and treatment method. The purpose of the analysis is to determine which of the independent variables best predicts the outcome measure. An ancillary calculation is known as the *hazard ratio*, which is simply the change in death rate associated with two values of a variable: drug vs.

placebo, overweight vs. normal weight, etc. In complex analyses, there is often interest in the hazard ratio between two adjacent values of an independent variable, such as drug dosage.

Many sets of data lend themselves to descriptive analysis using *time series*. Data plotted over successive intervals of time (days, months, etc.) are of this type, providing the intervals are continuous. Such data often exhibit variability from one point to the next. The purpose of time series analysis is to detect underlying patterns in the variability that may be causal. For example, consider data on daily referrals to the principal's office. Time series analyses might reveal trends and even permit predictions. Suppose the data show that the highest number of referrals every week occurs on Wednesday and the lowest number is typically on Monday. A school administrator might want to explore what is unique about those days. Alternatively, or additionally, the data might show a gradual increase in referrals as a holiday or vacation approaches. In either case, a time series analysis could help the administrator identify variables that influence the behaviors that lead teachers to refer students to the principal's office or make predictions that could justify hiring additional personnel or scheduling more frequent recess periods around those times, for example.

By their nature, the data points in a time series are not independent. Each data point is correlated with the next data point, the one after that, and so on. That is, an *autocorrelation* may exist. A simple way to detect the presence of an autocorrelation is to plot a data point followed by the point that is one point removed and so on. That is called lag 1 autocorrelation. One could plot the data for lag 2, lag 3, etc. in similar fashion. When a lag autocorrelation plot exhibits much less variability than the original plot, an autocorrelation has been detected. The investigator can then try to identify variables that might be involved. For example, if an autocorrelation plot indicates that the frequency of a child's tantrums tends to increase four hours after the last tantrum, the investigator might suspect a relation between tantrumming and feeding times or some other environmental event.

A time series analysis may detect the presence of an autocorrelation. As with any correlation, one must be careful not to attribute cause to either of the variables involved. Correlations indicate only whether two variables vary together. Only controlled experimentation can determine if one is functionally related to the other, or if both are influenced by some other variable(s).

Inferential Statistics

Terms and Reasoning. The basic purpose of inferential statistics is to make statements about characteristics of a population from which a sample has been drawn. For our purposes, the term *population* refers to the universe of all possible results of a measurement operation, and the term *sample* refers to a subset of the population. The sample characteristic is called the *statistic* and the corresponding property of the population is called the *parameter*. Sample statistics are used to estimate population parameters. We pointed out previously that that is appropriate in some circumstances, such as when poll-sters attempt to predict the outcome of an election on the basis of responses to questions by a sample of the voters. Another example comes from industrial quality control. A manager could sample products coming off an assembly line and note the proportion that is defective. From that statistic, the manager could estimate the proportion of the products in the entire run that will be found defective. It is not appropriate, however, to make inferences from the sample to the single case – for instance, to predict that the next item pulled off the assembly line will be defective.

The larger the number of cases in the sample, the better is the estimate of the parameter. If all the cases are included in the sample, the statistic and the parameter are the same. The variability around the sample statistic is given by the general formula standard error of $s = s/\sqrt{n}$. The larger the value of n, the smaller will be the standard error and hence the more accurate will be the statistic as an estimate of the parameter.

Confidence Intervals. Every time an investigator draws a sample and computes a sample statistic, she can also compute the *standard error* and use it to make a statement about the quality of her estimate of the popula-tion parameter. For example, the mathematics of the normal curve show that the true value of the parameter will lie between −2 and +2 standard errors approximately 95% of the time. Those limits are called the 95% confidence interval. That reasoning can be applied to any sample statistic – proportion, mean, correlation, etc. Again, as the sample size increases, the interval asso-ciated with a given confidence level decreases, and faith in the accuracy of the estimate of the parameter is enhanced. Confidence intervals are really descriptive statistics, but they form the basis of the more elaborate inferential procedures that are described next.

Two basic assumptions must be satisfied in order for the inferential process to be considered valid. First, the sample must be drawn at random from the population. Second, the observations must be independent of each other. Those assumptions are required because the inferential process depends on a model that is derived from the mathematics of probability, for which the assumptions are necessary. To take a familiar example, suppose you toss a coin 100 times. If the coin is unbiased, you would expect heads to come up 50 times or some number near 50. If you observed 95 heads, you might reasona-bly suspect the coin of being loaded. The 100 tosses are a random sample of the infinite number of possible tosses, and there is no reason to suspect that each toss influences the outcome of the next toss; that is, the observations are independent. Using a mathematical model based on equal probability of heads and tails, one can calculate the probability of each possible outcome from 0 to 100. If you converted each possible number of heads outcomes to a z-score and plotted the proportion of the corresponding values, you would produce something that approximates a *normal curve*. If the total area under the curve is set at 1.0 (the combined probability of all the outcomes) and you look at the areas under the curve, you can estimate the probability of any subset of observations as the proportion of the total area associated with that subset. For example, half of the observations will be above 50, half below. If you make a coin toss that is associated with a small probability value like .05, again you might conclude that there was something wrong with the coin or perhaps the way it was tossed.

Hypothesis Testing. This is a process that derives from the logical device known as proof by contradiction. The formal structure is as follows: (1) If A is true, B will be true, (2) Observe B is not true, (3) Conclude A is not true. In general, in the research approach that involves group designs and statistical analysis to evaluate treatments, at the outset of a study the investigator states the *null hypothesis (H_o)* that the treatment of interest has no real effect – that is, there will be no difference between the treatment and control groups when the study ends. He also specifies what is known as *alpha (α)*, or the region of rejection. That is the portion of the probability distribution that contains all the unlikely outcomes should the null hypothesis happen to be true. Relatedly, the investigator sets a *level of significance* known as the p value. It is often referred to as the probability that the obtained results occurred "by chance." By convention, p is usually set at .05 or .01. The study is conducted, and aggregated data from the treatment and control groups are compared statistically. A difference between them would be highly unlikely if the null hypothesis were true. Therefore, if there is a difference in favor of the treatment group and the p statistic falls within the pre-set region of rejection, the investigator concludes that the null hypothesis is false and that an effect was

---

BOX 15.2

More on Statistical Significance

If only to avoid embarrassment, behavior analysts should understand the difference between α and p. Alpha (α) is the region of rejection, while p is the result of the statistical calculation. Either p falls in the region of rejection or it does not, and the result is either statistically significant or it is not. Statistical significance, like pregnancy, is a binary event; that is, a result should not be described as more or less significant depending on the value of p. Nevertheless, it is common to see research reports in which several p values are presented with no explanation of the reasoning behind the selection of different values of alpha.

It is important to remember that a result that is statistically significant says nothing about its possible value or application in the real world. For example, a researcher might report that megadoses of vitamins had a statistically significant effect on the attending skills of a sample of children with autism, but that should not be taken as evidence that the vitamins had practically important effects on the attending behavior of any of the children in that treatment group. In fact, with large enough samples it is entirely possible to obtain statistically significant results when the actual effects of the independent variable are quite weak.

demonstrated. The reported results usually indicate that the post-treatment difference between the aggregate data of the two groups is statistically significant and the probability level at which the null hypothesis was rejected, e.g., $p < .05$.

To illustrate hypothesis testing using the previous coin-tossing example, the null hypothesis would be that the coin is unbiased, so the expected outcome of 100 tosses is 50 heads and 50 tails. If the model indicates that the probability of an outcome like 10 heads or fewer lies in the region of rejection specified by alpha (say, .05) but that outcome is obtained when the coin-tossing experiment is conducted, that would encourage rejection of the null hypothesis and a conclusion that the results were statistically significant. It would also support a suspicion that the coin is biased. But suppose the coin were truly unbiased and the result, though unlikely, was not due to bias. In that case, the null hypothesis would be true, and rejecting it would constitute what is called a *Type 1 error*. The approach taken in this book would entail replicating the experiment by tossing the coin again 100 times. If the result was similar to the first experiment, confidence in the original conclusion would be enhanced. If that happened a third time, the investigator should design a new experiment to try to isolate the source of the bias.

Very few experiments focus on the outcome of coin tossing, of course, but it is worth remembering that the origins of mathematical statistics are found in the gaming tables of 17th century Europe. The concept of chance is as central to an understanding of statistical procedures as it was to the early developers of those methods. "Chance" is a shorthand way of describing the fact that variability permeates all natural processes and is often used as a substitute explanation for events we do not fully understand. Thus the statement that the result of an experiment was "due to chance" is another way of saying that the investigator does not understand the causes of the variability. Inferential statistics make use of unexplained variability as a reference point for evaluating explained or imposed variability.

It is important to note that null-hypothesis significance testing has been roundly criticized for decades, increasingly so since about 1990. Among its many flaws are the facts that, contrary to popular belief, the technique does not yield information about the likelihood that results of a study will be replicated, the degree of confidence one can have in the findings, the probability that the obtained results were due to chance, the magnitude of treatment effects, or whether the statistically significant differences are important in any sense other than the statistical one (though they are often misconstrued to be significant clinically, theoretically, and in other ways). A number of researchers have called for describing results as "statistically different" rather than "significant" and abandoning null-hypothesis testing altogether in favor of other statistical techniques, such as confidence intervals (discussed previously) and calculations of indices of clinical or practical significance known as effect sizes (discussed later). Readers who are interested in more detailed information and discussions are referred to Branch (1999), Cumming (2012; 2014), and Cumming and Calin-Jageman (2017), and Lambdin (2012).

BOX 15.3

A Closer Look at the T-Test

The formula for the t-test is a ratio. The numerator is the observed difference between the group means minus the hypothesized difference between the population means, usually 0. The denominator is a quantity known as the standard error of the mean difference. It is a composite of the standard errors of the two means, which are themselves derived from the standard deviations of the two samples. In other words, it is from the observed variability in the data that a means of deciding whether the data came from the same or different populations is derived. To call such measures of variability "standard" is somewhat misleading in that they owe their existence entirely to the data they describe. Notice also that the sample sizes (n_1 and n_2) are involved in the denominator. The larger the values of n, the smaller will be the standard errors of the individual means and hence the standard error of the difference. As the sample sizes increase, the denominator of the *t* ratio decreases and the t value thereby increases, thus making it more likely to produce a small *p* value. That is why investigators often try to start their studies with large groups and may even run additional participants if the initial analysis fails to reach statistical significance in hopes of ultimately getting a p value that falls inside the sacred zone.

Differences between Means. Suppose an investigator wants to compare the performances of two similar groups of fifth-grade students, one drawn from an urban school and the other from a rural school, on a standardized math test. To answer that question, the investigator could perform a *t-test* for independent means. She might set alpha at .05, calculate the t value, and look it up in a t table. If the associated *p* value fell in the alpha range, the investigator would reject the null hypothesis of no difference and conclude instead that the samples came from different populations – that is, that the difference between the mean math test performances of the two groups was statistically significant.

The logic underlying the t-test can be extended to the case of multiple groups. Using a procedure called *analysis of variance (ANOVA)*, the means of several groups can be compared at once. A ratio (F) is formed with an estimate of the population variance furnished by the various means (between-groups variance) divided by the estimate of the population variance provided by the variance surrounding each of the means (within-group variance). Tables of probabilities associated with various F values are available for all possible combinations of numbers of group means and numbers of cases within the combined groups. These numbers are called *degrees of freedom* (df) and, as is the case with the t ratio, the larger the df in the denominator, the greater the likelihood the F ratio will reach statistical significance.

Reliability. Some authors state or imply that a statistically significant effect is an indication of the reliability or reproducibility of a study's findings. The

---

BOX 15.4

Variations on ANOVA

Analysis of variance (ANOVA) procedures are used in many different ways. For example, in the study involving boys and girls in a fifth grade math class, the investigator could have entered actual math test scores rather than tally marks in a 2 × 2 contingency table. She could also add a score for the sixth and seventh grades to create an array with two columns and three rows. That would produce three possible F ratios: one for the grades, one for the sexes, and one for the inter-action (G × S). If the interaction were statistically significant, it would suggest that the boy/girl difference is different from grade to grade. In all cases, the F ratio is formed between the population variance estimate furnished by the means (row, column, or cell) and the variance estimate furnished by the data surrounding those measures.

Another variant of ANOVA involves what is known as a mixed research design. A type of mixed design that is often used by behavior analysts involves repeated measures of the behavior of individuals in specific groups. For example, each of two or more groups of fifth-grade students might be assigned to expe-rience different math curricula. The accuracy with which students in both or all groups completed a set of math problems could be measured on successive days over a period of time and those scores analyzed using ANOVA. The overall within-subject effect of days would indicate whether performances improved over the course of the study. The overall between-subject effect of the different curricula would reveal whether they produced different performance levels. The investigator might also be interested in the days × curriculum interaction. If it were statistically significant, that would suggest that differential learning was induced by the curricula in some groups but not others. If the investigator found statistically significant effects of both days and groups but no interaction, she might infer that learning took place. That inference might be supported by the plot of the accuracy scores of all groups over days that showed an increas-ing trend across time. The groups effect tells the investigator that the curricula were different, but she already knew that. Suppose the investigator also found a statistically significant groups × days interaction. That tells her that the groups probably learned at different rates, but it doesn't tell her why. Socioeconomic factors, differential effects of the curricula, a combination of the two, or some other variable(s) could be responsible. Depending on her purpose, the investi-gator could either publish the statistically significant findings and move on to another problem or attempt to tease out experimentally what was actually going on in the study.

---

argument is that a p value of .05 or less implies that if the study were repeated a large number of times, the same results would be obtained at least 95% of the time. As Branch (1999) and others have pointed out, that is simply untrue. Recall that a p value indicates the likelihood of the obtained result given that the null hypothesis (no effect) is true. If the null hypothesis is not true, p becomes a statement of the probability of the null hypothesis being true given the obtained result – an entirely different concept. The proper approach to establishing the reliability of an obtained result is to repeat the study.

Measures of Clinical or Practical Significance: Effect Sizes

Many people have recognized that a statistically significant difference between or among sets of group aggregate data may not indicate anything about the magnitude of any treatment effect or the clinical or practical importance of a treatment for the participants in a study or others like them. To address that problem, some researchers report the size of treatment effects using fairly straightforward descriptive statistics, such as the mean amount of change on the dependent measure over the course of the study for the treatment and control or comparison groups or the number of participants in each group whose scores on the dependent measure reached a certain criterion or changed by a certain amount.

Several more sophisticated measures of *effect size* have been developed to quantify the size and magnitude of treatment effects in group-design studies in ways that allow comparisons across studies. Perhaps the most common is *Cohen's d* (also called the *standardized mean difference*). It and related statistics can be used when the independent variable is binary or dichotomous (e.g., treatment vs. no treatment; treatment 1 vs. treatment 2) and the dependent variable is ordered. The idea is that a more meaningful reference for assessing a difference between two group means is the standard deviations of the original populations from which the samples were drawn. When comparing two groups, d is computed by subtracting the mean of the second group from the mean of the first group and dividing by the pooled standard deviation of both groups. That quantity can range from minus to plus infinity, with zero indicating no effect.

Effect size can also be indexed by calculating the correlation between the independent variable (treatment) and dependent variable (measure of effect). The resulting r statistic indicates the strength of association between the variables, and ranges from -1.0 to $+1.0$ with zero representing no effect. Squaring the correlation coefficient gives the measure r^2, which can be interpreted as the percentage of variability shared by the two variables. The closer that value is to 1.0, the greater is the effect of the independent variable on the dependent variable. Sometimes the independent variable has only a few values, such as when it refers to the number of a phase change. Special correlation calculation procedures exist for that situation, but the interpretation remains the same. That is, if the value of r^2 approaches 1.0, it suggests that the phases account for most of the variability in the data.

Several measures of effect size that are often applied in studies comparing a treatment with no treatment or one treatment with another can be categorized as measures of *risk potency*. They are used when both the independent and dependent variable are binary, meaning that treatment effects are categorized on an either/or basis (e.g., success or failure; at risk of a negative outcome or not; improved by a specified amount or not). Details about calculating and interpreting those measures are beyond the scope of this chapter, but interested readers can find good basic descriptions in Faraone (2008) and Kraemer and colleagues (2003). Of those effect sizes, the one that may be most useful to behavior analysts is NNT. It is the number of individuals who must receive a specified treatment to produce one more success or one less failure than would result if all of those individuals received a comparison treatment. For instance, in a study comparing Treatment A with Treatment B, an NNT of 5 in favor of Treatment A means that for every 5 individuals who received that treatment, one additional individual succeeded who would not have succeeded with Treatment B. If every individual in the treatment group succeeds and everyone in the comparison group fails, the NNT is 1.0. The larger the NNT, the less effective is the treatment relative to the comparison. An illustration is provided in a meta-analysis (a set of techniques we discuss in the next section) of data on individual participants in 16 group-design studies of interventions for young children with autism by Eldevik and colleagues (2010). In those 16 studies collectively, 309 children received intensive behavior analytic intervention, 39 received intensive eclectic intervention, and 105 received standard early intervention services. The investigators set criteria for reliable changes on standardized measures of intellectual skills (IQ) and adaptive skills, and identified the percentages of children in each of the three groups who achieved those criteria. They found statistically significant differences in favor of behavior analytic intervention. Additionally, the investigators computed the NNTs for behavior analytic intervention to be 5 for intellectual skills and 7 for adaptive skills. Those results were comparable to NNTs for psychological and medical treatments for major depression, obsessive-compulsive disorders, and bulimia nervosa (Eldevik, Hastings, Hughes, Jahr, Eikeseth, & Cross, 2010).

Procedures exist for finding confidence intervals for effect size values (e.g., Hedges & Olkin, 1985). Details are beyond the scope of this chapter, but the concept should be familiar from our previous discussion. The larger the sample sizes, the greater the stability of the estimates of effect size and the smaller the variability of those estimates.

Meta-analysis of Group-Design Studies

Meta-analysis is the practice of combining the results of several studies and analyzing the pooled data in order to quantify the overall effect(s) of a particular independent variable on some common outcome measure or measures, such as academic achievement, health status, or survival. Effect sizes like those described above are usually calculated for each study, aggregated across all studies, and analyzed statistically.

It is best if those who conduct meta-analyses clearly specify their research question, criteria for including and excluding studies, and criteria and procedures they used to evaluate the methodological quality of each included study (participant selection and assessment, research design, measurement methods, data analysis methods, etc.). That information is essential for evaluating the credibility of the data that each study contributes to the meta-analysis. If the authors of a meta-analysis fail to provide that information in their report – or worse, fail to filter studies appropriately – the conclusions they draw should be taken with several grains of salt. (Computer programmers have an aphorism that describes that situation aptly: GIGO, which stands for "garbage in, garbage out"). In a similar vein, if a meta-analysis includes only a narrow swath of the potentially relevant research – for instance, only RCTs – its applicability is limited.

The impulse to conduct meta-analyses probably springs from the same well as the decision to resort to inferential statistics. The hope is that amidst all the variability there is truth to be found. As with any combinatorial process, however, valuable information may be lost when data from multiple studies are lumped together for meta-analysis. For instance, the findings of the individual component studies can be obscured. Importantly, effect sizes are often calculated by using the group aggregate statistics (such as means and standard deviations) that were reported by the authors of each study. That compounds the obfuscation of the effects of the treatment(s) on individuals. That problem can be mitigated to some extent by using data on the individual participants in each of the component studies, as in the meta-analysis of research on early behavioral intervention for autism that was discussed previously (Eldevik et al., 2010). The result is a more sensitive and powerful meta-analysis than could be obtained by using group aggregate data.

Cautions notwithstanding, meta-analysis has several benefits. For one, a good meta-analysis synthesizes the reported results of multiple studies in a particular area and quantifies them in ways that are not typical of other types of research reviews. That can save practitioners, researchers, and policymakers the time and effort of combing the research literature and digesting and integrating the findings of large numbers of studies. Another is that meta-analyses often result in large sample sizes, which enable some types of analyses and general conclusions that could not be derived from individual studies. The methods may be particularly useful for examining the effects of treatments that have been evaluated with relatively small samples of participants because the treatments are complex or target relatively rare conditions, for example. Additionally, combining measures from all studies weights evenly the contributions of small and large studies. In sum, meta-analyses can be useful for determining the best available evidence about a particular treatment, the overall comparative effectiveness of treatments, and the conditions under which a treatment is effective and with whom. Many policymakers and others rely on meta-analyses for drawing conclusions that can have profound effects on behavior analysts and their clients, such as which interventions have sufficient evidence to warrant official endorsement or funding, so you are encouraged to learn how to read and interpret them. For an introduction, see Baldwin and Shadish (2011).

External Validity and Generality

Previously we mentioned the concept of the validity of a study – the likelihood that the independent variable was responsible for the observed effect on the dependent variable (see Box 16.2). Researchers in the group-design tradition also invoke the concept of *external validity*, which is defined as the likelihood that the observed effect applies beyond the limits of the study sample. Often the term *generality* (with a modifier) is used to describe that aspect of the results of a study, as in "This effect seems to have wide generality" or "Until more research is done, we believe this finding has limited generality." In most cases, the term refers to members of a broader population than is strictly represented by the study sample and is assumed to be greater the larger the sample size (N). Studies involving small Ns, as in most behavior analytic research, are often assumed to lack generality to the larger population and therefore to have little value. That can be misleading because N can also refer to the number of observations obtained – a value that can be quite large even if only a few participants are involved.

Additionally, and very importantly, generality is approached very differently in behavior analysis than in fields that follow the group design/statistics tradition (see Chapter 16). It is established empirically by replicating the effects of independent variables across response classes, individuals, and conditions rather than by speculating that the effects observed with a study sample will be obtained with other individuals. Once a particular relation between independent and dependent variables has been observed repeatedly, its generality can be explored. For example, time out from reinforcement is a procedure that was first developed in animal laboratories in the 1950s. Multiple experiments showed that stimuli signaling the absence of reinforcement became aversive; animals behaved to terminate or avoid them. The same phenomenon was demonstrated to occur across experimental conditions and species, including humans, in hundreds of basic and applied studies. Nowadays time out is a staple of many parents, teachers, and others who have no idea of its origins. The generality of intermittent reinforcement and many other behavior analytic procedures has been established similarly, through countless replications in both laboratory and practical settings.

STATISTICAL ANALYSIS IN BEHAVIOR ANALYTIC RESEARCH AND PRACTICE

Descriptive and Inferential Statistics

Because behavior analysis focuses on the behavior of the individual measured directly and repeatedly, its primary approach to data analysis is visual inspection of graphed individual data rather than statistical analyses of group aggregate data. Visual inspection techniques have generally proved accurate and reliable for detecting moderate to large changes in behavior across control

BOX 15.5

Replication

Replication is the lifeblood of any science, for if its findings are not repeatable, no useful technology can emerge. Recently, a group of 270 collaborators undertook to replicate 100 studies published in reputable psychology journals (Open Science Collaboration, 2015). Ninety-seven percent of the original studies had statistically significant results, whereas that was true of only 36% of the replications. Only 39% of the replications were judged successful by subjective analysis. Those findings call into question the scientific and practical utility of the results of studies that rely on large-sample, statistical hypothesis testing methods. In response, many researchers have suggested stiffening the requirements for publication by increasing sample sizes or setting alpha at a lower level, say .001 instead of .05. Clearly, those tactics would serve to increase the cost of research while not assuring any increase in the reproducibility or applicability of research results.

An alternative solution has been proposed by Killeen and his colleagues (Killeen, 2015). It is a calculation of the **probability of replication,** p_{rep}. Its value is based on Cohen's d, so it depends on measures of variability inherent in the samples being compared. In that regard, it shares properties of p but does not depend for its interpretation on a faulty logical structure. The value of p_{rep} also depends on the sample sizes. For a given effect d, p_{rep} varies directly with n_1 and n_2, as one would expect. It also varies inversely with p. Unlike p, however, it is useful as a descriptive statistic indicating the estimated likelihood that a particular statistical difference would recur if the sampling were repeated. Use of p_{rep} could reduce the embarrassing frequency with which statistically significant results do not survive replication. It would also seem to be a better index of publication worthiness than p values because it estimates the degree to which a result contributes to the body of literature. Procedures for calculating p_{rep} are easily performed by anyone who has had a basic course in statistics.

and experimental phases. Under some conditions, however, certain descriptive statistics can be useful supplements to visual inspection. For instance, as noted at the beginning of this chapter, measures of central tendency and variability can help summarize and elucidate collections of observations in which changes are not obvious. Certain regression statistics may also be appropriate for analyzing changes in the levels, slopes, and trends in data series. Additionally, some behavior analysts have used some of the inferential statistics described previously to analyze aggregated observations of individual behavior within and across phases.

Behavior analytic data can also lend themselves to time series analyses, described previously. Jones, Vaught, and Weinrott (1977) illustrated such analyses with studies published in the *Journal of Applied Behavior Analysis*. All of the studies involved repeated measures designs with small groups of participants and at least one experimental condition or treatment. The authors used time series analyses to evaluate the effects of introducing treatments and the presence of trends and changes in trends across phases. In some cases, their analyses suggested the existence of effects that were not noticed by the original investigators.

Whenever a descriptive statistic is applied to a set of data, it is important to recognize that one value comes to serve in place of the several that comprise the original set. The careful investigator always studies the original data before applying any summarizing statistics. That is behavioral information in its purest form and is the hard-earned result of the measurement tactics described elsewhere in this book. It should not go to waste.

Measures of Effect Sizes

Several methods have been developed for quantifying the magnitude of effects in studies using single-subject research designs as an adjunct or supplement to visual inspection of graphed data. One that can be used in studies of behavior reduction procedures is *percentage reduction data* (PRD) or mean baseline reduction (MBR). It is calculated by subtracting the mean value of the last three data points in a treatment phase from the mean of the last three data points in the adjacent control phase, dividing that by the mean of the last three data points in the control phase, and multiplying by 100%. A measure of the extent to which an intervention completely suppresses a target behavior is *percentage of zero data* (PZD), calculated by identifying the first zero data point in a treatment phase and calculating the percentage of data points that remain at zero from that first zero data point on.

Perhaps the most commonly used effect size measure is the *percentage of non-overlapping data* (PND). It is the percentage of data points in a treatment phase that represent observed values that fall above the highest value (if behavior increase is expected) or below the lowest value (if behavior decrease is expected) in the adjacent control phase. The resulting PND statistic can range from 0 to 100%. The higher the PND, the larger the effect. A variation is the *percentage of all non-overlapping data* (PAND), which is calculated by counting the overlapping data points in adjacent treatment and control phases, dividing that sum by the total number of data points in both phases, and subtracting the result from 100%. A related measure is the *percentage of data points exceeding the median* (PEM). That is calculated by locating the median data point in the control phase, drawing a horizontal line through that point into the adjacent treatment phase, and dividing the number of data points in the treatment phase that are above or below that median line (depending on whether behavior increase or decrease is expected) by the total number of data points in the treatment phase. Again, the higher the PEM, the larger the effect size; anything less than 70% is generally considered evidence that the treatment was not effective.

An advantage of the methods just described is that the effect sizes can be calculated by hand and do not require much expertise in statistics, so they can be used by many practitioners. Each has limitations, however, that can make the resulting effect sizes misleading. For instance, PRD and PND use only some of the data in each phase; PND can be skewed by outlier values and cannot be used when control phase data are highly variable; PAND requires at least 20 data points; and PEM does not reflect the magnitude of data points above (or below) the median, among other limitations. Other methods that are beyond the scope of this chapter use measures of standardized mean differences, regression analyses to quantify changes in trends, levels, and slopes in data series across control and treatment phases, and multilevel statistical modeling procedures. They require assumptions about the nature of the data sets that are often not met by data from studies using single-subject research designs, as well as expertise in sophisticated statistical methods and the use of computer programs. Still other methods for calculating effect sizes are being developed or explored (see Onghena, Michiels, Jamshidi, Moeyaert, & Van den Noortgate, 2017; Parker & Vannest, 2009; Pustejovsky & Ferron, 2017; Shadish, Hedges, & Pustejovsky, 2014).

Meta-analysis of Single-Subject Design Studies

In recent years, increased use of single-subject research designs in several fields in addition to behavior analysis (e.g., special education, communication disorders, brain injury rehabilitation, psychology, behavioral health, medicine) and an increased emphasis on using research evidence to guide policy and clinical decisions have spurred the development of meta-analytic methods that are suited to these kinds of studies. In fact, some professional journals have devoted entire issues to this topic; for instance, see *Journal of Behavioral Education*, 2012, *21(3)*, *Remedial and Special Education*, 2017, *38(6)* and *Journal of School Psychology*, 2014, *52(2)*. As with group-design studies, conducting a good meta-analysis of studies using single-subject research designs starts by setting criteria for including and excluding studies and then carefully evaluating the methodological rigor of each included study. Because the focus is the relation between independent and dependent variables, particular attention is paid to design and measurement features that support strong inferences about that relation. Effect sizes are often calculated for each of the included studies and then combined or compared. Most research reports include graphed data representing measures of the dependent variable for individual participants, so raw data can be extracted and used to calculate effect sizes – a strength in comparison to meta-analyses of group-design studies where those calculations involve only group summary statistics. Some effect size measures were described in the preceding section. Although many others have been developed, much work remains to be done to determine which effect size statistics are best suited to each type of single-subject design and how to accommodate the flexibility that is a hallmark and strength of the research approach described in this book.

Most of the limitations and benefits of meta analyses that were discussed in the context of group-design studies apply to meta-analyses of single-subject design studies. The fact that they yield evidence about the effects of interventions on fairly large numbers of participants may be a particularly important benefit when it comes to communicating with those who make actuarial decisions about which interventions are worthy of support and others who are comfortable with large Ns and statistical analyses. In any case, the use of meta-analysis methods to summarize and synthesize results of multiple behavior analytic studies appears to be here to stay. Many meta-analyses of research on behavior analytic interventions have already been published and more are sure to come, so it behooves behavior analytic practitioners and researchers to learn about the methods. Interested readers might start with Pustejovsky and Ferron (2017).

CHAPTER SUMMARY

1. The majority of studies conducted by researchers in other disciplines involve group research designs and statistical analyses. In order to communicate and collaborate with members of other professions, use the research findings of other disciplines, advocate for policies that support behavior analysis, and fulfill their ethical responsibilities, behavior analysts need to be informed consumers of research using group designs and statistical analyses.

2. The use of statistics to supplement visual analyses of individual behavioral data seems to be increasing. Behavior analytic practitioners and researchers must be able to recognize when such analyses are appropriate, determine which statistical tools to use, and correctly interpret results.

3. In a randomized controlled or clinical trial (RCT), participants are randomly assigned to two or more groups. The experimental or treatment group is designated to receive a specific treatment while the other group (control or comparison group) receives no treatment, a placebo or sham treatment, "treatment as usual" (e.g., commonly available services), or a different specific treatment.

4. The pre- and post-treatment mean scores of each group are typically compared statistically to evaluate change within the group over the course of the study. It is important to note that findings of statistically significant differences in aggregate measures, whether between or within groups, provide no information about how the intervention(s) affected any individuals, including whether any individuals improved and if so, how much.

5. Limitations of RCTs for evaluating the effects of behavioral interventions include ethical constraints on randomly assigning participants to control groups where they will receive no intervention, a placebo, or an intervention that is likely to be less effective than the one received by the treatment group. Several logistical challenges are also inherent in conducting RCTs and other group-design studies.

6. In a non-randomized controlled trial, the participants are not randomly assigned to groups. Investigators often take steps to ensure that the

treatment and control groups are matched on key variables that could influence the study results by identifying pairs of similar individuals and assigning one member of each pair to the treatment group and the other to the control group. Alternatively, they could make sure the overall makeup of the group is comparable in terms of variables that are relevant to the research question (e.g., gender, chronological age, developmental level).

7. In single-group pretest-posttest or posttest-only designs, the mean group pre- and post-treatment scores or other aggregate data are compared statistically to determine if change occurred over the course of treatment. In some studies, the dependent measure is administered only after the participants have experienced the treatment; there is no pretest. These designs avoid some of the problems inherent in between-groups comparisons, since each participant serves as his or her own control.

8. One subcategory of studies that are sometimes termed observational by medical and epidemiological researchers is the cohort study. In a cohort study, a sample of people drawn from a specified population is identified, and specific data are collected in order to make comparisons. Although many cohort studies are purely descriptive rather than experimental, data from such studies are sometimes used to draw inferences about medical, educational, and behavioral treatments. It is important to recognize that extraneous factors could explain any observed differences within or between cohorts and that strong correlations between two variables do not indicate that one caused the other.

9. The three most commonly used measures of central tendency are the mean, median, and mode. The arithmetic mean, or average, is calculated by summing the values and dividing the result by the count. The median is the middle value in the data set. The mode is the value that occurs most often.

10. The two most commonly used measures of variability are the range and standard deviation. The range is calculated by subtracting the smallest value from the largest value in the collection. The standard deviation is derived from a measure called the variance, which is the average squared deviation of each value in the dataset from the mean. The standard deviation is the square root of the variance.

11. There are several statistical tools for determining if multiple measures of the same or different behavior are associated or correlated. By calculating a correlation coefficient (r), the researcher or practitioner can assess degree of independence between two measures. If there is a strong correlation between measures of two behaviors, it may be the case that applying contingencies to one will impact the other as well.

12. Behavior analysts working in or interpreting research results from certain medical fields may encounter a procedure known as logistical regression analysis. This is a correlation procedure in which the dependent variable is binary and the independent variable(s) must be on an interval or ratio scale.

13. The basic purpose of inferential statistics is to make statements about characteristics of a population from which a sample has been drawn. For our purposes, the term population refers to the universe of all possible results of a measurement operation, and the term sample refers to a subset of the population. The sample characteristic is called the statistic, and the corresponding property of the population is called the parameter. Sample statistics are used to estimate population parameters.

14. Two basic assumptions must be satisfied in order for the inferential process to be considered valid. First, the sample must be drawn at random from the population. Second, the observations must be independent of each other.

15. In general, in the research approach that involves group designs and statistical analysis to evaluate treatments, at the outset of the study the investigator states the null hypothesis (H_o) that the treatment of interest has no real effect (i.e., there will be no difference between the treatment and control groups when the study ends).

16. Null-hypothesis significance testing has been increasingly criticized. Among its flaws is that the technique does not yield information about the likelihood that results of a study will be replicated, the degree of confidence one can have in the findings, the probability that the obtained results were due to chance, the magnitude of treatment effects, or whether the statistically significant differences were actually significant clinically.

17. To address some of the issues raised above, many researchers now report effect size as a way to quantify the size and magnitude of treatment effects in group-design studies in ways that allow comparisons across studies. Perhaps the most common is Cohen's d (also called the standardized mean difference). It and related statistics can be used when the independent variable is binary or dichotomous and the dependent variable is ordered. When comparing two groups, d is computed by subtracting the mean of the second group from the mean of the first group and dividing by the pooled standard deviation of both groups.

18. Meta-analysis is the practice of combining the results of several studies and analyzing the pooled data in order to quantify the overall effect(s) of a particular independent variable on some common outcome measure(s). Effect sizes are usually calculated for each study, aggregated across all studies, and analyzed statistically.

19. Generality is approached very differently in behavior analysis than in fields that follow the group design/statistics tradition. It is established empirically by replicating the effects of independent variables across response classes, individuals, and conditions rather than by speculating that the effects observed with a study sample will be obtained with other individuals.

20. Because behavior analysis focuses on the behavior of the individual measured directly and repeatedly, its primary approach to data analysis is visual inspection of graphed individual data rather than statistical analyses of

group aggregate data. Under some conditions, certain descriptive and inferential statistics can be useful supplements to visual inspections.

21. Several methods have been developed for quantifying the magnitude of effects in studies using single-subject research designs. Perhaps the most commonly used effect size measure is the percentage of non-overlapping data (PND). It is the percentage of data points in a treatment phase that represent observed values that fall above the highest value (if behavior increase is expected) or below the lowest value (if behavior decrease is expected) in the adjacent control phase. The higher the PND, the larger the effect.

22. Most of the limitations and benefits of meta-analyses for group-design studies apply to meta-analyses of single-subject design studies. The fact that they yield evidence about the effects of interventions on fairly large numbers of participants may be a particularly important benefit when it comes to communicating with those who make actuarial decisions about which interventions are worthy of support and others who are more comfortable with large Ns and statistical analyses.

TEXT STUDY GUIDE

1. Describe the dominant research approach utilized by disciplines that utilize group research designs.

2. Why must behavior analysts be informed consumers of research using group designs and statistical analyses?

3. Identify and describe at least three external contingencies that may increase the likelihood that a behavior analyst may choose to use a group design and/or statistical analyses as part of their research.

4. Describe how a randomized controlled trial (RCT) is conducted.

5. What is random assignment and what purpose does it serve?

6. Describe in your own words what the authors mean when they state that a finding of statistical significance does not indicate that an intervention produced socially or clinically significant improvements.

7. Describe the potential sources of bias that are inherent in RCTs and possible ways in which these concerns can be minimized.

8. What are the limitations of RCTs for evaluating the effects of behavioral interventions?

9. How could researchers using a non-randomized controlled trial attempt to control for potential issues related to not randomly assigning participants to groups?

10. Describe the regression discontinuity design. How does it differ from a non-randomized controlled trial?

11. Outline what a research study might look like that utilizes a single-group pretest-posttest or posttest-only design.

12. Compare and contrast prospective cohort studies with retrospective cohort studies.

13. What is a case control study?

14. Identify, describe, and provide an example of the three most commonly used measures of central tendency.

15. What information does the range of a dataset provide the investigator?

16. Describe what information the standard deviation provides.

17. What is the semi-interquartile range?

18. What purpose do measures of variability serve?

19. What is a z-score, and why might it be calculated?

20. Describe what a correlation coefficient (r) tells us and how to interpret its value.

21. Why might it be beneficial to use a scatterplot when examining correlations?

22. Describe a contingency table and what the chi square statistic (X^2) may tell us about the variables in the table.

23. Describe logistical regression analysis and what purpose it serves.

24. What is a time series, and how are they related to autocorrelations?

25. Define the following terms: population, sample, statistic, and parameter.

26. What is a confidence interval?

27. What two basic assumptions must be satisfied in order for the inferential process to be considered valid?

28. Describe and provide an example of a null hypothesis (H_o). How does the null hypothesis relate to Type 1 error?

29. What is alpha (α), and how is it related to the level of significance?

30. List some of the criticisms that have been made regarding null-hypothesis significance testing.

31. Discuss when you would use a t-test as opposed to an analysis of variance (ANOVA).

32. Why is a statistically significant effect not an indication of the reliability or reproducibility of a study's findings?

33. What is an effect size? Describe why the NNT measure may be useful to behavior analysts.

34. Describe meta-analyses and their benefits.

35. What kinds of information may be lost when using meta-analyses, and how could you address this concern?

36. Briefly describe how generality is approached in behavior analysis as compared to other fields that typically utilize the group design/statistics approach.

37. Discuss how descriptive statistics could be used to supplement visual inspection of graphed data.

38. Describe the five different methods outlined by the authors that have been developed for quantifying the magnitude of effects in studies using single-subject research designs.
39. Discuss the benefits and limitations of meta-analyses of single-subject design studies.

BOX STUDY GUIDE

1. Describe the difference between α and p.
2. Does statistical significance correspond to clinical significance? Explain your answer.
3. Why do investigators often try to start their studies with large groups?
4. What is an ANOVA, and what kinds of information can it provide an investigator?
5. Briefly describe issues related to replication in psychological research. How might the probability of replication (p_{rep}) statistic help address this issue?

SUGGESTED READINGS

Ator, N. A. (1999). Statistical inference in behavior analysis: Environmental determinants? *The Behavior Analyst, 22,* 93-97.

Branch, M. N. (1999). Statistical inference in behavior analysis: Some things significance testing does and does not do. *The Behavior Analyst, 22,* 87-92.

Keenan, M., & Dillenburger, K. (2011). When all you have is a hammer: RCTs and hegemony in science. *Research in Autism Spectrum Disorders, 5,* 1-13.

Lambdin, C. (2012). Significance tests as sorcery: Science is empirical - significant tests are not. *Theory & Psychology, 22(1),* 67-90.

DISCUSSION TOPICS

1. Discuss possible examples of positive and negative correlations related to self-injurious behavior.
2. Select a published study in a behavioral journal that used inferential statistics to supplement their analysis. Discuss what kinds of statistics were used and how they supplemented the investigators' analysis.
3. Discuss the replication crisis in psychology and how the field of behavior analysis has been proactive in dealing with issues of reliability or reproducibility of findings.

EXERCISES

1. Calculate the mean, median, mode, and range of chapter length for this textbook.

2. After reading this chapter and articles from *The Behavior Analyst*'s special issue on statistical inference [1999, Volume 22(2)], prepare debating points on the advantages and disadvantages of using inferential statistics in behavior analytic investigations.

3. Find two examples from sources (e.g., social media, websites, advertisements) where statistically significant results are reported but may not be socially significant.

4. Select an article published in a behavioral journal that does not report inferential statistics. Describe how you could alter the study so that a group design would be utilized. Which kind of inferential statistic(s) might be appropriate to use?

CHAPTER SIXTEEN

Interpreting Research and Practical Projects

> *Across Target Behaviors*
> *Across Settings*
> *Across Species*
> Evidence
>   EVALUATING INTERPRETATIONS

INTERPRETIVE BEHAVIOR

Throughout this volume, we have viewed the actions of researchers and practitioners in the same conceptual framework we apply to the behavior of experimental and clinical participants. In this chapter, we focus this point of view on the interpretive behavior of researchers and practitioners. Although it might seem that the data are the most important outcome of a research project or practical intervention, this information is almost worthless unless it leads to interpretations by the investigator and others that prompt people to behave more effectively. In effect, when someone interprets a study, he or she translates the language of nature (quantitative data) into the language of the culture. This transformation enables people who were not involved with the project, especially those who have no training in the field, to interact success-fully with nature without having to accumulate personal experiences. This is how, for example, people can learn that smoking is unhealthy by reading about scientific findings without having to smoke for many years to discover that the hard way.

The primary challenge in interpreting a project, whether it is a formal research study or a practical intervention program, is to decide how each of its features might have affected the data. The investigator must then decide how each factor should influence interpretive statements about what the data seem to reveal. Interpreting a study therefore requires many judgments about how data collection procedures, the details of control and treatment conditions, and the resulting data themselves should influence statements about what has been learned. In making this assessment, we must start by considering each of the possible sources of control over the investigator's interpretive reactions. This exercise is also a good way to review and bring together the interests of prior chapters.

SOURCES OF CONTROL

Planning

Theory. Some influences on the investigator's interpretive behavior are likely to play a significant role when the study or treatment program is originally designed. For example, the investigator's theoretical or conceptual perspective toward behavior and the specific topic under investigation typically influences early decisions. How the research or practical questions are framed, measurement procedures are set up, research comparisons are arranged, and data are analyzed are all typically guided by the investigator's general approach to behavior as a subject matter. That influence therefore establishes and limits the procedures and data that are available for interpretation.

As a source of control over interpretations, the investigator's theoretical persuasion cannot be prejudged as inherently helpful or harmful. In one instance, it might prevent the researcher from seeing flaws in procedures. In another case, however, it may help by prompting reactions to the data that others might fail to detect. Whatever the impact of theoretical orientation, it would help if investigators could step back and appreciate how their perspective toward behavior could be influencing their reactions to a study. Perhaps not surprisingly, that self-reflective tendency is uncommon. If a practitioner tends to accommodate mentalistic fictions in framing an individual's behavioral issues, for example, it is not likely that he or she will recognize this as a problem and instead attempt a purely behavioral review of the issues. Seeing a child's misbehavior in school as the result of mental processes rather than environmental contingencies is likely to bias decisions about what is measured and how intervention protocols are designed, not to mention how data are interpreted.

Literature. The published literature concerning the question at issue influences how the researcher frames and designs the project (see Chapter 3). After the project is completed, the literature also provides a context for its results. For instance, how findings are described may partly depend on whether they support or conflict with published research. An important feature of this assessment is comparing the methods of the present study to those in the literature. If the results of the study seem to differ with those already published, these methodological dissimilarities would be considered in evaluating what the new study might contribute. So if a project compares two error correction procedures and gets results that contrast with published studies, how the data are interpreted will focus on differences between the literature and how the two procedures were designed and implemented.

Other Professional Contingencies. As we noted in Chapter 3, scientific research is not conducted in the sterile context many might suppose. There are many potential influences on a researcher's interpretations that have nothing to do with the study itself, and practitioners are susceptible to the same kinds of factors. It is important, though often difficult, to assess whether these influences are appropriate and helpful.

One possible problem is that by the time a study is completed, the investigator has usually invested considerable time, money, and effort. It may be as punishing to draw conclusions unfavorable to these interests as it is reinforcing to reach favorable conclusions. This kind of contingency can lead to what we have called advocacy research (see Box 3.1), in which the investigator biases the design and conduct of a study toward a preordained outcome. It is this kind of bias that makes it important for studies to be replicated by other investigators.

Another source of control over interpretive reactions is related to the degree of fame and fortune that may accrue to researchers who report certain outcomes. The fact that investigators may be deprived of both only means that such deprivations are easily satisfied. At the very least, publication in peer reviewed journals brings some measure of recognition, if not monetary reward. The riches may be institutional rather than personal. Obtaining or maintaining funding for a line of research is often contingent on a certain kind of finding. Access to research settings or participants can also depend on a project's outcomes.

These contingencies may be even more evident for practitioners. As the practitioner community has grown in recent years, opportunities for benefiting from promotion of a particular treatment model or procedure have become especially tempting. Being invited to present at conventions or conduct workshops can easily become a significant career objective, with the attendant benefits of recognition and monetary rewards.

We might agree that these influences on an investigator's conclusions can be problematic. However, that does not mean the planned uses of a study's findings should not be considered when deciding how results should be described. On the one hand, the procedures and data of a study should be interpreted on their own merits, regardless of how the findings might be used by others. Nevertheless, it could be argued that a study's outcomes might be described more or less conservatively depending on how they may be used. For example, if a study's results will be used to encourage nationwide dissemination of a new treatment procedure, it may be wise to be more cautious than if a study's conclusions are only going to guide further research.

Research Question. Chapter 3 considers the pervasive role of the research question in interpreting a study. The question concisely summarizes the investigator's interests, and determining how well the project is able to answer the question is therefore a natural focus of interpretation. This influence is an important constraint. Because the question presumably guided decisions about how the study was designed and conducted, it places certain limits on what the procedures and data can reveal. If interpretations exceed these limits, it may mean conclusions are too strongly influenced by other factors, such as those discussed in the previous section. On the other hand, too slavish a devotion to the research question can blind the investigator to the possibility of discovering outcomes that were not forecast by the question. Box 3.6 pointed out the importance of serendipity in science, and the question should not discourage examining the data for unanticipated discoveries.

Measurement

Target Behavior Definition. It is risky to interpret data without knowing exactly what they represent and how they were obtained. Each of the elements of behavioral measurement provides information essential to understanding

---

BOX 16.1

When You Can't Get There From Here

As Chapter 3 points out, one of psychology's biggest methodological headaches comes from asking questions that cannot be clearly answered. Such questions often share a focus on hypothesized "mental events." (The reason for putting "mental events" in quotes is because they are not real, physical events.) Questions about mental activity can only be approached by working with behavior and environmental variables, which are very much in the physical world. The problem with this approach is knowing whether the behavior measured in a study and the environmental variables actually manipulated have anything to do with the "mental events" that are the focus of the research question.

Consider as an example a question that asks whether self-esteem in previously unsuccessful students changes as a result of positive learning experiences. Self-esteem might be measured in multiple ways, such as with a questionnaire and by counting the occurrence of positive self-statements. The experimental procedure may involve arranging learning tasks in which success is assured.

What is actually measured in each case is not self-esteem, however, but verbal behavior. The researcher might like to assume the questionnaire and positive self-statements represent self-esteem, but how are we to know this? Although the experimental manipulations may be clear, all we can say with certainty is that they were followed by certain changes in questionnaire answering behavior and positive self-statements. This assessment does not answer our question about whether these changes represent self-esteem. In other words, questions about "phenomena" that are not known to exist force researchers to assume there is a relationship between the conceptual elements in the question and the operational elements in the study.

Asking questions about behavior, clearly a physical event, helps minimize this problem, although this approach does not always avoid it. When the question asks about behavior that is not directly measured, the same issue can arise. For instance, a question may ask about the impact of different ratios of work and leisure time on recycling behaviors such as separating trash. However, what if the study is conducted in a laboratory setting in which participants "work" by pushing buttons and "recycle" points under different ratios of "work" and "leisure" periods during each session? Although the investigator may want these conditions to represent what goes on in everyday life, it will not be clear whether the project really has anything to do with recycling.

---

what the data might reveal. Chapter 4 considered how different ways of defining target behaviors can affect the nature of the data.

There are a number of questions whose answers should be used to guide interpretations.

1. Was the selected target behavior appropriate and useful for answering the research question?

2. Did the definition capture the behavior of individual participants or some form of grouped behavior of multiple participants?

3. Was the target behavior defined in functional or topographical terms (or both)? What are the implications of this choice for interpretation?

4. Was the level of specificity in the definition appropriate for the study?

Dimensions and Units. Another influence on interpretations concerns the behavioral dimensions and units that were the focus of measurement. The treatment of these choices in Chapter 5 raises a number of questions that should be answered in considering what the data might reveal.

1. Was the chosen behavioral dimension adequately sensitive to treatment variables? Would different dimensions have been more appropriate?

2. What limits does the selected dimension place on the characteristics of responding that were observed?

3. Does the selected dimension reflect variability that is informative and useful?

4. If a ratio was used, is it important to look at the contributing dimensions separately?

5. Did the units of measurement used describe fixed amounts of the observed dimensions defined independently of what was measured? If not, what are the resulting constraints on interpretations?

Observing and Recording. The data available for interpretation depend on what was observed, and Chapter 6 considers this topic in detail. Here are some of the questions that must be answered.

1. Did the observation procedure accommodate the needs of the question and the characteristics of the target behavior?

2. Were the timing, frequency, and duration of observation periods adequate?

3. If incomplete observation procedures were used, what limitations should they place on interpretations?

4. If human observers were used, were they properly selected, trained, and evaluated?

5. What kind of evidence was gathered about the observation and recording process? Does the evidence reveal accuracy and reliability of observations or only agreement among observers?

Evaluating Measurement Procedures and Data. Finally, the investigator and others evaluating a study must be satisfied about the quality of the data generated by these measurement procedures. The investigator has presumably been making this assessment all along and by this late stage should be content with his or her decisions and their impact on the data. Others can only judge measurement procedures and the resulting data as a completed package.

Nevertheless, the decision must be multifaceted, taking into account all aspects of measurement. Anyone interpreting a study should be able to take a single data point and, in a single sentence, state precisely what it represents. For example, consider the two following statements:

1. This data point represents the average number of functionally defined compliance statements per minute (accuracy unknown) of a single participant recorded by a single observer during a 45-minute period in the clinic.

2. This data point represents the mean number of 20-second intervals out of consecutive 30-second periods for five participants scored as containing at least one topographically defined disruptive response (accuracy unknown) recorded by a single observer during a 15-minute period in a classroom setting.

This is not only a good exercise for students reviewing a published study, it is a realistic standard for experienced investigators as well. It requires a precise and comprehensive description of measurement components in a way that makes the basis for interpretive statements clear.

Behavioral Comparisons

Independent Variable. At this point, we will assume a study's measurement procedures and the resulting data have been judged acceptable and are therefore worthy of interpretation. Interest may now turn to (a) whether the independent variable is appropriate for the focus of the research or practical question at issue and (b) how well it was managed during the project. That assessment helps reveal whether comparing responding under the matched control and treatment conditions is likely to make any progress toward answering the question.

The first issue can sometimes be complex because there are no simple rules to guide an evaluation of whether the independent variable will help answer the question. As an example of this challenge, consider a series of studies trying to understand why consuming satiation quantities of food at meals has the effect of immediately and substantially reducing rates of post-meal ruminating in intellectually disabled individuals (Rast, Johnston, & Drum, 1984; Rast, Johnston, Drum, & Conrin, 1981; Rast, Johnston, Ellinger-Allen, & Lubin, 1988; Johnston, Greene, Rawal, Winston, Vazin, & Rossi, 1991). The basic research literature suggests that increases in oropharyngeal and esophageal stimulation from chewing and swallowing, the level of glycogen in the blood, and the degree of stomach distention might contribute to this effect. Each of these variables was therefore manipulated in separate studies, in each case requiring a procedure that would represent the variable in question. What complicated this challenge was that in order to separate the effects of these three variables each had to be manipulated while the other two were held constant.

To manipulate chewing and swallowing, the participants were encouraged to chew sugarless bubble gum before eating. Because these severely and profoundly intellectually disabled individuals would normally immediately swallow a piece of gum, it was placed in a strip of gauze, and staff held the ends of the gauze to prevent the gum from being swallowed. Staff also counted the number of chewing and swallowing responses (periodically swapping old gum for fresh) until they matched the average number of chews and swallows taken to consume a satiation quantity meal for each individual. This procedure did not affect the other two variables.

To evaluate the role of increased glycogen, participants were fed single portion meals that had the caloric density of a satiation-sized meal. This was done by preparing otherwise typical meals using high calorie ingredients. In other words, under this condition they experienced the effects of eating satiation quantities of food without increasing the amount of chewing and swallowing or the extent of stomach distention.

To assess the effects of increased stomach distention, participants were fed regular single portion meals followed by supplementary dietary fiber. The amount of fiber was calculated to mimic the stomach distention effect of satiation-sized meals.

These studies were intended to reveal whether each variable had an effect on rates of ruminating, which were measured as each condition was introduced and withdrawn. Although the data clearly showed a decrease in ruminating when each procedure was implemented, it is fair to ask if these effects were due to the intended independent variables. That is, although it was reasonably clear that the effects were due to the procedure, did the procedure properly represent the variables of interest? For example, perhaps feeding supplementary fiber did not properly mimic the stomach distending effect of consuming a very large meal. In other words, the fact that a procedure apparently changed behavior does not clarify why the change occurred or what it might mean for the research question.

The second issue, concerning how well the independent variable was managed during the study, is easier to assess. The primary concern is that the independent variable and other features of the intervention condition in which it is embedded were implemented as designed and that they were consistent from session to session. For research conducted in highly controlled settings such as laboratories, this fidelity and consistency is usually assured. Researchers using applied settings, on the other hand, often struggle to make sure that the procedures in both control and treatment conditions are implemented as intended. It is often the case, for instance, that these procedures require varied personnel to comply with specific protocols. As we suggested in Chapter 9, for instance, classroom teachers might have to follow detailed rules in how they interact with students serving as participants. Staff members in a group home might have to adhere to intervention rules seven days a week across two daily shifts. Under such circumstances, it is often useful to collect evidence specifically to verify that procedures happened as designed (Gresham, MacMillan, Beebe-Frankenberger, & Bocian, 2000; Peterson, Homer, & Wonderlick, 1982; Wheeler, Mayton, Carter, Chitiyo, Menendez, & Huang, 2009). For example, the investigator might measure the teachers' compliance with experimental protocols and present these data alongside those showing participant performance. Figure 16.1 shows an example of this practice.

Control Conditions and Extraneous Variables. It is not enough to determine that the independent variable was appropriate and properly implemented. The same issues of appropriateness and consistency must be addressed for the control condition. We discussed the role of the control condition in Chapter 11. It controls for all of the factors operating in an intervention condition except the independent variable. That is, if all of the variables present in the control condition are also present in an intervention condition, the only thing that differs between the two conditions will be the independent variable. This means the independent variable will be the only reasonable explanation for any differences in responding (the dependent variable) between the two conditions (ignoring the matter of extraneous influences).

That reasoning means that in interpreting a project it must first be clear that the control condition is appropriate for its task. As Chapter 11 noted, a control condition must (a) establish environmental conditions that are likely to help reveal the effects of the independent variable and (b) control for those factors present in the treatment condition that are not part of the independent variable. Anyone interpreting a study must evaluate the appropriateness of the control condition in serving these two functions.

In addition, as with the treatment condition, it is important that the control condition is implemented as designed and is consistent in its features from session to session. For example, even if it is clear that a control condition is well designed for its two functions, if it is also evident that the condition is not well managed by the investigator, the condition may not provide a good basis for evaluating the effects of the treatment condition. As we have already noted, insuring consistency in control or treatment conditions from session to session within a phase is often especially challenging in complex applied research settings. That is why researchers sometimes collect evidence about the fidelity of not only the treatment condition but the control condition as well. That information not only helps the investigator manage the study but also helps others evaluate the consistency of the conditions being compared.

Finally, how well the control and treatment conditions have been selected and managed is not the only interpretive concern about a study's procedures. Extraneous variables that are not taken into account by the control condition can come and go at any point during a project. For example, a participant may be sick one day or a school field trip in the morning one day may affect a student's behavior in an afternoon session. Whether such events influence an individual's performance is often not obvious. As we have already discussed, sometimes an apparently significant event will not evidently disrupt the usual performance, just as performance can be affected by more subtle extraneous factors.

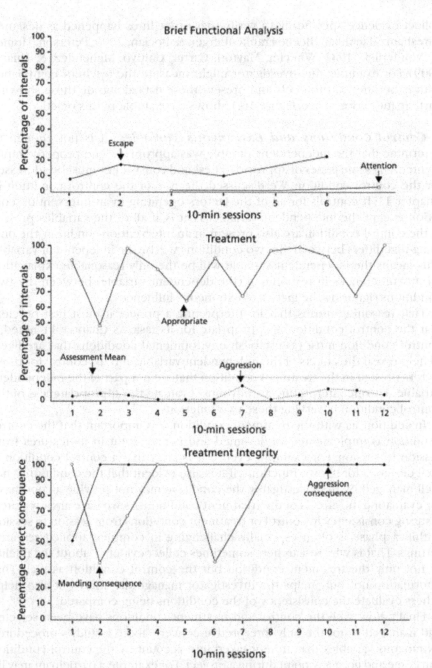

FIG. 16.1. Example of data showing participant outcomes (top two graphs) and teacher implementation of treatment procedures (bottom graph). Adapted from Northup, J., Wacker, D. P., Berg, W. K., Kelly, L., Sasso, G., & DeRaad, A. (1994). The treatment of severe behavior problems in school settings using a technical assistance model. *Journal of Applied Behavior Analysis, 27,* 33–47, p. 41. Copyright 1994 by the Society of the Experimental Analysis of Behavior, Inc. Used by permission.

Occasional extraneous anomalies are not necessarily a serious threat to sound comparisons of control and intervention conditions. Nevertheless, interpreting a study requires a judgment about whether extraneous factors had frequent and powerful effects on responding. If so, the data would intermingle their effects with those of the control and experimental conditions. This might encourage conclusions that fail to hold up when others attempt to use them.

Evaluating Behavioral Comparisons. When it is clear that the control and treatment conditions of the study were appropriately designed and well managed, attention can turn to assessing the available comparisons. In order to keep matters simple, we have so far been considering the simplest of studies examining the effects of a single independent variable with one control condition and its matched treatment condition. However, good research designs usually involve more than one treatment condition. Interpreting a study requires evaluating the nature of all of the resulting comparisons. One straightforward assessment concerns whether a particular comparison between a control and its matched treatment condition was repeated. As Chapters 12 and 13 pointed out, replications of control and treatment conditions provide additional opportunities to make comparisons, which in turn can strengthen confidence in the resulting conclusions. In other words, an ABAB design is inherently stronger than an AB design and, other things being equal, would merit more unambiguous conclusions.

In studies involving more than one independent variable, therefore, each must be evaluated in terms of the number of control-treatment comparisons available for that treatment condition. For example, if there is only a single AB comparison available, any conclusions must be very tentative, for reasons discussed in Chapter 11. In other words, it is important to remember that a study should be evaluated not on the basis of how many total replications are included but how many comparisons are available for each different independent variable or treatment condition under examination. (This was the point of the discussion in Chapter 13 concerning Figure 13.12.) A project examining two treatment conditions may allow three control-treatment comparisons for one of the interventions but only one such comparison for the other.

Finally, interpreting a study requires more than determining whether each particular control-treatment comparison was replicated and showed consistent results. There is also the matter of deciding what each comparison says about the influence of the independent variable and, more broadly, the research question. This is often a complex judgment, and no simple rules will help. This complexity is evident in the fact that the comparisons in a particular study may prompt somewhat different interpretations by different readers. That is why even reasonably clear findings should usually be expressed tentatively out of respect for what we may not yet know. Of course, one thing we do not know is whether a particular conclusion is correct. We learn this only with future investigations and applications.

BOX 16.2

Internal and External Validity

In 1966, Campbell and Stanley published a slim volume about experimental designs in which they introduced a distinction between internal and external validity. These terms caught on because they referred to important influences on the legitimacy of experimental inferences.

Internal validity refers to the appropriateness of attributing a causal role to independent variables. It can be threatened by a variety of extraneous factors, as we have described in different chapters. For example, the *history* that participants bring to a study, especially events in their lives during the course of the study, can influence their performance. *Maturational changes* can occur in studies that last long periods (for example, a two-year study with rats) and can confound the effects of treatment variables. If participants perform differently on a posttest because of their prior exposure to the pretest, then *testing* is another threat to internal validity. *Instrumentation* refers to the possibility that measurement operations may change over time, thus contributing error to the data. *Statistical regression* refers to the tendency of extreme scores to regress toward the mean with subsequent testing, a statistical phenomenon that means that they often become less extreme. *Selection biases* can plague between groups designs in which different participants are exposed to control and experimental conditions if participant characteristics are not properly matched. *Attrition* can also be a problem in group designs when participants drop out during the study, thereby creating the impression that the group performance has changed. *Diffusion of treatment* refers to situations in which control and experimental conditions do not remain distinct but become confounded in some way. This might be the case when a trainer is supposed to behave differently under two conditions but fails to comply fully.

External validity refers to the extent that the results of a study can be generalized to other circumstances. There are a number of questions that may be asked about whether features of the study limit generality. We have already discussed *generality across participants, settings, and target behaviors. Generality across time* refers to the possible influence of the time at which the experiment was conducted and whether variables associated with it contributed to the results and might therefore limit generality. *Generality across behavior change agents* asks the same kind of question about individuals who interacted with participants as part of experimental procedures. If individuals behave differently because of their status as participants, it is called *reactive experimental arrangements*. *Reactive assessment* refers to what is also called measurement reactivity, or the effects of the participant's performance of being measured. *Pretest sensitization* concerns the possibility that participants will react differently to the experimental condition because of the effects of a pretest. *Multiple-treatment interference* or sequence effects are possible if one condition influences responding in a subsequent condition.

Data

Analytical Procedures. In turning to the data as an influence over interpretive reactions, the first question is how data analysis procedures might affect our reactions. We examine this topic in some detail in Chapter 14, and it should be clear that how data are processed and presented might sway how readers interpret a study.

With the advantage of access to the raw data, investigators are able to consider all of the relevant options and choose analytical procedures that help reveal the data's message. Others are not obligated to agree with the researcher's analytical decisions, however. They may judge the selected quantitative or graphical techniques limiting in some way, for example, perhaps preventing them from making an analysis they would prefer. Although it is perfectly appropriate for them to request unpublished information about procedures and data from the investigator so they can conduct their own analysis, this involves a substantial investment in time and is not commonly done. More practically, the investigator's peers usually satisfy themselves with evaluating the impact of the investigator's analytical choices on their own interpretations.

Variability. After being confident that the study's analytical procedures will help identify sound interpretations, it is finally appropriate to evaluate the data. Before trying to understand what the data say about intervention conditions and the research question, however, it is important to look at the nature of the variability in the data.

One important consideration follows from having already evaluated the study's measurement and analytical procedures. It is possible that problems with these procedures produced data that do not represent what actually happened. As Chapter 6 discusses, the pattern of data points on a graph, for instance, can partly reflect observer error. There are also ways that discontinuous observing procedures generate misleading values. In addition, decisions about how to construct graphs can distort the displayed values, as Chapter 14 discusses. These possibilities make it important to decide the extent to which the data show variability that really happened versus variability that is merely illusory. Unfortunately, if that assessment is discouraging, there is often nothing that can be done, other than to put the study aside.

A second way of looking at the variability in the data follows from evaluating the pattern of responding within phases. Chapter 10 identified the most important issue – whether stable responding was adequately achieved in each phase. The evidence on this point is a marker for the level of experimental control attained and the extent to which extraneous factors intruded. As we have already stressed, whether differences in responding between control and treatment conditions justify conclusions about the effects of the treatment condition depends on not just the size of the differences but also the characteristics of responding in each of the two phases being compared.

Finally, if the study was well designed and conducted, the variability between phases presumably represents the effects of the independent variable.

The interpretive issues here concern the characteristics of the changes in responding as the intervention condition is initiated and withdrawn. Although it is common to focus on differences in the "level" of responding (how much increase or decrease was found), this is not the only feature that might be important. Changes in variability under control versus treatment conditions are often evident and might be relevant to the experimental question. For example, it might be that one effect of the treatment condition is to reduce session-to-session variability compared to the control condition. Such a change can have important practical implications. Another effect that can be important is the nature of the transition when initiating the treatment condition. Whether the transition to a stable pattern of responding is rapid or slow is often relevant to clinical interests, for instance. Figure 10.7 shows different kinds of transitions that may have practical consequences in different treatment scenarios.

Conclusions. At this point in the interpretive process, there is nothing left to do but judge what the data reveal about the effects of the independent variable and how these effects might help answer the research question. Before trying to draw these conclusions, however, a final, summary assessment is important.

Identifying a study's outcomes is only appropriate if the project's procedures and data are worthy of interpretation. Although all of the factors discussed in this chapter and explored in more detail in prior chapters bear on this decision, it comes down to a dichotomous judgment. All things considered, the study is either good enough to warrant conclusions or it is fatally flawed and therefore cannot support conclusions. There really is no middle ground. If the procedures are only somewhat weak in certain ways, proceeding to interpret the study may be worthwhile if conclusions are sufficiently qualified and cautious. If some aspects of measurement decisions and procedures are seriously problematic, however, ignoring these flaws and drawing conclusions anyway may only assure that the conclusions are misleading and not useful.

Deciding whether a study justifies conclusions is easy when it has been well done. However, after going to the trouble of carefully evaluating a study's features, it is often difficult to put it aside because of serious flaws in its procedures or data. This is especially true when you are interested in the topic and the particular question posed by the project. Our natural tendency is to accept the implicit opinion of the journal's reviewers and editors, who decided it was at least worth publishing, and draw conclusions about what the study showed, even though we know it has serious problems. It is no less tempting to accept the positions of colleagues presenting or promoting their findings at conventions and workshops.

Nevertheless, researchers and practitioners in all disciplines learn that publication in a peer-reviewed journal or an invitation to present at a meeting does not guarantee that a study is methodologically sound or that the author's conclusions are valid. It may be more difficult to appreciate that failing to recognize serious weaknesses in a study, or choosing to ignore them, risks conclusions that will not hold up when they are used in some way. In other words, although we may honestly believe (or at least hope) conclusions are reasonably

---

BOX 16.3

Do Attitudes Toward Interpretation Vary Across Disciplines?

There are many differences between the social sciences and the natural sciences (see Reading 1 in Johnston & Pennypacker, 1993b). The natural sciences have been around a good bit longer than the social sciences and have settled many methodological issues. They have accumulated a sophisticated literature describing how the world of matter works. They have learned that there is no point in using weak or inappropriate methods or drawing inaccurate and self-serving conclusions. In fact, they tend not to tolerate much conceptual, methodological, or interpretive sloppiness.

Their methodological progress has been rewarded by an increasingly broad and sound foundation of scientific laws. Scientists can see the relationship between good research methods and outcomes because they reap the benefits every day. As a result, interpretation seems to be approached with the highest concern about finding truth, whatever its consequences for theory or individuals. Although these are crude generalities with inevitable exceptions, the influence of theory, literature, and extra-experimental factors in the natural sciences seems distinctly secondary to research procedures and data.

Do the social sciences generally approach interpretation with different attitudes? After all, they are relatively young and are still struggling with the most basic methodological issues, such as the nature of their subject matter. Although their literatures are large, they do not yet reflect a sound, well developed, and broadly accepted understanding about how behavior works. In fact, they reveal diverse conceptual and methodological approaches to the same fundamental phenomena. The uncertain state of these literatures is reflected by the fact that there are few effective technologies that have emerged from a century of research (Estes, 1979), and progress seems to be represented by new literatures replacing, rather than building on, old ones.

It should not be surprising, therefore, that social scientists do not easily see a clear relationship between the quality of experimental methods and the likelihood of accurate and important findings. As a result, interpretation may more often be a self-serving exercise than in the natural sciences. The ideal of seeking truth often seems subservient to the influence of theory, literature, and extra-experimental factors. Because there is not yet much of a track record showing that the nature of research methods and interpretation makes a big difference in the advancement of the science, it may be understandable if social scientists approach interpretation somewhat differently than do natural scientists.

---

accurate, the real test comes when someone acts on them. If a practitioner improperly concludes that a study showed that a procedure was effective when it actually was not, for example, it may not work as expected when it is used in a treatment program.

More optimistically, let us assume that a study is at least generally sound and warrants our attention. Having examined the methodological features of a study, as well as its data, the remaining task is to decide what the data have to say about the effects of the independent variable. Of course, the independent variable was selected because it might shed light on the research question, so that assessment should license an attempt to answer the question.

Once again, there are no simple rules for coming up with this answer. One reason this is a complex process is that studies often lead to not a single answer but several. Even in a simple study with only a single independent variable, the data may reveal more than one kind of outcome. For example, measuring more than one target behavior or multiple behavioral dimensions creates the possibility that a treatment condition had somewhat different effects depending on which measures are examined (see Figure 14.2). One behavior may have increased during the treatment condition, but another may have decreased. The frequency or rate of responding may have decreased while the aggregate duration of responses increased. Of course, an additional reason conclusions tend to be multifaceted is that many studies investigate more than one treatment condition. This means conclusions must also take into account how the effects of each condition bear on the research question.

Even when a study's conclusions are clear, part of interpretation is considering what those conclusions mean in the context of the published literature. In comparing the study's findings with those of other studies, that judgment is even more complex. Furthermore, it is not unusual for researchers to agree on what a particular study shows but disagree about what those conclusions might mean for a certain issue or larger question. For instance, the first controlled study of intensive, comprehensive ABA treatment for young children with autism documented large increases in scores on measures of intellectual functioning (IQ tests) for just under half of the children in that treatment group (Lovaas, 1987). Some researchers questioned whether that outcome reflected real improvements in intellectual skills or just improved compliance with the testing procedures.

At this point in what is admittedly a complicated process, it would be understandable to wish for an approach to interpretation of research findings that is bound by firm rules. However, it is actually important that each reader bring his or her unique histories to this task. After all, even well done studies may generate misleading outcomes, and investigators have learned to avoid assuming that any one study proves some unimpeachable truth. When investigators disagree about the conclusions of a study or their implications for larger issues, it is often not clear who is right. Only more research will answer that kind of question. Such disagreements are an important feature of the scientific process.

In sum, interpreting a study is a complex skill with many influences; it is a skill that takes both training and experience to master. Perhaps the most valuable guidance is to remember that *the task is not just to interpret the data but to interpret the entire study*. It is often tempting to "read" an article by skipping ahead and looking at the graphs. However, data cannot be meaningfully interpreted without a detailed appreciation of all of the factors that led to the data and were involved in their analysis.

GENERALITY

Definition

Thus far, we have discussed interpretation only in terms of what happened in a study and what the results might mean for the question it addresses. The interests surrounding a research project or treatment program are usually broader than a single question might suggest, however. After all, if a study's results had no value outside of its unique features, there would be little point in having conducted the project. Extending a study's findings beyond the special circumstances that generated them is therefore an important part of interpretation. Deciding what a study showed is grounded in what was done and how that affected the target behavior. By contrast, speculating about what these findings might mean for somewhat different situations involves some risks and raises new issues. They concern what is called the **generality** of a study's effects.

> **Generality.** The meaningfulness of interpretations of a study under circumstances different from those that generated the data.

Generality has to do with the meaningfulness of interpretations under circumstances that are at least somewhat different from those that generated the data. Generality is not a characteristic of data, unlike variability, for example. It is simply a way of referring to the predictions inherent in interpretations that address future uses of research or practical findings. In a sense, data do not actually "mean" anything by themselves. Their only role, together with the details of experimental procedures, is to prompt investigators to say things about the relationship between the independent and dependent variables. In other words, when we talk about the generality of a study, we are not speculating about a quality of the data or even their meaning. We are talking about our predictions about what our interpretations of the study's findings might mean under different circumstances.

These predictions are sometimes fairly specific or narrow, such as when we speculate about whether the study's findings would hold if the same procedures were applied to participants with somewhat different characteristics. For example, will the findings of a project conducted with typical first graders also be obtained if the same procedures are used with 6-year-old children who are developmentally delayed? We might also guess what would happen if the procedures in a study were slightly modified or if their effects would be the same with a different target behavior.

Conjectures about a study's findings are often relatively broad, however. For instance, when a practitioner uses the findings from a published study in deciding on how to design a clinical intervention, he or she makes an implicit prediction about the applicability of the study to the clinical circumstances of interest. In such cases, there are probably many details in the clinical situation that differ from those in the research project. Factors associated with the

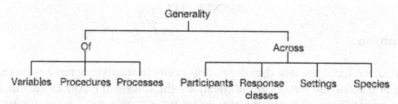

FIG. 16.2. Dimensions of generality.

setting, staff members, participants, and procedures will be determined by the practical situation and are likely to differ, sometimes substantially, from those of the research project.

In sum, asking about the generality of our interpretations addresses the question, "If research findings are applied under circumstances that are somewhat different, will the same kind of effects be obtained?" This question is similar to the question raised by curiosity about the reliability of a study's outcomes, but it is not the same. Reliability asks, "If experimental procedures are repeated, will the same effects be obtained?" We make this same distinction in discussing replication in Chapter 11. In both instances, we are making predictions, but the basis for these predictions is different. Concluding that a study's effects are reliable predicts that the same results would be obtained if the procedures were repeated exactly. Concluding that our interpretations are general predicts that the same kind of results would be obtained even if certain features of the study were somewhat different.

Interests in Generality

Generality Of and Generality Across. There are always two kinds of interests that make up our curiosity about generality. We are interested in the generality *of* some aspect of a study *across* changes in some other feature. In other words, in speculating about generality, there must be some elements of the study whose "generalness" is in question, and there must be other features of the study which if changed would provide a test of whether the element of interest is in fact general. Figure 16.2 summarizes these and other dimensions of generality.

Suppose, for example, that a practitioner is interested in using the findings of a published research study as a basis for developing an intervention procedure that will change an individual's behavior in some way. The practitioner might be able to faithfully duplicate the procedure described in the study. However,

TABLE 16.1
Distinguishing between the reliability and the generality of experimental findings

• Reliability	Asks about getting the same outcomes if procedures were repeated exactly
• Generality	Asks about getting the same outcomes if procedures were somewhat different

the question remains as to how much the reported outcomes depended on characteristics of the participants in the study. If their characteristics were a key influence on the results, the individual the practitioner is working with might not share all of those characteristics and therefore not show the same effects of the procedure. On the other hand, if the study's results did not depend on the characteristics of its participants, the practitioner might expect to get the same results. In this example, we would say that the practitioner was interested in the generality *of* a procedure *across* different individuals. As we have seen, this is a way of asking if the feature that differs between the original study and some other circumstance (such as a practical application) is critical to obtaining the same results.

Of Variables. Interest in the generality of variables helps to integrate and systematize a literature. When investigators can show that a particular variable is relevant beyond the confines of a certain study or even an area of literature, it advances our knowledge of behavior. Discovering such similarities is one of the goals of a science. Although differences are easier to discover, they are only signs of our ignorance.

A good example of a variable in the science of behavior is conditioned reinforcement (reinforcement by stimuli that have become conditioned reinforcers through pairings with other reinforcers). This variable has been shown to have excellent generality across species, individuals, response classes, settings, and other dimensions. The subject index of basic research journals such as the *Journal of the Experimental Analysis of Behavior* provides a long list of variables whose generality continues to be examined.

Of Procedures. Most behavioral research is directed toward the generality of methods of controlling behavior. This is the natural focus for applied research, of course, because the practical goal is often to develop techniques that will be effective in changing behavior under widely varying circumstances. Although this is an ideal outcome, a procedure can be quite valuable even though it is only effective under a narrow range of conditions. Whatever the range of effectiveness of a procedure, it is important to know its limits.

What determines the conditions under which a procedure will be effective is the status of its components, as well as the status of other factors operating when it is implemented. Learning about the generality of a procedure requires identifying which of its components may be varied and by how much without weakening the effectiveness of the procedure. It is possible that certain components are critical and must not be tampered with at all, whereas others are unimportant and could even be omitted without risking the procedure's effectiveness.

Behavior analytic treatment of severe feeding disorders in children is a case in point. Treatment often involves multiple components, including but not limited to differential reinforcement of alternative behavior (DRA), noncontingent reinforcer delivery, behavioral momentum, physical guidance, extinction of disruptive behaviors that interfere with eating, and escape extinction.

Analyses of the extensive research in this area show that escape extinction is essential for reducing disruptive behaviors that interfere with food acceptance (Sharp, Jaquess, Morton, & Herzinger, 2010; Volkert & Piazza, 2012).

Of Processes. A behavioral process may be defined as the result of an ordered series of steps. Sidman (1960) described two meanings of behavioral processes. First, behavior that results from the interactions of two or more different variables or procedures can be called a behavioral process. Perhaps the clearest example here is the process we call discrimination, which results from a combination of reinforcement and extinction procedures applied to certain behavioral features.

A second type of behavioral process results from repeated exposure to contingencies to promote certain performances, with the result that behavior changes more and more quickly as training progresses (often referred to as "learning set"). An example is the increased efficiency with which children with and without autism mastered new visual discriminations and reversals of those discriminations over the course of training on several discriminations and reversals (Lionello-DeNolf, McIlvane, Canovas, De Souza, & Barrios, 2008). The fact that the number of trials required to learn a new discrimination and reversal decreased over successive trainings makes that a behavioral process.

Across Individuals. Whether focusing on variables, procedures, or processes, perhaps the most common curiosity about generality concerns whether the findings will be obtained across individuals. This interest follows from the fact that each individual brings together many factors that can affect the impact of the variables that make up an intervention procedure. Even individuals who are similar in some obvious ways (for instance, children diagnosed with autism spectrum disorders) vary in gender and other biological features, reinforcement history of target behaviors, certain features of their repertoire, level of functioning, sensitivity to treatment variables, and many other characteristics. The question about generality is whether the results of a study substantially depended on the status of any of these factors among the participants. If this is true, and if individuals to whom these results are applied differ in these features from the study's participants, the study's results may not be consistently obtained in practice.

The discussion of replication in Chapter 11 suggested that generality across individuals can be assessed by repeating a study with different participants. Reproducing the original results may imply that they did not depend on participant characteristics. Failure to obtain the original results, however, might then require the more selective approach of systematically varying particular characteristics to see which ones are the key to research outcomes.

Across Target Behaviors. Although the target behavior used as the dependent variable in a study might be considered an individual characteristic, particular behaviors often have consistent characteristics across different individuals. That makes it reasonable to wonder if a study's results would still

BOX 16.4

Are We Preoccupied with Generality Across Individuals?

In most psychological research, the paramount interest in generality is whether the findings will hold for all individuals in a class (such as all individuals diagnosed with a certain mental illness) or even all human beings. This focus stems from the widespread use of inferential statistics, which reduces the search for generality across participants to an actuarial or sampling issue (see Reading 13 in Johnston & Pennypacker, 1993b). From this perspective, the question is how well the control and treatment group samples represent the population.

This preoccupation with generality across individuals also confuses our desire that a finding be as universal as possible with our obligation to establish generality through experimental manipulations of controlling variables. Parametric tests of statistical significance encourage the confusion by providing a simple method that appears to enhance generality while increasing the likelihood of getting a significant result – increasing the number of participants in control and treatment groups. Unfortunately, this only further discourages a distinction between assessing versus obtaining generality across individuals. The drive to evaluate generality across individuals at the conclusion of the study by making it a sampling question takes attention away from the more important matter of determining what needs to be learned from future studies about the role of individual characteristics.

Because behavior is an intraorganism phenomenon, our real interest should be in the individual, not the population. When we understand what factors produce a certain outcome at this level, we are in a much better position to assess whether that outcome will be obtained for other individuals or classes of individuals. Furthermore, it is important to understand that no aspect of generality can be fully resolved with a single study. Identifying the participant variables that influence the impact of a procedure requires a series of studies in which those variations are systematically manipulated. This approach also helps refocus attention away from an uncritical desire for generality across a broad range of individuals and toward an interest in identifying those characteristics that will reliably predict success or failure in each case.

It is interesting that in research conducted in the methodological framework of this book, generality across individuals is not regarded with special attention and is easily addressed as a matter of routine. This does not reflect a lack of interest in this aspect of generality but an appreciation of its proper place among our scientific curiosities. Furthermore, behavioral researchers have learned that when sufficient attention is given to issues of experimental control, generality across a study's participants (and eventually other individuals) is relatively easy to demonstrate. In fact, behavioral researchers are accustomed to finding that most, if not all, participants in a study show the same kind of effects.

In contrast, between groups designs tend to put the cart before the horse. The tactics of (a) exposing different levels of the independent variable to different groups, (b) insuring that these groups contain a large number of participants, and (c) treating their responses collectively provides comparisons that describe no member of any group. By failing to focus on individuals with careful attention to experimental control, these traditional methods greatly decrease the chances of discovering orderly relations in the first place. This makes the question of generality across individuals moot.

be obtained if a different target behavior were used. For example, functional communication training has been shown to be more effective for reducing problem behaviors when the communicative response that is targeted for strengthening is vocal-verbal than when it involves the use of augmentative and alternative communication systems, such as exchanging picture cards or touching symbols on a speech-generating device (Heath, Ganz, Parker, Burke, & Ninci, 2015).

It is clear why applied researchers and practitioners are often interested in the generality of findings across target behaviors. Although practitioners hope that behavior change procedures will be as broadly effective as possible, they must at least know about any limits on a procedure's generality across target behaviors. It is especially important to answer this question when the study at issue was conducted in a highly controlled setting and used arbitrary behaviors such as button pushing or touching a computer screen. These target behaviors are selected because they are simple, easily managed, and usually lack a meaningful reinforcement history. This may be an advantage in some basic research projects, but it often leaves applied researchers and practitioners wondering whether the same results would be obtained with more practically relevant behaviors.

Across Settings. Practitioners have a similar interest in the generality of findings across settings. Even in applied research projects, the circumstances of a study are usually somewhat different from the situations in which practical applications take place. In this context, "setting" is a broad reference not just to a physical location but also to everything that comes with that location. This might include social factors associated with individuals other than the person whose behavior is targeted for change (peers, for example), things going on in a setting that have nothing to do with the intervention procedure (a school fire drill), and the other behaviors of the individual that are not targeted for change.

So, a research publication may show that a parenting skills course was effective in getting foster parents to use certain procedures with their children in the home. The report indicates that the course was taught to six foster parents in the early afternoon at the county offices of the department of human resources by two trainers assisted by two graduate students in five, weekly three-hour classes. For the practitioner interested in using this parenting skills curriculum, the question is whether presenting the same curriculum will yield the same outcomes if the circumstances are somewhat different. What if the class is taught in the evening or there is only one trainer? What if the classes are only one hour long and taught over 15 weeks? What if they are held in a church basement? The question, then, is whether any of these features in the published study contributed to the effectiveness of the curriculum.

Across Species. Behavioral scientists are interested in discovering relationships that hold across the widest variety of circumstances, including different species. The most common form of this question is whether the findings of research conducted with nonhuman species will also be found when they are extended to humans. Overall, the basic processes of operant learning have shown strong generality across species. As a result, it has been possible to build a behavior change technology strongly rooted in basic science. Of course, the generality of specific studies with nonhuman species to human behavior depends on the details of each prediction.

Evidence

The best evidence about the generality of a study's findings should be the nature of the study's procedures and data. There are two aspects of a study that are important. First, the stronger a study's methods and data, the greater the foundation for predictions about its generality. If a study is methodologically weak or generates equivocal data, it should not encourage speculations about the generality of its outcomes. If those outcomes are themselves debatable, questions about generality should be put aside.

Second, the more directly a study addresses issues of generality, the greater the opportunity for speculations about how well its findings will hold under different conditions. For example, if a study included only a single set of control and intervention conditions, there may be little basis for proposing that its results should be obtained when certain features are varied. On the other hand, if a study included systematic variations in particular features of key proce-dures, there may be a solid basis for speculating about whether those features will be important under other circumstances. Similarly, if a project used only two very similar participants, there may be limited evidence about whether its results would be obtained with participants exhibiting varying characteristics.

That second feature of research projects and treatment programs raises a useful distinction in the basis for statements about generality. On the one hand, they may be largely speculative when there is little evidence in a project about whether its results should still be expected if some of its features are changed. In contrast, they may be well founded when a study includes systematic or even unsystematic variations in some of its features so that the data can provide support for certain predictions.

In other words, we might distinguish between interpretations that merely speculate about generality versus those that rest on clear evidence about gen-erality. Such evidence usually takes one of three forms: (a) showing that the same results are obtained even when a certain variable is changed, suggesting that it does not limit generality; (b) showing that the results change when a certain variable is changed, suggesting that it does limit generality; and (c) sys-tematically manipulating the variable and showing how it affects the results. The last option is usually the most convincing.

Finally, although this section focuses on generality, what we really want to know is how important certain variables are in obtaining a certain outcome. Once we know about the role of each factor, we will be in a good position to predict what will be required to obtain that same outcome under widely varying circumstances. That is, when we wonder about the generality of a

TABLE 16.2
Evidence for generality

Evidence	Conclusions
• Showing that the same results are obtained when a variable is changed	Variable does not limit generality
• Showing that the results change when a variable is changed	Variable does limit generality

study's findings, what we really want to know is how much each of its features contributed to its results. If we understand the role of these variables, we no longer have to ask about generality. We would then know what it takes to produce those results, as well as what would prevent obtaining those results.

In other words, the real objective is not to develop procedures or outcomes that are "general" but to understand the role of contributing variables. As a way of making this point, imagine that someone had discovered a technique that was highly effective for treating 25% of the cases of a particular kind of behavior. With this track record, we might say the technique had weak generality across individuals. However, what if we had identified the participant variables that allowed practitioners to determine in advance those individuals with whom the technique would always work. With this knowledge, how might we assess the generality of the procedure? We could now say that its generality to individuals sharing certain characteristics is excellent. That example makes the point that questions about the generality of research findings disappear when we understand the variables underlying research outcomes.

EVALUATING INTERPRETATIONS

When we interpret a research study, our statements about what happened and what it means probably fall short of perfect accuracy and completeness. We do not know how far short, of course, which often leads to disagreements among colleagues considering the same project. These differences of opinion might tempt some to search for fixed interpretive rules that require certain conclusions under certain conditions, but this approach would misunderstand the problem.

In fact, interpretive disagreements are an inevitable and important part of the scientific process. After all, science addresses questions that are at the limits of our knowledge, and individual experiments rarely provide completely unambiguous answers. When readers disagree in their interpretations, it is usually not clear who is right. Differing interpretations of a study are therefore not a problem so much as a prompt for additional research. Interpretive issues are eventually resolved as more is learned about the phenomenon.

This same point applies to interpretation of data from the delivery of practical services. When conclusions from treatment programs are shared with colleagues, whether locally or at a professional meeting, it should be expected that there would be some differences of opinion about the project's findings. Although project personnel may understandably prefer their own interpretations, it is important to consider the legitimacy of other points of view.

Does this mean there is no way to be sure if our interpretations of a project are correct? In a word, "Yes." When analyzing a study, the best that can be done is to be aware of the influences summarized in this chapter. Regardless of our level of confidence, there is no way to know whether our interpretations are correct, much less whether they will hold up under different circumstances. Interpretations are no more than the verbal behavior of individual researchers, practitioners, and others. Anyone's interpretations are influenced by many different factors and may not be accurate or complete. This assessment applies regardless of the general analytical approach or particular techniques used.

This does not mean we can draw whatever conclusions we like without concern about contradictions, however. There is a kind of yardstick that ultimately measures the soundness of all interpretations. This standard is the *reproducibility* of the original findings. Let us say, for instance, that a practitioner concludes that a published study showed that a particular procedure was effective in changing behavior in a certain way. If this interpretation is correct, when the practitioner uses that procedure there is a good chance the same result will be obtained. If so, being able to reproduce that result implies that the interpretation of the study was correct. If the procedure does not work as expected, it may suggest that the interpretation was incorrect in some way. Of course, things are not this simple. The practitioner's success will also depend on how well the application replicates the critical factors at work in the original study. In other words, this standard for evaluating interpretations is not perfect. It does not test our interpretations until we use them in some way, and even then the assessment is complicated by how they are used.

The standard of reproducibility is at least unavoidable, however. Even if an investigator does not replicate his or her own study, sooner or later others will use the findings in some way. Other investigators might base new studies on the original results, and practitioners might use the findings in service settings. These eventual replications create a public contingency between our interpretations and their consequences for others who use them. This contingency can lead to support for our interpretations or evidence that they do not hold up for others. These consequences encourage everyone to base their interpretations on a careful consideration of research methods and data.

This example of how the contingencies embedded in research methods influence the behavior of investigators has been a theme throughout this book. It reminds us that early researchers did not invent scientific methods through some rational process. The history of science shows that they slowly evolved one study at a time. Some practices were shaped and maintained because they often produced reinforcing consequences in the form of an increased ability to predict and control natural events. Other practices were abandoned because they failed to do so. In other words, what might appear as a set of rules about "how to do science" is really just a way of summarizing contingencies between the investigator's behavior and the subject matter.

Although the strategies and tactics outlined in this book are certainly important guidelines, following them will not guarantee success any more than violating them will assure failure. Each research or clinical challenge is unique, and creativity is often more important that blind compliance with methodological rules. Every methodological decision has its consequences, however, and skilled researchers are well aware of these relationships.

CHAPTER SUMMARY

1. The primary challenge in interpreting a project is to decide how each of its features might have affected the data. The investigator must then decide how each factor should influence interpretive statements about what the data seem to reveal. In making this assessment, the investigator must start by considering all of the possible sources of control over their interpretive reactions.

2. Some influences on the investigator's interpretive behavior are likely to play a significant role when the study or treatment program is originally designed. Variables such as an investigator's theoretical perspective, the scientific literature, and available resources are likely to have influenced how the research question has been framed.

3. Because the research question guides decisions about how the experiment is designed and conducted, it places certain limits on what the procedures and data can reveal. If interpretations exceed these limits, it may mean that conclusions are too strongly influenced by other factors, such as extra-experimental considerations. However, too slavish a devotion to the research question can blind the investigator to the possibility of discovering outcomes that were not forecast by the question.

4. In comparing responding under the matched control and treatment conditions, we are attempting to assess if any change in responding is due to the introduction of the independent variable. In deciding if this is the case, the reader must determine whether the independent variable was appropriate for the experimental question and how well it was managed during the project.

5. It is not enough to determine that the independent variable was appropriate and properly implemented. The same issues of appropriateness and consistency must be addressed for the control condition. Additionally, extraneous variables that are not taken into account by the control condition must be considered when evaluating the results.

6. Interpreting a project requires more than determining whether each particular control-treatment comparison was replicated and showed consistent results. There is also the matter of deciding what each comparison says

about the influence of the independent variable and, more broadly, the research question. This is often a complex judgment in which no simple rules will help.

7. In considering what the data say about intervention conditions, it is important to look at the nature of the variability in the data. It is possible that problems with the project's measurement and analytical procedures have produced data that do not accurately represent what actually occurred. However, if the study was well designed and conducted, the variability between phases presumably represents the effects of the independent variable. Once we are confident that this is the case, we can then judge what the data reveal about the effects of the independent variable and how these effects might help answer the research question.

8. Generality has to do with the meaningfulness of interpretations under circumstances that are at least somewhat different from those that generated the data. There are always two kinds of interests that make up our curiosity about generality. We are interested in the generality of some aspect of a study (e.g., variables, procedures, processes) across changes in some other feature (e.g., individuals, target behaviors, settings). Each area of interest contributes to our understanding of specific techniques and variables and aids us in integrating and expanding the literature on these topics.

9. When we interpret a research study, our statements about what happened and what it means probably fall short of perfect accuracy and completeness. This may lead to interpretive disagreements, which are an inevitable and important part of the scientific process. Differing interpretations of a study are not a problem so much as a prompt for replication and additional research.

10. Regardless of our level of confidence, there is no way to know whether our interpretations are correct, much less whether they will hold up under different circumstances. Interpretations are no more than the verbal behavior of individuals. They are influenced by many different factors and may or may not be accurate or complete. This assessment applies regardless of the general analytical approach or particular techniques used.

11. Although the strategies and tactics outlined in this book are certainly important guidelines, following them will not guarantee experimental success any more than violating them will assure failure. Each research or clinical challenge is unique, and an investigator's creativity is often more important and valuable than blind compliance with methodological rules. Every methodological decision has its consequences, however, and skilled investigators understand these relationships well.

HIGHLIGHTED TERMS

Generality. The meaningfulness of interpretations of a study under circumstances different from those that generated the data.

TEXT STUDY GUIDE

1. What is the primary challenge in interpreting a project?
2. How can an investigator's theoretical persuasion affect interpretations?
3. What are some other professional contingencies that may influence interpretations?
4. How can focusing on the research question sometimes be a harmful influence on interpretations?
5. What are some aspects of target behavior definitions that should guide interpretations?
6. What are some issues concerning dimensional quantities and units of measurement that are relevant to interpretations?
7. List some features of observing and recording that should be considered when drawing conclusions.
8. What is the point of the exercise of describing in one sentence what a single data point represents?
9. Under what experimental circumstances might it be important to measure how well the control and treatment conditions were implemented?
10. What are the requirements a control condition must satisfy?
11. Why does it matter how many instances of each control-treatment comparison are available?
12. What features of the data should be evaluated before drawing conclusions about what they mean?
13. Under what circumstances might you decide to reject a study because it does not warrant interpretation?
14. Explain the dictum "… the task is not just to interpret the data, but to interpret the entire experiment."
15. What is generality, and what is it not?
16. How is the generality of a study's findings different from its reliability?
17. Explain the two main interests in generality.
18. What is it that must be learned in order to predict the conditions under which a study's findings will or will not be obtained under other circumstances?
19. Explain the standard by which all interpretations are eventually evaluated.

BOX STUDY GUIDE

1. What is the main problem associated with experimental questions that ask about mental events?
2. Define and distinguish between internal and external validity.

3. Describe several factors that may influence internal validity.
4. Why might attitudes toward interpretation differ between the social sciences and the natural sciences?
5. How does a preoccupation with generality across individuals confuse interest in the broad applicability of a finding with the requirement to establish generality experimentally?
6. How will a sound understanding of individual characteristics that influence the effects of a procedure help to predict whether those effects will be found with other individuals?
7. Why is generality across individuals not the primary goal of experimentation for behavioral researchers?
8. Why can between-groups designs make it difficult to establish generality across individuals?

SUGGESTED READINGS

Johnston, J. M. (1979). On the relation between generality and generalization. *The Behavior Analyst*, *2*, 1–6.
Terrell, D. J., & Johnston, J. M. (1989). Logic, reasoning, and verbal behavior. *The Behavior Analyst*, *12*, 35–44.

DISCUSSION TOPICS

1. Select and study an empirical study published in a behavior analytic journal. Debate the interpretations given the methodology described in the article.
2. Discuss the contrast between generality as discussed in this chapter and how it is treated in research based on inferential statistics (see Chapter 15).

EXERCISES

1. Develop an example showing how an independent variable could be inappropriate for a research question.
2. Select an empirical study published in a behavior analytic journal. Assess the study in terms of the number of questions concerning target behavior definition, dimensional quantities and units, and observing and recording. How should this assessment affect interpretations of the data?
3. Choose an empirical study published in a behavior analytic journal and describe in a single sentence exactly what a single data point represents.

4. Review the first empirical study published in the most recent edition of your favorite behavior analytic journal. Did the study address issues related to generality, and, if so, what kind of generality?

5. Find an empirical behavior analytic article that did not address issues of generality. Why did the author(s) not address generality, and how could you modify the study to address this issue?

CHAPTER SEVENTEEN

Behavior Analysis Research Ethics

HISTORY

Federal Regulation

The contemporary focus on research ethics grew out of World War II. In 1946, an American military tribunal began criminal proceedings against German doctors for conducting medical experiments on concentration camp prisoners without their consent. The Allies proceeded to adopt the Nuremberg Code for research on human subjects in 1948, establishing the principle that subjects should give consent and that the benefits of research must outweigh the risks.

In 1964, the World Medical Association issued the Helsinki Declaration, concerning ethical principles for medical research using human subjects. That document has been revised a number of times over the years and remains the basis for Good Clinical Practices used today. The key features of those guidelines require that research with humans should be based on the results of laboratory and animal experimentation, that research should be reviewed by an independent committee before a project is begun, that informed consent is secured from participants, and that risks should not exceed benefits. The Helsinki Declaration added two important features to the principles of the Nuremburg Code: that the interests of the subject should always be placed above the interests of society and that every subject should receive the best-known treatment.

The Helsinki Declaration did not immediately resolve ongoing problems in the use of human subjects, however. Perhaps the most shameful example was the Tuskegee Syphilis Study. This project had been in operation since 1932, infecting 400 out of 600 African-American males with syphilis without their knowledge. Although they received free medical examinations, they were not told of their disease. They were monitored for 40 years and not given an effective treatment (penicillin) when it became available in the 1950s. In some cases, when other physicians diagnosed the disorder, researchers intervened to prevent treatment. Not surprisingly, the public was outraged when this project was discovered in 1972.

As a result of this and other scandals that had unfolded over the years, the United States congress passed the National Research Act in 1974, which authorized federal agencies to develop human research regulations. This act also created a National Commission for the Protection of Human Subjects of Biomedical and Behavioral Research. In 1979, the commission released The Belmont Report, which became the primary basis for human subject research ethics regulations. The report enshrined three basic ethical principles. "Respect for persons" meant that individuals should be treated as autonomous agents and that persons with diminished autonomy are entitled to protection. "Beneficence" meant that human subjects should not be harmed and that research should maximize possible benefits and minimize possible harm. "Justice" meant that the benefits and risks of the research must be distributed fairly.

In 1981, the Department of Health and Human Services (DHHS) issued the Code of Federal Regulations (CFR), Title 45 (public welfare), Part 46 (protection of human subjects). The Food and Drug Administration concurrently issued CFR Title 21 (food and drugs), Parts 50 (protection of human subjects) and 56 (Institutional Review Boards). In 1991, these core DHHS regulations were formally adopted by other federal departments and agencies that conduct or fund research involving human subjects as the Federal Policy for the Protection of Human Subjects, now referred to as the "Common Rule" (45 CFR 46). That policy includes requirements for assuring compliance by research institutions, for researchers obtaining and documenting informed consent, for Institutional Review Board operations, and for protections of certain vulnerable research subjects such as pregnant women, prisoners, and children. (See Rice, 2008 for more details of this history.)

BOX 17.1

Times Change

The days are long past when behavioral researchers could design and conduct a study with concern only for methodological niceties. Today, behavioral scientists using any vertebrate species in their studies must comply with a complex array of detailed regulations and guidelines. By design, these policies have a pervasive and often intrusive impact on the kinds of questions that may be asked and how they may be pursued with experimental procedures. In fact, their influence usually touches most features of a study, including how the characteristics of participants are selected, how individuals are acquired or recruited, the circumstances under which their participation may continue throughout the project, the procedures and conditions to which they may be exposed, and how they must be treated when the study is completed.

Research ethics are about cultural values. There are different ways of defining cultures and cultural values, but it is at least clear that there are widely varying views about science and how it should be conducted and used. For example, although some revere science and have high hopes for its accomplishments, others question what science can learn and the value of scientific knowledge. Most people are comfortable with humans using other animal species for food, products, and entertainment, but we may also know people who avoid eating meat, refuse to buy leather clothing, and view the animal acts at the circus as mistreatment. And when it comes to research, a sometimes vocal community believes it is immoral to use animals as subjects, especially when it involves any form of discomfort. Others are willing to use animals as subjects as long as the research can be justified in terms of its potential benefits for society.

The practical challenge is how to resolve these differences among various cultural convictions and interests. The laws and regulations governing behavioral research today are the result of not only governmental commissions, panels, bureaucratic procedures, and legislative actions but of public debate, citizen protests, and even terrorist activity against universities and individual scientists. Furthermore, these laws and regulations are not static. Cultures and cultural values change, and practices that were once acceptable may later become objectionable. For example, it was once common to design research procedures that involved deceiving human participants about not only the reasons for the procedures they would experience but what these procedures actually involved. Today the requirements for informing participants about the conditions they will experience and getting their consent greatly limit this kind of deception. The transitional nature of cultural values and regulations is particularly clear in animal research. For instance, society's interests in continuing to reduce or limit the use of animals in research are built into animal welfare policies and regulations.

In sum, compliance with research regulations demands careful study of the rules that apply to human and nonhuman species, consultation with regulatory bodies about the details of a proposed project, submitting required paperwork, obtaining necessary approvals, and conforming to the protocols that have been approved.

Behavior Analysis Research Ethics

The young field of behavior analysis contacted evolving regulations concerning research ethics largely through its long association with psychology. For many years, behavior analysts engaged in research were primarily employed in departments of psychology in colleges and universities. The American Psychological Association (APA) developed its own policies and regulations concerning research and clinical ethics consistent with federal rules (American Psychological Association, 2010). Behavior analyst investigators were therefore guided by APA research rules, as well as by federal regulations governing research conducted in higher education institutions.

As behavior analysis gradually progressed toward greater independence as an academic and clinical discipline, the need for a set of ethical standards addressing the distinct needs of behavior analytic researchers and practitioners became clear. That challenge was initially undertaken by John Jacobson, who as chair of the Professional Standards Committee of the Association for Behavior Analysis International (ABAI) was charged in 1998 with drafting a code of ethics for behavior analysts. Jacobson and his committee began by examining the ethics codes of nine organizations, including national organizations in psychology, sociology, anthropology, education, social work, and school psychology (Behavior Analyst Certification Board, 2016). The initial draft of the ethics code incorporated features of those codes that were especially pertinent to the interests of behavior analysts and was sent to scores of behavior analysts for review and suggested revisions. The final document was adopted by the Behavior Analyst Certification Board (BACB) in 1999 as its *Guidelines for Responsible Conduct of Behavior Analysts*. Compliance with the *Guidelines* was initially voluntary on the part of individuals who were credentialed by the BACB, though there was a separate set of disciplinary standards that the BACB enforced. The *Guidelines* were revised several times by subject matter experts. In 2014 they were revised to become the *Professional and Ethical Compliance Code for Behavior Analysts*, which has been fully enforced with all professionals and paraprofessionals who are credentialed by the BACB since January 1, 2016 (Behavior Analyst Certification Board, September 2014, 2016). That code is incorporated, in whole or in part, in many U.S. state laws to license behavior analysts. From its inception in 2007, the Association of Professional Behavior Analysts adopted the BACB *Guidelines* and then the *Compliance Code* for its members (Association of Professional Behavior Analysts, 2019). The Association for Behavior Analysis International's ethics policy states that "… each ABAI member should adhere to the ethical standards that have been defined for his or her profession" and lists several example ethics codes, one of which is the *BACB Professional and Ethical Compliance Code for Behavior Analysts* (Association for Behavior Analysis International, 2016).

In its present form, the Code encompasses ten sections. Section 9 concerns research activities.

TABLE 17.1
Sections of the Behavior Analysis Certification Board's Professional and
Ethical Compliance Code for Behavior Analysts

1. Responsible conduct of behavior analysts
2. Behavior analysts' responsibility to clients
3. Assessing behavior
4. Behavior analysts and the behavior-change program
5. Behavior analysts as supervisors
6. Behavior analysts' ethical responsibility to the profession of behavior analysts
7. Behavior analysts' ethical responsibility to colleagues
8. Public statements
9. Behavior analysts and research
10. Behavior analysts' ethical responsibility to the BACB

PROFESSIONAL AND ETHICAL COMPLIANCE CODE
FOR BEHAVIOR ANALYSTS

Article 9.0: Behavior Analysts and Research

*Behavior analysts design, conduct, and report research in accordance with
recognized standards of scientific competence and ethical research.*

Article 9.0 of the Code summarizes the breadth of the obligations of behavior
analysts who conduct research. It indirectly references all applicable ethics
policies that may apply to behavioral research and also encompasses the
content of all of the paragraphs of this section of the BACB Code. However,
this overarching statement hides an important question that must be answered
before considering the following sections of the Code. What are the defining
features of behavior analytic research that distinguish it from ABA practice?
This is an especially challenging question for behavior analysts because our
field explicitly blends many of the characteristics of research and practice. For
example, much of the field's research literature concerns applied issues and
is conducted in field settings using indigenous participants. Research projects
often focus not only on answering the research question but also on providing
some practical benefit to participants (Baer, Wolf, & Risley, 1968).

The fact that routine delivery of ABA services involves the same research
methods showcased in research publications, as previous chapters have
detailed, further integrates the characteristics of research and practice. The
fundamentals of measurement do not differentiate behavior analysis research
and practice, for instance, and even the features that allow researchers to make
comparisons of responding under different conditions are often shared by practitioners. Although we have noted that practitioners may sometimes be forced
to compromise ideal research standards in favor of practical constraints and
client priorities, this bias is not a good basis for defining behavioral research or
even separating it from practice. In behavior analysis, research cannot be distinguished from practice because it is sometimes more methodologically "pure."

A more fruitful approach to locating the line separating research and practice in behavior analysis considers the use to which findings might be put. Our frequent reference throughout the book to "investigators" as a descriptor of both researcher and practitioner roles should suggest that the common agenda is to learn what is going on with a target behavior. Although both kinds of activities are about discovery, the results tend to be used in different ways. Practitioners apply their discoveries by resolving everyday problems unique to each client in service to the individual's needs. In contrast, researchers are interested in making general statements that will hold for populations of individuals sharing certain characteristics. These are fundamentally different objectives, even though achieving them often requires much the same approach.

One sign of the difference between the objectives of research versus practice has to do with what is done with empirical outcomes. Although research findings must be communicated to others in order to be useful, practical findings can be useful without sharing them with colleagues at all. Practitioners may discuss their clinical projects with agency colleagues or even put together a presentation for broader dissemination at a professional meeting, but their objective is met when the client's behavioral issues are resolved. Researchers must communicate their findings to the field at large to achieve their objective, in part because building an effective body of knowledge requires the participation of other researchers.

So we may define research in behavior analysis as empirical activity consistent with the requirements of research methods that justifies general statements about behavior that apply to particular circumstances defined by the characteristics of individual, settings, procedures, and so forth. In contrast, whatever its similarities with research, behavior analytic practice focuses on serving the behavioral needs of individuals and therefore does not typically generate findings that warrant such general statements.

Are researchers obligated to be ethical in ways that may not be relevant to practitioners? An examination of the ten sections of the BACB Code suggests that there is considerable overlap in the ethical responsibilities of researchers and practitioners. Although there are certain details that may not usually be relevant to researchers (for instance, matters of fees, billing, and referrals), researchers conducting applied research cannot escape most of the obligations facing practitioners. In turn, practitioners may be less likely to need to worry about matters associated with plagiarism and publication of findings.

Article 9.01: Conforming with Laws and Regulations

Behavior analysts plan and conduct research in a manner consistent with all applicable laws and regulations, as well as professional standards governing the conduct of research. Behavior analysts also comply with other applicable laws and regulations relating to mandated-reporting requirements.

Article 9.01 clarifies the obligation of behavior analysts engaged in research to comply with "all applicable laws and regulations."This phrasing does not point to any particular source, which should suggest that any legal, regulatory, or ethical standards that apply to a particular investigator or project are part of this obligation.The possibilities include policies, rules, and regulations laid out by federal and state agencies, as well as by institutions such as colleges and universities, professional organizations, and employers.

The days in which all an investigator had to do was design and run a study are long past. Investigators now must comply with a maze of requirements - far more than this chapter can detail. For example, behavior analysts affiliated in any way with a higher education institution must comply with federal research rules, including obtaining advance approval of detailed project specifications from an Institutional Review Board and then conducting the project in accordance with the approved plans.A study that involves the participation of individuals served by state government - individuals with intellectual disabilities, for example - must obtain advance approval from one or more state entities of the particulars of the project and the involvement of the served individuals. Reference to "professional standards" includes not only the BACB's Code but also those that may come with other professional credentials, such as those associated with psychology, teaching, social work, and speech and language therapy.

The legal, regulatory, and ethical requirements for conducting research generally concern the justification for the project, the procedures that will be used, the characteristics of participants, the detailed nature of their selection and involvement, and a variety of safeguards associated with their treatment. Changes in the approved protocol at any point may require additional authorizations. Compliance with these rules should be taken seriously throughout the project.Violations of the terms of approval may require an investigator to terminate a project, reimburse project funds, or accept other administrative or legal consequences.

Article 9.02: Characteristics of Responsible Research

(a) *Behavior analysts conduct research only after approval by an independent, formal research review board.*

(b) *Behavior analysts conducting applied research conjointly with provision of clinical or human services must comply with requirements for both intervention and research involvement by client-participants.When research and clinical needs conflict, behavior analysts prioritize the welfare of the client.*

(c) *Behavior analysts conduct research competently and with due concern for the dignity and welfare of the participants.*

(d) *Behavior analysts plan their research so as to minimize the possibility that results will be misleading.*

(e) *Researchers and assistants are permitted to perform only those tasks for which they are appropriately trained and prepared. Behavior analysts are responsible for the ethical conduct of research conducted by assistants or by others under their supervision or oversight.*

(f) *If an ethical issue is unclear, behavior analysts seek to resolve the issue through consultation with independent, formal research review boards, peer consultations, or other proper mechanisms.*

(g) *Behavior analysts only conduct research independently after they have successfully conducted research under a supervisor in a defined relationship (e.g., thesis, dissertation, specific research project).*

(h) *Behavior analysts conducting research take necessary steps to maximize benefit and minimize risk to their clients, supervisees, research participants, students, and others with whom they work.*

(i) *Behavior analysts minimize the effects of personal, financial, social, organizational, or political factors that might lead to misuse of their research.*

(j) *If behavior analysts learn of misuse or misrepresentation of their individual work products, they take appropriate steps to correct the misuse or misrepresentation.*

(k) *Behavior analysts avoid conflicts of interest when conducting research.*

(l) *Behavior analysts minimize interference with the participants or environment in which research is conducted.*

Article 9.02 covers many aspects of behavior analytic research. Most of its paragraphs offer straightforward guidance. For instance, Paragraph (a) makes it clear that it is improper to initiate a research project without obtaining prior approval from applicable boards or committees; Paragraph (b) puts clinical responsibilities ahead of research interests, and so on.

Some of the mandates may seem uncomfortably vague, however. Paragraph (c) requires a "competent" effort and "due concern" for the "dignity and welfare" of participants but leaves these terms undefined. What seems to one investigator like a competent research protocol may be viewed by peers as falling well short of professional standards. What actions might be required to show "due concern?" What treatment of participants might be seen as violating the "dignity and welfare" of participants? Other paragraphs seem to call for similarly subjective judgments. What is appropriate training and preparation (Paragraph (e))? How far must an investigator go to maximize benefit and minimize risks (Paragraph (h))? What constitutes a conflict of interest (Paragraph (k))? Given that research protocols usually involve disturbing routine environmental circumstances, what constitutes minimal interference (Paragraph (l))?

These uncertainties can often be addressed by turning to peers. When questions arise about the proper course of action in planning and conducting a research project, the best resource is others who have comparable training and experience. This consultation starts with getting approval of the project from some sort of review board or committee, such as an Institutional Review Board. This body will often offer suggestions for improvements or even require modifications of research plans. The peer review process should also include co-workers or other colleagues, perhaps befriended in graduate school or at professional meetings. A colleague may point out how a measurement procedure that seems straightforward to an investigator is likely to yield misleading data.An investigator may see no problem in how participants are to be treated, but a colleague may have a different perspective and suggest ways of modifying procedures to avoid problems.

The key is that investigators consult with peers whose different histories will make their reactions to the questions raised by Article 9.02 valuable. Even seemingly straightforward research projects are likely to prompt questions that may not have clear answers, which is why research should not be a solitary venture. Paragraph (g) emphasizes this caution by requiring that investigators have explicit training and supervised experience in conducting research.

Not all practitioners are adequately prepared to conduct research projects – no more than all researchers are prepared to offer practical services. Nevertheless, sometimes practitioners may begin a project intending to do no more than provide a service but along the way become interested in its broader implications. The temptation to reconceptualize a practical effort as a research project once underway should generally be avoided, however. At that point, it is too late to obtain necessary prior review and approval from authorities, participants, and others. It may also be the case that approaching the effort from the outset as a research project rather than a clinical effort would lead to different decisions about some features of the protocol. For instance, measurement procedures might be more stringent and data collection more comprehensive.

Remember that research is distinguished from practice by its objective of obtaining and communicating general findings that will hold for a population of individuals. This objective often demands some methodological decisions that might not be necessary for purely practical purposes, particularly when it comes to arranging experimental comparisons. This caution about morphing practical services into research projects does not mean that practitioners should not share their findings with peers. However, formal presentations should be accompanied by appropriate caveats about any methodological limitations and their consequences for how the data are interpreted. The investigator should always take a conservative position in suggesting what the results might mean for circumstances beyond those in the project. As Chapter 16 suggests, practitioners may often find it difficult to comply with such caveats, particularly when a project was clinically successful. This is why it is important to approach a project as a research venture – with all of its cautions – from the outset.

Article 9.03: Informed Consent

Behavior analysts inform participants or their guardian or surrogate in understandable language about the nature of the research; that they are free to participate, to decline to participate, or to withdraw from the research at any time without penalty; about significant factors that may influence their willingness to participate; and answer any other questions participants may have about the research.

The Code's description of the requirements for obtaining informed consent from prospective participants is relatively standard across disciplines that conduct any type of research with people. Given the abuses mentioned in the first section of the chapter, it is understandable that these requirements favor the interests and protection of participants. Although Article 4.0 of the Code includes the requirement for practitioners to obtain appropriate consent for treatment protocols (see Paragraphs 4.02, 4.03, 4.04, 4.05, and 4.06), the details of Article 9.03 are somewhat different. Whereas practitioners must describe procedures in full detail, researchers need only describe the general nature of the research, presumably because explaining all of the procedural details might bias a participant's performance in certain types of studies. Instead, the article focuses on the conditions of the participant's consent, making sure that the options of declining or withdrawing without penalty are clear.

Article 9.04: Using Confidential Information for Didactic or Instructive Purposes

(a) *Behavior analysts do not disclose personally identifiable information concerning their individual or organizational clients, research participants, or other recipients of their services that they obtained during the course of their work, unless the person or organization has consented in writing or unless there is other legal authorization for doing so.*

(b) *Behavior analysts disguise confidential information concerning participants, whenever possible, so that they are not individually identifiable to others and so that discussions do not cause harm to identifiable participants.*

These two complementary paragraphs describe straightforward protections of confidentiality for research participants. Although it might seem that these requirements primarily concern showing data to colleagues or presenting findings at meetings, this caution is quite comprehensive. Anyone who is part of the research team will likely know the identity of participants, but no one else should have any form of access to this information. In other words, participants should not be identified by name or in any other way even in casual conversations with anyone not directly involved in the project, much less by including their name on graphs or any other documents that others might see.

Article 9.05: Debriefing

Behavior analysts inform the participant that debriefing will occur at the conclusion of the participant's involvement in the research.

Participants are typically informed of this option when they consent to involvement in a research project. Although they may not be fully informed of the details of the research protocol at the outset because of the risk that this information will affect their reactions to experimental procedures, there is no reason to avoid full disclosure when their role is concluded. In fact, it is the lack of complete candor prior to participation that requires post-experimental clarity.

Article 9.06: Grant and Journal Reviews

Behavior analysts who serve on grant review panels or as manuscript reviewers avoid conducting any research described in grant proposals or manuscripts that they reviewed, except as replications fully crediting the prior researchers.

This article cautions against the obvious potential for conflicts of interest in anyone who has detailed access to other researcher's proposed or completed research projects. This rule is particularly important because grant and journal reviewers are usually experts in the topic under review, so they are especially likely to appreciate the importance of submissions or to take advantage of what they may reveal. Grant review committees and journal editorial review processes customarily require reviewers to sign a non-disclosure agreement to emphasize this limitation on their access to reviewed material.

Article 9.07: Plagiarism

(a) *Behavior analysts fully cite the work of others where appropriate.*
(b) *Behavior analysts do not present portions or elements of another's work or data as their own.*

Although there is room for judgment in complying with these mandates, using the work of others without clearly acknowledging their efforts is widely prohibited not only in science but also more broadly in the culture. Most occasions for citing the work of others are straightforward, and style manuals provide detailed rules for how to do so (see American Psychological Association, 2010, which is widely used in the social and behavioral sciences). Researchers often realize that citing the work of others helps readers appreciate the breadth and depth of understanding that underlies the research project, which makes them look good. The risk is that it may sometimes seem to investigators that they would look even better if readers give them credit for making important points that they actually got from others.

The consequences for plagiarism are at least embarrassing and can be quite damaging to one's reputation. Employers understand that it hurts their reputation as well when it is shown that an employee plagiarized material. This prohibition is especially well respected in colleges and universities, where much research is conducted. Egregious instances of plagiarism can result in termination of employment.

Article 9.08: Acknowledging Contributions

Behavior analysts acknowledge the contributions of others to research by including them as co-authors or footnoting their contributions. Principal authorship and other publication credits accurately reflect the relative scientific or professional contributions of the individuals involved, regardless of their relative status. Minor contributions to the research or to the writing for publications are appropriately acknowledged, such as, in a footnote or introductory statement.

Research projects are often complex affairs involving not just a principal investigator but also others who contribute to planning and implementing a study. Deciding how to credit each person's contributions can be difficult. It is not just a matter of judging who deserves to be listed as an author and what priority of authorship is warranted. Those who contributed in supporting roles may also deserve recognition for their roles.

There is no reason to avoid being thorough and gracious in documenting the contributions of at least most of the people whose efforts were required to conduct a research project. Article 9.08 not only encourages this approach, it demands that the importance of each person's role be the criterion by which authorship and other credits are assigned. The matter of assigning authorship and the priority among authors has become especially important over the years in all sciences. It is now accepted that the sequence of multiple authors be largely determined by the nature and extent of each person's contribution to the project.

Article 9.09: Accuracy and Use of Data

(a) Behavior analysts do not fabricate data or falsify results in their publications. If behavior analysts discover errors in their published data, they take steps to correct such errors in a correction, retraction, erratum, or other appropriate publication means.

(b) Behavior analysts do not omit findings that might alter interpretations of their work.

(c) Behavior analysts do not publish, as original data, data that have been previously published. This does not preclude republishing data when they are accompanied by proper acknowledgment.

(d) After research results are published, behavior analysts do not withhold the data on which their conclusions are based from other competent professionals who seek to verify the substantive claims through reanalysis and who intend to use such data only for that purpose, provided that the confidentiality of the participants can be protected and unless legal rights concerning proprietary data preclude their release.

The prohibitions listed in Article 9.09 should be easy to understand. Paragraphs (a) and (b) are largely about being not just honest but scrupulously honest – even to the point of reporting any significant errors in the data. However, failing to acknowledge evidence that might be important to colleagues – errors of omission – may be an even more seductive temptation for researchers. Other chapters have made it clear that there are many ways to collect and analyze data, for example, and some procedures may mislead readers, who may have no way to know what data might have resulted from alternative procedures. Together, Paragraphs (a) and (b) make it clear that researchers must not take or fail to take any steps in conducting and reporting projects that involve knowingly misleading others.

Paragraph (d) articulates a key feature of scientific method – its public character. Not only must research be reviewed and shared, colleagues who wish to reanalyze published data must be given this opportunity, though with appropriate safeguards. It is not common for another investigator to request research data for this purpose, but it is in the larger interests of the field that researchers cooperate in this process. After all, if a reexamination of data using different analytical procedures revealed somewhat different findings, this should be no less interesting to the original research team than it is to others.

In sum, the section of the Professional and Ethical Compliance Code for Behavior Analysts dealing with research responsibilities is broad and somewhat limited in its details. As noted in Paragraph 9.01, however, researchers are also obligated to comply with all laws, regulations and professional ethical guidelines that apply with their credentials, employment, and the features of the planned research project. In total, such requirements are comprehensive and detailed in their guidance, and ignorance of their details is not a defense for any ethical missteps.

CHAPTER SUMMARY

1. The Federal Policy for the Protection of Human Subjects was formally adopted in 1991. Preceded and informed by the Nuremberg Code (1948), Helsinki Declaration (1964) and the Belmont Report (1979), this policy includes requirements for assuring compliance by research institutions, for researchers obtaining and documenting informed consent, for Institutional Review Board operations, and for protections of certain vulnerable research subjects such as pregnant women, prisoners, and children.

2. As behavior analysis gradually progressed toward greater independence as an academic and clinical discipline, the need for its own set of ethical standards addressing the needs of both researchers and practitioners became clear. Initial guidelines were adopted by the Behavior Analyst Certification Board (BACB) in 2001 and revised in 2016 into the Professional and Ethical Compliance Code for Behavior Analysts (hereafter referred to as the Code).

3. Article 9.0 of the Code summarizes the breadth of the obligations of behavior analysts who conduct research. It indirectly references all applicable ethics policies that may apply to behavioral research and also encompasses the content of all of the paragraphs of this section of the BACB Code.

4. In behavior analysis, research cannot be distinguished from practice because it is sometimes more methodologically "pure." One sign of the difference between the objectives of research versus practice has to do with what is done with empirical outcomes. Research findings must be communicated to others in order to be useful. However, practical findings can be useful without sharing them with colleagues at all.

5. We may define research in behavior analysis as empirical activity consistent with the requirements of research methods that justifies general statements about behavior that apply to populations of individuals sharing certain characteristics.

6. The legal, regulatory, and ethical requirements for conducting research generally concern the justification for the project, the procedures that will be used, the characteristics of participants, the detailed nature of their selection and involvement, and a variety of safeguards associated with treatment.

7. When questions arise about the proper course of action in planning and conducting a research project, the best resource is others who have comparable training and experience. This consultation starts with getting approval of the project from some sort of review board or committee. The key is that investigators consult with peers whose different histories will make their reactions to the questions raised by Article 9.02 (Characteristics of Responsible Research) valuable.

8. The morphing of practical services into research projects does not mean that practitioners should not share their findings with peers. However, formal presentations should be accompanied by appropriate caveats about any methodological limitations and their consequences for how the data are interpreted.

9. Whereas practitioners must describe procedures in full detail, researchers need only describe the general nature of the research, presumably because explaining all of the procedural details might bias a participant's performance in certain types of studies.

10. Participants should not be identified by name or in any other way even in casual conversations with anyone not directly involved in the project, much less by including their name on graphs or any other documents that others might see.

11. There is no reason to avoid being thorough and gracious in documenting the contributions of at least most of the people whose efforts were required to conduct a research project. It is now accepted that the sequence of multiple authors be largely determined by the nature and extent of each person's contribution to the project.

12. Investigators must not take or fail to take any steps in conducting and reporting projects that involve knowingly misleading others.

TEXT STUDY GUIDE

1. Briefly describe the key historical events related to the development of research ethics.
2. Describe the three basic ethical principles outlined in the Belmont Report.
3. Briefly discuss the development of ethical standards for the field of behavior analysis.
4. What are the defining features of behavior analytic research that distinguish it from ABA practice?
5. Discuss situations in which researchers may be obligated to ethical guidelines that do not impact practitioners.
6. Discuss situations in which practitioners may be obligated to ethical guidelines that do not impact researchers.
7. Briefly describe the relevance of Article 9.01: Conforming with Laws and Regulations to both researchers and practitioners.
8. How can some of the vagueness of terms used in Article 9.02 (e.g., competent, due concern) be addressed?
9. Describe how practitioners should address situations in which their services morph into a research project.
10. Identify and discuss any differences between informed consent provided during a research project versus informed consent provided as part of receiving behavior analytic services.
11. Describe how to address issues related to confidential information used for didactic or instructive purposes.
12. What is debriefing?
13. Why is it important to always cite the work of other individuals?
14. How is authorship order typically assigned in the field of behavior analysis?
15. Describe the importance of paragraph (d) in Article 9.09: Accuracy and Use of Data.

BOX STUDY GUIDE

1. What role does culture have in determining research ethics?

SUGGESTED READINGS

Bailey, J. S., & Burch, M. R. (2016). *Ethics for behavior analysts*, 3rd edition. New York: Routledge.
Behavior Analyst Certification Board (2016). *Professional and ethical compliance code for behavior analysts, Ver. January 20, 2016*. Littleton, CO: Author.

Bhutta, Z. A., & Crane, J. (2014). Should research fraud be a crime? *BMJ*, *349*, g4532.

DISCUSSION TOPICS

1. Article 1.02 in the Code discusses the importance of practicing/researching within your scope of competence. Discuss strategies that investigators can implement to maintain and expand professional competence.
2. Discuss situations in which delaying, withholding, or withdrawing a treatment in order to demonstrate experimental control would violate ethical guidelines. What solutions would an investigator have in this scenario?

EXERCISES

1. Visit your institution's Institutional Review Board (IRB) website, and review the necessary steps that investigators must follow in order to submit a protocol for review. Describe any requirements you found unclear or that were unexpected.
2. Behavior analytic research is conducted across the globe. Complete an internet search to identify any legal, regulatory, or ethical requirements for conducting research in countries other than the United States of America.
3. Read the article by Bhutta and Crane (2014) that discusses whether research misconduct should be considered a criminal offense. In what ways could publishing inaccurate data impact the field of behavior analysis? Do you think research fraud should be treated as a criminal offense (it already is in some countries) – why or why not?

GLOSSARY

AB comparison. A within-subject sequence of phases composed of one control and one experimental condition.

Accuracy. The extent to which observed values approximate the events that actually occurred. In metrology, the absence of consistent over- or underestimation of true values.

Alternate-form reliability. The extent to which the results of two different forms of the same assessment administered to the same group of individuals correlate.

Alternative explanation. A way of explaining the results of a control/treatment comparison that takes into account factors other than the independent variable.

Antecedent-behavior-consequence (ABC) recording. A procedure in which an observer records descriptions of all of an individual's behaviors and the conditions under which they occurred during a specified period of time.

Antecedent event. An environmental event that occurs immediately before a response. Used generically when it is not certain what function the event serves.

Applied behavior analysis. A phrase that may refer to (a) the area of research that focuses on developing and evaluating procedures for changing behavior for practical purposes, (b) the behavior change technology resulting from behavior analytic research, or (c) the field encompassed by both applied behavior analysis research and the delivery of applied behavior analysis services.

Baseline condition. A condition or phase of an experiment in which the independent variable is not present. Also referred to as a control condition.

Behavioral variability. Variations in features of responding within a single response class, as well as variations in summary measures of that class.

Believability. The extent to which the investigator can, in the absence of direct evidence, convince others to believe that the data are good enough for interpretation. Does not involve direct evidence about the relationship between data and the events they are intended to represent.

Between-groups design. A method of arranging comparisons between control and experimental (treatment) conditions in which different groups of subjects are exposed to control and experimental conditions. Data from the individual participants in each group are combined so that the data that are analyzed represent the combined performance of individual participants who have experienced only one of the conditions.

Blind. A reference to being unaware of the goals of an experiment, the nature of experimental or control conditions, or the outcomes of each condition. May apply to the investigator, observers, or participants. If both investigator and participants are blind, it is called a *double-blind* experiment.

Calibration. Evaluating the accuracy and reliability of data produced by a measurement procedure and, if necessary, using these findings to improve the procedure so that it meets desired standards.

Celeration. A dimension that describes change in the rate or frequency of responding over time.

Changing criterion design. A within-subject, single baseline design using AB and reversal sequences to identify effects of manipulating performance criteria.

Complete observation. A schedule of observation that allows detection of all occurrences of the target behavior.

Concurrent multiple baseline design. A within-subject design that uses two or more concurrent baselines that are coordinated in time to allow control-treatment comparisons both within and across baselines.

Concurrent validity. The extent to which results produced by a new assessment correspond with results of a well-established assessment of the same construct or domain.

Consequent event. An environmental event that occurs immediately after a response. Used generically when it is not certain what function the event serves.

Construct validity. The extent to which an instrument is shown to assess the construct that it purports to measure.

Content validity. The extent to which items on an assessment represent the content that the instrument purports to measure.

Contingency. A relationship between a class of responses (a behavior) and a class (or classes) or stimuli. Implies nothing about the nature of the relationship or its effects.

Continuous observation. Observation and recording procedures in which all occurrences of the target behavior can be detected during observation periods.

Control or baseline condition. A condition or phase of an experiment in which the independent variable is not present.

Countability or count. A dimension reflecting the occurrence of the event being measured, independent of any temporal features.

Covert behavior. Behavior that is similar to overt or public behavior but occurs at a reduced magnitude and is often detectable only by the behaving individual.

Criterion-referenced assessment. An assessment on which an individual's score is compared to a prespecified performance standard.

Cycle. A unit of measurement for the dimension of countability or count. In the study of behavior, "responses" is often used as a substitute label.

Cycles per unit time. The unit of measurement for the dimension of rate or frequency. In the study of behavior, minutes are most often the time unit used (e.g., 1.5 cycles per minute).

Cycles per unit time per unit time. The unit of measurement for celeration.

Cyclic variability. A repeating pattern of local variability, often involving sequences of increasing and decreasing trends.

Dead Man's Test. An informal test of whether a particular event is a behavior. The test is that if a dead man can do it, it is not behavior.

Dependent variable. In behavior analytic research, usually a response class, at least one dimension of which is measured throughout all phases of a study.

Dimension. A quantifiable aspect of a natural phenomenon.

Dimensional measurement. An approach to measurement that involves attaching a number representing the observed extent of a dimension to an appropriate unit of measurement.

Dimensionless ratio. A ratio of like dimensional measures that results in a unitless or scalar number.

Direct measurement. Measurement practices in which the events that are measured are exactly the same as those about which conclusions are drawn.

Discontinuous observation. Observation and recording procedures in which all occurrences of the target behavior are not necessarily detected and recorded during observation sessions.

Duration. A dimension that refers to the elapsed time between the beginning and ending of an event. In the study of behavior, the event may be a single response or a bout or episode of responding.

Environment. The physical circumstances in which the organism or referenced part of the organism exists. This includes any physical event or set of events that is not part of a behavior and may include other parts of the organism.

Episode (or bout). A relatively brief period of responding defined by the relatively frequent occurrence of one or more specific response classes and distinguished from other such episodes by relatively extended periods in which the target responses do not occur.

Event-response latency. In the study of behavior, a type of latency representing the time between an environmental event and a response.

Exact agreement procedure. A procedure for calculating interobserver agreement that involves dividing the observation period into intervals in which observers record the actual number of responses. In order to obtain percent agreement, only intervals in which the two observers agreed on the exact count are considered agreements.

Experimental condition. A condition or phase in which the independent variable is present. Also referred to as a *treatment, intervention,* or *independent variable condition.*

Experimental control. The management or control of different variables in a study, including the independent variable and extraneous variables.

Experimental (research) design. Arrangements of control and experimental conditions that permit comparisons that help identify the effects of the independent variable on the dependent variable.

Exploratory data analysis (EDA). An approach to data analysis emphasizing largely graphical techniques focusing on discovering order and structure in the data. EDA may be contrasted with confirmatory data analysis or hypothesis testing.

Extraneous variable. An environmental event that is not of interest to the researcher but that may influence the participant's behavior in ways that obscure the effects of the independent variable.

Extrinsic variability. The assumption that variability in behavior is describable, explainable, and predictable in terms of variation in other physical phenomena, whether biological or environmental. See *Intrinsic variability.*

Frequency or rate. A compound dimension describing the average number of events per unit of time. In the study of behavior, rate or frequency is calculated by dividing total count by either total IRT or the total time during which responses occurred.

Functional analysis (experimental functional analysis, analogue functional analysis). An assessment procedure in which environmental events that may influence a behavior are systematically and repeatedly presented and withdrawn one at a time while the behavior is observed and recorded.

Functional behavior assessment. A category of procedures for assessing relations between environmental events and behaviors.

Functional definition. A definition of a behavior based on the functional relations between its responses and classes of antecedent and consequent environmental events.

Functional relation. An experimentally determined relation that shows that the dependent variable depends on or is a function of particular variables – ideally the independent variable and nothing else.

Generality. The meaningfulness of interpretations of a study under circumstances different from those that generated the data.

Group behavior. Often inferred from the result of combining the data from multiple individuals who may be related in some way (e.g., sharing exposure to an experimental condition or applied intervention or interacting in some way). Does not refer to a natural phenomenon distinct from the behavior of individual organisms.

Ignored day. A plotting convention referring to days on which the target behavior could have occurred but was not measured. Data points bracketing such days should be connected in line graphs.

Incomplete observation. A schedule of observation that samples from all occurrences of the target behavior and may therefore fail to detect some responses.

Independent variable. An environmental event whose presence or absence is manipulated by the investigator in order to determine its effects on the dependent variable.

Independent variable condition. A condition or phase in which the independent variable is present. Also referred to as an *experimental, treatment,* or *intervention condition.*

Indirect measurement. Measurement practices in which the events that are measured are not the same as those about which conclusions will be drawn.

Interobserver agreement. A procedure for enhancing the believability of data that involves comparing simultaneous but independent observations from two or more observers. Provides no information about accuracy or reliability.

Interresponse time (IRT). A dimension referring to the elapsed time between two successive responses.

Intersubject variability. Differences in responding among participants.

Inter-tester (or inter-rater) reliability. The extent to which the scores recorded by several examiners on an assessment administered to a sample of individuals correlate with each other.

Interval agreement procedure. A procedure for calculating interobserver agreement when interval recording or time sampling is used. Each interval scored by both observers is counted as an agreement, and each interval that is scored by neither observer is also called an agreement. Intervals for which only one observer scored the behavior are counted as disagreements.

Interval-based recording. A category of discontinuous observation and recording procedures in which observation periods are divided into equal intervals, and occurrences of the target response are recorded by interval according to some rule.

Intervention condition. A condition or phase in which the independent variable is present. Also referred to as an *experimental, treatment,* or *independent variable condition.*

Intraorganism.   A reference to the individual organism as the level at which behavior occurs and can be studied, due to the fact that behavior depends on relations between the individual organism and its environment.

Intrinsic variability.   The assumption that variability in behavior is in one way or another inherent or built into the nature of organisms. See *Extrinsic variability*.

Latency.   A dimension that refers to the time between two events. In the study of behavior, the first event may be a response or an environmental event and the second event is usually a response.

Linear interval scale.   A measurement scale that allows descriptions of events that show how much they differ in terms of equal intervals between values.

Logarithmic interval scale.   A measurement scale that allows descriptions of events that show how much they differ in terms of equal ratios between values.

Measurement reactivity.   The effects of measurement procedures on a participant's behavior.

Mentalism.   Attributing the causes of behavior to events and processes said to occur in a mind or inner world that lacks physical dimensions.

Momentary time sampling (MTS).   A form of interval-based recording in which observation periods are divided into equal intervals but the observer only records whether the target response is occurring at the end of each interval.

Movement cycle.   The beginning, middle, and end of a single response such that the organism is in a position to emit another instance of that behavior.

Multi-element design.   A variation of a reversal design that exposes a participant to two or more conditions in some form of brief, repeated alternation. Also called an *alternating treatments* design.

No chance day.   A plotting convention referring to days on which the target behavior could not have occurred. Data points bracketing such days should not be connected in line graphs.

Non-concurrent multiple baseline design.   A within-subject design that uses two or more baselines in which matched control and treatment conditions are not operating concurrently and therefore do not permit control/treatment comparisons across baselines.

Norm-referenced assessment.   An assessment on which an individual's score is interpreted relative to the scores of other individuals in a defined group.

Observed values.   Values resulting from observation and recording procedures used to collect the data for a study.

Observer drift.   A change in an observer's performance, often gradual and for reasons that may not be obvious to the investigator.

Occurrence/nonoccurrence agreement.   A conservative approach to calculating interobserver agreement when interval recording or time sampling is used that involves calculating and reporting agreement separately for both occurrences (scored intervals) and nonoccurrences (unscored intervals).

Operant.   A class of responses (a behavior) defined by a functional relation with a class of consequent events that immediately follow those responses.

Parametric design.   A within-subject, single baseline design using AB and reversal sequences to identify effects of manipulating a specific parameter of a variable or procedure.

Partial interval recording (PIR).   A form of interval-based recording in which an occurrence is recorded if the target response (or even part of a response) was observed at any time during the interval. Only one occurrence is recorded even if multiple responses occurred during the interval.

Predictive or criterion-related validity.   The degree to which predictions about the behavior of individuals that are based on the results of an assessment conducted at one point in time are confirmed by measures of the later behavior of the same individuals.

Preference assessments.   A category of procedures for identifying stimuli that are preferred by an individual and so may function as reinforcers in behavior change contingencies.

Psychometrics.   The field of study whose subject matter is psychological testing and measurement.

Radical behaviorism.   The philosophy of science of behavior analysis, which focuses on behavior as a physical phenomenon and avoids mentalism in all forms.

Range.   A measure of variability defined by the highest and lowest values in a data set.

Rate or frequency.   A dimension describing the average number of events per unit of time. In the study of behavior, rate or frequency is calculated by dividing total count by either total IRT or the total time during which responses occurred.

Reliability.   In general, the stability of the relationship between observed values and the events that actually occurred. In psychometrics, the degree of measurement error in the results yielded by an assessment.

Replication.   Repetition of any parts of an experiment.

Replication across a condition or phase.   Repetition of an entire phase during the course of an experiment. Requires session-by-session display of data for each phase.

Replication across research literatures.   Repetition of phenomena under different conditions across different fields of science.

Replication across sessions.   Repetition of the same condition many times in succession throughout a phase. Requires session-by-session display of data.

Replication across trials.   Repetition of a basic element of procedure throughout each session. Requires trial-by-trial display of data.

Replication of entire studies.   Repetition of an earlier study, usually by other researchers.

Reproduction.   Repetition of results, usually as an outcome of repeating procedures.

Response class.   A collection of individual responses that have common sources of influence in the environment. Also called a behavior.

Response products.   The tangible or intangible environmental effects of responding that are more than transitory in duration.

Reversal design.   A within-subject experimental design minimally involving a pair of control and experimental conditions in which one or both conditions repeat at least once.

Scatter plot.   A record of observed occurrences of a behavior in a series of time intervals during a lengthy observation period over multiple days. The record is analyzed to determine if the behavior tends to occur more often at some times than at others. The term is used somewhat differently in statistical contexts.

Scientific method.   The established practices of scientific communities that have evolved over time because of their effectiveness in studying natural phenomena.

Sequence effect.   The effect of exposure to one condition on responding in a subsequent condition.

Standardized assessment.   An assessment instrument or procedure on which all components (contents, timing, administration and scoring procedures, etc.) are the same every time the assessment is administered.

Steady state.   A pattern of responding that shows relatively little variation in the dimension(s) of interest over some period of time.

Steady state strategy. An approach to making comparisons between the effects of two conditions on a target behavior that involves repeatedly measuring an individual's responding under each condition. It is essential for assessing and managing extraneous influences in order to get stable patterns of responding that represent the full effects of each condition.

Test-retest reliability. The extent to which the scores from two administrations of the same test correlate.

Time per cycle. The unit of measurement for interresponse time.

Topographical definition. A definition of a behavior based on the form of responses in three-dimensional space.

Total agreement procedure. A procedure for calculating interobserver agreement typically used with dimensions such as count, duration, and latency that involves summing the total count for each of the two observers, dividing the smaller total by the larger total, and multiplying the result by 100 to arrive at the percent agreement.

Transition state. A pattern of responding involving change from one steady state to a different steady state.

Transitory state. A pattern of responding involving a deviation from a steady state that ends in a return to the same steady state.

Treatment condition. A condition or phase in which the independent variable is present. Also referred to as an *experimental, intervention,* or *independent variable condition.*

Treatment integrity. The extent to which the independent variable or other key features of a condition are consistently implemented as designed. Also referred to as *procedural integrity* or *independent variable integrity.*

Trend. A relatively consistent change in the data in a single direction.

True (criterion) values. Values resulting from special observation and recording procedures that are somewhat different from those used to collect the data being evaluated and that involve special efforts to minimize error.

Unit of analysis. A constituent part of a whole phenomenon that serves as a basis for experimental study. In the study of behavior, the unit of analysis is the response class.

Unit of measurement. A determinate amount of a dimension of the phenomenon being measured.

Validity. In general, the extent to which observed values represent the events they are supposed to represent and that will be the focus of interpretation. In psychometric assessment, the appropriateness and usefulness of inferences that are drawn from assessment results.

Whole interval recording (WIR). A form of interval-based recording in which an occurrence is recorded if the target response occurs without ceasing throughout the entire interval.

Within-subject design. A method of arranging comparisons between control and experimental (treatment) conditions in which each subject is exposed to both control and experimental conditions in sequence and the data represent the performance of individual participants under both conditions.

References

Ahearn, W. H., Clark, K. M., MacDonald, R. P. F., & Chung, B. I. (2007). Assessing and treating vocal stereotypy in children with autism. *Journal of Applied Behavior Analysis, 40*, 263-275.

American Psychological Association (2010). *Publication manual of the American Psychological Association*, 6th edition. Washington DC.

Association for Behavior Analysis International (2016). *Policies. Code of Ethics*. https://www.abainternational.org/about-us/policies-and-positions.aspx, accessed January 3, 2019.

Association of Professional Behavior Analysts (2019). *Application for Membership*. https://www.apbahome.net/page/membership, accessed January 3, 2019.

Ator, N. A. (1999). Statistical inference in behavior analysis: Environmental determinants? *The Behavior Analyst, 22*, 93-97.

Austin, J., & Carr, J. E. (2000). *Handbook of applied behavior analysis*. Reno, NV: Context Press.

Azrin, N. H., Rubin, H., O'Brien, F., Ayllon, T., & Roll, D. (1968). Behavioral engineering: Postural control by a portable apparatus. *Journal of Applied Behavior Analysis, 1*, 99-108.

Baer, D. M., Wolf, M. M., & Risley, T. R. (1968). Some current dimensions of applied behavior analysis. *Journal of Applied Behavior Analysis, 1*, 91-97.

Bailey, J. S., & Burch, M. R. (2002). *Research methods in applied behavior analysis*. Thousand Oaks, CA: Sage Publications.

Bailey, J. S., & Burch, M. R. (2016). *Ethics for behavior analysts*, 3rd edition. New York: Routledge.

Baldwin, S. A., & Shadish, W. R. (2011). A primer on meta-analysis in clinical psychology. *Journal of Experimental Psychopathology, 2*, 294-317.

Barrett, B. H. (1962). Reduction in rate of multiple tics by free operant conditioning methods. *Journal of Nervous and Mental Disease, 135*, 187-195.

Bartlett, S. M., Rapp, J. T., & Henrickson, M. L. (2011). Detecting false positives in multielement designs: Implications for brief assessments. *Behavior Modification, 35*, 531-552.

Baum, W. M. (2005). *Understanding behaviorism*, 2nd edition. Malden, MA: Blackwell.

Beavers, G. A., Iwata, B. A., & Lerman, D. C. (2013). Thirty years of research on the functional analysis of problem behavior. *Journal of Applied Behavior Analysis, 46*, 1-21.

Behavior Analyst Certification Board, http://www.BACB.com.

Behavior Analyst Certification Board (September 2014). *BACB Newsletter - Special edition on ethics*. Littleton, CO: Author.

Behavior Analyst Certification Board (2016). *Professional and ethical compliance code for behavior analysts, Ver. January 20, 2016*. Littleton, CO: Author.

Bhutta, Z. A., & Crane, J. (2014). Should research fraud be a crime? *BMJ, 349*, g4532.

Bijou, S. W., Peterson, R. F., & Ault, M. H. (1968). A method to integrate descriptive and experimental field studies at the level of data and empirical concepts. *Journal of Applied Behavior Analysis, 1*, 175-191.

Bijou, S. W., Peterson, R. F., Harris, F. R., Allen, K. E., & Johnston, M. S. (1969). Methodology for experimental studies of young children in natural settings. *Psychological Record, 19*, 177-210.

Birnbrauer, J. S., & Leach, D. J. (1993). The Murdoch Early Intervention Program after 2 years. *Behaviour Change, 10(2)*, 63-74.

Brady, N. C., Fleming, K., Thiemann-Bourque, K., Olswang, L., Dowden, P., & Saunders, M. D. (2012). Development of the communication complexity scale. *American Journal of Speech-Language Pathology, 21(1)*, 16-28.

Branch, M. N. (1999). Statistical inference in behavior analysis: Some things significance testing does and does not do. *The Behavior Analyst, 22*, 87-92.

Branch, M., & Vollmer, T. (2004). Two suggestions for the verbal behavior(s) of organisms (i.e., authors). *The Behavior Analyst, 27*, 95-98.

Bridgman, P. W. (1927). *The logic of modern physics*. New York: Macmillan.

Bussman, J. B. J., Martens, W. L. J., Tulen, J. H. M., Schasfoort, F. C., Van den Berg-Emons, H. J. G., & Stam, H. J. (2001). Measuring daily behavior using ambulatory accelerometry: The activity monitor. *Behavior Research Methods, Instruments, & Computers, 33*, 349-356.

Calkin, A. B. (2009). An examination of inner (private) and outer (public) behaviors. *European Journal of Behavior Analysis, 10(1)*, 61-75.

Campbell, D. T., & Stanley, J. C. (1966). *Experimental and quasi-experimental designs for research*. Chicago: Rand McNally.

Canella, H. I., O'Reilly, M. F., & Lancioni, G. E. (2005). Choice and preference assessment research with people with severe to profound developmental disabilities: A review of the literature. *Research in Developmental Disabilities, 26*, 1-15.

Capriotti, M. R., Turkel, J. E., Johnson, R. A., Espil, F. M., & Woods, D. W. (2017). Comparing fixed-amount and progressive-amount DRO schedules for tic suppression in youth with chronic tic disorders. *Journal of Applied Behavior Analysis, 50*, 106-120.

Carey, M. K., & Bourret, J. C. (2014). Effects of data sampling on graphical depictions of learning. *Journal of Applied Behavior Analysis, 47*, 749-764.

Carey, T. A., & Stiles, W. B. (2016). Some problems with randomized controlled trials and some viable alternatives. *Clinical Psychology & Psychotherapy, 23*, 87-95.

Carr, A. (1966). Adaptation aspects of the scheduled travel of Chelonia. In *Annual orientation and navigation*. Corvallis: Oregon State University Press.

Carr, J. E. (2005). Recommendations for reporting multiple-baseline designs across participants. *Behavioral Interventions, 20(3)*, 219-224.

Carr, J. E., Nosik, M. R., & Luke, M. M. (2018). On the use of the term "frequency" in applied behavior analysis. *Journal of Applied Behavior Analysis, 51(2)*, 436-439.

Catania, A. C. (2013). *Learning*, 5th edition. Cornwall-On-Hudson, NY: Sloan Publishing.

Catania, A. C., Shimoff, E., & Mathews, B. A. (1989). An experimental analysis of rule- governed behavior. In S. C. Hayes (Ed.), *Rule-governed behavior: Cognition, contingencies, and instructional control* (pp. 119-150). New York: Plenum.

Connell, J. E., & Witt, J. C. (2004). Applications of computer-based instruction: Using specialized software to aid letter-name and letter-sound recognition. *Journal of Applied Behavior Analysis, 37*, 67-71.

Coon, J. C., & Rapp, J. T. (2017). Application of multiple baseline designs in behavior analytic research: Evidence for the influence of new guidelines. *Behavioral Interventions, 2017*, 1-13. https://doi.org/10.1002/bin.1510.

Cooper, J. O., Heron, T. E., & Heward, W. L. (2007). *Applied behavior analysis*. Upper Saddle River, NJ: Pearson.

Cumming, G. (2012). *Understanding the new statistics: Effect sizes, confidence intervals, and meta-analysis*. New York: Routledge.

Cumming, G. (2014). The new statistics: Why and how. *Psychological Science, 25(1)*, 7-29.

Cumming, G., & Calin-Jageman, R. (2017). *Introduction to the new statistics*. New York: Routledge.

Cummings, A. R., & Carr, J. E. (2009). Evaluating progress in behavioral programs for children with autism spectrum disorders via continuous and discontinuous measurement. *Journal of Applied Behavior Analysis, 42*, 57-71.

Devine, S. L., Rapp, J. T., Testa, J. R., Henrickson, M. L., & Schnerch, G. (2011). Detecting changes in simulated events using partial-interval recording and momentary time sampling III: Evaluating sensitivity as a function of session length. *Behavioral Interventions, 26*, 103-124.

Devlin, S., Healy, O., Leader, G., & Hughes, B. M. (2011). Comparison of behavioral intervention and sensory-integration therapy in the treatment of challenging behavior. *Journal of Autism and Developmental Disorders, 41*, 1303-1320.

Dollins, P., & Carbone, V. J. (2003, May). Using probe data recording methods to assess learner acquisition of skills. In V. J. Carbone (Chair), *Research related to Skinner's analysis of verbal behavior with children with autism*. Symposium conducted at the 29th annual convention of the Association for Behavior Analysis, San Francisco.

Dube, W. V., MacDonald, R. P. F., Mansfield, R. C., Holcomb, W. L., & Ahearn, W. H. (1994). Toward a behavioral analysis of joint attention. *The Behavior Analyst, 27*, 197-207.

Durbin, P. T. (1968). *Logic and scientific inquiry*. Milwaukee, WI: Brice Publishing.

Eikeseth, S., Smith, T., Jahr, E., & Eldevik, S. (2007). Outcome for children with autism who began intensive behavioral treatment between ages 4 and 7: A comparison controlled study. *Behavior Modification, 31*, 264-278.

Eldevik, S., Eikeseth, S., Jahr, E., & Smith, T. (2006). Effects of low-intensity behavioral treatment for children with autism and mental retardation. *Journal of Autism and Developmental Disorders, 36*, 211-224.

Eldevik, S., Hastings, R. P., Hughes, J. C., Jahr, E., Eikeseth, S., & Cross, S. (2010). Using participant data to extend the evidence for intensive behavioral intervention for children with autism. *American Journal on Intellectual and Developmental Disabilities, 115*, 381-405.

Epstein, R. (Ed.). (1980). *Notebooks, B. F. Skinner*. Englewood Cliffs, NJ: Prentice-Hall.

Ervin, R. A., Radford, P. M., Bertsch, K., Piper, A. L., Ehrhardt, K. E., & Poling, A. (2001). A descriptive analysis and critique of the empirical literature on school-based functional assessment. *School Psychology Review, 30*, 193-210.

Esch, B., Carr, J. E., & Grow, L. L. (2009). Evaluation of an enhanced stimulus-stimulus pairing procedure to increase early vocalizations of children with autism. *Journal of Applied Behavior Analysis, 42*, 225-241.

Estes, W. K. (1979). Experimental psychology: An overview. In E. Hearst (Ed.), *The first century of experimental psychology* (pp. 623-667). Hillsdale, NJ: Lawrence Erlbaum Associates.

Faraone, S. V. (2008). Interpreting estimates of treatment effects: Implications for managed care. *Pharmacy and Therapeutics, 33(12)*, 700-711.

Faux, S. F. (2002). Cognitive neuroscience from a behavioral perspective: A critique of chasing ghosts with Geiger counters. *The Behavior Analyst, 25(2)*, 161-173.

Fenske, E. C., Krantz, P. J., & McClannahan, L. E. (2001). Incidental teaching: A not-discrete trial teaching procedure. In C. Maurice, G. Green, & R. M. Foxx (Eds.), *Making a difference: Behavioral intervention for autism* (pp. 75-82). Austin, TX: Pro-Ed.

Ferguson, T. D., Briesch, A. M., Volpe, R. J., & Daniels, B. (2012). The influence of observation length on the dependability of data. *School Psychology Quarterly, 27*, 187-197.

Fisher, W. W., Piazza, C. C., & Roane, H. S. (Eds.) (2011). *Handbook of applied behavior analysis*. New York: The Guilford Press.

Fiske, K., & Delmolino, L. (2012). Use of discontinuous methods of data collection in behavioral intervention: Guidelines for practitioners. *Behavior Analysis in Practice, 5(2)*, 77-81.

Floyd, R. G., Phaneuf, R. L., & Wilczynski, S. M. (2005). Measurement properties of indirect assessment methods for functional behavioral assessment: A review of research. *School Psychology Review, 34*, 58-73.

Fryling, M. J. Wallace, M. D., & Yassine, J. N. (2012) Impact of treatment integrity on intervention effectiveness. *Journal of Applied Behavior Analysis, 45*, 449-453.

Gall, M. D., Gall, J. P., & Borg, W. R. (2006). *Educational research: An introduction*, 8th edition. Upper Saddle River, NJ: Pearson.

Garcia, D., Dukes, C., Brady, M. P., Scott, J., & Wilson, C. L. (2016). Using modeling and rehearsal to teach fire safety to children with autism. *Journal of Applied Behavior Analysis*, *49(3)*, 699-704.

Gardenier, N. C., MacDonald, R., & Green, G. (2004). Comparison of direct observational methods for measuring stereotypic behavior in children with autism spectrum disorders. *Research in Developmental Disabilities*, *25*, 99-118.

Giunta-Fede, T., Reeve, S. A., DeBar, R. M., Vladescu, J. C., & Reeve, K. F. (2016). Comparing continuous and discontinuous data collection during discrete trial teaching of tacting by children with autism. *Behavioral Interventions*, *31*, 311-331.

Glenn, I. M., & Dallery, J. (2007). Effects of internet-based voucher reinforcement and a transdermal nicotine patch on cigarette smoking. *Journal of Applied Behavior Analysis*, *40*, 1-13.

Goodwin, M. S., Intille, S. S., Albinali, F., & Velicer, W. F. (2010). Automated detection of stereotypical motor movements. *Journal of Autism and Developmental Disorders*, *41(6)*, 770-782.

Graff, R. B., & Green, G. (2004). Two methods for teaching simple visual discriminations to learners with severe disabilities. *Research in Developmental Disabilities*, *25*, 295-307.

Green, G., Brennan, L. C., & Fein, D. (2002). Intensive behavioral treatment for a toddler at high risk for autism. *Behavior Modification*, *26*, 69-102.

Green, V.A., Pituch, K.A., Itchon, A. C., O'Reilly, M., & Sigafoos, J. (2006). Internet survey of treatments used by parents of children with autism. *Research in Developmental Disabilities*, *27*, 70-84.

Gresham, F. M., MacMillan, D. L., Beebe-Frankenberger, M. E., & Bocian, K. M. (2000). Treatment integrity in learning disabilities intervention research: Do we really know how treatments are implemented? *Learning Disabilities: Research & Practice*, *15(4)*, 198-205.

Hall, R. V., Lund, D., & Jackson, D. (1968). Effects of teacher attention on study behavior. *Journal of Applied Behavior Analysis*, *1(1)*, 1-12.

Hanley, G. P. (2012) Functional assessment of problem behavior: Dispelling myths, overcoming implementation obstacles, and developing new lore. *Behavior Analysis in Practice*, *5(1)*, 54-72.

Hanley, G. P., Cammilleri, A. P., Tiger, J. H., & Ingvarsson, E.T. (2007). A method for describing preschoolers' activity preferences. *Journal of Applied Behavior Analysis*, *40*, 603-618.

Hanley, G. P., Iwata, B.A., & McCord, B. E. (2003). Functional analysis of problem behavior: A review. *Journal of Applied Behavior Analysis*, *36*, 147-185.

Harris, F. N., & Jenson, W. R. (1985). Comparisons of multiple-baseline across persons designs and AB designs with replication: Issues and confusions. *Behavioral Assessment*, *7*, 121-129.

Hart, B. M., & Risley, T. R. (1982). *How to use incidental teaching for elaborating language*. Austin, TX: Pro-Ed.

Harvey, M. T., May, M. E., & Kennedy, C. H. (2004). Noncurrent multiple baseline designs and the evaluation of educational systems. *Journal of Behavioral Education*, *13(4)*, 267-276.

Hawkins, R. P., & Dotson, V. A. (1975). Reliability scores that delude: An Alice In Wonderland trip through the misleading characteristics of interobserver agreement scores in interval recording. In E. Ramp & G. Semb (Eds.), *Behavior analysis: Areas of research and application* (pp. 359-376). Englewood Cliffs, NJ: Prentice-Hall.

Haynes, S. N., O'Brien, W. H., & Kaholokula, J. K. (2011). *Behavioral assessment and case formulation*. Hoboken, NJ: John Wiley & Sons.

Heath, A. K., Ganz, J. B., Parker, R., Burke, M., & Ninci, J. (2015). A meta-analytic review of functional communication training across mode of communication, age, and disability. *Review Journal of Autism and Developmental Disorders*, *2*, 155-166.

Hedges, L., & Olkin, I. (1985). *Statistical methods for meta-analysis*. New York: Academic Press.

Hefferline, R. F., & Keenan, B. (1963). Amplitude-induction gradient of a small-scale (covert) operant. *Journal of the Experimental Analysis of Behavior*, *6*, 307-315.

Heffernan, L., & Lyons, D. (2016). Differential reinforcement of other behavior for the reduction of severe nail biting. *Behavior Analysis in Practice*, *9*, 253-256.

Helton, M. R., & Ivy, J. W. (2016). A preliminary examination of a vocal generalized conditioned reinforcer. *Behavioral Interventions*, *31*, 62-69.

Henson, D. E., & Rubin, H. B. (1971). Voluntary control of eroticism. *Journal of Applied Behavior Analysis*, *4*, 37-44.

Hoaglin, D. C., Mosteller, R., & Tukey, J. W. (1985). *Exploring data tables, trends and shapes*. New York: Wiley.

Howard, J., Sparkman, C., Cohen, H., Green, G., & Stanislaw, H. (2005). A comparison of intensive behavior analytic and eclectic treatments for young children with autism. *Research in Developmental Disabilities, 26*, 359-383.

Howard, J. S., Stanislaw, H., Green, G., Sparkman, C. R., & Cohen, H. G. (2014). Comparison of behavior analytic and eclectic interventions for young children with autism after three years. *Research in Developmental Disabilities, 35*, 3326-3344.

Iwata, B. A., Vollmer, T. R., & Zarcone, J. R. (1990). The experimental (functional) analysis of behavior disorders: Methodology, applications, and limitations. In A. C. Repp & N. N. Singh (Eds.), *Perspectives on the use of nonaversive and aversive interventions for persons with developmental disabilities* (pp. 301-330). Sycamore, IL: Sycamore.

Jessel, J., Hanley, G. P., & Ghaemmaghami, M. (2016). Interview-informed synthesized contingency analyses: Thirty replications and reanalysis. *Journal of Applied Behavior Analysis, 49*, 1-22.

Johnson, L. M., & Morris, E. K. (1987). When speaking of probability in behavior analysis. *Behaviorism, 15*, 107-129.

Johnston, J. M. (1979). On the relation between generality and generalization. *The Behavior Analyst, 2*, 1-6.

Johnston, J. M. (1988). Strategic and tactical limits of comparison studies. *The Behavior Analyst, 11*, 1-9.

Johnston, J. M. (1993a). The development of behavioral research methods: Contributions of B. F. Skinner. In J. M. Johnston and H. S. Pennypacker (Eds.), *Readings for strategies and tactics of behavioral research* (pp. 8-17). Hillsdale, NJ: Lawrence Erlbaum Associates.

Johnston, J. M. (1993b). Why behavior analysis is a natural science. In *Readings for strategies and tactics of behavioral research*, 2nd edition. Hillsdale, NJ: Lawrence Erlbaum Associates.

Johnston, J. M. (1996). Distinguishing between applied research and practice. *The Behavior Analyst, 19*, 35-47.

Johnston, J. M. (2014, Sept. 22). The problem with problem behavior as communication. [Web Blog] Retrieved from talkingaboutbehavior.com.

Johnston, J. M. (2014). *Radical behaviorism for ABA practitioners*. Cornwall-on-Hudson, NY: Sloan Publishing.

Johnston, J. M. (2015, Jan. 12). It's about the evidence. [Web Blog] Retrieved from talkingaboutbe havior.com.

Johnston, J. M., Greene, K., Rawal, A., Winston, M., Vazin, T., & Rossi, M. (1991). The effects of caloric density on ruminating. *Journal of Applied Behavior Analysis, 24(3)*, 597-603.

Johnston, J. M., Mellichamp, F. H., Shook, G. L., & Carr, J. E. (2014). Determining BACB examination content and standards. *Behavior Analysis in Practice*, 7, 3-9. DOI 10.1007/s40617-014-003-6.

Johnston, J. M., & Pennypacker, H. S. (1993a). *Strategies and tactics of behavioral research*, 2nd edition. Hillsdale, NJ: Erlbaum Associates.

Johnston, J. M., & Pennypacker, H. S. (1993b). *Readings for strategies and tactics of behavioral research*. Hillsdale, NJ: Erlbaum Associates.

Johnston, J. M., & Pennypacker, H. S. (2009). *Strategies and tactics of behavioral research*, 3rd edition. New York: Routledge.

Jones, R., Vaught, R., & Weinrott, M. (1977). Time-series analysis in operant research. *Journal of Applied Behavior Analysis, 10*, 151-166.

Juni, P., Altman, D. G., & Egger, M. (2001). Assessing the quality of controlled clinical trials. *BMJ, 323*, 42-46.

Kahng, S. W., Iwata, B. A., Fischer, S. M., Page, T. J., Treadwell, K. R. H., Williams, D. E., & Smith, R. G. (1998). Temporal distributions of problem behavior based on scatter plot analysis. *Journal of Applied Behavior Analysis, 31*, 593-604.

Kang, S., O'Reilly, M., Lancioni, G., Falcomata, T. S., Sigafoos, J., & Xu, Z. (2013). Comparison of the predictive validity and consistency among preference assessment procedures: A review of the literature. *Research in Developmental Disabilities, 34(4)*, 1125-1133.

Kay, S., & Vyse, S. (2005). Helping parents separate the wheat from the chaff: Putting autism treatments to the test. In J. W. Jacobson, R. M. Foxx, & J. A. Mulick (Eds.), *Controversial therapies for developmental disabilities* (pp. 265-277). Mahwah, NJ: Erlbaum.

Keenan, M., & Dillenburger, K. (2011). When all you have is a hammer: RCTs and hegemony in science. *Research in Autism Spectrum Disorders, 5*, 1-13.

Kelley, M. E., LaRue, R. H., Roane, H. S., & Gadaire, D. M. (2011) Indirect behavioral assessments: Interviews and rating scales. In W. W. Fisher, C. C. Piazza, & H. S. Roane (Eds.), *Handbook of applied behavior analysis* (pp. 182-190). New York: The Guilford Press.

Kelly, S., Green, G., & Sidman, M. (1998). Visual identity matching and auditory-visual matching: A procedural note. *Journal of Applied Behavior Analysis, 31(2)*, 237-243.

Kennedy, C. H. (2005). *Single-case designs for educational research*. Boston: Pearson Education.

Killeen, P. R. (2015). P(rep): The probability of replicating an effect. *The Encyclopedia of Clinical Psychology*. New York: Wiley & Sons.

Klintwall, L., Eldevik, S., & Eikeseth, S. (2015). Narrowing the gap: Effects of intervention on developmental trajectories in autism. *Autism, 19*, 53-63.

Kostewicz, D. E., King, S. A., Datchuk, S. M., Brennan, K. M., & Casey, S. D. (2016). Data collection and measurement assessment in behavioral research: 1958-2013. *Behavior Analysis: Research and Practice, 16*, 19-33.

Kraemer, H. C., Morgan, G. A., Leech, N. L., Gliner, J. A., Vaske, J. J., & Harmon, R. J. (2003). Measures of clinical significance. *Journal of the American Academy of Child and Adolescent Psychiatry, 42*, 1524-1529.

Lambdin, C. (2012). Significance tests as sorcery: Science is empirical - significant tests are not. *Theory & Psychology, 22(1)*, 67-90.

Lancioni, G., Sigafoos, J., O'Reilly, M. F., & Singh, N. N. (2013). *Assistive technology*. New York: Springer.

Lang, R., Rispoli, M., Machalicek, W., White, P. J., Kang, S., Pierce, N., Mulloy, A., Fragale, T., O'Reilly, M., Sigafoos, J., & Lancioni, G. (2009). Treatment of elopement in individuals with developmental disabilities: A systematic review. *Research in Developmental Disabilities, 30*, 670-681.

Ledford, J. R., Ayres, K. M., Lane, J. D., & Lam, M. F. (2015). Identifying issues and concerns with the use of interval-based systems in single case research using a pilot simulation study. *The Journal of Special Education, 49(2)*, 104-117.

Ledford, J. R., & Gast, D. L. (2018). *Single case research methodology: Applications in special education and behavioral sciences*, 3rd edition. New York: Routledge.

Lee, V. L. (1981). Terminological and conceptual revision in the experimental analysis of language development: Why. *Behaviorism, 9*, 25-53.

Lerman, D. C., Dittlinger, L. H., Fentress, G., & Lanagan, T. (2011). A comparison of methods for collecting data on performance during discrete trial teaching. *Behavior Analysis in Practice, 4(1)*, 53-62.

Lerman, D. C., Tetreault, A., Hovanetz, A., Bellaci, E., Miller, J., Karp, H., Mahmood, A., Strobel, M., Mullen, S., Keyl, A., & Toupard, A. (2010). Applying signal-detection theory to the study of observer accuracy and bias in behavioral assessment. *Journal of Applied Behavior Analysis, 43*, 195-213.

Levin, K. A. (2007). Study design VII: Randomised controlled trials. *Evidence-Based Dentistry, 8*, 22-23.

Lindsley, O. R. (1966). An experiment with parents handling behavior at home. In J. Parnicky (Ed.), *Johnstone Bulletin, 9(1)*, 27-36.

Lionello-DeNolf, K. M., McIlvane, W. J., Canovas, D. S., De Souza, D. G., & Barros, R. S. (2008). Reversal learning set and functional equivalence in children with and without autism. *The Psychological Record, 58*, 15-36.

Lovaas, O. I. (1987). Behavioral treatment and normal educational and intellectual functioning in young autistic children. *Journal of Consulting and Clinical Psychology, 55*, 3-9.

Lowe, C. F. (1979). Determinants of human operant behaviour. In M. D. Zeiler & P. Harzem (Eds.), *Reinforcement and the organization of behaviour* (pp. 159-192). New York: John Wiley & Sons.

MacDonald, R., Anderson, J., Dube, W. V., Geckeler, A., Green, G., Holcomb, W., Mansfield, R., & Sanchez, J. (2006). Behavioral assessment of joint attention: A methodological report. *Research in Developmental Disabilities, 27*, 138-150.

Madden, G. J., & Bickel, W. (2010). *Impulsivity: The behavioral and neurological science of discounting*. Washington, DC: American Psychological Association.

McNamee, J., & Van der Mars, H. (2005). Accuracy of momentary time sampling: A comparison of varying interval lengths using SOFIT. *Journal of Teaching in Physical Education, 24*, 28-292.

Meany-Daboul, M. G., Roscoe, E. M., Bourret, J. C., & Ahearn, W. H. (2007). A comparison of momentary time sampling and partial-interval recording for evaluating functional relations. *Journal of Applied Behavior Analysis, 40*, 501-514.

Merbitz, C. T., Merbitz, N. H., & Pennypacker, H. S. (2016). On terms: Frequency and rate in applied behavior analysis. *The Behavior Analyst, 39*, 333-338.

Moore, J. (2008). *Conceptual foundations of radical behaviorism.* Cornwall-on-Hudson, NY: Sloan Publishing.

Moore, J. (2015). *From a behavioral point of view: A psychological primer.* Cornwall-on Hudson, NY: Sloan Publishing.

Morris, E. K., Altus, D. E., & Smith, N. G. (2013). A study in the founding of applied behavior analysis through its publications. *The Behavior Analyst, 36*, 73-107.

Mudford, O. C., Beale, I. L., & Singh, N. N. (1990). The representativeness of observational samples of different durations. *Journal of Applied Behavior Analysis, 23*, 323-331.

Mudford, O. C., Martin, N. T., Hui, J. K. Y., & Taylor, S. A. (2009). Assessing observer accuracy in continuous recording of rate and duration: Three algorithms compared. *Journal of Applied Behavior Analysis, 42*, 527-539.

Mudford, O. C., Taylor, S. A., & Martin, N. T. (2009). Continuous recording and interobserver agreement algorithms reported in the *Journal of Applied Behavior Analysis* (1995-2005). *Journal of Applied Behavior Analysis, 42*, 165-169.

Mudford, O. C., Zeleny, J. R., Fisher, W. W., Klum, M. E., & Owen, T. M. (2011). Calibration of observational measurement of rate of responding. *Journal of Applied Behavior Analysis, 44*, 571-586.

National Autism Center (2015). *Findings and conclusions: National standards project, Phase 2.* http://www.nationalautismcenter.org/national-standards-project/phase-2/.

Neef, N. A., & Peterson, S. M. (2007). Functional behavior assessment. In J. O. Cooper, T. E. Heron, & W. L. Heward (Eds.), *Applied Behavior Analysis,* 2nd edition. (pp. 500-524). Upper Saddle River, NJ: Pearson.

Northup, J., Wacker, D. P., Berg, W. K., Kelly, L., Sasso, G., & DeRaad, A. (1994). The treatment of severe behavior problems in school settings using a technical assistance model. *Journal of Applied Behavior Analysis, 27*, 33-47.

O'Brien, F., Azrin, N. H., & Bugle, C. (1972). Training profoundly retarded children to stop crawling. *Journal of Applied Behavior Analysis, 5*, 131-137.

Onghena, P., Michiels, B., Jamshidi, L., Moeyaert, M., & Van den Noortgate, W. (2017). One by one: Accumulating evidence by using meta-analytical procedures for single-case experiments. *Brain Impairment, 19(1)*, 33-58.

Ontario Association for Behaviour Analysis (2017). Evidence-based practices for individuals with autism spectrum disorder: Recommendation for caregivers, practitioners, and policy makers. Report of the Ontario Scientific Expert Task Force on the treatment of autism spectrum disorder. http://www.ontaba.org/pdf/ONTABA%20OSETTASD%20REPORT%20WEB.pdf.

Open Science Collaboration, Nosek, Brian A., Aarts, Alexander A., Anderson, Christopher J., Anderson, Joanna E., & Kappes, Heather Barry (2015) Estimating the reproducibility of psychological science. *Science, 349* (6251).

Parker, R. I., & Vannest, K. (2009). An improved effect size for single-case research: Nonoverlap of all pairs. *Behavior Therapy, 40*, 357-367.

Pelios, L., Morren, J., Tesch, D., & Axelrod, S. (1999). The impact of functional analysis methodology on treatment choice for self-injurious and aggressive behavior. *Journal of Applied Behavior Analysis, 32*, 185-195.

Pennypacker, H. S., Gutierrez, A., Jr., & Lindsley, O. R. (2003). *Handbook of the standard celeration chart.* Gainesville, AL: Author.

Peterson, H., Homer, A. L., & Wonderlick, S. A. (1982). The integrity of independent variables in behavior analysis. *Journal of Applied Behavior Analysis, 15*, 474-493.

Peterson, K. M., Piazza, C. C., & Volkert, V. M. (2016). A comparison of a modified sequential oral sensory approach to an applied behavior analytic approach in the treatment of food selectivity in children with autism spectrum disorders. *Journal of Applied Behavior Analysis, 49*, 1-27.

Petursdottir, A. I., & Aguilar, G. (2016). Order of stimulus presentation influences children's acquisition in receptive identification tasks. *Journal of Applied Behavior Analysis, 49*, 58-68.

Phillips, K. J., Mudford, O. C., Zeleny, J. R., & Elliffe, D. (2014). Using calibration and interobserver agreement algorithms to assess the accuracy and precision of data from electronic and pen-and-paper continuous recording methods. *Behavioral Interventions, 29*, 315-330.

Plotz, T., Hammerla, N. Y., Rozga, A., Reavis, A., Call, N., & Abowd, G. D. (2012). Automatic assessment of problem behavior in individuals with developmental disabilities. *Proceedings of the 2012 ACM Conference on Ubiquitous Computing*, 391-400.

Pustejovsky, J. E., & Ferron, J. M. (2017). Research synthesis and meta-analysis of single-case designs. In J. M. Kaufmann, D. P. Hallahan, & P. C. Pullen (Eds.), *Handbook of special education*, 2nd edition. New York: Routledge.

Radley, K. C., O'Handley, R. D., & Labrot, Z. C. (2015). A comparison of momentary time sampling and partial-interval recording for assessment of effects of social skills training. *Psychology in the Schools, 52(4)*, 363-378.

Rapp, J. T., Carr, J. E., Miltenberger, R. G., Dozier, C. L., & Kellum, K. K. (2001). Using real-time recording to enhance the analysis of within-session functional analysis data. *Behavior Modification, 25*, 79-93.

Rapp, J. T., Carroll, R. A., Stangeland, L., Swanson, G., & Higgins, W. J. (2011). A comparison of reliability measures for continuous and discontinuous recording methods: Inflated agreement scores with partial interval recording and momentary time sampling for duration events. *Behavior Modification, 35(4)*, 389-402.

Rapp, J. T., Colby, A. M., Vollmer, T. R., Roane, H. S., Lomas, J., & Britton, L. N. (2007). Interval recording for duration events: A re-evaluation. *Behavioral Interventions, 22*, 319-345.

Rapp, J. T., Colby-Dirksen, A. M., Michalski, D. N., Carroll, R. A., & Lindenberg, A. M. (2008). Detecting changes in simulated events using partial-interval recording and momentary time sampling. *Behavioral Interventions, 23*, 237-269.

Rast, J., Johnston, J. M., Drum, C., & Conrin, J. (1981). The relation of food quantity to rumination behavior. *Journal of Applied Behavior Analysis, 14*, 121-130.

Rast, J., Johnston, J. M., & Drum, C. (1984). A parametric analysis of the relationship between food quantity and rumination. *Journal of the Experimental Analysis of Behavior, 41(2)*, 125-134.

Rast, J., Johnston, J. M., Ellinger-Allen, J., & Drum, C. (1984). Effects of nutritional and mechanical properties of food on ruminative behavior. *Journal of the Experimental Analysis of Behavior, 44*, 195-206.

Rast, J., Johnston, J. M., Ellinger-Allen, J., & Lubin, D. (1988). Effects of pre-meal chewing on ruminative behavior. *American Journal of Mental Retardation, 93(1)*, 67-74.

Rice, T. W. (2008). The historical, ethical, and legal background of human-subjects research. *Respiratory Care, 53(10)*, 1325-1329.

Roane, H. W., Kelly, M. L., & Fisher, W. W. (2003). The effects of noncontingent access to food on the rate of object mouthing across three settings. *Journal of Applied Behavior Analysis, 36*, 579-582.

Sallows, G. O., & Graupner, T. D. (2005). Intensive behavioral treatment for children with autism: Four-year outcome and predictors. *American Journal on Mental Retardation, 110*, 417-438.

Salmon, W. C. (1966). *The conceptual foundations of scientific inference*. Pittsburgh: University of Pittsburgh Press.

Saunders, K. J., Pilgrim, C. A., & Pennypacker, H. S. (1986). Increased proficiency of search in breast self-examination. *Cancer, 58(11)*, 2531-2537.

Schlinger, H. D. (2008). Listening is behaving verbally. *The Behavior Analyst, 31(2)*, 145-161.

Schmidt, M. G., Rapp, J. T., Novotny, M. A., & Lood, E. A. (2013). Detecting changes in non-simulated events using partial interval recording and momentary time sampling: Evaluating false positives, false negatives, and trending. *Behavioral Interventions, 28*, 58-81.

Schneider, S. M. (2012). *The science of consequences: How they affect genes, change the brain, and impact our world*. Amherst, NY: Prometheus Books.

Schreck, K. A., Karunaratne, Y., Zane, T., & Wilford, H. (2016). Behavior analysts' use of and beliefs in treatments for people with autism: A 5-year follow-up. *Behavioral Interventions, 31*, 355-376.

Schwartz, B., & Gamzu, E. (1977). Pavlovian control of operant behavior. In W. K. Honig & J. E. R. Staddon (Eds.), *Handbook of operant behavior* (pp. 53-97). Englewood Cliffs, NJ: Plenum Press.

Shadish, W. R., Hedges, L. V., & Pustejovsky, J. E. (2014). Analysis and meta-analysis of single-case designs with a standardized mean difference statistic: A primer and applications. *Journal of School Psychology, 52(2)*, 123-147.

Sharp, R. A., Mudford, O. C., & Elliffe, D. (2015). Representativeness of direct observations selected using a work-sampling equation. *Journal of Applied Behavior Analysis, 48*, 153-166.

Sharp, W. G., Jaquess, D. L., Morton, J. F., & Herzinger, C. V. (2010). Pediatric feeding disorders: A quantitative synthesis of treatment outcomes. *Clinical Child and Family Psychology Review, 13*, 348-365.

Shook, G. L., Johnston, J. M., & Mellichamp, F. H. (2004). Determining essential content for applied behavior analyst practitioners. *The Behavior Analyst, 27(1)*, 67-94.

Sidman, M. (1960). *Tactics of scientific research*. New York: Basic Books.

Sidman, M. (1994). *Equivalence relations and behavior: A research story*. Boston, MA: Authors Cooperative.

Skinner, B. F. (1935). The generic nature of the concepts of stimulus and response. *Journal of General Psychology, 12*, 40-65.

Skinner, B. F. (1938). *The behavior of organisms*. New York: Applewon-Century-Crofts.

Skinner, B. F. (1945). Operational analysis of psychological terms. *Psychological Review, 52*, 270-281.

Skinner, B. F. (1953). *Science and human behavior*. New York: The Free Press.

Skinner, B. F. (1956). A case history in scientific method. *American Psychologist, 11*, 221-233.

Skinner, B. F. (1961). *Cumulative record*. New York: Appleton-Century-Crofts.

Skinner, B. F. (1971). *Beyond freedom and dignity*. New York: Alfred A. Knopf.

Skinner, B. F. (1974). *About behaviorism*. New York: Alfred A. Knopf.

Skinner, B. F. (1975). The shaping of phylogenic behavior. *Journal of the Experimental Analysis of Behavior, 24*, 117.

Skinner, B. F. (1976). *Particulars of my life*. New York: Alfred A. Knopf.

Skinner, B. F. (1979). *The shaping of a behaviorist*. New York: Alfred A. Knopf.

Skinner, B. F. (1983). *A matter of consequences*. New York: Alfred A. Knopf.

Skinner, B. F. (1989). *Recent issues in the analysis of behavior*. Columbus, OH: Merrill Publishing Company.

Smith, T. (2013). What is evidence-based behavior analysis? *The Behavior Analyst, 36*, 7-33.

Smith, T., & Antolovich, M. (2000). Parental perceptions of supplemental interventions received by young children with autism in intensive behavior analytic treatment. *Behavioral Interventions, 15*, 83-97.

Smith, T., Groen, A. D., & Wynn, J. W. (2000). Randomized trial of intensive early intervention for children with pervasive developmental disorder. *American Journal on Mental Retardation, 105(4)*, 269-285.

Smith, W. C. (2014). Estimating unbiased treatment effects in education using a regression discontinuity design. *Practical Assessment, Research, & Evaluation, 19(9)*, 1-9.

Spieler, C., & Miltenberger, R. (2017). Using awareness training to decrease nervous habits during public speaking. *Journal of Applied Behavior Analysis, 50*, 38-47.

Stephenson, J., & Imrie, J. (1998). Why do we need randomized controlled trials to assess behavioral interventions? *BMJ, 316*, 611-613.

Stoerzinger, A., Johnston, J. M., Pisor, K., & Monroe, C. M. (1978). Implementation and evaluation of a feedback system for employees in a salvage operation. *Journal of Organizational Behavior Management, 1*, 268-280.

Sundberg, M. L., & Hale, L. (2003, May). Using textual stimuli to teach vocal-intraverbal behaviors. In A. I. Petursdottir (Chair), *Methods for teaching intraverbal behavior to children*. Symposium conducted at the 29th annual convention of the Association for Behavior Analysis, San Francisco.

Terrell, D. J., & Johnston, J. M. (1989). Logic, reasoning, and verbal behavior. *The Behavior Analyst, 12*, 35-44.

Tiger, J. H., Miller, S. J., Mevers, J. L., Mintz, J. C., Scheithauer, M. C., & Alvarez, J. (2013). On the representativeness of behavior observation samples in classrooms. *Journal of Applied Behavior Analysis, 46*, 424-435.

Touchette, P. E., MacDonald, R. F., & Langer, S. N. (1985). A scatter plot for identifying stimulus control of problem behavior. *Journal of Applied Behavior Analysis, 1*, 343-351.

Tufte, E. R. (1983). *The visual display of quantitative information*. Cheshire, CN: Graphics Press.

Tufte, E. R. (1990). *Envisioning information*. Cheshire, CN: Graphics Press.

Tufte, E. R. (1997). *Visual explanations*. Cheshire, CN: Graphics Press.

Tufte, E. R. (2006). *Beautiful evidence*. Cheshire, CN: Graphics Press.

Tukey, J. W. (1977). *EDA: Exploratory data analysis*. Reading, MA: Addison-Wesley.

Tullis, C. A., Canella-Malone, H. I., Basbigill, A. R., Yeager, A., Fleming, C. V., Payne, D., & Wu, P. F. (2011). Review of the choice and preference assessment literature for individuals with severe to profound disabilities. *Education and Training in Autism and Developmental Disabilities, 46(4)*, 576-595.

Twohig, M. P., & Woods, D. W. (2001). Habit reversal as a treatment for chronic skin picking in typically developing adult male siblings. *Journal of Applied Behavior Analysis, 34*, 217-220.

Uttal, W. R. (2011). *Mind and brain: A critical appraisal of cognitive neuroscience*. Cambridge, MA: MIT Press.

Velleman, P., & Hoaglin, D. C. (1981). *The AB's of EDA: Applications, basics, and computing of exploratory data analysis*. Boston, MA: Duxbury.

Virues-Ortega, J., Pritchard, K., Grant, R. L., North, S., Hurtado-Parrado, C., Lee, M. S. H., Temple, B., Julio, F., & Yu, C. T. (2014). Clinical decision making and preference assessment for individuals with intellectual and developmental disabilities. *American Journal on Intellectual and Developmental Disabilities, 119(2)*, 151-170.

Volkert, V. M., & Piazza, C. C. (2012). Pediatric feeding disorders. In P. Sturmey & M. Hersen (Eds.), *Handbook of evidence-based practice in clinical psychology, Volume 1: Child and adolescent disorders* (pp. 323-337). Hoboken, NJ: Wiley.

Watson, P. J., & Workman, E. A. (1981). The non-concurrent multiple baseline across-individuals design: An extension of the tradition multiple baseline design. *Journal of Behavior Therapy and Experimental Psychiatry, 12*, 257-259.

Weeden, M., Ehrhardt, K., & Poling, A. (2010). Psychotropic drug treatments for people with autism and other developmental disorders: A primer for practicing behavior analysts. *Behavior Analysis in Practice, 3*, 4-12.

Wheeler, J. J., Mayton, M. R., Carter, S. L., Chitiyo, M., Menendez, A. L., & Huang, A. (2009). An assessment of treatment integrity in behavioral intervention studies conducted with persons with mental retardation. *Education and Training in Developmental Disabilities, 44(2)*, 187-195.

Wirth, O., Slaven, J., & Taylor, M. A. (2014). Interval sampling methods and measurement error: A computer simulation. *Journal of Applied Behavior Analysis, 47*, 83-100.

Wolf, M. M. (1978). Social validity: The case for subjective measurement or how applied behavior analysis is finding its heart. *Journal of Applied Behavior Analysis, 11(2)*, 203-214.

Wong, C., Odom, S. L., Hume, K., Cox, A. W., Fettig, A., Kucharczyk, S., Brock, M. E., Plavnick, J. B., Fleury, V. P, & Schutz, T. R. (2015). *Journal of Autism and Developmental Disorders, 45*, 1951-1966.

Zakszeski, B. N., Hojnoski, R. L., & Wood, B. K. (2017). Considerations for time sampling interval durations in the measurement of young children's classroom engagement. *Topics in Early Childhood Special Education, 37(1)*, 42-53.

Author Index

Page numbers in **bold** refer to figures, page numbers in *italic* refer to tables.

Subject Index

Page numbers in **bold** refer to figures, page numbers in *italic* refer to tables.